MW01356654

IMAGE EVALUATION
TEST TARGET (MT-3)

1.0 1.1 1.25 1.4 1.6 1.8 2.0 2.2 2.5 2.8

6"

©1986

Technical and Bibliographic Notes/Notes techniques et bibliographiques

The Institute has attempted to obtain the best original copy available for filming. Features of this copy which may be bibliographically unique, which may alter any of the images in the reproduction, or which may significantly change the usual method of filming, are checked below.

L'Institut a microfilmé le meilleur exemplaire qu'il lui a été possible de se procurer. Les détails de cet exemplaire qui sont peut-être uniques du point de vue bibliographique, qui peuvent modifier une image reproduite, ou qui peuvent exiger une modification dans la méthode normale de filmage sont indiqués ci-dessous.

- [ ] Coloured covers/ Couverture de couleur
- [ ] Covers damaged/ Couverture endommagée
- [ ] Covers restored and/or laminated/ Couverture restaurée et/ou pelliculée
- [ ] Cover title missing/ Le titre de couverture manque
- [ ] Coloured maps/ Cartes géographiques en couleur
- [ ] Coloured ink (i.e. other than blue or black)/ Encre de couleur (i.e. autre que bleue ou noire)
- [ ] Coloured plates and/or illustrations/ Planches et/ou illustrations en couleur
- [ ] Bound with other material/ Relié avec d'autres documents
- [ ] Tight binding may cause shadows or distortion along interior margin/ La reliure serrée peut causer de l'ombre ou de la distorsion le long de la marge intérieure
- [ ] Blank leaves added during restoration may appear within the text. Whenever possible, these have been omitted from filming/ Il se peut que certaines pages blanches ajoutées lors d'une restauration apparaissent dans le texte, mais, lorsque cela était possible, ces pages n'ont pas été filmées.
- [ ] Additional comments:/ Commentaires supplémentaires:

- [ ] Coloured pages/ Pages de couleur
- [ ] Pages damaged/ Pages endommagées
- [ ] Pages restored and/or laminated/ Pages restaurées et/ou pelliculées
- [x] Pages discoloured, stained or foxed/ Pages décolorées, tachetées ou piquées
- [ ] Pages detached/ Pages détachées
- [x] Showthrough/ Transparence
- [ ] Quality of print varies/ Qualité inégale de l'impression
- [ ] Includes supplementary material/ Comprend du matériel supplémentaire
- [ ] Only edition available/ Seule édition disponible
- [ ] Pages wholly or partially obscured by errata slips, tissues, etc., have been refilmed to ensure the best possible image/ Les pages totalement ou partiellement obscurcies par un feuillet d'errata, une pelure, etc., ont été filmées à nouveau de façon à obtenir la meilleure image possible.

This item is filmed at the reduction ratio checked below/
Ce document est filmé au taux de réduction indiqué ci-dessous.

10X 14X 18X 22X 26X 30X

12X 16X 20X 24X ✓ 28X 32X

e
étails
s du
nodifier
r une
image

is

errata
to

pelure,
n à

32X

The copy filmed here has been reproduced thanks to the generosity of:

D. B. Weldon Library
University of Western Ontario

The images appearing here are the best quality possible considering the condition and legibility of the original copy and in keeping with the filming contract specifications.

Original copies in printed paper covers are filmed beginning with the front cover and ending on the last page with a printed or illustrated impression, or the back cover when appropriate. All other original copies are filmed beginning on the first page with a printed or illustrated impression, and ending on the last page with a printed or illustrated impression.

The last recorded frame on each microfiche shall contain the symbol —► (meaning "CONTINUED"), or the symbol ▼ (meaning "END"), whichever applies.

Maps, plates, charts, etc., may be filmed at different reduction ratios. Those too large to be entirely included in one exposure are filmed beginning in the upper left hand corner, left to right and top to bottom, as many frames as required. The following diagrams illustrate the method:

L'exemplaire filmé fut reproduit grâce à la générosité de:

D. B. Weldon Library
University of Western Ontario

Les images suivantes ont été reproduites avec le plus grand soin, compte tenu de la condition et de la netteté de l'exemplaire filmé, et en conformité avec les conditions du contrat de filmage.

Les exemplaires originaux dont la couverture en papier est imprimée sont filmés en commençant par le premier plat et en terminant soit par la dernière page qui comporte une empreinte d'impression ou d'illustration, soit par le second plat, selon le cas. Tous les autres exemplaires originaux sont filmés en commençant par la première page qui comporte une empreinte d'impression ou d'illustration et en terminant par la dernière page qui comporte une telle empreinte.

Un des symboles suivants apparaîtra sur la dernière image de chaque microfiche, selon le cas: le symbole —► signifie "A SUIVRE", le symbole ▼ signifie "FIN".

Les cartes, planches, tableaux, etc., peuvent être filmés à des taux de réduction différents. Lorsque le document est trop grand pour être reproduit en un seul cliché, il est filmé à partir de l'angle supérieur gauche, de gauche à droite, et de haut en bas, en prenant le nombre d'images nécessaire. Les diagrammes suivants illustrent la méthode.

1	2	3

1
2
3

1	2	3
4	5	6

METHODIST

HYMN AND TUNE BOOK

COMPILED AND PUBLISHED BY AUTHORITY OF THE GENERAL CONFERENCE OF THE METHODIST CHURCH.

Speaking one to another in psalms and hymns and spiritual songs, singing and making melody with your heart to the Lord.—*Eph.* v. 19.

TORONTO:
METHODIST BOOK AND PUBLISHING HOUSE.

MONTREAL:
METHODIST BOOK-ROOM.

HALIFAX:
METHODIST BOOK-ROOM.

ELECTROTYPED AND PRINTED AT THE METHODIST BOOK AND PUBLISHING HOUSE, WESLEY BUILDINGS, TORONTO.

PREFACE TO THE HYMN AND TUNE BOOK.

TO meet a long-felt want of the Church for an edition of the HYMN BOOK WITH TUNES, the General Conference of 1890 authorized the Book Committee "to proceed with the publication of such a book."—*Journal*, page 146, sec. 12.

Committees were formed in Toronto, Montreal and Halifax respectively. That in Montreal was represented by Mr. C. W. Coates, whose valuable suggestions were of great service, and that in Halifax by Mr. A. E. Huestis, who, being in Toronto, was appointed its representative on the Toronto Committee, upon the members of which devolved the chief responsibility of bringing out the book.

Hundreds of tunes most in use in the churches were received from choir leaders and others prominent in musical circles throughout Canada, and from these fifty of different metres, and having the highest number of recommendations, were accepted. In addition, selections were made from a variety of sources, English and American as well as Canadian, and care was exercised in adjusting them so as to furnish the best expression for the thought contained in the hymn. Where the Committee could not reach a decision by consent, the matter was fully discussed and then settled by vote, and thus a common judgment prevailed over the individual opinion. The book is, therefore, not the product of one mind merely, but of several, familiar with the subject of music and hymn singing in the congregation.

The Committee believes it has avoided the serious errors of running into a rut, adopting only one standard of excellence, or of accepting tunes after the tastes and predilections of only one school of musicians, and that, thereby, a book has been produced that will be useful to the greater number, and, it is hoped, may become a favourite with both old and young, in the rural circuits, as well as the town and city congregations of Canadian Methodism. A firm purpose has been maintained to make it one of practical use for special as well as for regular services. Thus, while recognizing the demands of modern culture, the heart singing of the masses has not been overlooked, and so the familiar melody and the more difficult musical composition may be found side by side throughout the work.

Special attention is called to the explanations and suggestions of the musical editors, Messrs. F. H. Torrington and T. C. Jeffers, of the Metropolitan and Central Methodist Churches respectively. These gentlemen stand in the front rank of Canadian musicians, and are eminently qualified to speak with authority in such matters. They have also put the Church under obligation for the valuable professional services they have rendered as well as in bearing their share of responsibility, as members of the Committee, in selecting and allocating the tunes.

In the matter of copyright tunes, great care has been taken to secure consent to use them, where the name of the author or owner was known. In some cases a large price has been paid for the use of tunes, and in others permission has been freely *given*. If in any case acknowledgment has been overlooked, or not correctly made, it is hoped that it may be attributed to inadvertency, for it has been the aim of the Committee to render honour and right where these are due, as also to make such a book that any composer might feel it a compliment to have his tune included therein.

The Committee regrets to say that the use of some few familiar tunes, controlled by an English copyright, has been refused after repeated efforts to secure them, but believes that the tunes substituted will be equally acceptable when well known.

Many thanks are due to Messrs. F. Warrington, J. B. Baxter, and A. E. Huestis for their attention and labours as specialists in church music, and to Messrs. Richard Brown, T. G. Mason, W. H. Pearson, and J. B. Boustead as experienced and accomplished connoisseurs in choir and congregational singing, for their able services upon the Committee; as also to the Rev. John E. Lanceley and the musical editors; to Drs. Dewart, Sutherland, Withrow, Briggs and Lathern, and to many others whose cheering words and valuable assistance have done much to make the book what it is, and what it is hoped it will continue to be,—an important instrument in the spiritual progress of the people as they sing the praises of God in the sanctuary, the school, and the home.

It is now sent forth with many prayers and high hopes for its success in voicing the finer feelings of the human heart under the inspiration of a truly devotional spirit. "I will sing with the spirit, and I will sing with the understanding also."—1 Cor. xiv. 15. "In the midst of the congregation will I sing thy praise."—Heb. ii. 12.

On behalf of the Committee,

John Kay, *Chairman.*
A. C. Crews, *Secretary.*

Toronto, Sept. 1st, 1894.

MUSICAL EDITORS' PREFACE.

The musical editors are not responsible for the selection of the tunes, nor for their union with the respective hymns, beyond their votes as members of the Committee. The editors' task has largely consisted of a careful revision of the harmony, notation and adaptation, and a vigilant correction of the proofs.

In the case of most of the Gospel hymns, of course, much change was neither possible nor desirable. In a number of the old melodies, where changes in the harmony were necessary, they have generally been so managed that no confusion will arise even should the old arrangements at first be sung from memory by congregation or choir. All tunes which were formerly set too high have been transposed to a lower key. The editors have also to explain that the absence of separate stems for the notes of each part, is due to motives of economy, and the desire to bring the price of the book within the reach of all. (See note, page viii.)

It is true that no hymnal has yet appeared which is entirely free from typographical errors, but there is reason for hoping that this book will contain as few mistakes as any.

The hymns should be given to the choir-master at least twenty minutes before the service, or, if possible, on the choir practice night.

It has been suggested that if the pastor were to ask, *at every service*, for hearty congregational singing, much benefit would ensue.

Some definite method for learning new tunes should be adopted, and when a new tune has once been introduced, the pastor should set it down for the second hymn during the next three or four services, and thereafter make use of it at stated intervals until it becomes thoroughly familiar to the congregation.

It is recommended that the pastor and choir-master meet together at least once a month, to discuss their plans regarding the music of the services.

F. H. Torrington.
T. C. Jeffers.

The hearty thanks of the Committee are due to G. F. Chambers, Esq., for the tune "Maidstone"; Sir Arthur Sullivan, for "Bethlehem," "Samuel," and "Noel"; J. Walch, Esq., for "Sawley" and "Eagley"; Sir H. S. Oakeley, for "Abends"; Rev. T. Richard Matthews, B.A., for "Saxby"; Messrs. Burns, Oates & Co., for "St. Luke"; Messrs. Novello, Ewer & Co., for "St. Gertrude," "Barnby," "Supplication," and "Rapture," from the Hymnary; J. Nisbet & Co., for "Lancashire" and "Regent Square"; Arthur Henry Brown, Esq., for "Holy Cross," "St. Anatolius," and "Purleigh," from Hymns Ancient and Modern; Mr. F. G. Dykes, for "St. Agnes," "St. Oswald," and "Lux Benigna," tunes by the late Dr. Dykes; Mr. E. S. Elvey, for "St. Crispin" and "St. George," tunes by the late Sir George Elvey; Rev. F. G. Wesley, for "Aurelia" and "Faith," tunes by the late Dr. S. S. Wesley; Family of the late Dr. Gauntlett, for "Armageddon" and "St George"; Rev. E. W. Bullinger, for "Art Thou Weary"; H. J. E. Holmes, Esq., for "Pater Omnium"; Rev. Dr. Chope, for "St. Bees," "St. Sylvester," and the Chant used to the words "The Strain Upraise"; Dr. E. J. Hopkins, for "Sacrament"; Rev. W. J. Blew, for "St. Alphege," from the Church and Tune Book; T. C. Jeffers, Esq., for original tune "Bloor"; J. B. Baxter, for original tune "Queen Street"; Miss Kate McIntosh, for original tune "Sunset"; J. Masters & Co., for "Ajalon" and "Redhead"; Lady Carberry, for "Ellers"; Rev. G. C. White, for "St. Cross," from Hymns Ancient and Modern; Maynard, Merrill & Co., for "Foster," from the Church Hymnary; A. H. Mann, Esq., for "Lassus."

associations, having been for a century a source of consolation and strength to multitudes of God's people. The Committee, therefore, were unanimous in resolving to leave out no hymn which, by its adaptation to public worship, or private devotion, had vindicated a right to a place in the psalmody of the Church. But they felt that hymns which, after a trial of nearly a hundred years, had revealed little or no adaptation for use, might be safely omitted, to make place for others of greater practical value. Some long hymns have been divided, and others shortened to a moderate length, by omitting imperfect or inferior stanzas. In a few instances, where some solecism, or offensive confusion of figures, marred a beautiful hymn, it was thought better to adopt an appropriate emendation, than to perpetuate a blemish that could be removed without lessening the lyrical or devotional value of the hymn.

"In this book, all that constitutes the richness and attractive beauty of Wesleyan hymnology has been retained; and over three hundred of the choicest modern and ancient hymns have been added. In the selection of new hymns, particular attention has been given to increase the number of those suitable for public worship and special occasions, while having careful regard to lyrical harmony and doctrinal soundness. The unity and completeness of the classification, the number and excellence of the new hymns, and the carefully prepared headings, indicating the subject of every hymn, must greatly enhance the popularity and usefulness of this collection. The Committee, in presenting the result of their labours to the Church, cherish a confident hope that this Hymn-Book, with its rich variety of grand and inspiring songs of praise, will give a new impulse to the worship and devotion of our people; and that it will long continue to be an effective means of guiding sinners to the Saviour, and increasing the faith and love of the thousands who follow Christ under the banners of our Canadian Methodism."

The cordial thanks of the Committee are tendered to the following authors and publishers, for permission to insert hymns of which they possess the copyright:—The Right Rev. the Bishop of Lincoln; the Very Rev. the Dean of Westminster; the Rev. Horatius Bonar, D.D.; the Rev. W. M. Punshon, LL.D.; Miss M. V. G. Havergal; the Rev. J. Ellerton; the Rev. H. Twells, M.A.; James Nisbet & Co.; the Religious Tract Society; and other publishers of volumes from which hymns have been taken. If in any instance, from want of information, hymns have been inserted without formal permission, it is hoped such oversight will be forgiven by the authors or publishers concerned.

CONTENTS.

EDITORIAL NOTE.

Some prejudice may possibly exist against the extensive use of the quarter-note as the unit of value, in place of the older half-note system. Without this change, our hymnal would have been altogether too bulky, and would have lost in clearness and simplicity. It will, of course, be understood that the quarter-note (♩), in $\frac{2}{4}$, $\frac{3}{4}$ and $\frac{4}{4}$ rhythms, is of equal value to the half-note (𝅗𝅥), in $\frac{2}{2}$, $\frac{3}{2}$ and $\frac{4}{2}$ rhythms, and other notes accordingly.

ALPHABETICAL INDEX OF TUNES.

ALPHABETICAL INDEX OF TUNES.

METRICAL INDEX OF TUNES.

L. M.

Tune.	No. of Hymn.
Abends	259, 560, 672, 804, 932
Angels' Song	53, 340, 481
Angelus	153, 481, 712, 858
Bartholdy	482
Beethoven	10, 420
Bloor	809, 981
Crasselius	452
Crucifixion	151
Dresden	8, 103, 677
Duke Street	131, 203, 329, 674, 707, 889
Eden	67, 147, 207, 369, 483, 678, 704, 805
Ernan	101, 266, 633, 761, 806
Eucharist	848
Evening Hymn	808
Federal Street	172, 257, 385, 792, 850
Germany	65, 179, 263, 468, 846
Going Home	763
Grace Church	284, 480
Hamburg	192, 305, 393, 845
Happy Day	807
Hebron	200, 297, 916
Hesperus	261, 382, 646
Home	307, 533, 708, 718
Hursley	79, 644, 804, 849, 927
Intercession	711
Justification	627
Lassus	643, 679, 700, 886
Melcombe	229, 899, 902
Montgomery	847
Morning Hymn	807
Old Hundredth (in G)	7, 60, 669
Old Hundredth (in A)	706
Olives' Brow	485, 764, 852
Pentecost	130, 262
Percy	565
Retreat	384, 810
Rockingham	127, 152, 285, 680, 827
St. Alban	180, 421, 534, 642
St. Crispin	83, 193, 287, 409, 716
St. Cross	288, 532
St. Luke	129
Saxby	191, 327
Stanley Terrace	842
Stirling	55, 884
Symphony	82
Trinity	557
Ward	51, 81, 451, 885
Wareham	104, 367, 418, 668, 694
Warrington	63, 556, 600, 928
Woodworth	526
Worcester	467
Zephyr	230, 530

L. M. D.

Tune.	No. of Hymn.
Fillmore	806
Hayes	71
Wordsworth	72

C. M.

Tune.	No. of Hymn.
Abridge	44, 113, 139, 184, 237, 445, 906
Antioch	41, 111
Arlington	472
Arnold	182, 301, 559, 684
Ashley	847
Azmon	2
Balerma	364
Bedford	93, 136, 562, 911
Belmont	109, 359, 609, 645, 700, 747, 843
Byzantium	107, 518, 564, 912
Coronation	108
Dalehurst	576
Dublin	309, 310
Dundee	165, 290, 701, 840
Eagley	523, 900
Elim	278, 304, 623
Evan	242, 262, 491, 563, 608, 888, 895
Evangelist	471, 490, 890
Foster	646, 650, 751
Hallon	577, 729
Holy Cross	91, 219, 344, 470
Invitation	918, 925
Irish	46, 303, 360, 444, 842
Jerusalem	607
Lydia	610
Manchester	615
Manoah	86, 171, 282, 521
Marlow	820
Martyrdom	241, 289, 427, 514, 841, 913
Mear	235, 236
Miles' Lane	108
Ortonville	818
Peterborough	346, 387, 561, 578, 760
Prescott	923
St. Agnes	88, 110, 166, 492, 519, 601, 702
St. Ann's	90, 239, 446, 690
St. Bernard	48, 134, 566
St. Flavian	112
St. Magnus	713
St. Martin's	363, 424, 636, 689, 699
St. Mary's	304
St. Peter	186, 301, 362, 601, 709, 926
St. Stephen	308, 420, 670, 800
Sawley	6, 221, 276, 381, 390, 516, 815, 844
Serenity	503, 600, 658, 909
Siloam	693, 819
Spohr	167, 300
Tallis' Ordinal	1, 4, 42, 396, 934
Warwick	279, 648
Wiltshire	311, 332, 393, 671, 749
Winchester	728

C. M. D.

Tune.	No. of Hymn.
Bethlehem	138
Ellacombe	606
Noel	141

S. M.

Tune.	No. of Hymn.
Boylston	232, 420, 441, 494, 632, 738, 753, 854
Cambridge	157, 651
Dennis	691, 758
Laington	234, 528, 618
Leeds	159, 683, 754
Rhodes	756
St. George	428, 460, 921
St. Mark	14, 84, 602
St. Michael	240, 403, 895, 920
Sarah	733
Shawmut	917
Shirland	661
Silver Street	12, 938
Supplication	490
Thatcher	248, 459
Westenhanger	526

S. M. D.

Tune.	No. of Hymn.
Armageddon	430, 442, 454, 827
Aurelia	455, 461, 824, 784
Fairfield	401
Leominster	85, 250, 339, 616, 759, 853, 836
Massah	198
Nearer Home	96, 337, 402, 463, 615
Victory	457

6-8s.

Tune.	No. of Hymn.
Admah	269, 370, 587, 613
Barnby	74, 154, 203, 881, 697
Brighton	297, 894, 915, 930
Carey's	265, 488, 572, 640, 887
Confidence	296, 568, 570
Creation	98, 187, 374
Eaton	822, 323
Euphony	181, 638
Giessen	486, 551, 866
Halle	487
Luther's Hymn	16, 379, 484, 781
Middlesex	17, 132, 159, 582, 722
Mozart	73, 422, 575, 641
Pater Omnium	223, 207, 654, 793, 796
Rakem	76, 324, 730
Raleigh	465
St. Petersburg	447, 574, 933
Selena	155, 687, 887
Stella	19, 372, 549, 614, 797, 936

6-8s. (2nd metre.)

Tune.	No. of Hymn.
Lucerne	60, 423, 590
Monmouth	62
Nashville	579, 581, 659

5.5.5.11.

Tune.	No. of Hymn.
Sherbrook	229

5.5.5.11. D.

Tune.	No. of Hymn.
Excelsior	440, 630, 742

5.5.11, 5.5.11.

Tune.	No. of Hymn.
Houghton	163

6.4, 6.4.

Tune.	No. of Hymn.
Dependence	781

6.4, 6.4, 6.6.4.

Tune.	No. of Hymn.
Bethany	399
Devotion	398
Sunset	390

6.5, 6.5, 6.6.6.5.

Tune.	No. of Hymn.
Unity	760

6.6.4, 6.6.4.

Tune.	No. of Hymn.
Solemnity	862

6.6.4, 6.6.6.4.

Tune.	No. of Hymn.
Canada	839, 903
God Save the Queen	904
Italian Hymn	26
Newhaven	25, 203
Olivet	400

6s. (6 lines.)

Tune.	No. of Hymn.
Life	779
Life (new)	779

6s. (8 lines.)

Tune.	No. of Hymn.
Willing	501

6.6, 6.6, 8.8.

Tune.	No. of Hymn.
Caledon	178, 880
Darwell	612, 789
Lenox	123
Millennium	658, 891
Murray	588, 676
Queen Street	23, 121, 211, 737
Samuel	21
Steggall	119, 647, 657, 818
Warsaw	791

6.6, 7.7, 7.7.

Tune.	No. of Hymn.
Bangor	199, 877
Calvary	326
Eccles	69, 125, 538
Irene	626

6.6.8, 6.6.8.

Tune.	No. of Hymn.
Crusaders' Hymn	123

6.6, 8.6, 8.8.

Tune.	No. of Hymn.
Lucca	861

METRICAL INDEX OF TUNES.

METHODIST

HYMN AND TUNE BOOK.

SECTION I.

ADORATION.

TALLIS' ORDINAL. C. M. THOMAS TALLIS.

1 *Praise to the Redeemer.*

1 O FOR a thousand tongues to sing
My great Redeemer's praise,
The glories of my God and King,
The triumphs of his grace!

2 My gracious Master and my God,
Assist me to proclaim,
To spread through all the earth abroad
The honours of thy Name.

3 Jesus! the Name that charms our fears,
That bids our sorrows cease;
'Tis music in the sinner's ears,
'Tis life, and health, and peace.

4 He breaks the power of cancelled sin,
He sets the prisoner free;
His blood can make the foulest clean,
His blood availed for *me*.

5 He speaks, and, listening to his voice,
New life the dead receive;
The mournful, broken hearts rejoice;
The humble poor believe.

6 Hear him, ye deaf; his praise, ye dumb,
Your loosened tongues employ;
Ye blind, behold your Saviour come;
And leap, ye lame, for joy.

7 Look unto him, ye nations; own
Your God, ye fallen race;
Look, and be saved through faith alone,
Be justified by grace.

8 See all your sins on Jesus laid:
The Lamb of God was slain,
His soul was once an offering made
For every soul of man.

—Charles Wesley.

AZMON. C.M. CARL GOTTHELF GLASER, ARR. BY LOWELL MASON.

2 *Creation and Redemption.*

1 FATHER, how wide thy glory shines!
How high thy wonders rise!
Known through the earth by thousand signs,
By thousands through the skies.

2 Those mighty orbs proclaim thy power,
Their motions speak thy skill;
And on the wings of every hour
We read thy patience still.

3 Part of thy name divinely stands
On all thy creatures writ;
They show the labour of thy hands,
Or impress of thy feet.

4 But when we view thy strange design
To save rebellious worms,
Where justice and compassion join
In their divinest forms;

5 Here the whole Deity is known,
Nor dares a creature guess
Which of the glories brightest shone,
The justice, or the grace.

6 Now the full glories of the Lamb
Adorn the heavenly plains;
Bright seraphs learn Immanuel's name,
And try their choicest strains.

7 O may I bear some humble part
In that immortal song!
Wonder and joy shall tune my heart,
And love command my tongue.

—*Isaac Watts.*

3 *One God in Three Persons.*

1 HAIL! Father, Son, and Holy Ghost,
One God, in Persons Three!
Of thee we make our joyful boast,
Our songs we make of thee.

2 Thou neither canst be felt nor seen;
Thou art a Spirit pure;
Thou from eternity hast been,
And always shalt endure.

3 Present alike in every place,
Thy Godhead we adore;
Beyond the bounds of time and space,
Thou dwell'st for evermore.

4 In wisdom infinite thou art,
Thine eye doth all things see;
And every thought of every heart
Is fully known to thee.

5 Thou lov'st whate'er thy hands have made;
Thy goodness we rehearse,
In shining characters displayed
Throughout our universe.

6 Mercy, with love and endless grace,
O'er all thy works doth reign;
But mostly thou delight'st to bless
Thy favourite creature, Man.

7 Wherefore let every creature give
To thee the praise designed;
But chiefly, Lord, the thanks receive,
The hearts of all mankind.

—*Charles Wesley.*

TALLIS' ORDINAL. C.M. — Thomas Tallis, 1561.

4 *Angels and men praising the Trinity.*

1 A thousand oracles divine
Their common beams unite,
That sinners may with angels join
To worship God aright:

2 To praise a Trinity adored
By all the hosts above,
And one thrice-holy God and Lord
Through endless ages love.

3 Triumphant host! they never cease
To laud and magnify
The Triune God of holiness,
Whose glory fills the sky.

4 Whose glory to this earth extends,
When God himself imparts,
And the whole Trinity descends
Into our faithful hearts.

5 By faith the upper choir we meet;
And challenge them to sing
Jehovah on his shining seat,
Our Maker and our King.

6 But God made flesh is wholly ours,
And asks our nobler strain;
The Father of celestial powers,
The Friend of earth-born man.

7 Ye seraphs nearest to the throne,
With rapturous amaze
On us, poor ransomed worms, look down
For heaven's superior praise:

8 The King, whose glorious face ye see,
For us his crown resigned;
The fulness of the Deity,
He died for all mankind!

—*Charles Wesley.*

5 *Adoration of the Trinity.*

1 Hail! holy, holy, holy Lord!
Whom One in Three we know;
By all thy heavenly host adored,
By all thy church below.

2 One undivided Trinity
With triumph we proclaim;
Thy universe is full of thee,
And speaks thy glorious name.

3 Thee, Holy Father, we confess;
Thee, Holy Son, adore;
Thee, Spirit of Truth and Holiness,
We worship evermore.

4 Three Persons equally divine
We magnify and love;
And both the choirs ere long shall join,
To sing thy praise above.

5 Hail! holy, holy, holy Lord,
(Our heavenly song shall be,)
Supreme, essential One, adored
In co-eternal Three!

—*Charles Wesley.*

SAWLEY. C.M. — J. Walch.

6 *Blessing and light from the Trinity.*

1 Jehovah, God the Father, bless,
And thy own work defend;
With mercy's outstretched arms embrace
And keep us to the end.

2 Preserve the creatures of thy love,
By providential care
Conducted to the realms above,
To sing thy goodness there.

3 Jehovah, God the Son, reveal
The brightness of thy face;
And all thy pardoned people fill
With plenitude of grace.

4 Shine forth with all the Deity,
Which dwells in thee alone;
And lift us up, thy face to see
On thy eternal throne.

5 Jehovah, God the Spirit, shine,
Father and Son to show;
With bliss ineffable, divine,
Our ravished hearts o'erflow.

6 Sure earnest of that happiness
Which human hope transcends,
Be thou our everlasting peace,
When grace in glory ends.

—*Charles Wesley.*

OLD HUNDREDTH. L.M. G. FRANC, 1543.

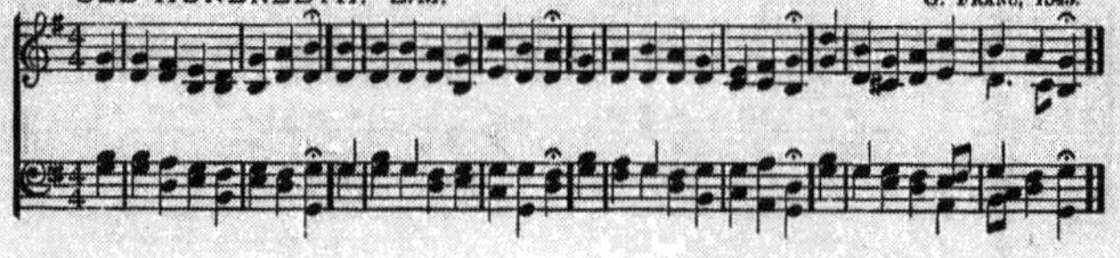

7

Psalm c.

1 BEFORE Jehovah's awful throne,
Ye nations bow with sacred joy;
Know that the Lord is God alone,
He can create, and he destroy.

2 His sovereign power, without our aid,
Made us of clay, and formed us men;
And when like wandering sheep we strayed,
He brought us to his fold again.

3 We'll crowd thy gates with thankful songs,
High as the heavens our voices raise;
And earth, with her ten thousand tongues,
Shall fill thy courts with sounding praise.

4 Wide as the world is thy command;
Vast as eternity thy love;
Firm as a rock thy truth shall stand,
When rolling years shall cease to move.

—*Isaac Watts.*

DRESDEN. L.M. FROM MOZART.

8

Adoration of the Divine Majesty.

1 ETERNAL Power, whose high abode
Becomes the grandeur of a God,
Infinite lengths beyond the bounds
Where stars revolve their little rounds!

2 Thee, while the first archangel sings,
He hides his face behind his wings;
And ranks of shining thrones around
Fall worshipping, and spread the ground.

3 Lord, what shall earth and ashes do?
We would adore our Maker too!
From sin and dust to thee we cry,
The Great, the Holy, and the High.

4 Earth from afar hath heard thy fame,
And worms have learned to lisp thy name:
But, O! the glories of thy mind
Leave all our soaring thoughts behind!

5 God is in heaven, and men below:
Be short our tunes, our words be few!
A solemn reverence checks our songs,
And praise sits silent on our tongues.

—*Isaac Watts.*

G. Franc, 1543.

thankful songs,
voices raise;
ousand tongues,
sounding praise.

ommand;
e;
iall stand,
cease to move.

—*Isaac Watts.*

From Mozart.

e cry,
e High.

thy fame,
lisp thy name:
ind
ts behind!

elow:
ls be few!
ur songs,
tongues.

—*Isaac Watts.*

TUNE: OLD HUNDREDTH. L.M. (See Hymn 7.)

9

Psalm cxvii.

1 From all that dwell below the skies
Let the Creator's praise arise;
Let the Redeemer's name be sung,
Through every land, by every tongue.

2 Eternal are thy mercies, Lord;
Eterna' truth attends thy word:
Thy praise shall sound from shore to shore,
Till suns shall rise and set no more.

3 Your lofty themes, ye mortals, bring;
In songs of praise divinely sing;
The great salvation loud proclaim,
And shout for joy the Saviour's name.

4 Praise God, from whom all blessings flow;
Praise him, all creatures here below;
Praise him above, ye heavenly host;
Praise Father, Son, and Holy Ghost!

—*Isaac Watts.*

BEETHOVEN. L.M.

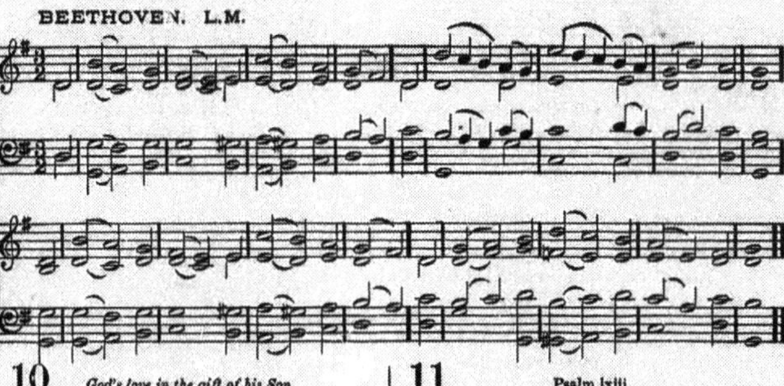

10

God's love in the gift of his Son.

1 Father, whose everlasting Love
Thy only Son for sinners gave,
Whose grace to all did freely move,
And sent him down the world to save:

2 Help us thy mercy to extol,
Immense, unfathomed, unconfined;
To praise the Lamb who died for all,
The general Saviour of mankind.

3 Thy undistinguishing regard
Was cast on Adam's fallen race;
For all thou hast in Christ prepared
Sufficient, sovereign, saving grace.

4 The world he suffered to redeem;
For all he hath atonement made;
For those that will not come to him,
The ransom of his life was paid.

5 Arise, O God! maintain thy cause;
The fulness of the Gentiles call;
Lift up the standard of thy cross,
And all shall own thou diedst for all.

—*Charles Wesley.*

11

Psalm lxiii.

1 Great God, indulge my humble claim,
Be thou my hope, my joy, my rest;
The glories that compose thy name
Stand all engaged to make me blest.

2 Thou great and good, thou just and wise,
Thou art my Father and my God;
And I am thine, by sacred ties,
Thy son, thy servant, bought with blood.

3 With fainting heart, and lifted hands,
For thee I long, to thee I look,
As travellers in thirsty lands
Pant for the cooling water-brook.

4 Should I from thee, my God, remove,
Life could no lasting bliss afford:
My joy, the sense of pardoning love;
My guard, the presence of my Lord.

5 I'll lift my hands, I'll raise my voice,
While I have breath to pray or praise;
This work shall make my heart rejoice,
And fill the circle of my days.

—*Isaac Watts.*

SILVER STREET. S.M. ISAAC SMITH.

12

A call to worship.

1 COME, sound his praise abroad,
And hymns of glory sing;
Jehovah is the sovereign God,
The universal King.

2 He formed the deeps unknown;
He gave the seas their bound;
The watery worlds are all his own,
And all the solid ground.

3 Come, worship at his throne;
Come, bow before the Lord;
We are his works, and not our own;
He formed us by his word.

4 To-day attend his voice,
Nor dare provoke his rod;
Come, as the people of his choice,
And own your gracious God.

—*Isaac Watts.*

13

Trust in God our Saviour.

1 To God the only wise,
Our Saviour and our King,
Let all the saints below the skies
Their humble praises bring.

2 'Tis his almighty love,
His counsel and his care,
Preserve us safe from sin and death,
And every hurtful snare.

3 He will present our souls,
Unblemished and complete,
Before the glory of his face,
With joys divinely great.

4 Then all the chosen seed
Shall meet around the throne,
Shall bless the conduct of his grace,
And make his wonders known.

5 To our Redeemer God
Wisdom and power belongs,
Immortal crowns of majesty,
And everlasting songs.

—*Isaac Watts.*

ST. MARK. S.M. GEO. KINGSLEY.

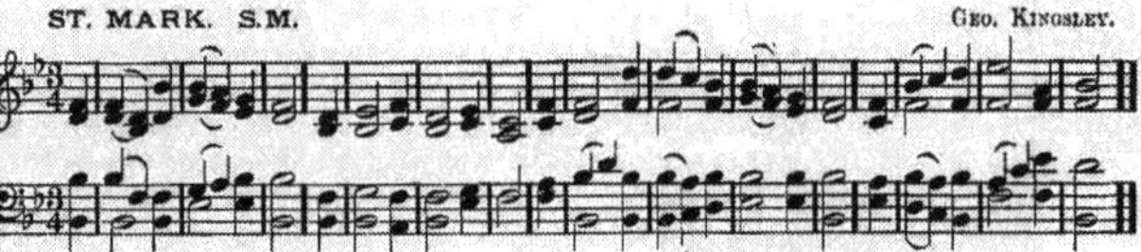

14

Song of Moses and the Lamb.

1 AWAKE, and sing the song
Of Moses and the Lamb;
Wake every heart and every tongue,
To praise the Saviour's name.

2 Sing of his dying love;
Sing of his rising power;
Sing how he intercedes above
For those whose sins he bore.

3 Sing on your heavenly way,
Ye ransomed sinners, sing;
Sing on, rejoicing every day
In Christ, the eternal King.

4 Soon shall ye hear him say,
"Ye blessed children, come;"
Soon will he call you hence away
To your eternal home.

5 There shall our raptured tongue
His endless praise proclaim,
And sweeter voices swell the song
Of Moses and the Lamb.

—*W. Hammond.*

TUNE: ST. MARK. S.M. (See Hymn 14.)

15

Creating love and redeeming grace.

1 Father, in whom we live,
In whom we are, and move,
The glory, power, and praise receive
Of thy creating love.

2 Let all the angel throng
Give thanks to God on high;
While earth repeats the joyful song,
And echoes through the sky.

3 Incarnate Deity,
Let all the ransomed race
Render in thanks their lives to thee,
For thy redeeming grace.

4 The grace to sinners showed,
Ye heavenly choirs, proclaim,
And cry, "Salvation to our God,
Salvation to the Lamb!"

5 Spirit of Holiness,
Let all thy saints adore
Thy sacred energy, and bless
Thy heart-renewing power.

6 Not angel tongues can tell
Thy love's ecstatic height,
The glorious joy unspeakable,
The beatific sight.

7 Eternal, Triune Lord!
Let all the hosts above,
Let all the sons of men, record
And dwell upon thy love

8 When heaven and earth are fled
Before thy glorious face,
Sing all the saints thy love hath made
Thine everlasting praise!

—Charles Wesley.

LUTHER'S HYMN. 6-8s. Martin Luther.

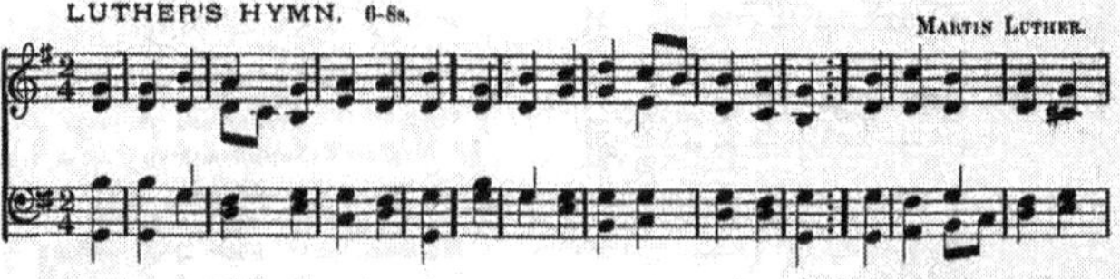

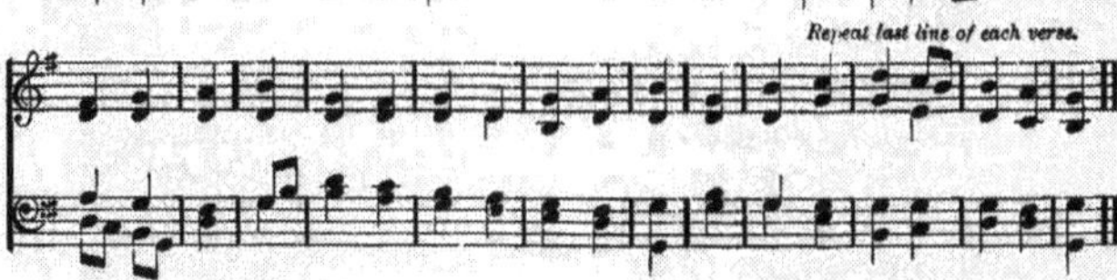
Repeat last line of each verse.

16

Genesis xxviii. 16, 17.

1 Lo! God is here! let us adore,
And own how dreadful is this place!
Let all within us feel his power,
And silent bow before his face;
Who know his power, his grace who prove,
Serve him with awe, with reverence love.

2 Lo! God is here! him day and night
United choirs of angels sing;
To him, enthroned above all height,
Heaven's host their noblest praises bring:
Disdain not, Lord, our meaner song,
Who praise thee with a stammering tongue.

3 Gladly the toys of earth we leave,
Wealth, pleasure, fame, for thee alone;
To thee our will, soul, flesh, we give;
O take, O seal them for thine own!
Thou art the God, thou art the Lord;
Be thou by all thy works adored.

4 Being of beings! may our praise
Thy courts with grateful fragrance fill;
Still may we stand before thy face,
Still hear and do thy sovereign will:
To thee may all our thoughts arise,
Ceaseless, accepted sacrifice.

5 As flowers their opening leaves display,
And glad drink in the solar fire,
So may we catch thy every ray,
So may thy influence us inspire;
Thou Beam of the eternal Beam,
Thou purging Fire, thou quickening Flame.

—From Tersteegen.
Translated by John Wesley.

MIDDLESEX. 6-8s.

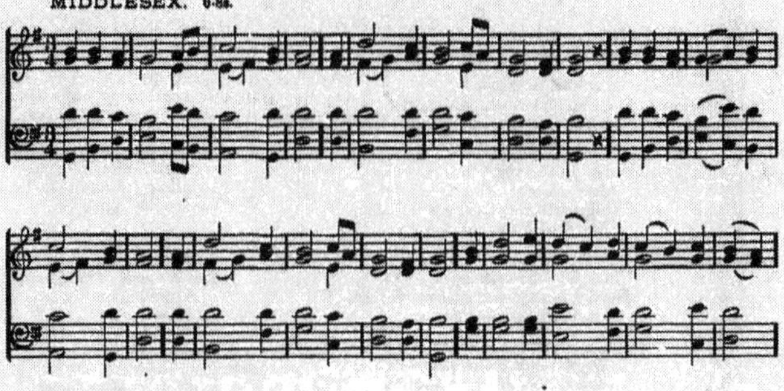

17

Psalm xvii.

1 My heart is fixed, O God, my heart
Is fixed to triumph in thy grace:
(Awake, my lute, and bear a part:)
My glory is to sing thy praise,
Till all thy nature I partake,
And bright in all thine image wake.

2 Thee will I praise among thine own;
Thee will I to the world extol,
And make thy truth and goodness known:
Thy goodness, Lord, is over all;
Thy truth and grace the heavens transcend;
Thy faithful mercies never end.

3 Be thou exalted, Lord, above
The highest name in earth or heaven;
Let angels sing thy glorious love,
And bless the Name to sinners given;
All earth and heaven their King proclaim;
Bow every knee to Jesus' name.

—*Charles Wesley.*

18

Psalm xlv.

1 My heart is full of Christ, and longs
Its glorious matter to declare;
Of him I make my loftier songs,
I cannot from his praise forbear;
My ready tongue makes haste to sing
The glories of my heavenly King.

2 Fairer than all the earth-born race,
Perfect in comeliness thou art;
Replenished are thy lips with grace,
And full of love thy tender heart:
God ever blest! we bow the knee,
And own all fulness dwells in thee.

3 Gird on thy thigh the Spirit's sword,
And take to thee thy power divine;
Stir up thy strength, almighty Lord,
All power and majesty are thine:
Assert thy worship and renown;
O all-redeeming God, come down!

4 Come, and maintain thy righteous cause,
And let thy glorious toil succeed;
Dispread the victory of thy cross,
Ride on, and prosper in thy deed;
Through earth triumphantly ride on,
And reign in every heart alone.

—*Charles Wesley.*

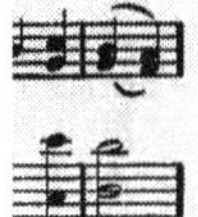

STELLA. 6-8s. From "Crown of Jesus."

19

Prayer to Jehovah in Three Persons.

1 Come, Father, Son, and Holy Ghost,
Whom one all-perfect God we own,
Restorer of thine image lost,
Thy various offices make known;
Display, our fallen souls to raise,
Thy whole economy of grace.

2 Jehovah in Three Persons, come,
And draw, and sprinkle us, and seal,
Poor, guilty, dying worms, in whom
Thou dost eternal life reveal;
The knowledge of thyself bestow,
And all thy glorious goodness show.

3 Soon as our pardoned hearts believe
That thou art pure, essential love,
The proof we in ourselves receive
Of the Three Witnesses above;
Sure, as the saints around thy throne,
That Father, Word, and Spirit, are One.

4 O that we now, in love renewed,
Might blameless in thy sight appear:
Wake we in thy similitude,
Stamped with the Triune character:
Flesh, spirit, soul, to thee resign;
And live and die entirely thine!

—*Charles Wesley.*

20

Psalm cxlvi.

1 My soul, inspired with sacred love,
The Lord thy God delight to praise;
His gifts I will for him improve,
To him devote my happy days;
To him my thanks and praises give,
And only for his glory live.

2 Long as my God shall lend me breath,
My every pulse shall beat for him;
And when my voice is lost in death,
My spirit shall resume the theme.
The gracious theme, for ever new,
Through all eternity pursue.

3 He, then, is blest, and only he,
Whose hope is in the Lord his God;
Who can to him for succour flee,
That spread the earth and heaven abroad;
That still the universe sustains,
And Lord of his creation reigns.

4 The Lord thy God, O Sion, reigns,
Supreme in mercy as in power,
The endless theme of heavenly strains,
When time and death shall be no more:
And all eternity shall prove
Too short to utter all his love.

—*Charles Wesley.*

SAMUEL. 6.6, 6.6, 8.8. SIR ARTHUR SULLIVAN.

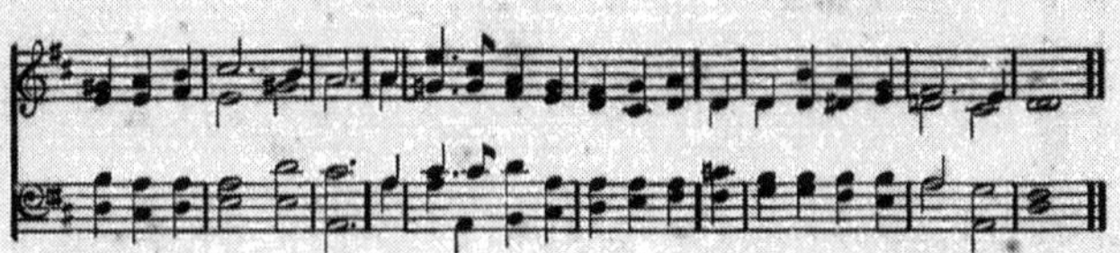

21 *Song of Praise to the Trinity.*

1 WE give immortal praise
  To God the Father's love,
For all our comforts here,
  And better hopes above;
He sent his own eternal Son,
To die for sins that man had done.

2 To God the Son belongs
  Immortal glory too,
Who bought us with his blood
  From everlasting woe:
And now he lives, and now he reigns,
And sees the fruit of all his pains.

3 To God the Spirit's name
  Immortal worship give,
Whose new-creating power
  Makes the dead sinner live;
His work completes the great design,
And fills the soul with joy divine.

4 Almighty God, to thee
  Be endless honours done;
The undivided Three,
  And the mysterious One:
Where reason fails with all her powers,
There faith prevails, and love adores.

—*Isaac Watts.*

22 *The greatness and condescension of God.*

1 THE Lord Jehovah reigns,
  His throne is built on high;
The garments he assumes
  Are light and majesty;
His glories shine with beams so bright,
No mortal eye can bear the sight.

2 The thunders of his hand
  Keep the wide world in awe;
His wrath and justice stand
  To guard his holy law;
And where his love resolves to bless,
His truth confirms and seals the grace.

3 Through all his mighty works
  Amazing wisdom shines;
Confounds the powers of hell,
  And breaks their dark designs;
Strong is his arm and shall fulfil
His great decrees and sovereign will.

4 And will this sovereign King
  Of glory condescend?
And will he write his name,
  My Father and my Friend?
I love his name, I love his word:
Join all my powers to praise the Lord!

—*Isaac Watts.*

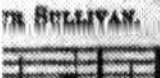

QUEEN STREET. 66,66,88. J. B. BAXTER.

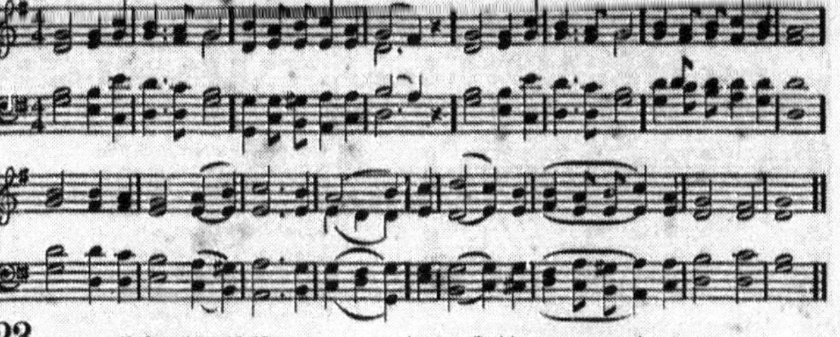

23

Psalm cxlviii. 12, 13.

1 YOUNG men and maidens, raise
 Your tuneful voices high;
Old men and children, praise
 The Lord of earth and sky;
Him Three in One, and One in Three,
Extol to all eternity.

2 The universal King
 Let all the world proclaim;
Let every creature sing
 His attributes and name!
Him Three in One, and One in Three,
Extol to all eternity.

3 In his great name alone
 All excellencies meet,
Who sits upon the throne,
 And shall forever sit:
Him Three in One, and One in Three,
Extol to all eternity.

4 Glory to God belongs;
 Glory to God be given,
Above the noblest songs
 Of all in earth or heaven!
Him Three in One, and One in Three,
Extol to all eternity.

—*Charles Wesley.*

HEBER. 11,12,12,10. A. STONE.

24

Praise to the blessed Trinity.

1 HOLY, holy, holy, Lord God Almighty!
Gratefully adoring our song shall rise to thee:
Holy, holy, holy, merciful and mighty,
God in Three Persons, blessed Trinity!

2 Holy, holy, holy! all the saints adore thee,
Casting down their golden crowns around the glassy sea;
Cherubim and Seraphim falling down before thee,
Who wert, and art, and evermore shall be.

3 Holy, holy, holy! though the darkness hide thee,
Though the eye of sinful man thy glory may not see,
Only thou art holy: there is none beside thee
Perfect in power, in love, and purity!

4 Holy, holy, holy, Lord God Almighty!
All thy works shall praise thy name, in earth and sky and sea:
Holy, holy, holy, merciful and mighty,
God in Three Persons, blessed Trinity!

—*Bishop Heber.*

NEWHAVEN. 6.6.4, 6.6.6.4. Dr. T. Hastings.

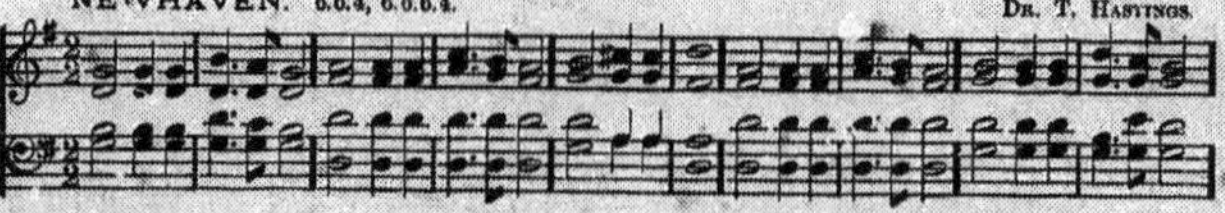

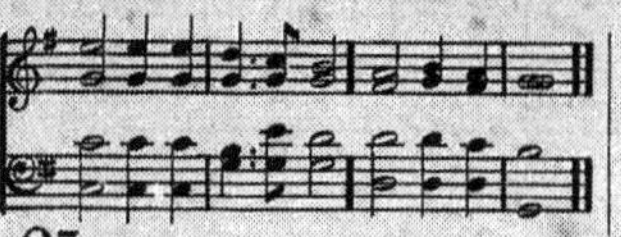

25 *"And God said, Let there be light."*

1 Thou, whose almighty Word
Chaos and darkness heard,
And took their flight,
Hear us, we humbly pray,
And where the gospel day
Sheds not its glorious ray,
Let there be light!

2 Thou, who didst come to bring
On thy redeeming wing
Healing and sight,
Health to the sick in mind,
Sight to the inly blind,—
O now to all mankind
Let there be light!

3 Spirit of truth and love,
Life-giving, holy Dove,
Speed forth thy flight;
Move on the waters' face,
Spreading the beams of grace,
And in earth's darkest place
Let there be light!

4 Blessed and holy Three,
Glorious Trinity,
Grace, love, and might,
Boundless as ocean's tide,
Rolling in fullest pride,
Through the world far and wide,
Let there be light!

—*J. Marriott.*

ITALIAN HYMN. 6.6.4, 6.6.6.4. F. Giardini.

26 *"Worthy is the Lamb that was slain."*

1 Glory to God on high!
Let heaven and earth reply,
Praise ye his name!
Angels, his love adore,
Who all our sorrows bore;
And saints, cry evermore,
Worthy the Lamb!

2 All they around the throne
Cheerfully join in one,
Praising his name:
We who have felt his blood
Sealing our peace with God,
Sound his high praise abroad;
Worthy the Lamb!

3 Join, all the ransomed race,
Our Lord and God to bless;
Praise ye his name!
In him we will rejoice,
Making a cheerful noise,
Shouting with heart and voice,
Worthy the Lamb!

4 Though we must change our place,
Yet shall we never cease
Praising his name:
To him we'll tribute bring,
Hail him our gracious King,
And without ceasing sing,
Worthy the Lamb!

—*Charles Wesley.*

TUNE: ITALIAN HYMN. 6.6.4, 6.6.6.4. (SEE HYMN 26.)

27

Invocation of the Trinity.

1 COME, thou almighty King,
Help us thy name to sing,
Help us to praise:
Father all-glorious,
O'er all victorious,
Come, and reign over us,
Ancient of days!

2 Come, thou incarnate Word,
Gird on thy mighty sword,
Our prayer attend:
Come, and thy people bless,
And give thy word success:
Spirit of Holiness,
On us descend!

3 Come, holy Comforter,
Thy sacred witness bear
In this glad hour:
Thou who almighty art,
Now rule in every heart,
And ne'er from us depart,
Spirit of power!

4 To thee, great One and Three,
Eternal praises be,
Hence, evermore:
Thy sovereign majesty
May we in glory see,
And to eternity
Love and adore!

—*Charles Wesley.*

ST. THOMAS. 8.7, 8.7, 4.7.

28

Psalm xcix.

1 GOD the Lord is King; before him,
Earth, with all thy nations, wait!
Where the cherubim adore him,
Sitteth he in royal state;
He is holy,
Blessed, only Potentate!

2 God the Lord is King of glory,
Zion, tell the world his fame;
Ancient Israel, the story
Of his faithfulness proclaim;
He is holy,
Holy is his awful name.

3 In old times when dangers darkened,
When, invoked by priest and seer,
To his people's cry he hearkened,
Answered them in all their fear;
He is holy,
As they called, they found him near.

4 Laws divine to them were spoken
From the pillar of the cloud;
Sacred precepts, quickly broken:
Fiercely then his vengeance flowed;
He is holy,
To the dust their hearts were bowed.

5 But their Father God forgave them,
When they sought his face once more;
Ever ready was to save them,
Tenderly did he restore;
He is holy,
We too will his grace implore.

6 God in Christ is all-forgiving,
Waits his promise to fulfil;
Come, exalt him all the living,
Come, ascend his holy hill;
He is holy,
Worship at his holy hill.

—*G. Rawson.*

HOUGHTON. 10,10,11,11. Dr. Gauntlett.

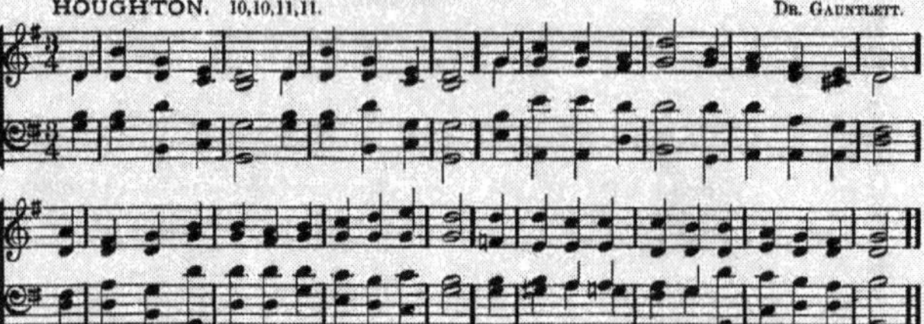

29

The glory of the heavenly King.

1 O worship the King all glorious above!
O gratefully sing his power and his love!
Our Shield and Defender, the Ancient of days,
Pavilioned in splendour, and girded with praise.

2 O tell of his might, O sing of his grace,
Whose robe is the light, whose canopy space;
His chariots of wrath the deep thunder-clouds form;
And dark is his path on the wings of the storm.

3 Thy bountiful care, what tongue can recite?
It breathes in the air, it shines in the light,
It streams from the hills, it descends to the plain,
And sweetly distils in the dew and the rain.

4 Frail children of dust, and feeble as frail,
In thee do we trust, nor find thee to fail:
Thy mercies, how tender, how firm to the end,
Our Maker, Defender, Redeemer, and Friend!

—*Sir R. Grant.*

TANTUM ERGO. 8.7, 8.7, 8.7, 8.7.

30

Psalm lxvi.

1 Earth, with all thy thousand voices,
Praise in songs the eternal King;
Praise his name, whose praise rejoices
Ears that hear, and tongues that sing.
Lord, from each far-peopled dwelling
Earth shall raise the glad acclaim;
All shall kneel, thy greatness telling,
Sing thy praise and bless thy name.

2 Come and hear the wondrous story,
How our mighty God of old,
In the terrors of his glory,
Back the flowing billows rolled:
Walked within the threatening waters,
Free we passed the upright wave;
Then was joy to Israel's daughters,
Loud they sang his power to save.

3 Bless the Lord, who ever liveth;
Sound his praise through every land,
Who our dying souls reviveth,
By whose arm upheld we stand.
Now upon this cheerful morrow
We thine altars will adorn,
And the gifts we vowed in sorrow
Pay on joy's returning morn.

4 Come, each faithful soul, who fearest
Him who fills the eternal throne:
Hear, rejoicing while thou hearest,
What our God for us hath done:
When we made our supplication,
When our voice in prayer was strong,
Then we found his glad salvation;
And his mercy fills our tongue.

—*E. Churton.*

can recite?
the light,
scends to the

d the rain.
as frail,
to fail:
m to the end,
and Friend!
—*Sir R. Grant.*

ry land,

nd.

ow

earest
one:
est,
ne:

s strong,
n;
e.
E. Churton.

TUNE: TANTUM ERGO. 8.7, 8.7, 8.7, 8.7. (SEE HYMN 30.)

31

Psalm cxlviii.

1 PRAISE the Lord! ye heavens, adore him;
Praise him, angels, in the height;
Sun and moon, rejoice before him;
Praise him, all ye stars of light;
Praise the Lord! for he hath spoken,
Worlds his mighty voice obeyed;
Laws that never shall be broken,
For their guidance he hath made.

2 Praise the Lord! for he is glorious;
Never shall his promise fail;
God hath made his saints victorious;
Sin and death shall not prevail.
Praise the God of our salvation!
Hosts on high, his power proclaim;
Heaven and earth, and all creation,
Laud and magnify his name.

—*J. Kempthorne.*

32

Psalm xcvi.

1 RAISE the psalm: let earth adoring,
Through each kindred, tribe, and tongue,
To her God his praise restoring,
Raise the new accordant song.
Bless his name, each farthest nation;
Sing his praise, his truth display:
Tell anew his high salvation
With each new return of day.

2 Tell it out beneath the heaven,
To each kindred, tribe, and tongue,
Tell it out from morn till even
In your unexhausted song:
Tell that God for ever reigneth,
He, who set the world so fast,
He, who still its state sustaineth
Till the day of doom to last.

3 Yea, the far-resounding ocean
Shall its thousand voices raise,
All its waves in glad commotion
Chant the fulness of his praise.
When the Judge, to earth descending,
Righteous judgment shall ordain,
Fraud and wrong shall then have ending,
Truth, immortal truth, shall reign.

—*E. Churton.*

BENEVENTO. 8.7's. S. WEBBE.

33

Praise to the Triune God.

1 HOLY, holy, holy Lord,
God the Father, and the Word,
God the Comforter, receive
Blessings more than we can give!
Mixed with those beyond the sky,
Chanters to the Lord Most High,
We our hearts and voices raise,
Echoing thy eternal praise.

2 One, inexplicably Three,
Three, in simplest Unity,
God, incline thy gracious ear,
Us, thy lisping creatures, hear!
Thee while man, the earth-born, sings,
Angels shrink within their wings;
Prostrate seraphim above
Breathe unutterable love.

3 Happy they who never rest,
With thy heavenly presence blest!
They the heights of glory see,
Sound the depths of Deity.
Fain with them our souls would vie,
Sink as low, and mount as high;
Fall o'erwhelmed with love, or soar,
Shout, or silently adore.

—*Charles Wesley.*

JUDAH. 7.7, 7.7. J. V. WATTS.

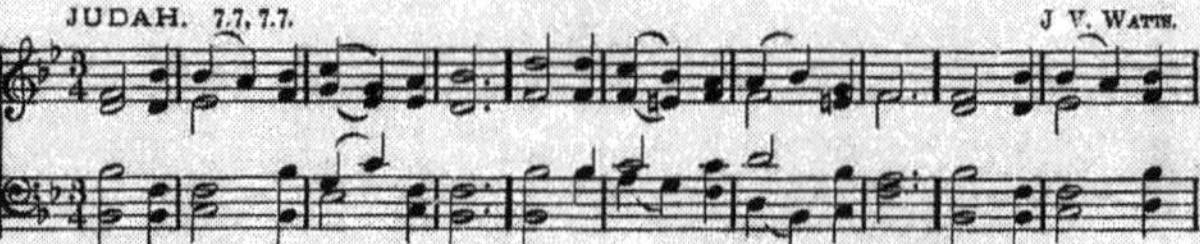

34 *Praise and prayer to the Trinity.*

1 GLORY be to God on high,
God whose glory fills the sky;
Peace on earth to man forgiven,
Man, the well-beloved of heaven.

2 Sovereign Father, heavenly King,
Thee we now presume to sing;
Glad, thine attributes confess,
Glorious all, and numberless.

3 Hail, by all thy works adored!
Hail, the everlasting Lord!
Thee with thankful hearts we prove
God of power, and God of love.

4 Christ our Lord and God we own,
Christ, the Father's only Son,
Lamb of God for sinners slain,
Saviour of offending man.

5 Bow thine ear, in mercy bow,
Hear, the world's atonement, thou!
Jesus, in thy name we pray,
Take, O take our sins away!

6 Hear, for thou, O Christ, alone,
Art with God the Father one,
One the Holy Ghost with thee,
One supreme, eternal THREE.

—*Charles Wesley.*

PURLEIGH. 8.8.6, 8.8.6. A. H. BROWN.

35 *The Omniscience of God.*

1 O THAT I could, in every place,
By faith behold Jehovah's face;
My strict Observer see
Present, my heart and reins to try;
And feel the influence of his eye
For ever fixed on me!

2 Discerning thee, my Saviour, stand
My Advocate at God's right hand,
I never shall remove;
I cannot fall, upheld by thee,
Or sin against the majesty
Of omnipresent Love.

3 Now, Saviour, now appear, appear,
And let me always see thee near,
And know as I am known:
My spirit to thyself unite,
And bear me through a sea of light
To that eternal throne.

—*Charles Wesley.*

36 *God's glorious presence.*

1 THOU God of power, thou God of love,
Whose glory fills the realms above,
Whose praise archangels sing,
And veil their faces while they cry,
"Thrice holy," to their God most high,
"Thrice holy," to their King;

2 Thee as our God we too would claim,
And bless the Saviour's precious name,
Through whom this grace is given:
He bore the curse to sinners due;
He forms their ruined souls anew,
And makes them heirs of heaven.

3 The veil that hides thy glory rend,
And here in saving power descend,
And fix thy blest abode;
Here to our hearts thyself reveal,
And let each waiting spirit feel
The presence of our God.

—*J. Walker.*

TUNE: PURLEIGH. 8.8.6, 8.8.6. (See Hymn 35.)

37

Praise for Divine goodness.

1 O THOU to whom archangels raise
A ceaseless song of perfect praise,
  Yet tremble as they sing;
To us incline thy gracious ear,
And while, with reverence, we draw near,
  Accept the praise we bring.

2 In vain with all the angel choir,
The ransomed hosts of heaven aspire,
  Thy glory to proclaim;
How then shall we approach thy throne?
How make thy countless mercies known,
  Or sing thine awful Name?

3 Thy love alone our stay hath been,
In every dark and changing scene
  Throughout the circling year;
Preserved by thine almighty hand,
Again before thy face we stand,
  And sing thy goodness here.

4 Father, for Jesus' sake receive
The praise which now we gladly give,
  Though with a stammering tongue;
Grant us at length to see thy face,
And join with all the ransomed race
  In heaven's eternal song.

LEONI. 6.6.8.4, 6.6.8.4. ANCIENT JEWISH MELODY.

38

"I am thy shield, and thy exceeding great reward."

1 THE God of Abraham praise,
  Who reigns enthroned above,
Ancient of everlasting days,
  And God of Love:
Jehovah, Great I AM,
  By earth and heaven confest;
I bow and bless the sacred Name,
  For ever blest.

2 The God of Abraham praise,
  At whose supreme command
From earth I rise, and seek the joys
  At his right hand:
I all on earth forsake,
  Its wisdom, fame and power;
And him my only portion make,
  My shield and tower.

3 The God of Abraham praise,
  Whose all-sufficient grace
Shall guide me all my happy days
  In all my ways.
He calls a worm his friend,
  He calls himself my God,
And he shall save me to the end,
  Through Jesus' blood.

4 He by himself hath sworn,
  I on his oath depend;
I shall, on eagle's wings upborne,
  To heaven ascend:
I shall behold his face,
  I shall his power adore,
And sing the wonders of his grace
  For evermore.

—*T. Olivers.*

HARVINGTON. 6.6.8.4, 6.6.8.4. A. E. KETTLE.

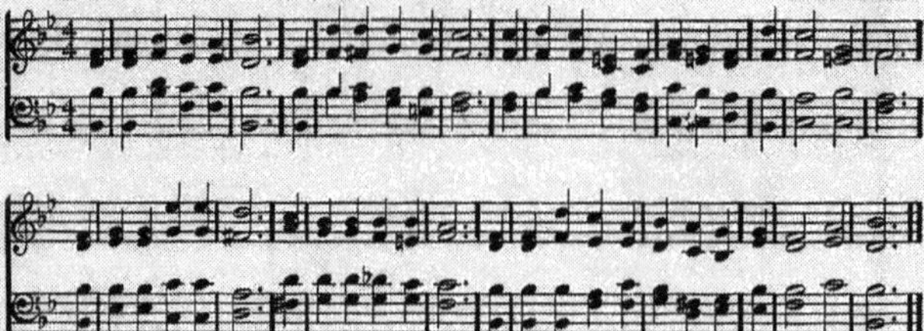

39

SECOND PART.

1 Though nature's strength decay,
And earth and hell withstand,
To Canaan's bounds I urge my way,
At his command.
The watery deep I pass,
With Jesus in my view;
And through the howling wilderness
My way pursue.

2 The goodly land I see,
With peace and plenty blest;
A land of sacred liberty,
And endless rest.
There milk and honey flow,
And oil and wine abound,
And trees of life for ever grow,
With mercy crowned.

3 There dwells the Lord our King,
The Lord our Righteousness,
Triumphant o'er the world and sin,
The Prince of Peace;
On Sion's sacred height
His kingdom still maintains;
And glorious with his saints in light
For ever reigns.

4 He keeps his own secure,
He guards them by his side,
Arrays in garments white and pure
His spotless bride:
With streams of sacred bliss,
With groves of living joys,
With all the fruits of Paradise,
He still supplies.

—*Thos. Olivers.*

40

THIRD PART.

1 Before the great Three-One,
They all exulting stand,
And tell the wonders he hath done,
Through all their land:
The listening spheres attend,
And swell the growing fame,
And sing, in songs which never end,
The wondrous Name.

2 The God who reigns on high
The great archangels sing;
And "Holy, holy, holy," cry,
"Almighty King!
Who was and is the same,
And evermore shall be;
Jehovah, Father, Great I AM,
We worship thee."

3 Before the Saviour's face
The ransomed nations bow;
O'erwhelmed at his almighty grace,
For ever new:
He shows his prints of love,—
They kindle to a flame,
And sound through all the worlds above,
The slaughtered Lamb.

4 The whole triumphant host
Give thanks to God on high;
"Hail, Father, Son, and Holy Ghost,"
They ever cry:
Hail, Abraham's God, and mine!
(I join the heavenly lays),
All might and majesty are thine,
And endless praise.

—*Thos. Olivers.*

ANTIOCH. C. M. — FROM HANDEL.

41

Worshipping the Lamb.

1 COME, let us join our cheerful songs,
With angels round the throne;
Ten thousand thousand are their tongues,
But all their joys are one.

2 "Worthy the Lamb that died," they cry,
"To be exalted thus!"
"Worthy the Lamb!" our hearts reply;
"For he was slain for us."

3 Jesus is worthy to receive
Honour and power divine;
And blessings, more than we can give,
Be Lord, for ever thine!

4 The whole creation join in one,
To bless the sacred name
Of him who sits upon the throne,
And to adore the Lamb!

—*Isaac Watts.*

TALLIS' ORDINAL. C. M. — THOMAS TALLIS, 1561.

42

Exodus xxxiv. 5, 6.

1 GREAT God! to me the sight afford
To him of old allowed;
And let my faith behold its Lord
Descending in a cloud.

2 In that revealing Spirit come down,
Thine attributes proclaim,
And to mine inmost soul make known
The glories of thy name.

3 Jehovah, Christ, I thee adore,
Who gavest my soul to be:
Fountain of being, and of power,
And great in majesty!

4 The Lord, the mighty God, thou art;
But let me rather prove
That name in-spoken to my heart,
That favourite name of Love.

5 Merciful God, thyself proclaim
In this polluted breast;
Mercy is thy distinguished name,
Which suits a sinner best.

6 Our misery doth for pity call,
Our sin implores thy grace;
And thou art merciful to all
Our lost apostate race.

—*Charles Wesley.*

43

SECOND PART.

1 THY ceaseless, unexhausted love,
Unmerited and free,
Delights our evil to remove,
And help our misery.

2 Thou waitest to be gracious still;
Thou dost with sinners bear;
That, saved, we may thy goodness feel,
And all thy grace declare.

3 Thy goodness and thy truth to me,
To every soul, abound!
A vast, unfathomable sea,
Where all our thoughts are drowned.

4 Its streams the whole creation reach,
So plenteous is the store;
Enough for all, enough for each,
Enough for evermore.

5 Faithful, O Lord, thy mercies are,
A rock that cannot move!
A thousand promises declare
Thy constancy of love.

6 Throughout the universe it reigns,
Unalterably sure;
And while the truth of God remains,
The goodness must endure.

—*Charles Wesley.*

ABRIDGE. C. M. ISAAC SMITH.

44

The fulness of God.

1 BEING of beings, God of Love!
To thee our hearts we raise;
Thy all-sustaining power we prove,
And gladly sing thy praise.

2 Thine, only thine, we pant to be;
Our sacrifice receive;
Made, and preserved, and saved by thee,
To thee ourselves we give.

3 Heavenward our every wish aspires;
For all thy mercies' store,
The sole return thy love requires
Is that we ask for more.

4 For more we ask; we open then
Our hearts to embrace thy will;
Turn, and revive us, Lord, again,
With all thy fulness fill.

5 Come, Holy Ghost, the Saviour's love
Shed in our hearts abroad!
So shall we ever live, and move,
And be, with Christ in God.

Charles Wesley.

45

God the only object of worship.

1 O GOD, our strength, to thee our song
With grateful hearts we raise;
To thee, and thee alone, belong,
All worship, love, and praise.

2 In trouble's dark and stormy hour
Thine ear hath heard our prayer;
And graciously thine arm of power
Hath saved us from despair.

3 And thou, O ever gracious Lord,
Wilt keep thy promise still,
If, meekly hearkening to thy word,
We seek to do thy will.

4 Led by the light thy grace imparts,
Ne'er may we bow the knee
To idols, which our wayward hearts,
Set up instead of thee.

5 So shall thy choicest gifts, O Lord,
Thy faithful people bless;
For them shall earth its stores afford,
And heaven its happiness.

—Harriet Auber.

IRISH. C. M. ARRANGED FROM ISAAC SMITH.

46

"Righteousness and peace and joy in the Holy Ghost."

1 FATHER of me, and all mankind,
And all the hosts above,
Let every understanding mind
Unite to praise thy love:

2 To know thy nature, and thy name,
One God in Persons Three;
And glorify the Great I AM,
Through all eternity.

3 Thy kingdom come, with power and grace,
To every heart of man;
Thy peace, and joy, and righteousness,
In all our bosoms reign.

4 The righteousness that never ends,
But makes an end of sin,
The joy that human thought transcends
Into our souls bring in:

5 The kingdom of established peace,
Which can no more remove;
The perfect power of godliness,
The omnipotence of love.

—Charles Wesley.

TUNE: IRISH. C. M. (See Hymn 46.)

47 *The faithfulness of God in his promises.*

1 Begin, my soul, some heavenly theme;
Awake, my voice, and sing
The mighty works, or mightier name,
Of our eternal King.

2 Tell of his wondrous faithfulness,
And sound his power abroad;
Sing the sweet promise of his grace,
And the performing God.

3 Proclaim salvation from the Lord
For wretched, dying men:
His hand hath writ the sacred word
With an immortal pen.

4 Engraved as in eternal brass,
The mighty promise shines;
Nor can the powers of darkness 'rase
Those everlasting lines.

5 His every word of grace is strong
As that which built the skies;
The voice that rolls the stars along
Speaks all the promises.

6 Now shall my fainting heart rejoice,
To know thy favour sure:
I trust the all-creating voice,
And faith desires no more.

—Isaac Watts.

ST. BERNARD. C. M. W. Richardson.

48 *God the source of power and blessing.*

1 Blest be our everlasting Lord,
Our Father, God, and King!
Thy sovereign goodness we record,
Thy glorious power we sing.

2 By thee the victory is given;
The majesty divine,
And strength, and might, and earth, and heaven,
And all therein, are thine.

3 The kingdom, Lord, is thine alone,
Who dost thy right maintain,
And, high on thine eternal throne,
O'er men and angels reign.

4 Riches, as seemeth good to thee,
Thou dost, and honour, give;
And kings their power and dignity
Out of thy hand receive.

5 Thou hast on us the grace bestowed
Thy greatness to proclaim;
And therefore now we thank our God,
And praise thy glorious name.

6 Thy glorious name and nature's powers
Thou dost to us make known;
And all the Deity is ours,
Through thy incarnate Son.

—Charles Wesley.

49 Psalm xviii. 9, 10.

1 The Lord descended from above,
And bowed the heavens most high,
And underneath his feet he cast
The darkness of the sky.

2 On cherubim and seraphim
Full royally he rode,
And on the wings of mighty winds
Came flying all abroad.

3 He sat serene upon the floods,
Their fury to restrain;
And he, as sovereign Lord and King,
For evermore shall reign.

4 Give glory to his awful name,
And honour him alone;
Give worship to his majesty
Upon his holy throne.

—T. Sternhold.

OLD HUNDREDTH. L. M. — G. Franc, 1543.

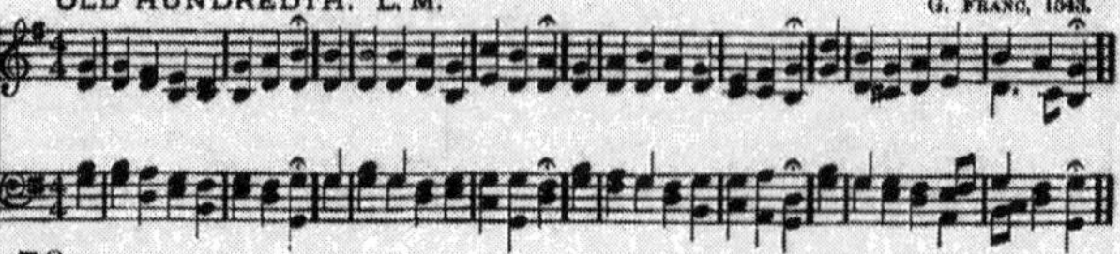

50 *Invitation to worship.*—Psalm c.

1 All people that on earth do dwell,
Sing to the Lord with cheerful voice:
Him serve with fear, his praise forth tell,
Come ye before him, and rejoice.

2 Know that the Lord is God indeed,
Without our aid he did us make;
We are his flock, he doth us feed,
And for his sheep he doth us take.

3 O enter then his gates with praise,
Approach with joy his courts unto:
Praise, laud, and bless his name always,
For it is seemly so to do.

4 For why? the Lord our God is good,
His mercy is forever sure;
His truth at all times firmly stood,
And shall from age to age endure.

—Kethe or Hopkins.

WARD. L. M. — Dr. L. Mason.

51 *All holiness derived from God.*

1 Holy as thou, O Lord, is none!
Thy holiness is all thy own;
A drop of that unbounded sea
Is ours, a drop derived from thee

2 And when thy purity we share,
Thy only glory we declare;
And, humbled into nothing, own
Holy and pure is God alone.

3 Sole, self-existing God and Lord,
By all thy heavenly hosts adored,
Let all on earth bow down to thee,
And own thy peerless majesty:

4 Thy power unparalleled confess,
Established on the Rock of Peace;
The Rock that never shall remove,
The Rock of pure, Almighty Love.

—Charles Wesley.

52 *Christ the Creator of all things.*

1 Let all that breathe, Jehovah praise;
Almighty, all-creating Lord!
Let earth and heaven his power confess,
Brought out of nothing by his word.

2 He spake the word, and it was done:
The universe his word obeyed;
His Word is his eternal Son,
And Christ the whole creation made.

3 Jesus, the Lord and God most high,
Maker of all mankind and me!
Me thou hast made to glorify,
To know, and love, and live to thee.

4 Wherefore to thee my heart I give,
For thou thyself dost give the power;
And if for thee on earth I live,
Thee I shall soon in heaven adore.

—Charles Wesley.

ANGELS' SONG. L. M. ORLANDO GIBBONS.

53 *The glory of God.*

1 God is a name my soul adores,
The almighty Three, the eternal One;
Nature and grace, with all their powers,
Confess the Infinite Unknown.

2 Thy voice produced the sea and spheres,
Bade the waves roar, the planets shine;
But nothing like thyself appears
Through all these spacious works of thine.

3 Still restless nature dies and grows,
From change to change the creatures run;
Thy being no succession knows,
And all thy vast designs are one.

4 A glance of thine runs through the globe,
Rules the bright worlds, and moves their frame;
Of light thou form'st thy dazzling robe,
Thy ministers are living flame.

5 How shall polluted mortals dare
To sing thy glory or thy grace?
Beneath thy feet we lie afar,
And see but shadows of thy face.

6 Who can behold the blazing light?
Who can approach consuming flame?
None but thy Wisdom knows thy might,
None but thy Word can speak thy name.

—*Isaac Watts.*

54 *Witnessing grace and success implored.*

1 What shall we offer our good Lord,
Poor nothings! for his boundless grace?
Fain would we his great name record,
And worthily set forth his praise.

2 Great object of our growing love,
To whom our more than all we owe,
Open the fountain from above,
And let it our full souls o'erflow.

3 So shall our lives thy power proclaim,
Thy grace for every sinner free;
Till all mankind shall learn thy name,
Shall all stretch out their hands to thee.

4 Open a door which earth and hell
May strive to shut, but strive in vain;
Let thy word richly in us dwell,
And let our gracious fruit remain.

5 O multiply the sower's seed!
And fruit we every hour shall bear,
Throughout the world thy gospel spread,
Thy everlasting truth declare.

6 We all, in perfect love renewed,
Shall know the greatness of thy power;
Stand in the temple of our God
As pillars, and go out no more.

—*John Wesley, translated from Spangenberg.*

STIRLING. L.M. R. Harrison.

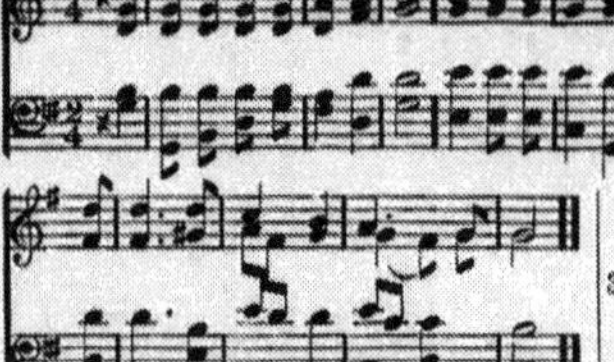

55

Christ glorified.

1 What equal honours shall we bring
To thee, O Lord our God, the Lamb?
Since all the notes that angels sing
Are far inferior to thy name.

2 Worthy is he that once was slain,
The Prince of Peace, that groaned and died;
Worthy to rise, and live, and reign
At his Almighty Father's side.

3 Power and dominion are his due
Who stood condemned at Pilate's bar;
Wisdom belongs to Jesus too,
Though he was charged with madness here.

4 Immortal praises must be paid,
Instead of scandal and of scorn;
While glory shines around his head,
And a bright crown without a thorn.

5 Honour for ever to the Lamb,
Who bore our sin, and curse, and pain;
Let angels bless his sacred name,
And every creature say, Amen!

—*Isaac Watts.*

WELD. 7.6.7.6, 7.7.7.6.

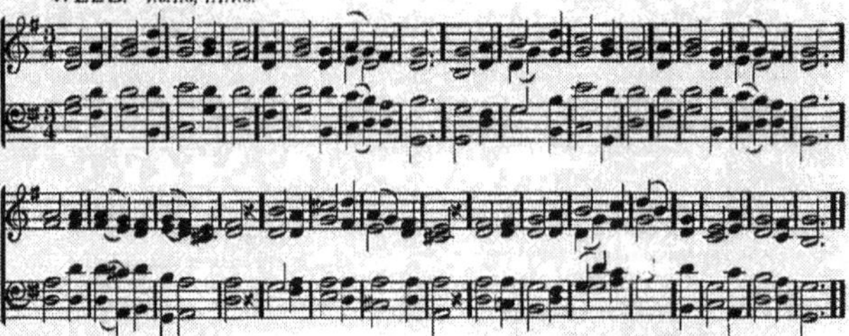

56

The Divine Perfections.

1 Glorious God, accept a heart
That pants to sing thy praise!
Thou without beginning art,
And without end of days:
Thou, a Spirit invisible,
Dost to none thy fulness show;
None thy majesty can tell,
Or all thy Godhead know.

2 All thine attributes we own,
Thy wisdom, power, and might,
Happy in thyself alone,
In goodness infinite,
Thou thy goodness hast displayed,
On thine every work imprest;
Lov'st whate'er thy hands have made,
But man thou lov'st the best.

3 Willing thou that all should know
Thy saving truth, and live,
Dost to each, or bliss or woe,
With strictest justice give:
Thou with perfect righteousness
Renderest every man his due;
Faithful in thy promises,
And in thy threatenings too.

4 Thou art merciful to all
Who truly turn to thee,
Hear me then for pardon call,
And show thy grace to me;
Me, through mercy reconciled,
Me, for Jesus' sake forgiven,
Me receive, thy favoured child,
To sing thy praise in heaven.

—*Charles Wesley.*

TUNE: WELD. 7.6.7.6, 7.7.7.6. (SEE HYMN 56.)

57

Earth and Heaven praising God.

1 MEET and right it is to sing,
  In every time and place,
Glory to our heavenly King,
  The God of truth and grace:
Join we then with sweet accord,
  All in one thanksgiving join,
Holy, holy, holy Lord,
  Eternal praise be thine!

2 Thee, the first-born sons of light,
  In choral symphonies,
Praise by day, day without night,
  And never, never cease:
Angels and archangels all
  Praise the mystic Three in One;
Sing, and stop, and gaze, and fall
  O'erwhelmed before thy throne

3 Vying with that happy choir,
  Who chant thy praise above,
We on eagles' wings aspire,
  The wings of faith and love;
Thee *they* sing with glory crowned,
  We extol the slaughtered Lamb;
Lower if our voices sound,
  Our subject is the same.

4 Father, God, thy love we praise,
  Which gave thy Son to die;
Jesus, full of truth and grace,
  Alike we glorify;
Spirit, Comforter divine,
  Praise by all to thee be given;
Till we in full chorus join,
  And earth is turned to heaven.

—*Charles Wesley.*

GILEAD. 7.6.7.6, 7.8.7.6.

Fine.

58

God's goodness and mercy unbounded.

1 GOOD thou art, and good thou dost,
  Thy mercies reach to all,
Chiefly those who on thee trust,
  And for thy mercy call;
New they every morning are;
  As fathers when their children cry,
Us thou dost in pity spare,
  And all our wants supply.

2 Mercy o'er thy works presides;
  Thy providence displayed
Still preserves, and still provides
  For all thy hands have made;
Keeps, with most distinguished care,
  The man who on thy love depends;
Watches every numbered hair,
  And all his steps attends.

3 Who can sound the depths unknown
  Of thy redeeming grace?
Grace that gave thine only Son
  To save a ruined race!
Millions of transgressors poor
  Thou hast for Jesus' sake forgiven,
Made them of thy favour sure,
  And snatched from hell to heaven.

4 Millions more thou ready art
  To save, and to forgive;
Every soul and every heart
  Of man thou wouldst receive;
Father, now accept of mine,
  Which now, through Christ, I offer thee;
Tell me now, in love divine,
  That thou hast pardoned me.—*Charles Wesley.*

59

"How unsearchable are his judgments, and his ways past finding out!"

1 THOU, the great, eternal God
  Art high above our thought!
Worthy to be feared, adored,
  By all thy hands have wrought:
None can with thyself compare;
  Thy glory fills both earth and sky;
We, and all thy creatures, are
  As nothing in thine eye.

2 Of thy great unbounded power
  To thee the praise we give,
Infinitely great, and more
  Than heart can e'er conceive:
When thou wilt to work proceed,
  Thy purpose firm none can withstand,
Frustrate the determined deed,
  Or stay the almighty hand.

3 Thou, O God, art wise alone;
  Thy counsel doth excel;
Wonderful thy works we own,
  Thy ways unsearchable:
Who can sound the mystery,
  Thy judgments' deep abyss explain,
Thine, whose eyes in darkness see,
  And search the heart of man?—*C. Wesley.*

LUCERNE. 8.8.8, 8.8.8. (2nd Metre.) German.

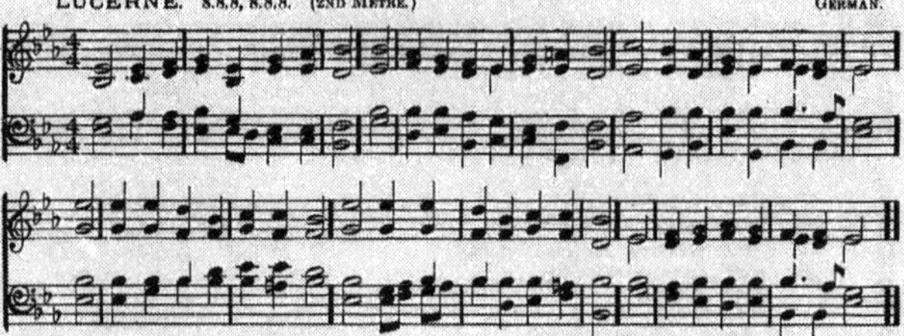

60

Divine greatness and goodness.

1 O God, of good the unfathomed Sea!
Who would not give his heart to thee?
Who would not love thee with his might?
O Jesus, Lover of mankind,
Who would not his whole soul and mind,
With all his strength, to thee unite?

2 Thou shin'st with everlasting rays;
Before the insufferable blaze
Angels with both wings veil their eyes;
Yet, free as air thy bounty streams
On all thy works; thy mercy's beams
Diffusive, as thy sun's, arise.

3 Astonished at thy frowning brow,
Earth, hell, and heaven's strong pillars bow;
Terrible majesty is thine!
Who then can that vast love express,
Which bows thee down to me, who less
Than nothing am, till thou art mine?

4 High throned on heaven's eternal hill,
In number, weight, and measure still
Thou sweetly orderest all that is:
And yet thou deign'st to come to me,
And guide my steps, that I, with thee
Enthroned, may reign in endless bliss.

5 Fountain of good, all blessing flows
From thee; no want thy fulness knows;
What but thyself canst thou desire?
Yet, self-sufficient as thou art,
Thou dost desire my worthless heart;
This, only this, dost thou require.

6 O God, of good the unfathomed Sea!
Who would not give his heart to thee?
Who would not love thee with his might?
O Jesus, Lover of mankind,
Who would not his whole soul and mind,
With all his strength, to thee unite?

—*Charles Wesley.*

61

The Spirit of Christ implored.

1 Father of everlasting grace,
Thy goodness and thy truth we praise,
Thy goodness and thy truth we prove;
Thou hast, in honour of thy Son,
The gift unspeakable sent down,
The Spirit of life, and power, and love.

2 Send us the Spirit of thy Son,
To make the depths of Godhead known,
To make us share the life divine;
Send him the sprinkled blood to apply,
Send him our souls to sanctify,
And show and seal us ever thine.

3 So shall we pray, and never cease;
So shall we thankfully confess
Thy wisdom, truth, and power, and love;
With joy unspeakable adore,
And bless and praise thee evermore,
And serve thee as thy hosts above;

4 Till, added to that heavenly choir,
We raise our songs of triumph higher,
And praise thee in a nobler strain,
Out-soar the first-born seraph's flight,
And sing, with all our friends in light,
Thy everlasting love to man.

—*Charles Wesley.*

MONMOUTH. 8.8.8, 8.8.8. (2nd Metre.) G. Davis.

MONMOUTH. *(Continued.)*

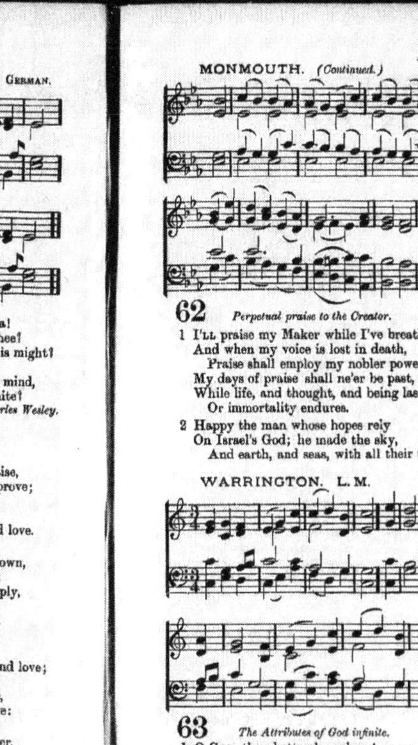

62

Perpetual praise to the Creator.

1 I'LL praise my Maker while I've breath,
And when my voice is lost in death,
Praise shall employ my nobler powers;
My days of praise shall ne'er be past,
While life, and thought, and being last,
Or immortality endures.

2 Happy the man whose hopes rely
On Israel's God; he made the sky,
And earth, and seas, with all their train;
His truth for ever stands secure,
He saves the opprest, he feeds the poor,
And none shall find his promise vain.

3 The Lord pours eyesight on the blind;
The Lord supports the fainting mind;
He sends the labouring conscience peace;
He helps the stranger in distress,
The widow and the fatherless,
And grants the prisoner sweet release.

4 I'll praise him while he lends me breath,
And when my voice is lost in death,
Praise shall employ my nobler powers;
My days of praise shall ne'er be past,
While life, and thought, and being last,
Or immortality endures.

—*Isaac Watts.*

WARRINGTON. L. M. REV. RALPH HARRISON.

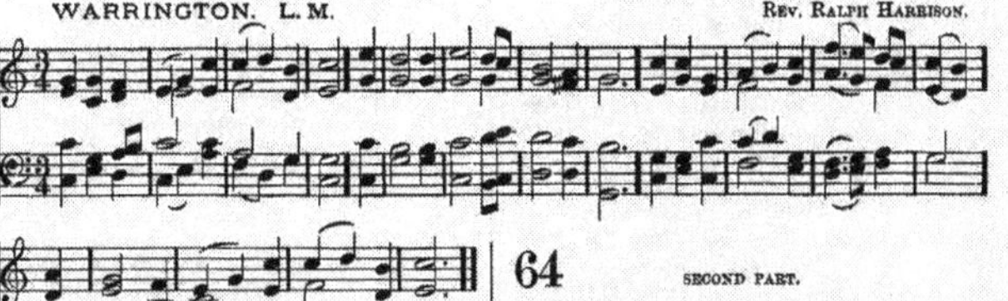

63

The Attributes of God infinite.

1 O GOD, thou bottomless abyss!
Thee to perfection who can know?
O height immense! What words suffice
Thy countless attributes to show?

2 Unfathomable depth thou art;
O plunge me in thy mercy's sea!
Void of true wisdom is my heart;
With love embrace and cover me.

3 Eternity thy fountain was,
Which, like thee, no beginning knew;
Thou wast ere time began his race,
Ere glowed with stars the ethereal blue.

4 Greatness unspeakable is thine,
Greatness, whose undiminished ray,
When short-lived worlds are lost, shall shine,
When earth and heaven are fled away.

—*Charles Wesley.*

64

SECOND PART.

1 UNCHANGEABLE, all-perfect Lord,
Essential life's unbounded sea,
What lives and moves, lives by thy word;
It lives, and moves, and is from thee.

2 High is thy power above all height;
Whate'er thy will decrees is done:
Thy wisdom, equal to thy might,
Only to thee, O God, is known!

3 Heaven's glory is thy awful throne,
Yet earth partakes thy gracious sway:
Vain man! thy wisdom folly own,
Lost is thy reason's feeble ray.

4 What our dim eye could never see,
Is plain and naked to thy sight;
What thickest darkness veils, to thee
Shines clearly as the morning light.

5 In light thou dwell'st; light that no shade,
No variation ever knew;
Heaven, earth, and hell, stand all displayed,
And open to thy piercing view.

—*Charles Wesley.*

GERMANY. L. M. BEETHOVEN.

65

THIRD PART.

1 Thou, true and only God, lead'st forth
The immortal armies of the sky;
Thou laugh'st to scorn the gods of earth,
Thou thunderest, and amazed they fly.

2 With downcast eye the angelic choir
Appear before thy awful face;
Trembling they strike the golden lyre,
And through heaven's vault resound thy praise.

3 Thine, Lord, is wisdom, thine alone;
Justice and truth before thee stand;
Yet, nearer to thy sacred throne,
Mercy withholds thy lifted hand.

4 Each evening shows thy tender love,
Each rising morn thy plenteous grace;
Thy wakened wrath doth slowly move,
Thy willing mercy flies apace.

5 To thy benign indulgent care,
Father, this light, this breath, we owe;
And all we have, and all we are,
From thee, great Source of being, flow.

—*John Wesley, from Lange.*

66

FOURTH PART.

1 Parent of Good, thy bounteous hand
Incessant blessings down distils,
And all in air, or sea, or land,
With plenteous food and gladness fills.

2 All things in thee live, move, and are;
Thy power infused doth all sustain;
Even those thy daily favours share,
Who thankless spurn thy easy reign.

3 The sun thou bidd'st his genial ray
Alike on all impartial pour;
To all, who hate or bless thy sway,
Thou bidd'st descend the fruitful shower.

4 Yet while, at length, who scorned thy might
Shall feel thee a consuming fire,
How sweet the joys, the crown how bright,
Of those who to thy love aspire!

5 All creatures, praise the eternal Name!
Ye hosts that to his court belong,
Cherubic choirs, seraphic flames,
Awake the everlasting song!

6 Thrice Holy! thine the kingdom is,
The power omnipotent is thine;
And when created nature dies,
Thy never-ceasing glories shine.

—*Charles Wesley.*

EDEN. L. M. Dr. L. Mason.

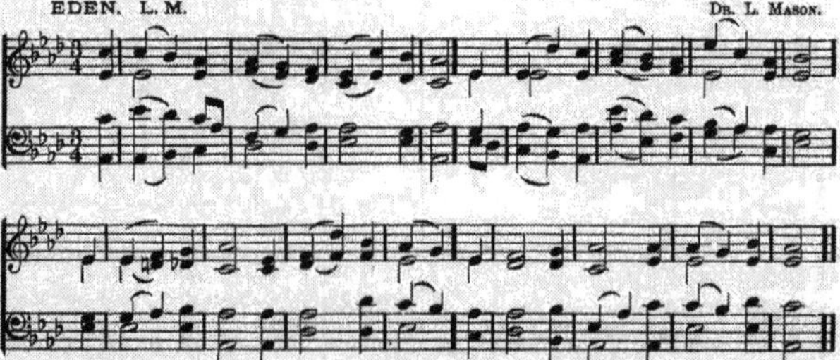

TUNE: EDEN. L. M.

67

The condescension of God.

1 Eternal depth of love divine,
In Jesus, God with us, displayed;
How bright thy beaming glories shine
How wide thy healing streams are spread!

2 To thy sure love, thy tender care,
Our flesh, soul, spirit, we resign;
O fix thy sacred presence there,
And seal the abode for ever thine.

3 O King of glory, thy rich grace
Our feeble thought surpasses far;
Yea, even our crimes, though numberless,
Less numerous than thy mercies are.

4 Still, Lord, thy saving health display,
And arm our souls with heavenly zeal;
So fearless shall we urge our way
Through all the powers of earth and hell.
—*Charles Wesley.*

68

Psalm xxiv.

1 The earth with all her fulness owns
Jehovah for her sovereign Lord;
The countless myriads of her sons
Rose into being at his word.
2 His word did out of nothing call
The world, and founded all that is;
Launched on the floods this solid ball,
And fixed it in the floating seas.
3 But who shall quit this low abode,
Who shall ascend the heavenly place,
And stand upon the mount of God,
And see his Maker face to face?
4 The man whose hands and heart are clean
That blessed portion shall receive;
Whoe'er by grace is saved from sin,
Hereafter shall in glory live.
5 He shall obtain the starry crown;
And, numbered with the saints above,
The God of his salvation own,
The God of his salvation love.—*C. Wesley.*

ECCLES. 6.6.7.7.7.7. BOGGETT.

69

The Trinity in Unity.

1 Hail, co-essential Three,
In mystic Unity!
Father, Son, and Spirit, hail!
God by heaven and earth adored,
God incomprehensible;
‖:One supreme, almighty Lord.:‖

2 Thou sittest on the throne,
Plurality in One;
Saints behold thine open face,
Bright, insufferably bright;
Angels tremble as they gaze,
‖:Sink into a sea of light.:‖

3 Ah! when shall we increase
Their heavenly ecstasies?
Chant, like them, the Lord Most High,
Fall like them who dare not move;
"Holy, holy, holy," cry,
‖:Breathe the praise of silent love?:‖

4 Come, Father, in the Son
And in the Spirit down;
Glorious Triune Majesty,
God through endless ages blest,
Make us meet thy face to see,
‖:Then receive us to thy breast.:‖
—*Charles Wesley.*

GODERICH. 11,8, 11,8. W. H. W. DARLEY.

70 *Thanksgiving in the Sanctuary.*

1 BE joyful in God, all ye lands of the earth;
O serve him with gladness and fear!
Exult in his presence with music and mirth,
||: With love and devotion draw near. :||

2 Jehovah is God, and Jehovah alone,
Creator and Ruler o'er all;
And we are his people, his sceptre we own,
||: His sheep, and we follow his call. :||

3 O enter his gates with thanksgiving and song!
Your vows in his temple proclaim;
His praise with melodious accordance prolong,
||: And bless his adorable name. :||

4 For good is the Lord, inexpressibly good,
And we are the work of his hand;
His mercy and truth from eternity stood,
||: And shall to eternity stand. :||

—*Montgomery.*

HAYES. L. M. D. FROM BEETHOVEN.

71 *The Lord's Prayer.*

1 FATHER of all, whose powerful voice
Called forth this universal frame!
Whose mercies over all rejoice,
Through endless ages still the same;
Thou by thy word upholdest all;
Thy bounteous love to all is showed;
Thou hear'st thy every creature's call,
And fillest every mouth with good.

2 In heaven thou reign'st enthroned in light,
Nature's expanse beneath thee spread;
Earth, air, and sea, before thy sight,
And hell's deep gloom, are open laid:
Wisdom, and might, and love are thine;
Prostrate before thy face we fall,
Confess thine attributes divine,
And hail thee sovereign Lord of all.

3 Thee sovereign Lord let all confess,
That move in earth, or air, or sky;
Revere thy power, thy goodness bless,
Tremble before thy piercing eye.
All ye, who owe to him your birth,
In praise your every hour employ:
Jehovah reigns! be glad, O earth!
And shout, ye morning stars, for joy.

—*Charles Wesley.*

WORDSWORTH. L. M. D.

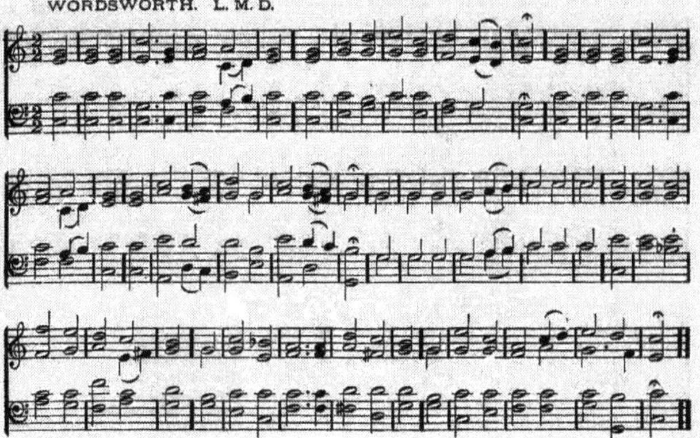

72

SECOND PART.

1 Son of thy Sire's eternal love,
Take to thyself thy mighty power,
Let all earth's sons thy mercy prove,
Let all thy boundless grace adore;
The triumphs of thy love display,
In every heart reign thou alone,
Till all thy foes confess thy sway,
And glory ends what grace begun.

2 Spirit of grace, and health, and power,
Fountain of light and love below,
Abroad thy healing influence shower,
O'er all the nations let it flow;
Inflame our hearts with perfect love,
In us the work of faith fulfil;
So not heaven's host shall swifter move
Than we on earth to do thy will.

3 Father, 'tis thine each day to yield
Thy children's wants a fresh supply,
Thou cloth'st the lilies of the field,
And hearest the young ravens cry:
On thee we cast our care; we live
Through thee, who know'st our every need;
O feed us with thy grace, and give
Our souls this day the living bread!

—John Wesley.

73

THIRD PART.

1 Eternal, spotless Lamb of God,
Before the world's foundation slain,
Sprinkle us ever with thy blood;
O cleanse, and keep us ever clean!
To every soul (all praise to thee!)
Our bowels of compassion move;
And all mankind by this may see
God is in us; for God is love.

2 Giver and Lord of life, whose power
And guardian care for all are free,
To thee, in fierce temptation's hour,
From sin and Satan let us flee;
Thine, Lord, we are, and ours thou art,
In us be all thy goodness showed;
Renew, enlarge, and fill our heart
With peace, and joy, and heaven, and God.

3 Blessing and honour, praise and love
Co-equal, co-eternal Three,
In earth below, and heaven above,
By all thy works, be paid to thee!
Thrice Holy! thine the kingdom is,
The power omnipotent is thine;
And when created nature dies,
Thy never-ceasing glories shine.

—Charles Wesley.

BARNBY. 6-8s. J. BARNBY.

By permission of Messrs. Novello, Ewer & Co.

74

"Te Deum laudamus."

1 INFINITE God, to thee we raise
Our hearts in solemn songs of praise;
By all thy works on earth adored,
We worship thee, the common Lord;
The everlasting Father own,
And bow our souls before thy throne.

2 Thee all the choir of angels sings,
The Lord of hosts, the King of kings;
Cherubs proclaim thy praise aloud,
And seraphs shout the Triune God;
And "Holy, holy, holy," cry,
"Thy glory fills both earth and sky!"

3 God of the patriarchal race,
The ancient seers record thy praise;
The goodly apostolic band
In highest joy and glory stand;
And all the saints and prophets join
To extol thy majesty divine.

4 Head of the martyrs' noble host,
Of thee they justly make their boast;
The church, to earth's remotest bounds,
Her heavenly Founder's praise resounds;
And strives with those around the throne,
To hymn the mystic Three in One.

5 Father of endless majesty,
All might and love they render thee;
Thy true and only Son adore,
The same in dignity and power;
And God the Holy Ghost declare,
The saints' eternal Comforter.

—*Charles Wesley.*

75

SECOND PART.

1 MESSIAH, joy of every heart,
Thou, thou the King of Glory art!
The Father's everlasting Son!
Thee it delights thy church to own;
For all our hopes on thee depend,
Whose glorious mercies never end.

2 Bent to redeem a sinful race,
Thou, Lord, with unexampled grace,
Into our lower world didst come,
And stoop to a poor virgin's womb;
Whom all the heavens cannot contain,
Our God appeared a child of man!

3 When thou hadst rendered up thy breath,
And dying drawn the sting of death,
Thou didst from earth triumphant rise,
And ope the portals of the skies,
That all who trust in thee alone
Might follow, and partake thy throne.

4 Seated at God's right hand again,
Thou dost in all his glory reign;
Thou dost, thy Father's image, shine
In all the attributes divine;
And thou with judgment clad shalt come
To seal our everlasting doom.

5 Wherefore we now for mercy pray;
O Saviour, take our sins away!
Before thou as our Judge appear,
In dreadful majesty severe,
Appear our Advocate with God,
And save the purchase of thy blood.

6 Hallow, and make thy servants meet,
And with thy saints in glory seat;
Sustain and bless us by thy sway,
And keep to that tremendous day,
When all thy church shall chant above
The new eternal song of love.

—*Charles Wesley.*

RAKEM. 6-8s. ISAAC BAKER WOODBURY.

Fine. *D. C.*

76

THIRD PART.

1 SAVIOUR, we now rejoice in hope,
That thou at last wilt take us up;
With daily triumph we proclaim,
And bless and magnify thy name;
And wait thy greatness to adore
When time and death shall be no more.

2 Till then with us vouchsafe to stay,
And keep us pure from sin to-day;
Thy great confirming grace bestow,
And guard us all our days below;
And ever mightily defend,
And save thy servants to the end.

3 Still let us, Lord, by thee be blest,
Who in thy guardian mercy rest:
Extend thy mercy's arms to me,
The weakest soul that trusts in thee;
And never let me lose thy love,
Till I, even I, am crowned above.

—*Charles Wesley.*

77

Prayer for convincing and converting grace.

1 FATHER of omnipresent grace,
We seem agreed to seek thy face;
But every soul assembled here
Doth naked in thy sight appear:
Thou know'st who only bows the knee,
And who in heart approaches thee.

2 Thy Spirit hath the difference made
Betwixt the living and the dead;
Thou now dost into some inspire
The pure, benevolent desire:
O that even now thy powerful call
May quicken and convert us all!

3 The sinners suddenly convince,
O'erwhelmed beneath their load of sins;
To-day, while it is called to-day,
Awake, and stir them up to pray,
Their dire captivity to own,
And from the iron furnace groan.

4 Then, then acknowledge, and set free
The people bought, O Lord, by thee!
The sheep for whom their Shepherd bled,
For whom we in thy Spirit plead:
Let all in thee redemption find,
And not a soul be left behind.

—*Charles Wesley.*

MOZART. 6-8s. FROM MOZART.

78

Prayer for light and forgiveness.

1 FATHER of everlasting grace,
Be mindful of thy changeless word;
We worship toward that holy place,
In which thou dost thy name record,
Dost make thy gracious nature known,
That living temple of thy Son.

2 Thou dost with sweet complacence see
The temple filled with light divine;
And art thou not well pleased that we,
Now turning to that heavenly shrine,
Through Jesus to thy throne apply,
Through Jesus for acceptance cry?

3 "Let there be light," again command,
And light there in our hearts shall be;
We then through faith shall understand
Thy great mysterious Majesty;
And, by the shining of thy grace,
Behold in Christ thy glorious face.

4 With all who for redemption groan,
Father, in Jesus' name we pray!
And still we cry and wrestle on,
Till mercy take our sins away:
Hear from thy dwelling-place in heaven,
And now pronounce our sins forgiven.

—*Charles Wesley.*

HURSLEY. L. M. — Huguenot Melody.

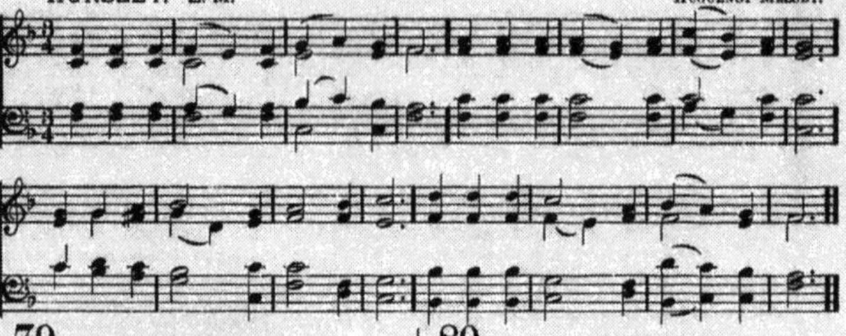

79

The joy of God's service.

1 Great God, attend, while Zion sings
The joy that from thy presence springs;
To spend one day with thee on earth
Exceeds a thousand days of mirth.

2 Might I enjoy the meanest place
Within thine house, O God of grace,
Not tents of ease, nor thrones of power,
Should tempt my feet to leave thy door

3 God is our sun, he makes our day;
God is our shield, he guards our way
From all the assaults of hell and sin,
From foes without, and foes within.

4 All needful grace will God bestow,
And crown that grace with glory too;
He gives us all things, and withholds
No real good from upright souls.

5 O God our King, whose sovereign sway
The glorious hosts of heaven obey,
And devils at thy presence flee,
Blest is the man that trusts in thee.

—*Isaac Watts.*

80

Psalm lxxxiv.

1 How pleasant, how divinely fair,
O Lord of hosts, thy dwellings are!
With strong desire my spirit faints
To meet the assemblies of thy saints.

2 Blest are the saints that sit on high,
Around thy throne of majesty;
Thy brightest glories shine above,
And all their work is praise and love.

3 Blest are the souls that find a place
Within the temple of thy grace;
Here they behold thy gentler rays,
And seek thy face, and learn thy praise.

4 Blest are the men whose hearts are set
To find the way to Zion's gate;
God is their strength, and through the road
They lean upon their helper God.

5 Cheerful they walk with growing strength,
Till all shall meet in heaven at length;
Till all before thy face appear,
And join in nobler worship there.

—*Isaac Watts.*

WARD. L. M. — Dr. L. Mason.

Slowly.

TUNE: WARD. L. M.

81

The realizing light of faith.

1 Author of faith, eternal Word,
Whose Spirit breathes the active flame;
Faith, like its Finisher and Lord,
To-day, as yesterday, the same.

2 To thee our humble hearts aspire,
And ask the gift unspeakable;
Increase in us the kindled fire,
In us the work of faith fulfil.

3 By faith we know thee strong to save;
Save us, a present Saviour thou!
Whate'er we hope, by faith we have,
Future and past subsisting now.

4 To him that in thy name believes
Eternal life with thee is given;
Into himself he all receives,
Pardon, and holiness, and heaven.

5 The things unknown to feeble sense,
Unseen by reason's glimmering ray,
With strong, commanding evidence,
Their heavenly origin display

6 Faith lends its realizing light,
The clouds disperse, the shadows fly;
The Invisible appears in sight,
And God is seen by mortal eye.

—*Charles Wesley.*

SYMPHONY. L. M. BEETHOVEN.

82

Praise to Christ our King.

1 Jesus, thou everlasting King,
Accept the tribute which we bring;
Accept thy well-deserved renown,
And wear our praises as thy crown.

2 Let every act of worship be
Like our espousals, Lord, to thee;
Like the glad hour when from above
We first received the pledge of love.

3 The gladness of that happy day,
O may it ever with us stay!
Nor let our faith forsake its hold,
Our hope decline, our love grow cold.

4 Let every moment, as it flies,
Increase thy praise, improve our joys,
Till we are raised to sing thy name,
At the great supper of the Lamb.

—*Isaac Watts.*

ST. CRISPIN. L. M. SIR G. J. ELVEY.

83

Trembling aspiration.

1 O thou, whom all thy saints adore,
We now with all thy saints agree,
And bow our inmost souls before
Thy glorious, awful Majesty.

2 We come, great God, to seek thy face,
And for thy loving-kindness wait;
And O how dreadful is this place!
'Tis God's own house, 'tis heaven's gate.

3 Tremble our hearts to find thee nigh;
To thee our trembling hearts aspire;
And lo! we see descend from high
The pillar and the flame of fire.

4 Still let it on the assembly stay,
And all the house with glory fill;
To Canaan's bounds point out the way,
And lead us to thy holy hill.

5 There let us all with Jesus stand,
And join the general Church above,
And take our seats at thy right hand,
And sing thine everlasting love.

—*Charles Wesley.*

ST. MARK. S. M. GEO. KINGSLEY.

84

The sacrifice of praise.

1 With joy we lift our eyes
To those bright realms above,
That glorious temple in the skies,
Where dwells eternal Love.

2 Before thy throne we bow,
O thou Almighty King;
Here we present the solemn vow,
And hymns of praise we sing.

3 While in thy house we kneel,
With trust and holy fear,
Thy mercy and thy truth reveal,
And lend a gracious ear.

4 Lord, teach our hearts to pray,
And tune our lips to sing;
Nor from thy presence cast away
The sacrifice we bring.

—*T. Jervis.*

LEOMINSTER. S. M. D. G. W. MARTIN.

85

The revealing Spirit invoked.

1 Spirit of faith, come down,
Reveal the things of God;
And make to us the Godhead known,
And witness with the blood:
'Tis thine the blood to apply,
And give us eyes to see,
Who did for every sinner die
Hath surely died for me.

2 No man can truly say
That Jesus is the Lord,
Unless thou take the veil away,
And breathe the living word;
Then, only then, we feel
Our interest in his blood,
And cry, with joy unspeakable,
"Thou art my Lord, my God!"

3 O that the world might know
The all-atoning Lamb!
Spirit of faith, descend, and show
The virtue of his Name;
The grace which all may find,
The saving power, impart!
And testify to all mankind,
And speak in every heart.

4 Inspire the living faith,
Which whosoe'er receives,
The witness in himself he hath,
And consciously believes;
The faith that conquers all,
And doth the mountain move,
And saves whoe'er on Jesus call,
And perfects them in love.

—*Charles Wesley.*

o. Kingsley.

el,

eal,

ray,

vay

-T. Jervis.

W. Martin.

w

ow

l,

les Wesley.

MANOAH. C. M. FROM MEHUL AND HAYDN.

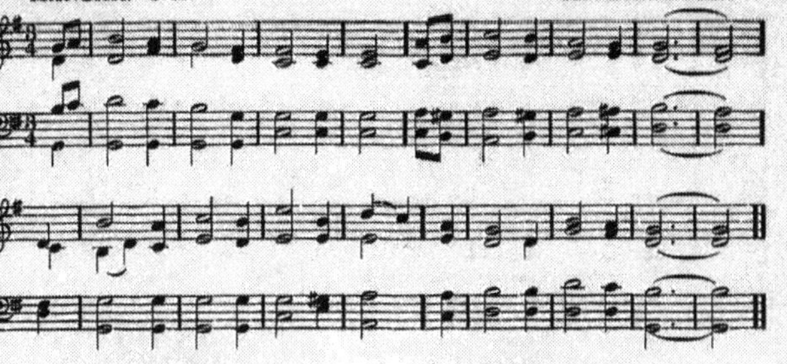

86 *Repentance and forgiveness implored.*

1 COME, O thou all-victorious Lord,
Thy power to us make known;
Strike with the hammer of thy word,
And break these hearts of stone!

2 O that we all might now begin
Our foolishness to mourn;
And turn at once from every sin,
And to our Saviour turn!

3 Give us ourselves and thee to know,
In this our gracious day;
Repentance unto life bestow,
And take our sins away.

4 Convince us first of unbelief,
And freely then release;
Fill every soul with sacred grief,
And then with sacred peace.

5 Impoverish, Lord, and then relieve,
And then enrich the poor;
The knowledge of our sickness give,
The knowledge of our cure.

6 That blessed sense of guilt impart,
And then remove the load;
Trouble, and wash the troubled heart
In the atoning blood.

—*Charles Wesley.*

87 *Prayer for the impenitent.*

1 THOU Son of God, whose flaming eyes
Our inmost thoughts perceive,
Accept the evening sacrifice
Which now to thee we give.

2 We bow before thy gracious throne,
And think ourselves sincere;
But show us, Lord, is every one
Thy real worshipper.

3 Is here a soul that knows thee not,
Nor feels his want of thee,
A stranger to the blood which bought
His pardon on the tree?

4 Convince him now of unbelief,
His desperate state explain;
And fill his heart with sacred grief,
And penitential pain.

5 Speak with that voice which wakes the dead,
And bid the sleeper rise!
And bid his guilty conscience dread
The death that never dies.

6 Extort the cry, "What must be done
To save a wretch like me?
How shall a trembling sinner shun
That endless misery?

7 "I must this instant now begin
Out of my sleep to wake,
And turn to God, and every sin
Continually forsake:

8 "I must for faith incessant cry,
And wrestle, Lord, with thee:
I must be born again, or die
To all eternity."

—*Charles Wesley.*

ST. AGNES. C. M. Dr. Dykes.

88 *Majesty and love of God.*

1 My God, how wonderful thou art,
Thy majesty how bright,
How glorious thy mercy-seat
In depths of burning light!

2 How dread are thine eternal years,
O everlasting Lord,
By prostrate spirits day and night
Incessantly adored!

3 No earthly father loves like thee,
No mother, e'er so mild,
Bears and forbears, as thou hast done
With me, thy wayward child.

4 O how I fear thee, living God,
With deepest, tenderest fears,
And worship thee with trembling hope,
And penitential tears!

5 Yet I may love thee too, O Lord,
Almighty as thou art;
For thou hast stooped to ask of me
The love of my poor heart.

—*F. W. Faber.*

89 *The Omniscience of God.*

1 In all my vast concerns with thee,
In vain my soul would try
To shun thy presence, Lord, or flee
The notice of thine eye.

2 Thy all-surrounding sight surveys
My rising and my rest,
My public walks, my private ways,
The secrets of my breast.

3 My thoughts lie open to thee, Lord,
Before they're formed within;
And, ere my lips pronounce the word,
Thou know'st the sense I mean.

4 O wondrous knowledge, deep and high!
Where can a creature hide?
Within thy circling arms I lie,
Beset on every side.

5 So let thy grace surround me still
And like a bulwark prove,
To guard my soul from every ill,
Secured by sovereign love.

—*Isaac Watts.*

Section II.

CREATION AND PROVIDENCE.

ST. ANN'S. C. M. Dr. Crofts.

TUNE: ST. ANN'S. C. M.

90

"Thy judgments are a great deep."

1 God moves in a mysterious way
His wonders to perform;
He plants his footsteps in the sea,
And rides upon the storm.

2 Deep in unfathomable mines
Of never-failing skill,
He treasures up his bright designs,
And works his sovereign will.

3 Ye fearful saints, fresh courage take!
The clouds ye so much dread
Are big with mercy, and shall break
In blessings on your head.

4 Judge not the Lord by feeble sense,
But trust him for his grace;
Behind a frowning providence
He hides a smiling face.

5 His purposes will ripen fast,
Unfolding every hour;
The bud may have a bitter taste,
But sweet will be the flower.

6 Blind unbelief is sure to err,
And scan his work in vain;
God is his own interpreter,
And he will make it plain.

—*Cowper.*

HOLY CROSS. C. M.

Arthur Henry Brown.

Slowly.

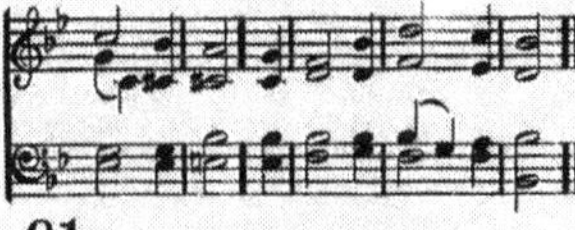

91

Divine guidance and protection.

1 O God of Bethel, by whose hand
Thy people still are fed;
Who through this weary pilgrimage
Hast all our fathers led;

2 Our vows, our prayers, we now present
Before thy throne of grace;
God of our fathers, be the God
Of their succeeding race!

3 Through each perplexing path of life
Our wandering footsteps guide;
Give us each day our daily bread,
And raiment fit provide.

4 O spread thy covering wings around,
Till all our wanderings cease,
And at our Father's loved abode
Our souls arrive in peace!

5 Such blessings from thy gracious hand
Our humble prayers implore;
And thou shalt be our chosen God
And portion evermore.

—*Doddridge.*

92

Thanksgiving for life's mercies.

1 When all thy mercies, O my God,
My rising soul surveys,
Transported with the view, I'm lost
In wonder, love, and praise.

2 Unnumbered comforts on my soul
Thy tender care bestowed,
Before my infant heart conceived
From whom those comforts flowed.

3 When in the slippery paths of youth
With heedless steps I ran,
Thine arm, unseen, conveyed me safe,
And led me up to man.

4 Through hidden dangers, toils, and deaths,
It gently cleared my way;
And through the pleasing snares of vice,
More to be feared than they.

5 Through every period of my life
Thy goodness I'll pursue;
And after death, in distant worlds,
The pleasing theme renew.

6 Through all eternity, to thee
A grateful song I'll raise;
But O eternity's too short
To utter all thy praise!

—*Addison.*

BEDFORD. C. M. W. WHEALL.

Slowly.

93

The goodness of God.

1 LET every tongue thy goodness speak,
Thou sovereign Lord of all;
Thy strengthening hands uphold the weak,
And raise the poor that fall.

2 When sorrow bows the spirit down,
Or virtue lies distressed,
Beneath the proud oppressor's frown,
Thou giv'st the mourner rest.

3 The Lord supports our infant days,
And guides our giddy youth;
Holy and just are all thy ways,
And all thy words are truth.

4 Thou know'st the pains thy servants feel,
Thou hear'st thy children cry;
And their best wishes to fulfil,
Thy grace is ever nigh.

5 Thy mercy never shall remove
From men of heart sincere;
Thou sav'st the souls whose humble love
Is joined with holy fear.

6 My lips shall dwell upon thy praise,
And spread thy fame abroad:
Let all the sons of Adam raise
The honours of their God!

—*Isaac Watts.*

94

These all wait upon thee; that thou mayest give them their meat in due season. —Psa. civ. 27.

1 SWEET is the memory of thy grace,
My God, my heavenly King;
Let age to age thy righteousness
In sounds of glory sing.

2 God reigns on high, but not confines
His bounty to the skies;
Through the whole earth his goodness shines,
And every want supplies.

3 With longing eyes the creatures wait
On thee for daily food;
Thy liberal hand provides them meat,
And fills their mouths with good.

4 How kind are thy compassions, Lord,
How slow thine anger moves!
But soon he sends his pardoning word,
To cheer the souls he loves.

5 Creatures, with all their endless race,
Thy power and praise proclaim;
But we, who taste thy richer grace,
Delight to bless thy name.

—*Isaac Watts.*

AUTUMN. 8.7, 8.7, 8.7, 8.7. SPANISH MELODY. FROM MARECHIO.

Fine.
D.S.

TUNE: AUTUMN. 8.7, 8.7, 8.7, 8.7.

95

Psalm xci.

1 Call Jehovah thy salvation,
Rest beneath the Almighty's shade;
In his secret habitation
Dwell, nor ever be dismayed;
There no tumult can alarm thee,
Thou shalt dread no hidden snare;
Guile nor violence can harm thee,
In eternal safety there.

2 From the sword at noon-day wasting,
From the noisome pestilence
In the depth of midnight blasting,
God shall be thy sure defence;
Fear thou not the deadly quiver,
When a thousand feel the blow;
Mercy shall thy soul deliver,
Though ten thousand be laid low.

3 Since, with pure and firm affection,
Thou on God hast set thy love,
With the wings of his protection
He will shield thee from above:
Thou shalt call on him in trouble,
He will hearken, he will save;
Here for grief reward thee double,
Crown with life beyond the grave.

Montgomery.

NEARER HOME. S. M. D. — Isaac Woodbury.

96

The call of Abraham.

1 In every time and place
Who serve the Lord most high,
Are called his sovereign will to embrace,
And still their own deny;
To follow his command,
On earth as pilgrims rove,
And seek an undiscovered land,
And house, and friends above.

2 Father, the narrow path
To that far country show;
And in the steps of Abraham's faith
Enable me to go,
A cheerful sojourner
Where'er thou bidd'st me roam,
Till, guided by thy Spirit here,
I reach my heavenly home.

—Charles Wesley.

(FIRST TUNE.) LUX BENIGNA. 10.4, 10.4, 10.10. REV. J. B. DYKES.

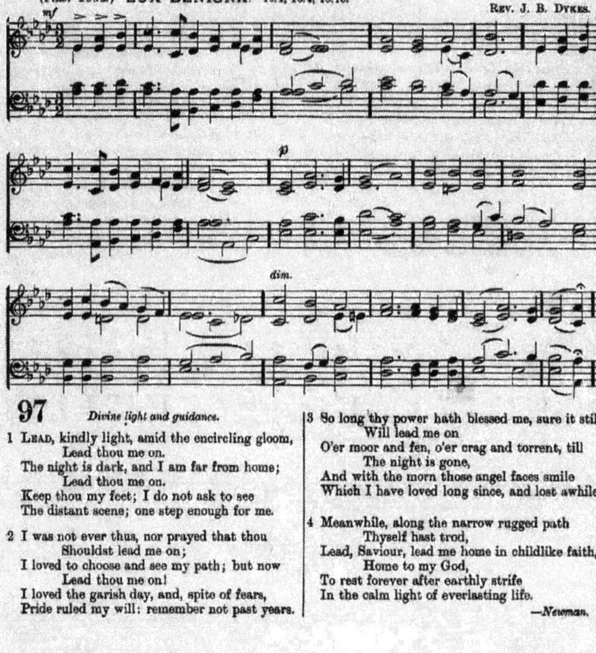
mf
p
dim.

97 *Divine light and guidance.*

1 LEAD, kindly light, amid the encircling gloom,
Lead thou me on.
The night is dark, and I am far from home;
Lead thou me on.
Keep thou my feet; I do not ask to see
The distant scene; one step enough for me.

2 I was not ever thus, nor prayed that thou
Shouldst lead me on;
I loved to choose and see my path; but now
Lead thou me on!
I loved the garish day, and, spite of fears,
Pride ruled my will: remember not past years.

3 So long thy power hath blessed me, sure it still
Will lead me on
O'er moor and fen, o'er crag and torrent, till
The night is gone,
And with the morn those angel faces smile
Which I have loved long since, and lost awhile.

4 Meanwhile, along the narrow rugged path
Thyself hast trod,
Lead, Saviour, lead me home in childlike faith,
Home to my God,
To rest forever after earthly strife
In the calm light of everlasting life.

—*Newman.*

(SECOND TUNE.) SANDON. 10.4, 10.4, 10.10. C. H. PURDAY.

CREATION. 6·8s. F. J. HAYDN.

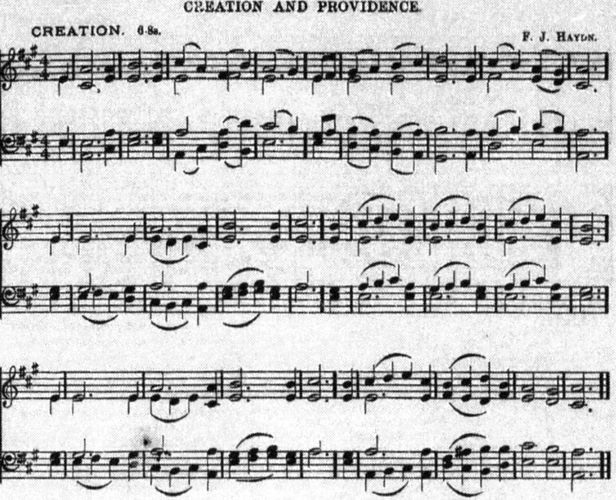

98

Confidence in Divine guidance.

1 CAPTAIN of Israel's host, and Guide
Of all who seek the land above,
Beneath thy shadow we abide,
The cloud of thy protecting love:
Our strength, thy grace; our rule, thy word;
Our end, the glory of the Lord.

2 By thine unerring Spirit led,
We shall not in the desert stray;
We shall not full direction need,
Nor miss our providential way;
As far from danger as from fear,
While love, almighty love, is near.

—*Charles Wesley.*

99

Psalm cxlv.

1 FAR as creation's bounds extend,
Thy mercies, heavenly Lord, descend;
One chorus of perpetual praise
To thee thy various works shall raise;
Thy saints to thee in hymns impart
The transports of a grateful heart.

2 They chant the splendours of thy name,
Delighted with the wondrous theme;
And bid the world's wide realm admire
The glories of the Almighty Sire,
Whose throne all nature's wreck survives,
Whose power through endless ages lives.

3 From thee, great God, while every eye
Expectant waits the wished supply,
Their bread proportioned to the day,
Thy opening hands to each convey;
In every sorrow of the heart
Eternal mercy bears a part.

4 Who ask thine aid with heart sincere
Shall find thy succours ever near;
To thee their prayer in each distress
Thy suffering servants, Lord, address;
And prove thee, verging on the grave,
Nor slow to hear, nor weak to save.

—*Merrick.*

BONN. 7.6, 7.6, 7.7, 7.6. ADAPTED FROM THE GERMAN.

100

Psalm cxxi.

1 To the hills I lift mine eyes,
The everlasting hills;
Streaming thence in fresh supplies,
My soul the Spirit feels.
Will he not his help afford?
Help, while yet I ask, is given:
God comes down; the God and Lord
That made both earth and heaven.

2 Faithful soul, pray always; pray,
And still in God confide;
He thy feeble steps shall stay,
Nor suffer thee to slide:
Lean on thy Redeemer's breast;
He thy quiet spirit keeps;
Rest in him, securely rest;
Thy Watchman never sleeps.

3 Neither sin, nor earth, nor hell
Thy Keeper can surprise;
Careless slumbers cannot steal
On his all-seeing eyes;
He is Israel's sure defence;
Israel all his care shall prove,
Kept by watchful providence,
And ever-waking love.

4 See the Lord, thy Keeper, stand
Omnipotently near!
Lo! he holds thee by thy hand,
And banishes thy fear;
Shadows with his wings thy head;
Guards from all impending harms;
Round thee and beneath are spread
The everlasting arms.

5 Christ shall bless thy going out,
Shall bless thy coming in;
Kindly compass thee about,
Till thou art saved from sin;
Like thy spotless Master, thou,
Filled with wisdom, love, and power,
Holy, pure, and perfect, now,
Henceforth, and evermore.

—Charles Wesley.

ERNAN. L. M. DR. L. MASON.

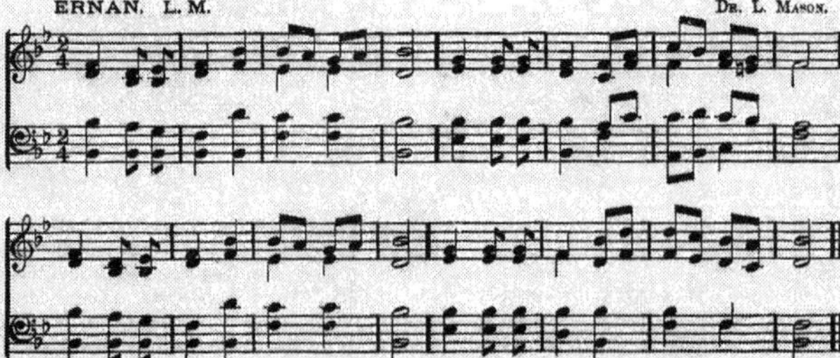

TUNE: ERNAN. L. M.

101 *God's presence with his people.*

1 When Israel, of the Lord beloved,
Out from the land of bondage came,
Her fathers' God before her moved,
An awful guide, in smoke and flame.

2 By day, along the astonished lands
The cloudy pillar glided slow;
By night, Arabia's crimsoned sands
Returned the fiery column's glow.

3 Thus present still, though now unseen,
When brightly shines the prosperous day,
Be thoughts of thee a cloudy screen,
To temper the deceitful ray.

4 And O, when gathers on our path,
In shade and storm, the frequent night,
Be thou, long suffering, slow to wrath,
A burning and a shining light!

—Sir W. Scott.

102 *Divine protection acknowledged.*

1 God of my life, whose gracious power
Through varied deaths my soul hath led,
Or turned aside the fatal hour,
Or lifted up my sinking head;

2 In all my ways thy hand I own,
Thy ruling Providence I see;
Assist me still my course to run,
And still direct my paths to thee.

3 Oft hath the sea confessed thy power,
And given me back at thy command;
It could not, Lord, my life devour,
Safe in the hollow of thine hand.

4 Oft from the margin of the grave
Thou, Lord, hast lifted up my head,
Sudden, I found thee near to save;
The fever owned thy touch, and fled.

5 Whither, O whither should I fly,
But to my loving Saviour's breast!
Secure within thine arms to lie,
And safe beneath thy wings to rest.

—Charles Wesley.

DRESDEN. L. M. From Mozart.

103 Psalm xxxvi.

1 High in the heavens, eternal God,
Thy goodness in full glory shines;
Thy truth shall break through every cloud
That veils and darkens thy designs.

2 For ever firm thy justice stands,
As mountains their foundations keep;
Wise are the wonders of thy hands;
Thy judgments are a mighty deep.

3 Thy providence is kind and large,
Both man and beast thy bounty share;
The whole creation is thy charge,
But saints are thy peculiar care.

4 My God, how excellent thy grace,
Whence all our hope and comfort springs!
The sons of Adam in distress
Fly to the shadow of thy wings.

5 Life, like a fountain rich and free,
Springs from the presence of the Lord;
And in thy light our souls shall see
The glories promised in thy word.

—Isaac Watts.

WAREHAM. L. M. W. KNAPP.

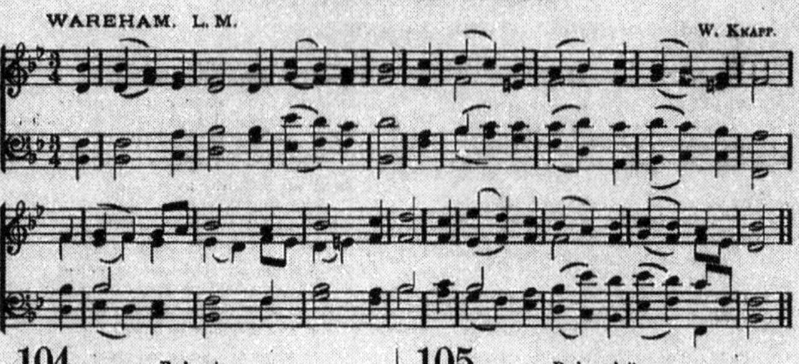

104

Psalm xix.

1 THE spacious firmament on high,
With all the blue ethereal sky,
And spangled heavens, a shining frame,
Their great Original proclaim.

2 The unwearied sun, from day to day,
Does his Creator's power display;
And publishes to every land
The work of an almighty hand.

3 Soon as the evening shades prevail,
The moon takes up the wondrous tale;
And nightly to the listening earth
Repeats the story of her birth:

4 Whilst all the stars that round her burn,
And all the planets in their turn,
Confirm the tidings as they roll,
And spread the truth from pole to pole.

5 What though, in solemn silence, all
Move round this dark terrestrial ball;
What though no real voice or sound
Amidst their radiant orbs be found;

6 In reason's ear they all rejoice,
And utter forth a glorious voice,
For ever singing, as they shine,
"The hand that made us is divine."

—*Addison.*

105

Psalm cxlvii.

1 PRAISE ye the Lord! 'tis good to raise
Your hearts and voices in his praise;
His nature and his works invite
To make this duty our delight.

2 He formed the stars, those heavenly flames,
He counts their numbers, calls their names;
His wisdom's vast, and knows no bound,
A deep where all our thoughts are drowned.

3 Sing to the Lord; exalt him high,
Who spreads his clouds along the sky,
There he prepares the fruitful rain,
Nor lets the drops descend in vain.

4 He makes the grass the hills adorn,
And clothes the smiling fields with corn;
The beasts with food his hands supply,
And the young ravens when they cry.

5 But saints are lovely in his sight,
He views his children with delight;
He sees their hope, he knows their fear,
And looks and loves his image there.

Isaac Watts.

MAIDSTONE. 8-7s. W. B. GILBERT.

MAIDSTONE. *(Continued.)*

106 *Thanksgiving for life's blessings.*

1 Happy man whom God doth aid!
God our souls and bodies made;
God on us, in gracious showers,
Blessings every moment pours;
Compasses with angel-bands,
Bids them bear us in their hands;
Parents, friends, 'twas God bestowed,
Life, and all, descend from God.

2 He this flowery carpet spread,
Made the earth on which we tread;
God refreshes in the air,
Covers with the clothes we wear,
Feeds us with the food we eat,
Cheers us by his light and heat,
Makes his sun on us to shine;
All our blessings are divine!

3 Give him then, and ever give,
Thanks for all that we receive;
Man we for his kindness love,
How much more our God above?
Worthy thou, our heavenly Lord,
To be honoured and adored;
God of all-creating grace,
Take the everlasting praise!

—*Charles Wesley.*

BYZANTIUM. C. M. W. Jackson.

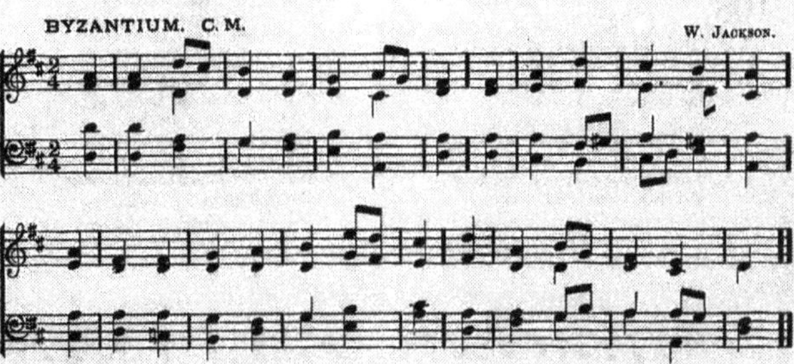

107 *"All thy works shall praise thee."*

1 I sing the almighty power of God,
That made the mountains rise,
That spread the flowing seas abroad,
And built the lofty skies.

2 I sing the wisdom that ordained
The sun to rule the day;
The moon shines full at his command,
And all the stars obey.

3 All creatures, numerous as they be,
Are subject to thy care;
There's not a place where we can flee,
But God is present there.

4 There's not a plant nor flower below
But makes thy glories known;
And clouds arise, and tempests blow
By order from thy throne.

5 His hand is my perpetual guard;
He keeps me with his eye:
Why should I, then, forget the Lord,
Who is for ever nigh?

—*Isaac Watts.*

Section III.

THE LORD JESUS CHRIST: HIS PERSON, OFFICES AND WORK.

CORONATION. C. M. (First Tune.)

108

The Coronation of Christ.

1 All hail the power of Jesus' name!
Let angels prostrate fall;
Bring forth the royal diadem,
And crown him Lord of all.

2 Ye seed of Israel's chosen race,
Ye ransomed from the fall,
Hail him who saves you by his grace,
And crown him Lord of all.

3 Sinners, whose love can ne'er forget
The wormwood and the gall;
Go, spread your trophies at his feet,
And crown him Lord of all.

4 Let every kindred, every tribe,
On this terrestrial ball,
To him all majesty ascribe,
And crown him Lord of all.

5 O that with yonder sacred throng
We at his feet may fall;
Join in the everlasting song,
And crown him Lord of all!

—*E. Perronet.*

MILES LANE. C. M. (Second Tune.) Shrubsole.

BELMONT. C. M. WEBBE.

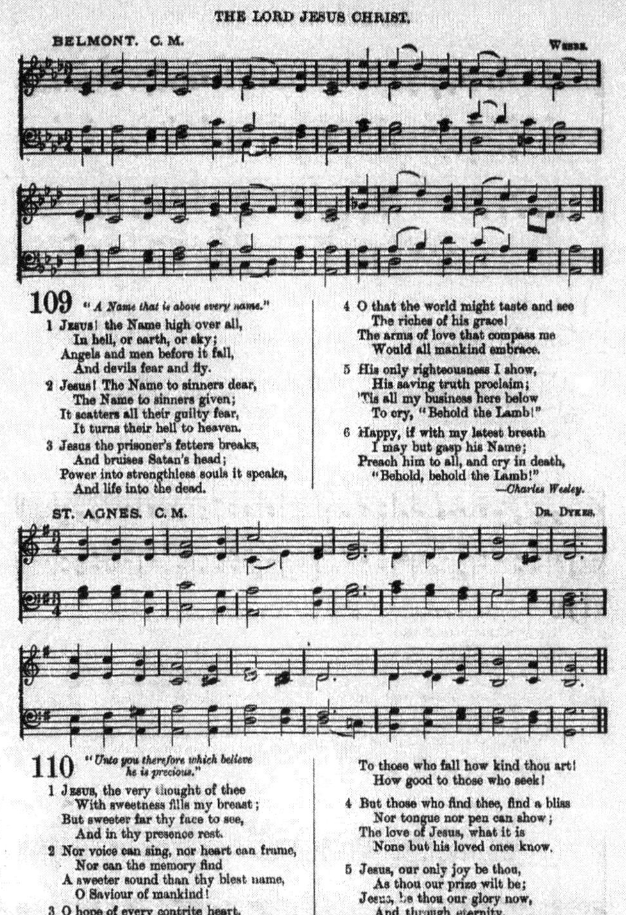

109 "A Name that is above every name."

1 JESUS! the Name high over all,
In hell, or earth, or sky;
Angels and men before it fall,
And devils fear and fly.

2 Jesus! The Name to sinners dear,
The Name to sinners given;
It scatters all their guilty fear,
It turns their hell to heaven.

3 Jesus the prisoner's fetters breaks,
And bruises Satan's head;
Power into strengthless souls it speaks,
And life into the dead.

4 O that the world might taste and see
The riches of his grace!
The arms of love that compass me
Would all mankind embrace.

5 His only righteousness I show,
His saving truth proclaim;
'Tis all my business here below
To cry, "Behold the Lamb!"

6 Happy, if with my latest breath
I may but gasp his Name;
Preach him to all, and cry in death,
"Behold, behold the Lamb!"

—Charles Wesley.

ST. AGNES. C. M. DR. DYKES.

110 "Unto you therefore which believe he is precious."

1 JESUS, the very thought of thee
With sweetness fills my breast;
But sweeter far thy face to see,
And in thy presence rest.

2 Nor voice can sing, nor heart can frame,
Nor can the memory find
A sweeter sound than thy blest name,
O Saviour of mankind!

3 O hope of every contrite heart,
O joy of all the meek,
To those who fall how kind thou art!
How good to those who seek!

4 But those who find thee, find a bliss
Nor tongue nor pen can show;
The love of Jesus, what it is
None but his loved ones know.

5 Jesus, our only joy be thou,
As thou our prize wilt be;
Jesus, be thou our glory now,
And through eternity.

—Bernard of Clairvaux.

ANTIOCH. C. M. FROM HANDEL.

111 *"The Lord reigneth, let the earth rejoice."*

1 Joy to the world! the Lord is come;
Let earth receive her King:
Let every heart prepare him room,
And heaven and nature sing.

2 Joy to the world! the Saviour reigns;
Let men their songs employ;
While fields and floods, rocks, hills and plains,
Repeat the sounding joy.

3 No more let sin and sorrow grow,
Nor thorns infest the ground;
He comes to make his blessings flow
Far as the curse is found.

4 He rules the world with truth and grace,
And makes the nations prove
The glories of his righteousness,
And wonders of his love.

—*Isaac Watts.*

ST. FLAVIAN. C. M.

112 *The name of Jesus.*

1 How sweet the name of Jesus sounds
In a believer's ear!
It soothes his sorrows, heals his wounds,
And drives away his fear.

2 Dear name! the rock on which I build,
My shield, and hiding-place,
My never-failing treasury, filled
With boundless stores of grace!

3 Jesus! my Shepherd, Brother, Friend,
My Prophet, Priest, and King;
My Lord, my Life, my Way, my End,
Accept the praise I bring.

4 Weak is the effort of my heart,
And cold my warmest thought;
But when I see thee as thou art,
I'll praise thee as I ought.

5 Till then I would thy love proclaim
With every fleeting breath;
And may the music of thy name
Refresh my soul in death.

—*J. Newton.*

ABRIDGE. C. M. ISAAC SMITH.

TUNE: ABRIDGE. C. M.

113 *Praise for redeeming love.*

1 PLUNGED in a gulf of dark despair
We wretched sinners lay,
Without one cheerful beam of hope,
Or spark of glimmering day.

2 With pitying eyes, the Prince of Peace
Beheld our helpless grief;
He saw, and, O amazing love!
He flew to our relief.

3 Down from the shining seats above
With joyful haste he sped;
Entered the grave in mortal flesh,
And dwelt among the dead.

4 O for this love let rocks and hills
Their lasting silence break;
And all harmonious human tongues
The Saviour's praises speak!

5 Angels, assist our mighty joys,
Strike all your harps of gold!
But when you raise your highest notes,
His love can ne'er be told.

—Isaac Watts.

114 *Hymn to God the Son.*

1 HAIL, God the Son, in glory crowned,
Ere time began to be;
Throned with thy Sire, through half the round
Of vast eternity!

2 Let heaven and earth's stupendous frame
Display their Author's power;
And each exalted seraph-flame,
Creator, thee adore.

3 Thy wondrous love the Godhead showed,
Contracted to a span,—
The co-eternal Son of God,
The mortal Son of man.

4 To save us from our lost estate,
Behold his life-blood stream:
Hail, Lord, almighty to create,
Almighty to redeem!

5 The Mediator's God-like sway
His church below sustains;
Till nature shall her Judge survey,
The King Messiah reigns.

6 Hail, with essential glory crowned,
When time shall cease to be;
Throned with thy Father, through the round
Of whole eternity!

—S. Wesley, jun.

ARIEL. 8.8.6, 8.8.6. DR. L. MASON.

115 *Grateful praise to the Saviour.*

1 O COULD I speak the matchless worth,
O could I sound the glories forth,
Which in my Saviour shine!
I'd soar and touch the heavenly strings,
And vie with Gabriel while he sings
||: In notes almost divine. :||

2 I'd sing the precious blood he spilt,
My ransom from the dreadful guilt
Of sin, and wrath divine;
I'd sing his glorious righteousness,
And magnify the wondrous grace
||: Which made salvation mine. :||

3 I'd sing the characters he bears,
And all the forms of love he wears,
Exalted on his throne;
In loftiest songs of sweetest praise,
I would to everlasting days
||: Make all his glories known. :||

4 Soon the delightful day will come
When my blest Lord will bring me home,
And I shall see his face;
Then with my Saviour, Brother, Friend,
A blest eternity I'll spend,
||: Triumphant in his grace. :||

—J. Medley.

REGENT SQUARE. 8.7.8.7.4.7. HENRY SMART.

116 "Whom having not seen ye love."

1 O THOU God of my salvation,
My Redeemer from all sin,
Moved by thy divine compassion,
Who hast died my heart to win,
‖:I will praise thee;:‖
Where shall I thy praise begin?

2 Though unseen, I love the Saviour;
He hath brought salvation near;
Manifests his pardoning favour;
And when Jesus doth appear,
‖:Soul and body:‖
Shall his glorious image bear.

3 While the angel choirs are crying,
"Glory to the great I AM,"
I with them will still be vying—
Glory! glory to the Lamb!
‖:O how precious:‖
Is the sound of Jesus' name!

4 Angels now are hovering round us
Unperceived among the throng;
Wondering at the love that crowned us,
Glad to join the holy song:
‖:Hallelujah!:‖
Love and praise to Christ belong!

—T. Olivers.

MARTYN. 8-7s. (FIRST TUNE.) S. B. MARSH.

Fine.
D.C.

TUNE: MARTYN. 8-7.

117 *Christ the soul's only refuge.*

mf 1 Jesus, Lover of my soul,
Let me to thy bosom fly,
While the nearer waters roll,
While the tempest still is high:
Hide me, O my Saviour, hide,
Till the storm of life be past;
dim. Safe into the haven guide,
pp O receive my soul at last!

mf 2 Other refuge have I none,
Hangs my helpless soul on thee;
Leave, ah! leave me not alone,
Still support and comfort me:
f All my trust on thee is stayed;
All my help from thee I bring;
dim. Cover my defenceless head
pp With the shadow of thy wing.

mf 3 Thou, O Christ, art all I want,
More than all in thee I find;
Raise the fallen, cheer the faint,
Heal the sick, and lead the blind.
Just and holy is thy name,
I am all unrighteousness;
False and full of sin I am,
Thou art full of truth and grace.

f 4 Plenteous grace with thee is found,
Grace to cover all my sin;
Let the healing streams abound,
Make and keep me pure within:
ff Thou of life the fountain art,
Freely let me take of thee;
Spring thou up within my heart,
Rise to all eternity.

—*Charles Wesley.*

REFUGE. 8-7s. (Second Tune.) Joseph P. Holbrook.

CHOPE. 4-7s. DR. CHOPE.

118

The Litany.

1 SAVIOUR, when in dust to thee
Low we bow the adoring knee;
When, repentant, to the skies,
Scarce we lift our weeping eyes,
O, by all thy pains and woe
Suffered once for man below,
Bending from thy throne on high,
Hear our solemn litany!

2 By thy helpless infant years,
By thy life of want and tears,
By thy fasting and distress
In the desert wilderness;
By the dread mysterious hour
Of the subtle tempter's power,
Turn, O turn a favouring eye,
Hear our solemn litany!

3 By the sacred grief that wept
O'er the grave where Lazarus slept;
By the gracious tears that flowed
Over Salem's loved abode;
By the mournful word that told
Treachery lurked within thy fold;
From thy seat above the sky,
Hear our solemn litany!

4 By thine hour of lone despair,
By thine agony of prayer,
By the purple robe of scorn,
By thy wounds, thy crown of thorn;
By the gloom that veiled the skies
O'er the dreadful sacrifice;
Listen to our humble cry,
Hear our solemn litany!

5 By thy deep expiring groan,
By the sealed sepulchral stone,
By the vault whose dark abode
Held in vain the rising God;
O from earth to heaven restored,
Mighty, re-ascended Lord,
Listen, listen to the cry
Of our solemn litany!

—*Sir R. Grant.*

STEGGALL. 6.6, 6.6, 8.8. DR. STEGGALL.

119

Jesus the joy of earth and heaven.

1 LET earth and heaven agree,
Angels and men be joined,
To celebrate with me
The Saviour of mankind;
To adore the all-atoning Lamb,
And bless the sound of Jesus' name.

2 Jesus, transporting sound!
The joy of earth and heaven;
No other help is found,
No other name is given,
By which we can salvation have;
But Jesus came the world to save.

3 Jesus, harmonious name!
It charms the hosts above;
They evermore proclaim
And wonder at his love;
'Tis all their happiness to gaze,
'Tis heaven to see our Jesus' face.

4 His name the sinner hears,
And is from sin set free;
'Tis music in his ears,
'Tis life and victory;
New songs do now his lips employ,
And dances his glad heart for joy.

5 Stung by the scorpion sin,
My poor expiring soul
The balmy sound drinks in,
And is at once made whole;
See there my Lord upon the tree!
I hear, I feel, he died for me.

6 O unexampled love!
O all-redeeming grace!
How swiftly didst thou move
To save a fallen race!
What shall I do to make it known
What thou for all mankind hast done?

7 O for a trumpet voice,
On all the world to call!
To bid their hearts rejoice
In him who died for all;
For all my Lord was crucified,
For all, for all my Saviour died!

—*Charles Wesley.*

TUNE: STEGGALL. 6.6, 6.6, 8.8. (SEE HYMN 119.)

120

The offices of Christ.

1 JOIN all the glorious names
Of wisdom, love, and power
That ever mortals knew,
That angels ever bore;
All are too mean to speak his worth,
Too mean to set our Saviour forth.

2 But O what gentle means,
What condescending ways,
Doth our Redeemer use
To teach his heavenly grace;
My soul, with joy and wonder see
What forms of love he bears for thee!

3 Arrayed in mortal flesh
The Covenant-Angel stands,
And holds the promises
And pardons in his hands;
Commissioned from his Father's throne
To make his grace to mortals known.

4 Be thou my Counsellor,
My Pattern, and my Guide;
And through this desert land
Still keep me near thy side;
O let my feet ne'er run astray,
Nor rove, nor seek the crooked way!

5 I love my Shepherd's voice;
His watchful eye shall keep
My wandering soul among
The thousands of his sheep;
He feeds his flock, he calls their names,
His bosom bears the tender lambs.

—*Isaac Watts.*

QUEEN STREET. 6.6, 6.6, 8.8. J. B. BAXTER.

121

SECOND PART.

1 GREAT Prophet of my God,
My lips shall bless thy name;
By thee the joyful news
Of our salvation came;
The joyful news of sins forgiven,
Of hell subdued, and peace with heaven.

2 Jesus, my great High Priest,
Offered his blood and died;
My guilty conscience seeks
No sacrifice beside;
His powerful blood did once atone,
And now it pleads before the throne.

3 O thou almighty Lord,
My Conqueror and my King!
Thy sceptre and thy sword,
Thy reign of grace, I sing;
Thine is the power; behold, I sit
In willing bonds before thy feet.

4 Now let my soul arise,
And tread the tempter down;
My Captain leads me forth
To conquest and a crown:
March on, nor fear to win the day,
Though death and hell obstruct the way.

5 Should all the hosts of death,
And powers of hell unknown,
Put their most dreadful forms
Of rage and malice on,
I shall be safe; for Christ displays
Superior power, and guardian grace.

—*Isaac Watts.*

LENOX. 6.6, 6.6, 8.8. LEWIS EDSON.

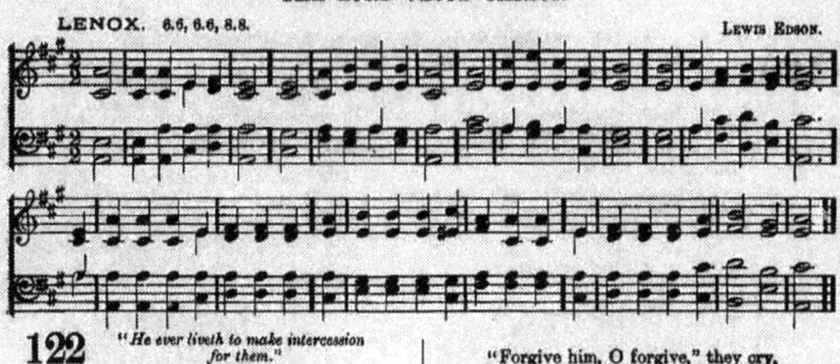

122 *"He ever liveth to make intercession for them."*

1 ARISE, my soul, arise,
Shake off thy guilty fears;
The bleeding sacrifice
In my behalf appears;
Before the throne my surety stands,
‖: My name is written on his hands. :‖

2 He ever lives above,
For me to intercede,
His all-redeeming love,
His precious blood, to plead;
His blood atoned for all our race,
‖: And sprinkles now the throne of grace. :‖

3 Five bleeding wounds he bears,
Received on Calvary;
They pour effectual prayers,
They strongly speak for me:
"Forgive him, O forgive," they cry,
‖: "Nor let that ransomed sinner die!" :‖

4 The Father hears him pray,
His dear anointed One;
He cannot turn away
The presence of his Son:
His Spirit answers to the blood,
‖: And tells me I am born of God. :‖

5 My God is reconciled,
His pardoning voice I hear,
He owns me for his child,
I can no longer fear;
With confidence I now draw nigh,
‖: And, Father, Abba, Father, cry! :‖

—*Charles Wesley.*

CRUSADER'S HYMN. 6.6.8, 6.6.8. 12TH CENTURY.

123 *"The Messiah, the Prince."*

1 MY heart and voice I raise,
To spread Messiah's praise;
Messiah's praise let all repeat;
The universal Lord,
By whose almighty word
Creation rose in form complete.

2 A servant's form he wore,
And in his body bore
Our dreadful curse on Calvary;
He like a victim stood,
And poured his sacred blood,
To set the guilty captives free.

3 But soon the Victor rose
Triumphant o'er his foes,
And led the vanquished host in chains;
He threw their empire down,
His foes compelled to own,
O'er all the great Messiah reigns.

4 With mercy's mildest grace,
He governs all our race
In wisdom, righteousness, and love;
Who to Messiah fly
Shall find redemption nigh,
And all his great salvation prove.

5 Hail, Saviour, Prince of Peace!
Thy kingdom shall increase,
Till all the world thy glory see;
And righteousness abound,
As the great deep profound,
And fill the earth with purity.

—*B. Rhodes.*

TUNE: CRUSADER'S HYMN. 6.6.8, 6.6.8. (See Hymn 123.)

124

SECOND PART.

1 Jerusalem divine,
When shall I call thee mine?
And to thy holy hill attain,
Where weary pilgrims rest,
And in thy glories blest,
With God Messiah ever reign?

2 There saints and angels join
In fellowship divine,
And rapture swells the solemn lay;
While all with one accord
Adore their glorious Lord,
And shout his praise in endless day.

3 May I but find the grace
To fill an humble place
In that inheritance above;
My tuneful voice I'll raise
In songs of loudest praise,
To spread thy fame, Redeeming Love!

4 Reign, true Messiah, reign!
Thy kingdom shall remain
When stars and sun no more shall shine;
Mysterious Deity,
Who ne'er began to be,
To sound thy endless praise be mine!

—*B. Rhodes.*

ECCLES. 6.6.7.7.7.7. BOGGETT.

125

Christ our Prophet, Priest and King.

1 Arise, my soul, arise,
Thy Saviour's sacrifice!
All the names that love could find,
All the forms that love could take,
Jesus in himself hath joined,
‖:Thee, my soul, his own to make.:‖

2 Prophet, to me reveal
Thy Father's perfect will;
Never mortal spake like thee,
Human Prophet, like divine;
Loud and strong their voices be,
‖:Small, and still, and inward thine!:‖

3 On thee, my Priest, I call;
Thy blood atoned for all:
Still the Lamb as slain appears,
Still thou stand'st before the throne,
Ever offering up my prayers,
‖:These presenting with thine own.:‖

4 Jesus, thou art my King,
From thee my strength I bring;
Shadowed by thy mighty hand,
Saviour, who shall pluck me thence?
Faith supports; by faith I stand,
‖:Strong in thy omnipotence.:‖

5 Hail! everlasting Lord,
Divine, incarnate Word!
Thee let all my powers confess;
Thee my latest breath proclaim;
Help, ye angel-choirs, to bless,
‖:Shout the loved Immanuel's name!:‖

—*Charles Wesley.*

RUTHERFORD. 7.6, 7.6, 7.6, 7.6. D'URHAN.

126

Preserving grace.

1 O LAMB of God! still keep me
Near to thy wounded side;
'Tis only there in safety
And peace I can abide.
What foes and snares surround me!
What lusts and fears within!
The grace that sought and found me
Alone can keep me clean.

2 'Tis only in thee hiding,
I know my life secure;
Only in thee abiding,
The conflict can endure;
Thine arm the victory gaineth
O'er every hurtful foe;
Thy love my heart sustaineth
In all its cares and woe.

3 Soon shall my eyes behold thee
With rapture, face to face;
One half hath not been told me
Of all thy power and grace;
Thy beauty, Lord, and glory,
The wonders of thy love,
Shall be the endless story
Of all thy saints above.

—*Charles Wesley.*

ROCKINGHAM. L. M. DR. MILLER.

127

Jesus the joy of loving hearts.

1 JESUS, thou Joy of loving hearts!
Thou Fount of life! thou Light of men!
From the best bliss that earth imparts,
We turn unfilled to thee again.

2 Thy truth unchanged hath ever stood;
Thou savest those that on thee call;
To them that seek thee, thou art good;
To them that find thee, all in all.

3 We taste thee, O thou Living Bread!
And long to feast upon thee still;
We drink of thee, the Fountain-head,
And thirst our souls from thee to fill.

4 Our restless spirits yearn for thee,
Where'er our changeful lot is cast;
Glad, when thy gracious smile we see;
Blest, when our faith can hold thee fast.

5 O Jesus, ever with us stay!
Make all our moments calm and bright;
Chase the dark night of sin away,
Shed o'er the world thy holy light!

—*Bernard of Clairvaux.*

128

"Who loved me and gave himself for me."

1 MY Saviour, how shall I proclaim,
How pay the mighty debt I owe!
Let all I have, and all I am,
Ceaseless to all thy glory show.

2 Too much to thee I cannot give;
Too much I cannot do for thee;
Let all thy love, and all thy grief,
Graven on my heart for ever be!

3 The meek, the still, the lowly mind,
O may I learn from thee, my God!
And love, with softest pity joined,
For those that trample on thy blood.

4 Still let thy tears, thy groans, thy sighs,
O'erflow my eyes, and heave my breast,
Till loose from flesh and earth I rise,
And ever in thy bosom rest.

—*Charles Wesley.*

ST. LUKE. L. M.

129 *Saints and angels praising Christ.*

1 Thee we adore, eternal Lord!
We praise thy name with one accord;
Thy saints, who here thy goodness see,
Through all the world do worship thee.

2 To thee aloud all angels cry,
And ceaseless raise their songs on high;
Both cherubim and seraphim,
The heavens and all the powers therein.

3 The apostles join the glorious throng;
The prophets swell the immortal song;
The martyrs' noble army raise
Eternal anthems to thy praise.

4 Thee, holy Prophet, Priest, and King!
Thee, Saviour of mankind, they sing:
Thus earth below, and heaven above,
Resound thy glory and thy love.

PENTECOST. L. M. WILLIAM BOYD.

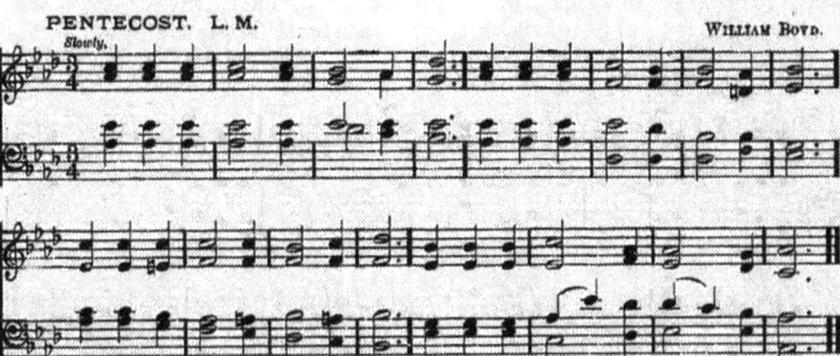
Slowly.

130 *Consecration to Christ.*

1 I come, thou wounded Lamb of God,
To wash me in thy cleansing blood;
To rest beneath thy cross, then pain
Is sweet, and life or death is gain.

2 Take my poor heart, and let it be
For ever closed to all but thee!
Seal thou my breast, and let me wear
That pledge of love for ever there.

3 How blest are they who still abide
Close sheltered at thy bleeding side!
Who life and strength from thee derive,
And by thee move, and in thee live.

4 What are our works but sin and death,
Till thou thy quickening Spirit breathe?
Thou giv'st the power thy grace to move:
O wondrous grace! O boundless love!

5 How can it be, thou heavenly King,
That thou shouldst us to glory bring?
Make slaves the partners of thy throne,
Decked with a never-fading crown?

6 First-born of many brethren thou!
To thee, lo! all our souls we bow;
To thee our hearts and hands we give:
Thine may we die, thine may we live!

—Translated from the German by J. Wesley.

DUKE STREET. L. M. JOHN HATTON.

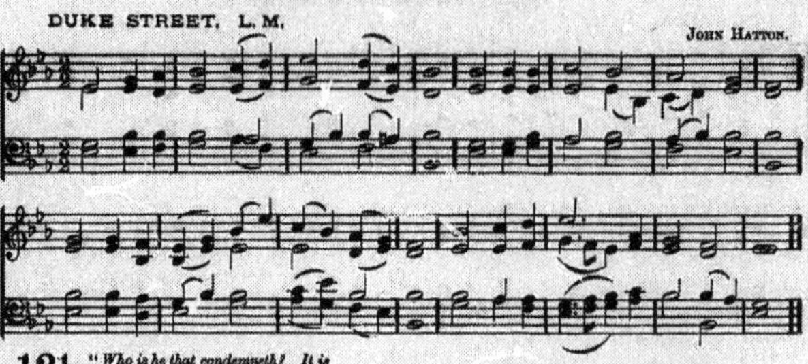

131 *"Who is he that condemneth? It is Christ that died."*

1 JESUS, thy blood and righteousness
My beauty are, my glorious dress;
'Midst flaming worlds, in these arrayed,
With joy shall I lift up my head.

2 Bold shall I stand in thy great day,
For who aught to my charge shall lay?
Fully absolved through these I am,
From sin and fear, from guilt and shame.

3 The holy, meek, unspotted Lamb,
Who from the Father's bosom came,
Who died for me, even me, to atone,
Now for my Lord and God I own.

4 Lord, I believe thy precious blood,
Which, at the mercy-seat of God,
For ever doth for sinners plead,
For me, even for my soul, was shed.

5 Lord, I believe, were sinners more
Than sands upon the ocean shore,
Thou hast for all a ransom paid,
For all a full atonement made.

6 When from the dust of death I rise,
To claim my mansion in the skies,
Even then, this shall be all my plea,
Jesus hath lived, hath died, for me.

—*Zinzendorf. Translated by J. Wesley.*

MIDDLESEX. 6-8s.

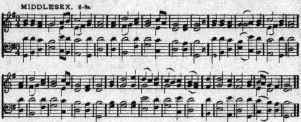

132 *Christ is all, and in all.*

1 THOU hidden Source of calm repose,
Thou all-sufficient Love Divine,
My help and refuge from my foes,
Secure I am, if thou art mine;
And lo! from sin, and grief, and shame,
I hide me, Jesus, in thy Name.

2 Thy mighty Name salvation is,
And keeps my happy soul above;
Comfort it brings, and power, and peace,
And joy, and everlasting love;
To me, with thy dear Name, are given
Pardon, and holiness, and heaven.

3 Jesus, my all in all thou art;
My rest in toil, my ease in pain,
The medicine of my broken heart;
In war my peace, in loss my gain,
My smile beneath the tyrant's frown,
In shame my glory and my crown:

4 In want my plentiful supply,
In weakness my almighty power;
In bonds my perfect liberty,
My light in Satan's darkest hour;
My joy in grief, my shield in strife,
In death my everlasting life.

—*Charles Wesley.*

TUNE: MIDDLESEX. 6-8s. (See Hymn 132.)

133 *Christ the Light of the world.*

1 Stupendous height of heavenly love,
Of pitying tenderness divine!
It brought the Saviour from above,
It caused the springing day to shine;
The Sun of Righteousness to appear,
And gild our gloomy hemisphere.

2 God did in Christ himself reveal,
To chase our darkness by his light,
Our sin and ignorance dispel,
Direct our wandering feet aright,
And bring our souls, with pardon blest,
To realms of everlasting rest.

3 Come then, O Lord, thy light impart,
The faith that bids our terrors cease;
Into thy love direct our heart,
Into thy way of perfect peace;
And cheer the souls of death afraid,
And guide them through the dreadful shade.

4 Answer thy mercy's whole design,
My God incarnated for me;
My spirit make thy radiant shrine,
My light and full salvation be;
And through the shades of death unknown
Conduct me to thy dazzling throne.

—*Charles Wesley.*

ST. BERNARD. C. M. W. Richardson.

134 *"I am the Way, the Truth, and the Life."*

1 Thou art the Way: to thee alone
From sin and death we flee;
And he who would the Father seek,
Must seek him, Lord, by thee.

2 Thou art the Truth: thy word alone
True wisdom can impart;
Thou only canst inform the mind,
And purify the heart.

3 Thou art the Life: the rending tomb
Proclaims thy conquering arm;
And those who put their trust in thee
Nor death nor hell shall harm.

4 Thou art the Way, the Truth, the Life;
Grant us that Way to know,
That Truth to keep, that Life to win,
Whose joys eternal flow.

—*G. W. Doane.*

135 *"The desire of our soul is to thy name."*

1 Thou great Redeemer, dying Lamb,
We love to hear of thee;
No music's like thy charming name,
Nor half so sweet can be.

2 O may we ever hear thy voice
In mercy to us speak!
In thee our Priest we will rejoice,
And thy salvation seek.

3 Our Jesus shall be still our theme,
While in this world we stay;
We'll sing the glories of his name,
When all things else decay.

4 When we appear in yonder cloud,
With all that favoured throng,
Then will we sing more sweet, more loud,
And Christ shall be our song.

—*J. Cennick.*

BEDFORD. C. M. W. WHEALL.

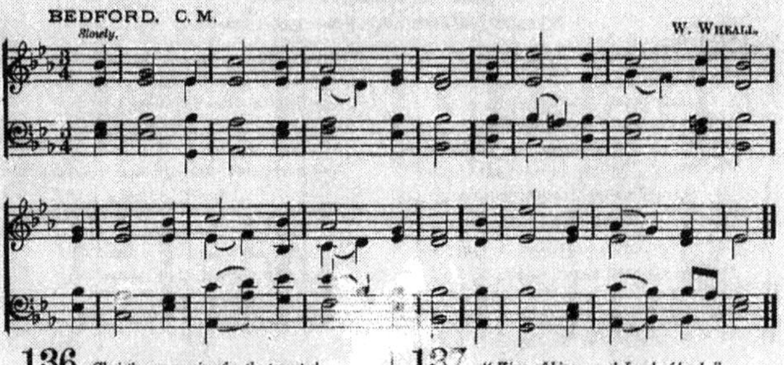
Slowly.

136 *Christ's compassion for the tempted.*

1 WITH joy we meditate the grace
Of our High Priest above;
His heart is made of tenderness,
And yearns with pitying love.

2 Touched with a sympathy within,
He knows our feeble frame;
He knows what sore temptations mean,
For he hath felt the same.

3 He in the days of feeble flesh
Poured out his cries and tears;
And, though exalted, feels afresh
What every member bears.

4 He'll never quench the smoking flax,
But raise it to a flame;
The bruised reed he never breaks,
Nor scorns the meanest name.

5 Then let our humble faith address
His mercy and his power;
We shall obtain delivering grace
In the distressing hour.

—Isaac Watts.

137 *"King of kings, and Lord of lords."*

1 THE head that once was crowned with thorns,
Is crowned with glory now;
A royal diadem adorns
The mighty Victor's brow.

2 The highest place that heaven affords,
Is to our Jesus given;
The King of kings, and Lord of lords,
He reigns o'er earth and heaven.

3 The joy of all who dwell above,
The joy of all below
To whom he manifests his love,
And grants his name to know.

4 To them the cross, with all its shame,
With all its grace, is given;
Their name, an everlasting name,
Their joy, the joy of heaven.

5 They suffer with their Lord below,
They reign with him above;
Their everlasting joy to know
The mystery of his love.

—T. Kelly.

BETHLEHEM. C. M. D. Old Melody, arranged by SIR A. SULLIVAN.

TUNE: BETHLEHEM. C. M. D.

138

Confidence in Christ.

1 Whom Jesus' blood doth sanctify,
Need neither sin nor fear;
Hid in our Saviour's hand we lie,
And laugh at danger near.
His guardian hand doth hold, protect,
And save, by ways unknown,
The little flock, the saints elect,
Who trust in him alone.

2 Our Prophet, Priest, and King, to thee
We joyfully submit;
And learn, in meek humility,
Our lesson at thy feet.
Spirit and life thy words impart,
And blessings from above;
And drop, in every listening heart
The manna of thy love.

—*Charles Wesley.*

ABRIDGE. C. M. Isaac Smith.

139

Luke iv. 18.

1 Hark! the glad sound, the Saviour comes!
The Saviour promised long;
Let every heart exult with joy,
And every voice be song!

2 On him the Spirit, largely shed,
Exerts its sacred fire;
Wisdom and might, and zeal and love,
His holy breast inspire.

3 He comes! the prisoners to release,
In Satan's bondage held;
The gates of brass before him burst,
The iron fetters yield.

4 He comes! from darkening scales of vice
To clear the inward sight;
And on the eyeballs of the blind
To pour celestial light.

5 He comes! the broken hearts to bind,
The bleeding souls to cure;
And with the treasures of his grace
To enrich the humble poor.

6 Our glad hosannas, Prince of Peace,
Thy welcome shall proclaim;
And heaven's exalted arches ring
With thy victorious name.

—*Doddridge.*

140

Joy at the Redeemer's birth.

1 Mortals, awake! with angels join,
And chant the solemn lay;
Joy, love, and gratitude combine
To hail the auspicious day.

2 In heaven the rapturous song began,
And sweet seraphic fire
Through all the shining legions ran,
And strung and tuned the lyre.

3 Swift through the vast expanse it flew,
And loud the echo rolled;
The theme, the song, the joy, was new;
'Twas more than heaven could hold.

4 Down through the portals of the sky
The impetuous torrent ran;
And angels flew, with eager joy,
To bear the news to man.

5 Hark! the cherubic armies shout,
And glory leads the song;
Good-will and peace are heard throughout
The vast celestial throng.

6 With joy the chorus we repeat,
"Glory to God on high!"
Good-will and peace are now complete,
Jesus was born to die.

7 Hail, Prince of Life, forever hail!
Redeemer, Brother, Friend!
Though earth, and time, and life shall fail,
Thy praise shall never end.

—*S. Medley.*

NOEL. C. M. D. Arranged by SIR ARTHUR SULLIVAN.

141 *"There was with the angel a multitude of the heavenly host praising God."*

1 IT came upon the midnight clear,
That glorious song of old,
From angels bending near the earth
To touch their harps of gold;
"Peace on the earth, good-will to men,
From heaven's all-gracious King!"
The world in solemn stillness lay
To hear the angels sing.

2 Still through the cloven skies they come,
With peaceful wings unfurled,
And still their heavenly music floats
O'er all the weary world;
Above its sad and lowly plains
They bend on hovering wing,
And ever o'er its Babel sounds
The blessed angels sing.

3 Yet with the woes of sin and strife
The world has suffered long;
Beneath the angel-strain have rolled
Two thousand years of wrong;
And man, at war with man, hears not
The love-song which they bring:
O hush the noise, ye men of strife,
And hear the angels sing!

4 And ye, beneath life's crushing load,
Whose forms are bending low,
Who toil along the climbing way,
With painful steps and slow,—
Look now, for glad and golden hours
Come swiftly on the wing;
O rest beside the weary road,
And hear the angels sing!

5 For lo! the days are hastening on
By prophet-bards foretold,
When with the ever-circling years
Comes round the age of gold;
When peace shall over all the earth
Its ancient splendours fling,
And the whole world give back the song
Which now the angels sing.

—*R. Sears.*

MENDELSSOHN. 8-7s. F. MENDELSSOHN.

MENDELSSOHN. *(Continued.)*

Hark! the herald-angels sing, "Glo - ry to the new-born King."
Organ Ped.

142 *"Glory to God in the highest."*

1 HARK! the herald-angels sing
"Glory to the new-born King,
Peace on earth, and mercy mild;
God and sinners reconciled."

2 Joyful, all ye nations, rise,
Join the triumph of the skies;
With angelic hosts proclaim,
"Christ is born in Bethlehem!"

3 Christ, by highest heaven adored,
Christ, the everlasting Lord;
Veiled in flesh the Godhead see;
Hail the incarnate Deity!

4 Mild he lays his glory by,
Born that man no more may die;
Born to raise the sons of earth,
Born to give them second birth.

5 Hail the heaven-born Prince of Peace!
Hail the Sun of righteousness!
Light and life to all he brings,
Risen with healing in his wings.

—*Charles Wesley.*

(Repeat first verse at end.)

CORNELL. 8.7, 8.7. J. H. CORNELL.

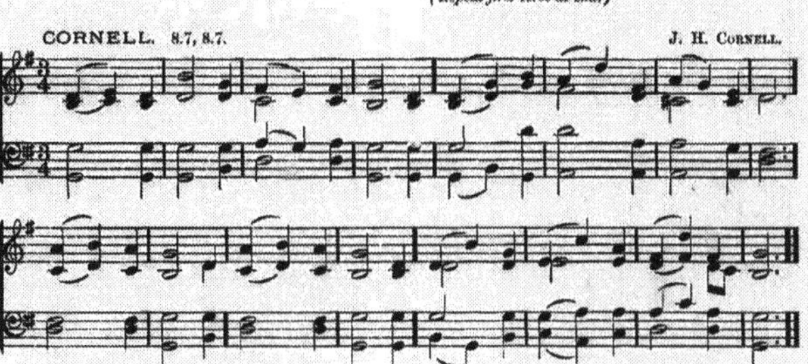

143 *"On earth peace, good-will toward men."*

1 HARK! what mean those holy voices,
Sweetly sounding through the skies?
Lo! the angelic host rejoices;
Heavenly hallelujahs rise.

2 Listen to the wondrous story,
Which they chant in hymns of joy:
"Glory in the highest, glory,
Glory be to God most high!"

3 Peace on earth, good-will from heaven,
Reaching far as man is found;
Souls redeemed, and sins forgiven,
Loud our golden harps shall sound.

4 Christ is born, the great Anointed;
Heaven and earth his praises sing;
O receive whom God appointed
For your Prophet, Priest, and King.

5 Hasten, mortals, to adore him;
Learn his name, and taste his joy;
Till in heaven ye sing before him,
"Glory be to God most high!"

—*J. Cawood.*

ST. OSWALD. 8.7, 8.7, 8.7, 8.7. DR. DYKES.

D.C.

144 "The desire of all nations shall come."

1 COME, thou long-expected Jesus,
Born to set thy people free,
From our fears and sins release us,
Let us find our rest in thee.
Israel's strength and consolation,
Hope of all the earth thou art;
Dear Desire of every nation,
Joy of every longing heart.

2 Born thy people to deliver,
Born a child and yet a king,
Born to reign in us forever,
Now thy gracious kingdom bring.
By thine own eternal Spirit
Rule in all our hearts alone;
By thine all-sufficient merit
Raise us to thy glorious throne.

—*Charles Wesley.*

REGENT SQUARE. 8.7.8.7.4.7. HENRY SMART.

145 *The Adoration of Christ.*

1 ANGELS, from the realms of glory,
Wing your flight o'er all the earth;
Ye who sang creation's story,
Now proclaim Messiah's birth:
||:Come and worship,:||
Worship Christ, the newborn King.

2 Shepherds, in the field abiding,
Watching o'er your flocks by night,
God with man is now residing;
Yonder shines the infant light:
||:Come and worship,:||
Worship Christ, the newborn King.

3 Sages, leave your contemplations,
Brighter visions beam afar;
Seek the great Desire of nations;
Ye have seen his natal star:
||:Come and worship,:||
Worship Christ, the newborn King.

4 Saints, before the altar bending,
Watching long in hope and fear,
Suddenly the Lord, descending,
In his temple shall appear:
||:Come and worship,:||
Worship Christ, the newborn King.

—*Montgomery.*

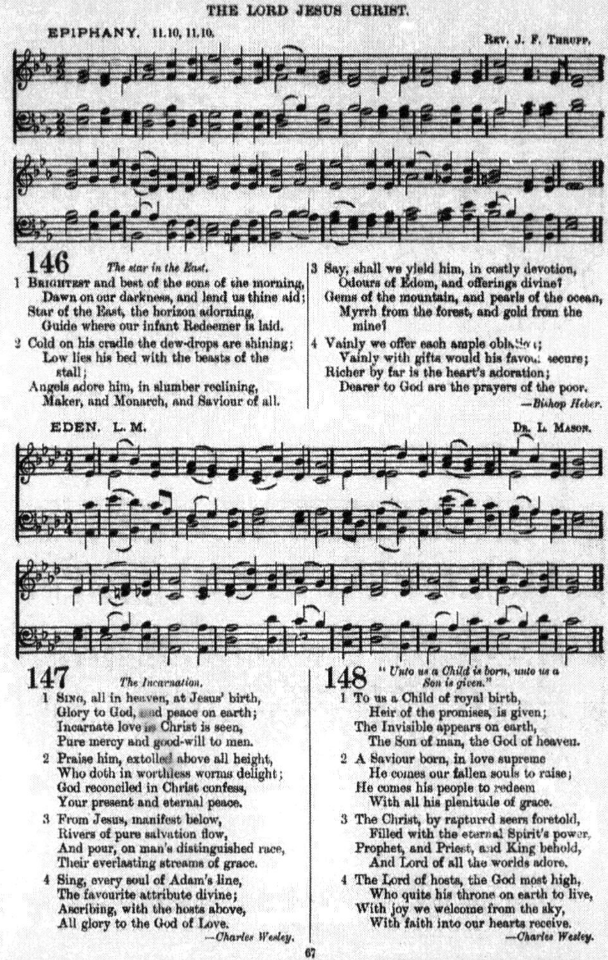

EPIPHANY. 11.10, 11.10. — REV. J. F. THRUPP.

146

The star in the East.

1 BRIGHTEST and best of the sons of the morning,
Dawn on our darkness, and lend us thine aid;
Star of the East, the horizon adorning,
Guide where our infant Redeemer is laid.

2 Cold on his cradle the dew-drops are shining;
Low lies his bed with the beasts of the stall;
Angels adore him, in slumber reclining,
Maker, and Monarch, and Saviour of all.

3 Say, shall we yield him, in costly devotion,
Odours of Edom, and offerings divine?
Gems of the mountain, and pearls of the ocean,
Myrrh from the forest, and gold from the mine?

4 Vainly we offer each ample oblation;
Vainly with gifts would his favour secure;
Richer by far is the heart's adoration;
Dearer to God are the prayers of the poor.

—*Bishop Heber.*

EDEN. L. M. — DR. L. MASON.

147

The Incarnation.

1 SING, all in heaven, at Jesus' birth,
Glory to God, and peace on earth;
Incarnate love in Christ is seen,
Pure mercy and good-will to men.

2 Praise him, extolled above all height,
Who doth in worthless worms delight;
God reconciled in Christ confess,
Your present and eternal peace.

3 From Jesus, manifest below,
Rivers of pure salvation flow,
And pour, on man's distinguished race,
Their everlasting streams of grace.

4 Sing, every soul of Adam's line,
The favourite attribute divine;
Ascribing, with the hosts above,
All glory to the God of Love.

—*Charles Wesley.*

148

"Unto us a Child is born, unto us a Son is given."

1 To us a Child of royal birth,
Heir of the promises, is given;
The Invisible appears on earth,
The Son of man, the God of heaven.

2 A Saviour born, in love supreme
He comes our fallen souls to raise;
He comes his people to redeem
With all his plenitude of grace.

3 The Christ, by raptured seers foretold,
Filled with the eternal Spirit's power,
Prophet, and Priest, and King behold,
And Lord of all the worlds adore.

4 The Lord of hosts, the God most high,
Who quits his throne on earth to live,
With joy we welcome from the sky,
With faith into our hearts receive.

—*Charles Wesley.*

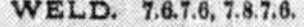
WELD. 7.6.7.6, 7.8.7.6.

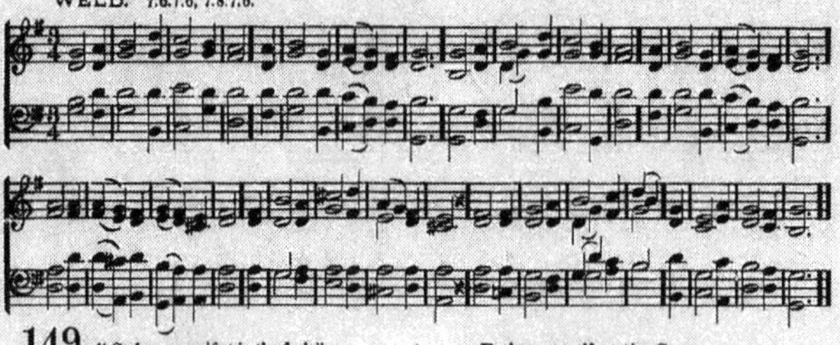

149 *"God was manifest in the flesh."*

1 Celebrate Immanuel's name,
 The Prince of Life and Peace;
God with us, our lips proclaim,
 Our faithful hearts confess:
God is in our flesh revealed;
 And earth and heaven in Jesus join;
Mortal with immortal filled,
 And human with divine.

2 Fulness of the Deity
 In our Immanuel dwells,
Dwells in all his saints and me,
 When God his Son reveals:
Father, manifest thy Son,
 And, conscious of the incarnate Word,
In our inmost souls make known
 The presence of the Lord.

3 Let the Spirit of our Head
 Through every member flow;
By our Lord inhabited,
 His saving power we know:
Then he doth his name express,
 And God in us we truly prove,
Filled with all the life of grace,
 And all the power of love.

—*Charles Wesley.*

FAITH. 7.6.7.6, 7.7.7.6. Dr. S. S. Wesley.

150 *Christ crucified.*

1 God of unexampled grace,
 Redeemer of mankind,
Matter of eternal praise
 We in thy passion find;
Still our choicest strains we bring,
 Still the joyful theme pursue,
Thee the Friend of sinners sing,
 Whose love is ever new.

2 Endless scenes of wonder rise
 From that mysterious tree,
Crucified before our eyes,
 Where we our Saviour see:
Jesus, Lord, what hast thou done?
 Publish we the death divine,
Stop, and gaze, and fall, and own
 Was never love like thine!

3 Never love nor sorrow was
 Like that my Saviour showed:
See him stretched on yonder cross,
 And crushed beneath our load!
Now discern the Deity,
 Now his heavenly birth declare!
Faith cries out, "'Tis he, 'tis he,
 My Lord, that suffers there!"

—*Charles Wesley.*

CRUCIFIXION. L. M.

151 *"He said, It is finished."*

1 'Tis finished! the Messiah dies,
Cut off for sins, but not his own;
Accomplished is the sacrifice,
The great redeeming work is done.

2 The veil is rent; in Christ alone
The living way to heaven is seen;
The middle wall is broken down,
And all mankind may enter in.

3 The types and figures are fulfilled;
Exacted is the legal pain;
The precious promises are sealed;
The spotless Lamb of God is slain.

4 The reign of sin and death is o'er,
And all may live from sin set free;
Satan hath lost his mortal power;
'Tis swallowed up in victory.

5 Death, hell, and sin are now subdued;
All grace is now to sinners given;
And, lo, we plead the atoning blood,
And in thy right we claim thy heaven.

—Charles Wesley.

ROCKINGHAM. L. M. Dr. Miller.

152 *"God forbid that I should glory, save in the cross of our Lord Jesus Christ."*

mf 1 When I survey the wondrous cross
On which the Prince of Glory died,
cres. My richest gain I count but loss,
And pour contempt on all my pride.

mf 2 Forbid it, Lord, that I should boast,
Save in the death of Christ, my God;
All the vain things that charm me most,
I sacrifice them to his blood.

p 3 See, from his head, his hands, his feet,
Sorrow and love flow mingled down;
Did e'er such love and sorrow meet,
dim. Or thorns compose so rich a crown!

f 4 Were the whole realm of nature mine,
That were a present far too small;
cres. Love so amazing, so divine,
ff Demands my soul, my life, my all.

—Isaac Watts.

ANGELUS. L. M. — J. SCHEFFLER.

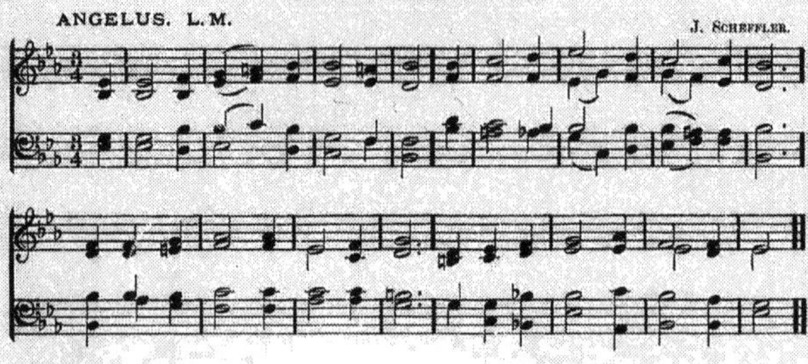

153 "*A shadow of good things to come.*"

1 O THOU, whose offering on the tree
 The legal offerings all foreshowed,
Borrowed their whole effect from thee,
 And drew their virtue from thy blood:

2 The blood of goats, and bullocks slain,
 Could never for one sin atone;
To purge the guilty offerer's stain,
 Thine was the work, and thine alone.

3 Vain in themselves their duties were;
 Their services could never please,
Till joined with thine, and made to share
 The merits of thy righteousness.

4 Forward they cast a faithful look
 On thy approaching sacrifice;
And thence their pleasing savour took,
 And rose accepted in the skies.

5 Those feeble types, and shadows old,
 Are all in thee, the Truth, fulfilled;
We in thy sacrifice behold
 The substance of those rites revealed.

6 Thy meritorious sufferings past,
 We see by faith to us brought back;
And on thy grand oblation cast,
 Its saving benefits partake.

—*Charles Wesley.*

BARNBY. 6-8s. — J. BARNBY.

TUNE: BARNBY. 6-8s.

154 *"Jesus Christ, and him crucified."*

1 O Love Divine! what hast thou done!
The incarnate God hath died for me!
The Father's co-eternal Son
Bore all my sins upon the tree:
The incarnate God for me hath died;
My Lord, my Love, is crucified.

2 Behold him, all ye that pass by,
The bleeding Prince of Life and Peace!
Come, sinners, see your Saviour die,
And say, was ever grief like his!
Come, feel with me his blood applied;
My Lord, my Love, is crucified.

3 Is crucified for me and you,
To bring us rebels back to God;
Believe, believe the record true;
Ye all are bought with Jesus' blood;
Pardon for all flows from his side;
My Lord, my Love, is crucified.

4 Then let us sit beneath his cross,
And gladly catch the healing stream;
All things for him account but loss,
And give up all our hearts to him;
Of nothing think or speak beside,—
"My Lord, my Love, is crucified."

—*Charles Wesley.*

SELENA. 6-8s. — Isaac Baker Woodbury.

155 *"While we were yet sinners, Christ died for us."*

1 Would Jesus have the sinner die?
Why hangs he then on yonder tree?
What means that strange expiring cry?
Sinners, he prays for you and me;
"Forgive them, Father, O forgive!
They know not that by me they live!"

2 Thou loving, all-atoning Lamb,
Thee—by thy painful agony,
Thy bloody sweat, thy grief and shame,
Thy cross and passion on the tree,
Thy precious death and life—I pray,
Take all, take all my sins away!

3 O let me kiss thy bleeding feet,
And bathe and wash them with my tears;
The story of thy love repeat
In every drooping sinner's ears;
That all may hear the quickening sound,
Since I, even I, have mercy found.

4 O let thy love my heart constrain,
Thy love for every sinner free;
That every fallen soul of man
May taste the grace that found out me;
That all mankind with me may prove
Thy sovereign, everlasting love.

—*Charles Wesley.*

156 *The Death of Christ.*

1 O thou eternal Victim, slain
A sacrifice for guilty man,
By the eternal Spirit made
An offering in the sinner's stead;
Our everlasting Priest art thou,
And plead'st thy death for sinners now.

2 Thy offering still continues new;
Thy vesture keeps its crimson hue;
Thou stand'st the ever-slaughtered Lamb;
Thy priesthood still remains the same;
Thy years, O God, can never fail,
Thy goodness is unchangeable.

3 O that our faith may never move,
But stand unshaken as thy love!
Sure evidence of things unseen,
Now let it pass the years between,
And view thee bleeding on the tree,
My God, who dies for me, for me!

—*Charles Wesley.*

CAMBRIDGE. S. M. REV. R. HARRISON.

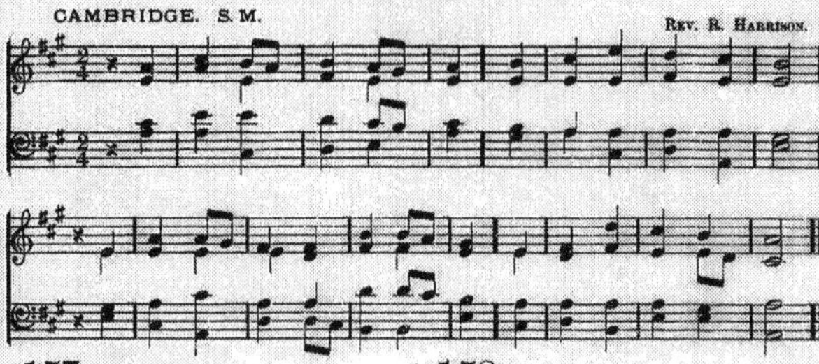

157 *Christ our only sacrifice.*

1 Not all the blood of beasts
On Jewish altars slain,
Could give the guilty conscience peace,
Or wash away our stain.

2 But Christ, the heavenly Lamb,
Takes all our sins away;
A sacrifice of nobler name,
And richer blood, than they.

3 Believing, we rejoice
To feel the curse remove;
We bless the Lamb, with cheerful voice,
And trust his bleeding love.

—*Isaac Watts.*

158 *"Behold, I send an Angel before thee."*

1 Thou very Paschal Lamb,
Whose blood for us was shed,
Through whom we out of bondage came,
Thy ransomed people led.

2 Angel of gospel grace,
Fulfil thy character;
To guard and feed the chosen race,
In Israel's camp appear.

3 Throughout the desert way,
Conduct us by thy light;
Be thou a cooling cloud by day,
A cheering fire by night.

4 Our fainting souls sustain
With blessings from above,
And ever on thy people rain
The manna of thy love.

—*Charles Wesley.*

LEEDS. S. M. SACRED HARMONY.

159 *"This is he that came not by water only, but by water and blood."*

1 This, this is he that came
By water and by blood;
Jesus is our atoning Lamb,
Our sanctifying God.

2 See from his wounded side
The mingled current flow!
The water and the blood applied
Shall wash us white as snow.

3 The water cannot cleanse,
Before the blood we feel,
To purge the guilt of all our sins,
And our forgiveness seal.

4 But both in Jesus join,
Who speaks our sins forgiven,
And gives the purity divine
That makes us meet for heaven.

—*Charles Wesley.*

AJALON. 6-7s. (First Tune.) — R. Redhead.

160

Christ the Rock of ages.

mp 1 Rock of ages, cleft for me,
Let me hide myself in thee,
Let the water and the blood
From thy wounded side which flowed,
Be of sin the double cure,
Save from wrath and make me pure.

mp 2 Could my tears for ever flow,
Could my zeal no languor know,
These for sin could not atone;
Thou must save and thou alone:
In my hand no price I bring,
Simply to thy cross I cling.

pp 3 While I draw this fleeting breath,
When my eyes shall close in death,
cres. When I rise to worlds unknown,
ff And behold thee on thy throne,
Rock of ages, cleft for me,
dim. Let me hide myself in thee.

—*Toplady.*

TOPLADY. 6-7s. (Second Tune.) — T. Hastings.

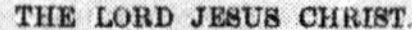

HOLLEY. 4-7s. G. Hews.

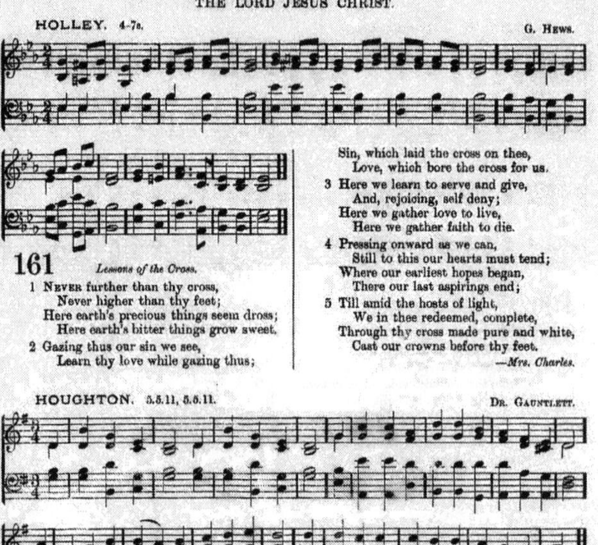

161

Lessons of the Cross.

1 Never further than thy cross,
Never higher than thy feet;
Here earth's precious things seem dross;
Here earth's bitter things grow sweet.

2 Gazing thus our sin we see,
Learn thy love while gazing thus;
Sin, which laid the cross on thee,
Love, which bore the cross for us.

3 Here we learn to serve and give,
And, rejoicing, self deny;
Here we gather love to live,
Here we gather faith to die.

4 Pressing onward as we can,
Still to this our hearts must tend;
Where our earliest hopes began,
There our last aspirings end;

5 Till amid the hosts of light,
We in thee redeemed, complete,
Through thy cross made pure and white,
Cast our crowns before thy feet.

—*Mrs. Charles.*

HOUGHTON. 5.5.11, 5.5.11. Dr. Gauntlett.

162

"Who was delivered for our offences."

1 All ye that pass by,
To Jesus draw nigh;
To you is it nothing that Jesus should die?
Your ransom and peace,
Your Saviour he is;
Come, see if there ever was sorrow like his.

2 He suffered for all;
O come at his call,
And low at his cross with astonishment fall.
But lift up your eyes
At Jesus's cries;
Impassive, he suffers; immortal, he dies.

3 For you and for me
He prayed on the tree;
The prayer is accepted, the sinner is free.
That sinner am I,
Who on Jesus rely,
And come for the pardon God will not deny.

4 My pardon I claim,
For a sinner I am,
A sinner believing in Jesus's name.
He purchased the grace
Which now I embrace;
O Father, thou know'st he hath died in my place.

5 His death is my plea;
My Advocate see,
And hear the blood speak that hath answered for me.
My ransom he was,
When he bled on the cross;
And by losing his life he hath carried my cause.

—*Charles Wesley.*

CHAMOUNI. 7.6, 7.6, 7.6, 7.6. C. E. KETTLE.

163

Christ crowned with thorns.

1 O LAMB of God, once wounded,
With grief and pain weighed down,
Thy sacred head surrounded
With thorns, thine only crown!
O Lamb of God, what glory,
What bliss, till now was thine!
Yet, though despised and gory,
I joy to call thee mine.

2 What thou, my Lord, hast suffered
Was all for sinners' gain;
Mine, mine was the transgression,
But thine the deadly pain.
Lo, here I fall, my Saviour!
'Tis I deserve thy place;
Look on me with thy favour,
Vouchsafe to me thy grace.

3 What language shall I borrow
To praise thee, dearest Friend,
For this, thy dying sorrow,
Thy pity without end?
O make me thine forever;
And should I fainting be,
Lord, let me never, never
Outlive my love to thee.

4 Be near me when I'm dying,
O show thyself to me;
And, for my succour flying,
Come, Lord, and set me free:
These eyes, new faith receiving,
From Jesus shall not move;
For he who dies believing,
Dies safely, through thy love.

—*Charles Wesley.*

BONAR. 8.8.7, 8.8.7. J. B. CALKIN.

164

"He was wounded for our transgressions."

1 DARKLY rose the guilty morning,
When, the King of Glory scorning,
Raged the fierce Jerusalem;
See the Christ, his cross up-bearing,
See him stricken, wounded, wearing
The thorn-platted diadem.

2 Not the crowd whose cries assailed him
Not the hands that rudely nailed him,
Slew him on the cursèd tree;
Ours the sin from heaven that called him,
Ours the sin whose burden galled him
In the sad Gethsemane.

3 For our sins, of glory emptied,
He was fasting, lone, and tempted,
He was slain on Calvary;
Yet he for his murderers pleaded:
Lord, by us that prayer is needed;
We have pierced, yet trust in thee.

4 In our joy or tribulation,
By thy precious cross and passion,
By thy blood and agony,
By thy glorious resurrection,
By thy Holy Ghost's protection,
Make us thine eternally.

DUNDEE. C. M. — SCOTCH PSALTER, 1615.

165

"There they crucified him."

1 BEHOLD the Saviour of mankind
Nailed to the shameful tree!
How vast the love that him inclined
To bleed and die for thee!

2 Hark, how he groans! while nature shakes,
And earth's strong pillars bend;
The temple's veil in sunder breaks,
The solid marbles rend.

3 'Tis done! the precious ransom's paid,
"Receive my soul!" he cries;
See where he bows his sacred head;
He bows his head, and dies!

4 But soon he'll break death's envious chain,
And in full glory shine:
O Lamb of God! was ever pain,
Was ever love, like thine!

—*S. Wesley, sen.*

ST. AGNES. C. M. — DR. DYKES.

166

Godly sorrow at the Cross.

1 ALAS! and did my Saviour bleed?
And did my Sovereign die?
Would he devote that sacred head
For such a worm as I?

2 Was it for crimes that I have done,
He groaned upon the tree?
Amazing pity! grace unknown!
And love beyond degree!

3 Well might the sun in darkness hide,
And shut his glories in,
When Christ, the mighty Maker, died
For man, the creature's sin.

4 Thus might I hide my blushing face
While his dear cross appears;
Dissolve my heart in thankfulness,
And melt mine eyes to tears.

5 But drops of grief can ne'er repay
The debt of love I owe;
Here, Lord, I give myself away,—
'Tis all that I can do.

—*Isaac Watts.*

SPOHR. C. M. — DR. L. SPOHR.

167 *Power of a crucified Saviour.*

1 JESUS, thou all-redeeming Lord,
Thy blessing we implore;
Open the door to preach thy word,
The great effectual door.

2 Gather the outcasts in, and save
From sin and Satan's power;
And let them now acceptance have,
And know their gracious hour.

3 Lover of souls, thou know'st to prize
What thou hast bought so dear;
Come then, and in thy people's eyes
With all thy wounds appear.

4 Appear, as when of old confest,
The suffering Son of God;
And let them see thee in thy vest
But newly dipt in blood.

5 The hardness from their hearts remove,
Thou who for all hast died;
Show them the tokens of thy love,
Thy feet, thy hands, thy side.

6 Thy side an open fountain is,
Where all may freely go,
And drink the living streams of bliss,
And wash them white as snow.

7 Ready thou art the blood to apply,
And prove the record true;
And all thy wounds to sinners cry,
"I suffered this for you!"

—*Charles Wesley.*

VERMONT. 8, 7, 8, 7. — WEBER.

168 *The Cross of Christ.*

1 SWEET the moments, rich in blessing,
Which before the cross I spend;
Life, and health, and peace possessing,
From the sinner's dying Friend.

2 Truly blessèd is the station,
Low before his cross to lie,
While I see divine compassion
Beaming from his gracious eye.

3 Here it is I find my heaven,
While upon the Lamb I gaze;
Love I much? I've much forgiven;
I'm a miracle of grace.

4 Love and grief my heart dividing,
With my tears his feet I'll bathe;
Constant still, in faith abiding,
Life deriving from his death.

5 Here in tender, grateful sorrow
With my Saviour will I stay;
Here new hope and strength will borrow;
Here will love my fears away.

—*Allen and Shirley.*

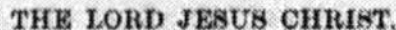

ST. OSWALD. 8.7, 8.7. Dr. Dykes.

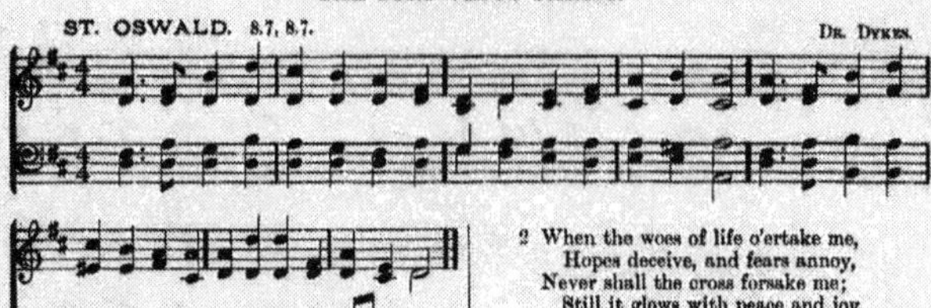

169

Glorying in the Cross.

1 In the cross of Christ I glory,
Towering o'er the wrecks of time;
All the light of sacred story
Gathers round its head sublime.

2 When the woes of life o'ertake me,
Hopes deceive, and fears annoy,
Never shall the cross forsake me;
Still it glows with peace and joy.

3 When the sun of bliss is beaming
Light and love upon my way,
From the cross the radiance streaming
Adds more lustre to the day.

4 Bane and blessing, pain and pleasure,
By the cross are sanctified;
Peace is there, that knows no measure,
Joys that evermore abide.

—*Sir John Bowring.*

SALVATOR. 8.7, 8.7, 8.7, 8.7. J. P. Judson.

170

Praise to the risen Saviour.

1 Hail! thou once despisèd Jesus!
Hail, thou Galilean King!
Thou didst suffer to release us;
Thou didst free salvation bring.
Hail, thou agonizing Saviour,
Bearer of our sin and shame!
By thy merits we find favour;
Life is given through thy name.

2 Paschal Lamb, by God appointed,
All our sins on thee were laid;
By almighty Love anointed,
Thou hast full atonement made.
All thy people are forgiven,
Through the virtue of thy blood;
Opened is the gate of heaven,
Peace is made 'twixt man and God.

3 Jesus, hail! enthroned in glory,
There for ever to abide;
All the heavenly host adore thee,
Seated at thy Father's side.
There for sinners thou art pleading,
There thou dost our place prepare;
Ever for us interceding,
Till in glory we appear.

4 Worship, honour, power, and blessing,
Thou art worthy to receive;
Loudest praises without ceasing,
Meet it is for us to give.
Help, ye bright angelic spirits!
Bring your sweetest, noblest lays;
Help to sing our Saviour's merits;
Help to chant Immanuel's praise.

—*J. Bakewell.*

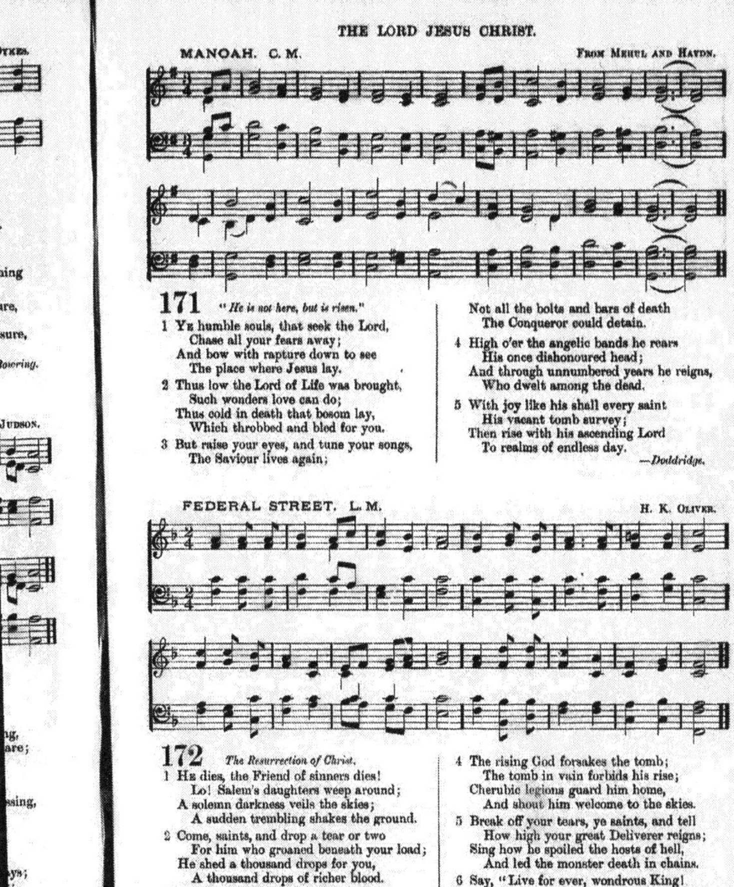

MANOAH. C. M. — From Mehul and Haydn.

171 "*He is not here, but is risen.*"

1 Ye humble souls, that seek the Lord,
Chase all your fears away;
And bow with rapture down to see
The place where Jesus lay.

2 Thus low the Lord of Life was brought,
Such wonders love can do;
Thus cold in death that bosom lay,
Which throbbed and bled for you.

3 But raise your eyes, and tune your songs,
The Saviour lives again;
Not all the bolts and bars of death
The Conqueror could detain.

4 High o'er the angelic bands he rears
His once dishonoured head;
And through unnumbered years he reigns,
Who dwelt among the dead.

5 With joy like his shall every saint
His vacant tomb survey;
Then rise with his ascending Lord
To realms of endless day.

—*Doddridge.*

FEDERAL STREET. L. M. — H. K. Oliver.

172 *The Resurrection of Christ.*

1 He dies, the Friend of sinners dies!
Lo! Salem's daughters weep around;
A solemn darkness veils the skies;
A sudden trembling shakes the ground.

2 Come, saints, and drop a tear or two
For him who groaned beneath your load;
He shed a thousand drops for you,
A thousand drops of richer blood.

3 Here's love and grief beyond degree;
The Lord of glory dies for man!
But, lo! what sudden joys I see,
Jesus, the dead, revives again!

4 The rising God forsakes the tomb;
The tomb in vain forbids his rise;
Cherubic legions guard him home,
And shout him welcome to the skies.

5 Break off your tears, ye saints, and tell
How high your great Deliverer reigns;
Sing how he spoiled the hosts of hell,
And led the monster death in chains.

6 Say, "Live for ever, wondrous King!
Born to redeem, and strong to save;"
Then ask the monster, "Where's thy sting?"
And, "Where's thy victory, boasting grave?"

—*Isaac Watts.*

PILTON. 4-7s.

173 *Salvation through the risen Saviour.*

1 Sons of God, triumphant rise,
Shout the finished sacrifice!
Shout your sins in Christ forgiven,
Sons of God and heirs of heaven.

2 Ye that round our altars throng,
Listening angels, join the song;
Sing with us, ye heavenly powers,
Pardon, grace, and glory ours!

3 Love's mysterious work is done;
Greet we now the atoning Son;
Healed and quickened by his blood,
Joined to Christ, and one with God.

4 Him by faith we taste below,
Mightier joys ordained to know,
When his utmost grace we prove,
Rise to heaven by perfect love.

5 There we shall with thee remain,
Partners of thy endless reign;
There thy face unclouded see,
Find our heaven of heavens in thee.

—*Charles Wesley.*

EASTER HYMN. 4-7s. CAREY.

Hal . . . . . . le . . . . lu . jah!
Hal . . . . le . . . lu . . jah!
Hal . . . . . . le . . . . . lu . . . jah!

EASTER HYMN. *(Continued.)*

Hal . . . . . . le . . lu . . jah!

174 *"Because I live, ye shall live also."*

1 "CHRIST, the Lord, is risen to-day,"
Sons of men and angels say;
Raise your joys and triumphs high;
Sing, ye heavens; thou earth, reply.

2 Love's redeeming work is done;
Fought the fight, the battle won;
Lo! the sun's eclipse is o'er,
Lo! he sets in blood no more.

3 Vain the stone, the watch, the seal,
Christ hath burst the gates of hell;
Death in vain forbids his rise,
Christ hath opened Paradise.

4 Lives again our glorious King,
Where, O death, is now thy sting?
Once he died our souls to save;
Where's thy victory, boasting grave?

5 Soar we now where Christ hath led,
Following our exalted Head;
Made like him, like him we rise,
Ours the cross, the grave, the skies.

6 King of glory! Soul of bliss!
Everlasting life is this,—
Thee to know, thy power to prove,
Thus to sing, and thus to love.

—*Charles Wesley.*

REGENT SQUARE. 8.7, 8.7, 4.7. HENRY SMART.

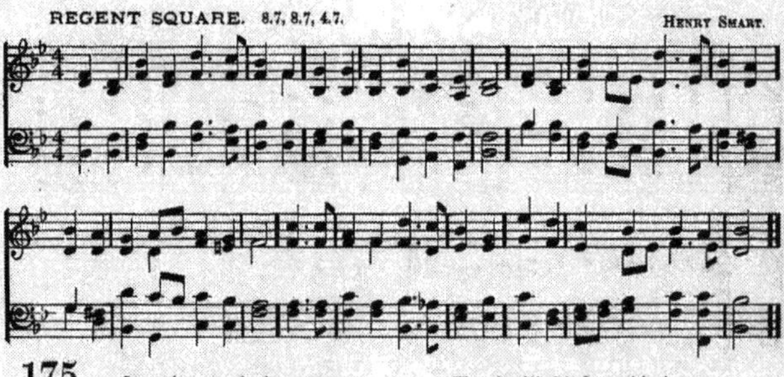

175 *Jesus, victor over death.*

1 COME, ye saints, look here and wonder,
See the place where Jesus lay;
He has burst his bands asunder;
He has borne our sins away;
‖:Joyful tidings!:‖
Yes, the Lord has risen to-day.

2 Jesus triumphs! sing ye praises;
By his death he overcame;
Thus the Lord his glory raises,
Thus he fills his foes with shame:
‖:Sing ye praises!:‖
Praises to the Victor's name.

3 Jesus triumphs! countless legions
Come from heaven to meet their King;
Soon, in yonder blessed regions,
They shall join his praise to sing
‖:Songs eternal:‖
Shall through heaven's high arches ring.

—*T. Kelly.*

ESSEX. 4-7s. THOMAS CLARKE.

176

"The Lord is risen indeed."

1 CHRIST, the Lord, is risen again,
Christ hath broken every chain;
Hark! angelic voices cry,
Singing evermore on high,
Hallelujah! Praise the Lord!

2 He who gave for us his life,
Who for us endured the strife,
Is our Paschal Lamb to-day;
We, too, sing for joy, and say,
Hallelujah! Praise the Lord!

3 He who bore all pain and loss,
Comfortless, upon the cross,
Lives in glory now on high,
Pleads for us, and hears our cry;
Hallelujah! Praise the Lord!

4 Now he bids us tell abroad
How the lost may be restored,
How the penitent forgiven,
How we, too, may enter heaven;
Hallelujah! Praise the Lord!

—*M. Weisse.*

VIENNA. 4-7s. J. H. KNECHT.

177

Eph. iv. 8.

1 HAIL, the day that sees him rise
To his throne above the skies;
Christ the Lamb for sinners given,
Enters now the highest heaven.

2 There for him high triumph waits;
Lift your heads, eternal gates;
He hath conquered death and sin,
Take the King of glory in.

3 Lo! the heaven its Lord receives;
Yet he loves the earth he leaves;
Though returning to his throne,
Still he calls mankind his own.

4 See, he lifts his hands above;
See, he shows the prints of love;
Hark! his gracious lips bestow
Blessings on his church below.

5 Still for us he intercedes,
His prevailing death he pleads;
Near himself prepares our place,
He, the first-fruits of our race.

6 Lord, though parted from our sight,
Far above the starry height,
Grant our hearts may thither rise,
Seeking thee above the skies.

—*Charles Wesley.*

CALEDON. 6.6, 6.6, 8.8.

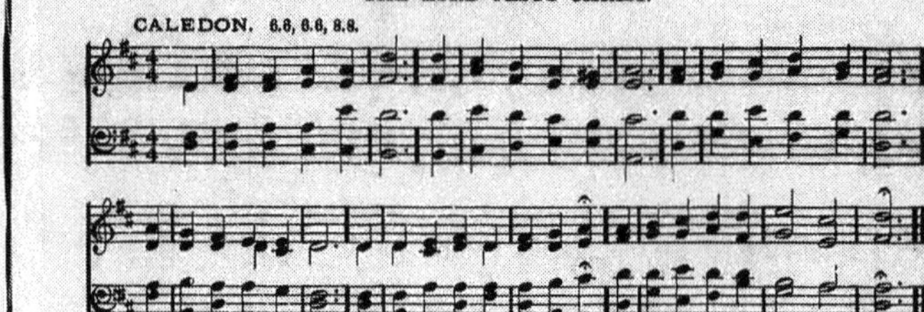

178 "*All power is given unto me.*"

1 God is gone up on high,
With a triumphant noise;
The clarions of the sky
Proclaim the angelic joys:
Join all on earth, rejoice and sing;
Glory ascribe to glory's King.

2 All power to our great Lord
Is by the Father given;
By angel-hosts adored,
He reigns supreme in heaven:
Join all on earth, rejoice and sing;
Glory ascribe to glory's King.

3 High on his holy seat,
He bears the righteous sway;
His foes beneath his feet
Shall sink and die away;
Join all on earth, rejoice and sing;
Glory ascribe to glory's King.

4 His foes and ours are one,
Satan, the world, and sin;
But he shall tread them down,
And bring his kingdom in:
Join all on earth, rejoice and sing;
Glory ascribe to glory's King.

5 Till all the earth, renewed
In righteousness divine,
With all the hosts of God
In one great chorus join;
Join all on earth, rejoice and sing;
Glory ascribe to glory's King.

—*Charles Wesley.*

GERMANY. L. M. BEETHOVEN.

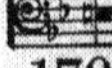

179 *The Ascension of Christ.*

1 Our Lord is risen from the dead,
Our Jesus is gone up on high;
The powers of hell are captive led,
Dragged to the portals of the sky.

2 There his triumphal chariot waits,
And angels chant the solemn lay:
Lift up your heads, ye heavenly gates;
Ye everlasting doors, give way!

3 Loose all your bars of massy light,
And wide unfold the ethereal scene;
He claims these mansions as his right;
Receive the King of glory in!

4 Who is the King of glory? Who?
The Lord that all our foes o'ercame;
The world, sin, death, and hell o'erthrew;
And Jesus is the Conqueror's name.

5 Lo! his triumphal chariot waits,
And angels chant the solemn lay:
Lift up your heads, ye heavenly gates;
Ye everlasting doors, give way!

6 Who is the King of glory? Who?
The Lord, of glorious power possessed;
The King of saints, and angels too,
God over all, for ever blessed!

—*Charles Wesley.*

ST. ALBAN. L. M. ST. ALBAN'S TUNE BOOK.

180 *Christ a sympathizing High Priest.*

1 WHERE high the heavenly temple stands,
The house of God not made with hands,
A great High Priest our nature wears,
The Guardian of mankind appears.

2 He who for men their surety stood,
And poured on earth his precious blood,
Pursues in heaven his mighty plan,
The Saviour and the Friend of man.

3 Though now ascended up on high,
He bends on earth a brother's eye;
Partaker of the human name,
He knows the frailty of our frame.

4 Our fellow-sufferer yet retains
A fellow-feeling of our pains;
And still remembers in the skies
His tears, his agonies, his cries.

5 In every pang that rends the heart,
The Man of sorrows had a part;
Touched with the feeling of our grief,
He to the sufferer sends relief.

6 With boldness, therefore, at the throne,
Let us make all our sorrows known;
And ask the aid of heavenly power
To help us in the evil hour.

—*M. Bruce.*

EUPHONY. 6-8s. T. SINGLETON.

TUNE: EUPHONY. 6-8s.

181 *The Priesthood of Christ.*

1 ENTERED the holy place above,
Covered with meritorious scars,
The tokens of his dying love
Our great High Priest in glory bears;
He pleads his passion on the tree,
‖:He shows himself to God for me.:‖

2 Before the throne my Saviour stands,
My Friend and Advocate appears;
My name is graven on his hands,
And him the Father always hears;
While low at Jesus' cross I bow,
‖:He hears the blood of sprinkling now.:‖

3 This instant now I may receive
The answer of his powerful prayer;
This instant now by him I live,
His prevalence with God declare;
And soon my spirit, in his hands,
‖:Shall stand where my Forerunner stands.:‖

—*Charles Wesley.*

SECTION IV.

THE HOLY SPIRIT.

ARNOLD. C. M. — DR. S. ARNOLD.

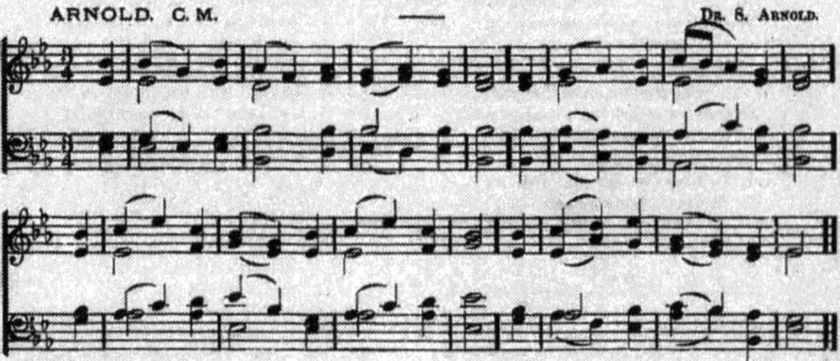

182 *Praise to the Holy Spirit.*

1 HAIL, Holy Ghost, Jehovah, Third
In order of the Three;
Sprung from the Father and the Word
From all eternity!

2 Thy Godhead brooding o'er the abyss
Of formless waters lay;
Spoke into order all that is,
And darkness into day.

3 God's image, which our sins destroy,
Thy grace restores below;
And truth, and holiness, and joy,
From thee, their Fountain, flow.

4 Hail, Holy Ghost, Jehovah, Third
In order of the Three;
Sprung from the Father and the Word
From all eternity!

—*S. Wesley, jr.*

183 *The Divine Spirit's influences.*

1 SPIRIT divine, attend our prayers,
And make this house thy home;
Descend with all thy gracious powers,
O come, great Spirit, come!

2 Come as the light! to us reveal
Our emptiness and woe;
And lead us in those paths of life
Where all the righteous go.

3 Come as the fire! and purge our hearts
Like sacrificial flame;
Let our whole soul an offering be
To our Redeemer's name.

4 Come as the dew! and sweetly bless
This consecrated hour,
May barrenness rejoice to own
Thy fertilizing power.

5 Come as the dove! and spread thy wings,
The wings of peaceful love;
And let thy church on earth become
Blest as the church above.

6 Come as the wind, with rushing sound
And Pentecostal grace!
That all of woman born may see
The glory of thy face.

7 Spirit divine, attend our prayers,
Make a lost world thy home;
Descend with all thy gracious powers,
O come, great Spirit, come!

—*Dr. A. Reed.*

ABRIDGE. C.M. — Isaac Smith.

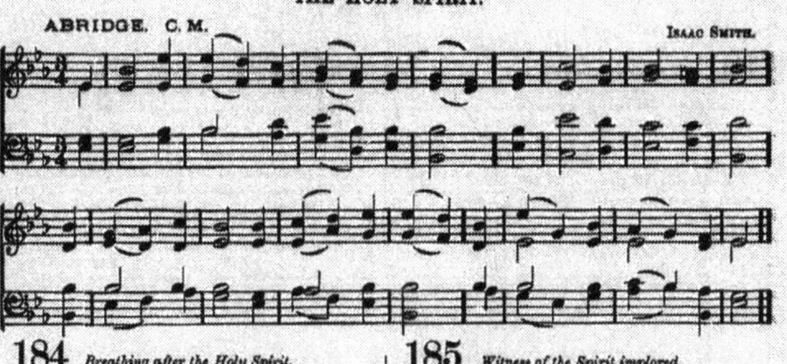

184 *Breathing after the Holy Spirit.*

1 Come, Holy Spirit, heavenly Dove,
With all thy quickening powers;
Kindle a flame of sacred love
In these cold hearts of ours.

2 In vain we tune our formal songs,
In vain we strive to rise;
Hosannas languish on our tongues,
And our devotion dies.

3 And shall we then for ever live
At this poor dying rate?
Our love so faint, so cold to thee,
And thine to us so great!

4 Come, Holy Spirit, heavenly Dove,
With all thy quickening powers;
Come, shed abroad the Saviour's love,
And that shall kindle ours.

—*Isaac Watts.*

185 *Witness of the Spirit implored.*

1 Why should the children of a king
Go mourning all their days?
Great Comforter, descend, and bring
The tokens of thy grace.

2 Dost thou not dwell in all thy saints,
And seal the heirs of heaven?
When wilt thou banish my complaints,
And show my sins forgiven?

3 Assure my conscience of its part
In the Redeemer's blood;
And bear thy witness with my heart,
That I am born of God.

4 Thou art the earnest of his love,
The pledge of joys to come:
May thy blest wings, celestial Dove,
Safely convey me home!

—*Isaac Watts.*

ST. PETER. C.M. — A. R. Reinagle.

186 *The Spirit of Adoption.*

1 Sovereign of all the worlds on high,
Allow my humble claim;
Nor, while unworthy I draw nigh,
Disdain a Father's name.

2 "My Father God!" that gracious sound
Dispels my guilty fear;
Not all the harmony of heaven
Could so delight my ear.

3 Come, Holy Spirit, seal the grace
On my expanding heart;
And show that in the Father's love
I share a filial part.

4 Cheered by a witness so divine,
Unwavering I believe;
And, "Abba, Father," humbly cry;
Nor can the sign deceive.

—*Doddridge.*

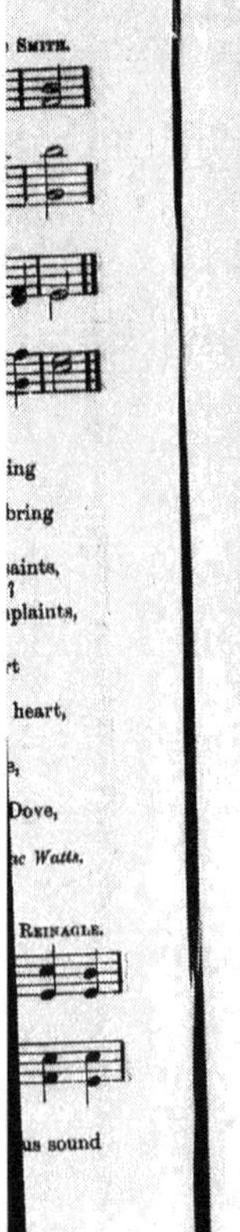

CREATION. 6-8s. F. J. HAYDN.

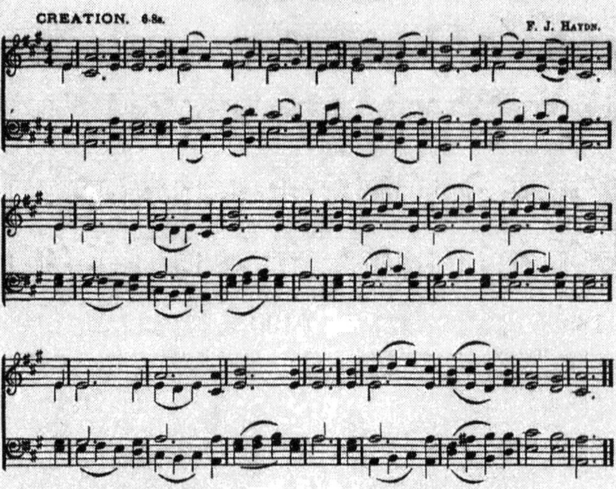

187

Veni, Creator.

1 Creator, Spirit, by whose aid
The world's foundations first were laid,
Come visit every waiting mind,
Come pour thy joys on human kind;
From sin and sorrow set us free,
And make thy temples worthy thee.

2 O Source of uncreated heat,
The Father's promised Paraclete!
Thrice holy Fount, immortal Fire,
Our hearts with heavenly love inspire:
Come, and thy sacred unction bring,
To sanctify us while we sing.

3 Plenteous of grace, descend from high,
Rich in thy sevenfold energy!
Thou strength of his almighty hand,
Whose power does heaven and earth command,
Refine and purge our earthly parts,
And stamp thine image on our hearts.

4 Create all new; our wills control,
Subdue the rebel in our soul;
Chase from our minds the subtle foe,
And peace, the fruit of faith, bestow;
And, lest again we go astray,
Protect and guide us in the way.

5 Immortal honours, endless fame,
Attend the Almighty Father's name;
The Saviour Son be glorified,
Who for lost man's redemption died;
And equal adoration be,
Eternal Comforter, to thee!

—*Dryden.*

188

Ordination Hymn.

1 Come, Holy Ghost, our souls inspire,
And lighten with celestial fire!
Thou the anointing Spirit art,
Who dost thy sevenfold gifts impart;
Thy blessèd unction from above
Is comfort, life, and fire of love.

2 Enable with perpetual light
The dulness of our blinded sight;
Anoint and cheer our soilèd face
With the abundance of thy grace;
Keep far our foes, give peace at home;
Where thou art guide no ill can come.

3 Teach us to know the Father, Son,
And thee, of both, to be but One;
That through the ages all along
This, this may be our endless song,
All praise to thy eternal merit,
O Father, Son, and Holy Spirit!

—*Charles Wesley.*

MIDDLESEX. 6-8s.

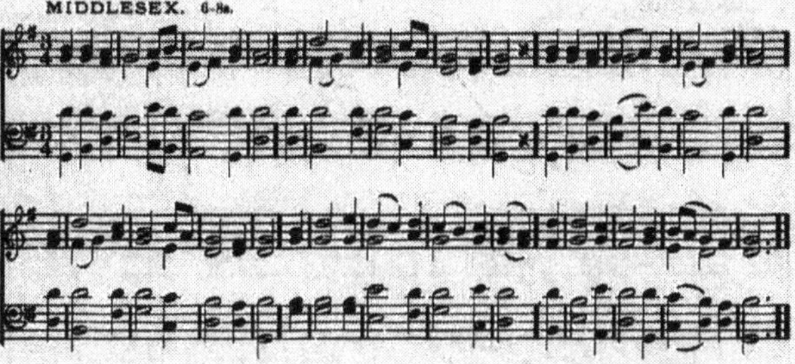

189 *Praying for the Spirit.*

1 Come, Holy Ghost, all-quickening fire,
Come, and in me delight to rest;
Drawn by the lure of strong desire,
O come and consecrate my breast!
The temple of my soul prepare,
And fix thy sacred presence there.

2 If now thy influence I feel,
If now in thee begin to live,
Still to my heart thyself reveal;
Give me thyself, for ever give:
A point my good, a drop my store,
Eager I ask, I pant for more.

3 Eager for thee I ask and pant,
So strong the principle divine
Carries me out, with sweet constraint,
Till all my hallowed soul is thine;
Plunged in the Godhead's deepest sea,
And lost in thine immensity.

4 My peace, my life, my comfort thou,
My treasure, and my all thou art;
True witness of my sonship, now
Engraving pardon on my heart;
Seal of my sins in Christ forgiven,
Earnest of love, and pledge of heaven.

5 Come then, my God, mark out thine heir,
Of heaven a larger earnest give;
With clearer light thy witness bear,
More sensibly within me live;
Let all my powers thy entrance feel,
And deeper stamp thyself the seal.

—Charles Wesley.

190 *The Spirit as Comforter and Witness.*

1 I want the Spirit of power within,
Of love, and of a healthful mind;
Of power, to conquer inbred sin;
Of love, to thee and all mankind;
Of health, that pain and death defies,
Most vigorous when the body dies.

2 When shall I hear the inward voice,
Which only faithful souls can hear?
Pardon, and peace, and heavenly joys,
Attend the promised Comforter;
O come, and righteousness divine,
And Christ, and all with Christ, are mine!

3 O that the Comforter would come,
Nor visit as a transient guest;
But fix in me his constant home,
And take possession of my breast;
And fix in me his loved abode,
The temple of indwelling God!

4 Come, Holy Ghost, my heart inspire,
Attest that I am born again;
Come, and baptize me now with fire,
Nor let thy former gifts be vain:
I cannot rest in sins forgiven;
Where is the earnest of my heaven?

5 Where the indubitable seal
That ascertains the kingdom mine?
The powerful stamp I long to feel,
The signature of love divine;
O shed it in my heart abroad,
Fulness of love, of heaven, of God!

—Charles Wesley.

SAXBY. L. M. — Rev. T. Richard Matthews, B.A.

191 *The promised Comforter.*

1 Jesus, we on the words depend,
Spoken by thee while present here,—
"The Father in my name shall send
The Holy Ghost, the Comforter."

2 That promise made to Adam's race,
Now, Lord, in us, even us, fulfil;
And give the Spirit of thy grace,
To teach us all thy perfect will.

3 That heavenly Teacher of mankind,
That Guide infallible impart,
To bring thy sayings to our mind,
And write them on our faithful heart.

4 He only can the words apply,
Through which we endless life possess;
And deal to each his legacy,
Our Lord's unutterable peace.

5 That peace of God, that peace of thine,
O might he now to us bring in,
And fill our souls with power divine,
And make an end of fear and sin.

6 The length and breadth of love reveal,
The height and depth of Deity;
And all the sons of glory seal,
And change, and make us all like thee.

—*Charles Wesley.*

HAMBURG. L. M. — Dr. L. Mason.

Slowly.

192 *Claiming the promise of the Spirit.*

1 Father, if justly still we claim
To us and ours the promise made,
To us be graciously the same,
And crown with living fire our head.

2 Our claim admit, and from above
Of holiness the Spirit shower;
Of wise discernment, humble love,
And zeal, and unity, and power.

3 The Spirit of convincing speech,
Of power demonstrative impart;
Such as may every conscience reach,
And sound the unbelieving heart:

4 The Spirit of refining fire,
Searching the inmost of the mind,
To purge all fierce and foul desire,
And kindle life more pure and kind:

5 The Spirit of faith, in this thy day,
To break the power of cancelled sin,
Tread down its strength, o'erturn its sway,
And still the conquest more than win.

6 The Spirit breathe of inward life,
Which in our hearts thy laws may write:
Then grief expires, and pain, and strife—
'Tis nature all, and all delight.

—*Altered from Dr. H. Moore.*

ST. CRISPIN. L. M. — Sir G. J. Elvey.

193 *Power and unction of the Spirit.*

1 O Spirit of the living God,
In all thy plenitude of grace,
Where'er the foot of man hath trod,
Descend on our apostate race.

2 Give tongues of fire and hearts of love,
To preach the reconciling word;
Give power and unction from above,
Where'er the joyful sound is heard.

3 Be darkness, at thy coming, light;
Confusion—order, in thy path;
Souls without strength inspire with might;
Bid mercy triumph over wrath.

4 Baptize the nations; far and nigh
The triumphs of the cross record;
The name of Jesus glorify,
Till every kindred call him Lord.

—Montgomery.

194 *The day of Pentecost.*

1 Come, Holy Spirit, raise our songs
To reach the wonders of the day,
When with thy fiery cloven tongues
Thou didst those glorious scenes display.

2 O 'twas a most auspicious hour,
Season of grace and sweet delight,
When thou didst come with mighty power,
And light of truth divinely bright!

3 By this the blest disciples knew
Their risen Head had entered heaven;
Had now obtained the promise due,
Fully by God the Father given.

4 Lord, we believe to us and ours
The apostolic promise given;
We wait the Pentecostal powers,
The Holy Ghost sent down from heaven.

5 Assembled here with one accord,
Calmly we wait the promised grace,
The purchase of our dying Lord:
Come, Holy Ghost, and fill the place.

6 If every one that asks may find,
If still thou dost on sinners fall,
Come as a mighty rushing wind;
Great grace be now upon us all.

—Charles Wesley.

DIX. 6-7s. — C. Kocher.

195 *Prayer for the Comforter.*

1 Father, glorify thy Son,
Answering his all-powerful prayer;
Send the Intercessor down,—
Send that other Comforter,
Whom believingly we claim,
Whom we ask in Jesus' name.

2 Then by faith we know and feel
Him, the Spirit of truth and grace;
With us he vouchsafes to dwell,
With us while unseen he stays;
All our help and good, we own,
Freely flows from him alone.

3 Wilt thou not the promise seal,
Good and faithful as thou art,
Send the Comforter to dwell
Every moment in our heart?
Yes, thou wilt the grace bestow;
Christ hath said it shall be so.

—Charles Wesley.

MERCY. 4-7s. L. M. GOTTSCHALK.

Slowly.

196 *The Spirit the earnest of endless rest.*

1 GRACIOUS Spirit, Love divine,
Let thy light within me shine!
All my guilty fears remove;
Fill me with thy heavenly love.

2 Speak thy pardoning grace to me
Set the burdened sinner free;
Lead me to the Lamb of God;
Wash me in his precious blood.

3 Life and peace to me impart;
Seal salvation on my heart;
Breathe thyself into my breast,
Earnest of eternal rest.

4 Let me never from thee stray;
Keep me in the narrow way;
Fill my soul with joy divine;
Keep me, Lord, forever thine.

—*J. Stalker.*

197 *The Spirit enlightening, cleansing, healing.*

1 HOLY Ghost, with light divine,
Shine upon this heart of mine;
Chase the shades of night away,
Turn my darkness into day.

2 Holy Ghost, with power divine,
Cleanse this guilty heart of mine;
Long hath sin, without control,
Held dominion o'er my soul.

3 Holy Ghost, with joy divine,
Cheer this saddened heart of mine;
Bid my many woes depart,
Heal my wounded, bleeding heart.

4 Holy Spirit, all divine,
Dwell within this heart of mine;
Cast down every idol-throne,
Reign supreme, and reign alone.

—*A. Reed.*

MASSAH. S. M. D. HAVERGAL.

198 *"They were all filled with the Holy Ghost."*

1 LORD God, the Holy Ghost,
In this accepted hour,
As on the day of Pentecost,
Descend in all thy power.
We meet with one accord
In our appointed place,
And wait the promise of our Lord,
The Spirit of all grace.

2 Like mighty rushing wind,
Upon the waves beneath,
Move with one impulse every mind;
One soul, one feeling, breathe;
The young, the old, inspire
With wisdom from above;
And give us hearts and tongues of fire
To pray, and praise, and love.

3 Spirit of light, explore
And chase our gloom away,
With lustre shining more and more
Unto the perfect day.
Spirit of truth, be thou
In life and death our guide;
O Spirit of adoption, now
May we be sanctified.

—*Montgomery.*

BANGOR. 6.6, 7.7, 7.7.

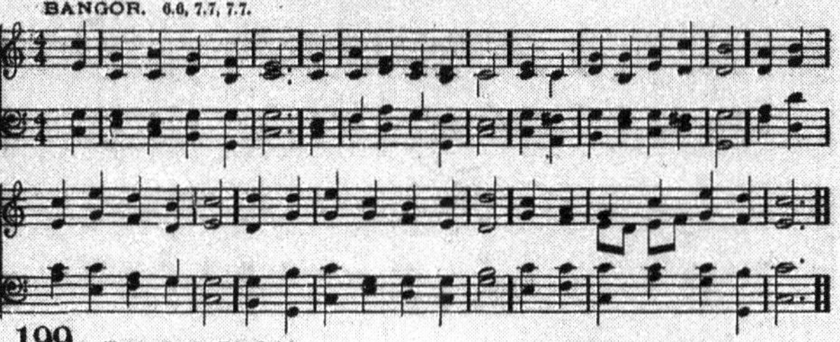

199

Waiting for the Holy Spirit.

1 Eternal Spirit, come
Into thy meanest home;
From thy high and holy place,
Where thou dost in glory reign,
Stoop in condescending grace,
Stoop to the poor heart of man.

2 For thee our hearts we lift,
And wait the heavenly gift;
Giver, Lord of life divine,
To our dying souls appear;
Grant the grace for which we pine,
Give thyself, the Comforter.

3 Our ruined souls repair,
And fix thy mansion there;
Claim us for thy constant shrine,
All thy glorious self reveal;
Life, and power, and love divine,
God in us for ever dwell.—*C. Wesley.*

200

Pentecostal blessings for all.

1 Sinners, your hearts lift up,
Partakers of your hope!
This, the day of Pentecost;
Ask, and ye shall all receive;
Surely now the Holy Ghost
God to all that ask shall give.

2 Ye all may freely take
The grace for Jesus' sake;
He for every man hath died,
He for all hath risen again;
Jesus now is glorified;
Gifts he hath received for men.

3 Blessings on all he pours,
In never-ceasing showers;
All he waters from above;
Offers all his joy and peace,
Settled comfort, perfect love,
Everlasting righteousness.

4 All may from him receive
A power to turn and live;
Grace for every soul is free;
All may hear the Spirit's call;
All the Light and Life may see;
All may feel he died for all.

5 Father, behold, we claim
The gift in Jesus' name!
Now the promised Comforter
Into all our spirits pour;
Let him fix his mansion here,
Come, and never leave us more.
—*Charles Wesley.*

CORNELL. 8.7, 8.7. J. H. Cornell.

TUNE: CORNELL. 8.7.8.7.

201 *The Spirit the source of consolation.*

1 Holy Ghost, dispel our sadness,
Pierce the clouds of nature's night;
Come, thou Source of joy and gladness,
Breathe thy life, and spread thy light.

2 From the height which knows no measure,
As a gracious shower descend,
Bringing down the richest treasure
Man can wish, or God can send.

3 Author of the new creation,
Come with unction and with power;
Make our hearts thy habitation;
On our souls thy graces shower.

4 Hear, O hear our supplication,
Blessèd Spirit, God of peace!
Rest upon this congregation,
With the fulness of thy grace.

—*P. Gerhardt.*

SHERBROOK. 5.5.5, 11. D.

202 *"Joy in the Holy Ghost."*

1 Away with our fears,
Our troubles and tears!
The Spirit is come,
The witness of Jesus returned to his home;
The pledge of our Lord
To his heaven restored
Is sent from the sky,
And tells us our Head is exalted on high.

2 Our Advocate there
By his blood and his prayer
The gift hath obtained,
For us he hath prayed, and the Comforter gained;
Our glorified Head
His Spirit hath shed,
With his people to stay,
And never again will he take him away.

3 Our heavenly Guide
With us shall abide,
His comforts impart,
And set up his kingdom of love in the heart.
The heart that believes
His kingdom receives,
His power and his peace,
His life, and his joy's everlasting increase.

4 The presence divine
Doth inwardly shine,
The Shechinah shall rest
On all our assemblies, and glow in our breast;
By day and by night
The pillar of light
Our steps shall attend,
And convoy us safe to our prosperous end.

5 Then let us rejoice
In heart and in voice,
Our Leader pursue,
And shout as we travel the wilderness through;
With the Spirit remove
To Zion above,
Triumphant arise,
And walk with our God, till we fly to the skies.

—*Charles Wesley.*

NEWHAVEN. 6.6.4, 6.6.6.4. — Dr. T. Hastings.

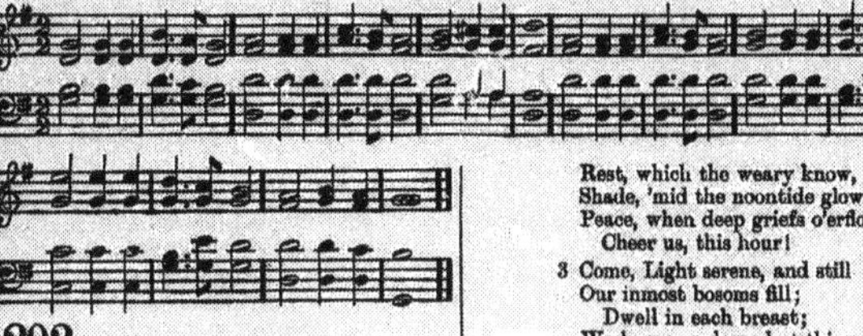

203

Invocation of the Holy Spirit.

1 Come, Holy Ghost, in love,
Shed on us from above
Thine own bright ray!
Divinely good thou art;
Thy sacred gifts impart
To gladden each sad heart:
O come to-day!

2 Come, tenderest Friend, and best,
Our most delightful Guest,
With soothing power:
Rest, which the weary know,
Shade, 'mid the noontide glow,
Peace, when deep griefs o'erflow,
Cheer us, this hour!

3 Come, Light serene, and still
Our inmost bosoms fill;
Dwell in each breast;
We know no dawn but thine,
Send forth thy beams divine,
On our dark souls to shine,
And make us blest!

4 Come, all the faithful bless;
Let all who Christ confess
His praise employ:
Give virtue's rich reward;
Victorious death accord,
And, with our glorious Lord,
Eternal joy!

—*Robert II. of France.*

ST. PHILIP. 7.7.7.

204

Veni, Sancte Spiritus.

1 Holy Ghost, my Comforter,
Now from highest heaven appear,
Shed thy gracious radiance here.

2 Blessèd Sun of grace, o'er all
Faithful hearts who on thee call
Let thy light and solace fall.

3 What without thy aid is wrought,
Skilful deed or wisest thought,
God will count but vain and nought.

4 Cleanse us, Lord, from sinful stain,
On the parchèd spirit rain,
Heal the wounded of its pain.

5 Bend the stubborn will to thine,
Melt the cold with fire divine,
Erring hearts to right incline.

6 Grant us, Lord, who cry to thee
Steadfast in the faith to be,
Give thy gift of charity.

7 May we live in holiness,
And in death find happiness,
And abide with thee in bliss.

—*Miss Winkworth,*
from Robert II. of France.

"LIVING WATER." 8.8, 7.7. — German.

"LIVING WATER." *(Continued.)*

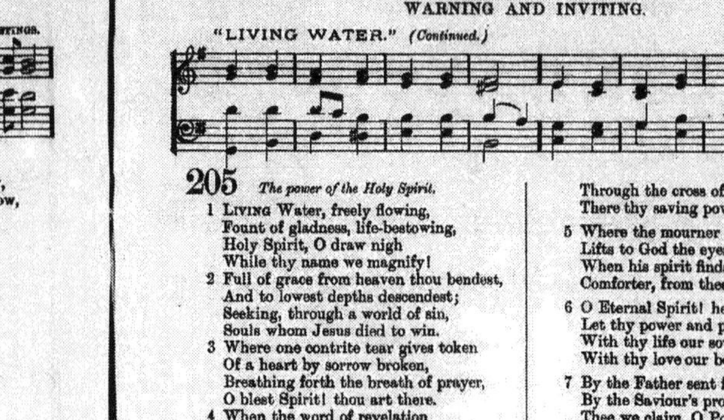

205 *The power of the Holy Spirit.*

1 Living Water, freely flowing,
Fount of gladness, life-bestowing,
Holy Spirit, O draw nigh
While thy name we magnify!

2 Full of grace from heaven thou bendest,
And to lowest depths descendest;
Seeking, through a world of sin,
Souls whom Jesus died to win.

3 Where one contrite tear gives token
Of a heart by sorrow broken,
Breathing forth the breath of prayer,
O blest Spirit! thou art there.

4 When the word of revelation
Glows with tidings of salvation,
Through the cross of Christ made known,
There thy saving power is shown.

5 Where the mourner in his anguish
Lifts to God the eyes that languish:
When his spirit finds repose,
Comforter, from thee it flows.

6 O Eternal Spirit! hear us;
Let thy power and presence cheer us;
With thy life our souls inspire;
With thy love our bosoms fire.

7 By the Father sent from heaven,
By the Saviour's promise given,
Thee we claim, O Power Divine!
Come, and make our hearts thy shrine.

Section V.

REPENTANCE AND CONVERSION.

1.—WARNING AND INVITING.

ERNAN. L. M. — Dr. L. Mason.

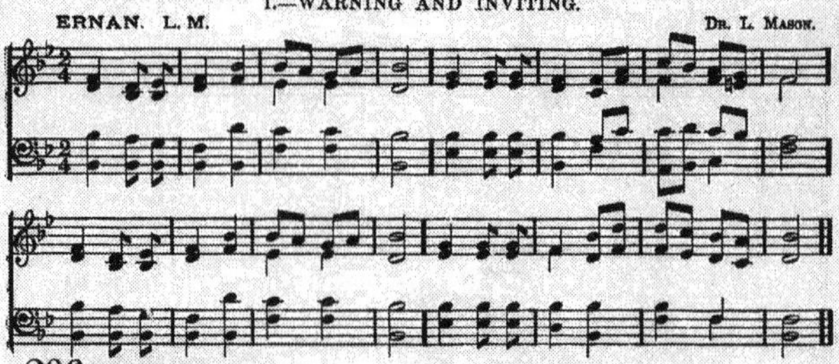

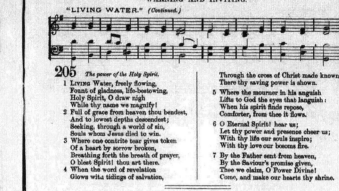

206 *Sinners invited to the gospel feast.*

1 Come, sinners, to the gospel feast,
Let every soul be Jesus' guest;
Ye need not one be left behind,
For God hath bidden all mankind.

2 Sent by my Lord, on you I call,
The invitation is to all;
Come, all the world; come, sinner, thou;
All things in Christ are ready now.

3 Come, all ye souls by sin oppress,
Ye restless wanderers after rest,
Ye poor, and maimed, and halt, and blind,
In Christ a hearty welcome find.

4 My message as from God receive;
Ye all may come to Christ, and live;
O let his love your hearts constrain,
Nor suffer him to die in vain!

5 His love is mighty to compel;
His conquering love consent to feel;
Yield to his love's resistless power,
And fight against your God no more.

6 See him set forth before your eyes,
That precious, bleeding Sacrifice!
His offered benefits embrace,
And freely now be saved by grace

7 This is the time, no more delay;
This is the acceptable day;
Come in this moment, at his call,
And live for him who died for all.

—*Charles Wesley.*

EDEN. L. M. DR. L. MASON.

207

Isaiah lv. 1, 2, 3.

1 Ho! every one that thirsts, draw nigh;
'Tis God invites the fallen race;
Mercy and free salvation buy;
Buy wine, and milk, and gospel grace.

2 Come to the living waters, come!
Sinners, obey your Maker's call;
Return, ye weary wanderers, home,
And find my grace is free for all.

3 See from the Rock a fountain rise!
For you in healing streams it rolls;
Money ye need not bring, nor price,
Ye labouring, burdened, sin-sick souls.

4 Nothing ye in exchange shall give,
Leave all you have and are behind;
Frankly the gift of God receive,
Pardon and peace in Jesus find.

5 "I bid you all my goodness prove;
My promises for all are free;
Come, taste the manna of my love,
And let your souls delight in ME.

6 "Your willing ear and heart incline,
My words believingly receive;
Quickened your souls by faith divine,
An everlasting life shall live."

—*J. Wesley.*

DUKE STREET. L. M. JOHN HATTON.

208

"Come, for all things are now ready."

1 SINNERS, obey the gospel-word,
Haste to the supper of your Lord!
Be wise to know your gracious day;
All things are ready, come away!

2 Ready the Father is to own
And kiss his late-returning son;
Ready your loving Saviour stands,
And spreads for you his bleeding hands.

3 Ready the Spirit of his love
Just now the hardness to remove,
To apply, and witness with the blood,
And wash and seal the sons of God.

4 Ready for you the angels wait,
To triumph in your blest estate;
Tuning their harps, they long to praise
The wonders of redeeming grace.

5 The Father, Son, and Holy Ghost
Are ready, with their shining host:
All heaven is ready to resound,
"The dead's alive! the lost is found!"

—*Charles Wesley.*

HEBRON. L. M. Dr. L. Mason.

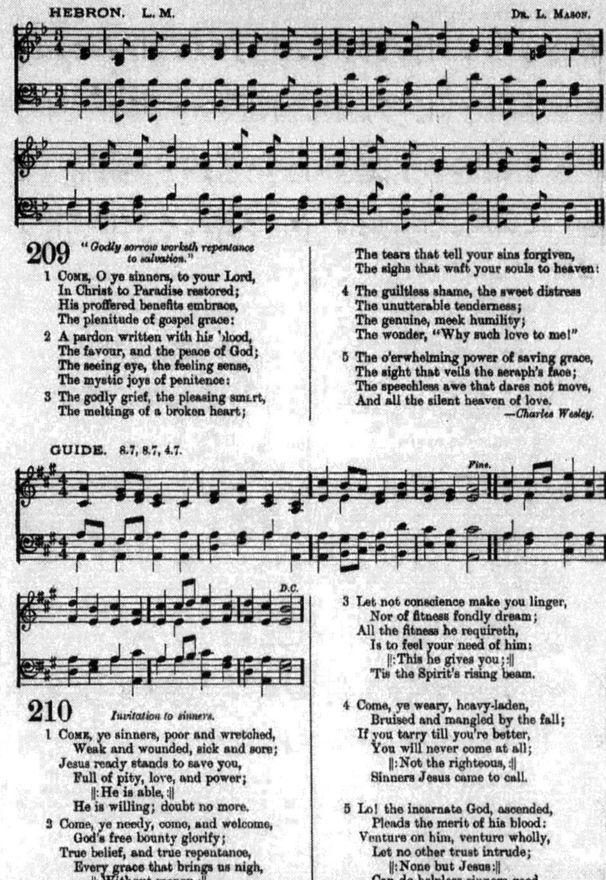

209 "Godly sorrow worketh repentance to salvation."

1 Come, O ye sinners, to your Lord,
In Christ to Paradise restored;
His proffered benefits embrace,
The plenitude of gospel grace:

2 A pardon written with his blood,
The favour, and the peace of God;
The seeing eye, the feeling sense,
The mystic joys of penitence:

3 The godly grief, the pleasing smart,
The meltings of a broken heart;
The tears that tell your sins forgiven,
The sighs that waft your souls to heaven:

4 The guiltless shame, the sweet distress
The unutterable tenderness;
The genuine, meek humility;
The wonder, "Why such love to me!"

5 The o'erwhelming power of saving grace,
The sight that veils the seraph's face;
The speechless awe that dares not move,
And all the silent heaven of love.

—*Charles Wesley.*

GUIDE. 8.7, 8.7, 4.7.

Fine.
D.C.

210 *Invitation to sinners.*

1 Come, ye sinners, poor and wretched,
Weak and wounded, sick and sore;
Jesus ready stands to save you,
Full of pity, love, and power;
‖: He is able, :‖
He is willing; doubt no more.

2 Come, ye needy, come, and welcome,
God's free bounty glorify;
True belief, and true repentance,
Every grace that brings us nigh,
‖: Without money, :‖
Come to Jesus Christ and buy.

3 Let not conscience make you linger,
Nor of fitness fondly dream;
All the fitness he requireth,
Is to feel your need of him:
‖: This he gives you; :‖
'Tis the Spirit's rising beam.

4 Come, ye weary, heavy-laden,
Bruised and mangled by the fall;
If you tarry till you're better,
You will never come at all;
‖: Not the righteous, :‖
Sinners Jesus came to call.

5 Lo! the incarnate God, ascended,
Pleads the merit of his blood:
Venture on him, venture wholly,
Let no other trust intrude;
‖: None but Jesus :‖
Can do helpless sinners good.

—*J. Hart.*

QUEEN STREET. 6.6, 6.6, 8.8. J. B. BAXTER.

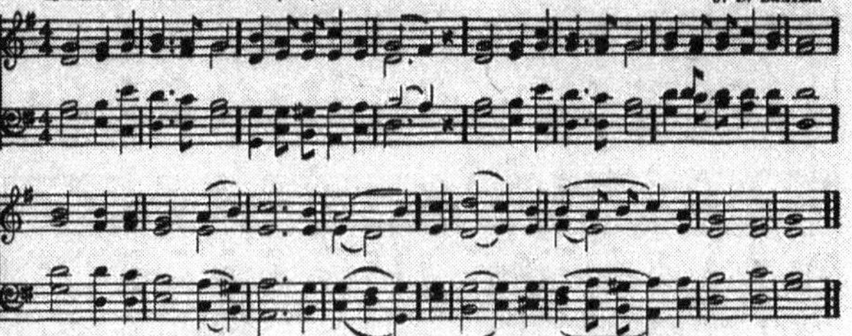

211 *The Year of Jubilee.*

1 Blow ye the trumpet, blow,
The gladly solemn sound;
Let all the nations know,
To earth's remotest bound,
The year of Jubilee is come!
Return, ye ransomed sinners, home.

2 Jesus, our great High Priest,
Hath full atonement made;
Ye weary spirits, rest;
Ye mournful souls, be glad;
The year of Jubilee is come!
Return, ye ransomed sinners, home.

3 Extol the Lamb of God,
The all-atoning Lamb;
Redemption through his blood
Throughout the world proclaim:
The year of Jubilee is come!
Return, ye ransomed sinners, home.

4 Ye slaves of sin and hell,
Your liberty receive;
And safe in Jesus dwell,
And blest in Jesus live:
The year of Jubilee is come!
Return, ye ransomed sinners, home.

5 Ye who have sold for nought
Your heritage above,
Receive it back unbought,
The gift of Jesus' love:
The year of Jubilee is come!
Return, ye ransomed sinners, home.

6 The gospel trumpet hear,
The news of heavenly grace;
And, saved from earth, appear
Before your Saviour's face:
The year of Jubilee is come!
Return, ye ransomed sinners, home.

—*Charles Wesley.*

"EVEN ME." 8.7, 8.7, 3. W. B. BRADBURY.

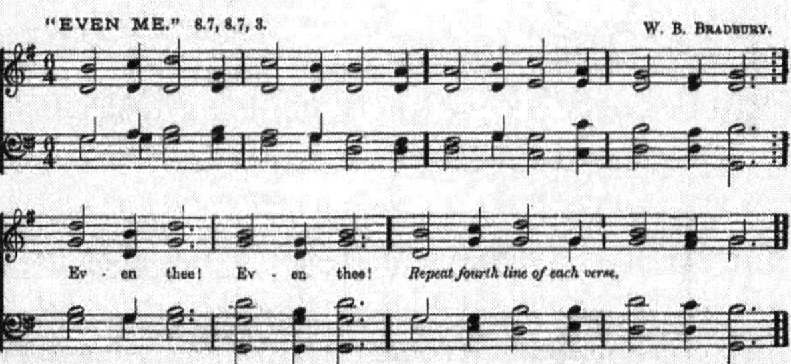
Ev - en thee! Ev - en thee!
Repeat fourth line of each verse.

B. Baxter.

home.

ht

home.

ace;

bear

e:

home.

arles Wesley.

Bradbury.

TUNE: "EVEN ME." 8.7, 8.7, 3.

212

"Him that cometh to me, I will in no wise cast out."

1 Hark! the Saviour's voice from heaven
Speaks a pardon full and free;
Come, and thou shalt be forgiven;
Boundless mercy flows for thee—
||: Even thee! :||

2 See the healing fountain springing
From the Saviour on the tree;
Pardon, peace, and cleansing bringing,
Lost one, loved one, 'tis for thee—
||: Even thee! :||

3 Hear his love and mercy speaking,
"Come, and lay thy soul on me;
Though thy heart for sin be breaking,
I have rest and peace for thee—
||: Even thee!" :||

4 Sinner, come, to Jesus flying,
From thy sin and woe be free;
Burdened, guilty, wounded, dying,
Gladly will he welcome thee—
||: Even thee! :||

5 Every sin shall be forgiven,
Thou, through grace, a child shalt be;
Child of God, and heir of heaven,
Yes, a mansion waits for thee—
||: Even thee! :||

6 Then in love for ever dwelling,
Jesus all thy joy shall be;
And thy song shall still be telling
All his mercy did for thee—
||: Even thee! :||

"ART THOU WEARY?" 8.5, 8.3. (First Tune.) E. W. Bullinger.

Slowly.

213

Christ the rest of the weary.

1 Art thou weary, heavy-laden?
Art thou sore distrest?
"Come to me," saith One, "and coming,
Be at rest."

2 Hath he marks to lead me to him,
If he be my Guide?
"In his feet and hands are wound-prints,
And his side."

3 Hath he diadem, as Monarch,
That his brow adorns?
"Yea, a crown, in very surety,
But of thorns."

4 If I find him, if I follow,
What his guerdon here?
"Many a sorrow, many a labour,
Many a tear."

5 If I still hold closely to him,
What hath he at last?
"Sorrow vanquished, labour ended,
Jordan past."

6 If I ask him to receive me,
Will he say me nay?
"Not till earth, and not till heaven
Pass away."

7 Finding, following, keeping, struggling,
Is he sure to bless?
Saints, apostles, prophets, martyrs,
Answer, "Yes."

—*Dr. Neale.*

ORIENT. 8.5, 8.3. (Second Tune.) From "Hymns of the Eastern Church."

"COME, YE DISCONSOLATE." 11.10, 11.10. WEBBE.

214 *Heavenly balm for earthly woes.*

1 COME, ye disconsolate, where'er ye languish;
Come to the mercy-seat, fervently kneel;
Here bring your wounded hearts, here tell your anguish;
Earth has no sorrow that Heaven cannot heal.

2 Joy of the desolate, Light of the straying,
Hope of the penitent, fadeless and pure,
Here speaks the Comforter, tenderly saying,
"Earth has no sorrow that Heaven cannot cure."

3 Here see the bread of life; see waters flowing
Forth from the throne of God, pure from above;
Come to the feast of love; come ever knowing
Earth has no sorrow but Heaven can remove.

—*T. Moore.*

REQUIES. 8-7s. BLUMENTHAL.

TUNE: REQUIES. 8-7s.

215 *"Why will ye die, O house of Israel?"*

1 Sinners, turn, why will ye die?
God, your Maker, asks you why:
God, who did your being give,
Made you with himself to live;
He the fatal cause demands,
Asks the work of his own hands,
Why, ye thankless creatures, why
Will ye cross his love, and die?

2 Sinners, turn, why will ye die?
God, your Saviour, asks you why:
God, who did your souls retrieve,
Died himself, that ye might live;
Will you let him die in vain?
Crucify your Lord again?
Why, ye ransomed sinners, why
Will ye slight his grace, and die?

3 Sinners, turn, why will ye die?
God, the Spirit, asks you why:
He who all your lives hath strove,
Wooed you to embrace his love;
Will you not his grace receive?
Will you still refuse to live?
Why, ye long-sought sinners, why
Will ye grieve your God, and die?

—*Charles Wesley.*

216 SECOND PART.

1 What could your Redeemer do,
More than he hath done for you?
To procure your peace with God,
Could he more than shed his blood?
After all his waste of love,
All his drawings from above,
Why will you your Lord deny?
Why will you resolve to die?

2 Turn, he cries, ye sinners, turn;
By his life your God hath sworn,
He would have you turn and live,
He would all the world receive.
If your death were his delight,
Would he you to life invite?
Would he ask, entreat, and cry,
Why will you resolve to die?

3 Sinners, turn, while God is near;
Dare not think him insincere:
Now, even now, your Saviour stands;
All day long he spreads his hands;
Cries, "Ye will not happy be!
No, ye will not come to me!
Me, who life to none deny:
Why will you resolve to die?"

4 Can you doubt if God is love?
If to all his mercies move?
Will you not his *word* receive?
Will you not his OATH believe?
See! the suffering God appears!
Jesus weeps; believe his tears!
Mingled with his blood, they cry,
"Why will you resolve to die?"

—*Charles Wesley.*

GERMAN HYMN. 4-7s. Pleyel.

217 *The wanderer exhorted to return.*

1 Brother, hast thou wandered far
From thy Father's happy home,
With thyself and God at war?
Turn thee, brother; homeward come.

2 Hast thou wasted all the powers
God for noble uses gave?
Squandered life's most golden hours?
Turn thee, brother; God can save!

3 Is a mighty famine now
In thy heart and in thy soul?
Discontent upon thy brow?
Turn thee; God will make thee whole.

4 He can heal thy bitterest wound,
He thy gentlest prayer can hear;
Seek him, for he may be found;
Call upon him; he is near.

—*J. F. Clarke.*

MAIDSTONE. 8.7s. W. B. GILBERT.

218 *"Come unto me, all ye that labour and are heavy laden, and I will give you rest."*

1 COME, ye weary sinners, come,
All who groan beneath your load,
Jesus calls his wanderers home;
Hasten to your pardoning God!
Come, ye guilty spirits, oppressed,
Answer to the Saviour's call:
"Come, and I will give you rest;
Come, and I will save you all."

2 Jesus, full of truth and love,
We thy kindest word obey;
Faithful let thy mercies prove;
Take our load of guilt away.
Fain we would on thee rely,
Cast on thee our every care;
To thine arms of mercy fly,
Find our lasting quiet there.

3 Burdened with a world of grief,
Burdened with our sinful load,
Burdened with this unbelief,
Burdened with the wrath of God;
Lo! we come to thee for ease,
True and gracious as thou art;
Now our groaning souls release,
Write forgiveness on our heart.

—*Charles Wesley.*

HOLY CROSS. C. M. ARTHUR HENRY BROWN.

Slowly.

TUNE: HOLY CROSS. C. M.

219 *"Remember now thy Creator in the days of thy youth."*

1 In life's gay morn, when sprightly youth
With vital ardour glows,
And shines in all the fairest charms
Which beauty can disclose;

2 Deep on thy soul, before its powers
Are yet by vice enslaved,
Be thy Creator's glorious name
And character engraved.

3 For soon the shades of grief shall cloud
The sunshine of thy days,
And cares and toils, in endless round,
Encompass all thy ways.

4 Soon shall thy heart the woes of age
In mournful sighs deplore,
And sadly muse on former joys,
That now return no more.

220 *"Let him return unto the Lord."*

1 Return, O wanderer, to thy home,
Thy Father calls for thee;
No longer now an exile roam
In guilt and misery.

2 Return, O wanderer, to thy home,
'Tis Jesus calls for thee:
The Spirit and the Bride say, Come;
O now for refuge flee.

3 Return, O wanderer, to thy home,
'Tis madness to delay;
There are no pardons in the tomb,
And brief is mercy's day.

—*Dr. Hastings.*

SAWLEY. C. M.

J. Walch.

221 *Christ waiting to be gracious.*

1 Jesus, Redeemer of mankind,
Display thy saving power;
Thy mercy let the sinner find,
And know his gracious hour.

2 Who thee beneath their feet have trod,
And crucified afresh,
Touch with thine all-victorious blood,
And turn the stone to flesh.

3 Open their eyes thy cross to see,
Their ears, to hear thy cries:
Sinner, thy Saviour weeps for thee,
For thee he weeps and dies.

4 All the day long he waiting stands,
His rebels to receive;
And shows his wounds, and spreads his hands,
And bids you turn and live.

5 Turn, and your sins of deepest dye
He will with blood efface;
Even now he waits the blood to apply;
Be saved, be saved by grace.

—*Charles Wesley.*

AJALON. 6-7s. R. REDHEAD.

222 *Redemption through his blood.*

1 WEARY souls, that wander wide
From the central point of bliss,
Turn to Jesus crucified,
Fly to those dear wounds of his:
Sink into the purple flood;
Rise into the life of God.

2 Find in Christ the way of peace,
Peace unspeakable, unknown;
By his pain he gives you ease,
Life by his expiring groan:
Rise, exalted by his fall;
Find in Christ your all in all.

3 O believe the record true,
God to you his Son hath given!
Ye may now be happy too,
Find on earth the life of heaven:
Live the life of heaven above,
All the life of glorious love.

4 This the universal bliss,
Bliss for every soul designed;
God's original promise this,
God's great gift to all mankind:
Blest in Christ this moment be!
Blest to all eternity!

—*Charles Wesley.*

PATER OMNIUM. 6-8s. H. J. E. HOLMES.

TUNE: PATER OMNIUM. 6-8s.

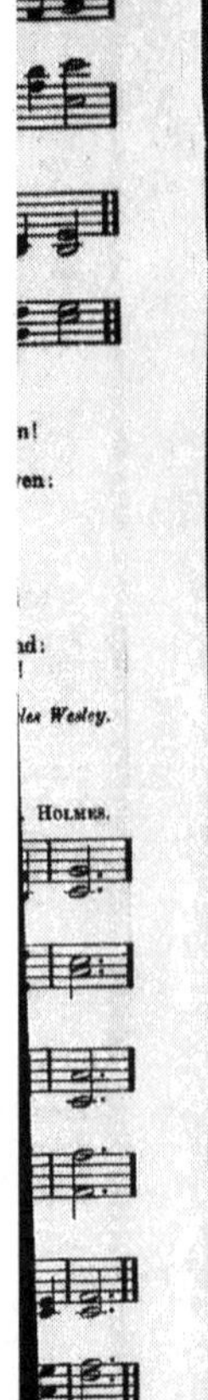

223 *Praise for redeeming love.*

1 Where shall my wondering soul begin?
How shall I all to heaven aspire?
A slave redeemed from death and sin,
A brand plucked from eternal fire,
How shall I equal triumphs raise,
Or sing my great Deliverer's praise?

2 O how shall I the goodness tell,
Father, which thou to me hast showed,—
That I, a child of wrath and hell,
I should be called a child of God,
Should know, should feel my sins forgiven,
Blest with this antepast of heaven?

3 Come, O my guilty brethren, come,
Groaning beneath your load of sin;
His bleeding heart shall make you room,
His open side shall take you in;
He calls you now, invites you home;
Come, O my guilty brethren, come!

4 For you the purple current flowed
In pardons from his wounded side;
Languished for you the incarnate God,
For you the Prince of glory died:
Believe, and all your sin's forgiven;
Only believe, and yours is heaven.

—*Charles Wesley.*

224 *"God is love."*

1 See, sinners, in the gospel glass,
The Friend and Saviour of mankind!
Not one of all the apostate race
But may in him salvation find.
His thoughts and words and actions prove—
His life and death—that God is love!

2 Behold the Lamb of God, who bears
The sins of all the world away!
A servant's form he meekly wears,
He sojourns in a house of clay;
His glory is no longer seen,
But God with God is man with men.

3 See where the God incarnate stands,
And calls his wandering creatures home;
He all day long spreads out his hands:
"Come, weary souls, to Jesus come!
Ye all may hide you in my breast;
Believe, and I will give you rest.

4 "Ah! do not of my goodness doubt;
My saving grace for all is free;
I will in nowise cast him out
That comes a sinner unto me:
I can to none myself deny;
Why, sinners, will ye perish, why?"

—*Charles Wesley.*

CORNELL. 8.7, 8.7. J. H. Cornell.

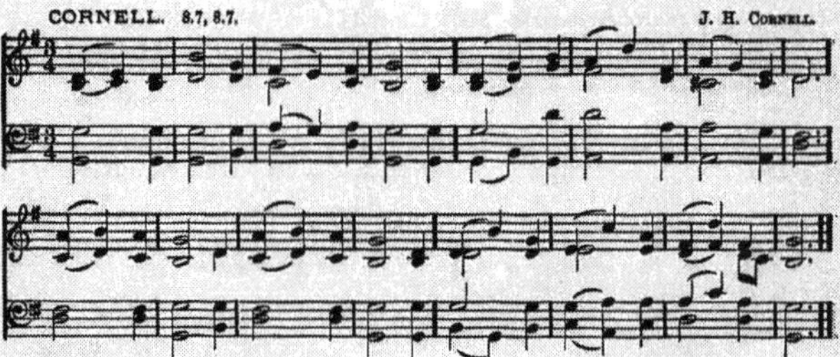

225 *The vastness of God's mercy.*

1 There's a wideness in God's mercy,
Like the wideness of the sea;
There's a kindness in his justice,
Which is more than liberty.

2 There is welcome for the sinner,
And more graces for the good;
There is mercy with the Saviour;
There is healing in his blood.

3 For the love of God is broader
Than the measure of man's mind;
And the heart of the Eternal
Is most wonderfully kind.

4 If our love were but more simple,
We should take him at his word;
And our lives would be all sunshine
In the favour of our Lord.

—*F. W. Faber.*

PORTUGUESE HYMN. 10.10.11.11. J. READING.

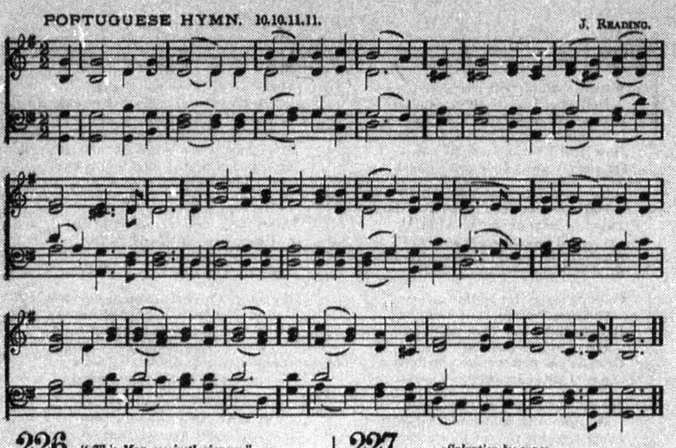

226 *"This Man receiveth sinners."*

1 THY faithfulness, Lord, each moment we find,
So true to thy word, so loving and kind;
Thy mercy so tender to all the lost race,
‖:The vilest offender may turn and find grace.:‖

2 The mercy I feel, to others I show,
I set to my seal that Jesus is true:
Ye all may find favour, who come at his call;
‖:O come to my Saviour, his grace is for ALL.:‖

3 To save what was lost, from heaven he came;
Come, sinners, and trust in Jesus's name!
He offers you pardon; he bids you be free:
‖:"If sin be your burden, O come unto me!":‖

4 O let me commend my Saviour to you,
The publican's Friend and Advocate too;
For you he is pleading his merits and death,
‖:With God interceding for sinners beneath.:‖

5 Then let us submit his grace to receive,
Fall down at his feet and gladly believe:
We all are forgiven for Jesus's sake;
‖:Our title to heaven his merits we take.:‖

—*Charles Wesley.*

227 *Salvation by grace.*

1 YE thirsty for God, to Jesus give ear,
And take, through his blood, a power to draw near:
His kind invitation, ye sinners, embrace,
‖:Accepting salvation, salvation by grace.:‖

2 Sent down from above, who governs the skies,
In vehement love to sinners he cries,
"Drink into my Spirit, who happy would be,
‖:And all things inherit, by coming to me.":‖

3 O Saviour of all, thy word we believe,
And come at thy call, thy grace to receive:
The blessing is given, wherever thou art;
‖:The earnest of heaven is love in the heart.:‖

4 To us at thy feet the Comforter give,
Who gasp to admit thy Spirit, and live;
The weakest believers acknowledge for thine,
‖:And fill us with rivers of water divine.:‖

—*Charles Wesley.*

HANOVER. 10.10.11.11. DR. CROFT.

HANOVER. *(Continued.)*

228 *Miracles of healing.*

1 Ye neighbours and friends, to Jesus draw near;
His love condescends, by titles so dear,
To call and invite you his triumph to prove,
And freely delight you in Jesus's love.

2 The Shepherd who died his sheep to redeem,
On every side are gathered to him
The weary and burdened, the reprobate race;
And wait to be pardoned through Jesus's grace.

3 The blind are restored through Jesus's name;
They see their dear Lord, and follow the Lamb:
The halt they are walking, and running their
race;
The dumb they are talking of Jesus's grace.

4 The deaf hear his voice, and comforting word,
It bids them rejoice in Jesus their Lord:
"Thy sins are forgiven, accepted thou art;"
They listen, and heaven springs up in their
heart.

5 The lepers from all their spots are made clean;
The dead by his call are raised from their sin;
In Jesus' compassion the sick find a cure,
And gospel salvation is preached to the poor.

6 O Jesus, ride on, till all are subdued;
Thy mercy make known, and sprinkle thy
blood;
Display thy salvation, and teach the new song
To every nation, and people, and tongue.

—*Charles Wesley.*

MELCOMBE. L. M. S. Webbe.

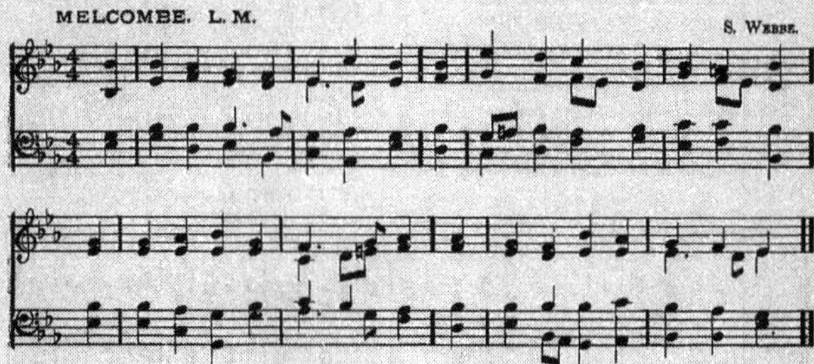

229 *"We pray you in Christ's stead, be ye reconciled to God."*

1 God, the offended God Most High,
Ambassadors to rebels sends;
His messengers his place supply,
And Jesus begs us to be friends.

2 Us, in the stead of Christ, they pray,
Us, in the stead of God, entreat
To cast our arms, our sins, away,
And find forgiveness at his feet.

3 Our God in Christ! thine embassy
And proffered mercy we embrace;
And gladly reconciled to thee,
Thy condescending goodness praise.

4 Poor debtors, by our Lord's request,
A full acquittance we receive;
And criminals, with pardon blest,
We, at our Judge's instance, live.

—*Charles Wesley.*

ZEPHYR. L. M. BRADBURY.

230 *Joy in heaven over a sinner repenting.*

1 Who can describe the joys that rise
Through all the courts of paradise
To see a prodigal return
To see an heir of glory born!

2 With joy the Father doth approve
The fruit of his eternal love;
The Son with joy looks down, and sees
The purchase of his agonies.

3 The Spirit takes delight to view
The contrite soul he forms anew;
And saints and angels join to sing
The growing empire of their King.
—*Isaac Watts.*

231 Isaiah lxi. 1, 2, 3.

1 The Spirit of the Lord our God,
Spirit of power, and health, and love,
The Father hath on Christ bestowed,
And sent him from his throne above.

2 Prophet, and Priest, and King of Peace,
Anointed to declare his will,
To minister his pardoning grace,
And every sin-sick soul to heal.

3 Sinners, obey the heavenly call,
Your prison-doors stand open wide;
Go forth, for he hath ransomed all,
For every soul of man hath died.

4 'Tis his the drooping soul to raise,
To rescue all by sin oppressed,
To clothe them with the robes of praise,
And give their weary spirits rest;

5 To help their grovelling unbelief,
Beauty for ashes to confer,
The oil of joy for abject grief,
Triumphant joy for sad despair;

6 To make them trees of righteousness,
The planting of the Lord below,
To spread the honour of his grace,
And on to full perfection grow.
—*Charles Wesley.*

BOYLSTON. S. M. DR. MASON.

232 *Repent, believe, obey!*

1 Return, and come to God,
Cast all your sins away;
Seek ye the Saviour's cleansing blood:
Repent, believe, obey!

2 Say not ye cannot come,
For Jesus bled and died,
That none who ask in humble faith
Should ever be denied

3 Say not ye will not come;
'Tis God vouchsafes to call;
And fearful will their end be found
On whom his wrath shall fall.

4 Come, then, whoever will;
Come, while 'tis called to-day;
Seek ye the Saviour's cleansing blood:
Repent, believe, obey!
—*Charles Wesley.*

TUNE: BOYLSTON. S. M. (See Hymn 232.)

233

Redeeming the time.

1 Make haste, O man, to live,
For thou so soon must die;
Time hurries past thee like the breeze;
How swift its moments fly!

2 Make haste, O man, to do
Whatever must be done;
Thou hast no time to lose in sloth,
Thy day will soon be gone.

3 Up, then, with speed, and work;
Fling ease and self away;
This is no time for thee to sleep,
Up, watch, and work, and pray!

4 Make haste, O man, to live,
Thy time is almost o'er;
O sleep not, dream not, but arise,
The Judge is at the door.

—*H. Bonar.*

LANGTON. S. M. Adapted by Streatfield.

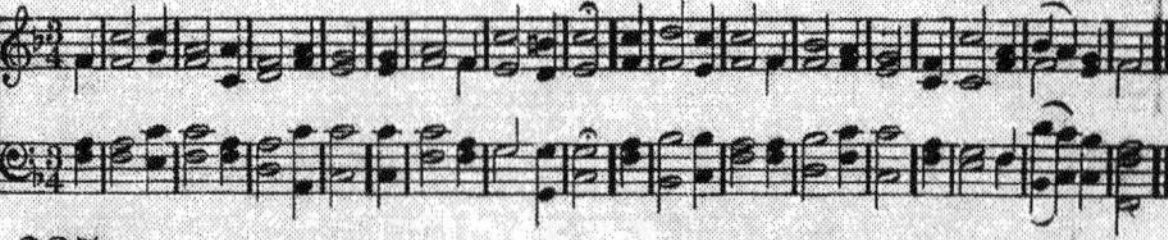

234

Rest found only in God.

1 O where shall rest be found,
Rest for the weary soul?
'Twere vain the ocean's depths to sound,
Or seek from pole to pole.

2 The world can never give
The bliss for which we sigh;
'Tis not the whole of life to live,
Nor all of death to die.

3 Beyond this vale of tears
There is a life above,
Unmeasured by the flight of years,
And all that life is love.

4 There is a death, whose pang
Outlasts the fleeting breath;
O what eternal horrors hang
Around the second death!

5 Thou God of truth and grace,
Teach us that death to shun,
Lest we be banished from thy face,
For evermore undone.

6 Here would we end our quest;
We find alone in thee
The life of perfect love, the rest
Of immortality.

—*Montgomery.*

MEAR. C. M. Welsh Air. Aaron Williams.

235

"The wrath to come."

1 Woe to the men on earth who dwell,
Nor dread the Almighty's frown,
When God doth all his wrath reveal,
And shower his judgments down!

2 Sinners, expect those heaviest showers;
To meet your God prepare!
For, lo! the seventh angel pours
His vial in the air.

3 Who then shall live, and face the throne,
And face the Judge severe?
When heaven and earth are fled and gone,
O where shall I appear?

4 Now, only now, against that hour
We may a place provide;
Beyond the grave, beyond the power
Of hell, our spirits hide:

5 Firm in the all-destroying shock,
May view the final scene;
For, lo! the everlasting Rock
Is cleft to take us in.

—*Charles Wesley.*

MEAR. C.M.  WELSH AIR. AARON WILLIAMS.

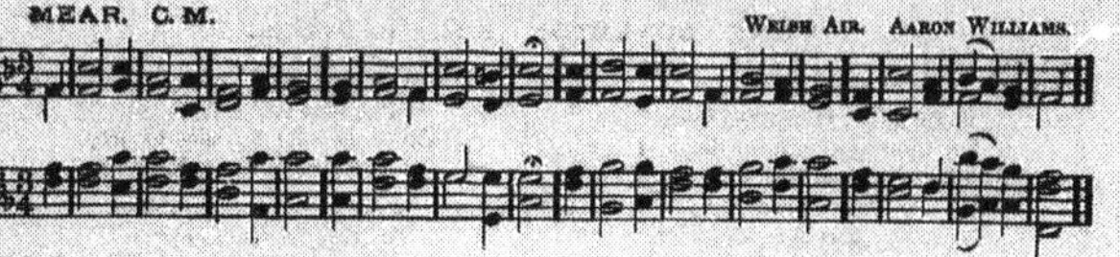

236 *The last judgment anticipated.*

1 TERRIBLE thought! shall I alone—
Who may be saved—shall I,
Of all, alas! whom I have known,
Through sin for ever die?

2 While all my old companions dear,
With whom I once did live,
Joyful at God's right hand appear,
A blessing to receive:

3 Shall I, amidst a ghastly band,
Dragged to the judgment-seat,
Far on the left with horror stand,
My fearful doom to meet?

4 Ah, no! I still may turn and live,
For still his wrath delays;
He now vouchsafes a kind reprieve,
And offers me his grace.

5 I will accept his offers now,
From every sin depart;
Perform my oft-repeated vow,
And render him my heart.

6 I will improve what I receive,
The grace through Jesus given;
Sure, if with God on earth I live,
To live with him in heaven.

—*Charles Wesley.*

2.—PENITENCE AND TRUST.

ABRIDGE. C.M. ISAAC SMITH.

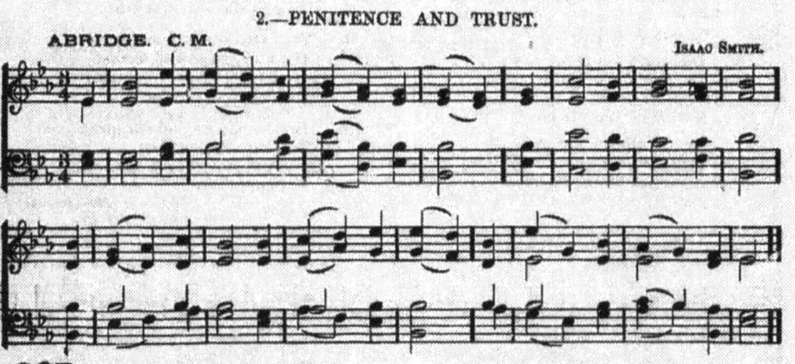

237 *"Mighty to save."*

1 JESUS! Redeemer, Saviour, Lord,
The weary sinner's Friend,
Come to my help, pronounce the word,
And bid my troubles end.

2 Deliverance to my soul proclaim,
And life and liberty;
Shed forth the virtue of thy Name,
And Jesus prove to me!

3 Salvation in that Name is found,
Balm of my grief and care;
A medicine for my every wound,
All, all I want is there.

4 Faith to be healed thou know'st I have,
For thou that faith hast given;
Thou canst, thou wilt the sinner save,
And make me meet for heaven.

5 Thou canst o'ercome this heart of mine;
Thou wilt victorious prove;
For everlasting strength is thine,
And everlasting love.

6 Thy powerful Spirit shall subdue
Unconquerable sin;
Cleanse this foul heart, and make it new,
And write thy law within.

7 Bound down with twice ten thousand ties,
Yet let me hear thy call,
My soul in confidence shall rise,
Shall rise and break through all.

—*Charles Wesley.*

TUNE: ABRIDGE. C. M. (See Hymn 237.)

238 *"Jesus Christ maketh thee whole."*

1 While dead in trespasses I lie,
Thy quickening Spirit give;
Call me, thou Son of God, that I
May hear thy voice, and live.

2 While, full of anguish and disease
My weak distempered soul
Thy love compassionately sees,
O let it make me whole!

3 To Jesus' Name, if all things now
A trembling homage pay,
O let my stubborn spirit bow,
My stiff-necked will obey!

4 Impotent, deaf, and dumb, and blind,
And sick, and poor I am;
But sure a remedy to find
For all in Jesus' Name.

—Charles Wesley.

ST. ANN'S. C. M. — Dr. Croft.

239 *All fulness in Christ.*

1 Jesus, in thee all fulness dwells,
And all for wretched man;
Fill every want my spirit feels,
And break off every chain!

2 If thou impart thyself to me,
No other good I need;
If thou, the Son, shalt make me free,
I shall be free indeed.

3 I cannot rest till in thy blood
I full redemption have;
But thou, through whom I come to God,
Canst to the utmost save.

4 From sin, the guilt, the power, the pain,
Thou wilt redeem my soul:
Lord, I believe, and not in vain;
My faith shall make me whole.

5 I too, with thee, shall walk in white;
With all thy saints shall prove
What is the length, and breadth, and height,
And depth of perfect love.

—Charles Wesley.

240 *"Who went about doing good."*

1 Jesus, if still thou art to-day
As yesterday the same,
Present to heal, in me display
The virtue of thy Name.

2 If still thou goest about to do
Thy needy creatures good,
On me, that I thy praise may show,
Be all thy wonders showed.

3 Now, Lord, to whom for help I call,
Thy miracles repeat;
With pitying eyes behold me fall
A leper at thy feet.

4 Loathsome, and vile, and self-abhorred,
I sink beneath my sin;
But, if thou wilt, a gracious word
Of thine can make me clean.

5 Thou seest me deaf to thy command;
Open, O Lord, my ear;
Bid me stretch out my withered hand,
And lift it up in prayer.

6 Blind from my birth to guilt and thee,
And dark I am within;
The love of God I cannot see,
The sinfulness of sin.

7 But thou, they say, art passing by;
O let me find thee near!
Jesus, in mercy hear my cry;
Thou Son of David, hear!

8 Behold me waiting in the way
For thee, the heavenly Light;
Command me to be brought, and say,
"Sinner, receive thy sight!"

—Charles Wesley.

MARTYRDOM. C. M. — Hugh Wilson.

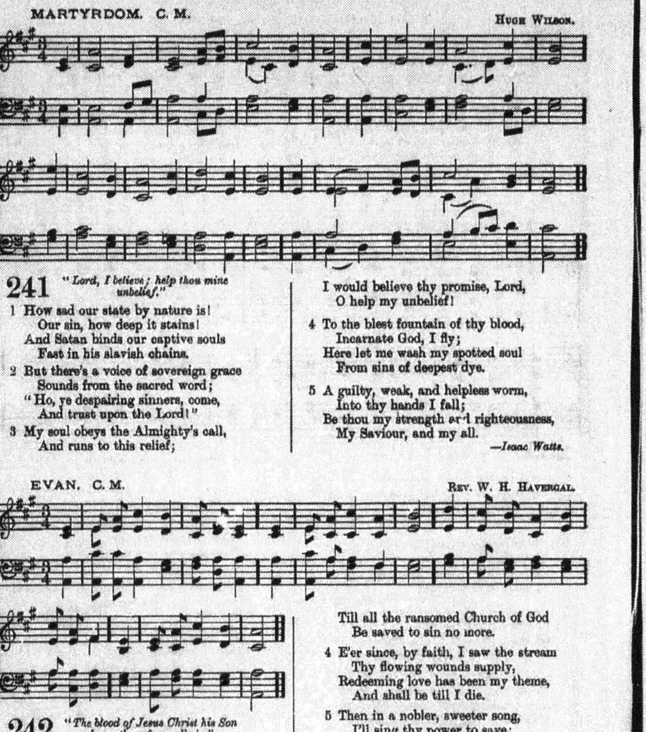

241 *"Lord, I believe; help thou mine unbelief."*

1 How sad our state by nature is!
Our sin, how deep it stains!
And Satan binds our captive souls
Fast in his slavish chains.

2 But there's a voice of sovereign grace
Sounds from the sacred word;
"Ho, ye despairing sinners, come,
And trust upon the Lord!"

3 My soul obeys the Almighty's call,
And runs to this relief;
I would believe thy promise, Lord,
O help my unbelief!

4 To the blest fountain of thy blood,
Incarnate God, I fly;
Here let me wash my spotted soul
From sins of deepest dye.

5 A guilty, weak, and helpless worm,
Into thy hands I fall;
Be thou my strength and righteousness,
My Saviour, and my all.

—*Isaac Watts.*

EVAN. C. M. — Rev. W. H. Havergal.

242 *"The blood of Jesus Christ his Son cleanseth us from all sin."*

1 There is a fountain filled with blood
Drawn from Immanuel's veins;
And sinners, plunged beneath that flood,
Lose all their guilty stains.

2 The dying thief rejoiced to see
That fountain in his day;
And there may I, though vile as he,
Wash all my sins away.

3 O dying Lamb, thy precious blood
Shall never lose its power,
Till all the ransomed Church of God
Be saved to sin no more.

4 E'er since, by faith, I saw the stream
Thy flowing wounds supply,
Redeeming love has been my theme,
And shall be till I die.

5 Then in a nobler, sweeter song,
I'll sing thy power to save;
When this poor lisping, stammering tongue
Lies silent in the grave.

6 Lord, I believe thou hast prepared,
Unworthy though I be,
For me a blood-bought free reward,
A golden harp for me!

7 'Tis strung and tuned for endless years,
And formed by power divine,
To sound in God the Father's ears
No other name but thine.

—*W. Cowper.*

Wilson.

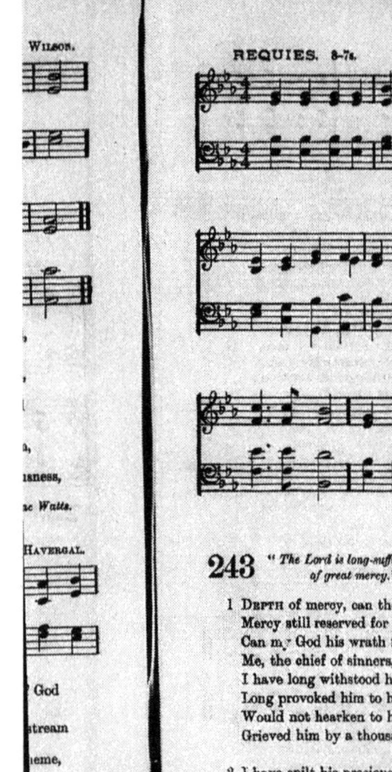

n,

usness,

ac Watts.

Havergal.

God

stream

heme,

ring tongue

red,

ard,

es years,

ars

Cowper.

REQUIES. 8-7s. BLUMENTHAL.

243

"The Lord is long-suffering and of great mercy."

1 Depth of mercy, can there be
Mercy still reserved for me?
Can my God his wrath forbear?
Me, the chief of sinners, spare?
I have long withstood his grace,
Long provoked him to his face;
Would not hearken to his calls,
Grieved him by a thousand falls.

2 I have spilt his precious blood,
Trampled on the Son of God,
Filled with pangs unspeakable,
I, who yet am not in hell!
Whence to me this waste of love?
Ask my Advocate above;
See the cause in Jesus' face,
Now before the throne of grace.

3 Lo! I cumber still the ground;
Lo! an Advocate is found;
"Hasten not to cut him down;
Let this barren soul alone."
There for me the Saviour stands,
Shows his wounds, and spreads his hands;
God is love! I know, I feel;
Jesus weeps, and loves me still!

4 Jesus, answer from above,
Is not all thy nature love?
Wilt thou not the wrong forget,
Suffer me to kiss thy feet?
If I rightly read thy heart,
If thou all compassion art,
Bow thine ear, in mercy bow,
Pardon and accept me now.

5 Pity from thine eye let fall,
By a look my soul recall;
Now the stone to flesh convert,
Cast a look, and break my heart.
Now incline me to repent,
Let me now my fall lament,
Now my foul revolt deplore,
Weep, believe, and sin no more.

—*Charles Wesley.*

SEYMOUR. 4-7s. C. M. VON WEBER.

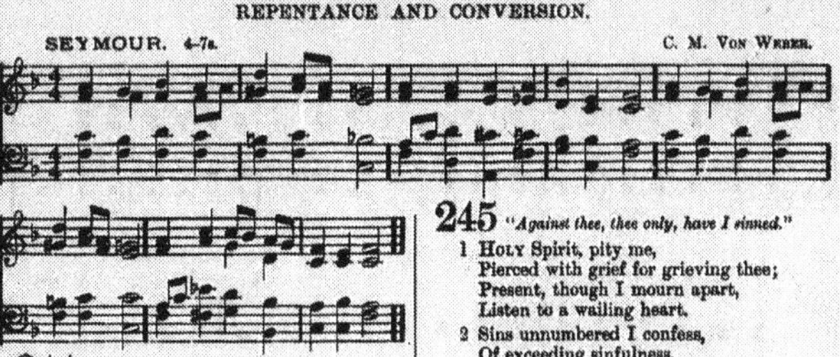

244 "Go in peace and sin no more."

1 AFTER all that I have done,
Saviour, art thou pacified?
Whither shall my vileness run?
Hide me, earth, the sinner hide!

2 Let me sink into the dust,
Full of holy shame adore;
Jesus Christ, the Good, the Just,
Bids me go and sin no more.

3 O confirm the gracious word,
Jesus, Son of God and man!
Let me never grieve thee, Lord,
Never turn to sin again.

4 Till my all in all thou art,
Till thou bring thy nature in,
Keep this feeble, trembling heart;
Save me, save me, Lord, from sin!

—*Charles Wesley.*

245 "Against thee, thee only, have I sinned."

1 HOLY Spirit, pity me,
Pierced with grief for grieving thee;
Present, though I mourn apart,
Listen to a wailing heart.

2 Sins unnumbered I confess,
Of exceeding sinfulness,
Sins against thyself alone,
Only to Omniscience known:

3 Deafness to thy whispered calls,
Rashness midst remembered falls,
Transient fears beneath the rod,
Treacherous trifling with my God;

4 Tasting that the Lord is good,
Pining then for poisoned food;
At the fountains of the skies,
Craving creaturely supplies;

5 Worldly cares at worship-time,
Grovelling aims in works sublime;
Pride, when God is passing by,
Sloth, when souls in darkness die.

6 O be merciful to me,
Now in bitterness for thee!
Father, pardon through thy Son
Sins against thy Spirit done!

—*W. M. Bunting.*

ST. MICHAEL. S. M. DAY'S PSALTER, 1588.

246 Guilty delay in coming to Christ.

1 AH! whither should I go,
Burdened, and sick, and faint?
To whom should I my trouble show,
And pour out my complaint?

2 My Saviour bids me come,
Ah! why do I delay?
He calls the weary sinner home,
And yet from him I stay!

3 What is it keeps me back,
From which I cannot part;
Which will not let my Saviour take
Possession of my heart?

4 Some cursèd thing unknown
Must surely lurk within;
Some idol, which I will not own,
Some secret bosom-sin.

5 Jesus, the hindrance, show
Which I have feared to see;
Yet let me now consent to know
What keeps me out of thee.

6 Searcher of hearts, in mine
Thy trying power display;
Into its darkest corners shine,
And take the veil away.

7 I now believe in thee
Compassion reigns alone;
According to my faith, to me
O let it, Lord, be done!

8 In me is all the bar,
Which thou wouldst fain remove;
Remove it, and I shall declare
That God is only Love.

—*Charles Wesley.*

TUNE: ST. MICHAEL. S. M. (SEE HYMN 246.)

247

"The love of Christ constraineth us."

1 WHEN shall thy love constrain,
And force me to thy breast?
When shall my soul return again
To her eternal rest?

2 Ah! what avails my strife,
My wandering to and fro?
Thou hast the words of endless life;
Ah! whither should I go?

3 Thy condescending grace
To me did freely move;
It calls me still to seek thy face,
And stoops to ask my love.

4 Lord, at thy feet I fall;
I groan to be set free;
I fain would now obey the call,
And give up all for thee.

5 My sinful heart to gain,
The God of all that breathe
Was found in fashion as a man,
And died a cursèd death.

6 And can I yet delay
My little all to give?
To tear my soul from earth away,
For Jesus to receive?

7 Nay, but I yield, I yield!
I can hold out no more;
I sink, by dying love compelled,
And own thee conqueror.

8 Though late, I all forsake,
My friends, my all resign;
Gracious Redeemer, take, O take,
And seal me ever thine!

—*Charles Wesley.*

THATCHER. S. M. HANDEL.

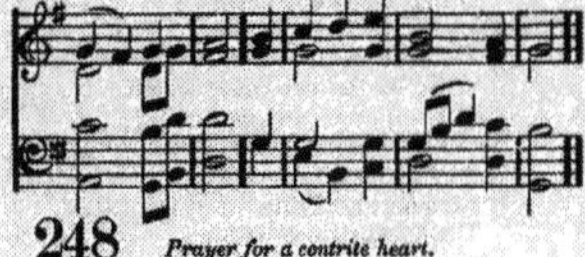

248

Prayer for a contrite heart.

1 O THAT I could repent,
With all my idols part,
And to thy gracious eyes present
A humble, contrite heart!

2 A heart with grief opprest
For having grieved my God;
A troubled heart that cannot rest,
Till sprinkled with thy blood.

3 Jesus, on me bestow
The penitent desire;
With true sincerity of woe
My aching breast inspire;

4 With softening pity look,
And melt my hardness down;
Strike with thy love's resistless stroke,
And break this heart of stone!

—*Charles Wesley.*

249

Hope in God's mercy.

1 O UNEXHAUSTED grace!
O love unsearchable!
I am not gone to my own place,
I am not yet in hell!

2 Earth doth not open yet,
My soul to swallow up;
And, hanging o'er the burning pit,
I still am forced to hope.

3 I hope at last to find
The kingdom from above,
The settled peace, the constant mind,
The everlasting love;

4 The sanctifying grace
That makes me meet for home;
I hope to see thy glorious face,
Where sin can never come.

5 What shall I do to keep
The blessed hope I feel?
Still let me pray, and watch, and weep,
And serve thy pleasure still.

6 O may I never grieve
My kind, long-suffering Lord!
But steadfastly to Jesus cleave,
And answer all his word.

7 Lord, if thou hast bestowed
On me this gracious fear,
This horror of offending God,
O keep it always here!

8 And that I never more
May from thy ways depart,
Enter with all thy mercy's power,
And dwell within my heart.

—*Charles Wesley.*

LEOMINSTER. S. M. D. G. W. MARTIN.

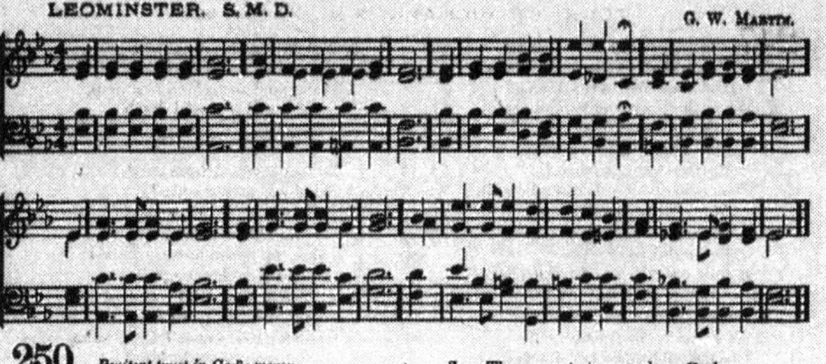

250 *Penitent trust in God's mercy.*

1 O MY offended God,
If now at last I see
That I have trampled on thy blood,
And done despite to thee;
If I begin to wake
Out of my deadly sleep,
Into thy arms of mercy take,
And there for ever keep.

2 Thy death hath bought the power
For every sinful soul,
That all may know the gracious hour,
And be by faith made whole.
Thou hast for sinners died,
That all may come to God;
The covenant thou hast ratified
And sealed it with thy blood.

3 He that believes in thee,
And doth till death endure,
He shall be saved eternally;
The covenant is sure.
The mountains shall give place,
Thy covenant cannot move,
The covenant of thy general grace,
Thy all-redeeming love.

—*Charles Wesley.*

251 *Prayer for a deeper sense of sin.*

1 O THAT I could revere
My much-offended God!
O that I could but stand in fear
Of thy afflicting rod!
If mercy cannot draw,
Thou by thy threatenings move
And keep an abject soul in awe,
That will not yield to love.

2 Show me the naked sword
Impending o'er my head;
O let me tremble at thy word,
And to my ways take heed!
With sacred horror fly
From every sinful snare;
Nor ever, in my Judge's eye,
My Judge's anger dare.

3 Thou great, tremendous God,
The conscious awe impart;
The grace be now on me bestowed,
The tender, fleshly heart.
For Jesus' sake alone
The stony heart remove,
And melt at last, O melt me down
Into the mould of love!

—*Charles Wesley.*

252 *Repentance and faith implored.*

1 O THAT I could repent!
O that I could believe!
Thou by thy voice the marble rend,
The rock in sunder cleave!
Thou, by thy two-edged sword,
My soul and spirit part;
Strike with the hammer of thy word,
And break my stubborn heart!

2 Saviour, and Prince of peace,
The double grace bestow:
Unloose the bands of wickedness,
And let the captive go;
Grant me my sins to feel,
And then the load remove;
Wound, and pour in, my wounds to heal,
The balm of pardoning love.

3 For thy own mercy's sake,
The cursèd thing remove;
And into thy protection take
The prisoner of thy love.
In every trying hour,
Stand by my feeble soul;
And screen me from my nature's power,
Till thou hast made me whole.

4 This is thy will, I know,
That I should holy be,
Should let my sin this moment go,
This moment turn to thee.
O might I now embrace
Thy all-sufficient power;
And never more to sin give place,
And never grieve thee more.

—*Charles Wesley.*

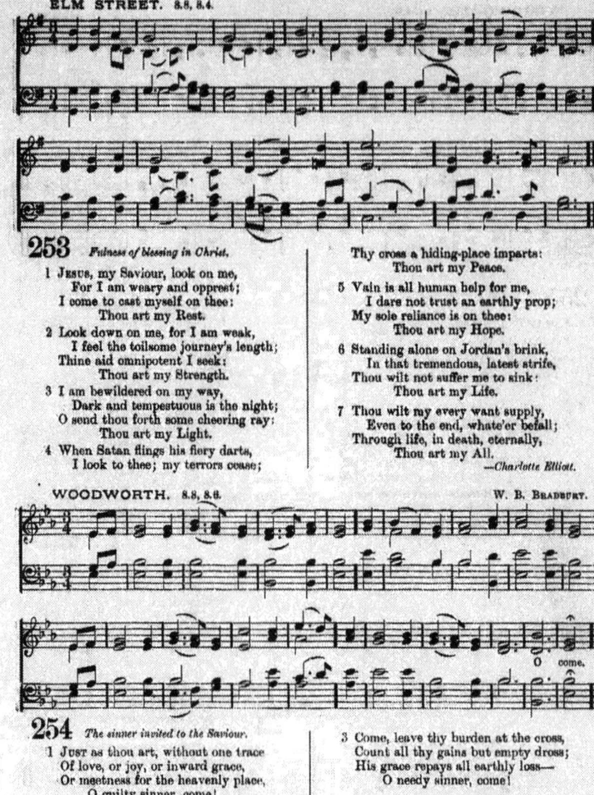
ELM STREET. 8.8, 8.4.
WOODWORTH. 8.8, 8.6.
W. B. Bradbury.
O come.

253 *Fulness of blessing in Christ.*

1 Jesus, my Saviour, look on me,
For I am weary and opprest;
I come to cast myself on thee:
Thou art my Rest.

2 Look down on me, for I am weak,
I feel the toilsome journey's length;
Thine aid omnipotent I seek:
Thou art my Strength.

3 I am bewildered on my way,
Dark and tempestuous is the night;
O send thou forth some cheering ray:
Thou art my Light.

4 When Satan flings his fiery darts,
I look to thee; my terrors cease;
Thy cross a hiding-place imparts:
Thou art my Peace.

5 Vain is all human help for me,
I dare not trust an earthly prop;
My sole reliance is on thee:
Thou art my Hope.

6 Standing alone on Jordan's brink,
In that tremendous, latest strife,
Thou wilt not suffer me to sink:
Thou art my Life.

7 Thou wilt my every want supply,
Even to the end, whate'er befall;
Through life, in death, eternally,
Thou art my All.

—Charlotte Elliott.

254 *The sinner invited to the Saviour.*

1 Just as thou art, without one trace
Of love, or joy, or inward grace,
Or meetness for the heavenly place,
O guilty sinner, come!

2 Burdened with guilt, wouldst thou be blest?
Trust not the world; it gives no rest;
Christ gives relief to hearts opprest—
O weary sinner, come!

3 Come, leave thy burden at the cross,
Count all thy gains but empty dross;
His grace repays all earthly loss—
O needy sinner, come!

4 Come, hither bring thy boding fears,
Thy aching heart, thy mournful tears;
'Tis mercy's voice salutes thine ears—
O trembling sinner, come!

—Russel S. Cook.

WOODWORTH. 8.8, 8.6. W. B. BRADBURY.

I come!

255

"Just as I am."

1 JUST as I am, without one plea
But that thy blood was shed for me,
And that thou bidd'st me come to thee,
O Lamb of God, I come!

2 Just as I am, and waiting not
To rid my soul of one dark blot,
To thee, whose blood can cleanse each spot,
O Lamb of God, I come!

3 Just as I am, though tossed about
With many a conflict, many a doubt,
With fears within, and foes without,
O Lamb of God, I come!

4 Just as I am, poor, wretched, blind;
Sight, riches, healing of the mind,
Yea, all I need, in thee to find,
O Lamb of God, I come!

5 Just as I am, thou wilt receive,
Wilt welcome, pardon, cleanse, relieve;
Because thy promise I believe,
O Lamb of God, I come!

6 Just as I am,—thy love unknown
Has broken every barrier down;
Now to be thine, yea, thine alone,
O Lamb of God, I come!

—*Charlotte Elliott.*

"EVEN ME." 8.7, 8.7, 3. W. B. BRADBURY.

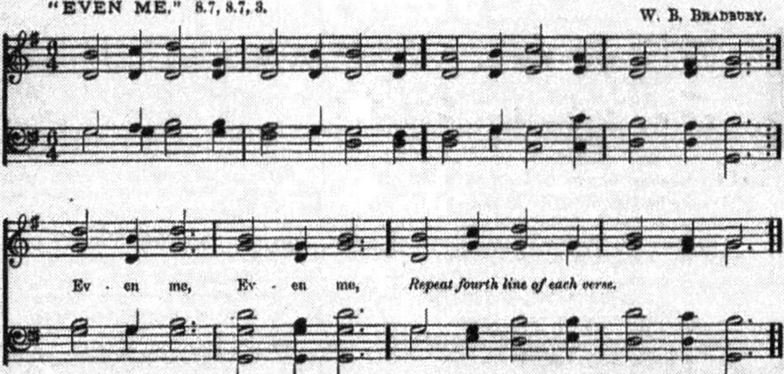
Ev - en me, Ev - en me,
Repeat fourth line of each verse.

TUNE: "EVEN ME." 8.7, 8.7, 3.

256 *Prayer for a personal blessing.*

1 Lord, I hear of showers of blessing
Thou art scattering, full and free—
Showers, the thirsty land refreshing;
Let some drops now fall on me—
Even me.

2 Pass me not, O God, our Father,
Sinful though my heart may be!
Thou might'st leave me, but the rather
Let thy mercy fall on me—
Even me.

3 Pass me not, O gracious Saviour,
Let me live and cling to thee!
I am longing for thy favour;
Whilst thou'rt calling, O call me!
Even me.

4 Pass me not, O mighty Spirit,
Thou canst make the blind to see;
Witnesser of Jesus' merit,
Speak some word of power to me—
Even me.

5 Love of God so pure and changeless,
Blood of Christ so rich and free,
Grace of God so strong and boundless,
Magnify it all in me—
Even me. —*Mrs. Codner.*

FEDERAL STREET. L. M. H. K. Oliver.

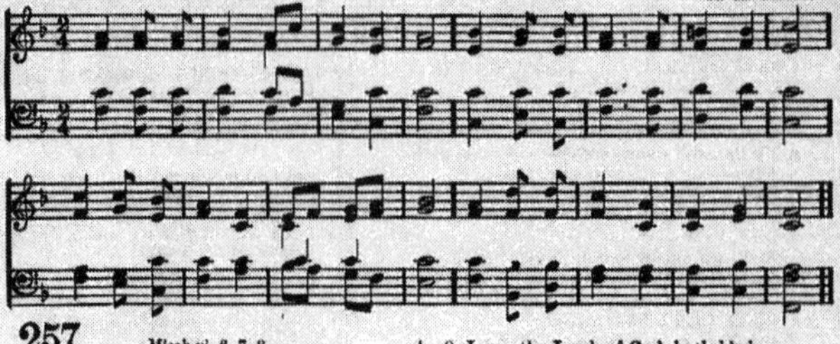

257 Micah vi. 6, 7, 8.

1 Wherewith, O God, shall I draw near,
And bow myself before thy face?
How in thy purer eyes appear?
What shall I bring to gain thy grace?

2 Will gifts delight the Lord Most High?
Will multiplied oblations please?
Thousands of rams his favour buy,
Or slaughtered hecatombs appease?

3 Can these avert the wrath of God?
Can these wash out my guilty stain?
Rivers of oil, and seas of blood,
Alas! they all must flow in vain.

4 Whoe'er to thee themselves approve,
Must take the path thy word hath showed;
Justice pursue, and mercy love,
And humbly walk by faith with God.

5 But though my life henceforth be thine,
Present for past can ne'er atone;
Though I to thee the whole resign,
I only give thee back thine own.

6 What have I then wherein to trust?
I nothing have, I nothing am;
Excluded is my every boast,
My glory swallowed up in shame.

7 Guilty I stand before thy face;
On me I feel thy wrath abide;
'Tis just the sentence should take place;
'Tis just—but O thy Son hath died!

8 Jesus, the Lamb of God, hath bled;
He bore our sins upon the tree;
Beneath our curse he bowed his head;
'Tis finished! he hath died for me!

9 See where before the throne he stands,
And pours the all-prevailing prayer!
Points to his side, and lifts his hands,
And shows that I am graven there.
—*Charles Wesley.*

258 *"Salvation is of the Lord."*

1 Lord, I despair myself to heal;
I see my sin, but cannot feel;
I cannot, till thy Spirit blow,
And bid the obedient waters flow.

2 'Tis thine a heart of flesh to give;
Thy gifts I only can receive;
Here, then, to thee I all resign;
To draw, redeem, and seal, is thine.

3 With simple faith on thee I call,
My Light, my Life, my Lord, my All;
I wait the moving of the pool;
I wait the word that speaks me whole.

4 Speak, gracious Lord, my sickness cure,
Make my infected nature pure;
Peace, righteousness, and joy impart,
And pour thyself into my heart.
—*Charles Wesley.*

ABENDS. L. M. SIR H. S. OAKLEY.

259

Psalm li.

1 SHOW pity, Lord; O Lord, forgive!
Let a repenting rebel live;
Are not thy mercies large and free?
May not a sinner trust in thee?

2 My lips with shame my sins confess
Against thy law, against thy grace;
Lord, should thy judgment be severe,
I am condemned, but thou art clear.

3 Lord, I am vile, conceived in sin,
And born unholy and unclean,
Sprung from the man whose guilty fall
Corrupts the race and taints us all.

4 Behold I fall before thy face,
My only refuge is thy grace;
No outward form can make me clean,
The leprosy lies deep within.

5 Yet save a trembling sinner, Lord,
Whose hope, still hovering round thy word,
Would light on some sweet promise there,
Some sure support against despair.

6 A broken heart, my God, my King,
Is all the sacrifice I bring;
The God of grace will ne'er despise
A broken heart for sacrifice.

—*Isaac Watts.*

260

Jesus the sinner's Friend.

1 JESUS, the sinner's Friend, to thee,
Lost and undone, for aid I flee;
Weary of earth, myself, and sin,
Open thine arms, and take me in!

2 Pity and heal my sin-sick soul;
'Tis thou alone canst make me whole;
Fallen, till in me thine image shine,
And lost I am, till thou art mine.

3 The mansion for thyself prepare;
Dispose my heart by entering there;
'Tis this alone can make me clean;
'Tis this alone can cast out sin.

4 At last I own it cannot be
That I should fit myself for thee;
Here, then, to thee I all resign;
Thine is the work, and only thine.

5 What shall I say thy grace to move?
Lord, I am sin, but thou art love;
I give up every plea beside,—
"Lord, I am lost, but thou hast died."

—*Charles Wesley.*

HESPERUS. L. M. H. BAKER, Mus. Bac.

TUNE: HESPERUS. L. M.

261

Confession of sin.

1 O THOU that hear'st when sinners cry,
Though all my crimes before thee lie,
Behold me not with angry look,
But blot their memory from thy book!

2 Create my nature pure within,
And form my soul averse from sin;
Let thy good Spirit ne'er depart,
Nor hide thy presence from my heart.

3 I cannot live without thy light,
Cast out and banished from thy sight;
Thy saving strength, O Lord, restore,
And guard me that I fall no more.

4 Though I have grieved thy Spirit, Lord,
His help and comfort still afford;
And let a wretch come near thy throne,
To plead the merits of thy Son.

5 My soul lies humbled in the dust,
And owns thy dreadful sentence just;
Look down, O Lord, with pitying eye,
And save the soul condemned to die.

6 Then will I teach the world thy ways;
Sinners shall learn thy sovereign grace;
I'll lead them to my Saviour's blood,
And they shall praise a pardoning God.

7 O may thy love inspire my tongue!
Salvation shall be all my song,
And all my powers shall join to bless
The Lord my strength and righteousness.

—*Isaac Watts.*

PENTECOST. L. M. WILLIAM BOYD.

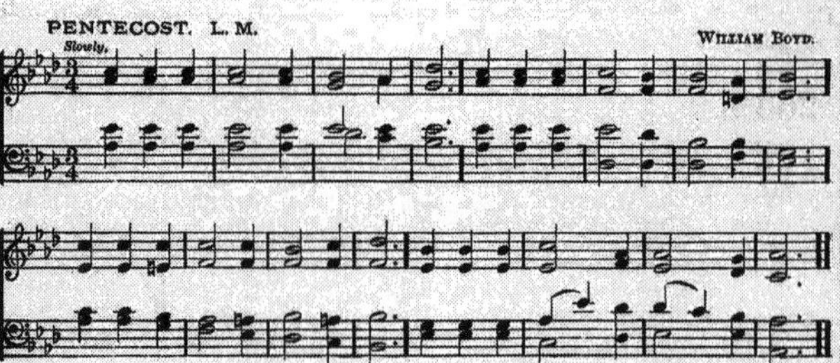
Slowly.

262

"God be merciful to me a sinner."

1 WITH broken heart and contrite sigh,
A trembling sinner, Lord, I cry;
Thy pardoning grace is rich and free:
O God, be merciful to me!

2 I smite upon my troubled breast,
With deep and conscious guilt oppressed;
Christ and his cross my only plea:
O God, be merciful to me!

3 Far off I stand with tearful eyes,
Nor dare uplift them to the skies;
But thou dost all my anguish see:
O God, be merciful to me!

4 Nor alms, nor deeds that I have done,
Can for a single sin atone;
To Calvary alone I flee:
O God, be merciful to me!

5 And when, redeemed from sin and hell,
With all the ransomed throng I dwell,
My raptured song shall ever be,
That God was merciful to me!

—*Elven.*

BARNBY. 6-8s. J. BARNBY.

By permission of Messrs. Novello, Ewer & Co.

263 *The wanderer returning to God.*

1 JESUS, in whom the weary find
Their late but permanent repose,
Physician of the sin-sick mind,
Relieve my wants, assuage my woes;
And let my soul on thee be cast
Till life's fierce tyranny be past.

2 Loosed from my God, and far removed,
Long have I wandered to and fro;
O'er earth in endless circles roved,
Nor found whereon to rest below:
Back to my God at last I fly,
For O the waters still are high!

3 Selfish pursuits, and nature's maze,
The things of earth for thee I leave;
Put forth thy hand, thy hand of grace,
Into the ark of love receive;
Take this poor fluttering soul to rest,
And lodge it, Saviour, in thy breast.

4 Fill with inviolable peace,
'Stablish and keep my settled heart;
In thee may all my wanderings cease,
From thee no more may I depart;
Thy utmost goodness called to prove,
Loved with an everlasting love!

—*Charles Wesley.*

264 *Prayer for the light of faith.*

1 FATHER of Jesus Christ, the Just,
My Friend and Advocate with thee,
Pity a soul that fain would trust
In him who lived and died for me;
But only thou canst make him known,
And in my heart reveal thy Son.

2 If, drawn by thine alluring grace,
My want of living faith I feel,
Show me in Christ thy smiling face;
What flesh and blood can ne'er reveal,
Thy co-eternal Son, display,
And turn my darkness into day.

3 The gift unspeakable impart;
Command the light of faith to shine,
To shine in my dark drooping heart,
And fill me with the life divine;
Now bid the new creation be:
O God, let there be faith in me!

—*Charles Wesley.*

CAREY'S. 6-8s. HENRY CAREY.

265 *Jacob wrestling with the Angel.*

1 COME, O thou Traveller unknown,
 Whom still I hold, but cannot see!
My company before is gone,
 And I am left alone with thee;
With thee all night I mean to stay,
And wrestle till the break of day.

2 I need not tell thee who I am,
 My misery and sin declare;
Thyself hast called me by my name,
 Look on thy hands, and read it there;
But who, I ask thee, who art thou?
Tell me thy name, and tell me now.

3 In vain thou strugglest to get free,
 I never will unloose my hold!
Art thou the man that died for me?
 The secret of thy love unfold;
Wrestling, I will not let thee go,
Till I thy name, thy nature know.

4 Wilt thou not yet to me reveal
 Thy new, unutterable name?
Tell me, I still beseech thee, tell;
 To know it now resolved I am;
Wrestling, I will not let thee go,
Till I thy name, thy nature know.

5 What though my shrinking flesh complain,
 And murmur to contend so long?
I rise superior to my pain,
 When I am weak, then I am strong;
And when my all of strength shall fail,
I shall with the God-man prevail.

—*Charles Wesley.*

266 SECOND PART.

1 YIELD to me now, for I am weak,
 But confident in self-despair;
Speak to my heart, in blessings speak,
 Be conquered by my instant prayer;
Speak, or thou never hence shalt move,
And tell me if thy Name is Love.

2 'Tis Love! 'tis Love! thou diedst for me!
 I hear thy whisper in my heart;
The morning breaks, the shadows flee,
 Pure, universal love thou art:
To me, to all, thy mercies move,
Thy Nature and thy Name is Love.

3 My prayer hath power with God; the grace
 Unspeakable I now receive;
Through faith I see thee face to face;
 I see thee face to face, and live!
In vain I have not wept and strove;
Thy Nature and thy Name is Love.

4 I know thee, Saviour, who thou art,
 Jesus, the feeble sinner's Friend;
Nor wilt thou with the night depart,
 But stay and love me to the end;
Thy mercies never shall remove;
Thy Nature and thy Name is Love.

5 The Sun of Righteousness on me
 Hath risen, with healing in his wings;
Withered my nature's strength, from thee
 My soul its life and succour brings;
My help is all laid up above;
Thy Nature and thy Name is Love.

6 Contented now upon my thigh
 I halt, till life's short journey end;
All helplessness, all weakness, I
 On thee alone for strength depend;
Nor have I power from thee to move;
Thy Nature and thy Name is Love.

7 Lame as I am, I take the prey;
 Hell, earth, and sin, with ease o'ercome,
I leap for joy, pursue my way,
 And, as a bounding hart, fly home,
Through all eternity to prove
Thy Nature and thy Name is Love.

—*Charles Wesley.*

PATER OMNIUM. 6-8s. H. J. E. HOLMES.

267

Prayer for forgiveness of backsliding.

1 WEARY of wandering from my God,
And now made willing to return,
I hear, and bow me to the rod;
For thee, not without hope, I mourn:
I have an Advocate above,
A Friend before the throne of Love.

2 O Jesus, full of truth and grace,
More full of grace than I of sin,
Yet once again I seek thy face;
Open thine arms and take me in,
And freely my backslidings heal,
And love the faithless sinner still.

3 Thou know'st the way to bring me back,
My fallen spirit to restore;
O for thy truth and mercy's sake,
Forgive, and bid me sin no more!
The ruins of my soul repair,
And make my heart a house of prayer.

4 The stone to flesh again convert;
The veil of sin again remove;
Sprinkle thy blood upon my heart,
And melt it by thy dying love;
This rebel heart by love subdue,
And make it soft, and make it new.

5 Ah! give me, Lord, the tender heart
That trembles at the approach of sin;
A godly fear of sin impart;
Implant and root it deep within,
That I may dread thy gracious power,
And never dare to offend thee more.

—*Charles Wesley.*

268

Hungering and thirsting for God.

1 JESUS, if still the same thou art,
If all thy promises are sure,
Set up thy kingdom in my heart,
And make me rich, for I am poor;
To me be all thy treasures given,
The kingdom of an inward heaven.

2 Thou hast pronounced the mourners blest,
And, lo! for thee I ever mourn;
I cannot, no, I will not rest,
Till thou, my only rest, return;
Till thou, the Prince of peace, appear,
And I receive the Comforter.

3 Where is the blessedness bestowed
On all that hunger after thee?
I hunger now, I thirst for God;
See the poor fainting sinner, see,
And satisfy with endless peace,
And fill me with thy righteousness.

4 Ah! Lord, if thou art in that sigh,
Then hear thyself within me pray;
Hear in my heart thy Spirit's cry,
Mark what my labouring soul would say;
Answer the deep unuttered groan,
And show that thou and I are one.

5 Shine on thy work, disperse the gloom,
Light in thy light I then shall see;
Say to my soul, "Thy light is come,
Glory divine is risen on thee;
Thy warfare's past, thy mourning's o'er;
Look up, for thou shalt weep no more."

6 Lord, I believe the promise sure,
And trust thou wilt not long delay,
Hungry, and sorrowful, and poor,
Upon thy word myself I stay;
Into thine hands my all resign,
And wait till all thou art is mine.—*C. Wesley.*

ADMAH. 6-8s. LOWELL MASON.

269

Matthew ix. 20-22.

1 UNCLEAN, of life and heart unclean,
How shall I in his sight appear?
Conscious of my inveterate sin
I blush and tremble to draw near;
Yet, through the garment of his word,
I humbly seek to touch my Lord.

Turn then, thou good Physician, turn,
Thou Source of unexhausted love;
Sole Comforter of souls forlorn,
Who only canst my plague remove,
O cast a pitying look on me
Who dare not lift mine eyes to thee!

3 Yet will I in my God confide,
Who comes to meet my seeking soul;
I wait to feel thy blood applied,
Thy blood applied shall make me whole;
And, lo! I trust thy gracious power
To touch, to heal me, in this hour.

—*John Wesley.*

SEVILLE. 6-7s. SPANISH CHANT.

270

Christ the true light.

1 CHRIST, whose glory fills the skies,
Christ, the true, the only Light,
Sun of Righteousness, arise,
Triumph o'er the shades of night;
Day-spring from on high, be near;
Day-star, in my heart appear!

2 Dark and cheerless is the morn,
Unaccompanied by thee;
Joyless is the day's return,
Till thy mercy's beams I see;
Till thou inward light impart,
Glad my eyes, and warm my heart.

3 Visit then this soul of mine,
Pierce the gloom of sin and grief;
Fill me, Radiancy Divine!
Scatter all my unbelief;
More and more thyself display,
Shining to the perfect day!

—*Charles Wesley.*

SEVILLE. 6-7s. SPANISH CHANT.

271 *Prayer for converting grace.*

1 JESUS, I believe thee near,
Now my fallen soul restore;
Now my guilty conscience clear;
Give me back my peace and power;
Stone to flesh again convert,
Write forgiveness on my heart.

2 I believe thy pardoning grace,
As at the beginning, free;
Open are thy arms to embrace
Me, the worst of rebels, me;
In me all the hindrance lies;
Called,—I still refuse to rise.

3 Now the gracious work begin;
Now for good some token give;
Give me now to feel my sin,
Give me now my sin to leave;
Bid me look on thee and mourn,
Bid me to thy arms return.

4 Take this heart of stone away,
Melt me into gracious tears;
Grant me power to watch and pray,
Till thy lovely face appears,
Till thy favour I retrieve,
Till by faith again I live.

—Charles Wesley.

AJALON. 6-7s. R. REDHEAD.

272 *Prayer for pardon and salvation.*

1 SAVIOUR, cast a pitying eye,
Bid my sins and sorrows end;
Whither should a sinner fly?
Art not thou the sinner's Friend?
Rest in thee I long to find,
Wretched I, and poor, and blind.

2 Haste, O haste, to my relief!
From the iron furnace take;
Rid me of my sin and grief,
For thy love and mercy's sake;
Set my heart at liberty,
Show forth all thy power in me.

3 Me, the vilest of the race,
Most unholy, most unclean;
Me, the farthest from thy face,
Full of misery and sin:
Me with arms of love receive,
Me, of sinners chief, forgive.

4 Jesus, on thine only name
For salvation I depend;
In thy gracious hands I am,
Save me, save me, to the end;
Let the utmost grace be given,
Save me quite from hell to heaven.

—Charles Wesley.

TUNE: AJALON. 6-7s. (SEE HYMN 272.)

273

True contrition implored.

1 SAVIOUR, Prince of Israel's race,
See me from thy lofty throne;
Give the sweet relenting grace,
Soften this obdurate stone;
Stone to flesh, O God, convert!
Cast a look, and break my heart.

2 By thy Spirit, Lord, reprove,
All my inmost sins reveal;
Sins against thy light and love
Let me see, and let me feel;
Sins that crucified my God,
Spilt again thy precious blood.

3 Jesus, seek thy wandering sheep,
Make me restless to return;
Bid me look on thee, and weep,
Bitterly as Peter mourn,
Till I say, by grace restored,
"Now thou know'st I love thee, Lord!"

4 Might I in thy sight appear,
As the publican distrest;
Stand, not daring to draw near,
Smite on my unworthy breast;
Groan the sinner's only plea,
"God be merciful to me!"

5 O remember me for good,
Passing through the mortal vale;
Show me the atoning blood,
When my strength and spirit fail;
Give my fainting soul to see
Jesus crucified for me.

—*Charles Wesley.*

TOPLADY. 6-7s. T. HASTINGS.

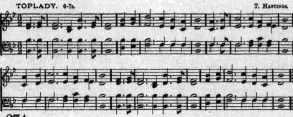

274

Inconstancy confessed.

1 JESUS, Shepherd of the sheep,
Pity my unsettled soul!
Guide, and nourish me, and keep,
Till thy love shall make me whole:
Give me perfect soundness, give,
Make me steadfastly believe.

2 I am never at one stay,
Changing every hour I am;
But thou art, as yesterday,
Now and evermore the same:
Constancy to me impart,
'Stablish with thy grace my heart.

3 Give me faith to hold me up,
Walking over life's rough sea,
Holy, purifying hope
Still my soul's sure anchor be;
That I may be always thine,
Perfect me in love divine.

—*Charles Wesley.*

275

A present salvation.

1 WHY not now, my God, my God!
Ready if thou always art,
Make in me thy mean abode,
Take possession of my heart;
If thou canst so greatly bow,
Friend of sinners, why not now?

2 God of love, in this my day,
For thyself to thee I cry;
Dying, if thou still delay,
Must I not for ever die!
Enter now thy poorest home,
Now, my utmost Saviour, come!

—*Charles Wesley.*

SAWLEY. C. M. J. WALCH.

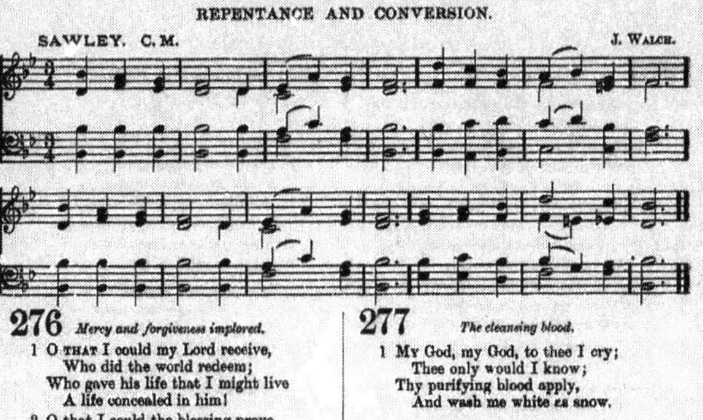

276 *Mercy and forgiveness implored.*

1 O THAT I could my Lord receive,
Who did the world redeem;
Who gave his life that I might live
A life concealed in him!

2 O that I could the blessing prove,
My heart's extreme desire,
Live happy in my Saviour's love,
And in his arms expire.

3 Mercy I ask to seal my peace,
That, kept by mercy's power,
I may from every evil cease,
And never grieve thee more.

4 Now, if thy gracious will it be,
Even now, my sins remove,
And set my soul at liberty
By thy victorious love.

5 In answer to ten thousand prayers,
Thou pardoning God, descend;
Number me with salvation's heirs,
My sins and troubles end.

6 Nothing I ask or want beside,
Of all in earth or heaven,
But let me feel thy blood applied,
And live and die forgiven.

—*Charles Wesley.*

277 *The cleansing blood.*

1 MY God, my God, to thee I cry;
Thee only would I know;
Thy purifying blood apply,
And wash me white as snow.

2 Touch me, and make the leper clean,
Purge my iniquity;
Unless thou wash my soul from sin,
I have no part in thee.

3 But art thou not already mine?
Answer, if mine thou art;
Witness within, thou Love divine,
And cheer my drooping heart.

4 Behold, for me the Victim bleeds,
His wounds are opened wide;
For me the blood of sprinkling pleads,
And speaks me justified.

5 O let me lose myself in thee,
The depth of mercy prove,
Thou vast, unfathomable sea
Of unexhausted love!

—*Charles Wesley.*

ELIM. C. M. H. W. GREATOREX.

TUNE: ELIM. C. M.

278 *Backsliding from God lamented.*

1 O why did I my Saviour leave,
So soon unfaithful prove?
How could I thy good Spirit grieve,
And sin against thy love?

2 I forced thee first to disappear,
I turned thee first aside;
Ah! Lord, if thou hadst still been here,
Thy servant had not died.

3 But O, how soon thy wrath is o'er,
And pardoning love takes place!
Assist me, Saviour, to adore
The riches of thy grace.

4 My humbled soul, when thou art near,
In dust and ashes lies;
How shall a sinful worm appear,
Or meet thy purer eyes?

5 I loathe myself when God I see,
And into nothing fall;
Content if thou exalted be,
And Christ be all in all.

—Charles Wesley.

WARWICK. C. M. SAMUEL STANLEY.

279 *Wanderings from God lamented.*

1 Infinite Power, eternal Lord,
How sovereign is thy hand!
All nature rose to obey thy word,
And moves at thy command.

2 With steady course the shining sun
Keeps his appointed way;
And all the hours obedient run
The circle of the day.

3 But, ah! how wide my spirit flies,
And wanders from her God!
My soul forgets the heavenly prize,
And treads the downward road.

4 The raging fire and stormy sea
Perform thy awful will;
And every beast and every tree
Thy great design fulfil.

5 Shall creatures of a meaner frame
Pay all their dues to thee—
Creatures that never knew thy name,
That ne'er were loved like me?

6 Great God, create my soul anew,
Conform my heart to thine!
Melt down my will, and let it flow,
And take the mould divine.

7 Then shall my feet no more depart,
Nor my affections rove;
Devotion shall be all my heart,
And all my passions, love.

—Isaac Watts.

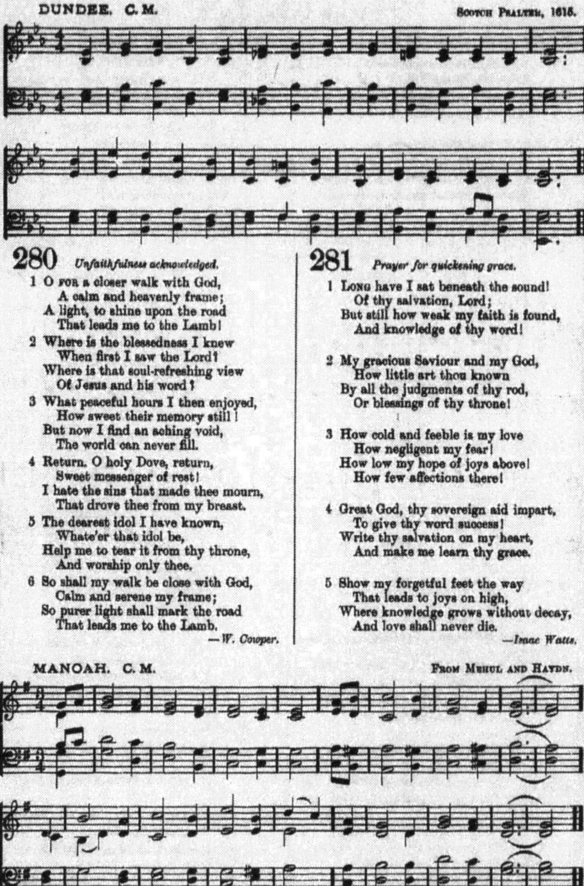
DUNDEE. C. M.
Scotch Psalter, 1615.
MANOAH. C. M.
From Mehul and Haydn.

280 *Unfaithfulness acknowledged.*

1 O for a closer walk with God,
A calm and heavenly frame;
A light, to shine upon the road
That leads me to the Lamb!

2 Where is the blessedness I knew
When first I saw the Lord?
Where is that soul-refreshing view
Of Jesus and his word?

3 What peaceful hours I then enjoyed,
How sweet their memory still!
But now I find an aching void,
The world can never fill.

4 Return, O holy Dove, return,
Sweet messenger of rest!
I hate the sins that made thee mourn,
That drove thee from my breast.

5 The dearest idol I have known,
Whate'er that idol be,
Help me to tear it from thy throne,
And worship only thee.

6 So shall my walk be close with God,
Calm and serene my frame;
So purer light shall mark the road
That leads me to the Lamb.

—*W. Cowper.*

281 *Prayer for quickening grace.*

1 Long have I sat beneath the sound!
Of thy salvation, Lord;
But still how weak my faith is found,
And knowledge of thy word!

2 My gracious Saviour and my God,
How little art thou known
By all the judgments of thy rod,
Or blessings of thy throne!

3 How cold and feeble is my love
How negligent my fear!
How low my hope of joys above!
How few affections there!

4 Great God, thy sovereign aid impart,
To give thy word success!
Write thy salvation on my heart,
And make me learn thy grace.

5 Show my forgetful feet the way
That leads to joys on high,
Where knowledge grows without decay,
And love shall never die.

—*Isaac Watts.*

TUNE: MANOAH. C. M.

282 *A prayer for living faith.*

1 Father, I stretch my hands to thee,
No other help I know;
If thou withdraw thyself from me,
Ah! whither shall I go?

2 What did thy only Son endure
Before I drew my breath;
What pain, what labour, to secure
My soul from endless death!

3 O Jesus, could I this believe,
I now should feel thy power;
Now all my wants thou wouldst relieve
In this the accepted hour.

4 Author of faith, to thee I lift
My weary, longing eyes;
O let me now receive that gift!
My soul without it dies.

5 Surely thou canst not let me die;
O speak, and I shall live!
For here I will unwearied lie,
Till thou thy Spirit give.

6 How would my fainting soul rejoice,
Could I but see thy face!
Now let me hear thy quickening voice,
And taste thy pardoning grace.

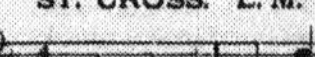

ST. CROSS. L. M. J. B. Dykes, Mus. Doc.

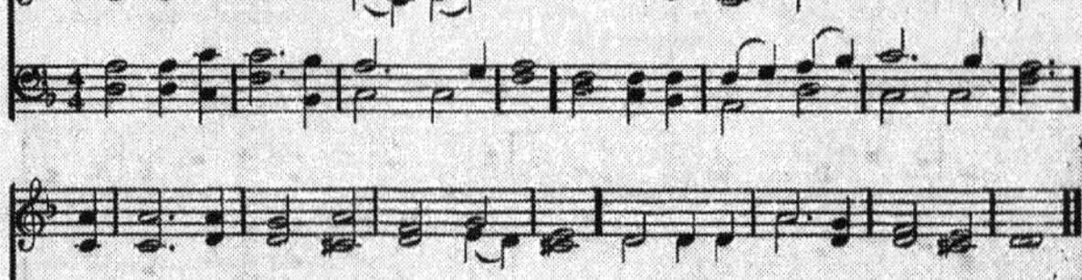

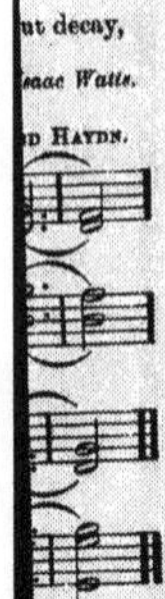

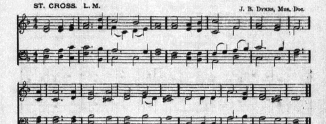

283 *A suffering and faithful Saviour.*

1 My sufferings all to thee are known,
Tempted in every point like me;
Regard my grief, regard thy own;
Jesus, remember Calvary!

2 O call to mind thy earnest prayers,
Thy agony, and sweat of blood,
Thy strong and bitter cries and tears,
Thy mortal groan, "My God! my God!"

3 For whom didst thou the cross endure?
Who nailed thy body to the tree?
Did not thy death my life procure?
O let thy mercy answer me!

4 Have I not heard, have I not known,
That thou, the everlasting Lord,
Whom heaven and earth their Maker own,
Art always faithful to thy word?

5 Thou wilt not break a bruisèd reed,
Or quench the smallest spark of grace,
Till through the soul thy power is spread,
Thy all-victorious righteousness.

6 The day of small and feeble things
I know thou never wilt despise;
I know, with healing in his wings,
The Sun of Righteousness shall rise.

—Charles Wesley.

GRACE CHURCH. L. M. IGNACE PLEYEL.

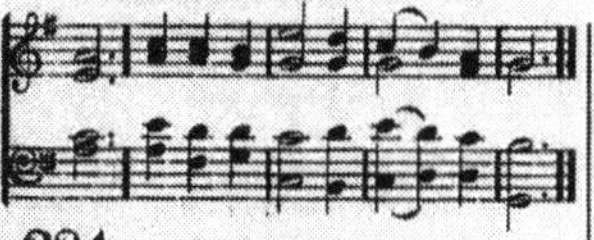

284 *Light and healing implored.*

1 WHEN, gracious Lord, when shall it be,
That I shall find my all in thee!
The fulness of thy promise prove,
The seal of thine eternal love!

2 Thee, only thee, I fain would find,
And cast the world and flesh behind;
Thou, only thou, to me be given,
Of all thou hast in earth or heaven.

3 Whom man forsakes, thou wilt not leave,
Ready the outcasts to receive;
Though all my sinfulness I own,
And all my faults to thee are known.

4 Ah, wherefore did I ever doubt!
Thou wilt in no wise cast me out,
A helpless soul that comes to thee,
With only sin and misery.

5 Lord, I am sick,—my sickness cure;
I want,—do thou enrich the poor;
Under thy mighty hand I stoop,—
O lift the abject sinner up!

6 Lord, I am blind,—be thou my sight;
Lord, I am weak,—be thou my might;
A helper of the helpless be,
And let me find my all in thee.

—*Charles Wesley.*

ROCKINGHAM. L. M. DR. MILLER.

285 *"And hath done despite unto the Spirit of grace."*

1 STAY, thou insulted Spirit, stay,
Though I have done thee such despite,
Nor cast the sinner quite away,
Nor take thine everlasting flight.

2 Though I have steeled my stubborn heart,
And still shook off my guilty fears,
And vexed, and urged thee to depart,
For many long rebellious years;

3 Though I have most unfaithful been
Of all who e'er thy grace received,
Ten thousand times thy goodness seen,
Ten thousand times thy goodness grieved;

4 Yet, O the chief of sinners spare!
In honour of my great High Priest,
Nor in thy righteous anger swear
To exclude me from thy people's rest.

5 Now, Lord, my weary soul release,
Up-raise me with thy gracious hand;
And guide into thy perfect peace,
And bring me to the promised land.

—*Charles Wesley.*

TUNE: ROCKINGHAM. L. M. (See Hymn 285.)

286 *Backsliding confessed and deplored.*

1 Saviour, I now with shame confess
My thirst for creature happiness;
By base desires I wronged thy love,
And forced thy mercy to remove.

2 Yet would I not regard thy stroke;
But when thou didst thy grace revoke,
And when thou didst thy face conceal,
Thy absence I refused to feel.

3 I knew not that the Lord was gone,
In my own froward will went on,
And lived to the desires of men;
But thou hast all my wanderings seen.

4 Yet, O the riches of thy grace!
Thou, who hast seen my evil ways,
Wilt freely my backslidings heal,
And pardon on my conscience seal.

5 Far off, yet at thy feet I lie,
Till thou again thy blood apply;
Till thou repeat my sins forgiven,
As far from God as hell from heaven.

6 But for thy truth and mercy's sake,
My comfort thou wilt give me back,
And lead me on from grace to grace,
In all the paths of righteousness;

7 Till, throughly saved, my new-born soul,
And perfectly by faith made whole,
Doth bright in thy full image rise,
To share thy glory in the skies.

—*Charles Wesley.*

ST. CRISPIN. L. M. Sir G. J. Elvey.

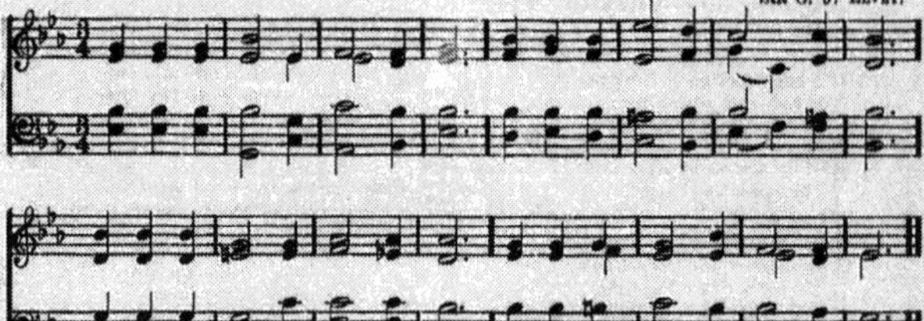

287 *"The dead shall hear the voice of the Son of God."*

1 My God, if I may call thee mine,
From heaven and thee removed so far,
Draw nigh, thy pitying ear incline,
And cast not out my languid prayer.

2 Gently the weak thou lov'st to lead,
Thou lov'st to prop the feeble knee;
O break not then a bruiséd reed,
Nor quench the smoking flax in me!

3 Buried in sin, thy voice I hear,
And burst the barriers of my tomb;
In all the marks of death appear,—
Forth at thy call, though bound, I come.

4 Give me, O give me, fully, Lord,
Thy resurrection's power to know;
Free me indeed, repeat the word,
And loose my bands, and let me go.

5 Fain would I go to thee, my God,
Thy mercies and my wants to tell;
To feel my pardon sealed in blood,
Saviour, thy love I wait to feel.

6 Freed from the power of cancelled sin,
When shall my soul triumphant prove?
Why breaks not out the fire within
In flames of joy, and praise, and love?

—*Charles Wesley.*

MERIBAH. 8.8.6, 8.8.6. DR. MASON.

288 *The witness of pardon and adoption.*

1 THOU great mysterious God unknown,
Whose love hath gently led me on,
Even from my infant days;
Mine inmost soul expose to view,
And tell me if I ever knew
Thy justifying grace.

2 If I have only known thy fear,
And followed, with a heart sincere,
Thy drawings from above,—
Now, now the further grace bestow,
And let my sprinkled conscience know
Thy sweet forgiving love.

3 Short of thy love I would not stop,
A stranger to the Gospel hope,
The sense of sin forgiven;
I would not, Lord, my soul deceive,
Without the inward witness live,
That antepast of heaven.

4 If now the witness were in me,
Would he not testify of thee
In Jesus reconciled?
And should I not with faith draw nigh,
And boldly, Abba, Father, cry,
And know myself thy child?

5 Whate'er obstructs thy pardoning love,—
Or sin, or righteousness,—remove,
Thy glory to display;
Mine heart of unbelief convince,
And now absolve me from my sins,
And take them all away.

6 Father, in me reveal thy Son,
And to my inmost soul make known
How merciful thou art;
The secret of thy love reveal,
And by thine hallowing Spirit dwell
For ever in my heart.

—*Charles Wesley.*

289 *Prayer for saving faith.*

1 AUTHOR of faith, to thee I cry,
To thee who wouldst not have me die,
But know the truth and live;
Open mine eyes to see thy face,
Work in my heart thy saving grace,
The life eternal give.

2 Shut up in unbelief I groan,
And blindly serve a God unknown,
Till thou the veil remove;
The gift unspeakable impart,
And write thy name upon my heart,
And manifest thy love.

3 I know the work is only thine,
The gift of faith is all divine;
But, if on thee we call,
Thou wilt the benefit bestow,
And give us hearts to feel and know
That thou hast died for all.

4 Thou bidd'st us knock and enter in,
Come unto thee, and rest from sin,
The blessing seek and find;
Thou bidd'st us ask thy grace, and have;
Thou canst, thou wouldst, this moment save
Both me and all mankind.

5 Be it according to thy word;
Now let me find my pardoning Lord,
Let what I ask be given;
The bar of unbelief remove,
Open the door of faith and love,
And take me into heaven.

—*Charles Wesley.*

HULL. 8.8.6, 8.8.6. OLD MELODY.

290 Exodus xxxiv. 5, 6, 7.

1 THEE, Jesus, thee, the sinner's Friend,
I follow on to apprehend,
Renew the glorious strife;
Divinely confident and bold,
With faith's strong arm on thee lay hold,
Thee, my eternal life.

2 Give me the grace, the love I claim;
Thy Spirit now demands thy Name,
Thou know'st the Spirit's will;
He helps my soul's infirmity,
And strongly intercedes for me
With groans unspeakable.

3 Prisoner of hope, to thee I turn,
And, calmly confident, I mourn,
And pray, and weep for thee;
Tell me thy love, thy secret tell,
Thy mystic Name in me reveal,
Reveal thyself in me.

4 Descend, pass by me, and proclaim,
O Lord of Hosts, thy glorious name,—
The Lord, the gracious Lord,
Long-suffering, merciful, and kind,
The God who always bears in mind
His everlasting word.

5 Plenteous he is in truth and grace;
He wills that all the fallen race
Should turn, repent, and live;
His pardoning grace for all is free;
Transgression, sin, iniquity,
He freely doth forgive.

6 Mercy he doth for thousands keep;
He goes and seeks the one lost sheep,
And brings his wanderer home;
And every soul that sheep might be;
Come, then, my Lord, and gather me,
My Jesus, quickly come.

—*Charles Wesley.*

291 *"I will take away the stony heart."*

1 O JESUS, let me bless thy Name!
All sin, alas! thou know'st I am,
But thou all pity art;
Turn into flesh my heart of stone;
Such power belongs to thee alone;
Turn into flesh my heart.

2 O let thy Spirit shed abroad
The love, the perfect love of God,
In this poor heart of mine!
O might he now descend, and rest,
And dwell for ever in my breast,
And make it all divine!

3 What shall I do my suit to gain?
O Lamb of God, for sinners slain,
I plead what thou hast done!
Didst thou not die the death for me?
Jesus, remember Calvary,
And break my heart of stone.

—*Charles Wesley.*

292 *A prayer for subduing love.*

1 STILL, Lord, I languish for thy grace:
Reveal the beauties of thy face,
The middle wall remove;
Appear, and banish my complaint;
Come, and supply my only want,
Fill all my soul with love.

2 O conquer this rebellious will;
Willing thou art, and ready still,
Thy help is always nigh;
The hardness from my heart remove,
And give me, Lord, O give me love,
Or at thy feet I die.

3 To thee I lift my mournful eye;
Why am I thus?—O tell me why
I cannot love my God!
The hindrance must be all in me;
It cannot in my Saviour be;
Witness that streaming blood.

4 It cost thy blood my heart to win,
To buy me from the power of sin,
And make me love again;
Come, then, my Lord, thy right assert,
Take to thyself my ransomed heart;
Nor bleed, nor die in vain.

—*Charles Wesley.*

NEW SONG. 8.8.6, 8.8.6. T. TURVEY.

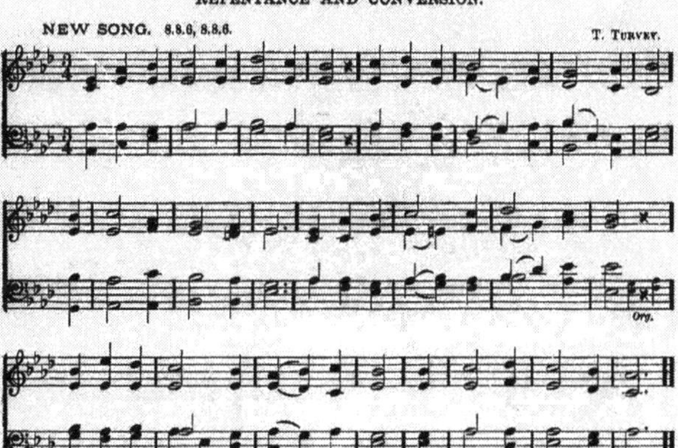
Org.

293 "They shall look upon me whom they have pierced."

1 O THOU who hast our sorrows borne,
Help us to look on thee and mourn,
On thee whom we have slain!
Have pierced a thousand thousand times,
And by reiterated crimes
Renewed thy mortal pain.

2 Vouchsafe us eyes of faith to see
The man transfixed on Calvary;
To know thee, who thou art,
The One Eternal God and true;
And let the sight affect, subdue,
And break my stubborn heart.

3 Lover of souls, to rescue mine,
Reveal the charity divine,
That suffered in my stead;
That made thy soul a sacrifice,
And quenched in death those flaming eyes,
And bowed that sacred head.

4 The veil of unbelief remove,
And by thy manifested love,
And by thy sprinkled blood,
Destroy the love of sin in me,
And get thyself the victory,
And bring me back to God.

5 Now let thy dying love constrain
My soul to love its God again,
Its God to glorify;
And, lo! I come thy cross to share,
Echo thy sacrificial prayer,
And with my Saviour die.

—*Charles Wesley.*

294 "Thou triest me every moment."

1 BY secret influence from above,
Me thou dost every moment prove,
And labour to convert;
Ready to save, I feel thee nigh,
And still I hear thy Spirit cry,
"My son, give me thy heart."

2 Why do I not the call obey,
Cast my besetting sin away,
With every useless load?
Why cannot I this moment give
The heart thou waitest to receive,
And love my loving God?

3 My loving God, the hindrance show,
Which nature dreads, alas! to know,
And lingers to remove;
Stronger than sin, thy grace exert,
And seize, and change, and fill my heart
With all the powers of love.

4 Then shall I answer thy design,
No longer, Lord, my own, but thine;
Till all thy will be done,
Humbly I pass my trial here,
And ripe in holiness appear
With boldness at thy throne.

—*Charles Wesley.*

CONFIDENCE. 6-8s.

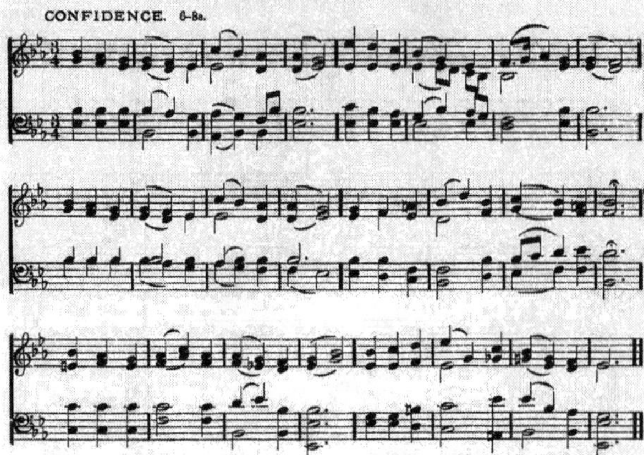

295 *Imploring a deeper sense of sin.*

1 Father of lights, from whom proceeds
Whate'er thy every creature needs;
Whose goodness, providently nigh,
Feeds the young ravens when they cry;
To thee I look; my heart prepare;
Suggest, and hearken to my prayer.

2 Since by thy light myself I see
Naked, and poor, and void of thee,
Thine eyes must all my thoughts survey,
Preventing what my lips would say;
Thou seest my wants, for help they call,
And, ere I speak, thou know'st them all.

3 Thou know'st the baseness of my mind,
Wayward, and impotent, and blind;
Thou know'st how unsubdued my will,
Averse from good, and prone to ill;
Thou know'st how wide my passions rove,
Nor checked by fear, nor charmed by love.

4 Fain would I know, as known by thee,
And feel the indigence I see;
Fain would I all my vileness own,
And deep beneath the burden groan;
Abhor the pride that lurks within,
Detest and loathe myself and sin.

5 Ah! give me, Lord, myself to feel;
My total misery reveal;
Ah! give me, Lord, I still would say,
A heart to mourn, a heart to pray;
My business this, my only care,
My life, my every breath, be prayer.

—*Charles Wesley.*

296 *"Lord, show us the Father."*

1 O thou, whom fain my soul would love,
Whom I would gladly die to know,
This veil of unbelief remove,
And show me,—all thy goodness show;
Jesus, thyself in me reveal,
Tell me thy name, thy nature tell.

2 Hast thou been with me, Lord, so long,
Yet thee, my Lord, have I not known?
I claim thee with a faltering tongue;
I pray thee, in a feeble groan,
Tell me, O tell me, who thou art,
And speak thy name into my heart!

3 If now thou talkest by the way
With such an abject worm as me,
Thy mystery of grace display;
Open mine eyes that I may see,
That I may understand thy word,
And now cry out, "It is the Lord!"

—*Charles Wesley.*

BRIGHTON. 6-8s.

297 *"I will arise and go to my Father."*

1 Yes, from this instant now, I will
To my offended Father cry;
My base ingratitude I feel;
Vilest of all thy children, I,
Not worthy to be called thy son;
Yet will I thee my Father own.

2 Guide of my life hast thou not been,
And rescued me from passion's power?
Ten thousand times preserved from sin,
Nor let the greedy grave devour?
And wilt thou now thy wrath retain,
Nor ever love thy child again?

3 Ah! canst thou find it in thy heart
To give me up, so long pursued?
Ah! canst thou finally depart,
And leave thy creature in his blood;
Leave me, out of thy presence cast,
To perish in my sins at last?

4 If thou hast willed me to return,
If weeping at thy feet I fall,
The prodigal thou wilt not spurn,
But pity, and forgive me all,
In answer to my Friend above,
In honour of his bleeding love.

—*Charles Wesley.*

298 *Sin hiding God's face.*

1 Thou God unsearchable, unknown,
Who still conceal'st thyself from me,
Hear an apostate spirit groan,
Broke off, and vanished far from thee;
But conscious of my fall I mourn,
And fain I would to thee return.

2 Send forth one ray of heavenly light,
Of gospel hope, of humble fear,
To guide me through the gulf of night,
My poor desponding soul to cheer,
Till thou my unbelief remove,
And show me all thy glorious love.

3 A hidden God indeed thou art!
Thy absence I this moment feel;
Yet must I own it from my heart,
Concealed, thou art a Saviour still;
And though thy face I cannot see,
I know thine eye is fixed on me.

4 My Saviour thou, not yet revealed,
Yet will I thee my Saviour call;
Adore thy hand, from sin withheld;
Thy hand shall save me from my fall;
Now, Lord, throughout my darkness shine,
And show thyself for ever mine.

—*Charles Wesley.*

299 *Salvation a miracle of love.*

1 Lay to thy hand, O God of grace!
O God, the work is worthy thee!
See at thy feet of all the race
The chief, the vilest sinner see;
And let me all thy mercy prove,
Thine utmost miracle of love.

2 Thee I shall then for ever praise,
In spirit and in truth adore;
While all I am declares thy grace,
And, born of God, I sin no more;
Thy pure and heavenly nature share,
And fruit unto perfection bear.

—*Charles Wesley.*

SPOHR. C. M. Dr. L. Spohr.

300 Psalm xlii.

1 As pants the hart for cooling streams,
When heated in the chase,
So longs my soul, O God, for thee,
And thy refreshing grace.

2 For thee, my God, the living God,
My thirsty soul doth pine;
O when shall I behold thy face,
Thou Majesty divine!

3 God of my strength, how long shall I,
Like one forgotten, mourn?
Forlorn, forsaken, and exposed
To the oppressor's scorn.

4 I sigh to think of happier days,
When thou, O Lord, wast nigh;
When every heart was tuned to praise,
And none more blest than I.

5 Why restless, why cast down, my soul?
Hope still, and thou shalt sing
The praise of him who is thy God,
Thy Saviour, and thy King.

—Tate and Brady.

ST. PETER. C. M. A. R. Reinagle.

301 Hosea vi. 1, 2, 3.

1 Come, let us to the Lord our God
With contrite hearts return;
Our God is gracious, nor will leave
The desolate to mourn.

2 His voice commands the tempest forth,
And stills the stormy wave;
His arm, though it be strong to smite,
Is also strong to save.

3 Our hearts, if God we seek to know,
Shall know him and rejoice;
His coming like the morn shall be,
Like morning songs his voice.

4 As dew upon the tender herb,
Diffusing fragrance round;
As showers that usher in the spring,
And cheer the thirsty ground;

5 So shall his presence bless our souls,
And shed a joyful light;
That hallowed morn shall chase away
The sorrows of the night.

—J. Morrison.

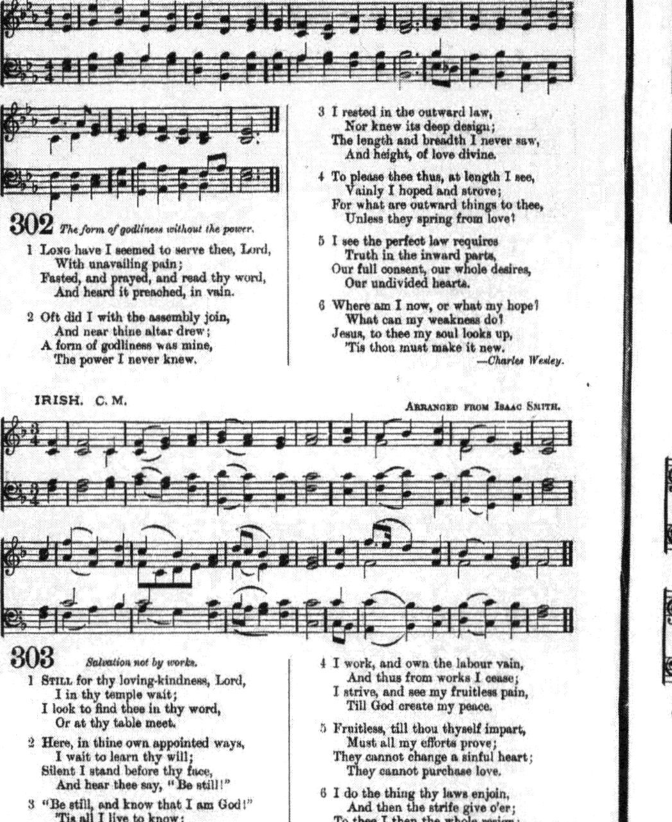

ST. PETER. C. M. — A. R. REINAGLE.

302 *The form of godliness without the power.*

1 LONG have I seemed to serve thee, Lord,
With unavailing pain;
Fasted, and prayed, and read thy word,
And heard it preached, in vain.

2 Oft did I with the assembly join,
And near thine altar drew;
A form of godliness was mine,
The power I never knew.

3 I rested in the outward law,
Nor knew its deep design;
The length and breadth I never saw,
And height, of love divine.

4 To please thee thus, at length I see,
Vainly I hoped and strove;
For what are outward things to thee,
Unless they spring from love?

5 I see the perfect law requires
Truth in the inward parts,
Our full consent, our whole desires,
Our undivided hearts.

6 Where am I now, or what my hope?
What can my weakness do?
Jesus, to thee my soul looks up,
'Tis thou must make it new.

—*Charles Wesley.*

IRISH. C. M. — ARRANGED FROM ISAAC SMITH.

303 *Salvation not by works.*

1 STILL for thy loving-kindness, Lord,
I in thy temple wait;
I look to find thee in thy word,
Or at thy table meet.

2 Here, in thine own appointed ways,
I wait to learn thy will;
Silent I stand before thy face,
And hear thee say, "Be still!"

3 "Be still, and know that I am God!"
'Tis all I live to know;
To feel the virtue of thy blood,
And spread its praise below.

4 I work, and own the labour vain,
And thus from works I cease;
I strive, and see my fruitless pain,
Till God create my peace.

5 Fruitless, till thou thyself impart,
Must all my efforts prove;
They cannot change a sinful heart;
They cannot purchase love.

6 I do the thing thy laws enjoin,
And then the strife give o'er;
To thee I then the whole resign;
I trust in means no more.

—*Charles Wesley.*

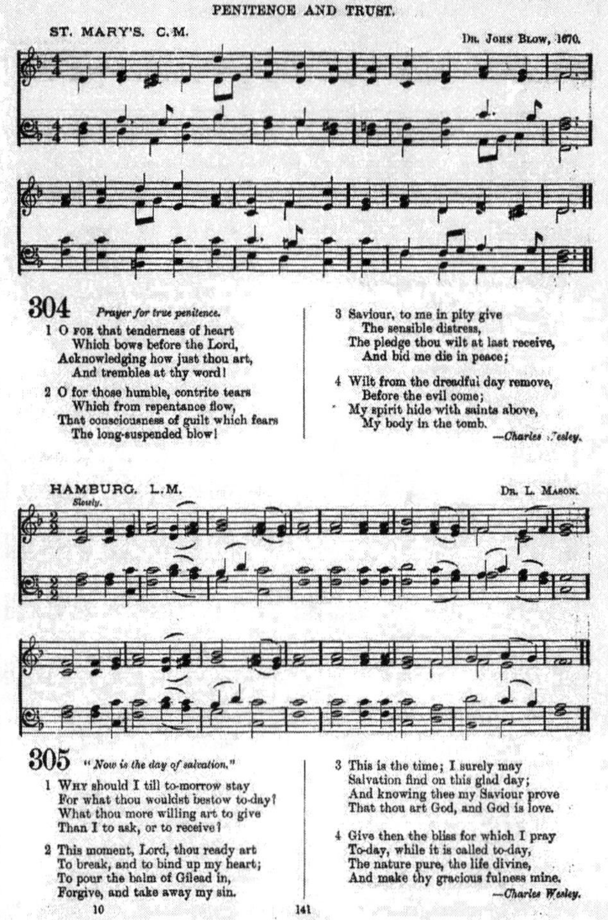
ST. MARY'S. C.M.
Dr. John Blow, 1670.
Slowly.
HAMBURG. L.M.
Dr. L. Mason.

304 *Prayer for true penitence.*

1 O for that tenderness of heart
Which bows before the Lord,
Acknowledging how just thou art,
And trembles at thy word!

2 O for those humble, contrite tears
Which from repentance flow,
That consciousness of guilt which fears
The long-suspended blow!

3 Saviour, to me in pity give
The sensible distress,
The pledge thou wilt at last receive,
And bid me die in peace;

4 Wilt from the dreadful day remove,
Before the evil come;
My spirit hide with saints above,
My body in the tomb.

—*Charles Wesley.*

305 *"Now is the day of salvation."*

1 Why should I till to-morrow stay
For what thou wouldst bestow to-day?
What thou more willing art to give
Than I to ask, or to receive?

2 This moment, Lord, thou ready art
To break, and to bind up my heart;
To pour the balm of Gilead in,
Forgive, and take away my sin.

3 This is the time; I surely may
Salvation find on this glad day;
And knowing thee my Saviour prove
That thou art God, and God is love.

4 Give then the bliss for which I pray
To-day, while it is called to-day,
The nature pure, the life divine,
And make thy gracious fulness mine.

—*Charles Wesley.*

FILLMORE. L. M. D. JEREMIAH INGALLS.

Fine.
D. C.

306 *Light, love, and life in Christ.*

1 Jesus, my Advocate above,
My Friend before the throne of love,
If now for me prevails thy prayer,
If now I find thee pleading there,
If thou the secret wish convey,
And sweetly prompt my heart to pray;
Hear, and my weak petitions join,
Almighty Advocate, to thine.

2 Fain would I know my utmost ill,
And groan my nature's weight to feel,
To feel the clouds that round me roll,
The night that hangs upon my soul,
The darkness of my carnal mind,
My will perverse, my passions blind,
Scattered o'er all the earth abroad,
Immeasurably far from God.

3 O Sovereign Love, to thee I cry,
Give me thyself, or else I die!
Save me from death, from hell set free;
Death, hell, are but the want of thee,
Quickened by thy imparted flame,
Saved, when possessed of thee, I am;
My life, my only heaven thou art,
O might I feel thee in my heart.

—*Charles Wesley.*

HOME. L. M. FROM MOZART.

307 *"The eyes of your understanding being enlightened."*

1 Jesus, whose glory's streaming rays,
Though duteous to thy high command,
Not seraphs view with open face,
But veiled before thy presence stand!

2 How shall weak eyes of flesh, weighed down
With sin, and dim with error's night,
Dare to behold thy awful throne,
Or view thy unapproachèd light?

3 Restore my sight; let thy free grace
An entrance to the holiest give:
Open mine eyes of faith; thy face
So shall I see, yet seeing live.

4 Thy golden sceptre from above
Reach forth; lo! my whole heart I bow,
Say to my soul, "Thou art my love;
My chosen 'midst ten thousand, thou."

5 O Jesus, full of grace, the sighs
Of a sick heart with pity view!
Hark! how my silence speaks, and cries,
"Mercy, thou God of mercy, show!"

6 I know thou canst not but be good;
How shouldst thou, Lord, thy grace restrain?
Thou, Lord, whose blood so freely flowed,
To save me from all guilt and pain.

—*Charles Wesley.*

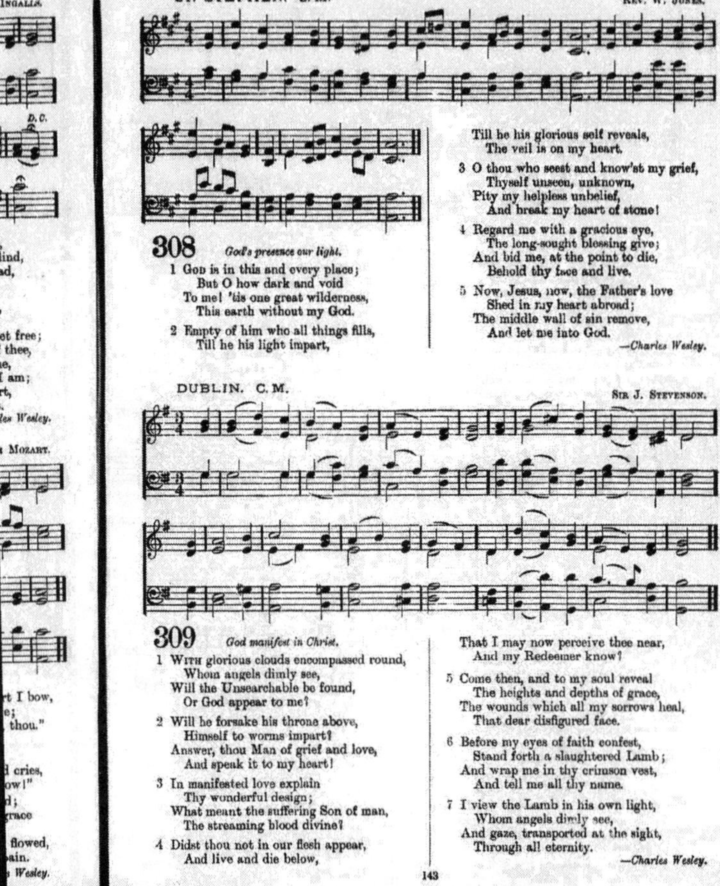

ST. STEPHEN. C. M. — Rev. W. Jones.

308

God's presence our light.

1 God is in this and every place;
But O how dark and void
To me! 'tis one great wilderness,
This earth without my God.

2 Empty of him who all things fills,
Till he his light impart,
Till he his glorious self reveals,
The veil is on my heart.

3 O thou who seest and know'st my grief,
Thyself unseen, unknown,
Pity my helpless unbelief,
And break my heart of stone!

4 Regard me with a gracious eye,
The long-sought blessing give;
And bid me, at the point to die,
Behold thy face and live.

5 Now, Jesus, now, the Father's love
Shed in my heart abroad;
The middle wall of sin remove,
And let me into God.

—*Charles Wesley.*

DUBLIN. C. M. — Sir J. Stevenson.

309

God manifest in Christ.

1 With glorious clouds encompassed round,
Whom angels dimly see,
Will the Unsearchable be found,
Or God appear to me?

2 Will he forsake his throne above,
Himself to worms impart?
Answer, thou Man of grief and love,
And speak it to my heart!

3 In manifested love explain
Thy wonderful design;
What meant the suffering Son of man,
The streaming blood divine?

4 Didst thou not in our flesh appear,
And live and die below,
That I may now perceive thee near,
And my Redeemer know?

5 Come then, and to my soul reveal
The heights and depths of grace,
The wounds which all my sorrows heal,
That dear disfigured face.

6 Before my eyes of faith confest,
Stand forth a slaughtered Lamb;
And wrap me in thy crimson vest,
And tell me all thy name.

7 I view the Lamb in his own light,
Whom angels dimly see,
And gaze, transported at the sight,
Through all eternity.

—*Charles Wesley.*

DUBLIN. C.M. SIR J. STEVENSON.

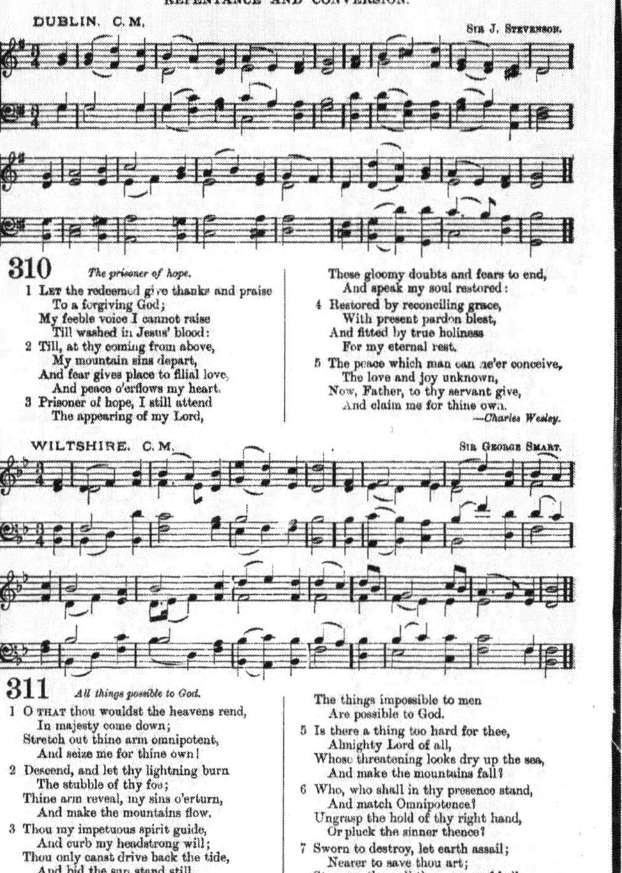

310 *The prisoner of hope.*

1 LET the redeemed give thanks and praise
  To a forgiving God;
My feeble voice I cannot raise
  Till washed in Jesus' blood:

2 Till, at thy coming from above,
  My mountain sins depart,
And fear gives place to filial love,
  And peace o'erflows my heart.

3 Prisoner of hope, I still attend
  The appearing of my Lord,
These gloomy doubts and fears to end,
  And speak my soul restored:

4 Restored by reconciling grace,
  With present pardon blest,
And fitted by true holiness
  For my eternal rest.

5 The peace which man can ne'er conceive,
  The love and joy unknown,
Now, Father, to thy servant give,
  And claim me for thine own.

—*Charles Wesley.*

WILTSHIRE. C.M. SIR GEORGE SMART.

311 *All things possible to God.*

1 O THAT thou wouldst the heavens rend,
  In majesty come down;
Stretch out thine arm omnipotent,
  And seize me for thine own!

2 Descend, and let thy lightning burn
  The stubble of thy foe;
Thine arm reveal, my sins o'erturn,
  And make the mountains flow.

3 Thou my impetuous spirit guide,
  And curb my headstrong will;
Thou only canst drive back the tide,
  And bid the sun stand still.

4 What though I cannot break my chain,
  Or e'er throw off my load,
The things impossible to men
  Are possible to God.

5 Is there a thing too hard for thee,
  Almighty Lord of all,
Whose threatening looks dry up the sea,
  And make the mountains fall?

6 Who, who shall in thy presence stand,
  And match Omnipotence?
Ungrasp the hold of thy right hand,
  Or pluck the sinner thence?

7 Sworn to destroy, let earth assail;
  Nearer to save thou art;
Stronger than all the powers of hell,
  And greater than my heart.

—*Charles Wesley.*

TUNE: WILTSHIRE. C.M. (SEE HYMN 311.)

312 *Prayer for revealing grace.*

1 THOU hidden God, for whom I groan,—
  Till thou thyself declare,
God inaccessible, unknown,—
  Regard a sinner's prayer!

2 An unregenerate child of man,
  To thee for faith I call;
Pity thy fallen creature's pain,
  And raise me from my fall.

3 Thou wilt in me reveal thy name,
  Thou wilt thy light afford;
Bound and oppressed, yet thine I am,
  The prisoner of the Lord.

4 Now, Lord, if thou art power, descend,
  The mountain sin remove;
My unbelief and troubles end,
  If thou art Truth and Love.

5 Show me the blood that bought my peace,
  The covenant blood apply,
And all my griefs at once shall cease,
  And all my sins shall die.

—*Charles Wesley.*

ST. DAVID'S. 8-8s. HANDEL.

D.C.

313 *Restoration through the Spirit.*

1 COME, holy, celestial Dove,
  To visit a sorrowful breast,
My burden of guilt to remove,
  And bring me assurance and rest.
Thou only hast power to relieve
  A sinner o'erwhelmed with his load,
The sense of acceptance to give,
  And sprinkle his heart with the blood.

2 Thy call if I ever have known,
  And sighed from myself to get free,
And groaned the unspeakable groan,
  And longed to be happy in thee;
Fulfil the imperfect desire,
  Thy peace to my conscience reveal,
The sense of thy favour inspire,
  And give me my pardon to feel.

3 Most merciful Spirit of grace,
  Relieve me again, and restore;
My spirit in holiness raise,
  To fall and to suffer no more.
Come, heavenly Comforter, come,
  True Witness of mercy divine,
And make me thy permanent home,
  And seal me eternally thine.

—*Charles Wesley.*

314 *Prayer for restoration from backsliding.*

1 How shall a lost sinner in pain
  Recover his forfeited peace?
When brought into bondage again,
  What hope of a second release?
Will mercy itself be so kind
  To spare such a rebel as me?
And O can I possibly find
  Such plenteous redemption in thee?

2 O Jesus, in pity draw near,
  Come quickly to help a lost soul;
To comfort a mourner appear,
  And make a poor Lazarus whole!
The balm of thy mercy apply;
  Thou seest the sore anguish I feel;
Save, Lord, or I perish, I die!
  O save, or I sink into hell!

3 I sink, if thou longer delay
  Thy pardoning mercy to show;
Come quickly, and kindly display
  The power of thy passion below.
The help of thy Spirit restore,
  And show me the life-giving blood,
And pardon a sinner once more,
  And bring me again unto God.

—*Charles Wesley.*

BROMLEY. 7.6, 7.6, 7.6, 7.6. LONDON TUNE BOOK.

315 *Coming to the Lamb of God.*

1 LAMB of God, for sinners slain,
To thee I feebly pray;
Heal me of my grief and pain,
O take my sins away!
From this bondage, Lord, release;
No longer let me be opprest:
Jesus, Master, seal my peace,
And take me to thy breast!

2 Wilt thou cast a sinner out,
Who humbly comes to thee?
No, my God, I cannot doubt,
Thy mercy is for me;
Let me then obtain the grace,
And be of paradise possest:
Jesus, Master, seal my peace,
And take me to thy breast!

3 Worldly good I do not want,
Be that to others given;
Only for thy love I pant,
My all in earth and heaven;
This the crown I fain would seize,
The good wherewith I would be blest:
Jesus, Master, seal my peace,
And take me to thy breast!

4 This delight I fain would prove,
And then resign my breath:
Join the happy few whose love
Was mightier than death.
Let it not my Lord displease,
That I would die to be thy guest:
Jesus, Master, seal my peace,
And take me to thy breast!

—*Charles Wesley.*

316 *"Go in peace, and sin no more."*

1 JESUS, Friend of sinners, hear,
Yet once again I pray;
From my debt of sin set clear,
For I have nought to pay;
Speak, O speak, the kind release,
A poor backsliding soul restore;
Love me freely, seal my peace,
And bid me sin no more.

2 For my selfishness and pride,
Thou hast withdrawn thy grace;
Left me long to wander wide,
An outcast from thy face;
But I now my sins confess,
And mercy, mercy, I implore;
Love me freely, seal my peace,
And bid me sin no more.

3 Though my sins as mountains rise,
And swell and reach to heaven,
Mercy is above the skies,
I may be still forgiven;
Infinite my sins' increase,
But greater is thy mercy's store;
Love me freely, seal my peace,
And bid me sin no more.

4 Sin's deceitfulness hath spread
A hardness o'er my heart;
But if thou thy Spirit shed,
The hardness shall depart;
Shed thy love, thy tenderness,
And let me feel thy softening power;
Love me freely, seal my peace,
And bid me sin no more.

5 For this only thing I pray,
And this will I require,
Take the power of sin away,
Fill me with pure desire;
Perfect me in holiness,
Thine image to my soul restore;
Love me freely, seal my peace,
And bid me sin no more.

—*Charles Wesley.*

SHERBOURNE. 7.6, 7.6, 7.8, 7.6. BEETHOVEN.

317 *Christ's death the sinner's plea.*

1 Let the world their virtue boast,
   Their works of righteousness,
I, a wretch undone and lost,
   Am freely saved by grace;
Other title I disclaim;
This, only this, is all my plea:
   I the chief of sinners am,
   But Jesus died for me.

2 I, like Gideon's fleece, am found
   Unwatered still, and dry,
While the dew on all around
   Falls plenteous from the sky;
Yet my Lord I cannot blame,
The Saviour's grace for all is free:
   I the chief of sinners am,
   But Jesus died for me.

3 Surely he will lift me up,
   For I of him have need;
I cannot give up my hope,
   Though I am cold and dead;
To bring fire on earth he came;
O that it now might kindled be!
   I the chief of sinners am,
   But Jesus died for me.

4 Jesus, thou for me hast died,
   And thou in me wilt live;
I shall feel thy death applied,
   I shall thy life receive;
Yet, when melted in the flame
Of love, this shall be all my plea;
   I the chief of sinners am,
   But Jesus died for me.

—*Charles Wesley.*

318 *The joy of forgiveness.*

1 Lord, and is thine anger gone?
   And art thou pacified?
After all that I have done,
   Dost thou no longer chide?
Infinite thy mercies are;
Beneath the weight I cannot move;
   O 'tis more than I can bear,
   The sense of pardoning love!

2 Let it still my heart constrain,
   And all my passions sway;
Keep me, lest I turn again
   Out of the narrow way;
Force my violence to be still,
And captivate my every thought;
   Charm, and melt, and change my will,
   And bring me down to nought.

3 See my utter helplessness,
   And leave me not alone;
O preserve in perfect peace,
   And seal me for thine own!
More and more thyself reveal,
Thy presence let me always find;
   Comfort, and confirm, and heal
   My feeble, sin-sick mind.

4 As the apple of an eye
   Thy weakest servant keep;
Help me at thy feet to lie,
   And there for ever weep;
Tears of joy mine eyes o'erflow,
That I have any hope of heaven;
   Much of love I ought to know,
   For I have much forgiven.

—*Charles Wesley.*

RICHMOND. 7.6, 7.6, 7.8, 7.6.

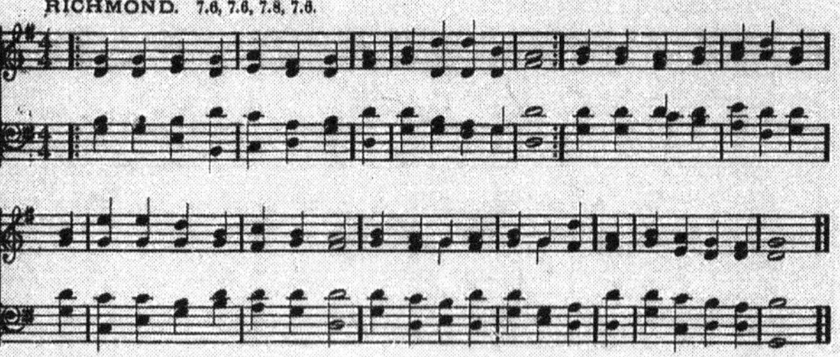

319 *The Woman of Canaan.*

1 Lord, regard my earnest cry,
A potsherd of the earth;
A poor guilty worm am I,
A Canaanite by birth;
Save me from this tyranny,
From all the power of Satan save;
Mercy, mercy upon me,
Thou Son of David, have!

2 Nothing am I in thy sight,
Nothing have I to plead;
Unto dogs it is not right
To cast the children's bread;
Yet the dogs the crumbs may eat,
That from the master's table fall;
Let the fragments be my meat;
Thy grace is free for all.

3 Give me, Lord, the victory,
My heart's desire fulfil;
Let it now be done to me
According to my will!
Give me living bread to eat,
And say, in answer to my call,
"Canaanite, thy faith is great;
My grace is free for all!"

4 If thy grace for all is free,
Thy call now let me hear;
Show this token upon me,
And bring salvation near;
Now the gracious word repeat,
The word of healing to my soul;
"Canaanite, thy faith is great;
Thy faith hath made thee whole!"

—*Charles Wesley.*

320 *"The Lord turned and looked upon Peter."*

1 Jesus, let thy pitying eye
Call back a wandering sheep;
False to thee, like Peter, I
Would fain, like Peter, weep;
Let me be by grace restored,
On me be all long-suffering shown;
Turn, and look upon me, Lord,
And break my heart of stone.

2 Saviour, Prince, enthroned above,
Repentance to impart,
Give me, through thy dying love,
The humble, contrite heart;
Speak the reconciling word,
And let thy mercy melt me down;
Turn, and look upon me, Lord,
And break my heart of stone.

3 For thine own compassion's sake
The gracious wonder show;
Cast my sins behind thy back,
And wash me white as snow;
Speak my paradise restored,
Redeem me by thy grace alone;
Turn, and look upon me, Lord,
And break my heart of stone.

4 Look, as when thy languid eye
Was closed, that we might live;
"Father," at the point to die
My Saviour gasped, "forgive!"
Surely, with that dying word,
He turns, and looks, and cries, "'Tis done!"
O my bleeding, loving Lord,
Thou break'st my heart of stone!

—*Charles Wesley.*

GILEAD. 7.6.7.6, 7.8.7.6.

Fine.
D.S.

321 *Healing and purity in Christ.*

1 WRETCHED, helpless, and distrest,
Ah! whither shall I fly?
Ever seeking after rest,
I cannot find it nigh;
Naked, sick, and poor, and blind,
Fast bound in sin and misery,
Friend of sinners, let me find
My help, my all, in thee!

2 I am sinful and unclean,
Thy purity I want;
My whole head is sick with sin,
And my whole heart is faint;
Full of putrefying sores,
Of bruises, and of wounds, my soul
Looks to Jesus, help implores,
And gasps to be made whole.

3 In the wilderness I stray,
My foolish heart is blind;
Nothing do I know; the way
Of peace I cannot find;
Jesus, Lord, restore my sight,
And take, O take, the veil away!
Turn my darkness into light,
My midnight into day.

4 Jesus, full of truth and grace,
In thee is all I want;
Be the wanderer's resting-place,
A cordial to the faint;
Make me rich, for I am poor;
In thee may I my Eden find;
To the dying health restore,
And eye-sight to the blind.

5 Clothe me with thy holiness,
Thy meek humility;
Put on me my glorious dress,
Endue my soul with thee;
Let thine image be restored,
Thy name and nature let me prove,
With thy fulness, fill me, Lord,
And perfect me in love.

—*Charles Wesley.*

EATON. 6-8s. ZERUBBABEL WYVILL.

322 *Repentance, faith, and pardon sought.*

1 O 'TIS enough, my God, my God!
Here let me give my wanderings o'er;
No longer trample on thy blood,
And grieve thy gentleness no more;
No more thy lingering anger move,
Or sin against thy light and love.

2 O Lord, if mercy is with thee,
Now let it all on me be shown;
On me, the chief of sinners, me,
Who humbly for thy mercy groan;
Me to thy Father's grace restore,
Nor let me ever grieve thee more!

3 Fountain of unexhausted love,
Of infinite compassions, hear!
My Saviour and my Prince above,
Once more in my behalf appear;
Repentance, faith, and pardon give;
O let me turn again and live!—*C. Wesley.*

EATON. 6-8s. ZERUBBABEL WYVILL.

323

Prayer for salvation by grace.

1 O God, if thou art love indeed,
Let it once more be proved in me,
That I thy mercy's praise may spread,
For every child of Adam free;
O let me now the gift embrace!
O let me now be saved by grace!

2 If all long-suffering thou hast shown
On me, that others may believe,
Now make thy loving-kindness known;
Now the all-conquering Spirit give,
Spirit of victory and power,
That I may never grieve thee more.

3 Grant my importunate request;
It is not my desire, but thine;
Since thou wouldst have the sinner blest,
Now let me in thine image shine;
Nor ever from thy footsteps move,
But more than conquer through thy love.

4 Be it according to thy will;
Set my imprisoned spirit free;
The counsel of thy grace fulfil;
Into thy glorious liberty
My spirit, soul, and flesh restore,
And I shall never grieve thee more.

—*Charles Wesley.*

RAKEM. 6-8s. ISAAC BAKER WOODBURY.

Fine. D. C.

324

The wanderer returning to Christ.

1 Jesus, thou know'st my sinfulness,
My faults are not concealed from thee;
A sinner in my last distress,
To thy dear wounds I fain would flee
And never, never thence depart,
Close sheltered in thy loving heart.

2 How shall I find the living way,
Lost, and confused, and dark, and blind?
Ah! Lord, my soul is gone astray;
Ah! Shepherd, seek my soul, and find,
And in thine arms of mercy take,
And bring the weary wanderer back.

3 Weary and sick of sin I am;
I hate it, Lord, and yet I love;
When wilt thou rid me of my shame?
When wilt thou all my load remove?
Destroy the fiend that lurks within,
And speak the word of power, "Be clean!"

4 Sin only let me not commit,
Sin never can advance thy praise;
And, lo! I lay me at thy feet,
And wait unwearied all my days,
Till my appointed time shall come,
And thou shalt call thine exile home.

—*Charles Wesley.*

TUNE: RAKEM. 6-8s. (SEE HYMN 324.)

325 *Pleading with Christ for salvation.*

1 REGARDLESS now of things below,
Jesus, to thee my heart aspires,
Determined thee alone to know,
Author and end of my desires;
Fill me with righteousness divine;
To end, as to begin, is thine.

2 Ah! show me, Lord, my depth of sin;
Ah! Lord, thy depth of mercy show;
End, Jesus, end this war within:
No rest my Spirit e'er shall know,
Till thou thy quickening influence give;
Breathe, Lord, and these dry bones shall live.

3 There, still before the throne thou art,
The Lamb ere earth's foundation slain;
Take thou, O take this guilty heart!
Thy blood will wash out every stain;
No cross, no sufferings I decline;
Only let all my heart be thine.
—*Charles Wesley.*

CALVARY. 6.6, 7.7, 7.7. T. TURVEY.

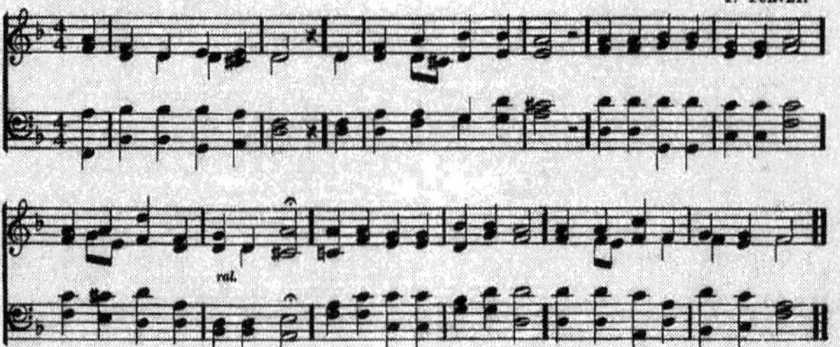

326 *"Out of the depths have I cried unto thee."*

1 OUT of the deep I cry,
Just at the point to die;
Hastening to eternal pain,
Jesus, Lord, I cry to thee;
Help a feeble child of man,
Show forth all thy power in me.

2 On thee I ever call,
Saviour and Friend of all;
Well thou know'st my desperate case;
Thou my curse and sin remove,
Save me by thy richest grace,
Save me by thy pardoning love.

3 I will not let thee go,
Till I thy mercy know;
Let me hear the welcome sound;
Speak, if still thou canst forgive;
Speak, and let the lost be found;
Speak, and let the dying live.

4 Thy love is all my plea,
Thy passion speaks for me;
By thy pangs and bloody sweat,
By thy depth of grief unknown,
Save me, fainting at thy feet,
Save, O save, thy ransomed one!

5 What hast thou done for me!
O think on Calvary!
By thy mortal groans and sighs,
By thy precious death, I pray,
Hear my dying spirit's cries,
Take, O take, my sins away!
—*Charles Wesley.*

SAXBY. L. M. REV. T. RICHARD MATTHEWS, B.A.

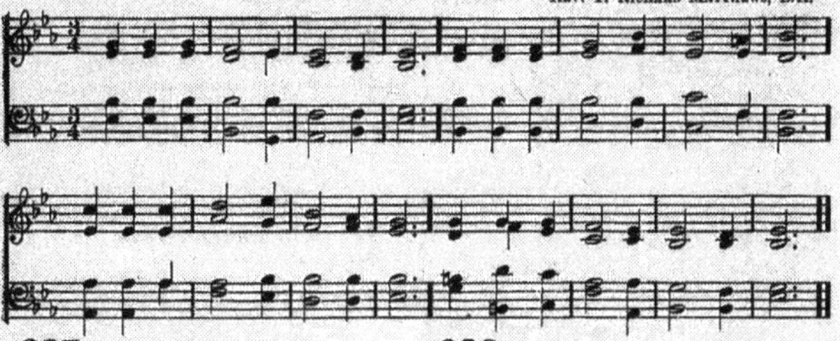

327 *The fear of Divine wrath.*

1 THOU Man of griefs, remember me,
Who never canst thyself forget,—
Thy last mysterious agony,
Thy fainting pangs and bloody sweat!

2 Father, if I may call thee so,
Regard my fearful heart's desire;
Remove this load of guilty woe,
Nor let me in my sins expire.

3 I tremble lest the wrath divine,
Which bruises now my sinful soul,
Should bruise this wretched soul of mine
Long as eternal ages roll.

4 To thee my last distress I bring,
The heightened fear of death I find;
The tyrant, brandishing his sting,
Appears, and hell is close behind.

5 I deprecate that death alone,
That endless banishment from thee;
O save, and give me to thy Son,
Who trembled, wept, and bled for me!

—*Charles Wesley.*

328 *Christ the soul's Physician.*

1 O THOU, whom once they flocked to hear,
Thy words to hear, thy power to feel;
Suffer the sinners to draw near,
And graciously receive us still.

2 They that be whole, thyself hast said,
No need of a physician have;
But I am sick, and want thine aid,
And want thine utmost power to save.

3 Thy power, and truth, and love divine,
The same from age to age endure;
A word, a gracious word of thine,
The most inveterate plague can cure.

4 Helpless howe'er my spirit lies,
And long hath languished at the pool,
A word of thine shall make me rise,
And speak me in a moment whole.

5 Make this the acceptable hour;
Come, O my soul's Physician, thou,
Display thy sanctifying power,
And show me thy salvation now!

—*Charles Wesley.*

DUKE STREET. L. M. JOHN HATTON.

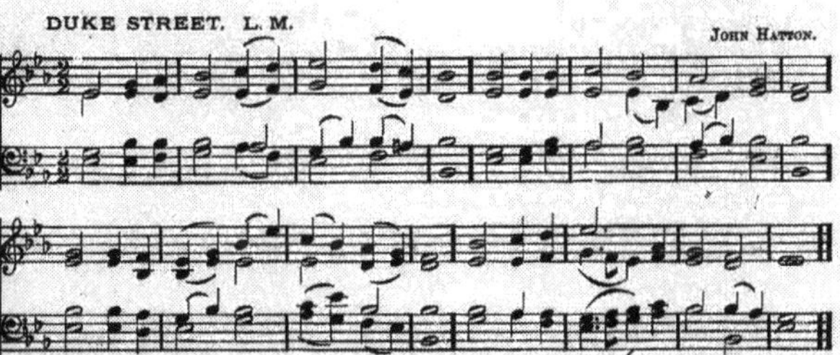

TUNE: DUKE STREET. L. M.

329 *Jesus an unchangeable Saviour.*

1 Jesus, thy far-extended fame
My drooping soul exults to hear;
Thy name, thy all-restoring name,
Is music in a sinner's ear.

2 Sinners of old thou didst receive
With comfortable words and kind,
Their sorrows cheer, their wants relieve,
Heal the diseased, and cure the blind.

3 And art thou not the Saviour still,
In every place and age the same?
Hast thou forgot thy gracious skill,
Or lost the virtue of thy name?

4 Faith in thy changeless name I have;
The good, the kind Physician, thou
Art able now our souls to save,
Art willing to restore them now.

5 All my disease, my every sin,
To thee, O Jesus, I confess;
In pardon, Lord, my cure begin,
And perfect it in holiness.

6 That token of thine utmost good
Now, Saviour, now on me bestow;
And purge my conscience with thy blood,
And wash my nature white as snow.
—Charles Wesley.

330 *Prayer of a sin-sick soul.*

1 O God, to whom, in flesh revealed,
The helpless all for succour came,
The sick to be relieved and healed,
And found salvation in thy name,—

2 Thou seest me helpless and distrest,
Feeble, and faint, and blind, and poor;
Weary, I come to thee for rest,
And sick of sin, implore a cure.

3 A touch, a word, a look from thee,
Can turn my heart, and make it clean;
Purge the foul, inbred leprosy,
And save me from my bosom sin.

4 Lord, if thou wilt, I do believe
Thou canst the saving grace impart;
Thou canst this instant now forgive,
And stamp thine image on my heart.

5 Be it according to thy word,
Accomplish now thy work in me;
And let my soul, to health restored,
Devote its little all to thee.
—Charles Wesley.

GILEAD. 7.6.7.6, 7.8.7.6.

Fine.
D.S.

331 *The Pool of Bethesda.*

1 Jesus, take my sins away,
And make me know thy name;
Thou art now, as yesterday
And evermore, the same.
Thou my true Bethesda be;
I know within thine arms is room;
All the world may unto thee,
Their House of Mercy, come.

2 Mercy then there is for me,
Away my doubts and fears!
Plagued with an infirmity
For many tedious years.
Jesus, cast a pitying eye!
Thou long hast known my desperate case;
Poor and helpless here I lie,
And wait the healing grace.

3 Long hath thy good Spirit strove
With my distempered soul,
But I still refused thy love,
And would not be made whole:
Hardly now at last I yield,
I yield with all my sins to part;
Let my soul be fully healed,
And throughly cleansed my heart.
—Charles Wesley.

GILEAD. 7.6.7.6, 7.8.7.6.

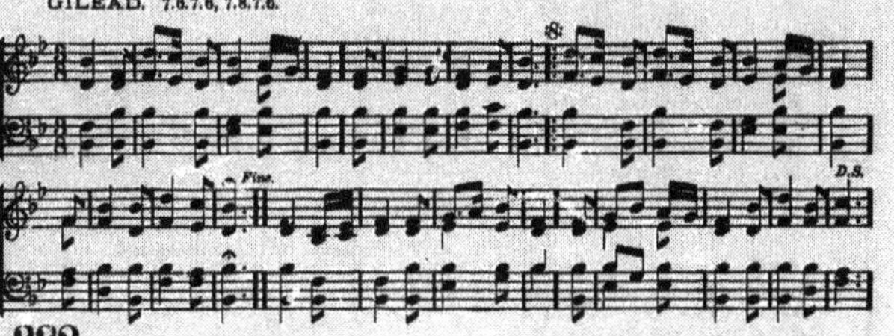
Fine.
D.S.

332 *Pleading the blood of the Lamb.*

1 God of my salvation, hear,
And help me to believe!
Simply do I now draw near,
Thy blessing to receive:
Full of sin, alas! I am,
But to thy wounds for refuge flee:
Friend of sinners, spotless Lamb,
Thy blood was shed for me.

2 Standing now as newly slain,
To thee I lift mine eye;
Balm of all my grief and pain,
Thy grace is always nigh;
Now, as yesterday, the same
Thou art, and wilt forever be:
Friend of sinners, spotless Lamb,
Thy blood was shed for me.

3 Nothing have I, Lord, to pay,
Nor can thy grace procure;
Empty send me not away,
For I, thou know'st, am poor;
Dust and ashes is my name,
My all is sin and misery:
Friend of sinners, spotless Lamb,
Thy blood was shed for me.

4 No good word, or work, or thought,
Bring I to gain thy grace;
Pardon I accept unbought,
Thy proffer I embrace;
Coming, as at first I came,
To take, and not bestow on thee:
Friend of sinners, spotless Lamb,
Thy blood was shed for me.

5 Saviour, from thy wounded side
I never will depart;
Here will I my spirit hide
When I am pure in heart;
Till my place above I claim,
This only shall be all my plea,
Friend of sinners, spotless Lamb,
Thy blood was shed for me.

—*Charles Wesley.*

AMSTERDAM. 7.6, 7.6, 7.8, 7.6. Dr. Nares.

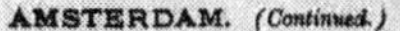

AMSTERDAM. *(Continued.)*

333 *Chastisement leading to repentance.*

1 Father, if thou must reprove,
For all that I have done,
Not in anger, but in love
Chastise thine humbled son;
Use the rod, and not the sword,
Correct with kind severity;
Bring me not to nothing, Lord,
But bring me home to thee.

2 True and faithful as thou art,
To all thy Church and me,
Give a new, believing heart,
That knows and cleaves to thee.
Freely our backslidings heal,
And, by thy precious blood restored,
Grant that every soul may feel,
"Thou art my pardoning Lord!"

3 Might we now with pure desire
Thine only love request;
Now, with willing heart entire,
Return to Christ our rest.
When we our whole hearts resign,
O Jesus, to be filled with thee,
Thou art ours, and we are thine,
Through all eternity.

—Charles Wesley.

334 *"Keep me, O Lord."*

1 Son of God, if thy free grace
Again hath raised me up,
Called me still to seek thy face,
And given me back my hope;
Still thy timely help afford,
And all thy loving-kindness show:
Keep me, keep me, gracious Lord,
And never let me go!

2 By me, O my Saviour, stand,
In sore temptation's hour;
Save me with thine outstretched hand,
And show forth all thy power;
O be mindful of thy word,
Thy all-sufficient grace bestow:
Keep me, keep me, gracious Lord,
And never let me go!

3 Give me, Lord, a holy fear,
And fix it in my heart,
That I may from evil near
With timely care depart;
Sin be more than hell abhorred;
Till thou destroy the tyrant foe,
Keep me, keep me, gracious Lord,
And never let me go!

4 Never let me leave thy breast,
From thee, my Saviour, stray;
Thou art my support and rest,
My true and living way;
My exceeding great reward,
In heaven above, and earth below:
Keep me, keep me, gracious Lord,
And never let me go!

—Charles Wesley.

SHERBOURNE. 7.6, 7.6, 7.8, 7.6. BEETHOVEN.

335 *The Good Samaritan.*

1 O THOU good Samaritan,
In thee is all my hope!
Only thou canst succour man,
And raise the fallen up;
Hearken to my dying cry;
My wounds compassionately see;
Me, a sinner, pass not by,
Who gasps for help from thee.

2 Saviour of my soul, draw nigh,
In mercy haste to me;
At the point of death I lie,
And cannot come to thee;
Now thy kind relief afford,
The wine and oil of grace pour in;
Good Physician, speak the word,
And heal my soul of sin.

3 Pity to my dying cries
Hath drawn thee from above;
Hovering over me, with eyes
Of tenderness and love,
Now, ev'n now, I see thy face,
The balm of Gilead I receive;
Thou hast saved me by thy grace
And bade the sinner live.

4 Perfect, then, the work begun,
And make the sinner whole;
All thy will on me be done,
My body, spirit, soul;
Still preserve me safe from harms,
And kindly for thy patient care;
Take me, Jesus, to thine arms,
And keep me ever there.

—*Charles Wesley.*

WELD. 7.6, 7.6, 7.7, 7.6.

336

TUNE: WELD. 7.6, 7.6, 7.7, 7.6.

Pardon for sins against light and love.

1 I WILL hearken what the Lord
Will say concerning me;
Hast thou not a gracious word
For one who waits on thee!
Speak it to my soul, that I
May in thee have peace and power,
Never from my Saviour fly,
And never grieve thee more.

2 How have I thy Spirit grieved
Since first with me he strove,
Obstinately disbelieved,
And trampled on thy love.
I have sinned against the light;
I have broke from thy embrace;
No, I would not, when I might,
Be freely saved by grace.

3 After all that I have done
To drive thee from my heart,
Still thou wilt not leave thine own,
Thou wilt not yet depart;
Wilt not give the sinner o'er;
Ready art thou now to save;
Bidd'st me to come, as heretofore
That I thy life may have.

4 O thou meek and gentle Lamb,
Fury is not in thee!
Thou continuest still the same,
And still thy grace is free;
Still thine arms are open wide,
Wretched sinners to receive;
Thou hast once for sinners died,
That all may turn and live.

5 Lo! I take thee at thy word;
My foolishness I mourn;
Unto thee, my loving Lord,
However late, I turn;
Yes, I yield, I yield at last,
Listen to thy speaking blood;
Me, with all my sins, I ca[illegible]
On my atoning God!

—Ch[illegible] Wesley.

SECTION VI.

THE CHRISTIAN LIFE.

1.—BELIEVERS REJOICING.

NEARER HOME. S. M. D. — ISAAC WOODBURY.

337

"Come before his presence with singing."

1 COME, ye that love the Lord,
And let your joys be known,
Join in a song with sweet accord,
While ye surround his throne.
Let those refuse to sing
Who never knew our God;
But servants of the heavenly King
May speak their joys abroad.

2 The God that rules on high,
That all the earth surveys,
That rides upon the stormy sky,
And calms the roaring seas;
This awful God is ours,
Our Father and our Love;
He will send down his heavenly powers
To carry us above.

3 There we shall see his face,
And never, never sin;
There, from the rivers of his grace,
Drink endless pleasures in;
Yea, and before we rise
To that immortal state,
The thoughts of such amazing bliss,
Should constant joys create.

4 The men of grace have found
Glory begun below;
Celestial fruit on earthly ground
From faith and hope may grow
Then let our songs abound,
And every tear be dry;
We're marching through Immanuel's ground,
To fairer worlds on high.

—Isaac Watts.

SILVER STREET. S.M. ISAAC SMITH.

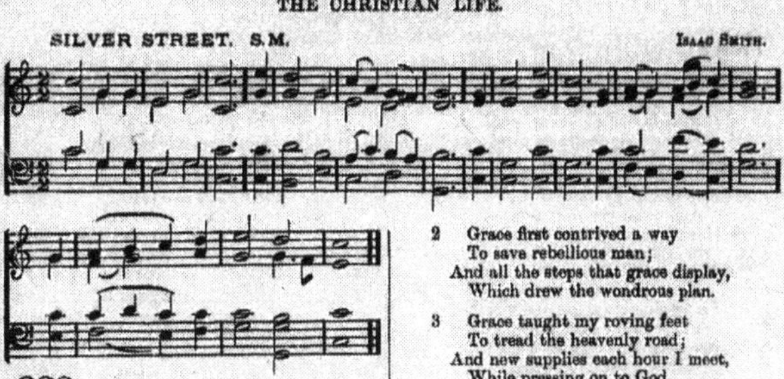

338 *"By grace are ye saved."*

1 GRACE! 'tis a charming sound,
Harmonious to the ear;
Heaven with the echo shall resound,
And all the earth shall hear.

2 Grace first contrived a way
To save rebellious man;
And all the steps that grace display,
Which drew the wondrous plan.

3 Grace taught my roving feet
To tread the heavenly road;
And new supplies each hour I meet,
While pressing on to God.

4 Grace all the work shall crown
Through everlasting days;
It lays in heaven the topmost stone,
And well deserves our praise.

—*Doddridge.*

LEOMINSTER. S.M.D. G. W. MARTIN.

339 *The assurance of forgiveness.*

1 How can a sinner know
His sins on earth forgiven?
How can my gracious Saviour show
My name inscribed in heaven?
What we have felt and seen,
With confidence we tell,
And publish to the sons of men
The signs infallible.

2 We who in Christ believe
That he for us hath died,
We all his unknown peace receive,
And feel his blood applied;
Exults our rising soul,
Disburdened of her load,
And swells unutterably full
Of glory and of God.

3 His love, surpassing far
The love of all beneath,
We find within our hearts, and dare
The pointless darts of death.
Stronger than death and hell,
The mystic power we prove;
And, conquerors of the world, we dwell
In heaven, who dwell in love.

4 We by his Spirit prove
And know the things of God,
The things which freely of his love
He hath on us bestowed;
His glory our design,
We live our God to please;
And rise, with filial fear divine,
To perfect holiness.

—*Charles Wesley.*

ANGELS' SONG. L. M.

ORLANDO GIBBONS.

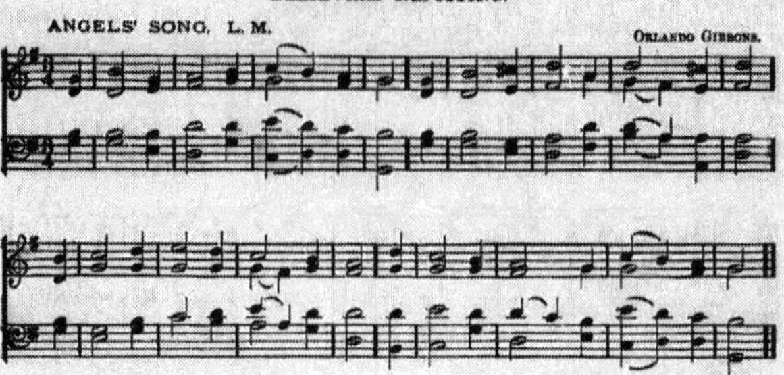

340 *The ways of Wisdom.*

1 HAPPY the man who finds the grace,
The blessing of God's chosen race,
The wisdom coming from above,
The faith that sweetly works by love.

2 Happy beyond description he
Who knows the Saviour died for me,
The gift unspeakable obtains,
And heavenly understanding gains.

3 Wisdom divine! who tells the price
Of wisdom's costly merchandise?
Wisdom to silver we prefer,
And gold is dross compared to her.

4 Her hands are filled with length of days,
True riches, and immortal praise,
Riches of Christ on all bestowed,
And honour that descends from God.

5 To purest joys she all invites,
Chaste, holy, spiritual delights;
Her ways are ways of pleasantness,
And all her flowery paths are peace.

6 Happy the man who wisdom gains;
Thrice happy, who his guest retains;
He owns, and shall forever own,
Wisdom, and Christ, and heaven, are one.

—Charles Wesley.

341 *The Beatitudes.*

1 BLEST are the humble souls that see
Their emptiness and poverty;
Treasures of grace to them are given,
And crowns of joy laid up in heaven.

2 Blest are the men of broken heart,
Who mourn for sin with inward smart;
The blood of Christ divinely flows,
A healing balm for all their woes.

3 Blest are the souls that long for grace,
Hunger and thirst for righteousness;
They shall be well supplied and fed,
With living streams, and living bread.

4 Blest are the pure, whose hearts are clean
From the defiling power of sin;
With endless pleasure they shall see
The God of spotless purity.

5 Blest are the sufferers, who partake
Of pain and shame for Jesus' sake;
Their souls shall triumph in the Lord;
Glory and joy are their reward.

6 There are the men, the holy race,
Who seek the God of Jacob's face;
These shall enjoy that blissful sight,
And dwell in everlasting light.

—Isaac Watts.

STANLEY TERRACE. L. M.

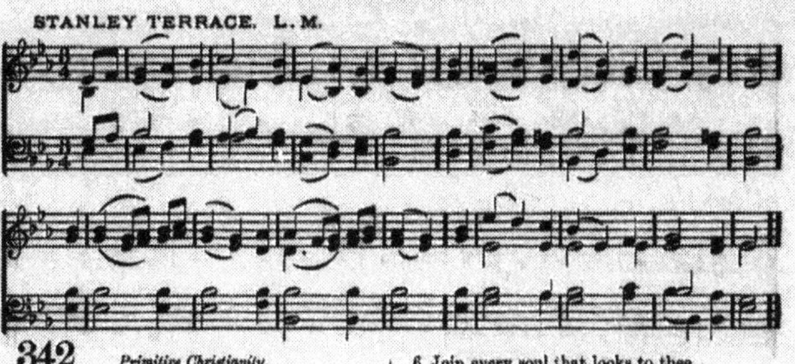

342

Primitive Christianity.

1 Happy the souls that first believed,
To Jesus and each other cleaved,
Joined by the unction from above,
In mystic fellowship of love.

2 Meek, simple followers of the Lamb,
They lived, and spake, and thought the same;
They joyfully conspired to raise
Their ceaseless sacrifice of praise.

3 With grace abundantly endued,
A pure, believing multitude,
They all were of one heart and soul,
And only love inspired the whole.

4 O what an age of golden days!
O what a choice, peculiar race!
Washed in the Lamb's all-cleansing blood,
Anointed kings and priests to God!

5 The gates of hell cannot prevail;
The Church on earth can never fail;
We, too, may power and grace receive,
Thy faithful witnesses to live.

6 Join every soul that looks to thee,
In bonds of perfect charity;
The fulness of thy love impart,
To make and keep us one in heart.

—*Charles Wesley.*

343

"He that glorieth, let him glory in the Lord."

1 Let not the wise his wisdom boast,
The mighty glory in his might,
The rich in flattering riches trust,
Which take their everlasting flight.

2 The rush of numerous years bears down
The most gigantic strength of man;
And where is all his wisdom gone,
When dust he turns to dust again?

3 One only gift can justify
The boasting soul that knows his God;
When Jesus doth his blood apply,
I glory in his sprinkled blood.

4 The Lord my Righteousness I praise;
I triumph in the love divine,
The wisdom, wealth, and strength of grace,
In Christ to endless ages mine.

—*Charles Wesley.*

HOLY CROSS. C. M. — Arthur Henry Brown.

Slowly.

TUNE: HOLY CROSS. C. M.

344 *"The greatest of these is Charity."*

1 Happy the heart where graces reign,
Where love inspires the breast;
Love is the brightest of the train,
And perfects all the rest.

2 Knowledge, alone, is all in vain,
And all in vain our fear;
Our stubborn sins will fight and reign,
If love be absent there.

3 'Tis love that makes our cheerful feet
In swift obedience move;
The devils know, and tremble too,
But Satan cannot love.

4 This is the grace that lives and sings,
When faith and hope shall cease;
'Tis this shall strike our joyful strings
In the sweet realms of bliss.

5 Before we quite forsake our clay,
Or leave this dark abode,
The wings of love bear us away
To see our gracious God.

—Isaac Watts.

345 *Unity and happiness of the Church.*

1 Happy the souls to Jesus joined,
And saved by grace alone;
Walking in all his ways, they find
Their heaven on earth begun.

2 The Church triumphant in thy love,
Their mighty joys we know;
They sing the Lamb in hymns above,
And we in hymns below.

3 Thee in thy glorious realm they praise,
And bow before thy throne;
We in the kingdom of thy grace:
The kingdoms are but one.

4 The holy to the holiest leads,
From thence our spirits rise;
And he that in thy statutes treads
Shall meet thee in the skies.

—Charles Wesley.

PETERBOROUGH. C. M. — Rev. Ralph Harrison.

346 Rev. iii. 20.

1 Come, let us, who in Christ believe,
Our common Saviour praise,
To him with joyful voices give
The glory of his grace.

2 He now stands knocking at the door
Of every sinner's heart;
The worst need keep him out no more,
Or force him to depart.

3 Through grace we hearken to thy voice,
Yield to be saved from sin;
In sure and certain hope rejoice
That thou wilt enter in.

4 Come quickly in, thou heavenly Guest,
Nor ever hence remove;
But sup with us, and let the feast
Be everlasting love.

—Charles Wesley.

ASHLEY. C. M. — Rev. M. Madan.

CHORUS.
Glo - ry, honour, praise and pow - er, Be un - to the Lamb for ev - er; Jesus Christ is
our Redeemer, Hal - le - lu - jah, Hal - le - lu - jah, Hal - le - lu - jah, praise the Lord.

347 *The joyful sound of salvation.*

1 Salvation! O the joyful sound!
What pleasure to our ears!
A sovereign balm for every wound,
A cordial for our fears.—Cho.

2 Salvation! let the echo fly
The spacious earth around;
While all the armies of the sky
Conspire to raise the sound.—Cho.

3 Salvation! O thou bleeding Lamb!
To thee the praise belongs!
Salvation shall inspire our hearts,
And dwell upon our tongues.—Cho.

—Isaac Watts.

HOUGHTON. 10,10,11,11. — Dr. Gauntlett.

348 TUNE: HOUGHTON. 10,10,11,11.

"The joy of thy salvation."

1 O WHAT shall I do my Saviour to praise,
So faithful and true, so plenteous in grace,
So strong to deliver, so good to redeem,
The weakest believer that hangs upon him!

2 How happy the man whose heart is set free,
The people that can be joyful in thee!
Their joy is to walk in the light of thy face,
And still they are talking of Jesus's grace.

3 For thou art their boast, their glory and power;
And I also trust to see the glad hour,
My soul's new creation, a life from the dead,
The day of salvation, that lifts up my head.

4 For Jesus, my Lord, is now my defence;
I trust in his word, none plucks me from thence;
Since I have found favour, he all things will do;
My King and my Saviour shall make me anew.

5 Yes, Lord, I shall see the bliss of thine own,
Thy secret to me shall soon be made known;
For sorrow and sadness I joy shall receive,
And share in the gladness of all that believe.

—*Charles Wesley.*

349

Thanksgiving for Divine goodness.

1 O HEAVENLY King, look down from above!
Assist us to sing thy mercy and love;
So sweetly o'erflowing, so plenteous the store,
Thou still art bestowing, and giving us more.

2 O God of our life, we hallow thy Name!
Our business and strife is thee to proclaim;
Accept our thanksgiving for creating grace;
The living, the living shall show forth thy praise.

3 Our Father and Lord, almighty art thou;
Preserved by thy word, we worship thee now;
The bountiful Donor of all we enjoy,
Our tongues to thine honour, and lives we
employ.

4 But oh! above all, thy kindness we praise,
From sin and from thrall which saves the
lost race;
Thy Son thou hast given the world to redeem,
And bring us to heaven, whose trust is in him.

5 Wherefore of thy love we sing and rejoice,
With angels above we lift up our voice;
Thy love each believer shall gladly adore,
For ever and ever, when time is no more.

—*Charles Wesley.*

350

The teaching of Christ.

1 LET all men rejoice, by Jesus restored!
We lift up our voice, and call him our Lord;
His joy is to bless us, and free us from thrall;
From all that oppress us, he rescues us all.

2 Him Prophet, and King, and Priest we
proclaim;
We triumph and sing of Jesus's name;
Poor sinners he teaches to show forth his praise,
And tell of the riches of Jesus's grace.

3 No matter how dull the scholar whom he
Takes into his school and gives him to see;
A wonderful fashion of teaching he hath,
And wise to salvation he makes us through
faith.

4 The wayfaring men, though fools, shall not
stray,
His method so plain, so easy the way;
The simplest believer his promise may prove,
And drink of the river of Jesus's love.

5 Poor outcasts of men, whose souls were
despised,
And left with disdain, by Jesus are prized;
His gracious creation in us he makes known,
And brings us salvation, and calls us his own.

—*Charles Wesley.*

COMFORT. 11,12,11,12.

351

"Joy unspeakable and full of glory."

1 MY God, I am thine! what a comfort divine,
What a blessing to know that my Jesus is mine!
In the heavenly Lamb, thrice happy I am,
And my heart it doth dance at the sound of
his Name.

2 True pleasures abound in the rapturous sound;
And whoever hath found it, hath paradise found.
My Jesus to know, and feel his blood flow,
'Tis life everlasting, 'tis heaven below.

3 Yet onward I haste to the heavenly feast;
That, that is the fulness, but this is the taste.
And this I shall prove, till with joy I remove
To the heaven of heavens in Jesus's love.

—*Charles Wesley.*

DUNDAS. 6.6.9, 6.6.9.

352 *"In whom believing ye rejoice."*

1 O how happy are they
Who the Saviour obey,
And have laid up their treasure above!
Tongue can never express
The sweet comfort and peace
||: Of a soul in its earliest love. :||

2 That sweet comfort was mine,
When the favour divine
I received through the blood of the Lamb;
When my heart first believed,
What a joy I received,
||: What a heaven in Jesus's name! :||

3 'Twas a heaven below
My Redeemer to know,
And the angels could do nothing more
Than to fall at his feet,
And the story repeat,
||: And the Lover of sinners adore. :||

4 Jesus all the day long
Was my joy and my song;
O that all his salvation might see!
"He hath loved me," I cried,
"He hath suffered and died,
||: To redeem such a rebel as me." :||

5 O the rapturous height
Of that holy delight
Which I felt in the life-giving blood!
Of my Saviour possest,
I was perfectly blest
||: As if filled with the fulness of God. :||

—*Charles Wesley.*

353 *The joy of faith an earnest of heaven.*

1 O how happy are we,
Who in Jesus agree
To expect his return from above!
We sit under our Vine
And delightfully join
||: In the praise of his excellent love. :||

2 O how pleasant and sweet,
In his Name when we meet,
Is his fruit to our spiritual taste!
We are banqueting here
On angelical cheer,
||: And the joys that eternally last. :||

3 All invited by him,
We now drink of the stream
Ever flowing in bliss from the throne;
Who in Jesus believe,
We the Spirit receive
||: That proceeds from the Father and Son. :||

4 The unspeakable grace
He obtained for our race,
And the spirit of faith he imparts;
Even here we conceive
How in heaven they live,
||: By the kingdom of God in our hearts. :||

5 We remember the word
Of our crucified Lord,
When he went to prepare us a place;
"I will come in that day,
And transport you away,
||: And admit to a sight of my face." :||

6 With most earnest desire
After thee we aspire,
And long thy appearing to see;
Till our souls thou receive
In thy presence to live,
||: And be perfectly happy in thee. :||

7 Come, O Lord, from the skies,
And command us to rise,
To the mansions of glory above;
With our Head to ascend
And eternity spend
||: In a rapture of heavenly love. :||

—*Charles Wesley.*

TUNE: DUNDAS. 6.6.9, 6.6.9. (SEE HYMN 352.)

354

Birthday Hymn.

1 COME away to the skies,
My beloved, arise,
And rejoice in the day thou wast born;
On this festival day,
Come exulting away,
‖:And with singing to Zion return.:‖

2 We have laid up our love
And our treasure above,
Though our bodies continue below;
The redeemed of the Lord,
We remember his word,
‖:And with singing to Paradise go.:‖

3 For thy glory we are
All created to share
Both the nature and kingdom divine;
But created again,
That our souls may remain
‖:In time and eternity thine.:‖

4 With thanks we approve
The design of thy love,
Which has joined us in Jesus's name;
So united in heart,
That we never can part,
‖:Till we meet at the feast of the Lamb.:‖

5 Hallelujah we sing,
To our Father and King,
And his rapturous praises repeat;
To the Lamb that was slain,
Hallelujah again,
‖:Sing all heaven, and fall at his feet!:‖

6 In assurance of hope
We to Jesus look up,
Till his banner unfurled in the air
From our graves we shall see,
And cry out, "It is he!"
‖:And fly up to acknowledge him there.:‖

—*Charles Wesley.*

DE FLEURY. 8-8s.

Fine.

D.C.

355

"The Lord is my Shepherd."

1 THOU Shepherd of Israel, and mine,
The joy and desire of my heart,
For closer communion I pine,
I long to reside where thou art;
The pasture I languish to find,
Where all who their Shepherd obey
Are fed, on thy bosom reclined,
And screened from the heat of the day.

2 Ah! show me that happiest place,
The place of thy people's abode,
Where saints in an ecstasy gaze,
And hang on their crucified Lord;
Thy love for a sinner declare,
Thy passion and death on the tree;
My spirit to Calvary bear,
To suffer and triumph with thee.

3 'Tis there, with the lambs of thy flock,
There only, I covet to rest,
To lie at the foot of the rock,
Or rise to be hid in thy breast;
'Tis there I would always abide,
And never a moment depart;
Concealed in the cleft of thy side,
Eternally held in thy heart.

—*Charles Wesley.*

356

God our trust.

1 THIS, this is the God we adore,
Our faithful, unchangeable Friend;
Whose love is as great as his power,
And neither knows measure nor end.
'Tis Jesus the First and the Last,
Whose Spirit shall guide us safe home;
We'll praise him for all that is past,
And trust him for all that's to come.

—*J. Hart.*

PURLEIGH. 8.8.6, 8.8.6. A. H. BROWN.

357 *Labour, prayer, and praise.*

1 How happy, gracious Lord, are we,
Divinely drawn to follow thee,
Whose hours divided are
Betwixt the mount and multitude;
Our day is spent in doing good,
Our night in praise and prayer.

2 With us no melancholy void,
No period lingers unemployed,
Or unimproved, below;
Our weariness of life is gone,
Who live to serve our God alone,
And only thee to know.

3 The winter's night and summer's day
Glide imperceptibly away,
Too short to sing thy praise;
Too few we find the happy hours,
And haste to join those heavenly powers,
In everlasting lays.

4 With all who chant thy Name on high,
And, "Holy, Holy, Holy," cry,
A bright harmonious throng,
We long thy praises to repeat,
And restless sing around thy seat
The new, eternal song.

—*Charles Wesley.*

358 *The spirit of praise.*

1 JESUS, thou soul of all our joys,
For whom we now lift up our voice,
And all our strength exert,
Vouchsafe the grace we humbly claim,
Compose into a thankful frame,
And tune thy people's heart.

2 While in the heavenly work we join,
Thy glory be our whole design,
Thy glory, not our own;
Still let us keep this end in view,
And still the pleasing task pursue,
To please our God alone.

3 Thee let us praise, our common Lord,
And sweetly join, with one accord
Thy goodness to proclaim;
Jesus, thyself in us reveal,
And all our faculties shall feel
Thy harmonizing Name.

4 With calmly-reverential joy,
O let us all our lives employ
In setting forth thy love;
And raise in death our triumph higher,
And sing, with all the heavenly choir,
That endless song above!

—*Charles Wesley.*

BELMONT. C. M. WEBBE.

BELMONT. *(Continued.)*

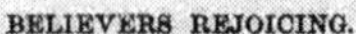

359

The joy of God's presence.

1 My God, the spring of all my joys,
The life of my delights,
The glory of my brightest days,
And comfort of my nights!

2 In darkest shades, if thou appear,
My dawning is begun;
Thou art my soul's bright morning star
And thou my rising sun.

3 The opening heavens around me shine,
With beams of sacred bliss,
If Jesus shows his mercy mine,
And whispers I am his.

4 My soul would leave this heavy clay
At that transporting word;
Run up with joy the shining way,
To see and praise my Lord.

5 Fearless of hell and ghastly death,
I'd break through every foe;
The wings of love, and arms of faith,
Would bear me conqueror through.

—*Charles Wesley.*

IRISH. C. M. ARRANGED FROM ISAAC SMITH.

360

Communion with God.

1 TALK with us, Lord, thyself reveal,
While here o'er earth we rove;
Speak to our hearts, and let us feel
The kindling of thy love.

2 With thee conversing, we forget
All time, and toil, and care;
Labour is rest, and pain is sweet,
If thou, my God, art here.

3 Here then, my God, vouchsafe to stay,
And bid my heart rejoice;
My bounding heart shall own thy sway,
And echo to thy voice.

4 Thou callest me to seek thy face;
'Tis all I wish to seek;
To attend the whispers of thy grace,
And hear thee inly speak.

5 Let this my every hour employ,
Till I thy glory see;
Enter into my Master's joy,
And find my heaven in thee.

—*Charles Wesley.*

SAWLEY. C. M. D. J. WALCH.

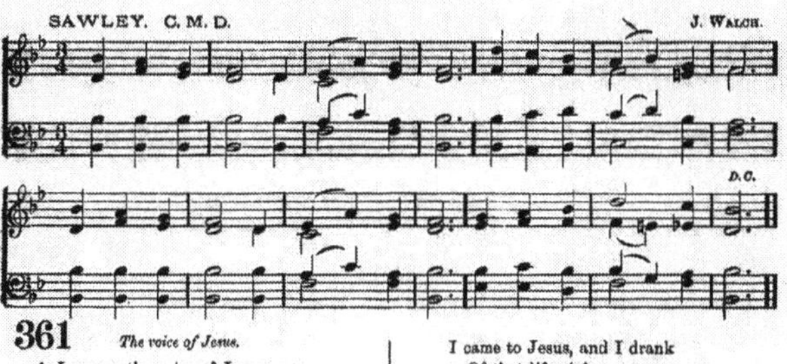
D.C.

361

The voice of Jesus.

1 I HEARD the voice of Jesus say,
"Come unto me and rest;
Lay down, thou weary one, lay down
Thy head upon my breast!"
I came to Jesus as I was,
Weary, and worn, and sad,
I found in him a resting-place,
And he hath made me glad.

2 I heard the voice of Jesus say,
"Behold, I freely give
The living water; thirsty one,
Stoop down, and drink, and live!"
I came to Jesus, and I drank
Of that life-giving stream;
My thirst was quenched, my soul revived,
And now I live in him.

3 I heard the voice of Jesus say,
"I am this dark world's light;
Look unto me, thy morn shall rise
And all thy day be bright!"
I looked to Jesus, and I found
In him my Star, my Sun;
And in that light of life I'll walk,
Till all my journey's done.

—*H. Bonar.*

EVAN. C. M. REV. W. H. HAVERGAL.

362

Psalm xxiii.

1 MY Shepherd will supply my need,
JEHOVAH is his name;
In pastures fresh he makes me feed,
Beside the living stream.

2 He brings my wandering spirit back,
When I forsake his ways;
And leads me, for his mercy's sake,
In paths of truth and grace.

3 When I walk through the shades of death,
Thy presence is my stay;
A word of thy supporting breath
Drives all my fears away.

4 Thy hand, in sight of all my foes,
Doth now my table spread;
My cup with blessings overflows,
Thine oil anoints my head.

5 The sure provisions of my God
Attend me all my days;
O may thine house be mine abode,
And all my work be praise!

—*Isaac Watts.*

ST. MARTIN'S. C. M. — TANSUR.

363 Psalm xxiii.—*Another Version.*

1 The Lord's my Shepherd, I'll not want,
He makes me down to lie
In pastures green; he leadeth me
The quiet waters by.

2 My soul he doth restore again,
And me to walk doth make
Within the paths of righteousness,
Even for his own name's sake.

3 Yes, though I walk in death's dark vale,
Yet will I fear no ill;
For thou art with me, and thy rod
And staff me comfort still.

4 My table thou hast furnishèd
In presence of my foes;
My head thou dost with oil anoint,
And my cup overflows.

5 Goodness and mercy all my life
Shall surely follow me,
And in God's house forever more
My dwelling-place shall be.

—*Scottish Version.*

BALERMA. C. M. — Adapted by R. SIMPSON.

364 *The blessings of salvation.*

1 Come, Father, Son, and Holy Ghost,
One God in Persons Three,
Bring back the heavenly blessing, lost
By all mankind and me.

2 Thy favour, and thy nature too,
To me, to all restore;
Forgive, and after God renew,
And keep us evermore.

3 Eternal Sun of Righteousness,
Display thy beams divine,
And cause the glories of thy face
Upon my heart to shine.

4 Light in thy light O may I see,
Thy grace and mercy prove;
Revived, and cheered, and blessed by thee,
The God of pardoning love!

5 Lift up thy countenance serene,
And let thy happy child
Behold, without a cloud between,
The Godhead reconciled.

6 That all-comprising peace bestow
On me, through grace forgiven;
The joys of holiness below,
And then the joys of heaven.

—*Charles Wesley.*

GERMANY. L. M. BEETHOVEN.

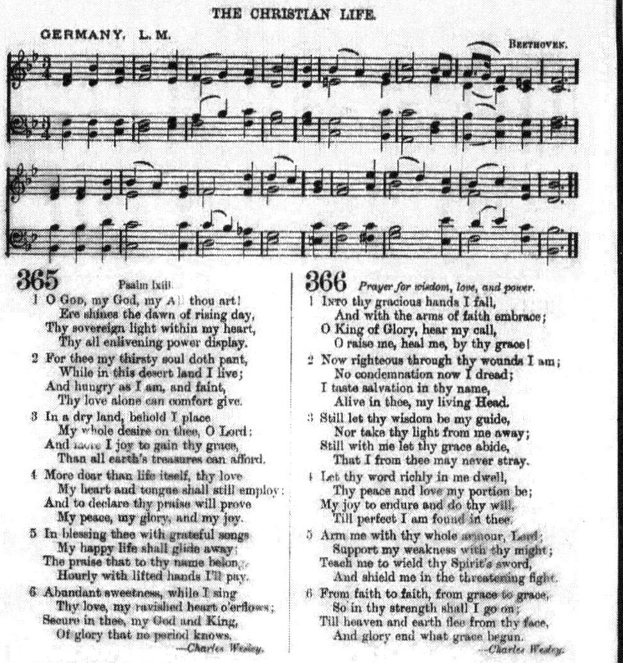

365

Psalm lxiii.

1 O God, my God, my All thou art!
Ere shines the dawn of rising day,
Thy sovereign light within my heart,
Thy all enlivening power display.

2 For thee my thirsty soul doth pant,
While in this desert land I live;
And hungry as I am, and faint,
Thy love alone can comfort give.

3 In a dry land, behold I place
My whole desire on thee, O Lord;
And more I joy to gain thy grace,
Than all earth's treasures can afford.

4 More dear than life itself, thy love
My heart and tongue shall still employ:
And to declare thy praise will prove
My peace, my glory, and my joy.

5 In blessing thee with grateful songs
My happy life shall glide away;
The praise that to thy name belongs,
Hourly with lifted hands I'll pay.

6 Abundant sweetness, while I sing
Thy love, my ravished heart o'erflows;
Secure in thee, my God and King,
Of glory that no period knows.

—*Charles Wesley.*

366

Prayer for wisdom, love, and power.

1 Into thy gracious hands I fall,
And with the arms of faith embrace;
O King of Glory, hear my call,
O raise me, heal me, by thy grace!

2 Now righteous through thy wounds I am;
No condemnation now I dread;
I taste salvation in thy name,
Alive in thee, my living Head.

3 Still let thy wisdom be my guide,
Nor take thy light from me away;
Still with me let thy grace abide,
That I from thee may never stray.

4 Let thy word richly in me dwell,
Thy peace and love my portion be;
My joy to endure and do thy will,
Till perfect I am found in thee.

5 Arm me with thy whole armour, Lord;
Support my weakness with thy might;
Teach me to wield thy Spirit's sword,
And shield me in the threatening fight.

6 From faith to faith, from grace to grace,
So in thy strength shall I go on;
Till heaven and earth flee from thy face,
And glory end what grace begun.

—*Charles Wesley.*

WAREHAM. L. M. W. KNAPP.

TUNE: WAREHAM. L. M.

367 *Ascribing salvation to God.*

1 Glory to God, whose sovereign grace
Hath animated lifeless stones;
Called us to stand before his face,
And raised us into Abraham's sons!

2 The people that in darkness lay,
In sin and error's deadly shade,
Have seen a glorious gospel day,
In Jesus' lovely face displayed.

3 Thou only, Lord, the work hast done,
And bared thine arm in all our sight;
Hast made the reprobates thine own,
And claimed the outcasts as thy right.

4 Thy single arm, almighty Lord,
To us the great salvation brought,
Thy Word, thy all-creating Word,
That spake at first a world from nought.

5 For this the saints lift up their voice,
And ceaseless praise to thee is given;
For this the hosts above rejoice,
We raise the happiness of heaven.
—*Charles Wesley.*

368 *"They that wait upon the Lord shall renew their strength."*

1 Awake, our souls! away, our fears!
Let every trembling thought be gone!
Awake, and run the heavenly race!
And put a cheerful courage on.

2 True, 'tis a strait and thorny road,
And mortal spirits tire and faint;
But they forget the mighty God,
That feeds the strength of every saint.

3 O mighty God, thy matchless power
Is ever new, and ever young,
And firm endures, while endless years
Their everlasting circles run!

4 From thee, the ever-flowing Spring,
Our souls shall drink a fresh supply;
While such as trust their native strength
Shall melt away, and droop, and die.

5 Swift as the eagle cuts the air,
We'll mount aloft to thine abode;
On wings of love our souls shall fly,
Nor tire along the heavenly road.
—*Isaac Watts.*

EDEN. L. M. Dr. L. Mason.

369 *"I will give thanks unto thee for ever."*

1 God of my life, through all my days,
My grateful powers shall sound thy praise;
My song shall wake with opening light,
And cheer the dark and silent night.

2 When anxious cares would break my rest,
And griefs would tear my throbbing breast,
Thy tuneful praises raised on high,
Shall check the murmur and the sigh.

3 When death o'er nature shall prevail,
And all the powers of language fail,
Joy through my swimming eyes shall break,
And mean the thanks I cannot speak.

4 But O when that last conflict's o'er,
And I am chained to earth no more,
With what glad accents shall I rise
To join the music of the skies!

5 Soon shall I learn the exalted strains
Which echo through the heavenly plains;
And emulate, with joy unknown,
The glowing seraphs round the throne.

6 The cheerful tribute will I give,
Long as a deathless soul shall live;
A work so sweet, a theme so high,
Demands and crowns eternity.
—*Doddridge.*

ADMAH. 6-8s. LOWELL MASON.

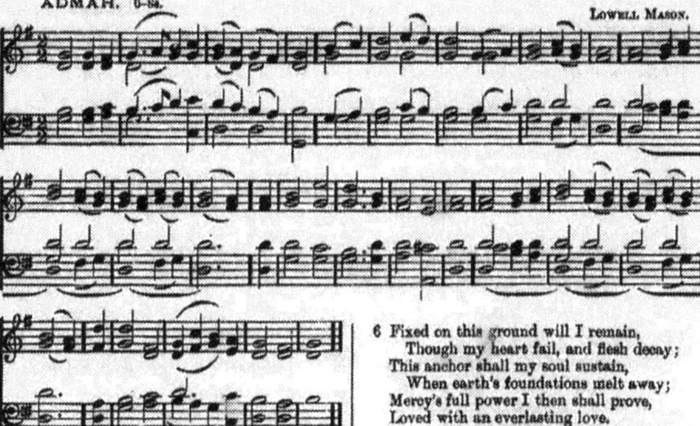

370 *Joy and peace through believing.*

1 Now I have found the ground wherein
Sure my soul's anchor may remain,
The wounds of Jesus for my sin
Before the world's foundation slain;
Whose mercy shall unshaken stay,
When heaven and earth are fled away.

2 Father, thine everlasting grace
Our scanty thought surpasses far;
Thy heart still melts with tenderness,
Thy arms of love still open are,
Returning sinners to receive,
That mercy they may taste and live.

3 O Love, thou bottomless abyss,
My sins are swallowed up in thee!
Covered is my unrighteousness,
Nor spot of guilt remains on me,
While Jesus' blood, through earth and skies,
Mercy, free, boundless mercy, cries.

4 With faith I plunge me in this sea,
Here is my hope, my joy, my rest;
Hither, when hell assails, I flee,
I look into my Saviour's breast;
Away, sad doubt, and anxious fear!
Mercy is all that's written there.

5 Though waves and storms go o'er my head,
Though strength, and health, and friends be gone,
Though joys be withered all and dead,
Though every comfort be withdrawn,
On this my steadfast soul relies,—
Father, thy mercy never dies.

6 Fixed on this ground will I remain,
Though my heart fail, and flesh decay;
This anchor shall my soul sustain,
When earth's foundations melt away;
Mercy's full power I then shall prove,
Loved with an everlasting love.

—Translated by John Wesley from Rothe.

371 *"I will love thee, O Lord, my strength."*

1 Thee will I love, my strength, my tower;
Thee will I love, my joy, my crown;
Thee will I love, with all my power,
In all thy works, and thee alone;
Thee will I love, till the pure fire
Fills my whole soul with chaste desire.

2 I thank thee, uncreated Sun,
That thy bright beams on me have shined;
I thank thee, who hast overthrown
My foes, and healed my wounded mind;
I thank thee, whose enlivening voice
Bids my freed heart in thee rejoice.

3 Uphold me in the doubtful race,
Nor suffer me again to stray;
Strengthen my feet with steady pace
Still to press forward in thy way;
My soul and flesh, O Lord of might,
Fill, satiate, with thy heavenly light.

4 Give to mine eyes refreshing tears;
Give to my heart pure, hallowed fires;
Give to my soul, with filial fears,
The love that all heaven's host inspires;
That all my powers, with all their might,
In thy sole glory may unite.

5 Thee will I love, my joy, my crown;
Thee will I love, my Lord, my God;
Thee will I love, beneath thy frown,
Or smile,—thy sceptre, or thy rod;
What though my flesh and heart decay?
Thee shall I love in endless day!

—Translated by John Wesley from Scheffler.

STELLA. 6-8s. From "Crown of Jesus."

372 *Thanksgiving for pardoning mercy.*

1 What am I, O thou glorious God;
  And what my father's house to thee,
That thou such mercies hast bestowed
  On me, the chief of sinners, me!
I take the blessing from above,
And wonder at thy boundless love.

2 Honour, and might, and thanks, and praise,
  I render to my pardoning God,
Extol the riches of thy grace,
  And spread thy saving name abroad,
That only name to sinners given,
Which lifts poor dying worms to heaven.

3 Jesus, I bless thy gracious power,
  And all within me shouts thy name;
Thy name let every soul adore,
  Thy power let every tongue proclaim;
Thy grace let every sinner know,
And find with me their heaven below.

—*Charles Wesley.*

373 Isaiah ix. 2-5.

1 The people that in darkness lay,
  The confines of eternal night,
Have seen a joyful gospel day,
  The glorious beams of heavenly light;
His Spirit in our hearts hath shone,
And showed the Father in the Son.

2 Father of everlasting grace,
  Thou hast in us thy arm revealed,
Hast multiplied the faithful race,
  Who, conscious of their pardon sealed,
Of joy unspeakable possest,
Anticipate their heavenly rest.

3 In tears we sowed, in joy we reap,
  And praise thy goodness all day long;
Him in our eye of faith we keep,
  Who gives us our triumphal song,
And doth his gifts to all divide,
A lot among the sanctified.

4 Not like the warring sons of men,
  With shouts and garments rolled in blood,
Our Captain doth the fight maintain;
  But, lo! the burning Spirit of God
Kindles in each a secret fire,
And all our sins as smoke expire.

—*Charles Wesley.*

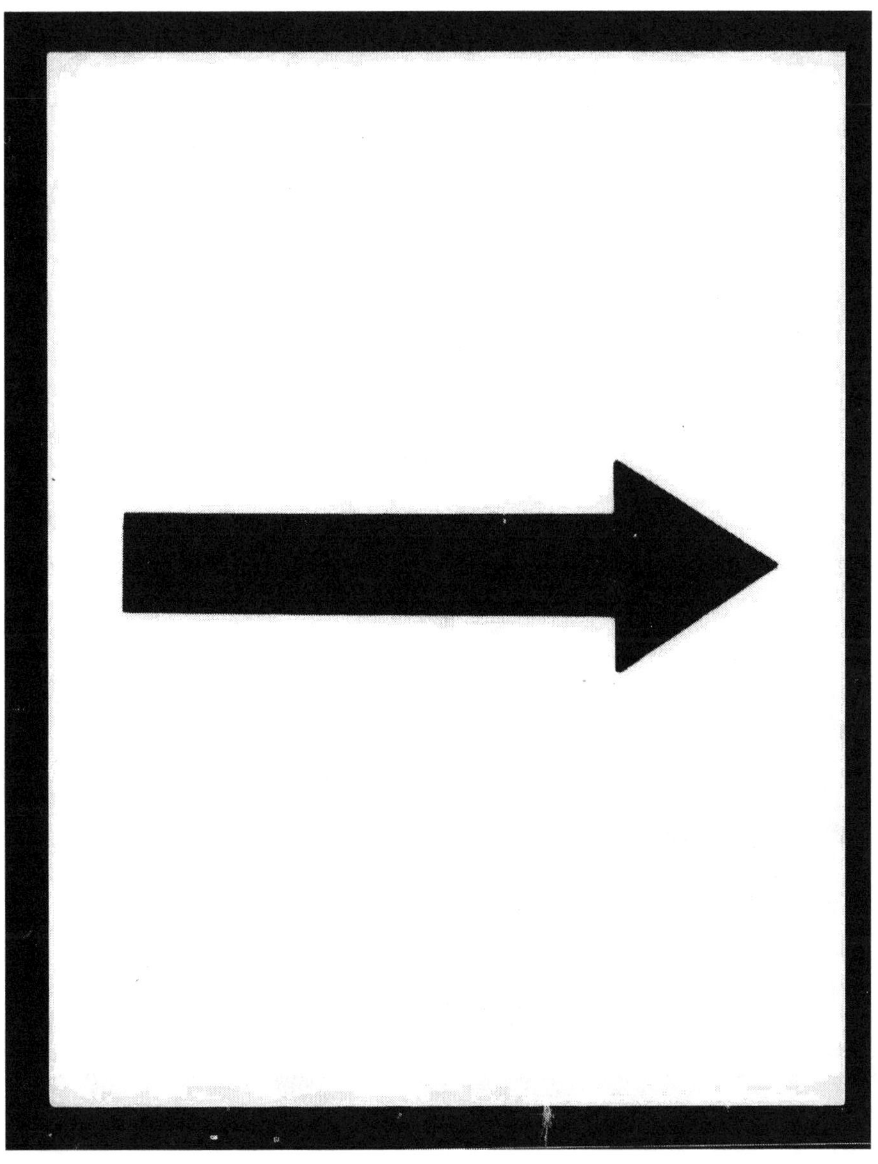

IMAGE EVALUATION TEST TARGET (MT-3)

Photographic Sciences Corporation

23 WEST MAIN STREET
WEBSTER, N.Y. 14580
(716) 872-4503

CREATION. 8-8s. HAYDN.

374 *Praise for pardoning grace.*

1 GREAT God of wonders! all thy ways
Display the attributes divine;
But countless acts of pardoning grace
Beyond thine other wonders shine:
Who is a pardoning God like thee?
Or who has grace so rich and free?

2 Crimes of such horror to forgive,
Such vile and guilty worms to spare,
This is thy grand prerogative,
And none may in this honour share:
Who is a pardoning God like thee?
Or who has grace so rich and free?

3 In wonder lost, with trembling joy
We take the pardon of our God;
Pardon for crimes of deepest dye,
A pardon bought with Jesus' blood:
Who is a pardoning God like thee?
Or who has grace so rich and free?

4 O may this strange, this wondrous grace,
This matchless miracle of love,
Fill the wide earth with grateful praise,
As now it fills the choirs above!
Who is a pardoning God like thee?
Or who has grace so rich and free?

—*Pres. Davies.*

REQUIES. 8-7s. BLUMENTHAL.

REQUIES. *(Continued.)*

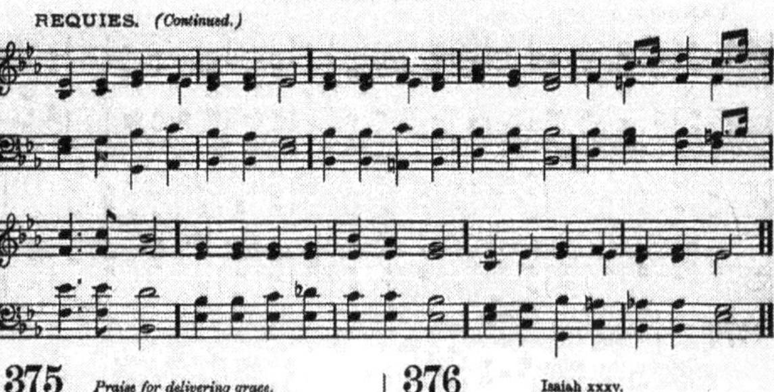

375 *Praise for delivering grace.*

1 MEET and right it is to praise
God, the Giver of all grace,
God, whose mercies are bestowed
On the evil and the good;
He foresees his creatures' call,
Kind and merciful to all;
Makes his sun on sinners rise,
Showers his blessings from the skies.

2 Least of all thy creatures, we
Daily thy salvation see;
As by heavenly manna fed,
Through a world of dangers led;
Through a wilderness of cares,
Through ten thousand thousand snares;
More than now our hearts conceive,
More than we could know and live!

3 Here, as in the lion's den,
Undevoured we still remain
Pass secure the watery flood,
Hanging on the arm of God;
Here we raise our voices higher,
Shout in the refiner's fire;
Clap our hands amidst the flame,
Glory give to Jesus' name.

4 Jesus' name in Satan's hour,
Stands our refuge and our tower;
Jesus doth his own defend,
Love, and save us to the end.
Love shall make us persevere
Till our conquering Lord appear,
Bear us to our thrones above,
Crown us with his heavenly love.

—*Charles Wesley.*

376 Isaiah xxxv.

1 HARK! the wastes have found a voice,
Lonely deserts now rejoice,
Gladsome hallelujahs sing,
All around with praises ring;
Lo! for us the wilds are glad,
All in cheerful green arrayed;
Opening sweets they all disclose,
Bud and blossom as the rose.

2 Ye that tremble at his frown,
He shall lift your hands cast down;
Christ, who all your weakness sees,
He shall prop your feeble knees.
Ye of fearful hearts be strong;
Jesus will not tarry long;
Fear not lest his truth should fail;
Jesus is unchangeable.

3 God, your God, shall surely come,
Quell your foes, and seal their doom;
He shall come and save you too;
We, O Lord, have found thee true!
Blind we were, but now we see;
Deaf, we hearken now to thee;
Dumb, for thee our tongues employ;
Lame, and lo! we leap for joy.

4 Faint we were, and parched with drought,
Water at thy word gushed out;
Streams of grace our thirst repress,
Starting from the wilderness;
Still we gasp thy grace to know,
Here forever let it flow,
Make the thirsty land a pool;
Fix the Spirit in our soul.

—*Charles Wesley.*

BANGOR. 6.6, 7.7, 7.7.

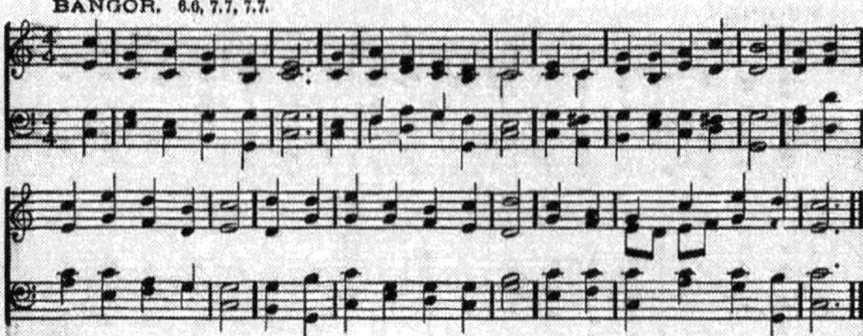

377

The Living Way opened.

1 Jesus, to thee we fly,
On thee for help rely;
Thou our only refuge art,
Thou dost all our fears control,
Rest of every troubled heart,
Life of every dying soul.

2 We lift our joyful eyes,
And see the dazzling prize,
See the purchase of thy blood,
Freely now to sinners given;
Thou the living way hast showed,
Thou to us hast opened heaven.

3 We now, divinely bold,
Of thy reward lay hold;
All thy glorious joy is ours,
All the treasures of thy love;
Now we taste the heavenly powers,
Now we reign with thee above.

4 Our anchor sure and fast
Within the veil is cast;
Stands our never-failing hope
Grounded in the holy place;
We shall after thee mount up,
See the Godhead face to face.

—*Charles Wesley.*

GILEAD. 7.6.7.6, 7.8.7.6.

Fine.
D.S.

378

Rev. i. 4, 5.

1 True and faithful Witness, thee,
O Jesus, we receive;
Fulness of the Deity,
In all thy people live!
First-begotten from the dead,
Call forth thy living witnesses;
King of saints, thine empire spread
O'er all the ransomed race.

2 Grace, the fountain of all good,
Ye happy saints, receive,
With the streams of peace o'erflowed,
With all that God can give;
He who is, and was, in peace,
And grace, and plenitude of power,
Comes, your favoured souls to bless,
And never leave you more.

3 Let the Spirit before his throne,
Mysterious One and Seven,
In his various gifts sent down,
Be to the churches given;
Let the pure seraphic joy
From Jesus Christ, the Just, descend;
Holiness without alloy,
And bliss that ne'er shall end.

—*Charles Wesley.*

LUTHER'S HYMN. 6-8s. MARTIN LUTHER.

Repeat last line of each verse.

379 *"The Spirit of grace and of supplications."*

1 JESUS, thou sovereign Lord of all,
The same through one eternal day,
Attend thy feeblest followers' call,
And O instruct us how to pray!
Pour out the supplicating grace,
And stir us up to seek thy face.

2 We cannot think a gracious thought,
We cannot feel a good desire,
Till thou, who call'dst a world from nought,
The power into our hearts inspire;
And then we in thy Spirit groan,
And then we give thee back thine own.

3 Jesus, regard the joint complaint
Of all thy tempted followers here,
And now supply the common want,
And send us down the Comforter;
The spirit of ceaseless prayer impart,
And fix thy Agent in our heart.

4 To help our soul's infirmity,
To heal thy sin-sick people's care,
To urge our all-prevailing plea,
And make our hearts a house of prayer,
The promised Intercessor give,
And let us now thyself receive.

5 Come in thy pleading Spirit down
To us who for thy coming stay;
Of all thy gifts we ask but one,
We ask the constant power to pray;
Indulge us, Lord, in this request,
Thou canst not then deny the rest.
—*Charles Wesley.*

380 *The power of faithful prayer.*

1 O WONDROUS power of faithful prayer,
What tongue can tell the almighty grace!
God's hands or bound or open are,
As Moses or Elijah prays:
Let Moses in the spirit groan,
And God cries out, "Let me alone!"

2 "Let me alone, that all my wrath
May rise the wicked to consume!
While justice hears thy praying faith,
It cannot seal the sinner's doom;
My Son is in my servant's prayer,
And Jesus forces me to spare."

3 Father, we ask in Jesus' name,
In Jesus' power and spirit pray;
Divert thy vengeful thunder's aim,
O turn thy threatening wrath away!
Our guilt and punishment remove,
And magnify thy pardoning love.

4 Father, regard thy pleading Son!
Accept his all-availing prayer,
And send a peaceful answer down,
In honour of our Spokesman there;
Whose blood proclaims our sins forgiven,
And speaks thy rebels up to heaven.
—*Charles Wesley.*

BARNBY. 6-8s. J. BARNBY.

By permission of Messrs. Novello, Ewer & Co.

381 *Compassion for the suffering.*

1 Let God, who comforts the distrest,
Let Israel's Consolation hear!
Hear, Holy Ghost, our joint request,
And show thyself the Comforter;
And swell the unutterable groan,
And breathe our wishes to the throne!

2 We weep for those that weep below,
And, burdened for the afflicted, sigh;
The various forms of human woe
Excite our softest sympathy,
Fill every heart with mournful care,
And draw out all our souls in prayer.

3 We wrestle for the ruined race,
By sin eternally undone,
Unless thou magnify thy grace,
And make thy richest mercy known,
And make thy vanquished rebels find
Pardon in Christ for all mankind.

4 Father of everlasting love,
To every soul thy Son reveal,
Our guilt and sufferings to remove,
Our deep, original wound to heal;
And bid the fallen race arise,
And turn our earth to Paradise.

—*Charles Wesley.*

HESPERUS. L. M. H. BAKER, Mus. Bac.

TUNE: HESPERUS. L. M.

382 *Prayer for young converts.*

1 Author of faith, we seek thy face
For all who feel thy work begun;
Confirm and strengthen them in grace,
And bring thy feeblest children on.

2 Thou seest their wants, thou know'st their names,
Be mindful of thy youngest care;
Be tender of thy new-born lambs,
And gently in thy bosom bear.

3 The lion roaring for his prey,
And ravening wolves on every side,
Watch over them to tear and slay,
If found one moment from their guide.

4 Satan his thousand arts essays,
His agents all their powers employ,
To blast the blooming work of grace,
The heavenly offspring to destroy.

5 Baffle the crooked Serpent's skill,
And turn his sharpest dart aside;
Hide from their eyes the deadly ill,
O save them from the demon, Pride!

6 In safety lead thy little flock,
From hell, the world, and sin secure;
And set their feet upon the rock,
And make in thee their goings sure.
—*Charles Wesley.*

383 *Prayer for the penitent.*

1 O let the prisoners' mournful cries
As incense in thy sight appear!
Their humble wailings pierce the skies,
If haply they may feel thee near.

2 The captive exiles make their moans,
From sin impatient to be free;
Call home, call home thy banished ones!
Lead captive their captivity!

3 Show them the blood that bought their peace,
The anchor of their steadfast hope;
And bid their guilty terrors cease,
And bring the ransomed prisoners up.

4 Out of the deep regard their cries,
The fallen raise, the mourners cheer;
O Sun of Righteousness, arise,
And scatter all their doubt and fear!

5 Pity the day of feeble things;
O gather every halting soul!
And drop salvation from thy wings,
And make the contrite sinner whole.
—*Charles Wesley.*

RETREAT. L. M. Thomas Hastings.

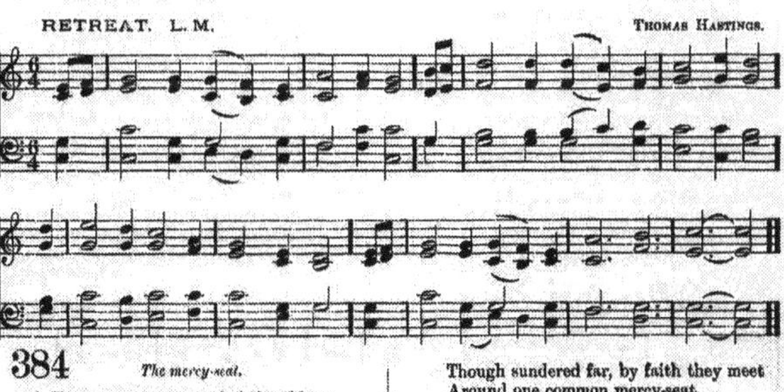

384 *The mercy-seat.*

1 From every stormy wind that blows,
From every swelling tide of woes,
There is a calm, a sure retreat;
'Tis found beneath the mercy-seat.

2 There is a place where Jesus sheds
The oil of gladness on our heads,
A place than all besides more sweet;
It is the blood-bought mercy-seat.

3 There is a place where spirits blend,
Where friend holds fellowship with friend;
Though sundered far, by faith they meet
Around one common mercy-seat.

4 Ah! whither could we flee for aid,
When tempted, desolate, dismayed?
Or how the hosts of hell defeat,
Had suffering saints no mercy-seat?

5 There, there on eagle wings we soar,
And sin and sense molest no more;
And heaven comes down our souls to greet,
While glory crowns the mercy-seat.
—*H. Stowell.*

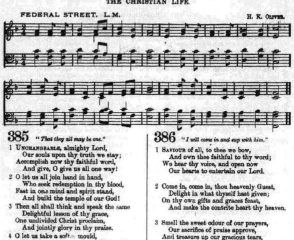

FEDERAL STREET. L. M. H. K. OLIVER.

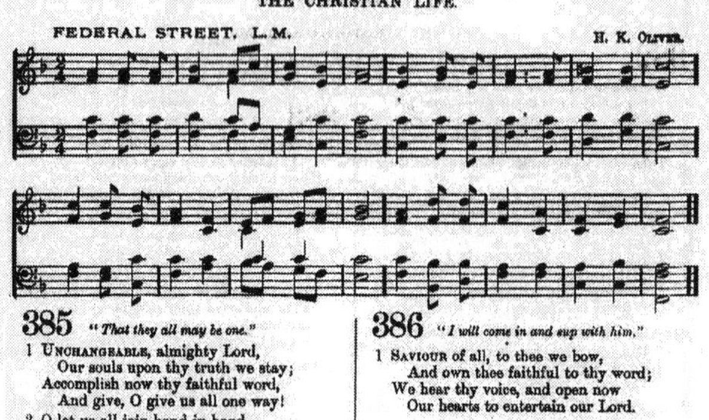

385 *"That they all may be one."*

1 UNCHANGEABLE, almighty Lord,
Our souls upon thy truth we stay;
Accomplish now thy faithful word,
And give, O give us all one way!

2 O let us all join hand in hand,
Who seek redemption in thy blood,
Fast in one mind and spirit stand,
And build the temple of our God!

3 Then all shall think and speak the same
Delightful lesson of thy grace,
One undivided Christ proclaim,
And jointly glory in thy praise.

4 O let us take a softer mould,
Blended and gathered into thee;
Under one Shepherd make one fold,
Where all is love and harmony!

5 Regard thine own eternal prayer,
And send a peaceful answer down;
To us thy Father's name declare;
Unite and perfect us in one.

6 So shall the world believe and know,
That God hath sent thee from above,
When thou art seen in us below,
And every soul displays thy love.

—*Charles Wesley.*

386 *"I will come in and sup with him."*

1 SAVIOUR of all, to thee we bow,
And own thee faithful to thy word;
We hear thy voice, and open now
Our hearts to entertain our Lord.

2 Come in, come in, thou heavenly Guest,
Delight in what thyself hast given;
On thy own gifts and graces feast,
And make the contrite heart thy heaven.

3 Smell the sweet odour of our prayers,
Our sacrifice of praise approve,
And treasure up our gracious tears,
And rest in thy redeeming love.

4 Beneath thy shadow let us sit,
Call us thy friends, and love, and bride,
And bid us freely drink and eat
Thy dainties, and be satisfied.

5 The heavenly manna faith imparts,
Faith makes thy fulness all our own;
We feed upon thee in our hearts,
And find that heaven and thou art one.

—*Charles Wesley.*

PETERBOROUGH. C. M. REV. RALPH HARRISON.

TUNE: PETERBOROUGH. C. M.

387

"I am the good Shepherd."

1 Jesus, great Shepherd of the sheep,
To thee for help we fly;
Thy little flock in safety keep;
For, oh! the wolf is nigh.

2 Us into thy protection take,
And gather with thy arm;
Unless the fold we first forsake,
The wolf can never harm.

3 We laugh to scorn his cruel power,
While by our Shepherd's side;
The sheep he never can devour,
Unless he first divide.

4 O do not suffer him to part
The souls that here agree;
But make us of one mind and heart,
And keep us one in thee!

5 Together let us sweetly live,
Together let us die;
And each a starry crown receive,
And reign above the sky.

—*Charles Wesley.*

388

"Continue ye in my love."

1 Jesus, united by thy grace,
And each to each endeared,
With confidence we seek thy face,
And know our prayer is heard.

2 Still let us own our common Lord,
And bear thine easy yoke,
A band of love, a threefold cord,
Which never can be broke.

3 Make us into one spirit drink;
Baptize into thy name;
And let us always kindly think,
And sweetly speak, the same.

4 Touched by the loadstone of thy love,
Let all our hearts agree,
And ever towards each other move,
And ever move towards thee.

5 To thee inseparably joined,
Let all our spirits cleave;
O may we all the loving mind
That was in thee receive!

6 Grant this, and then from all below
Insensibly remove;
Our souls their change shall scarcely know,
Made perfect first in love!

7 Yet when the fullest joy is given,
The same delight we prove,
In earth, in paradise, in heaven,
Our all in all is love.

—*Charles Wesley.*

MARTYRDOM. C. M. Hugh Wilson.

389

Prayer for growth in grace.

1 Try us, O God, and search the ground
Of every sinful heart;
Whate'er of sin in us is found,
O bid it all depart!

2 When to the right or left we stray,
Leave us not comfortless;
But guide our feet into the way,
Of everlasting peace.

3 Help us to help each other, Lord,
Each other's cross to bear;
Let each his friendly aid afford,
And feel his brother's care.

4 Help us to build each other up,
Our little stock improve;
Increase our faith, confirm our hope,
And perfect us in love.

5 Up into thee, our living Head,
Let us in all things grow,
Till thou hast made us free indeed,
And spotless here below.

6 Then, when the mighty work is wrought,
Receive thy ready bride;
Give us in heaven a happy lot
With all the sanctified.

—*Charles Wesley.*

SAWLEY. C. M. J. WALCH.

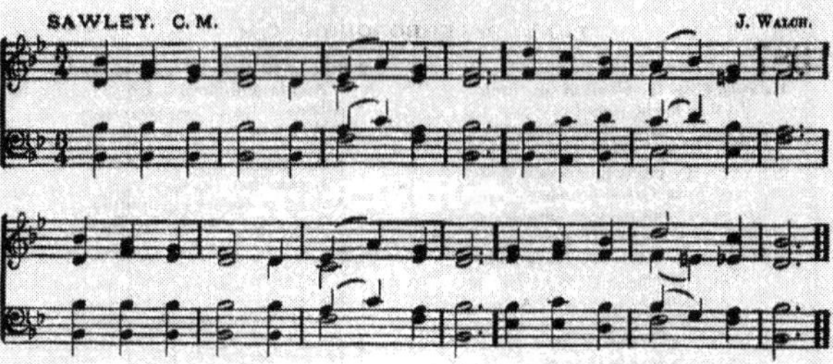

390 *"I will not let thee go unless thou bless me."*

1 SHEPHERD Divine, our wants relieve,
In this our evil day,
To all thy tempted followers give
The power to watch and pray.

2 Long as our fiery trials last,
Long as the cross we bear,
O let our souls on thee be cast
In never-ceasing prayer!

3 The Spirit of interceding grace
Give us in faith to claim,
To wrestle till we see thy face,
And know thy hidden name.

4 Till thou thy perfect love impart,
Till thou thyself bestow,
Be this the cry of every heart,
"I will not let thee go:

5 "I will not let thee go, unless
Thou tell thy name to me,
With all thy great salvation bless,
And make me all like thee.

6 "Then let me on the mountain-top
Behold thy open face,
Where faith in sight is swallowed up,
And prayer in endless praise."
—*Charles Wesley.*

ARNOLD. C. M. DR. S. ARNOLD.

TUNE: ARNOLD. C. M.

391

Secret prayer.

1 FATHER of Jesus Christ, my Lord,
I humbly seek thy face,
Encouraged by the Saviour's word
To ask thy pardoning grace.

2 Entering into my closet, I
The busy world exclude,
In secret prayer for mercy cry,
And groan to be renewed.

3 Far from the paths of men, to thee
I solemnly retire;
See, thou who dost in secret see,
And grant my heart's desire.

4 Thy grace I languish to receive,
The Spirit of love and power,
Blameless before thy face to live,
To live and sin no more.

5 Fain would I all thy goodness feel,
And know my sins forgiven,
And do on earth thy perfect will
As angels do in heaven.

6 O Father, glorify thy Son,
And grant what I require;
For Jesus' sake the gift send down,
And answer me by fire.

7 Kindle the flame of love within,
Which may to heaven ascend;
And now the work of grace begin,
Which shall in glory end.

—*Charles Wesley.*

WILTSHIRE. C. M. SIR GEORGE SMART.

392

"God is Light."

1 O SUN of Righteousness, arise,
With healing in thy wing!
To my diseased, my fainting soul,
Life and salvation bring.

2 These clouds of pride and sin dispel,
By thy all-piercing beam;
Lighten my eyes with faith, my heart
With holy hope inflame.

3 My mind, by thy all-quickening power,
From low desires set free;
Unite my scattered thoughts, and fix
My love entire on thee.

4 Father, thy long-lost son receive;
Saviour, thy purchase own;
Blest Comforter, with peace and joy
Thy new-made creature crown.

5 Eternal, undivided Lord,
Co-equal One and Three,
On thee, all faith, all hope be placed;
All love be paid to thee.

—*John Wesley.*

WILTSHIRE. C. M. — SIR GEORGE SMART.

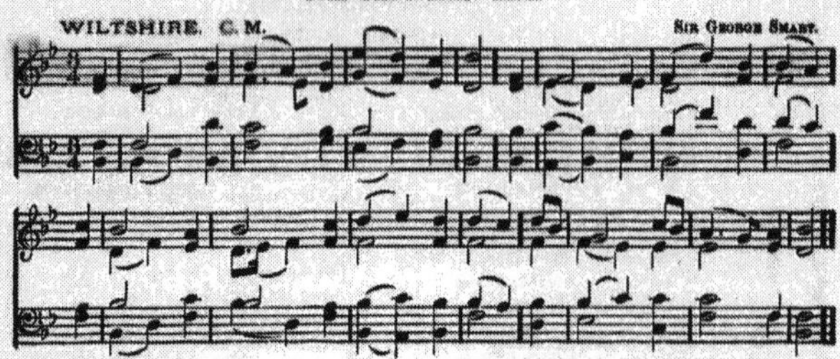

393 *Coming to the throne of grace.*

1 LORD, I approach the mercy-seat
Where thou dost answer prayer;
There humbly fall before thy feet,
For none can perish there.

2 Thy promise is my only plea,
With this I venture nigh;
Thou callest burdened souls to thee,
And such, O Lord, am I.

3 Bowed down beneath a load of sin,
By Satan sorely pressed,
By war without, and fears within,
I come to thee for rest.

4 Be thou my shield and hiding-place,
That, sheltered near thy side,
I may my fierce accuser face,
And tell him thou hast died.

5 O wondrous love! to bleed and die,
To bear the cross and shame,
That guilty sinners such as I
Might plead thy gracious name.

—*J. Newton.*

ELIM. C. M. — H. W. GREATOREX.

394 *Prayer for sincerity.*

1 LORD, when we bend before thy throne,
And our confessions pour,
Teach us to feel the sins we own,
And hate what we deplore.

2 Our broken spirits, pitying, see;
And penitence impart;
And let a kindling glance from thee
Beam hope upon the heart.

3 When we disclose our wants in prayer,
May we our wills resign,
And not a thought our bosom share
That is not wholly thine.

4 May faith each weak petition fill,
And waft it to the skies;
And teach our hearts 'tis goodness still
That grants it, or denies.

—*J. D. Carlyle.*

TUNE: ELIM. C. M. (SEE HYMN 394.)

395

"Lord, increase our faith."

1 INCREASE our faith, almighty L.
For thou alone canst give
The faith that takes thee at thy word,
The faith by which we live.

2 Increase our faith, that we may claim
Each starry promise sure;
And always triumph in thy name,
And to the end endure.

3 Increase our faith, O Lord, we pray,
That we may not depart
From thy commands, but all obey
With free and faithful heart.

4 Increase our faith, that never dim
Or faltering it may be;
Crowned with the perfect peace of him
Whose mind is stayed on thee.

5 Increase our faith, that unto thee
More fruit may still abound;
That in the harvest time may be
To thy great glory found.

6 Increase our faith, O Saviour dear,
By thy rich sovereign grace,
Till, changing faith for vision clear,
We see thee face to face.

—*Miss Havergal.*

TALLIS' ORDINAL. C. M. THOMAS TALLIS.

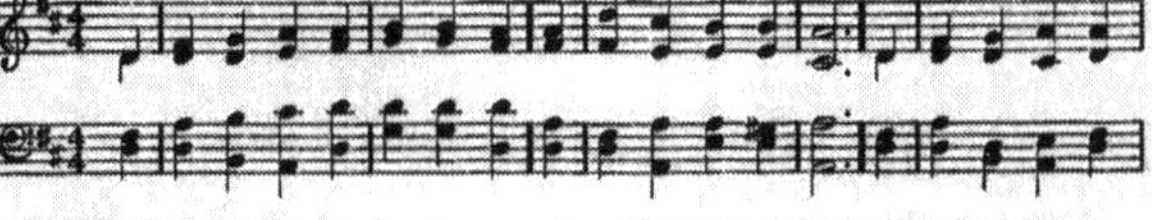

396

The Lord's Prayer.

1 OUR Father, God, who art in heaven,
All hallowed be thy name;
Thy kingdom come; thy will be done
In heaven and earth the same.

2 Give us this day our daily bread;
And, as we those forgive
Who sin against us, so may we
Forgiving grace receive.

3 Into temptation lead us not;
From evil set us free;
And thine the kingdom, thine the power,
And glory, ever be.

—*A. Judson.*

397

"Lord, teach us to pray."

1 PRAYER is the soul's sincere desire,
Uttered or unexpressed;
The motion of a hidden fire,
That trembles in the breast.

2 Prayer is the burden of a sigh,
The falling of a tear;
The upward glancing of an eye,
When none but God is near.

3 Prayer is the simplest form of speech
That infant lips can try;
Prayer the sublimest strains that reach
The Majesty on high.

4 Prayer is the contrite sinner's voice
Returning from his ways;
While angels in their songs rejoice,
And cry, "Behold he prays!"

5 Prayer is the Christian's vital breath,
The Christian's native air;
His watchword at the gates of death;
He enters heaven with prayer.

6 The saints in prayer appear as one,
In word, in deed, and mind;
While with the Father and the Son
Sweet fellowship they find.

7 Nor prayer is made on earth alone;
The Holy Spirit pleads;
And Jesus, on the eternal throne,
For sinners intercedes.

8 O thou by whom we come to God,
The Life, the Truth, the Way!
The path of prayer thyself hast trod;
Lord, teach us how to pray.

—*Montgomery.*

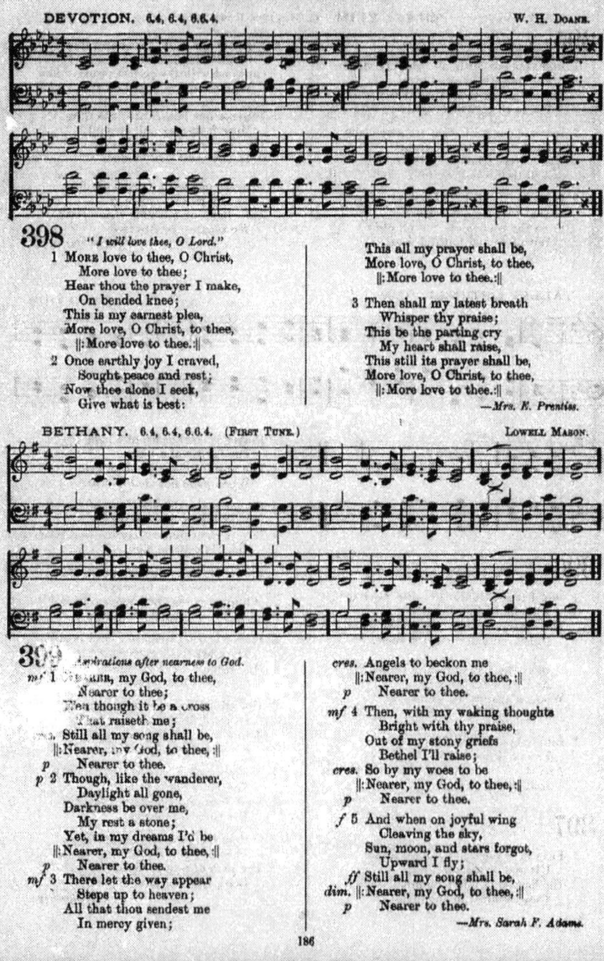

DEVOTION. 6.4, 6.4, 6.6.4. W. H. DOANE.

398

"I will love thee, O Lord."

1 More love to thee, O Christ,
More love to thee;
Hear thou the prayer I make,
On bended knee;
This is my earnest plea,
More love, O Christ, to thee,
‖: More love to thee. :‖

2 Once earthly joy I craved,
Sought peace and rest;
Now thee alone I seek,
Give what is best:
This all my prayer shall be,
More love, O Christ, to thee,
‖: More love to thee. :‖

3 Then shall my latest breath
Whisper thy praise;
This be the parting cry
My heart shall raise,
This still its prayer shall be,
More love, O Christ, to thee,
‖: More love to thee. :‖

—*Mrs. E. Prentiss.*

BETHANY. 6.4, 6.4, 6.6.4. (FIRST TUNE.) LOWELL MASON.

399

Aspirations after nearness to God.

mf 1 Nearer, my God, to thee,
Nearer to thee;
Even though it be a cross
That raiseth me;
cres. Still all my song shall be,
‖: Nearer, my God, to thee, :‖
p Nearer to thee.

p 2 Though, like the wanderer,
Daylight all gone,
Darkness be over me,
My rest a stone;
Yet, in my dreams I'd be
‖: Nearer, my God, to thee, :‖
p Nearer to thee.

mf 3 There let the way appear
Steps up to heaven;
All that thou sendest me
In mercy given;
cres. Angels to beckon me
‖: Nearer, my God, to thee, :‖
p Nearer to thee.

mf 4 Then, with my waking thoughts
Bright with thy praise,
Out of my stony griefs
Bethel I'll raise;
cres. So by my woes to be
‖: Nearer, my God, to thee, :‖
p Nearer to thee.

f 5 And when on joyful wing
Cleaving the sky,
Sun, moon, and stars forgot,
Upward I fly;
ff Still all my song shall be,
dim. ‖: Nearer, my God, to thee, :‖
p Nearer to thee.

—*Mrs. Sarah F. Adams.*

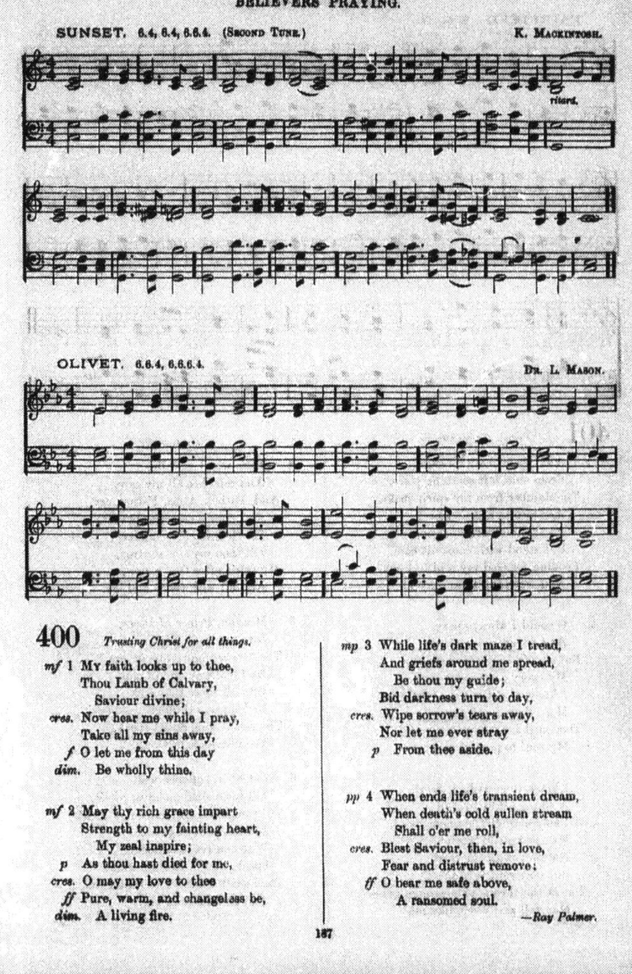
SUNSET. 6.4, 6.4, 6.6.4. (Second Tune.)
K. Mackintosh.
ritard.
OLIVET. 6.6.4, 6.6.6.4.
Dr. L. Mason.

400 *Trusting Christ for all things.*

mf 1 My faith looks up to thee,
Thou Lamb of Calvary,
Saviour divine;
cres. Now hear me while I pray,
Take all my sins away,
f O let me from this day
dim. Be wholly thine.

mf 2 May thy rich grace impart
Strength to my fainting heart,
My zeal inspire;
p As thou hast died for me,
cres. O may my love to thee
ff Pure, warm, and changeless be,
dim. A living fire.

mp 3 While life's dark maze I tread,
And griefs around me spread,
Be thou my guide;
Bid darkness turn to day,
cres. Wipe sorrow's tears away,
Nor let me ever stray
p From thee aside.

pp 4 When ends life's transient dream,
When death's cold sullen stream
Shall o'er me roll,
cres. Blest Saviour, then, in love,
Fear and distrust remove;
ff O bear me safe above,
A ransomed soul.

—*Ray Palmer.*

FAIRFIELD. S. M. D. LA TROBE.

401

Prayer for repentance.

1 AH! when shall I awake
From sin's soft-soothing power,
The slumber from my spirit shake,
And rise to fall no more!
Awake, no more to sleep,
But stand with constant care,
Looking for God my soul to keep,
And watching unto prayer!

2 O could I always pray,
And never, never faint,
But simply to my God display
My every care and want!
I know that thou would'st give
More than I can request;
Thou still art ready to receive
My soul to perfect rest.

3 I know thee willing, Lord,
A sinful world to save;
All may obey thy gracious word,
May peace and pardon have;
Not one of all the race
But may return to thee,
But at the throne of sovereign grace
May fall and weep, like me.

SECOND PART.

4 Here will I ever lie,
And tell thee all my care,
And, Father, Abba, Father, cry,
And pour a ceaseless prayer;
Till thou my sins subdue,
Till thou my sins destroy,
My spirit after God renew,
And fill with peace and joy.

5 Messiah, Prince of Peace,
Into my soul bring in
The everlasting righteousness
And make an end of sin.
Into all those that seek
Redemption through thy blood,
The sanctifying Spirit speak,
The plenitude of God.

6 Let us in patience wait
Till faith shall make us whole,
Till thou shalt all things new create,
In each believing soul.
Who can resist thy will?
Speak, and it shall be done!
Thou shalt the work of faith fulfil
And perfect us in one.

—*Charles Wesley.*

NEARER HOME. S. M. D. ISAAC WOODBURY.

402 *Prayer for entire consecration.*

1 Jesus, my strength, my hope,
On thee I cast my care;
With humble confidence look up,
And know thou hear'st my prayer.
Give me on thee to wait,
Till I can all things do;
On thee, almighty to create,
Almighty to renew.

2 I want a sober mind,
A self-renouncing will,
That tramples down and casts behind
The baits of pleasing ill;
A soul unmoved by pain,
By hardship, grief, or loss,
Bold to take up, firm to sustain,
The consecrated cross.

3 I want a godly fear,
A quick-discerning eye,
That looks to thee when sin is near,
And sees the Tempter fly;
A spirit still prepared,
And armed with jealous care,
Forever standing on its guard,
And watching unto prayer.

SECOND PART.

4 I want a heart to pray,
To pray and never cease;
Never to murmur at thy stay,
Or wish my sufferings less.
This blessing, above all,
Always to pray, I want,
Out of the deep on thee to call,
And never, never faint.

5 I want a true regard,
A single, steady aim,
Unmoved by threatening or reward,
To thee and thy great name;
A jealous, just concern
For thine immortal praise;
A pure desire that all may learn
And glorify thy grace.

6 I rest upon thy word,
The promise is for me;
My succour and salvation, Lord,
Shall surely come from thee;
But let me still abide,
Nor from my hope remove,
Till thou my patient spirit guide
Into thy perfect love.

—*Charles Wesley.*

ST. MICHAEL. S. M. D. — DAY'S PSALTER, 1588.

D.C.

403

"Watch and pray."

1 THE praying Spirit breathe,
The watching power impart,
From all entanglements beneath
Call off my anxious heart.
My feeble mind sustain,
By worldly thoughts opprest;
Appear, and bid me turn again
To my eternal rest.

2 Swift to my rescue come,
Thy own this moment seize;
Gather my wandering spirit home,
And keep in perfect peace:
Suffered no more to rove
O'er all the earth abroad,
Arrest the prisoner of thy love,
And shut me up in God.

—*Charles Wesley.*

HENDON. 4-7s. — MALAN.

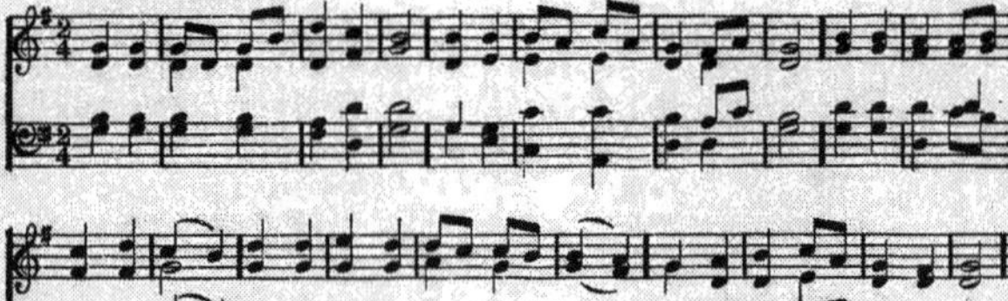

404

"Come boldly unto the throne of grace."

1 COME, my soul, thy suit prepare,
Jesus loves to answer prayer;
He himself has bid thee pray,
‖:Therefore will not say thee nay.:‖

2 Thou art coming to a King,
Large petitions with thee bring;
For his grace and power are such,
‖:None can ever ask too much.:‖

3 With my burden I begin,
Lord, remove this load of sin!
Let thy blood for sinners spilt
‖:Set my conscience free from guilt.:‖

4 Lord, I come to thee for rest,
Take possession of my breast;
There thy blood-bought right maintain,
‖:And without a rival reign.:‖

5 While I am a pilgrim here,
Let thy love my spirit cheer;
As my Guide, my Guard, my Friend,
‖:Lead me to my journey's end.:‖

—*J. Newton.*

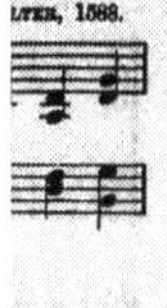

MARTYN. 8-7s. S. B. MARSH.

Fine. D.C.

405 *"Be not conformed to this world."*

1 GOD of love, who hearest prayer,
Kindly for thy people care,
Who on thee alone depend;
Love us, save us to the end.
Save us, in the prosperous hour,
From the flattering Tempter's power,
From his unsuspected wiles,
From the world's pernicious smiles.

2 Cut off our dependence vain
On the help of feeble man;
Every arm of flesh remove;
Stay us on thy only love.
Save us from the great and wise,
Till they sink in their own eyes,
Meekly to thy yoke submit,
Lay their honours at thy feet.

3 Never let the world break in;
Fix a mighty gulf between;
Keep us little and unknown,
Prized and loved by God alone.
Let us still to thee look up,
Thee, thy Israel's Strength and Hope;
Nothing know, or seek, beside
Jesus, and him crucified.
—Charles Wesley.

PRAYER. 4-7s. A. ABBOTT.

406 *Prayer for godly simplicity.*

1 LORD, that I may learn of thee,
Give me true simplicity;
Wean my soul, and keep it low,
Willing thee alone to know.

2 Let me cast my reeds aside,
All that feeds my knowing pride;
Not to man, but God submit,
Lay my reasonings at thy feet;

3 Of my boasted wisdom spoiled,
Docile, helpless as a child;
Only seeing in thy light,
Only walking in thy might.

4 Then infuse the teaching grace,
Spirit of truth and righteousness;
Knowledge, love divine, impart,
Life eternal, to my heart.
—Charles Wesley.

407 *Prayer for unity.*

1 JESUS, Lord, we look to thee,
Let us in thy name agree;
Show thyself the Prince of Peace;
Bid our jars forever cease.

2 By thy reconciling love,
Every stumbling-block remove;
Each to each unite, endear;
Come, and spread thy banner here.

3 Make us of one heart and mind,
Courteous, pitying, and kind,
Lowly, meek, in thought and word,
Altogether like our Lord.

4 Let us for each other care,
Each the other's burden bear;
To thy church the pattern give,
Show how true believers live.

5 Free from anger and from pride,
Let us thus in God abide;
All the depths of love express,
All the heights of holiness.
—Charles Wesley.

MAIDSTONE. 8-7s. W. B. GILBERT.

408

Christ the good Shepherd.

1 HAPPY soul, that, free from harms,
Rests within his Shepherd's arms!
Who his quiet shall molest?
Who shall violate his rest?
Jesus doth his spirit bear;
Jesus takes his every care;
He who found the wandering sheep,
Jesus, still delights to keep.

2 O that I might so believe,
Steadfastly to Jesus cleave;
On his only love rely,
Smile at the destroyer nigh;
Free from sin and servile fear,
Have my Jesus ever near;
All his care rejoice to prove,
All his paradise of love!

3 Jesus, seek thy wandering sheep;
Bring me back, and lead, and keep;
Take on thee my every care;
Bear me, on thy bosom bear;
Let me know my Shepherd's voice,
More and more in thee rejoice;
More and more of thee receive;
Ever in thy Spirit live.

4 Live, till all thy life I know,
Perfect, through my Lord, below;
Gladly then from earth remove,
Gathered to the fold above;
O that I at last may stand
With the sheep at thy right hand;
Take the crown so freely given,
Enter in by thee to heaven!

—*Charles Wesley.*

ST. BEES. 4-7s. DR. DYKES.

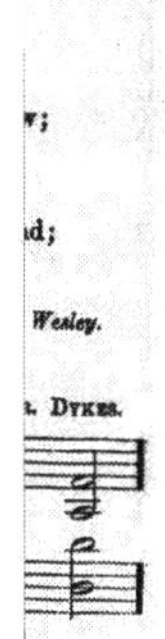

TUNE: ST. BEES. 4-7s.

409

Prayer for unity and peace.

1 Father, at thy footstool see
Those who now are one in thee;
Draw us by thy grace alone,
Give, O give us to thy Son!

2 Jesus, Friend of human kind,
Let us in thy name be joined;
Each to each unite and bless;
Keep us still in perfect peace.

3 Heavenly, all-alluring Dove,
Shed thy over-shadowing love,
Love, the sealing grace, impart;
Dwell within our single heart.

4 Father, Son, and Holy Ghost,
Be to us what Adam lost;
Let us in thine image rise,
Give us back our paradise.

—*Charles Wesley.*

410

The communion of saints.

1 Father, Son, and Spirit, hear
Faith's effectual fervent prayer;
Hear, and our petitions seal,
Let us now the answer feel.

2 Still our fellowship increase;
Knit us in the bond of peace;
Join our new-born spirits, join
Each to each, and all to thine.

3 Build us in one body up,
Called in one high calling's hope;
One the Spirit whom we claim;
One the pure baptismal flame.

4 One the faith, and common Lord;
One the Father lives adored;
Over, through, and in us all,
God incomprehensible.

—*Charles Wesley.*

MERCY. 4-7s. L. M. Gottschalk.

Slowly.

411

SECOND PART.

1 Other ground can no man lay,
Jesus takes our sins away;
Jesus the foundation is,
This shall stand, and only this;

2 Fitly framed in him we are,
All the building rises fair;
Let it to a temple rise,
Worthy him who fills the skies.

3 Husband of the church below,
Christ, if thee our Lord we know,
Unto thee, betrothed in love,
Always let us faithful prove;

4 Never rob thee of our heart,
Never give the creature part;
Only thou possess the whole;
Take our body, spirit, soul.

—*Charles Wesley.*

412

THIRD PART.

1 Christ, our Head, gone up on high,
Be thou in thy Spirit nigh;
Advocate with God, give ear
To thine own effectual prayer.

2 One the Father is with thee;
Knit us in like unity;
Make us, O uniting Son,
One as thou and he are one.

3 Still, O Lord, for thine we are,
Still to us his name declare;
Thy revealing Spirit give,
Whom the world cannot receive.

4 Fill us with the Father's love;
Never from our souls remove;
Dwell in us, and we shall be
Thine through all eternity.

—*Charles Wesley.*

AMSTERDAM. 7.6, 7.6, 7.8, 7.6. DR. NARES.

413

"Pray without ceasing."

1 COME, ye followers of the Lord,
In Jesus' service join,
Jesus gives the sacred word,
The ordinance divine;
Let us his command obey,
And ask and have whate'er we want:
Pray we, every moment pray,
And never, never faint.

2 Be it weariness and pain
To slothful flesh and blood,
Yet we will the cross sustain,
And bless the welcome load;
All our griefs to God display,
And humbly pour out our complaint:
Pray we, every moment pray,
And never, never faint.

3 Let us patiently endure,
And still our wants declare;
All the promises are sure
To persevering prayer;
Till we see the perfect day,
And each wakes up a sinless saint,
Pray we, every moment pray,
And never, never faint.

4 Pray we on when all renewed,
And perfected in love;
Till we see the Saviour God
Descending from above,
All his heavenly charms survey,
Beyond what angel minds can paint,
Pray we, every moment pray,
And never, never faint.

—*Charles Wesley.*

414

"Men ought always to pray and not faint."

1 JESUS, thou hast bid us pray,
Pray always and not faint;
With the word a power convey
To utter our complaint;
Quiet shalt thou never know,
Till we from sin are fully freed:
O avenge us of our foe,
And bruise the Serpent's head!

2 We have now begun to cry,
And we will never end,
Till we find salvation nigh,
And grasp the sinner's Friend:
Day and night we'll speak our woe,
With thee importunately plead:
O avenge us of our foe,
And bruise the Serpent's head!

3 Speak the word, and we shall be
From all our bands released;
Only thou canst set us free,
By Satan long oppressed;
Now thy power almighty show,
Arise, the Woman's conquering Seed!
O avenge us of our foe,
And bruise the Serpent's head!

4 To the never-ceasing cries
Of thine elect attend;
Send deliverance from the skies,
The mighty Spirit send;
Though to man thou seemest slow,
Our cries thou seemest not to heed,
O avenge us of our foe,
And bruise the Serpent's head!

—*Charles Wesley.*

FAITH. 7.6.7.6, 7.7.7.6. Dr. S. S. Wesley.

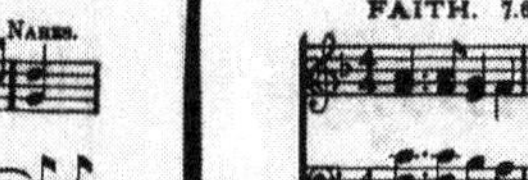

415 *Prayer for the promised Comforter.*

1 Father of our dying Lord,
Remember us for good;
O fulfil his faithful word,
And hear his speaking blood!
Give us that for which he prays;
Father, glorify thy Son!
Show his truth, and power, and grace,
And send the promise down.

2 True and faithful Witness, thou,
O Christ, thy Spirit give!
Hast thou not received him now,
That we might now receive?
Art thou not our living Head?
To thy members life impart;
Shed thy love, thy Spirit shed
In every waiting heart.

3 Holy Ghost, the Comforter,
The gift of Jesus, come;
Glows our heart to find thee near,
And swells to make thee room;
Present with us thee we feel,
Come, O come, and in us be!
With us, in us, live and dwell,
To all eternity.

—*Charles Wesley.*

RICHMOND. 7.6, 7.6, 7.8, 7.6.

416 Ezekiel xxxiv. 26, 27.

1 Us, who climb thy holy hill,
A general blessing make;
Let the world our influence feel,
Our gospel grace partake;
Grace, to help in time of need,
Pour out on sinners from above;
All thy Spirit's fulness shed,
In showers of heavenly love.

2 Make our earthly souls a field
Which God delights to bless;
Let us in due season yield
The fruits of righteousness;
Make us trees of paradise,
Which more and more thy praise may show,
Deeper sink, and higher rise,
And to perfection grow.

—*Charles Wesley.*

SALVATOR. 8.7, 8.7, 8.7, 8.7. J. P. JUDSON.

417 *Prayer for the sanctifying Spirit.*

1 COME, thou all-inspiring Spirit,
Into every longing heart!
Bought for us by Jesus' merit,
Now thy blissful self impart;
Sign our uncontested pardon;
Wash us in the atoning blood;
Make our hearts a watered garden;
Fill our spotless souls with God.

2 If thou gav'st the enlarged desire
Which for thee we ever feel,
Now our longing souls inspire,
Now our cancelled sin reveal;
Claim us for thy habitation;
Dwell within each hallowed breast;
Seal us heirs of full salvation,
Fitted for our heavenly rest.

3 Give us quietly to tarry,
Till for all thy glory meet,
Waiting, like attentive Mary,
Happy at the Saviour's feet;
Keep us from the world unspotted,
From all earthly passions free,
Wholly to thyself devoted,
Fixed to live and die for thee.

4 Wrestling on in mighty prayer,
Lord, we will not let thee go,
Till thou all thy mind declare,
All thy grace on us bestow;
Peace, the seal of sin forgiven,
Joy, and perfect love, impart,
Present, everlasting heaven,
All thou hast, and all thou art!

—*Charles Wesley.*

3.—BELIEVERS WORKING.

WAREHAM. L. M. W. KNAPP.

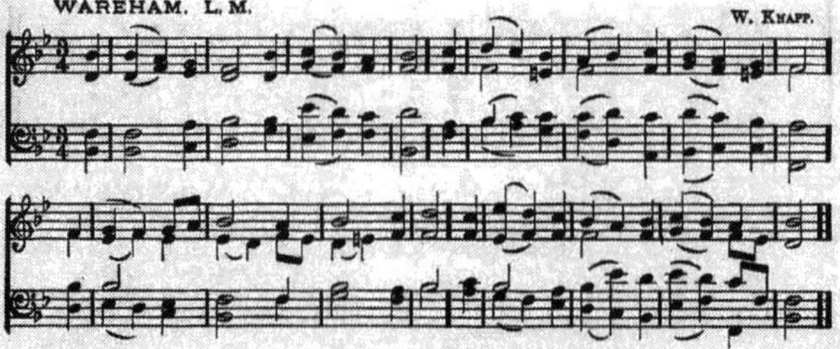

TUNE: WAREHAM. L.M.

418 *Consecration to Christ's service.*

1 O THOU who camest from above
The pure celestial fire to impart,
Kindle a flame of sacred love
On the mean altar of my heart.

2 There let it for thy glory burn
With inextinguishable blaze;
And trembling to its source return,
In humble prayer and fervent praise.

3 Jesus, confirm my heart's desire
To work, and speak, and think for thee;
Still let me guard the holy fire,
And still stir up thy gift in me.

4 Ready for all thy perfect will,
My acts of faith and love repeat,
Till death thy endless mercies seal,
And make the sacrifice complete.

—Charles Wesley.

419 *Daily consecration.*

1 FORTH in thy name, O Lord, I go,
My daily labour to pursue,
Thee, only thee, resolved to know,
In all I think, or speak, or do.

2 The task thy wisdom hath assigned,
O let me cheerfully fulfil,
In all my works thy presence find,
And prove thy acceptable will.

3 Thee may I set at my right hand,
Whose eyes my inmost substance see;
And labour on at thy command,
And offer all my works to thee.

4 Give me to bear thy easy yoke,
And every moment watch and pray,
And still to things eternal look,
And hasten to thy glorious day.

5 For thee delightfully employ
Whate'er thy bounteous grace hath given;
And run my course with even joy,
And closely walk with thee to heaven.

—Charles Wesley.

BEETHOVEN. L.M. FROM BEETHOVEN.

420 *Living to Christ.*

1 MY gracious Lord, I own thy right
To every service I can pay,
And call it my supreme delight
To hear thy counsels and obey.

2 What is my being but for thee,
Its sure support, its noblest end?
'Tis my delight thy face to see,
And serve the cause of such a Friend.

3 I would not sigh for worldly joy,
Or to increase my worldly good;
Nor future days nor powers employ
To spread a sounding name abroad.

4 To Christ my Saviour I would live,
To him who for my ransom died;
Nor could all worldly honour give
Such bliss as crowns me at his side.

5 His work my hoary age shall bless,
When youthful vigour is no more;
And my last hour of life confess
His dying love, his saving power.

—Doddridge.

ST. ALBAN. L.M. — St. Alban's Tune Book.

421 *"Go work in my vineyard."*

1 Go labour on; spend and be spent,
Thy joy to do the Father's will;
It is the way the Master went,
Should not the servant tread it still?

2 Go labour on; 'tis not for nought,
Thy earthly loss is heavenly gain;
Men heed thee, love thee, praise thee not;
The Master praises; what are men?

3 Go labour on, while it is day,
The world's dark night is hastening on;
Speed, speed thy work, cast sloth away;
It is not thus that souls are won.

4 Men die in darkness at thy side
Without a hope to cheer the tomb;
Take up the torch, and wave it wide,
The torch that lights time's thickest gloom.

5 Toil on, faint not, keep watch, and pray;
Be wise, the erring soul to win;
Go forth into the world's highway,
Compel the wanderer to come in.

6 Toil on, and in thy toil rejoice;
For toil comes rest, for exile home;
Soon shalt thou hear the Bridegroom's voice,
The midnight peal, "Behold I come!"

—*H. Bonar.*

MOZART. 6-8s. — From Mozart.

422 *"Teach me thy way, O Lord."*

1 Behold the servant of the Lord!
I wait thy guiding eye to feel,
To hear and keep thy every word,
To prove and do thy perfect will;
Joyful from my own works to cease,
Glad to fulfil all righteousness.

2 Me, if thy grace vouchsafe to use,
The least of all thy creatures, me,
The deed, the time, the manner choose,
Let all my fruit be found of thee;
Let all my works in thee be wrought,
By thee to full perfection brought.

3 Here then to thee thy own I give,
Mould as thou wilt thy passive clay;
But let me all thy stamp receive,
And let me all thy words obey;
Serve with a single heart and eye,
And to thy glory live and die.

—*Charles Wesley.*

LUCERNE. 6-8s. (2nd Metre.) GERMAN.

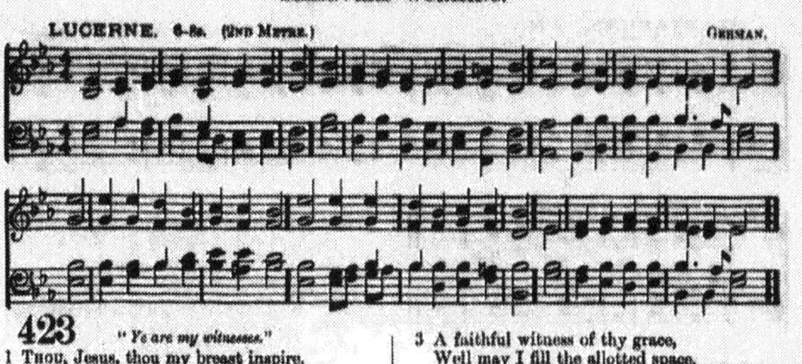

423 "Ye are my witnesses."

1 Thou, Jesus, thou my breast inspire,
And touch my lips with hallowed fire,
And loose thy stammering servant's tongue;
Prepare the vessel of thy grace,
Adorn me with the robes of praise,
And mercy shall be all my song:

2 Mercy for all who know not God,
Mercy for all in Jesus' blood,
Mercy that earth and heaven transcends;
Love, that o'erwhelms the saints in light,
The length, and breadth, and depth, and height
Of love divine, which never ends.

3 A faithful witness of thy grace,
Well may I fill the allotted space,
And answer all thy great design;
Walk in the paths by thee prepared;
And find annexed the vast reward,
The crown of righteousness divine.

4 When I have lived to thee alone,
Pronounce the welcome word, "Well done!"
And let me take my place above;
Enter into my Master's joy,
And all eternity employ,
In praise, and ecstasy, and love.

—*Charles Wesley.*

ST. MARTIN'S. C. M. TANSUR.

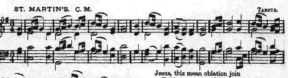

424 Renewed consecration to work.

1 Summoned my labour to renew,
And glad to act my part,
Lord, in thy name my work I do,
And with a single heart.

2 End of my every action thou,
In all things thee I see;
Accept my hallowed labour now,
I do it unto thee.

3 Whate'er the Father views as thine,
He views with gracious eyes;
Jesus, this mean oblation join
To thy great sacrifice.

4 Stamped with an infinite desert,
My work he then shall own;
Well pleased with me, when mine thou art,
And I his favoured son.

—*Charles Wesley.*

425 Christ an example of service.

1 Servant of all, to toil for man
Thou didst not, Lord, refuse;
Thy majesty did not disdain
To be employed for us.

2 Thy bright example I pursue,
To thee in all things rise;
And all I think, or speak, or do,
Is one great sacrifice.

3 Careless through outward cares I go,
From all distraction free;
My hands are but engaged below,
My heart is still with thee.

—*Charles Wesley.*

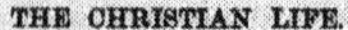

ST. STEPHEN. C. M. REV. W. JONES.

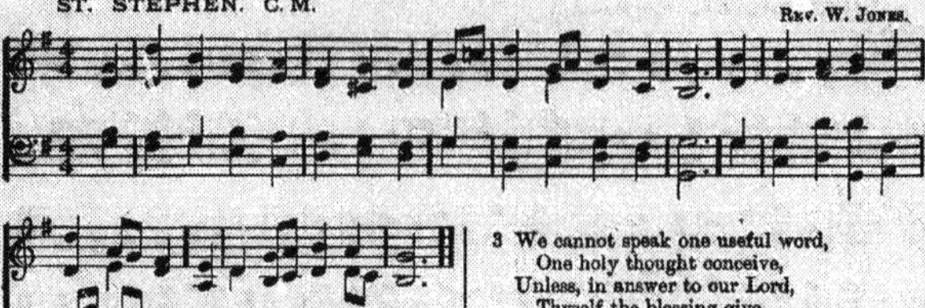

426 *"Thou hast wrought all our works in us."*

1 FATHER, to thee my soul I lift,
My soul on thee depends,
Convinced that every perfect gift
From thee alone descends.

2 Mercy and grace are thine alone,
And power and wisdom too;
Without the Spirit of thy Son
We nothing good can do.

3 We cannot speak one useful word,
One holy thought conceive,
Unless, in answer to our Lord,
Thyself the blessing give.

4 His blood demands the purchased grace;
His blood's availing plea
Obtained the help for all our race,
And sends it down to me.

5 Thou all our works in us hast wrought;
Our good is all divine;
The praise of every virtuous thought,
And righteous word, is thine.

6 From thee, through Jesus, we receive
The power on thee to call,
In whom we are, and move, and live;
Our God is all in all!

—*Charles Wesley.*

MARTYRDOM. C. M. HUGH WILSON.

427 *Bearing the cross patiently.*

1 LORD, as to thy dear cross we flee,
And pray to be forgiven,
O let thy life our pattern be,
And form our souls for heaven.

2 Help us, through good report and ill,
Our daily cross to bear;
Like thee to do our Father's will,
Our brother's griefs to share.

3 Let grace our selfishness expel,
Our earthliness refine;
And kindness in our bosoms dwell
As free and true as thine.

4 If joy shall at thy bidding fly,
And grief's dark day come on,
We, in our turn, would meekly cry,
"Father, thy will be done!"

5 Kept peaceful in the midst of strife,
Forgiving and forgiven,
O may we lead the pilgrim's life,
And follow thee to heaven!

—*J. H. Gurney.*

ST. GEORGE. S. M. — H. J. GAUNTLETT, Mus. Doc.

428 *The recompense of toil.*

1 SERVANTS of Christ, arise,
And gird you for the toil!
The dew of promise from the skies
Already cheers the soil.

2 Go where the sick recline,
Where mourning hearts deplore;
And where the sons of sorrow pine,
Dispense your hallowed store.

3 Be faith, which looks above,
With prayer, your constant guest;
And wrap the Saviour's changeless love
A mantle round your breast.

4 So shall you share the wealth
That earth may ne'er despoil,
And the blest gospel's saving health
Repay your arduous toil.

—Mrs. Sigourney.

BOYLSTON. S. M. — DR. L. MASON.

429 *"The field is the world."*

1 Sow in the morn thy seed,
At eve hold not thine hand;
To doubt and fear give thou no heed,
Broadcast it o'er the land.

2 Beside all waters sow,
The highway furrows stock,
Drop it where thorns and thistles grow,
Scatter it on the rock.

3 Thou know'st not which may thrive,
The late or early sown;
Grace keeps the precious germs alive,
When and wherever strown.

4 And duly shall appear,
In verdure, beauty, strength,
The tender blade, the stalk, the ear,
And the full corn at length.

5 Thou canst not toil in vain;
Cold, heat, and moist, and dry,
Shall foster and mature the grain
For garners in the sky.

6 Thence, when the glorious end,
The day of God, is come,
The angel-reapers shall descend,
And heaven shout "Harvest-home!"

—J. Montgomery.

ARMAGEDDON. S. M. D. DR. GAUNTLETT.

430

"Do all to the glory of God."

1 God of almighty love,
By whose sufficient grace
I lift my heart to things above,
And humbly seek thy face;
Through Jesus Christ the Just,
My faint desires receive,
And let me in thy goodness trust,
And to thy glory live.

2 Whate'er I say or do,
Thy glory be my aim;
My offerings all be offered through
The ever-blessed Name.
Jesus, my single eye
Be fixed on thee alone;
Thy name be praised on earth, on high;
Thy will by all be done.

3 Spirit of faith, inspire
My consecrated heart;
Fill me with pure, celestial fire,
With all thou hast, and art;
My feeble mind transform,
And perfectly renewed,
Into a saint exalt a worm,
A worm exalt to God!

—*Charles Wesley.*

TICHFIELD. 8-7s. R. W. BEATY.

TUNE: TICHFIELD. 8-7s.

431 *Following Christ's example.*

1 HOLY Lamb, who thee confess
Followers of thy holiness,
Thee they ever keep in view,
Ever ask, "What shall we do?"
Governed by thy only will,
All thy words we would fulfil;
Would in all thy footsteps go,
Walk as Jesus walked below.

2 While thou didst on earth appear,
Servant to thy servants here,
Mindful of thy place above,
All thy life was prayer and love.
Such our whole employment be,
Works of faith and charity;
Works of love on man bestowed,
Secret intercourse with God.

3 Early in the temple met,
Let us still our Saviour greet;
Nightly to the mount repair,
Join our praying Pattern there.
There by wrestling faith obtain
Power to work for God again,
Power his image to retrieve,
Power, like thee, our Lord, to live.

4 Vessels, instruments of grace,
Pass we thus our happy days
'Twixt the mount and multitude,
Doing or receiving good;
Glad to pray and labour on,
Till our earthly course is run,
Till, our sufferings ended, we
Bow the head and die like thee.
—Charles Wesley.

DIX. 8-7s. C. KOCHER.

432 *"Whose I am, and whom I serve."*

1 JESUS, Master, whom I serve,
Though so feebly and so ill,
Strengthen hand and heart and nerve
All thy bidding to fulfil;
Open thou mine eyes to see
All the work thou hast for me.

2 Lord, thou needest not, I know,
Service such as I can bring;
Yet I long to prove and show
Full allegiance to my King:
Thou art light and life to me,
Let me be a praise to thee.

3 Jesus, Master, wilt thou use
One who owes thee more than all?
As thou wilt, I would not choose,
Only let me hear thy call:
Jesus, let me always be
In thy service glad and free.
—Miss Havergal.

433 *Entire consecration to God's service.*

1 FATHER, Son, and Holy Ghost,
One in Three, and Three in One,
As by the celestial host,
Let thy will on earth be done;
Praise by all to thee be given,
Glorious Lord of earth and heaven!

2 Vilest of the sinful race,
Lo! I answer to thy call;
Meanest vessel of thy grace,
Grace divinely free for all,
Lo! I come to do thy will,
All thy counsel to fulfil.

3 If so poor a worm as I
May to thy great glory live,
All my actions sanctify,
All my words and thoughts receive;
Claim me for thy service, claim
All I have, and all I am.

4 Take my soul and body's powers;
Take my memory, mind, and will;
All my goods, and all my hours,
All I know, and all I feel,
All I think, or speak, or do;
Take my heart;—but make it new!

5 Now, O God, thine own I am;
Now I give thee back thine own;
Freedom, friends, and health, and fame,
Consecrate to thee alone;
Thine I live, thrice happy I,
Happier still if thine I die! *—C. Wesley.*

GOUNOD. 8.7, 8.7, 7.7. C. GOUNOD.

434 *Christ our living Head.*

1 Joined to Christ in mystic union—
We thy members, thou our Head—
Sealed by deep and true communion,
Risen with thee, who once were dead—
Saviour, we would humbly claim
All the power of this thy name.

2 Constant sympathy to brighten
All their weakness and their woe,
Guiding grace their way to lighten
Shall thy loving members know;
All their sorrows thou dost bear,
All thy gladness they shall share.

3 Make thy members every hour
For thy blessèd service meet;
Earnest tongues, and arms of power,
Skilful hands, and willing feet,
Ever ready to fulfil
All thy word and all thy will.

4 Everlasting life thou givest,
Everlasting love to see;
They shall live because thou livest,
And their life is hid with thee.
Safe thy members shall be found,
When their glorious Head is crowned.

—*Miss Havergal.*

GILEAD. 7.6.7.6, 7.8.7.6.

Fine.
D.S.

TUNE: GILEAD. 7.6.7.6, 7.8.7.6.

435 *"I delight to do thy will, O God."*

1 Lo! I come with joy to do
The Master's blessèd will;
Him in outward works pursue,
And serve his pleasure still.
Faithful to my Lord's commands,
I still would choose the better part;
Serve with careful Martha's hands,
And loving Mary's heart.

2 Careful without care I am,
Nor feel my happy toil,
Kept in peace by Jesus' name,
Supported by his smile;
Joyful thus my faith to show,
I find his service my reward;
Every work I do below,
I do it to the Lord.

3 Thou, O Lord, in tender love,
Dost all my burdens bear;
Lift my heart to things above,
And fix it ever there.
Calm on tumult's wheel I sit,
'Midst busy multitudes alone,
Sweetly waiting at thy feet,
Till all thy will be done.

4 Thou, O Lord, my portion art,
Before I hence remove;
Now my treasure and my heart
Are all laid up above;
Far above all earthly things,
While yet my hands are here employed,
Sees my soul the King of kings,
And freely talks with God.

5 O that all the art might know
Of living thus to thee!
Find their heaven begun below,
And here thy glory see;
Walk in all the works prepared
By thee to exercise their grace,
Till they gain their full reward,
And see thy glorious face.

—*Charles Wesley.*

AUTUMN. 8.7, 8.7, 8.7, 8.7. SPANISH MELODY. FROM MARECHIO.

Fine.
D.S.

436 *The Master calling.*

1 Hark, the voice of Jesus calling,
"Who will go and work to-day?
Fields are white, and harvests waiting,
Who will bear the sheaves away?"
Loud and long the Master calleth,
Rich reward he offers free;
Who will answer, gladly saying,
"Here am I, O Lord, send me"?

2 Let none hear you idly saying,
"There is nothing I can do,"
While the souls of men are dying,
And the Master calls for you;
Take the task he gives you gladly;
Let his work your pleasure be;
Answer quickly when he calleth,
"Here am I, O Lord, send me."

—*D. March.*

CORNELL. 8.7, 8.7. J. H. CORNELL.

437 *Now and afterward.*

1 Now, the sowing and the weeping,
Working hard, and waiting long;
Afterward, the golden reaping,
Harvest-home and grateful song.

2 Now, the long and toilsome duty,
Stone by stone to carve and bring;
Afterward, the perfect beauty
Of the palace of the King.

3 Now, the spirit conflict-riven,
Wounded heart, and painful strife;
Afterward, the triumph given,
And the victor's crown of life.

4 Now, the training, hard and lowly,
Weary feet and aching brow;
Afterward, the service holy,
And the Master's "Enter thou!"

—*Miss Havergal.*

THE PILGRIM'S MISSION. P. M. PHILIP PHILLIPS.

THE PILGRIM'S MISSION. *(Continued.)*

Rit.
CHORUS.
Then work, brothers, work, let us slum - ber no long - er, For God's call to
la - bour grows stronger and stronger; The light of this life shall be
Rit.
darkened full soon, But the light of the bet - ter life resteth at noon.

438

A call to labour.

1 Listen! the Master beseecheth,
Calling each one by his name;
His voice to each loving heart reacheth,
Its cheerfullest service to claim.
Go where the vineyard demandeth
Vinedressers' nurture and care;
Or go where the white harvest standeth,
The joy of the reaper to share.—Cho.

2 Seek those of evil behaviour,
Bid them their lives to amend;
Go, point the lost world to the Saviour,
And be to the friendless a friend.
Still be the lone heart of anguish,
Soothed by the pity of thine;
By waysides, if wounded ones languish,
Go, pour in the oil and the wine.—Cho.

3 Work for the good that is nighest,
Dream not of greatness afar;
That glory is ever the highest
Which shines upon men as they are.
Work, though the world may defeat you,
Heed not its slander and scorn;
Nor weary till angels shall greet you
With smiles through the gates of the morn.
—Cho.

4 Offer thy life on the altar,
In the high purpose be strong;
And if the tired spirit should falter,
Then sweeten thy labour with song.
What if the poor heart complaineth,
Soon shall its wailing be o'er;
For there, in the rest that remaineth,
It shall grieve and be weary no more.—Cho.

—*W. M. Punshon.*

MERIBAH. 8.8.6, 8.8.6. Dr. Mason.

439

Working and witnessing.

1 Except the Lord conduct the plan,
The best concerted schemes are vain,
And never can succeed;
We spend our wretched strength for nought;
But if our works in thee be wrought,
They shall be blest indeed.

2 Lord, if thou didst thyself inspire
Our souls with this intense desire
Thy goodness to proclaim,
Thy glory if we now intend,
O let our deed begin and end
Complete in Jesus' name!

3 Not in the tombs we pine to dwell,
Not in the dark monastic cell,
By vows and grates confined;
Freely to all ourselves we give,
Constrained by Jesus' love to live
The servants of mankind.

4 Now, Jesus, now thy love impart,
To govern each devoted heart,
And fit us for thy will;
Deep founded in the truth of grace,
Build up thy rising church, and place
The city on the hill.

5 O let our faith and love abound!
O let our lives to all around
With purest lustre shine!
That all the world our works may see
And give the glory, Lord, to thee,
The heavenly Light Divine.

—*Charles Wesley.*

EXCELSIOR. 5.5.5.11. D. Samuel Webbe.

TUNE: EXCELSIOR. 5.5.5.11. D.

440 *The relief of want and suffering.*

1 Come, let us arise,
And press to the skies;
The summons obey,
My friends, my beloved, and hasten away.
The Master of all
For our service doth call,
And deigns to approve,
With smiles of acceptance, our labour of love.

2 His burden who bear,
We alone can declare
How easy his yoke,
While to love and good works we each other provoke;
By word and by deed,
The bodies in need,
The souls to relieve,
And freely as Jesus hath given to give.

3 Then let us attend
Our heavenly Friend,
In his members distrest,
By want, or affliction, or sickness opprest:
The prisoner relieve,
The stranger receive;
Supply all their wants,
And spend and be spent in assisting his saints.

4 Thus while we bestow
Our moments below,
Ourselves we forsake
And refuge in Jesus's righteousness take.
His passion alone
The foundation we own;
And pardon we claim,
And eternal redemption, in Jesus's name.

—*Charles Wesley.*

4.—BELIEVERS WATCHING.

BOYLSTON. S. M. Dr. L. Mason.

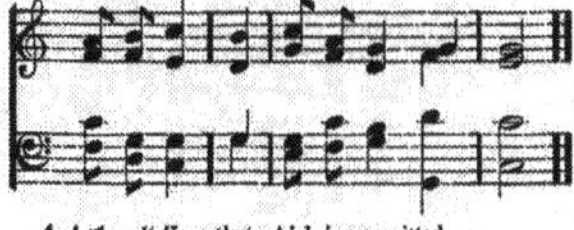

441 *"Keep that which is committed to thy trust."*

1 A charge to keep I have,
A God to glorify,
A never-dying soul to save,
And fit it for the sky:

2 To serve the present age,
My calling to fulfil;
O may it all my powers engage
To do my Master's will!

3 Arm me with jealous care,
As in thy sight to live;
And O, thy servant, Lord, prepare
A strict account to give!

4 Help me to watch and pray,
And on thyself rely;
Assured, if I my trust betray,
I shall forever die.

—*Charles Wesley.*

ARMAGEDDON. S. M. D.

DR. GAUNTLETT.

442 *"Could ye not watch with me one hour?"*

1 GRACIOUS Redeemer, shake
This slumber from my soul!
Say to me now, "Awake, awake!
And Christ shall make thee whole."
Lay to thy mighty hand,
Alarm me in this hour;
And make me fully understand
The thunder of thy power.

2 Give me on thee to call,
Always to watch and pray,
Lest I into temptation fall,
And cast my shield away.
For each assault prepared
And ready may I be,
Forever standing on my guard,
And looking up to thee.

3 O do thou always warn
My soul of danger near!
When to the right or left I turn,
Thy voice still let me hear:
"Come back, this is the way!
Come back, and walk herein!"
O may I hearken and obey,
And shun the paths of sin!

4 Myself I cannot save,
Myself I cannot keep;
But strength in thee I surely have,
Whose eyelids never sleep:
My soul to thee alone
Now therefore I commend;
Thou, Jesus, love me as thy own,
And love me to the end.

—*Charles Wesley.*

443 *"Watch unto prayer."*

1 BID me of men beware,
And to my ways take heed;
Discern their every secret snare,
And circumspectly tread.
O may I calmly wait
Thy succours from above;
And stand against their open hate
And well-dissembled love!

2 But, above all, afraid
Of my own bosom-foe,
Still let me seek to thee for aid,
To thee my weakness show;
Hang on thine arm alone,
With self-distrusting care,
And deeply in the spirit groan
The never-ceasing prayer.

3 Give me a sober mind,
A quick-discerning eye,
The first approach of sin to find,
And all occasions fly.
Still may I cleave to thee,
And never more depart,
But watch with godly jealousy
Over my evil heart.

4 Thus may I pass my days
Of sojourning beneath,
And languish to conclude my race,
And render up my breath;
In humble love and fear,
Thine image to regain,
And see thee in the clouds appear,
And rise with thee to reign.

—*Charles Wesley.*

IRISH. C. M. — ARRANGED FROM ISAAC SMITH.

444 *Prayer for a tender conscience.*

1 I WANT a principle within
Of jealous, godly fear,
A sensibility of sin,
A pain to feel it near.

2 I want the first approach to feel
Of pride, or fond desire,
To catch the wandering of my will,
And quench the kindling fire.

3 That I from thee no more may part,
No more thy goodness grieve,
The filial awe, the contrite heart,
The tender conscience give.

4 If to the right or left I stray,
That moment, Lord, reprove,
And let me weep my life away,
For having grieved thy love.

5 Quick as the apple of an eye,
O God, my conscience make!
Awake my soul, when sin is nigh,
And keep it still awake.

6 O may the least omission pain
My well-instructed soul,
And drive me to the blood again,
Which makes the wounded whole!

—Charles Wesley.

ABRIDGE. C. M. — ISAAC SMITH.

445 *On returning home.*

1 THOU, Lord, hast blest my going out;
O bless my coming in!
Compass my weakness round about,
And keep me safe from sin.

2 Still hide me in thy secret place,
Thy tabernacle spread;
Shelter me with preserving grace
And screen my naked head.

3 To thee for refuge may I run
From sin's alluring snare;
Ready its first approach to shun,
And watching unto prayer.

4 O that I never, never more
Might from thy ways depart!
Here let me give my wanderings o'er,
By giving thee my heart.

5 Fix my new heart on things above,
And then from earth release;
I ask not life, but let me love,
And lay me down in peace.

—Charles Wesley.

ST. ANN'S. C. M. DR. CROFT.

446

Prayer for filial fear.

1 God of all grace and majesty,
Supremely great and good!
If I have mercy found with thee,
Through the atoning blood;

2 The guard of all thy mercies give,
And to my pardon join
A fear lest I should ever grieve
The gracious Spirit Divine.

3 Rather I would, in painful awe,
Beneath thine anger move,
Than sin against the gospel law
Of liberty and love.

4 But, O thou wouldst not have me live
In bondage, grief, or pain;
Thou dost not take delight to grieve
The helpless sons of men.

5 Thy will is my salvation, Lord;
O let it now take place!
And let me tremble at the word
Of reconciling grace.

6 Still may I walk as in thy sight,
My strict Observer see;
And thou by reverent love unite,
My child-like heart to thee.

7 Still let me, till my days are past,
At Jesus' feet abide;
So shall he lift me up at last,
And seat me by his side.

—*Charles Wesley.*

ST. PETERSBURG. 6-8s. DIMITRI S. BORTNIANSKY.

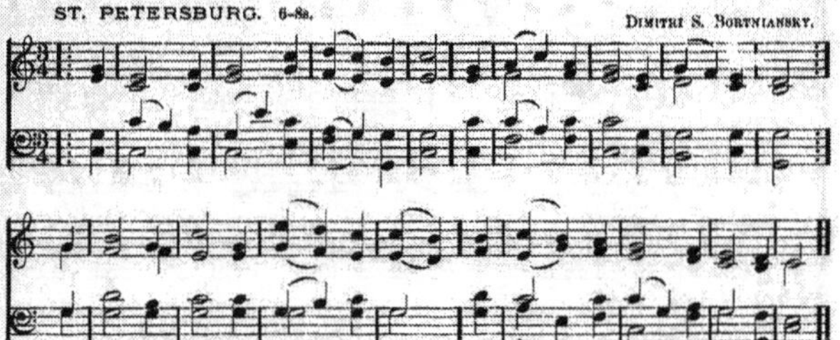

447

Christians under the eye of the world.

1 Watched by the world's malignant eye,
Who load us with reproach and shame,
As servants of the Lord Most High,
As zealous for his glorious name,
We ought in all his paths to move,
With holy fear and humble love.

2 That wisdom, Lord, on us bestow,
From every evil to depart;
To stop the mouth of every foe,
While, upright both in life and heart,
The proofs of godly fear we give,
And show them how the Christians live.

—*Charles Wesley.*

TUNE: ST. PETERSBURG. 6-8s. (SEE HYMN 447.)

448

The humble, watchful spirit.

1 FATHER, to thee I lift mine eyes,
  My longing eyes, and restless heart;
Before the morning watch I rise,
  And wait to taste how good thou art,
To obtain the grace I humbly claim,
The saving power of Jesus' name.

2 This slumber from my soul, O shake!
  Warn by thy Spirit's inward call;
Let me to righteousness awake,
  And pray that I no more may fall,
Or give to sin or Satan place,
But walk in all thy righteous ways.

3 O wouldst thou, Lord, thy servant guard,
  Against each known or secret foe!
A mind for all assaults prepared,
  A sober, vigilant mind bestow,
Ever apprized of danger nigh,
And when to fight, and when to fly.

4 O never suffer me to sleep
  Secure upon the verge of hell!
But still my watchful spirit keep
  In lowly awe and loving zeal;
And bless me with a godly fear,
And plant that guardian-angel here.

5 Attended by the sacred dread,
  And wise from evil to depart,
Let me from strength to strength proceed,
  And rise to purity of heart;
Through all the paths of duty move,
From humble faith to perfect love.

—*Charles Wesley.*

HARWOOD. 8.8.6, 8.8.6. HARWOOD.

449

Watching against sin.

1 BE it my only wisdom here,
To serve the Lord with filial fear,
    With loving gratitude;
Superior sense may I display,
By shunning every evil way,
    And walking in the good.

2 O may I still from sin depart!
A wise and understanding heart,
    Jesus, to me be given;
And let me through thy Spirit know,
To glorify my God below,
    And find my way to heaven.

—*Charles Wesley.*

450

"Lord, save, or I perish."

1 HELP, Lord, to whom for help I fly,
And still my tempted soul stand by
    Throughout the evil day;
The sacred watchfulness impart,
And keep the issues of my heart,
    And stir me up to pray.

2 My soul with thy whole armour arm;
In each approach of sin alarm,
    And show the danger near;
Surround, sustain, and strengthen me,
And fill with godly jealousy,
    And sanctifying fear.

3 Whene'er my careless hands hang down,
O let me see thy gathering frown,
    And feel thy warning eye;
And starting cry, from ruin's brink,
Save, Jesus, or I yield, I sink,
    O save me, or I die!

4 If near the pit I rashly stray,
Before I wholly fa'l away,
    The keen conviction dart!
Recall me by that pitying look,
That kind, upbraiding glance, which broke
    Unfaithful Peter's heart.

5 In me thine utmost mercy show,
And make me like thyself below,
    Unblamable in grace;
Ready prepared, and fitted here,
By perfect holiness to appear
    Before thy glorious face.—*C. Wesley.*

WARD. L. M. Dr. L. Mason.

Slowly.

451 *Watching against falling from grace.*

1 Ah! Lord, with trembling I confess,
A gracious soul may fall from grace;
The salt may lose its seasoning power,
And never, never find it more.

2 Lest that my fearful case should be,
Each moment knit my soul to thee;
And lead me to the mount above,
Through the low vale of humble love.

—*Charles Wesley.*

CRASSELIUS. L. M. Crasselius.

452 *"My grace is sufficient for thee."*

1 Jesus, my Saviour, Brother, Friend,
On whom I cast my every care,
On whom for all things I depend,
Inspire, and then accept, my prayer.

2 If I have tasted of thy grace,
The grace that sure salvation brings,
If with me now thy Spirit stays,
And hovering hides me in his wings,

3 Still let him with my weakness stay,
Nor for a moment's space depart,
Evil and danger turn away,
And keep till he renews my heart.

4 When to the right or left I stray,
His voice behind me may I hear,
"Return, and walk in Christ thy way;
Fly back to Christ; for sin is near."

5 His sacred unction from above
Be still my comforter and guide;
Till all the hardness he remove,
And in my loving heart reside.

6 Jesus, I fain would walk in thee,
From nature's every path retreat;
Thou art my Way, my Leader be,
And set upon the rock my feet.

7 Uphold me, Saviour, or I fall,
O reach me out thy gracious hand!
Only on thee for help I call,
Only by faith in thee I stand.

—*Charles Wesley.*

TUNE: WARD. L. M. (See Hymn 451.)

453 *"Let the fear of the Lord be upon you."*

1 Lord, fill me with an humble fear;
My utter helplessness reveal!
Satan and sin are always near,
Thee may I always nearer feel.

2 O that to thee my constant mind
Might with an even flame aspire,
Pride in its earliest motions find,
And mark the risings of desire!

3 O that my tender soul might fly
The first abhorred approach of ill,
Quick as the apple of an eye,
The slightest touch of sin to feel!

4 Till thou anew my soul create,
Still may I strive, and watch, and pray,
Humbly and confidently wait,
And long to see the perfect day.

—*Charles Wesley.*

5.—CONFLICT AND SUFFERING.

ARMAGEDDON. S. M. D. Dr. Gauntlett.

454 *"A good soldier of Jesus Christ."*

1 Soldiers of Christ, arise,
And put your armour on;
Strong in the strength which God supplies
Through his eternal Son;
Strong in the Lord of Hosts,
And in his mighty power,
Who in the strength of Jesus trusts,
Is more than conqueror.

2 Stand then in his great might,
With all his strength endued;
But take to arm you for the fight,
The panoply of God;
That having all things done,
And all your conflicts passed,
Ye may o'ercome, through Christ alone,
And stand entire at last.

3 Stand then against your foes,
In close and firm array;
Legions of wily fiends oppose
Throughout the evil day;
But meet the sons of night,
But mock their vain design,
Armed in the arms of heavenly light,
Of righteousness divine.

4 Leave no unguarded place,
No weakness of the soul;
Take every virtue, every grace,
And fortify the whole;
Indissolubly joined,
To battle all proceed;
But arm yourselves with all the mind
That was in Christ, your Head.

—*Charles Wesley.*

AURELIA. S. M. D. Dr. S. S. Wesley.

455

SECOND PART.

1 But, above all, lay hold
On faith's victorious shield;
Armed with that adamant and gold,
Be sure to win the field;
If faith surround your heart,
Satan shall be subdued;
Repelled his every fiery dart,
And quenched with Jesus' blood.

2 Jesus hath died for you!
What can his love withstand?
Believe, hold fast, your shield, and who
Shall pluck you from his hand?
Believe that Jesus reigns;
All power to him is given;
Believe, till freed from sin's remains;
Believe yourselves to heaven!

3 To keep your armour bright,
Attend with constant care,
Still walking in your Captain's sight,
And watching unto prayer.
Ready for all alarms,
Steadfastly set your face,
And always exercise your arms,
And use your every grace.

4 Pray, without ceasing, pray;
Your Captain gives the word;
His summons cheerfully obey,
And call upon the Lord;
To God your every want
In instant prayer display;
Pray always; pray, and never faint;
Pray, without ceasing, pray!

—Charles Wesley.

456

THIRD PART.

1 In fellowship, alone,
To God with faith draw near;
Approach his courts, besiege his throne
With all the powers of prayer;
Go to his temple, go,
Nor from his altar move;
Let every house his worship know,
And every heart his love.

2 To God your spirits dart;
Your souls in words declare;
Or groan, to him who reads the heart,
The unutterable prayer;
His mercy now implore,
And now show forth his praise;
In shouts, or silent awe, adore
His miracles of grace.

3 Pour out your souls to God,
And bow them with your knees;
And spread your heart and hands abroad,
And pray for Sion's peace;
Your guides and brethren bear
Forever on your mind;
Extend the arms of mighty prayer,
In grasping all mankind.

4 From strength to strength go on,
Wrestle, and fight, and pray;
Tread all the powers of darkness down,
And win the well-fought day;
Still let the Spirit cry
In all his soldiers, "Come;"
Till Christ the Lord descend from high,
And take the conquerors home.

—Charles Wesley.

VICTORY. S. M. D.

457 *The Christian soldier's prayer.*

1 EQUIP me for the war,
And teach my hands to fight;
My simple, upright heart prepare,
And guide my words aright;
Control my every thought;
My whole of sin remove;
Let all my works in thee be wrought,
Let all be wrought in love.

2 O arm me with the mind,
Meek Lamb! which was in thee;
And let my knowing zeal be joined
With perfect charity;
With calm and tempered zeal
Let me enforce thy call;
And vindicate thy gracious will,
Which offers life to all.

3 O do not let me trust
In any arm but thine!
Humble, O humble to the dust,
This stubborn soul of mine!
A feeble thing of nought,
With lowly shame I own,
The help which upon earth is wrought,
Thou dost it all alone.

4 O may I love like thee!
In all thy footsteps tread;
Thou hatest all iniquity,
But nothing thou hast made.
O may I learn the art,
With meekness to reprove;
To hate the sin with all my heart,
But still the sinner love.

—*Charles Wesley.*

458 *The Captain of our salvation.*

1 JESUS, the Conqueror reigns,
In glorious strength arrayed;
His kingdom over all maintains,
And bids the earth be glad.
Ye sons of men, rejoice
In Jesus' mighty love;
Lift up your heart, lift up your voice,
To him who rules above.

2 Extol his kingly power;
Kiss the exalted Son,
Who died, and lives, to die no more,
High on his Father's throne;
Our Advocate with God,
He undertakes our cause;
And spreads through all the earth abroad
The victory of his cross.

3 That bloody banner see,
And, in your Captain's sight,
Fight the good fight of faith with me,
My fellow-soldiers, fight!
In mighty phalanx joined,
To battle all proceed;
Armed with the unconquerable mind
Which was in Christ, your Head.

—*Charles Wesley.*

THATCHER. S. M. D. HANDEL.

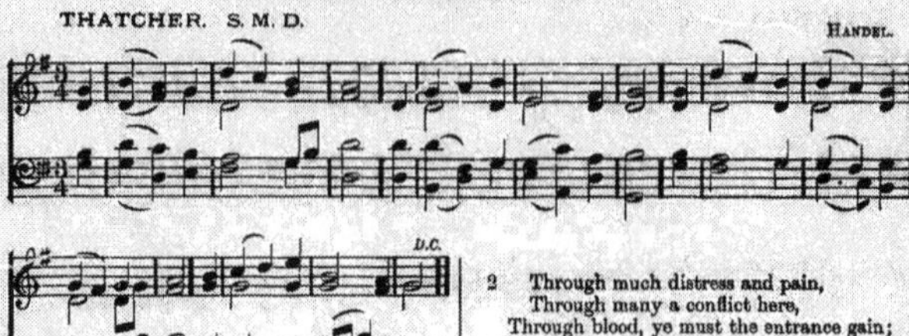
D.C.

459

SECOND PART.

1 URGE on your rapid course,
Ye blood-besprinkled bands;
The heavenly kingdom suffers force;
'Tis seized by violent hands;
See there the starry crown
That glitters in the skies!
Satan, the world, and sin tread down,
And take the glorious prize!

2 Through much distress and pain,
Through many a conflict here,
Through blood, ye must the entrance gain;
Yet, O disdain to fear!
"Courage," your Captain cries,
Who all your toil foreknew;
"Toil ye shall have; yet all despise.
I have o'ercome for you."

3 The world cannot withstand
Its ancient Conqueror;
The world must sink beneath the hand
Which arms us for the war:
This is our victory!
Before our faith they fall;
Jesus hath died for you and me;
Believe, and conquer all.

—*Charles Wesley.*

ST. GEORGE. S. M. H. J. GAUNTLETT, Mus. Doc.

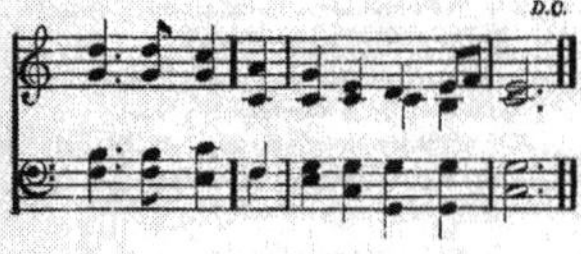
D.C.

460

Conflict with spiritual foes.

1 HARK, how the watchmen cry,
Attend the trumpet's sound!
Stand to your arms, the foe is nigh,
The powers of hell surround:
Who bow to Christ's command,
Your arms and hearts prepare;
The day of battle is at hand!
Go forth to glorious war!

2 See, in the mountain-top,
The standard of your God!
In Jesus' name I lift it up,
All stained with hallowed blood.
His standard-bearer, I
To all the nations call;
Let all to Jesus' cross draw nigh!
He bore the cross for all.

3 Go up with Christ, your Head;
Your Captain's footsteps see;
Follow your Captain, and be led
To certain victory.
All power to him is given;
He ever reigns the same;
Salvation, happiness, and heaven
Are all in Jesus' name.

—*Charles Wesley.*

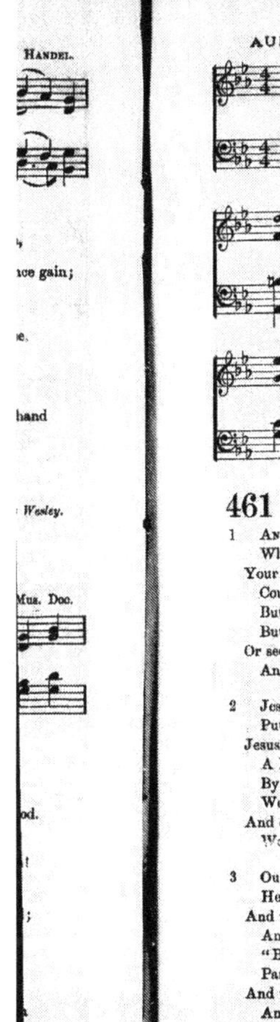

AURELIA. S. M. D. — DR. S. S. WESLEY.

461

SECOND PART.

1 ANGELS your march oppose,
Who still in strength excel,
Your secret, sworn, eternal foes,
Countless, invisible:
But shall believers fear?
But shall believers fly?
Or see the bloody cross appear,
And all their powers defy?

2 Jesus' tremendous name
Puts all our foes to flight;
Jesus, the meek, the angry Lamb,
A Lion is in fight.
By all hell's host withstood,
We all hell's host o'erthrow;
And conquering them, through Jesus' blood,
We still to conquer go.

3 Our Captain leads us on;
He beckons from the skies,
And reaches out a starry crown,
And bids us take the prize:
"Be faithful unto death;
Partake my victory;
And thou shalt wear this glorious wreath,
And thou shalt reign with me."

—*Charles Wesley.*

462

"As the mountains are round about Jerusalem, so the Lord is round about his people."

1 WHO in the Lord confide,
And feel his sprinkled blood,
In storms and hurricanes abide,
Firm as the mount of God;
Steadfast, and fixed, and sure,
His Zion cannot move;
His faithful people stand secure
In Jesus' guardian love.

2 As round Jerusalem
The hilly bulwarks rise,
So God protects and covers them
From all their enemies.
On every side he stands,
And for his Israel cares;
And safe in his almighty hands
Their souls forever bears.

3 But let them still abide
In thee, all-gracious Lord,
Till every soul is sanctified,
And perfectly restored;
The men of heart sincere
Continue to defend;
And do them good, and save them here,
And love them to the end.

—*Charles Wesley.*

NEARER HOME. S. M. D. — Isaac Woodbury.

463

2 Tim. iv. 7.

1 "I the good fight have fought,"
O when shall I declare!
The victory by my Saviour got,
I long with Paul to share.
O may I triumph so,
When all my warfare's past;
And, dying, find my latest foe
Under my feet at last!

2 This blessed word be mine
Just as the port is gained,
"Kept by the power of grace divine,
I have the faith maintained."
The Apostles of my Lord,
To whom it first was given,
They could not speak a greater word,
Nor all the saints in heaven.

—*Charles Wesley.*

LUTHER'S HYMN. 6-8s. — Martin Luther.

TUNE: LUTHER'S HYMN. 6-8s.

464

"Though an host should encamp against me, my heart shall not fear."

1 Surrounded by a host of foes,
Stormed by a host of foes within,
Nor swift to flee, nor strong to oppose,
Single against hell, earth, and sin,
Single, yet undismayed, I am;
‖:I dare believe in Jesus' name.:‖

2 What though a thousand hosts engage,
A thousand worlds, my soul to shake?
I have a shield shall quell their rage,
And drive the alien armies back;
Portrayed it bears a bleeding Lamb;
‖:I dare believe in Jesus' name.:‖

3 Me to retrieve from Satan's hands,
Me from this evil world to free,
To purge my sins, and loose my bands,
And save from all iniquity,
My Lord and God from heaven he came;
‖:I dare believe in Jesus' name.:‖

4 Salvation in his name there is;
Salvation from sin, death, and hell;
Salvation into glorious bliss;
How great salvation, who can tell?
But all he hath for mine I claim;
‖:I dare believe in Jesus' name.:‖

—*Charles Wesley.*

RALEIGH. 6-8s. W. S. Gilbert.

465

Deliverance from trouble.

1 Jesus, to thee our hearts we lift,
(May all our hearts with love o'erflow!)
With thanks for thy continued gift,
That still thy precious name we know,
Retain our sense of sin forgiven,
And wait for all our inward heaven.

2 What mighty troubles hast thou shown
Thy feeble, tempted followers here!
We have through fire and water gone,
But saw thee on the floods appear,
But felt thee present in the flame,
And shouted our Deliverer's name.

3 Thou who hast kept us to this hour,
O keep us faithful to the end!
When, robed with majesty and power,
Our Jesus shall from heaven descend,
His friends and witnesses to own,
And seat us on his glorious throne.

—*Charles Wesley.*

466

"Be thou faithful unto death."

1 Thou, Lord, on whom I still depend,
Shalt keep me faithful to the end;
I trust thy truth, and love, and power,
Shall save me to the latest hour;
And when I lay this body down,
Reward with an immortal crown.

2 Jesus, in thy great name I go
To conquer death, my final foe!
And when I quit this cumbrous clay,
And soar on angels' wings away,
My soul the second death defies,
And reigns eternal in the skies.

3 Eye hath not seen, nor ear hath heard,
What Christ hath for his saints prepared,
Who conquer through their Saviour's might,
Who sink into perfection's height,
And trample death beneath their feet,
And gladly die their Lord to meet.

4 Dost thou desire to know and see,
What thy mysterious name shall be?
Contending for thy heavenly home,
Thy latest foe in death o'ercome;
Till then thou searchest out in vain,
What only conquest can explain.

—*Charles Wesley.*

WORCESTER. L. M.

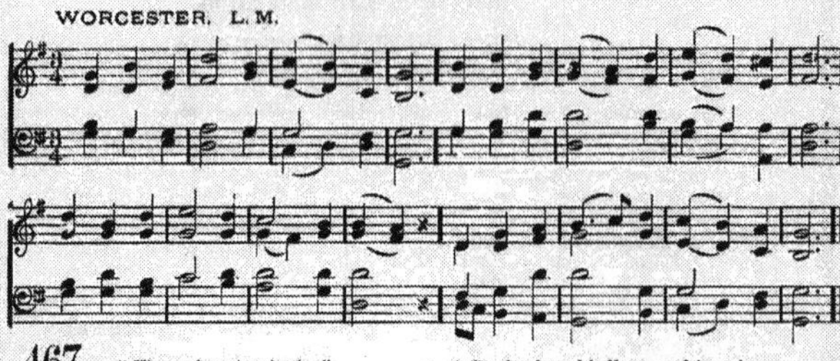

467 *"His arm brought salvation."*

1 Arm of the Lord, awake, awake!
Thine own immortal strength put on!
With terror clothed, hell's kingdom shake,
And cast thy foes with fury down!

2 As in the ancient days appear;
The sacred annals speak thy fame;
Be now omnipotently near,
To endless ages still the same.

3 Thine arm, Lord, is not shortened now;
It wants not now the power to save;
Still present with thy people, thou
Bear'st them through life's disparted wave.

4 By death and hell pursued in vain,
To thee the ransomed seed shall come;
Shouting, their heavenly Zion gain,
And pass through death triumphant home.

5 The pain of life shall there be o'er,
The anguish and distracting care;
There sighing grief shall weep no more,
And sin shall never enter there.

6 Where pure, essential joy is found,
The Lord's redeemed their heads shall raise,
With everlasting gladness crowned,
And filled with love, and lost in praise.

—*Charles Wesley.*

GERMANY. L. M. BEETHOVEN.

468 Psalm xlvi.

1 God is the refuge of his saints,
When storms of sharp distress invade;
Ere we can offer our complaints,
Behold him present with his aid!

2 Let mountains from their seats be hurled
Down to the deep, and buried there,
Convulsions shake the solid world,
Our faith shall never yield to fear.

3 Loud may the troubled ocean roar;
In sacred peace our souls abide;
While every nation, every shore,
Trembles, and dreads the swelling tide.

4 There is a stream whose gentle flow
Supplies the city of our God;
Life, love, and joy still gliding through,
And watering our divine abode.

5 That sacred stream, thy living word,
Thus all our anxious fear controls;
Sweet peace thy promises afford,
And give new strength to fainting souls.

6 Zion enjoys her Monarch's love,
Secure against the threatening hour;
Nor can her firm foundation move,
Built on his faithfulness and power.

—*Isaac Watts.*

ST. CRISPIN. L. M. — SIR G. J. ELVEY.

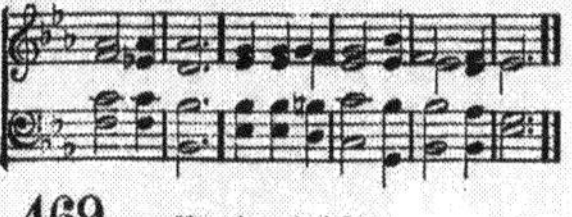

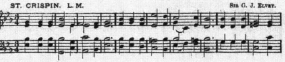

469 *Not ashamed of Jesus.*

1 JESUS, and shall it ever be,
A mortal man ashamed of thee!
Ashamed of thee, whom angels praise,
Whose glories shine through endless days!

2 Ashamed of Jesus! sooner far
Let evening blush to own a star;
He sheds the beams of light divine
O'er this benighted soul of mine.

3 Ashamed of Jesus! just as soon
Let midnight be ashamed of noon;
'Tis midnight with my soul till he,
Bright Morning Star, bid darkness flee.

4 Ashamed of Jesus! that dear Friend
On whom my hopes of heaven depend!
No; when I blush, be this my shame,
That I no more revere his name.

5 Ashamed of Jesus! yes, I may,
When I've no guilt to wash away;
No tear to wipe, no good to crave,
No fears to quell, no soul to save.

6 Till then—nor is my boasting vain—
Till then, I boast a Saviour slain;
And oh! may this my glory be,
That Christ is not ashamed of me!

—*Joseph Grigg.*

HOLY CROSS. C. M. — ARTHUR HENRY BROWN.

Slowly.

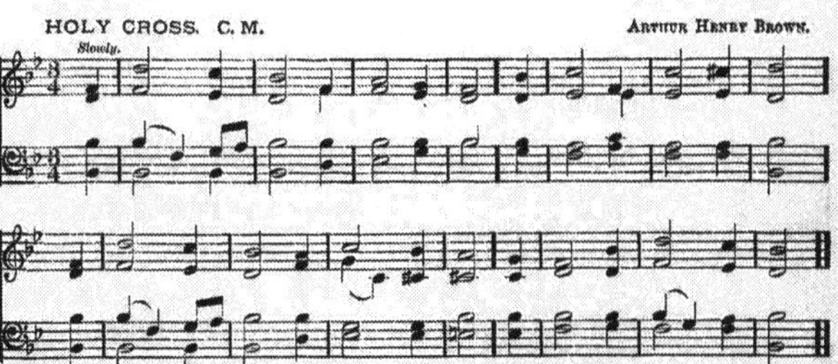

470 *Prayer for victorious faith.*

1 O FOR a faith that will not shrink,
Though pressed by every foe!
That will not tremble on the brink
Of any earthly woe;

2 That will not murmur or complain
Beneath the chastening rod,
But, in the hour of grief or pain,
Will lean upon its God:

3 A faith that shines more bright and clear
When tempests rage without;
That when in danger knows no fear,
In darkness feels no doubt:

4 That bears, unmoved, the world's dread frown,
Nor heeds its scornful smile;
That seas of trouble cannot drown,
Or Satan's arts beguile:

5 A faith that keeps the narrow way
Till life's last hour is fled,
And with a pure and heavenly ray
Illumes a dying bed.

6 Lord, give us such a faith as this,
And then, whate'er may come,
We'll taste, while here, the hallowed bliss
Of an eternal home.

—*W. H. Bathurst.*

EVANGELIST. C. M. FROM MENDELSSOHN.

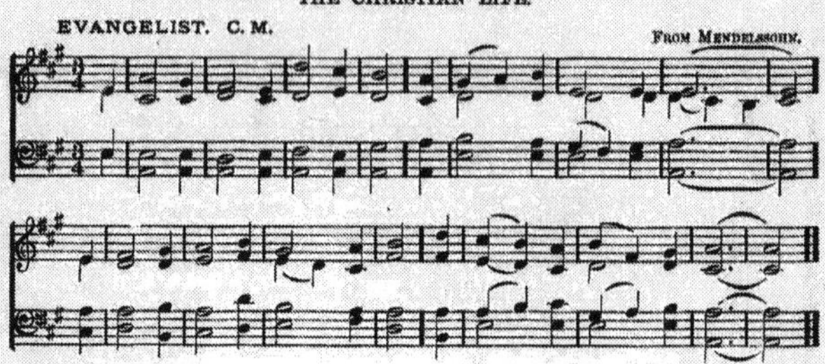

471 *"I know whom I have believed."*

1 I'M not ashamed to own my Lord,
Or to defend his cause,
Maintain the honour of his word,
The glory of his cross.

2 Jesus, my God! I know his name;
His name is all my trust;
Nor will he put my soul to shame,
Nor let my hope be lost.

3 Firm as his throne his promise stands,
And he can well secure
What I've committed to his hands,
Till the decisive hour.

4 Then will he own my worthless name
Before his Father's face;
And in the new Jerusalem
Appoint my soul a place.

—*Isaac Watts.*

ARLINGTON. C. M. ARNE.

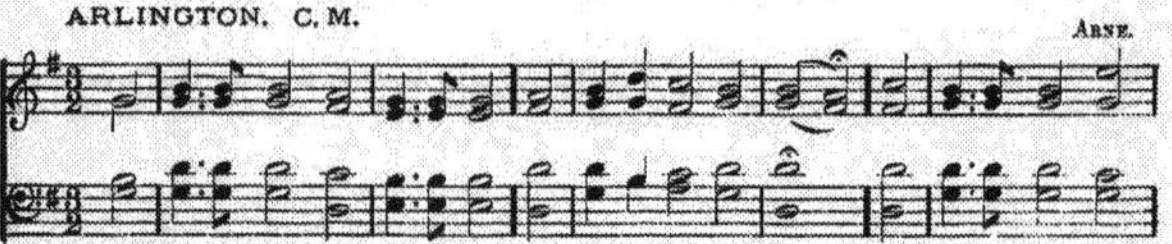

472 *"Fight the good fight of faith."*

1 AM I a soldier of the cross,
A follower of the Lamb,
And shall I fear to own his cause,
Or blush to speak his name?

2 Must I be carried to the skies
On flowery beds of ease,
While others fought to win the prize,
Or sailed through bloody seas?

3 Are there no foes for me to face?
Must I not stem the flood?
Is this vile world a friend to grace,
To help me on to God?

4 Sure I must fight, if I would reign;
Increase my courage, Lord;
I'll bear the toil, endure the pain,
Supported by thy word.

5 Thy saints in all this glorious war
Shall conquer, though they die;
They see the triumph from afar,
By faith they bring it nigh.

6 When that illustrious day shall rise,
And all thy armies shine
In robes of victory through the skies,
The glory shall be thine.

—*Isaac Watts.*

WORSHIP. 7.7, 8.7, 7.7, 8.7. MICHAEL HAYDN.

473 *Praising Christ in times of trouble.*

1 HEAD of thy Church triumphant,
We joyfully adore thee;
Till thou appear, thy members here
Shall sing like those in glory.
We lift our hearts and voices,
With blest anticipation,
And cry aloud, and give to God
The praise of our salvation.

2 While in affliction's furnace,
And passing through the fire,
Thy love we praise, which knows our days,
And ever brings us nigher.
We clap our hands exulting
In thine almighty favour;
The love divine which made us thine
Shall keep us thine forever.

3 Thou dost conduct thy people
Through torrents of temptation,
Nor will we fear, while thou art near,
The fire of tribulation.
The world with sin and Satan
In vain our march opposes;
Through thee we shall break through them all,
And sing the song of Moses.

4 By faith we see the glory
To which thou shalt restore us,
The cross despise for that high prize
Which thou hast set before us.
And if thou count us worthy,
We each, as dying Stephen,
Shall see thee stand at God's right hand,
To take us up to heaven.

—*Charles Wesley.*

474 *Christ an Almighty Saviour.*

1 WORSHIP, and thanks, and blessing,
And strength ascribe to Jesus!
Jesus alone defends his own,
When earth and hell oppress us.
Jesus with joy we witness
Almighty to deliver;
Our seals set to, that God is true,
And reigns a King for ever.

2 Omnipotent Redeemer,
Our ransomed souls adore thee;
Our Saviour thou, we find it now,
And give thee all the glory.
We sing thine arm unshortened,
Brought through our sore temptation;
With heart and voice in thee rejoice,
The God of our salvation.

3 Thine arm hath safely brought us
A way no more expected,
Then when thy sheep passed through the deep,
By crystal walls protected.
Thy glory was our rearward,
Thy hand our lives did cover,
And we, even we, have passed the sea,
And marched triumphant over.

4 The world's and Satan's malice
Thou, Jesus, hast confounded;
And, by thy grace, with songs of praise
Our happy souls resounded.
Accepting our deliverance,
We triumph in thy favour,
And for the love which now we prove,
Shall praise thy name for ever.

—*Charles Wesley.*

AUSTRIA. 8.7, 8.7, 8.7, 8.7. HAYDN, 1809.

475

Bearing the Cross.

1 JESUS, I my cross have taken,
All to leave and follow thee;
Destitute, despised, forsaken,
Thou, from hence, my all shalt be.
Perish every fond ambition,
All I've sought, and hoped, and known;
Yet how rich is my condition,
God and heaven are still my own!

2 Let the world despise and leave me,
They have left my Saviour, too;
Human hearts and looks deceive me;
Thou art not, like man, untrue;
And, while thou shalt smile upon me,
God of wisdom, love, and might,
Foes may hate, and friends may shun me;
Show thy face, and all is bright.

3 Man may trouble and distress me,
'Twill but drive me to thy breast;
Life with trials hard may press me,
Heaven will bring me sweeter rest.
Know, my soul, thy full salvation;
Rise o'er sin, and fear, and care;
Joy to find in every station
Something still to do or bear.

4 Haste thee on from grace to glory,
Armed by faith, and winged by prayer;
Heaven's eternal day's before thee,
God's own hand shall guide thee there.
Soon shall close thy earthly mission;
Swift shall pass thy pilgrim days;
Hope shall change to glad fruition,
Faith to sight, and prayer to praise.

—*H. F. Lyte.*

SALVATOR. 8.7, 8.7, 8.7, 8.7. J. P. JUDSON.

TUNE: SALVATOR. 8.7, 8.7, 8.7, 8.7.

476

Trust in sorrow.

1 Lord of life, when foes assail us,
And our hearts are bowed in pain,
Earthly friends can not deliver;
Swords and bucklers, all are vain.
Be our buckler, thou whose pity
Bore the shame upon the tree:
Man of Sorrows! in our sorrows
We can only trust in thee.

2 On the darkly heaving billows,
Thou didst walk, and they were still;
Thou canst stay the ills that press us,
They are servants to thy will.
Thou alone art King of nations,
Lord of life and victory:
Man of Sorrows! in our sorrows
We can only trust in thee.

3 O subdue our heart's rebellion,
That we faint not nor repine;
Nought of evil can befall us,
That comes down from hand of thine.
May we, like thy great disciple,
Meet thee on the swelling sea:
Man of Sorrows! in our sorrows
We can only trust in thee.

—*Hunter Dodds.*

EWING. 7.6, 7.6, 7.6, 7.6. ALEXANDER EWING.

477

Psalm xxvii. 1, 2, 3.

1 God is my strong salvation;
What foe have I to fear?
In darkness and temptation,
My light, my help, is near;
Though hosts encamp around me,
Firm in the fight I stand;
What terror can confound me,
With God at my right hand?

2 Place on the Lord reliance;
My soul, with courage wait;
His truth be thine affiance,
When faint and desolate;
His might thy heart shall strengthen,
His love thy joy increase;
Mercy thy days shall lengthen;
The Lord will give thee peace.

—*J. Montgomery.*

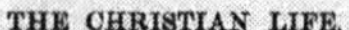

HANOVER. 10.10.11.11. Dr. Croft.

478 *Victory through Christ.*

1 Omnipotent Lord, my Saviour and King,
Thy succour afford, thy righteousness bring;
Thy promises bind thee compassion to have;
Now, now let me find thee almighty to save.

2 Rejoicing in hope, and patient in grief,
To thee I look up for certain relief;
I fear no denial, no danger I fear,
Nor start from the trial, while Jesus is near.

3 For God is above men, devils, and sin;
My Jesus's love the battle shall win;
So terribly glorious his coming shall be,
His love all-victorious shall conquer for me.

4 He all shall break through; his truth and his grace
Shall bring me into the plentiful place,
Through much tribulation, through water and fire,
Through floods of temptation, and flames of desire.

5 On Jesus, my power, till then I rely;
All evil before his presence shall fly;
When I have my Saviour, my sin shall depart,
And Jesus for ever shall reign in my heart.

—*Charles Wesley.*

PORTUGUESE HYMN. 4-11s. J. Reading.

TUNE: PORTUGUESE HYMN. 4-11s.

479 *God's promises a firm foundation.*

1 How firm a foundation, ye saints of the Lord,
Is laid for your faith in his excellent word!
What more can he say, than to you he hath said,
‖:To you, who for refuge to Jesus have fled?:‖

2 "Fear not, I am with thee; O be not dismayed!
For I am thy God, I will still give thee aid;
I'll strengthen thee, help thee, and cause thee to stand,
‖:Upheld by my gracious, omnipotent hand.:‖

3 "When through the deep waters I call thee to go,
The rivers of sorrow shall not overflow;
For I will be with thee thy trials to bless,
‖:And sanctify to thee thy deepest distress.:‖

4 "When through fiery trials thy pathway shall lie,
My grace, all-sufficient, shall be thy supply;
The flame shall not hurt thee; I only design
‖:Thy dross to consume, and thy gold to refine.:‖

5 "E'en down to old age all my people shall prove
My sovereign, eternal, unchangeable love;
And when hoary hairs shall their temples adorn,
‖:Like lambs they shall still in my bosom be borne.:‖

6 "The soul that on Jesus doth lean for repose,
I will not, in danger, desert to his foes;
That soul, though all hell should endeavour to shake,
‖:I'll never,—no never,—no never forsake!":‖

—*G. Keith.*

GRACE CHURCH. L. M. Ignace Pleyel.

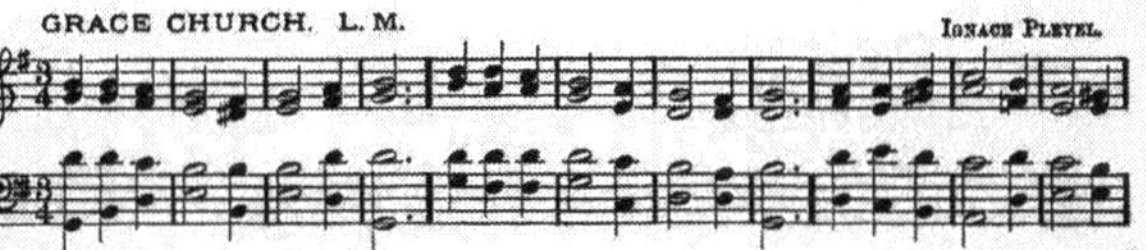

480 *Abraham offering up Isaac.*

1 Abraham, when severely tried,
His faith by his obedience showed;
He with the harsh command complied,
And gave his Isaac back to God.

2 His son the father offered up,
Son of his age, his only son,
Object of all his joy and hope,
And less beloved than God alone.

3 O for a faith like his, that we
The bright example may pursue;
May gladly give up all to thee,
To whom our more than all is due!

4 Now, Lord, to thee our all we leave;
Our willing soul thy call obeys;
Pleasure, and wealth, and fame we give,
Freedom, and life, to win thy grace.

5 Is there a thing than life more dear?
A thing from which we cannot part?
We can, we now rejoice to tear
The idol from our bleeding heart.

6 Jesus, accept our sacrifice;
All things for thee we count but loss;
Lo! at thy word our Isaac dies,
Dies on the altar of thy cross.

—*Charles Wesley.*

ANGELS' SONG. L. M. ORLANDO GIBBONS.

481 *Christ our Helper in sore trial.*

1 Eternal Beam of Light Divine,
Fountain of unexhausted love,
In whom the Father's glories shine,
Through earth beneath, and heaven above;

2 Jesus, the weary wanderer's rest,
Give me thy easy yoke to bear;
With steadfast patience arm my breast;
With spotless love and lowly fear.

3 Thankful I take the cup from thee,
Prepared and mingled by thy skill;
Though bitter to the taste it be,
Powerful the wounded soul to heal.

4 Be thou, O Rock of Ages, nigh!
So shall each murmuring thought be gone;
And grief, and fear, and care shall fly,
As clouds before the mid-day sun.

5 Speak to my warring passions, "Peace!"
Say to my trembling heart, "Be still!"
Thy power my strength and fortress is,
For all things serve thy sovereign will.

6 O Death! where is thy sting? Where now
Thy boasted victory, O Grave?
Who shall contend with God? or who
Can hurt whom God delights to save?

—*Charles Wesley.*

BARTHOLDY. L. M. MENDELSSOHN.

482 *Conflict with love of the world.*

1 Fondly my foolish heart essays
To augment the source of perfect bliss,
Love's all-sufficient sea to raise
With drops of creature happiness.

2 O Love, thy sovereign aid impart,
And guard the gift thyself hast given!
My portion thou, my treasure, art,
And life, and happiness, and heaven.

3 Would aught on earth my wishes share,
Though dear as life the idol be,
The idol from my breast I'd tear,
Resolved to seek my all in thee.

4 Whate'er I fondly counted mine,
To thee, my Lord, I here restore;
Gladly I all for thee resign;
Give me thyself, I ask no more.

—*Charles Wesley.*

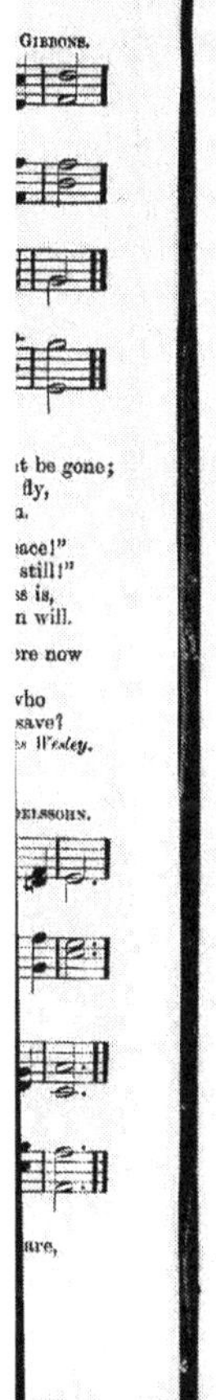

EDEN. L. M. — Dr. L. Mason.

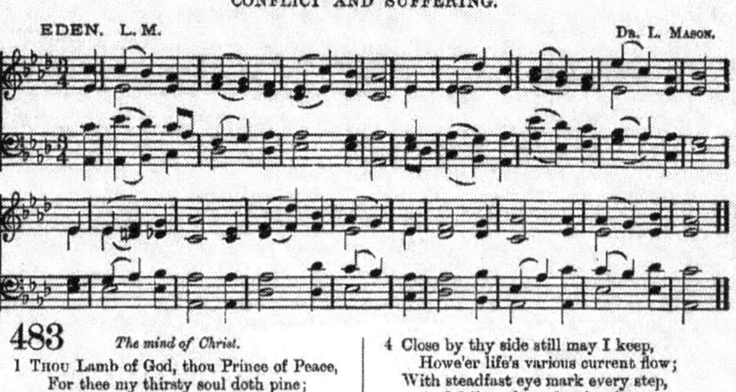

483 *The mind of Christ.*

1 Thou Lamb of God, thou Prince of Peace,
For thee my thirsty soul doth pine;
My longing heart implores thy grace;
O make me in thy likeness shine!

2 With fraudless, even, humble mind,
Thy will in all things may I see;
In love be every wish resigned,
And hallowed my whole heart to thee.

3 When pain o'er my weak flesh prevails,
With lamb-like patience arm my breast;
When grief my wounded soul assails,
In lowly meekness may I rest.

4 Close by thy side still may I keep,
Howe'er life's various current flow;
With steadfast eye mark every step,
And follow thee where'er thou go.

5 Thou, Lord, the dreadful fight hast won;
Alone thou hast the winepress trod;
In me thy strengthening grace be shown;
O may I conquer through thy blood!

6 So, when on Zion thou shalt stand,
And all heaven's host adore their King,
Shall I be found at thy right hand,
And free from pain thy glories sing.

—*J. Wesley, from Richter.*

ANGELUS. L. M. — J. Scheffler.

484 *Walking with Christ through suffering.*

1 O thou, to whose all-searching sight
The darkness shineth as the light,
Search, prove my heart; it pants for thee;
O burst these bonds, and set it free!

2 Wash out its stains, refine its dross,
Nail my affections to the cross;
Hallow each thought; let all within
Be clean, as thou, my Lord, art clean!

3 If in this darksome wild I stray,
Be thou my Light, be thou my Way;
No foes, no violence I fear,
No fraud, while thou, my God, art near.

4 When rising floods my soul o'erflow,
When sinks my heart in waves of woe,
Jesus, thy timely aid impart,
And raise my head, and cheer my heart.

5 Saviour, where'er thy steps I see,
Dauntless, untired, I follow thee;
O let thy hand support me still,
And lead me to thy holy hill!

6 If rough and thorny be the way,
My strength proportion to my day;
Till toil, and grief, and pain shall cease,
Where all is calm, and joy, and peace.

—*Charles Wesley.*

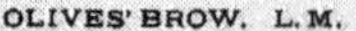

OLIVES' BROW. L. M. — W. B. Bradbury.

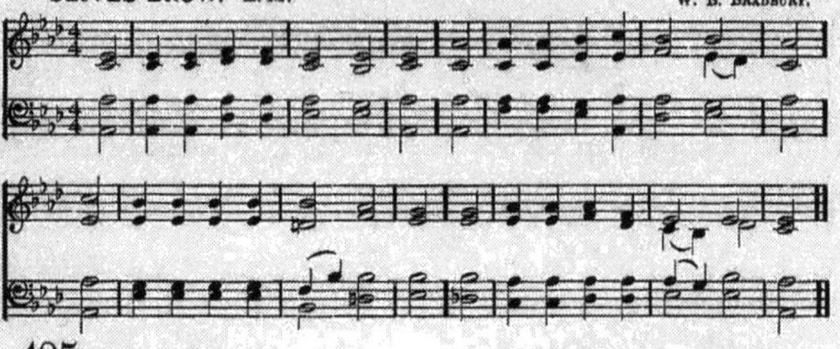

485 *"Blessed are they that mourn."*

1 Deem not that they are blest alone
Whose days a peaceful tenor keep;
The anointed Son of God makes known
A blessing for the eyes that weep.

2 The light of smiles shall fill again
The lids that overflow with tears;
And weary hours of woe and pain
Are promises of happier years.

3 There is a day of sunny rest
For every dark and troubled night;
Though grief may bide an evening guest,
Yet joy shall come with early light.

4 Nor let the good man's trust depart,
Though life its common gifts deny,
Though with a pierced and broken heart,
And spurned of men, he goes to die.

5 For God has marked each sorrowing day,
And numbered every secret tear;
And heaven's long age of bliss shall pay
For all his children suffer here.

—*W. C. Bryant.*

GIESSEN. 6-8s.

TUNE: GIESSEN. 6-8s.

486 *Christ's sympathy in suffering.*

1 When gathering clouds around I view,
And days are dark, and friends are few,
On him I lean, who not in vain
Experienced every human pain;
He knows my wants, allays my fears,
And counts and treasures up my tears.

2 If aught should tempt my soul to stray
From heavenly wisdom's narrow way,
To fly the good I would pursue,
Or do the thing I would not do;
Still he, who felt temptation's power,
Shall guard me in that dangerous hour.

3 If wounded love my bosom swell,
Deceived by those I prized too well,
He shall his pitying aid bestow,
Who felt on earth severer woe,—
At once betrayed, denied, or fled,
By those who shared his daily bread.

4 And oh! when I have safely passed
Through every conflict but the last,
Still, still unchanging, watch beside
My dying bed—for thou hast died;
Then point to realms of cloudless day,
And wipe the latest tear away.

—*Sir R. Grant.*

HALLE. 6-8s. Kugelmann. Harm. by J. S. Bach.

487 *"Comfort ye, comfort ye my people."*

1 Comfort, ye ministers of grace,
Comfort my people, saith your God!
Ye soon shall see his smiling face,
His golden sceptre, not his rod;
And own when now the cloud's removed,
He only chastened whom he loved.

2 Who sow in tears, in joy shall reap,
The Lord shall comfort all that mourn;
Who now go on their way and weep,
With joy they doubtless shall return,
And bring their sheaves with vast increase,
And have their fruit to holiness.

—*Charles Wesley.*

CAREY'S. 6-8s. HENRY CAREY.

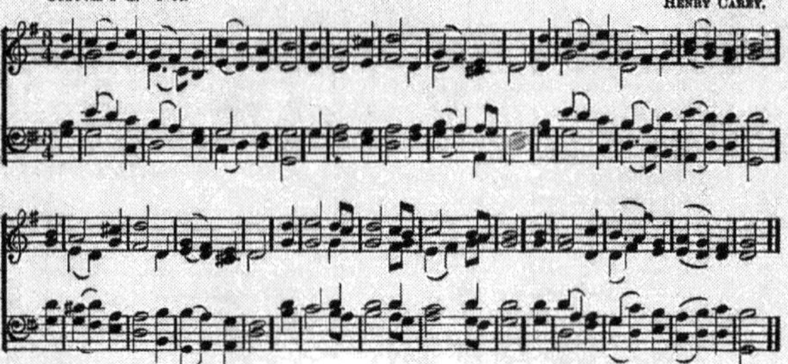

488 *"If we suffer, we shall also reign with him."*

1 SAVIOUR of all, what hast thou done,
What hast thou suffered on the tree?
Why didst thou groan thy mortal groan,
Obedient unto death for me?
The mystery of thy passion show,
The end of all thy griefs below.

2 Pardon, and grace, and heaven to buy,
My bleeding Sacrifice expired;
But didst thou not my Pattern die,
That, by thy glorious Spirit fired,
Faithful to death I might endure,
And make the crown by suffering sure?

3 Thy every suffering servant, Lord,
Shall as his patient Master be;
To all thy inward life restored,
And outwardly conformed to thee,
Out of thy grave the saint shall rise,
And grasp, through death, the glorious prize.

4 This is the strait and royal way,
That leads us to the courts above;
Here let me ever, ever stay,
Till, on the wings of perfect love,
I take my last triumphant flight,
From Calvary's to Zion's height.

—*Charles Wesley.*

489 *The presence of Christ in affliction.*

1 PEACE! doubting heart; my God's I am;
Who formed me man, forbids my fear;
The Lord hath called me by my name;
The Lord protects, for ever near;
His blood for me did once atone,
And still he loves and guards his own.

2 When passing through the watery deep,
I ask in faith his promised aid,
The waves an awful distance keep,
And shrink from my devoted head;
Fearless their violence I dare;
They cannot harm, for God is there!

3 To him mine eye of faith I turn,
And through the fire pursue my way;
The fire forgets its power to burn,
The lambent flames around me play;
I own his power, accept the sign,
And shout to prove the Saviour mine.

4 When darkness intercepts the skies,
And sorrow's waves around me roll,
When high the storms of passion rise,
And half o'erwhelm my sinking soul,
My soul a sudden calm shall feel,
And hear a whisper, "Peace; be still!"

5 Still nigh me, O my Saviour, stand!
And guard in fierce temptation's hour;
Hide in the hollow of thy hand;
Show forth in me thy saving power;
Still be thy arms my sure defence;
Nor earth nor hell shall pluck me thence.

—*Charles Wesley.*

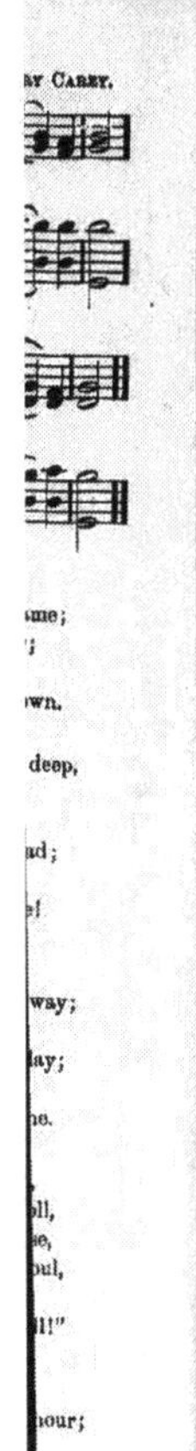

EVANGELIST. C. M. FROM MENDELSSOHN.

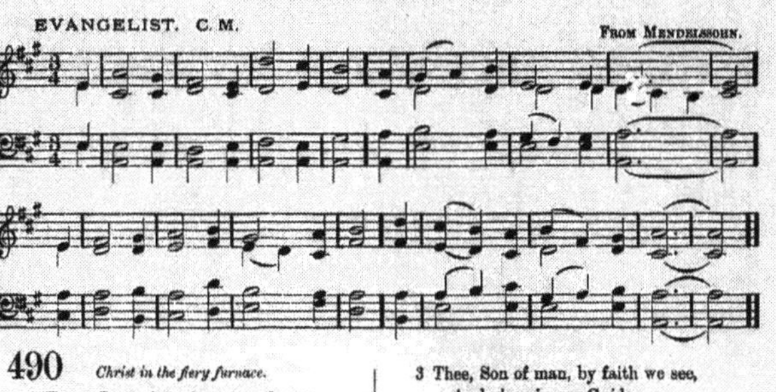

490 *Christ in the fiery furnace.*

1 THEE, Jesus, full of truth and grace,
Thee, Saviour, we adore;
Thee in affliction's furnace praise,
And magnify thy power.

2 Thy power, in human weakness shown,
Shall make us all entire;
We now thy guardian presence own,
And walk unburned in fire.

3 Thee, Son of man, by faith we see,
And glory in our Guide;
Surrounded and upheld by thee,
The fiery test abide.

4 The fire our graces shall refine,
Till, moulded from above,
We bear the character divine,
The stamp of perfect love.

—*Charles Wesley.*

EVAN. C. M. REV. W. H. HAVERGAL.

491 *A title to heavenly mansions.*

1 WHEN I can read my title clear
To mansions in the skies,
I'll bid farewell to every fear,
And wipe my weeping eyes.

2 Should earth against my soul engage,
And fiery darts be hurled,
Then I can smile at Satan's rage,
And face a frowning world.

3 Let cares like a wild deluge come,
Let storms of sorrow fall,
So I but safely reach my home,
My God, my heaven, my all!

4 There I shall bathe my weary soul
In seas of heavenly rest,
And not a wave of trouble roll
Across my peaceful breast.

—*Isaac Watts.*

ST. AGNES. C. M. — Dr. Dykes.

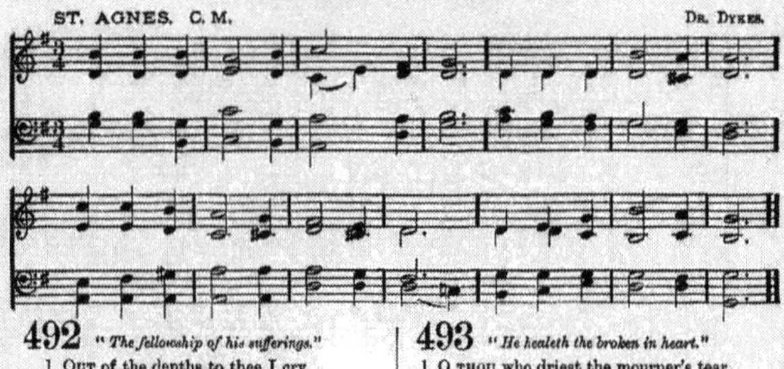

492 *"The fellowship of his sufferings."*

1 Out of the depths to thee I cry,
Whose fainting footsteps trod
The paths of our humanity,
Incarnate Son of God!

2 Thou Man of grief, who once apart
Didst all our sorrows bear,
The trembling hand, the fainting heart,
The agony, and prayer!

3 This is the consecrated dower
Thy chosen ones obtain,
To know thy resurrection power
Through fellowship of pain.

4 Then, O my soul, in silence wait!
Faint not, O faltering feet!
Press onward to that blest estate,
In righteousness complete.

5 Let faith transcend the passing hour,
The transient pain and strife;
Upraised by an immortal power,
The power of endless life.

—*Mrs. E. E. Marcy.*

493 *"He healeth the broken in heart."*

1 O thou who driest the mourner's tear,
How dark this world would be,
If, when deceived and wounded here,
We could not fly to thee!

2 The friends who in our sunshine live,
When winter comes, are flown;
And he who has but tears to give,
Must weep those tears alone.

3 But thou wilt heal that broken heart,
Which, like the plants that throw
Their fragrance from the wounded part,
Breathes sweetness out of woe.

4 O who could bear life's stormy doom,
Did not thy wing of love
Come brightly wafting through the gloom,
Our peace-branch from above!

5 Then sorrow, touched by thee, grows bright
With more than rapture's ray;
As darkness shows us worlds of light
We never saw by day.

—*T. Moore.*

BOYLSTON. S. M. — Dr. L. Mason.

494 *Trust in Providence.*

1 Commit thou all thy griefs
And ways into his hands,
To his sure truth and tender care,
Who earth and heaven commands.

2 Who points the clouds their course,
Whom winds and seas obey,
He shall direct thy wandering feet,
He shall prepare thy way.

3 Thou on the Lord rely,
So safe shalt thou go on;
Fix on his work thy steadfast eye,
So shall thy work be done.

4 No profit canst thou gain
By self-consuming care;
To him commend thy cause, his ear
Attends the softest prayer.

5 Thy everlasting truth,
Father, thy ceaseless love,
Sees all thy children's wants, and knows
What best for each will prove.

—*J. Wesley, from Gerhardt.*

TUNE: BOYLSTON. S.M. (SEE HYMN 494.)

495

SECOND PART.

1 GIVE to the winds thy fears;
Hope, and be undismayed:
God hears thy sighs, and counts thy tears;
God shall lift up thy head.

2 Through waves, and clouds, and storms,
He gently clears thy way:
Wait thou his time, so shall this night
Soon end in joyous day.

3 Still heavy is thy heart?
Still sink thy spirits down?
Cast off the weight, let fear depart,
Bid every care be gone.

4 What though thou rulest not?
Yet heaven, and earth, and hell
Proclaim, God sitteth on the throne,
And ruleth all things well!

5 Leave to his sovereign sway
To choose and to command;
So shalt thou wondering own his way,
How wise, how strong his hand.

6 Far, far above thy thought
His counsel shall appear,
When fully he the work hath wrought
That caused thy needless fear.

7 Thou seest our weakness, Lord;
Our hearts are known to thee;
O lift thou up the sinking hand,
Confirm the feeble knee!

8 Let us in life, in death,
Thy steadfast truth declare,
And publish with our latest breath
Thy love and guardian care.

—*J. Wesley, from Gerhardt.*

SUPPLICATION. S.M. JOSEPH BARNBY.

By permission of Messrs. Novello, Ewer & Co.

496

"My times are in thy hand."

1 "MY times are in thy hand;"
My God, I wish them there;
My life, my friends, my soul, I leave
Entirely to thy care.

2 "My times are in thy hand,"
Whatever they may be;
Pleasing or painful, dark or bright,
As best may seem to thee.

3 "My times are in thy hand;"
Why should I doubt or fear?
My Father's hand will never cause
His child a needless tear.

4 "My times are in thy hand,"
Jesus, the crucified!
The hand my cruel sins had pierced
Is now my guard and guide.

5 "My times are in thy hand;"
I'll always trust in thee;
And, after death, at thy right hand
I shall forever be.

—*W. F. Lloyd.*

497

"The counsel of the Lord standeth forever."

1 AWAY, my needless fears,
And doubts no longer mine;
A ray of heavenly light appears,
A messenger divine.

2 Thrice comfortable hope,
That calms my troubled breast;
My Father's hand prepares the cup,
And what he wills is best.

3 If what I wish is good,
And suits the will divine,
By earth and hell in vain withstood,
I know it shall be mine.

4 Still let them counsel take
To frustrate his decree,
They cannot keep a blessing back,
By Heaven designed for me.

5 Here then I doubt no more,
But in his pleasure rest,
Whose wisdom, love, and truth, and power,
Engage to make me blest.

6 To accomplish his design
The creatures all agree,
And all the attributes divine
Are now at work for me.

—*Charles Wesley.*

GUIDE. 8.7, 8.7, 4.7.

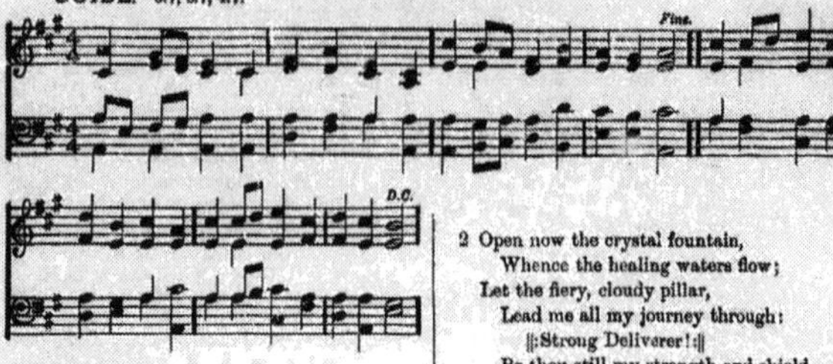
Fine.

D.C.

498 *Jehovah the pilgrim's Guide.*

1 Guide me, O thou great Jehovah,
Pilgrim through this barren land;
I am weak, but thou art mighty;
Hold me with thy powerful hand:
‖:Bread of heaven!:‖
Feed me till I want no more.

2 Open now the crystal fountain,
Whence the healing waters flow;
Let the fiery, cloudy pillar,
Lead me all my journey through:
‖:Strong Deliverer!:‖
Be thou still my strength and shield.

3 When I tread the verge of Jordan,
Bid my anxious fears subside;
Bear me through the swelling current;
Land me safe on Canaan's side:
‖:Songs of praises:‖
I will ever give to thee.

—*Wm. Williams.*

VERMONT. 8.7, 8.7. WEBER.

499 *"Lead me in a plain path."*

1 Gently, Lord, O gently lead us
Through this gloomy vale of tears;
And, O Lord, in mercy give us
Thy rich grace in all our fears.

2 When temptation's darts assail us,
When in devious paths we stray,
Let thy goodness never fail us,
Lead us in thy perfect way.

3 In the hour of pain and anguish,
In the hour when death draws near,
Suffer not our hearts to languish,
Suffer not our souls to fear.

4 When this mortal life is ended,
Bid us in thine arms to rest,
Till, by angel-bands attended,
We awake among the blest.

—*T. Hastings.*

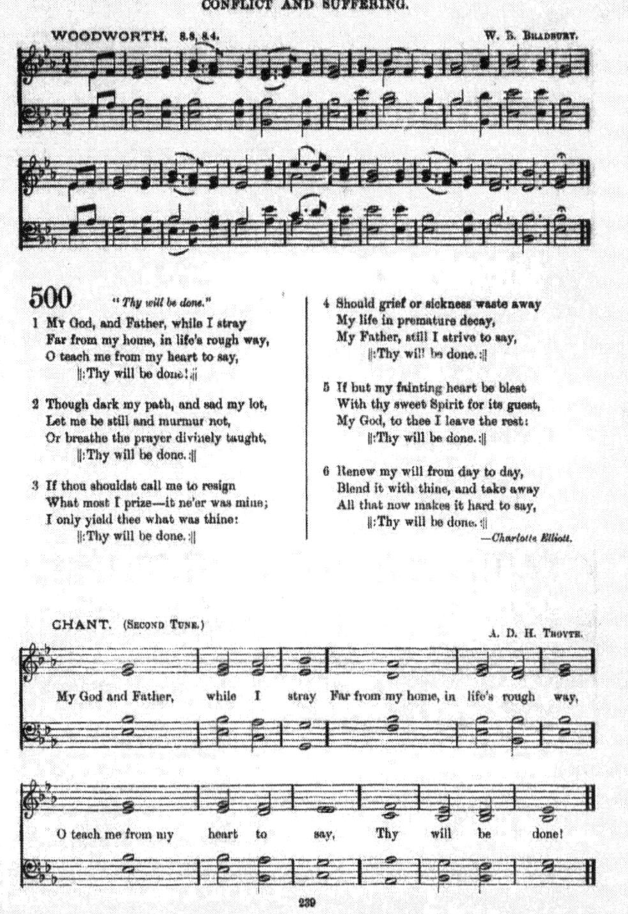

WOODWORTH. 8.8, 8.4. W. B. BRADBURY.

500

"Thy will be done."

1 MY God, and Father, while I stray
Far from my home, in life's rough way,
O teach me from my heart to say,
‖:Thy will be done!:‖

2 Though dark my path, and sad my lot,
Let me be still and murmur not,
Or breathe the prayer divinely taught,
‖:Thy will be done.:‖

3 If thou shouldst call me to resign
What most I prize—it ne'er was mine;
I only yield thee what was thine:
‖:Thy will be done.:‖

4 Should grief or sickness waste away
My life in premature decay,
My Father, still I strive to say,
‖:Thy will be done.:‖

5 If but my fainting heart be blest
With thy sweet Spirit for its guest,
My God, to thee I leave the rest:
‖:Thy will be done.:‖

6 Renew my will from day to day,
Blend it with thine, and take away
All that now makes it hard to say,
‖:Thy will be done.:‖

—*Charlotte Elliott.*

CHANT. (SECOND TUNE.) A. D. H. TROYTE.

My God and Father, while I stray Far from my home, in life's rough way,
O teach me from my heart to say, Thy will be done!

WILLING. 8-6s. C. E. WILLING.

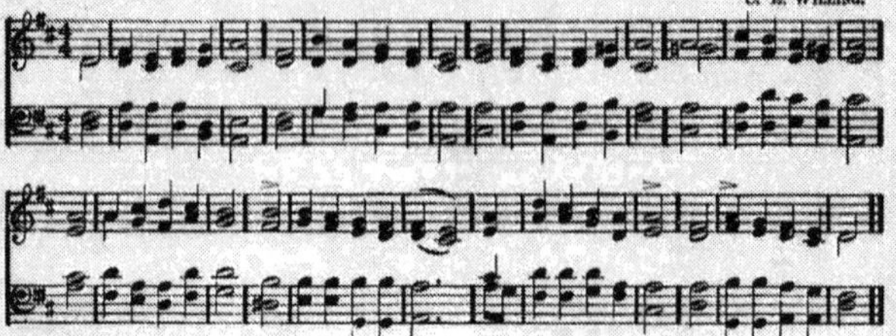

501

"Teach me thy way."

1 THY way, not mine, O Lord,
However dark it be!
Lead me by thine own hand,
Choose out the path for me;
Smooth let it be or rough,
It still will be the best,
Winding or straight, it leads
Right onward to thy rest.

2 I dare not choose my lot;
I would not, if I might:
Choose thou for me, my God,
So shall I walk aright.
The kingdom that I seek
Is thine; so let the way
That leads to it be thine,
Else I must surely stray.

3 Take thou my cup, and it
With joy or sorrow fill,
As best to thee may seem;
Choose thou my good and ill.
Not mine, not mine the choice,
In things or great or small;
Be thou my guide, my strength,
My wisdom, and my all.

—H. Bonar.

HOLLEY. 4-7s. G. HEWS.

502

"As thy days so shall thy strength be."

1 As thy day thy strength shall be—
This should be enough for thee;
He who knows thy frame will spare
Burdens more than thou canst bear.

2 When thy days are veiled in night,
Christ shall give thee heavenly light;
Are they wearisome and long?
Yet in him thou shalt be strong.

3 Cold and wintry though they prove,
Thine the sunshine of his love;
If with fervid heat opprest,
In his shadow thou shalt rest.

4 When thy days on earth are past,
Christ shall call thee home at last,
His redeeming love to praise,
Who hath strengthened all thy days.

—Miss Havergal.

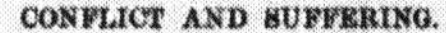

REDHEAD. 4-7s. R. REDHEAD.

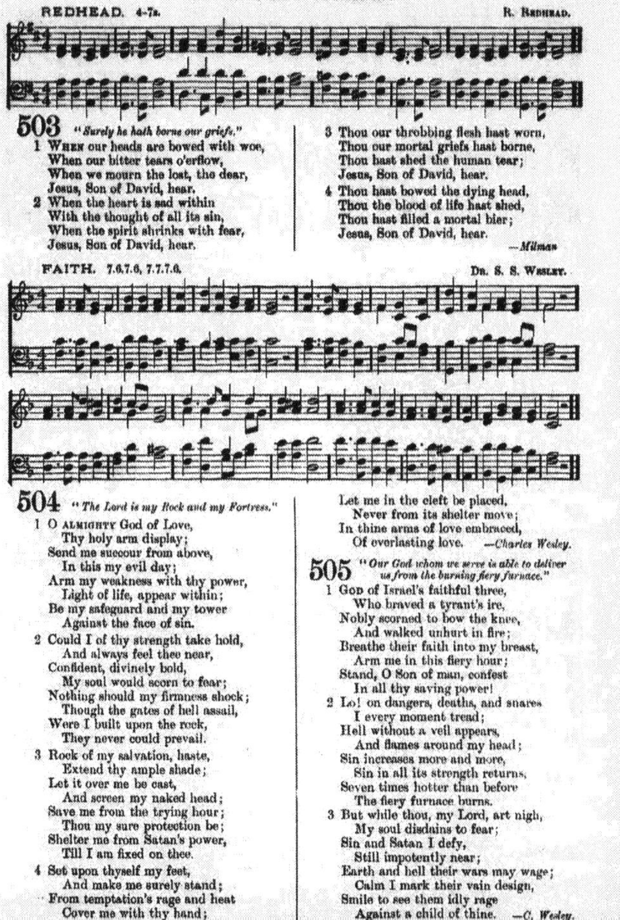

503 *"Surely he hath borne our griefs."*

1 When our heads are bowed with woe,
When our bitter tears o'erflow,
When we mourn the lost, the dear,
Jesus, Son of David, hear.

2 When the heart is sad within
With the thought of all its sin,
When the spirit shrinks with fear,
Jesus, Son of David, hear.

3 Thou our throbbing flesh hast worn,
Thou our mortal griefs hast borne,
Thou hast shed the human tear;
Jesus, Son of David, hear.

4 Thou hast bowed the dying head,
Thou the blood of life hast shed,
Thou hast filled a mortal bier;
Jesus, Son of David, hear.

—*Milman*

FAITH. 7.6.7.6, 7.7.7.6. DR. S. S. WESLEY.

504 *"The Lord is my Rock and my Fortress."*

1 O almighty God of Love,
Thy holy arm display;
Send me succour from above,
In this my evil day;
Arm my weakness with thy power,
Light of life, appear within;
Be my safeguard and my tower
Against the face of sin.

2 Could I of thy strength take hold,
And always feel thee near,
Confident, divinely bold,
My soul would scorn to fear;
Nothing should my firmness shock;
Though the gates of hell assail,
Were I built upon the rock,
They never could prevail.

3 Rock of my salvation, haste,
Extend thy ample shade;
Let it over me be cast,
And screen my naked head;
Save me from the trying hour;
Thou my sure protection be;
Shelter me from Satan's power,
Till I am fixed on thee.

4 Set upon thyself my feet,
And make me surely stand;
From temptation's rage and heat
Cover me with thy hand;
Let me in the cleft be placed,
Never from its shelter move;
In thine arms of love embraced,
Of everlasting love.

—*Charles Wesley.*

505 *"Our God whom we serve is able to deliver us from the burning fiery furnace."*

1 God of Israel's faithful three,
Who braved a tyrant's ire,
Nobly scorned to bow the knee,
And walked unhurt in fire;
Breathe their faith into my breast,
Arm me in this fiery hour;
Stand, O Son of man, confest
In all thy saving power!

2 Lo! on dangers, deaths, and snares
I every moment tread;
Hell without a veil appears,
And flames around my head;
Sin increases more and more,
Sin in all its strength returns,
Seven times hotter than before
The fiery furnace burns.

3 But while thou, my Lord, art nigh,
My soul disdains to fear;
Sin and Satan I defy,
Still impotently near;
Earth and hell their wars may wage;
Calm I mark their vain design,
Smile to see them idly rage
Against a child of thine.

—*C. Wesley.*

WORMS. 8.7, 8.7, 6.6, 6.6.7. MARTIN LUTHER.

506 *"A strong tower from the enemy."*

1 A MIGHTY fortress is our God,
A bulwark never failing;
Our Helper he, amid the flood
Of mortal ills prevailing.
For still our ancient foe
Doth seek to work us woe;
His craft and power are great,
And, armed with cruel hate,
On earth is not his equal.

2 Did we in our own strength confide,
Our striving would be losing;
Were not the right man on our side,
The man of God's own choosing.
Dost ask who that may be?
Christ Jesus, it is he;
Lord Sabaoth is his name,
From age to age the same,
And he must win the battle.

3 And though this world, with devils filled,
Should threaten to undo us;
We will not fear, for God hath willed
His truth to triumph through us.
The prince of darkness grim,
We tremble not for him;
His rage we can endure,
For lo! his doom is sure,
One little word shall fell him.

4 That word above all earthly powers—
No thanks to them—abideth;
The Spirit and the gifts are ours
Through him who with us sideth.
Let goods and kindred go,
This mortal life also;
The body they may kill;
God's truth abideth still,
His kingdom is forever.

—*Hedge, from Luther.*

BONN. 7.6, 7.6, 7.7, 7.6. ADAPTED FROM THE GERMAN.

507 *Joy in sorrow.*

1 FATHER, in the name I pray
Of thy incarnate Love;
Humbly ask, that as my day
My suffering strength may prove;
When my sorrows most increase,
Let thy strongest joys be given;
Jesus, come with my distress,
And agony is heaven!

2 Father, Son, and Holy Ghost,
For good remember me!
Me whom thou hast caused to trust
For more than life on thee;
With me in the fire remain,
Till like burnished gold I shine,
Meet, through consecrated pain,
To see the face divine.

—*Charles Wesley.*

AMSTERDAM. 7.6, 7.6, 7.8, 7.6. Dr. Nares.

508

Isaiah xxxii. 2.

1 To the haven of thy breast,
O Son of man, I fly!
Be my refuge and my rest,
For O the storm is high!
Save me from the furious blast;
A covert from the tempest be;
Hide me, Jesus, till o'erpast
The storm of sin I see.

2 Welcome as the water-spring
To a dry, barren place,
O descend on me, and bring
Thy sweet refreshing grace!
O'er a parched and weary land
As a great rock extends its shade,
Hide me, Saviour, with thine hand,
And screen my naked head.

3 In the time of my distress
Thou hast my succour been,
In my utter helplessness
Restraining me from sin;
O how swiftly didst thou move
To save me in the trying hour!
Still protect me with thy love,
And shield me with thy power.

4 First and last in me perform
The work thou hast begun;
Be my shelter from the storm,
My shadow from the sun;
Weary, parched with thirst, and faint,
Till thou the abiding Spirit breathe,
Every moment, Lord, I want
The merit of thy death.

—Charles Wesley.

509

The faithfulness of Christ.

1 Cast on the fidelity
Of my redeeming Lord,
I shall his salvation see,
According to his word;
Credence to his word I give;
My Saviour in distresses past
Will not now his servant leave,
But bring me through at last.

2 Better than my boding fears,
To me thou oft hast proved;
Oft observed my silent tears,
And challenged thy beloved;
Mercy to my rescue flew,
And death ungrasped his fainting prey;
Pain before thy face withdrew,
And sorrow fled away.

3 Now as yesterday the same,
In all my troubles nigh,
Jesus, on thy Word and Name
I steadfastly rely;
Sure as now the grief I feel,
The promised joy I soon shall have;
Saved again, to sinners tell
Thy power and will to save.

4 To thy blessèd will resigned,
And stayed on that alone,
I thy perfect strength shall find,
Thy faithful mercies own;
Compassed round with songs of praise,
My all to my Redeemer give,
Spread thy miracles of grace,
And to thy glory live.

—Charles Wesley.

PURLEIGH. 8.8.6, 8.8.6. A. H. BROWN.

510 *Christ our refuge in trouble.*

1 How happy are the little flock,
Who, safe beneath their guardian-rock,
In all commotions rest!
When war's and tumult's waves run high,
Unmoved above the storm they lie,
They lodge in Jesus' breast.

2 Such happiness, O Lord, have we,
By mercy gathered into thee,
Before the floods descend;
And while the bursting cloud comes down,
We mark the vengeful day begun,
And calmly wait the end.

3 Whatever ills the world befall,
A pledge of endless good we call,
A sign of Jesus near:
His chariot will not long delay;
We hear the rumbling wheels, and pray,
Triumphant Lord, appear!

—Charles Wesley.

511 *"Thou art my Deliverer."*

1 O GOD, thy faithfulness I plead,
My helplessness in time of need,
My great Deliverer, thou!
Haste to my aid, thine ear incline,
And rescue this poor soul of mine;
I claim the promise now!

2 Where is the way? Ah, show me where,
That I thy mercy may declare,
The power that sets me free;
How can I my destruction shun?
How can I from my nature run?
Answer, O God, for me!

3 For thou, O Lord, art full of grace;
Thy love can find a thousand ways
To foolish man unknown;
My soul upon thy love I cast;
I rest me, till the storm is past,
Upon thy love alone.

4 Thy faithful, wise, and mighty love
Shall every stumbling-block remove,
And make an open way;
Thy love shall burst the shades of death,
And bear me from the gulf beneath,
To everlasting day.

Charles Wesley.

HARWOOD. 8.8.6, 8.8.6. HARWOOD.

512 *The faithfulness and power of Christ.*

1 Light of the world! thy beams I bless!
On thee, bright Sun of Righteousness,
My faith hath fixed its eye;
Guided by thee, through all I go,
Nor fear the ruin spread below,
For thou art always nigh.

2 Ten thousand snares my path beset;
Yet will I, Lord, the work complete,
Which thou to me hast given;
Regardless of the pains I feel,
Close by the gates of death and hell,
I urge my way to heaven.

3 In thee, O Lord, I put my trust,
Mighty, and merciful, and just;
Thy sacred word is passed;
And I, who dare thy word receive,
Without committing sin shall live,
Shall live to God at last.

4 I rest in thine almighty power;
The name of Jesus is a tower,
That hides my life above;
Thou canst, thou wilt my Helper be;
My confidence is all in thee,
The faithful God of Love.

5 Wherefore, in never-ceasing prayer,
My soul to thy continual care
I faithfully commend,
Assured that thou through life shalt save,
And show thyself beyond the grave
My everlasting Friend.

—Charles Wesley.

513 *Present suffering and future glory.*

1 Come on, my partners in distress,
My comrades through the wilderness,
Who still your bodies feel;
Awhile forget your griefs and fears,
And look beyond this vale of tears,
To that celestial hill.

2 Beyond the bounds of time and space,
Look forward to that heavenly place,
The saints' secure abode;
On faith's strong eagle-pinions rise,
And force your passage to the skies,
And scale the mount of God.

3 Who suffer with our Master here,
We shall before his face appear,
And by his side sit down;
To patient faith the prize is sure;
And all that to the end endure
The cross, shall wear the crown.

4 Thrice blessèd, bliss-inspiring hope!
It lifts the fainting spirits up;
It brings to life the dead;
Our conflicts here shall soon be past,
And you and I ascend at last,
Triumphant with our Head.

5 The great mysterious Deity
We soon with open face shall see;
The beatific sight
Shall fill heaven's sounding courts with praise,
And wide diffuse the golden blaze
Of everlasting light.

6 The Father shining on his throne,
The glorious, co-eternal Son,
The Spirit, one and seven,
Conspire our rapture to complete;
And, lo! we fall before his feet,
And silence heightens heaven.

7 In hope of that ecstatic pause,
Jesus, we now sustain the cross,
And at thy footstool fall;
Till thou our hidden life reveal,
Till thou our ravished spirits fill,
And God is all in all!

—Charles Wesley.

6.—FULL SALVATION.

MARTYRDOM. C. M. HUGH WILSON.

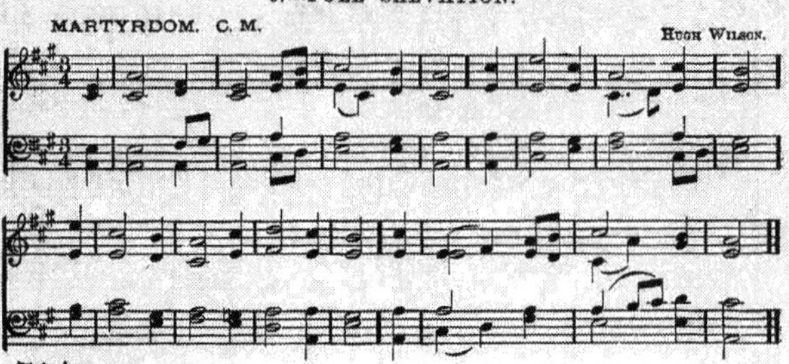

514 *"Create in me a clean heart, O God."*

1 O FOR a heart to praise my God,
A heart from sin set free!
A heart that always feels thy blood
So freely spilt for me!

2 A heart resigned, submissive, meek,
My great Redeemer's throne,
Where only Christ is heard to speak,
Where Jesus reigns alone:

3 A humble, lowly, contrite heart,
Believing, true, and clean;
Which neither life nor death can part
From him that dwells within:

4 A heart in every thought renewed,
And full of love divine;
Perfect, and right, and pure, and good,
A copy, Lord, of thine!

5 Thy tender heart is still the same,
And melts at human woe:
Jesus, for thee distressed I am,
I want thy love to know.

6 My heart, thou know'st, can never rest,
Till thou create my peace;
Till, of my Eden re-possest,
From every sin I cease.

7 Thy nature, gracious Lord, impart;
Come quickly from above;
Write thy new name upon my heart,
Thy new, best name of love.

—*Charles Wesley.*

MANCHESTER. C. M. DR. R. WAINWRIGHT.

TUNE: MANCHESTER. C. M.

515 *"Where sin abounded, grace did much more abound."*

1 What shall I do my God to love?
My loving God to praise?
The length, and breadth, and height to prove,
And depth of sovereign grace?

2 Thy sovereign grace to all extends,
Immense and unconfined;
From age to age it never ends;
It reaches all mankind.

3 Throughout the world its breadth is known,
Wide as infinity;
So wide, it never passed by one,
Or it had passed by me.

4 My trespass was grown up to heaven;
But far above the skies,
In Christ abundantly forgiven,
I see thy mercies rise.

5 The depth of all-redeeming love,
What angel-tongue can tell!
O may I to the utmost prove
The gift unspeakable!

6 Deeper than hell, it plucked me thence;
Deeper than inbred sin,
His love my sinful heart shall cleanse,
When Jesus enters in.

7 Come quickly, gracious Lord, and take
Possession of thine own;
My longing heart vouchsafe to make
Thine everlasting throne!

8 Assert thy claim, maintain thy right,
Come quickly from above;
And sink me to perfection's height,
The depth of humble love.

—*Charles Wesley.*

SAWLEY. C. M. J. Walch.

516 *Jesus the Saviour from sin.*

1 Jesus, to thee I now can fly,
On whom my help is laid;
Oppressed by sins, I lift my eye,
And see the shadows fade.

2 Believing on my Lord, I find
A sure and present aid;
On thee alone my constant mind
Be every moment stayed.

3 Whate'er in me seems wise, or good,
Or strong, I here disclaim;
I wash my garments in the blood
Of the atoning Lamb.

4 Jesus, my Strength, my Life, my Rest,
On thee will I depend,
Till summoned to the marriage-feast,
When faith in sight shall end.

—*Charles Wesley.*

517 *The rest of faith.*

1 Lord, I believe a rest remains,
To all thy people known;
A rest where pure enjoyment reigns,
And thou art loved alone:

2 A rest, where all our soul's desire
Is fixed on things above;
Where fear, and sin, and grief expire,
Cast out by perfect love.

3 O that I now the rest might know,
Believe, and enter in!
Now, Saviour, now the power bestow,
And let me cease from sin.

4 Remove this hardness from my heart,
This unbelief remove;
To me the rest of faith impart,
The Sabbath of thy love.

5 I would be thine, thou know'st I would,
And have thee all my own;
Thee, O my all-sufficient Good!
I want, and thee alone.

6 Thy name to me, thy nature grant;
This, only this be given;
Nothing beside my God I want;
Nothing in earth or heaven.

7 Come, Father, Son, and Holy Ghost,
And seal me thine abode;
Let all I am in thee be lost;
Let all be lost in God.

—*Charles Wesley.*

BYZANTIUM. C. M. W. JACKSON.

518

"That Christ may dwell in your hearts by faith."

1 O JOYFUL sound of gospel grace!
Christ shall in me appear;
I, even I, shall see his face;
I shall be holy here.

2 This heart shall be his constant home;
I hear his Spirit's cry;
"Surely," he saith, "I quickly come;"
He saith, who cannot lie.

3 The glorious crown of righteousness
To me reached out I view;
Conqueror through him, I soon shall seize,
And wear it as my due.

4 The promised land, from Pisgah's top,
I now exult to see;
My hope is full—O glorious hope!—
Of immortality.

5 He visits now the house of clay;
He shakes his future home;
O wouldst thou, Lord, on this glad day,
Into thy temple come!

6 With me I know, I feel, thou art;
But this cannot suffice,
Unless thou plantest in my heart
A constant paradise.

7 Come, O my God, thyself reveal,
Fill all this mighty void;
Thou only canst my spirit fill;
Come, O my God, my God!

—*Charles Wesley.*

ST. AGNES. C. M. DR. DYKES.

519

"The unspeakable gift."

1 JESUS hath died that I might live,
Might live to God alone;
In him eternal life receive,
And be in spirit one.

2 Saviour, I thank thee for the grace,
The gift unspeakable!
And wait with arms of faith to embrace,
And all thy love to feel.

3 My soul breaks out in strong desire
The perfect bliss to prove;
My longing heart is all on fire
To be dissolved in love.

4 Give me thyself; from every boast,
From every wish set free:
Let all I am in thee be lost;
But give thyself to me.

5 Thy gifts, alone, cannot suffice;
O let thyself be given!
Thy presence makes my paradise,
And where thou art is heaven.

—*Charles Wesley.*

TUNE: ST. AGNES. (SEE HYMN 519.)

520

"The hope of our calling."

1 WHAT is our calling's glorious hope,
But inward holiness?
For this to Jesus I look up,
I calmly wait for this.

2 I wait, till he shall touch me clean,
Shall life and power impart,
Give me the faith that casts out sin
And purifies the heart.

3 This is the dear redeeming grace,
For every sinner free;
Surely it shall on me take place,
The chief of sinners, me.

4 From all iniquity, from all,
He shall my soul redeem;
In Jesus I believe, and shall
Believe myself to him.

5 When Jesus makes my heart his home,
My sin shall all depart;
And, lo! he saith, "I quickly come,
To fill and rule thy heart!"

6 Be it according to thy word!
Redeem me from all sin;
My heart would now receive thee, Lord;
Come in, my Lord, come in!

—*Charles Wesley.*

MANOAH. C. M. FROM MEHUL AND HAYDN.

521

The gift of righteousness.

1 I ASK the gift of righteousness,
The sin-subduing power,
Power to believe, and go in peace,
And never grieve thee more.

2 I ask the blood-bought pardon sealed,
The liberty from sin,
The grace infused, the love revealed,
The kingdom fixed within.

3 Thou hear'st me for salvation pray;
Thou seest my heart's desire;
Made ready in thy powerful day,
Thy fulness I require.

4 My vehement soul cries out, opprest,
Impatient to be freed;
Nor can I, Lord, nor will I rest,
Till I am saved indeed.

5 Art thou not able to convert?
Art thou not willing too?
To change this old rebellious heart,
To conquer and renew?

6 Thou canst, thou wilt, I dare believe,
So arm me with thy power,
That I to sin shall never cleave,
Shall never feel it more.—*Charles Wesley.*

522

"Now is the day of salvation."

1 COME, O my God, the promise seal,
This mountain, sin, remove;
Now in my gasping soul reveal
The virtue of thy love.

2 I want thy life, thy purity,
Thy righteousness, brought in;
I ask, desire, and trust in thee,
To be redeemed from sin.

3 Anger and sloth, desire and pride,
This moment be subdued;
Be cast into the crimson tide
Of my Redeemer's blood.

4 Saviour, to thee my soul looks up,
My present Saviour, thou!
In all the confidence of hope,
I claim the blessing now.

5 'Tis done: thou dost this moment save,
With full salvation bless;
Redemption through thy blood I have,
And spotless love and peace.

—*Charles Wesley.*

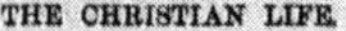

EAGLEY. C. M. J. WALCH.

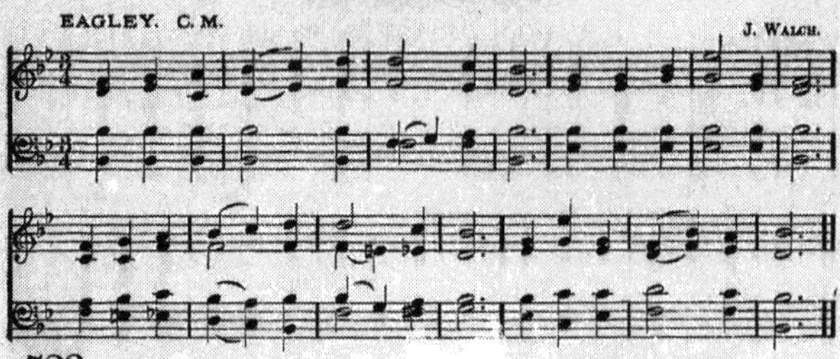

523

Living in union with Christ.

1 JESUS, the all-restoring Word,
My fallen spirit's hope,
After thy lovely likeness, Lord,
Ah! when shall I wake up?

2 Thou, O my God, thou only art
The Life, the Truth, the Way;
Quicken my soul, instruct my heart,
My sinking footsteps stay.

3 Of all thou hast in earth below,
In heaven above, to give,
Give me thy only love to know,
In thee to walk and live.

4 Fill me with all the life of love;
In mystic union join
Me to thyself, and let me prove
The fellowship divine.

5 Open the intercourse between
My longing soul and thee;
Never to be broke off again
To all eternity.

—*Charles Wesley.*

AURELIA. S. M. D. DR. S. S. WESLEY.

TUNE: AURELIA. S. M. D.

524

The law of love.

1 The thing my God doth hate
That I no more may do,
Thy creature, Lord, again create,
And all my soul renew:
My soul shall then, like thine,
Abhor the thing unclean,
And, sanctified by love divine,
For ever cease from sin.

2 That blessed law of thine,
Jesus, to me impart;
The Spirit's law of life divine,
O write it in my heart!
Implant it deep within,
Whence it may ne'er remove,
The law of liberty from sin,
The perfect law of love.

3 Thy nature be my law,
Thy spotless sanctity;
And sweetly every moment draw
My happy soul to thee.
Soul of my soul remain,
Who didst for all fulfil,
In me, O Lord, fulfil again
Thy heavenly Father's will.

—Charles Wesley.

525

The cleansing blood.

1 Father, I dare believe
Thee merciful and true;
Thou wilt my guilty soul forgive,
My fallen soul renew.
Come, then, for Jesus' sake,
And bid my heart be clean;
An end of all my troubles make,
An end of all my sin.

2 I will, through grace, I will,
I do, return to thee;
Empty my heart, O Lord, and fill
With perfect purity!
For power I feebly pray;
Thy kingdom now restore,
To-day, while it is called to-day,
And I shall sin no more.

3 I cannot wash my heart,
But by believing thee,
And waiting for thy blood to impart
The spotless purity;
While at thy cross I lie,
Jesus, thy grace bestow,
Now thy all-cleansing blood apply,
And I am white as snow.

—Charles Wesley.

WESTENHANGER. S. M. — C. W. Poole.

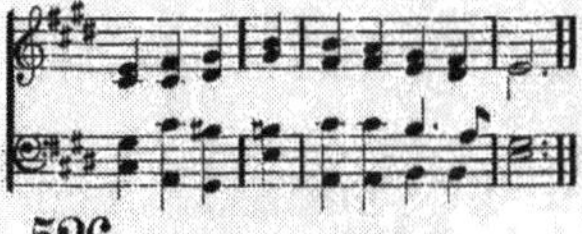

526

"Redemption in Christ Jesus."

1 Jesus, my Truth, my Way,
My sure, unerring Light,
On thee my feeble steps I stay,
Which thou wilt guide aright.

2 My Wisdom and my Guide,
My Counsellor thou art;
O never let me leave thy side,
Or from thy paths depart!

3 Never will I remove
Out of thy hands my cause;
But rest in thy redeeming love,
And hang upon thy cross.

4 Teach me the happy art
In all things to depend
On thee; O never, Lord, depart,
But love me to the end!

5 Through fire and water bring
Into the wealthy place;
And teach me the new song to sing,
When perfected in grace!

6 O make me all like thee,
Before I hence remove!
Settle, confirm, and stablish me,
And build me up in love.

7 Let me thy witness live,
When sin is all destroyed;
And then my spotless soul receive,
And take me home to God.

—Charles Wesley.

ARMAGEDDON. S. M. D. — Dr. Gauntlett.

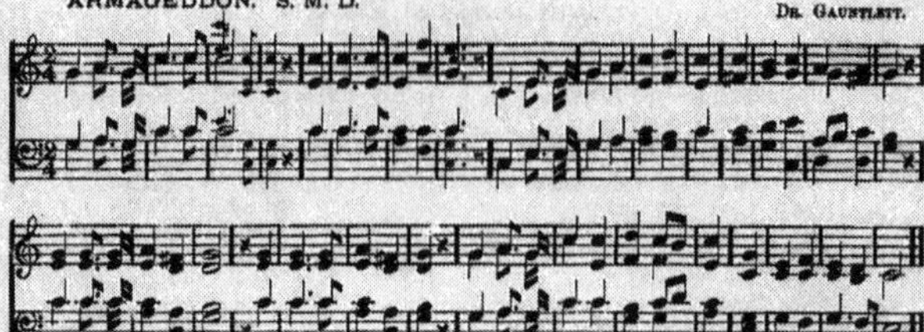

527 *"Redemption through his blood."*

1 Prisoners of hope, arise,
And see your Lord appear;
Lo! on the wings of love he flies,
And brings redemption near.
Redemption in his blood
He calls you to receive:
"Look unto me, the pardoning God;
Believe," he cries, "believe!"

2 The reconciling word
We thankfully embrace;
Rejoice in our redeeming Lord,
A blood-besprinkled race.
We yield to be set free;
Thy counsel we approve;
Salvation, praise, ascribe to thee,
And glory in thy love.

3 Jesus, to thee we look,
Till saved from sin's remains;
Reject the inbred tyrant's yoke,
And cast away his chains.
Our nature shall no more
O'er us dominion have;
By faith we apprehend the power
Which shall for ever save.

—*Charles Wesley.*

LANGTON. S. M. — Adapted by Streatfield.

528 *Purity of heart.*

1 Blest are the pure in heart,
For they shall see our God;
The secret of the Lord is theirs;
Their soul is his abode.

2 The Lord who left the heavens
His life and peace to bring,
Who dwelt in lowliness with men,
Their Pattern, and their King;

3 He to the lowly soul
Doth still himself impart,
And for his temple and his throne
Selects the pure in heart.

4 Lord, we thy presence seek,
May ours this blessing be;
O give the pure and lowly heart
A temple meet for thee!

—*J. Keble.*

TUNE: ARMAGEDDON. S. M. D. (See Hymn 527.)

529 *The Spirit of power and holiness.*

1 O come, and dwell in me,
Spirit of power within!
And bring the glorious liberty
From sorrow, fear, and sin.
The seed of sin's disease,
Spirit of health, remove,
Spirit of finished holiness,
Spirit of perfect love.

2 Hasten the joyful day,
Which shall my sins consume,
When old things shall be passed away,
And all things new become.
The original offence
Out of my soul erase;
Enter thyself, and drive it hence,
And take up all the place.

3 I want the witness, Lord,
That all I do is right,
According to thy will and word,
Well-pleasing in thy sight:
I ask no higher state;
Indulge me but in this,
And soon or later then translate
To my eternal bliss.

—*Charles Wesley.*

ZEPHYR. L. M. BRADBURY.

530 *The mind that was in Christ.*

1 What! never speak one evil word,
Or rash, or idle, or unkind!
O how shall I, most gracious Lord,
This mark of true perfection find!

2 Thy sinless mind in me reveal,
Thy Spirit's plenitude impart;
And all my spotless life shall tell
The abundance of a loving heart.

3 Saviour, I long to testify
The fulness of thy saving grace;
O might thy Spirit the blood apply,
Which bought for me the sacred peace!

4 Forgive and make my nature whole;
My inbred malady remove;
To perfect health restore my soul,
To perfect holiness and love.

—*Charles Wesley.*

531 *Full consecration to Christ.*

1 Come, Saviour, Jesus, from above!
Assist me with thy heavenly grace,
Empty my heart of earthly love,
And for thyself prepare the place.

2 O let thy sacred presence fill,
And set my longing spirit free,
Which pants to have no other will,
But day and night to feast on thee!

3 While in this region here below,
No other good will I pursue;
I'll bid this world of noise and show,
With all its glittering snares, adieu!

4 That path with humble speed I'll seek,
In which my Saviour's footsteps shine;
Nor will I hear, nor will I speak,
Of any other love but thine.

5 Henceforth may no profane delight
Divide this consecrated soul;
Possess it thou, who hast the right,
As Lord and Master of the whole.

6 Wealth, honour, pleasure, and what else
This short-enduring world can give,
Tempt as ye will, my soul repels,
To Christ alone resolved to live.

7 Nothing on earth do I desire,
But thy pure love within my breast;
This, only this, will I require,
And freely give up all the rest.

—*Dr. Byrom.*

ST. CROSS. L. M. Dr. Dykes.

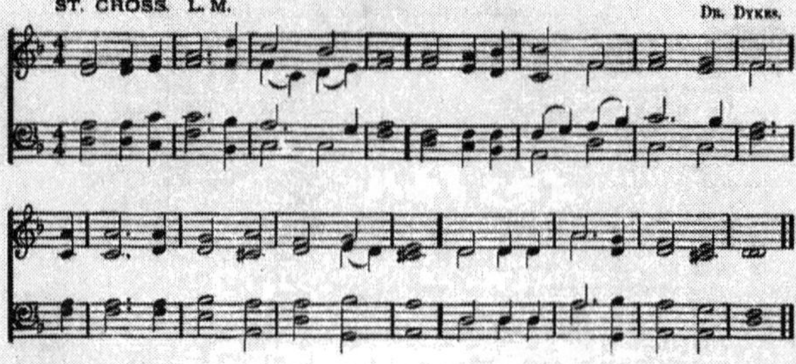

532 *Freedom from the bondage of sin.*

1 O that my load of sin were gone!
O that I could at last submit
At Jesus' feet to lay it down,
To lay my soul at Jesus' feet!

2 When shall mine eyes behold the Lamb?
The God of my salvation see?
Weary, O Lord, thou know'st I am;
Yet still I cannot come to thee.

3 Rest for my soul I long to find:
Saviour of all, if mine thou art,
Give me thy meek and lowly mind,
And stamp thine image on my heart.

4 Break off the yoke of inbred sin,
And fully set my spirit free;
I cannot rest till pure within,
Till I am wholly lost in thee.

5 Fain would I learn of thee, my God;
Thy light and easy burden prove,
The cross, all stained with hallowed blood,
The labour of thy dying love.

6 I would, but thou must give the power,
My heart from every sin release;
Bring near, O Lord, the joyful hour,
And fill me with thy perfect peace.

7 Come, Lord, the drooping sinner cheer,
Nor let thy chariot wheels delay;
Appear, in my poor heart appear!
My God, my Saviour, come away!

—*Charles Wesley.*

HOME. L. M. From Mozart.

TUNE: HOME. L. M.

533 *"A glorious Church, not having spot or wrinkle."*

1 Jesus, from whom all blessings flow,
Great Builder of thy Church below,
If now thy Spirit moves my breast,
Hear, and fulfil thine own request.
2 The few that truly call thee Lord,
And wait thy sanctifying word,
And thee their utmost Saviour own,
Unite and perfect them in one.
3 O let them all thy mind express,
Stand forth thy chosen witnesses;
Thy power unto salvation show,
And perfect holiness below!
4 Call them into thy wondrous light,
Worthy to walk with thee in white;
Make up thy jewels, Lord, and show
Thy glorious, spotless Church below.
5 From every sinful wrinkle free,
Redeemed from all iniquity,
The fellowship of saints make known,
And, O my God, may I be one!
6 Lord, if I now thy drawings feel,
And ask according to thy will,
Confirm the prayer, the seal impart,
And speak the answer to my heart.
7 Tell me, or thou shalt never go,
"Thy prayer is heard; it shall be so;"
The word hath passed thy lips, and I
Shall with thy people live and die.

—*Charles Wesley.*

ST. ALBAN. L. M. St. Alban's Tune Book.

534 *"The very God of peace sanctify you wholly."*

1 O thou, our Saviour, Brother, Friend,
Behold a cloud of incense rise!
The prayers of saints to heaven ascend,
Grateful, accepted sacrifice.
2 Regard our prayers for Zion's peace;
Shed in our hearts thy love abroad;
Thy gifts abundantly increase;
Enlarge, and fill us all with God.
3 Before thy sheep, great Shepherd, go,
And guide into thy perfect will;
Cause us thy hallowed name to know,
The work of faith in us fulfil.
4 Help us to make our calling sure;
O let us all be saints indeed,
And pure as thou thyself art pure,
Conformed in all things to our Head.
5 Take the dear purchase of thy blood;
Thy blood shall wash us white as snow,
Present us sanctified to God,
And perfected in love below.
6 That blood which cleanses from all sin,
That efficacious blood apply,
And wash, and make us wholly clean,
And change, and throughly sanctify.
7 From all iniquity redeem,
Cleanse by the water and the word,
And free from every spot of blame,
And make the servant as his Lord!

—*Charles Wesley.*

535 *The consecration of the life.*

1 God of my life, what just return
Can sinful dust and ashes give?
I only live my sin to mourn;
To love my God I only live.
2 To thee, benign and saving Power,
I consecrate my lengthened days;
While, marked with blessings, every hour
Shall speak thy co-extended praise.
3 Be all my added life employed
Thine image in my soul to see;
Fill with thyself the mighty void;
Enlarge my heart to compass thee.
4 The blessing of thy love bestow;
For this my cries shall never fail;
Wrestling, I will not let thee go,
I will not, till my suit prevail.
5 Come then, my Hope, my Life, my Lord,
And fix in me thy lasting home;
Be mindful of thy gracious word;
Thou with thy promised Father come.
6 Prepare, and then possess my heart;
O take me, seize me from above;
Thee may I love, for God thou art;
Thee may I feel, for God is Love.

—*Charles Wesley.*

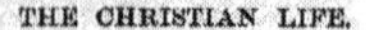

WOODWORTH. L. M. W. B. BRADBURY.

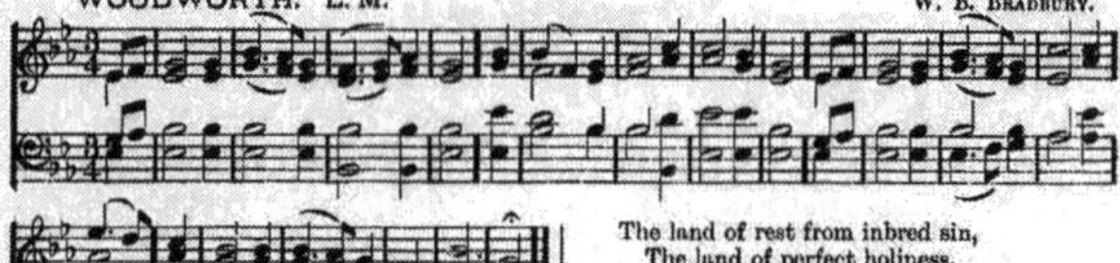

536 *"This is the will of God, even your sanctification."*

1 HE wills that I should holy be;
  That holiness I long to feel;
That full divine conformity
  To all my Saviour's righteous will.

2 See, Lord, the travail of thy soul
  Accomplished in the change of mine,
And plunge me, every whit made whole,
  In all the depths of love divine.

3 On thee, O God, my soul is stayed,
  And waits to prove thine utmost will;
The promise, by thy mercy made,
  Thou canst, thou wilt, in me fulfil.

4 No more I stagger at thy power,
  Or doubt thy truth, which cannot move;
Hasten the long-expected hour,
  And bless me with thy perfect love.

5 Jesus, thy loving Spirit alone
  Can lead me forth, and make me free;
Burst every bond through which I groan,
  And set my heart at liberty.

6 Now let thy Spirit bring me in;
  And give thy servant to possess
The land of rest from inbred sin,
  The land of perfect holiness.

7 Lord, I believe thy power the same;
  The same thy truth and grace endure;
And in thy blessèd hands I am,
  And trust thee for a perfect cure.

8 Come, Saviour, come, and make me whole;
  Entirely all my sins remove;
To perfect health restore my soul,
  To perfect holiness and love.

—*Charles Wesley.*

537 *Prayer for a faithful, tender heart.*

1 O JESUS, let thy dying cry
  Pierce to the bottom of my heart,
Its evils cure, its wants supply,
  And bid my unbelief depart.

2 Slay the dire root and seed of sin;
  Prepare for thee the holiest place;
Then, O essential Love, come in,
  And fill thy house with endless praise!

3 Let me, according to thy word,
  A tender, contrite heart receive,
Which grieves at having grieved its Lord,
  And never can itself forgive:

4 A heart thy joys and griefs to feel,
  A heart that cannot faithless prove,
A heart where Christ alone may dwell,
  All praise, all meekness, and all love.

—*Charles Wesley.*

ECCLES. 6.6.7.7.7.7. BOGGETT.

TUNE: ECCLES. 6.6.7.7.7.7.

538 *The kingdom of Christ within.*

1 Jesus, thou art my King!
To me thy succour bring;
Christ, the mighty One, art thou,
Help for all on thee is laid;
This the word; I claim it now,
‖:Send me now the promised aid.:‖

2 High on thy Father's throne,
O look with pity down!
Help, O help, attend my call,
Captive lead captivity;
King of glory, Lord of all,
‖:Christ, be Lord, be King to me!:‖

3 I pant to feel thy sway,
And only thee obey;
Thee my spirit gasps to meet;
This my one, my ceaseless prayer,
Make, O make my heart thy seat,
‖:O set up thy kingdom there!:‖

4 Triumph and reign in me,
And spread thy victory;
Hell, and death, and sin control,
Pride, and wrath, and every foe,
All subdue; through all my soul
‖:Conquering, and to conquer go.:‖
—*Charles Wesley.*

539 *Looking to Christ.*

1 Author of faith, appear;
Be thou its finisher!
Upward still for this we gaze,
Till we feel the stamp divine,
Thee behold with open face,
‖:Bright in all thy glory shine.:‖

2 Leave not thy work undone,
But ever love thine own;
Let us all thy goodness prove,
Let us to the end believe;
Show thine everlasting love,
‖:Save us, to the utmost save.:‖

3 O that our life might be
One looking up to thee!
Ever hastening to the day
When our eyes shall see thee near;
Come, Redeemer, come away,
‖:Glorious in thy saints appear.:‖
—*Charles Wesley.*

AUSTRIA. 8.7, 8.7, 8.7, 8.7. F. J. Haydn.

540 *"Created in Christ Jesus unto good works."*

1 Love Divine, all loves excelling,
Joy of heaven, to earth come down;
Fix in us thy humble dwelling,
All thy faithful mercies crown.
Jesus, thou art all compassion,
Pure, unbounded love thou art;
Visit us with thy salvation,
Enter every trembling heart.

2 Come, almighty to deliver,
Let us all thy grace receive;
Suddenly return, and never,
Never more, thy temples leave.
Thee we would be always blessing,
Serve thee as thy hosts above,
Pray, and praise thee, without ceasing,
Glory in thy perfect love.

3 Finish, then, thy new creation,
Pure and spotless let us be;
Let us see thy great salvation,
Perfectly restored in thee.
Changed from glory into glory,
Till in heaven we take our place,
Till we cast our crowns before thee,
Lost in wonder, love, and praise.
—*Charles Wesley.*

AJALON. 6-7s. R. Redhead.

541

Freedom from sin.

1 Since the Son hath made me free,
Let me taste my liberty;
Thee behold with open face,
Triumph in thy saving grace;
Thy great will delight to prove,
Glory in thy perfect love.

2 Abba, Father! hear thy child,
Late in Jesus reconciled;
Hear, and all the graces shower,
All the joy, and peace, and power;
All my Saviour asks above,
All the life and heaven of love.

3 Lord, I will not let thee go,
Till the blessing thou bestow;
Hear my Advocate divine;
Lo! to his my suit I join;
Joined to his, it cannot fail;
Bless me; for I will prevail!

4 Holy Ghost, no more delay;
Come, and in thy temple stay!
Now thine inward witness bear,
Strong, and permanent, and clear;
Spring of Life, thyself impart;
Rise eternal in my heart!

—*Charles Wesley.*

BROMLEY. 7.6, 7.6, 7.7, 7.6. London Tune Book.

542

The still small voice.

1 Open, Lord, my inward ear,
And bid my heart rejoice;
Bid my quiet spirit hear
Thy comfortable voice:
Never in the whirlwind found,
Or where earthquakes rock the place,
Still and silent is the sound,
The whisper of thy grace.

2 From the world of sin, and noise,
And hurry, I withdraw;
For the small and inward voice
I wait with humble awe:
Silent am I now and still,
Dare not in thy presence move;
To my waiting soul reveal
The secret of thy love.

3 Show me, as my soul can bear,
The depth of inbred sin;
All the unbelief declare,
The pride that lurks within:
Take me whom thyself hast bought,
Bring into captivity
Every high aspiring thought,
That would not stoop to thee.

4 Lord, my time is in thy hand;
My soul to thee convert;
Thou canst make me understand,
Though I am slow of heart:
Thine, in whom I live and move,
Thine the work, the praise is thine;
Thou art Wisdom, Power, and Love,
And all thou art is mine.

—*Charles Wesley.*

TUNE: BROMLEY. 7.6, 7.6, 7.7, 7.6. (SEE HYMN 542.)

543

Deut. xxxiii. 26-29.

1 NONE is like Jeshurun's God,
So great, so strong, so high,
Lo! he spreads his wings abroad,
He rides upon the sky;
Israel is his first-born son;
God, the Almighty God, is thine;
See him to thy help come down,
The excellence divine.

2 Thee the great Jehovah deigns
To succour and defend;
Thee the eternal God sustains,
Thy Maker and thy Friend;
Israel, what hast thou to dread?
Safe from all impending harms,
Round thee and beneath are spread
The everlasting arms.

3 God is thine; disdain to fear
The enemy within;
God shall in thy flesh appear,
And make an end of sin:
God the man of sin shall slay,
Fill thee with triumphant joy;
God shall thrust him out and say,
"Destroy them all, destroy!"

4 All the struggle then is o'er,
And wars and fightings cease;
Israel then shall sin no more,
But dwell in perfect peace:
All his enemies are gone;
Sin shall have in him no part;
Israel now shall dwell alone,
With Jesus in his heart.

5 Blest, O Israel, art thou;
What people is like thee?
Saved from sin, by Jesus, now
Thou art, and still shalt be:
Jesus is thy seven-fold shield,
Jesus is thy flaming sword,
Earth, and hell, and sin shall yield,
To God's almighty word.

—*Charles Wesley.*

WELD. 7.6, 7.6, 7.7, 7.6.

544

"Purifying their hearts by faith."

1 Now, even now, I yield, I yield,
With all my sins to part;
Jesus, speak my pardon sealed,
And purify my heart;
Purge the love of sin away,
Then I into nothing fall;
Then I see the perfect day,
And Christ is all in all.

2 Jesus, now our hearts inspire
With that pure love of thine;
Kindle now the heavenly fire,
To brighten and refine;
Purify our faith like gold;
All the dross of sin remove;
Melt our spirits down, and mould
Into thy perfect love.

—*Charles Wesley.*

BONN. 7.6, 7.6, 7.7, 7.6. ADAPTED FROM THE GERMAN.

545 *"Ye are the temple of the living God."*

1 WHO hath slighted or contemned
The day of feeble things?
I shall be by grace redeemed;
'Tis grace salvation brings:
When to me my Lord shall come,
Sin for ever shall depart;
Jesus takes up all the room
In a believing heart.

2 Son of God, arise, arise,
And to thy temple come!
Look, and with thy flaming eyes
The man of sin consume:
Slay him with thy Spirit, Lord;
Reign thou in my heart alone;
Speak the sanctifying word,
And seal me all thine own.

—*Charles Wesley.*

RICHMOND. 7.6, 7.6, 7.8, 7.6.

546 *"Perfect love casteth out fear."*

1 EVER fainting with desire,
For thee, O Christ, I call;
Thee I restlessly require,
I want my God, my All!
Jesus, dear redeeming Lord,
I wait thy coming from above:
Help me, Saviour, speak the word,
And perfect me in love.

2 Wilt thou suffer me to go
Lamenting all my days?
Shall I never, never know
Thy sanctifying grace?
Wilt thou not the light afford,
The darkness from my soul remove?
Help me, Saviour, speak the word,
And perfect me in love.

3 Thou, my Life, my treasure be,
My portion here below;
Nothing would I seek but thee,
Thee only would I know,
My exceeding great Reward,
My Heaven on earth, my Heaven above:
Help me, Saviour, speak the word,
And perfect me in love.

4 Grant me now the bliss to feel
Of those that are in thee;
Son of God, thyself reveal,
Engrave thy name on me;
As in heaven be here adored,
And let me now the promise prove:
Help me, Saviour, speak the word,
And perfect me in love.

—*Charles Wesley.*

TUNE: RICHMOND. 7.6, 7.6, 7.8, 7.6. (See Hymn 546.)

547

"I determined not to know any thing among you, save Jesus Christ, and him crucified."

1 Vain, delusive world, adieu,
With all of creature-good!
Only Jesus I pursue,
Who bought me with his blood;
All thy pleasures I forego,
I trample on thy wealth and pride:
Only Jesus will I know,
And Jesus crucified.

2 Other knowledge I disdain,
'Tis all but vanity;
Christ, the Lamb of God, was slain,
He tasted death for me.
Me to save from endless woe,
The sin-atoning Victim died:
Only Jesus will I know,
And Jesus crucified.

3 Turning to my rest again,
The Saviour I adore;
He relieves my grief and pain,
And bids me weep no more.
Rivers of salvation flow
From out his head, his hands, his side:
Only Jesus will I know,
And Jesus crucified.

4 Here will I set up my rest;
My fluctuating heart
From the haven of his breast
Shall never more depart.
Whither should a sinner go?
His wounds for me stand open wide:
Only Jesus will I know,
And Jesus crucified.

—*Charles Wesley.*

LEAMINGTON. 7.6, 7.6, 7.8, 7.6. J. B. Sale.

548

God manifest in the flesh.

1 Once thou didst on earth appear,
For all mankind to atone;
Now be manifested here,
And bid our sin be gone!
Come, and by thy presence chase
Its nature with its guilt and power;
Jesus, show thy open face,
And sin shall be no more.

2 Then my soul, with strange delight,
Shall comprehend and feel
What the length, and breadth, and height
Of love unspeakable:
Then I shall the secret know,
Which angels would search out in vain;
God was man, and served below,
That man with God might reign!

3 Father, Son, and Spirit, come,
And with thine own abide;
Holy Ghost, to make thee room,
Our hearts we open wide;
Thee, and only thee request,
To every asking sinner given;
Come, our life, and peace, and rest,
Our all in earth and heaven.

—*Charles Wesley.*

STELLA. 6-8s. FROM "CROWN OF JESUS."

549 *Confidence in God's faithfulness.*

1 PRISONERS of hope, lift up your heads!
The day of liberty draws near;
Jesus, who on the serpent treads,
Shall soon in your behalf appear:
The Lord will to his temple come,
Prepare your hearts to make him room.

2 Ye all shall find, whom in his word
Himself hath caused to put your trust,
The Father of our dying Lord
Is ever to his promise just;
Faithful, if we our sins confess,
To cleanse from all unrighteousness.

3 Yes, Lord, we must believe thee kind,
Thou never canst unfaithful prove;
Surely we shall thy mercy find;
Who ask, shall all receive thy love;
Nor canst thou it to me deny,
I ask, the chief of sinners, I.

4 O ye of fearful hearts, be strong!
Your downcast eyes and hands lift up;
Ye shall not be forgotten long;
Hope to the end, in Jesus hope!
Tell him, ye wait his grace to prove,
And cannot fail, if God is love.

—*Charles Wesley.*

550 SECOND PART.

1 PRISONERS of hope, be strong, be bold!
Cast off your doubts, disdain to fear!
Dare to believe; on Christ lay hold;
Wrestle with Christ in mighty prayer;
Tell him, "We will not let thee go,
Till we thy name, thy nature know."

2 Lord, we believe, and wait the hour
Which all thy great salvation brings;
The Spirit of love, and health, and power,
Shall come, and make us priests and kings;
Thou wilt perform thy faithful word,
"The servant shall be as his Lord."

3 The promise stands for ever sure,
And we shall in thine image shine,
Partakers of a nature pure,
Holy, angelical, divine;
In spirit joined to thee the Son,
As thou art with thy Father one.

4 Faithful and True, we now receive
The promise ratified by thee;
To thee the *when* and *how* we leave,
In time and in eternity;
We only hang upon thy word,
"The servant shall be as his Lord."

—*Charles Wesley.*

GIESSEN. 6-8s.

551 *The covenant of forgiveness.*

1 Forgive us for thy mercy's sake,
Our multitude of sins forgive!
And for thy own possession take,
And bid us to thy glory live;
Live in thy sight, and gladly prove
Our faith, by our obedient love.

2 The covenant of forgiveness seal,
And all thy mighty wonders show;
Our inbred enemies expel,
And conquering them to conquer go,
Till all of pride and wrath be slain,
And not one evil thought remain.

3 O put it in our inward parts,
The living law of perfect love!
Write the new precept in our hearts;
We shall not then from thee remove,
Who in thy glorious image shine,
Thy people, and for ever thine.

—Charles Wesley.

552 *The living water.*

1 Jesus, the gift divine I know,
The gift divine I ask of thee;
That living water now bestow,
Thy Spirit and thyself, on me;
Thou, Lord, of life the fountain art;
Now let me find thee in my heart.

2 Thee let me drink, and thirst no more
For drops of finite happiness;
Spring up, O Well, in heavenly power,
In streams of pure perennial peace,
In joy, that none can take away,
In life, which shall for ever stay.

3 Thy mind throughout my life be shown,
While listening to the sufferer's cry,
The widow's and the orphan's groan,
On mercy's wings I swiftly fly,
The poor and helpless to relieve,
My life, my all, for them to give.

4 Thus may I show the Spirit within,
Which purges me from every stain;
Unspotted from the world and sin,
My faith's integrity maintain;
The truth of my religion prove,
By perfect purity and love.

—Charles Wesley

CONFIDENCE. 6-8s.

553 *Forgiveness and sanctification through Christ.*

1 O God of our forefathers, hear,
And make thy faithful mercies known!
To thee, through Jesus, we draw near,
Thy suffering, well-belovéd Son,
In whom thy smiling face we see,
In whom thou art well pleased with me.

2 With solemn faith we offer up,
And spread before thy glorious eyes,
That only ground of all our hope,
That precious, bleeding Sacrifice,
Which brings thy grace on sinners down,
And perfects all our souls in one.

3 Acceptance through his only name,
Forgiveness in his blood, we have;
But more abundant life we claim
Through him who died our souls to save,
To sanctify us by his blood,
And fill with all the life of God.

4 Father, behold thy dying Son,
And hear the blood that speaks above!
On us let all thy grace be shown:
Peace, righteousness, and joy, and love,
Thy kingdom come to every heart,
And all thou hast, and all thou art.

—*Charles Wesley.*

554 Mark ix. 23.

1 All things are possible to him
That can in Jesus' name believe:
Lord, I no more thy truth blaspheme,
Thy truth I lovingly receive;
I can, I do believe in thee,
All things are possible to me.

2 The most impossible of all
Is, that I e'er from sin should cease;
Yet shall it be, I know it shall;
Jesus, I trust thy faithfulness!
If nothing is too hard for thee,
All things are possible to me.

3 Though earth and hell the word gainsay,
The word of God can never fail;
The Lamb shall take my sins away;
'Tis certain, though impossible;
The thing impossible shall be;
All things are possible to me.

4 Thy mouth, O Lord, hath spoke, hath sworn,
That I shall serve thee without fear,
Shall find the pearl which others spurn;
Holy, and pure, and perfect here,
The servant as his Lord shall be;
All things are possible to me.

5 All things are possible to God,
To Christ, the power of God in man,
To me, when I am all renewed,
When I in Christ am formed again,
And witness, from all sin set free,
All things are possible to me.

—*Charles Wesley.*

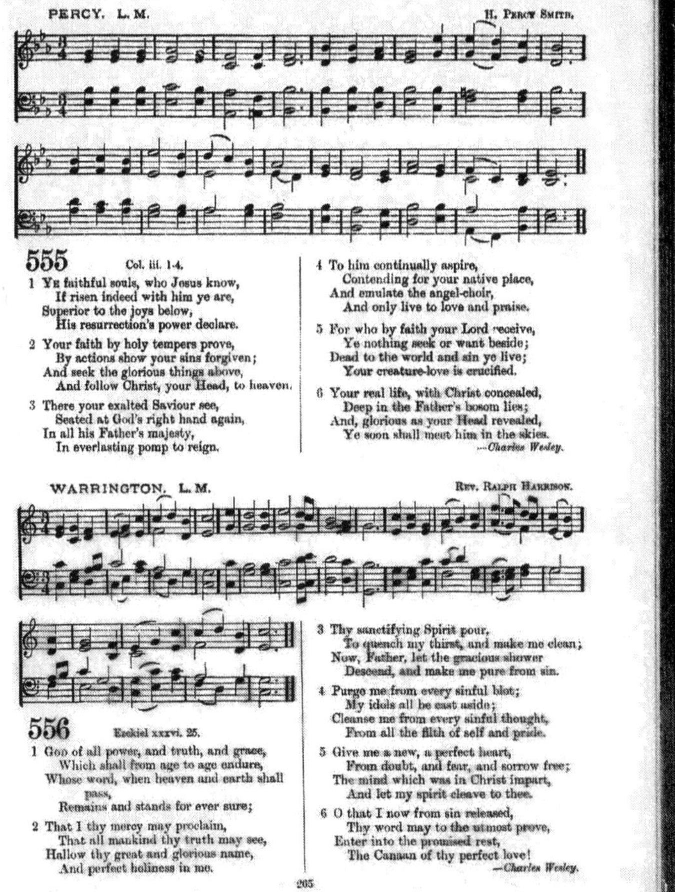

PERCY. L. M. — H. Percy Smith.

555 Col. iii. 1-4.

1 Ye faithful souls, who Jesus know,
If risen indeed with him ye are,
Superior to the joys below,
His resurrection's power declare.

2 Your faith by holy tempers prove,
By actions show your sins forgiven;
And seek the glorious things above,
And follow Christ, your Head, to heaven.

3 There your exalted Saviour see,
Seated at God's right hand again,
In all his Father's majesty,
In everlasting pomp to reign.

4 To him continually aspire,
Contending for your native place,
And emulate the angel-choir,
And only live to love and praise.

5 For who by faith your Lord receive,
Ye nothing seek or want beside;
Dead to the world and sin ye live;
Your creature-love is crucified.

6 Your real life, with Christ concealed,
Deep in the Father's bosom lies;
And, glorious as your Head revealed,
Ye soon shall meet him in the skies.
—*Charles Wesley.*

WARRINGTON. L. M. — Rev. Ralph Harrison.

556 Ezekiel xxxvi. 25.

1 God of all power, and truth, and grace,
Which shall from age to age endure,
Whose word, when heaven and earth shall pass,
Remains and stands for ever sure;

2 That I thy mercy may proclaim,
That all mankind thy truth may see,
Hallow thy great and glorious name,
And perfect holiness in me.

3 Thy sanctifying Spirit pour,
To quench my thirst, and make me clean;
Now, Father, let the gracious shower
Descend, and make me pure from sin.

4 Purge me from every sinful blot;
My idols all be cast aside;
Cleanse me from every sinful thought,
From all the filth of self and pride.

5 Give me a new, a perfect heart,
From doubt, and fear, and sorrow free;
The mind which was in Christ impart,
And let my spirit cleave to thee.

6 O that I now from sin released,
Thy word may to the utmost prove,
Enter into the promised rest,
The Canaan of thy perfect love!
—*Charles Wesley.*

TRINITY. L. M. PIERACCINI.

557

"The God that answereth by fire, let him be God."

1 Thou God that answerest by fire,
  On thee in Jesus' name we call;
Fulfil our faithful hearts' desire,
  And let on us thy Spirit fall.

2 Bound on the altar of thy cross,
  Our old offending nature lies;
Now, for the honour of thy cause,
  Come, and consume the sacrifice!

3 O that the fire from heaven might fall,
  Our sins its ready victims find,
Seize on our sins, and burn up all,
  Nor leave the least remains behind!

4 Then shall our prostrate souls adore,
  The Lord, he is the God, confess;
He is the God of saving power;
  He is the God of hallowing grace.

—*Charles Wesley.*

558

SECOND PART.

1 Holy, and true, and righteous Lord,
  I wait to prove thy perfect will;
Be mindful of thy gracious word,
  And stamp me with thy Spirit's seal.

2 Open my faith's interior eye;
  Display thy glory from above;
And all I am shall sink and die,
  Lost in astonishment and love.

3 Confound, o'erpower me by thy grace;
  I would be by myself abhorred;
All might, all majesty, all praise,
  All glory be to Christ my Lord.

4 Now let me gain perfection's height;
  Now let me into nothing fall;
As less than nothing in thy sight,
  And feel that Christ is all in all.

—*Charles Wesley.*

ARNOLD. C. M. DR. S. ARNOLD.

559

"If I wash thee not, thou hast no part with me."

1 For ever here my rest shall be,
  Close to thy bleeding side;
This all my hope, and all my plea,
  For me the Saviour died!

2 My dying Saviour, and my God,
  Fountain for guilt and sin,
Sprinkle me ever with thy blood,
  And cleanse, and keep me clean.

3 Wash me, and make me thus thine own;
  Wash me, and mine thou art;
Wash me, but not my feet alone,
  My hands, my head, my heart.

4 The atonement of thy blood apply,
  Till faith to sight improve,
Till hope in full fruition die,
  And all my soul be love.

—*Charles Wesley.*

ABENDS. L. M. — Sir H. S. Oakley.

560

Ezekiel xvi. 62, 63.

1 O God, most merciful and true,
Thy nature to my soul impart;
Stablish with me the covenant new,
And write perfection on my heart!

2 To real holiness restored,
O let me gain my Saviour's mind;
And, in the knowledge of my Lord,
Fulness of life eternal find.

3 Remember, Lord, my sins no more,
That them I may no more forget;
But sunk in guiltless shame adore,
With speechless wonder, at thy feet.

4 O'erwhelmed with thy stupendous grace,
I shall not in thy presence move;
But breathe unutterable praise,
And rapturous awe, and silent love.

5 Pardoned for all that I have done,
My mouth as in the dust I hide;
And glory give to God alone,
My God for ever pacified!

—*Charles Wesley.*

PETERBOROUGH. C. M. — Rev. Ralph Harrison.

561

"Ye are Christ's."

1 Let him to whom we now belong
His sovereign right assert,
And take up every thankful song,
And every loving heart.

2 He justly claims us for his own,
Who bought us with a price;
The Christian lives to Christ alone,
To Christ alone he dies.

3 Jesus, thine own at last receive,
Fulfil our hearts' desire,
And let us to thy glory live,
And in thy cause expire.

4 Our souls and bodies we resign;
With joy we render thee
Our all, no longer ours, but thine
To all eternity.

—*Charles Wesley.*

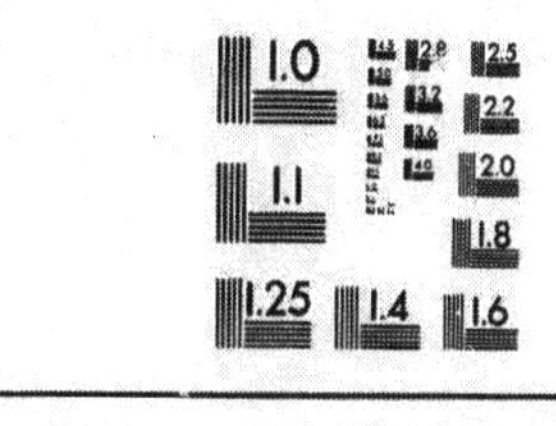

BEDFORD. C. M. W. WHEALL.

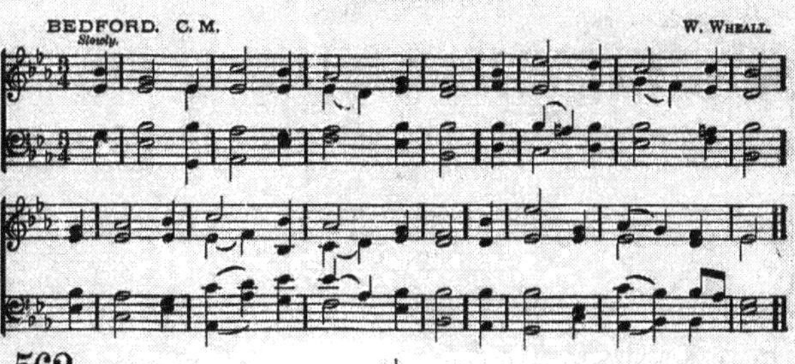
Slowly.

562

Prayer for cleansing.

1 O JESUS, at thy feet we wait,
Till thou shalt bid us rise,
Restored to our unsinning state,
To love's sweet paradise.

2 Saviour from sin, we thee receive,
From all indwelling sin;
Thy blood, we steadfastly believe,
Shall make us throughly clean.

3 Since thou wouldst have us free from sin,
And pure as those above,
Make haste to bring thy nature in,
And perfect us in love.

4 The counsel of thy love fulfil;
Come quickly, gracious Lord,
Be it according to thy will,
According to thy word!

5 O that the perfect grace were given,
The love diffused abroad!
O that our hearts were all a heaven,
For ever filled with God!

—*Charles Wesley.*

SERENITY. C. M. W. V. WALLACE.

563

Matt. iii. 12.

1 COME, thou omniscient Son of Man,
Display thy sifting power;
Come with thy Spirit's winnowing fan,
And throughly purge thy floor.

2 The chaff of sin, the accursèd thing,
Far from our souls be driven!
The wheat into thy garner bring,
And lay us up for heaven.

3 Look through me with thy eyes of flame,
The clouds and darkness chase;
And tell me what by sin I am,
And what I am by grace.

4 Whate'er offends thy glorious eyes,
Far from our hearts remove;
As dust before the whirlwind flies
Disperse it by thy love.

5 Then let us all thy fulness know,
From every sin set free;
Saved to the utmost, saved below,
And perfectly like thee.

—*Charles Wesley.*

WHEALL.

in,

iven,

aven,

Wesley.

WALLACE.

Wesley.

BYZANTIUM. C. M. — W. JACKSON.

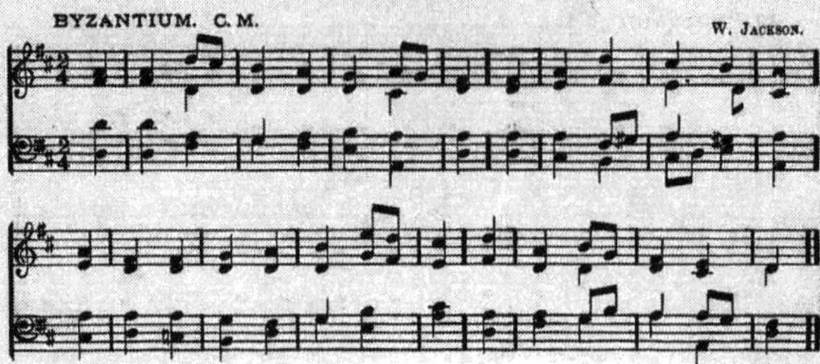

564 *The baptism of the Holy Ghost and fire.*

1 MY God! I know, I feel thee mine,
And will not quit my claim,
Till all I have is lost in thine,
And all renewed I am.

2 I hold thee with a trembling hand,
But will not let thee go,
Till steadfastly by faith I stand,
And all thy goodness know.

3 When shall I see the welcome hour,
That plants my God in me!
Spirit of health, and life, and power,
And perfect liberty!

4 Jesus, thine all-victorious love
Shed in my heart abroad;
Then shall my feet no longer rove,
Rooted and fixed in God.

5 Love can bow down the stubborn neck,
The stone to flesh convert,
Soften, and melt, and pierce, and break,
An adamantine heart.

6 O that in me the sacred fire
Might now begin to glow,
Burn up the dross of base desire,
And make the mountains flow!

7 C that it now from heaven might fall,
And all my sins consume!
Come, Holy Ghost, for thee I call,
Spirit of burning, come!

8 Refining fire, go through my heart,
Illuminate my soul;
Scatter thy life through every part,
And sanctify the whole.

—*Charles Wesley.*

565 *The power of faith.*

1 GOD of eternal truth and grace,
Thy faithful promise seal!
Thy word, thy oath, to Abraham's race,
In us, even us, fulfil.

2 Let us, to perfect love restored,
Thy image here retrieve,
And in the presence of our Lord
The life of angels live.

3 That mighty faith on me bestow,
Which cannot ask in vain;
Which holds, and will not let thee go,
Till I my suit obtain:

4 Till thou into my soul inspire
The perfect love unknown,
And tell my infinite desire,
"Whate'er thou wilt, be done."

5 But is it possible that I
Should live and sin no more?
Lord, if on thee I dare rely,
The faith shall bring the power.

6 On me that faith divine bestow,
Which doth the mountain move;
And all my spotless life shall show,
The omnipotence of love.

—*Charles Wesley.*

ST. BERNARD. C.M. W. RICHARDSON.

566 *Salvation through faith in Christ.*

1 FATHER of Jesus Christ, my Lord,
My Saviour, and my Head,
I trust in thee, whose powerful word
Hath raised him from the dead.

2 Thou know'st for my offence he died,
And rose again for me;
Fully and freely justified,
That I might live to thee.

3 Eternal life to all mankind
Thou hast in Jesus given;
And all who seek, in him shall find
The happiness of heaven.

4 In hope, against all human hope,
Self-desperate, I believe;
Thy quickening word shall raise me up,
Thou shalt thy Spirit give.

5 The thing surpasses all my thought,
But faithful is my Lord;
Through unbelief I stagger not,
For God hath spoke the word.

6 Faith, mighty faith, the promise sees,
And looks to that alone;
Laughs at impossibilities,
And cries, "It shall be done!"

7 Obedient faith, that waits on thee,
Thou never wilt reprove;
But thou wilt form thy Son in me,
And perfect me in love.
—Charles Wesley.

567 *"Let us go on to perfection."*

1 DEEPEN the wound thy hands have made
In this weak, helpless soul,
Till mercy, with its balmy aid,
Descends to make me whole.

2 The sharpness of thy two-edged sword
Enable me to endure,
Till bold to say, My hallowing Lord
Hath wrought a perfect cure.

3 I see the exceeding broad command,
Which all contains in one;
Enlarge my heart to understand
The mystery unknown.

4 O that with all thy saints I might
By sweet experience prove,
What is the length, and breadth, and height,
And depth, of perfect love!
—Charles Wesley.

EVAN. C.M. REV. W. H. HAVERGAL.

TUNE: EVAN. C. M.

568

The great salvation.

1 I KNOW that my Redeemer lives,
And ever prays for me;
A token of his love he gives,
A pledge of liberty.

2 I find him lifting up my head,
He brings salvation near;
His presence makes me free indeed,
And he will soon appear.

3 He wills that I should holy be,
What can withstand his will?
The counsel of his grace in me
He surely shall fulfil.

4 Jesus, I hang upon thy word;
I steadfastly believe
Thou wilt return and claim me, Lord,
And to thyself receive.

5 When God is mine, and I am his,
Of paradise possest,
I taste unutterable bliss,
And everlasting rest.

6 The bliss of those that fully dwell,
Fully in thee believe,
'Tis more than angel tongues can tell,
Or angel minds conceive.

7 Thou only know'st, who didst obtain,
And die to make it known;
The great salvation now explain,
And perfect us in one.

—*Charles Wesley.*

SERENITY. C. M. W. V. WALLACE.

569

All power given to Christ.

1 JESUS, my Lord, mighty to save,
What can my hopes withstand,
While thee my Advocate I have,
Enthroned at God's right hand?

2 Nature is subject to thy word;
All power to thee is given,
The uncontrolled, almighty Lord
Of hell, and earth, and heaven.

3 And shall my sins thy will oppose?
Master, thy right maintain;
O let not thy usurping foes
In me thy servant reign!

4 Come, then, and claim me for thine own;
Saviour, thy right assert;
Come, gracious Lord, set up thy throne,
And reign within my heart!

5 So shall I bless thy pleasing sway,
And, sitting at thy feet,
Thy laws with all my heart obey,
With all my soul submit.

6 So shall I do thy will below,
As angels do above;
The virtue of thy passion show,
The triumphs of thy love.

—*Charles Wesley.*

CONFIDENCE. 6-8s.

570

The love of Christ.

1 Jesus, thy boundless love to me
No thought can reach, no tongue declare;
O knit my thankful heart to thee,
And reign without a rival there!
Thine wholly, thine alone, I am,
Be thou alone my constant flame.

2 O grant that nothing in my soul
May dwell, but thy pure love alone:
O may thy love possess me whole,
My joy, my treasure, and my crown:
Strange flames far from my heart remove;
My every act, word, thought, be love!

3 O Love, how cheering is thy ray;
All pain before thy presence flies,
Care, anguish, sorrow, melt away,
Where'er thy healing beams arise;
O Jesus, nothing may I see,
Nothing desire, or seek, but thee!

4 Unwearied may I this pursue,
Dauntless to the high prize aspire;
Hourly within my soul renew
This holy flame, this heavenly fire;
And day and night be all my care
To guard the sacred treasure there.
—*Charles Wesley.*

571

SECOND PART.

1 O Saviour, thou thy love to me
In shame, in want, in pain, hast showed;
For me on the accursèd tree,
Thou pouredst forth thy guiltless blood;
Thy wounds upon my heart impress,
Nor aught shall the loved stamp efface.

2 More hard than marble is my heart,
And foul with sins of deepest stain;
But thou the mighty Saviour art,
Nor flowed thy cleansing blood in vain;
Ah! soften, melt this rock, and may
Thy blood wash all these stains away!

3 O that I, as a little child,
May follow thee, and never rest
Till sweetly thou hast breathed thy mild
And lowly mind into my breast!
Nor ever may we parted be,
Till I become one spirit with thee.

4 Still let thy love point out my way;
How wondrous things thy love hath wrought!
Still lead me, lest I go astray;
Direct my word, inspire my thought;
And if I fall, soon may I hear
Thy voice, and know that love is near.

5 In suffering be thy love my peace;
In weakness be thy love my power;
And when the storms of life shall cease,
Jesus, in that important hour,
In death as life be thou my guide,
And save me, who for me hast died.
—*Charles Wesley.*

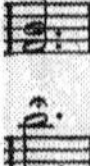

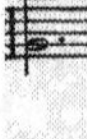

blood;
ace.
n;
vain;
y!
mild
h
t;
r.
;
se,
sley.

CAREY'S. 6-8s. HENRY CAREY.

572 *The fulness of love.*

1 O LOVE, I languish at thy stay!
I pine for thee with lingering smart;
Weary and faint through long delay,
When wilt thou come into my heart?
From sin and sorrow set me free,
And swallow up my soul in thee?

2 Come, O thou universal Good!
Balm of the wounded conscience, come!
The hungry, dying spirit's food,
The weary, wandering pilgrim's home;
Haven to take the shipwrecked in;
My everlasting rest from sin.

3 Be thou, O Love, whate'er I want;
Support my feebleness of mind;
Relieve the thirsty soul, the faint
Revive, illuminate the blind;
The mournful cheer, the drooping lead,
And heal the sick, and raise the dead.

4 Come, O my comfort and delight!
My strength and health, my shield and sun;
My boast, and confidence, and might,
My joy, my glory, and my crown;
My gospel hope, my calling's prize,
My tree of life, my paradise!

5 The secret of the Lord thou art,
The mystery so long unknown;
Christ in a pure and perfect heart,
The name inscribed in the white stone,
The life divine, the little leaven,
My precious pearl, my present heaven.

—*Charles Wesley.*

573 *Rest in the love of Christ.*

1 THOU hidden love of God, whose height,
Whose depth unfathomed, no man knows
I see from far thy beauteous light,
Inly I sigh for thy repose;
My heart is pained, nor can it be
At rest, till it finds rest in thee.

2 Thy secret voice invites me still
The sweetness of thy yoke to prove;
And fain I would; but though my will
Seems fixed, yet wide my passions rove;
Yet hindrances strew all the way;
I aim at thee, yet from thee stray.

3 'Tis mercy all, that thou hast brought
My mind to seek her peace in thee;
Yet while I seek, but find thee not,
No peace my wandering soul shall see;
O when shall all my wanderings end,
And all my steps to thee-ward tend?

4 Is there a thing beneath the sun
That strives with thee my heart to share?
Ah! tear it thence, and reign alone,
The Lord of every motion there;
Then shall my heart from earth be free,
When it hath found repose in thee.

—*John Wesley, from Tersteegen.*

ST. PETERSBURG. 6-8s. — Dimitri S. Bortniansky.

574

Exodus xxxiii. 18-23.

1 O God, my hope, my heavenly rest,
My all of happiness below,
Grant my importunate request,
To me thy power and goodness show;
Thy beatific face display,
The brightness of eternal day.

2 Before my faith's enlightened eyes
Make all thy gracious goodness pass;
Thy goodness is the sight I prize;
O may I see thy smiling face!
Thy nature in my soul proclaim,
Reveal thy love, thy glorious name.

3 There, in the place beside thy throne,
Where all that find acceptance stand,
Receive me up into thy Son;
Cover me with thy mighty hand;
Set me upon the Rock, and hide
My soul in Jesus' wounded side.

4 O put me in the cleft; empower
My soul the glorious sight to bear!
Descend in this accepted hour;
Pass by me and thy name declare;
Thy wrath withdraw, thy hand remove,
And show thyself the God of Love.

—*Charles Wesley.*

MOZART. 6-8s. — From Mozart.

575

SECOND PART.

1 To thee, great God of Love, I bow,
And prostrate in thy sight adore;
By faith I see thee passing now;
I have, but still I ask for more;
A glimpse of love cannot suffice,
My soul for all thy presence cries.

2 The fulness of my vast reward
A blest eternity shall be;
But hast thou not on earth prepared
Some better thing than this for me?
What, but one drop! one transient sight!
I want a sun, a sea of light.

3 More favoured than the saints of old,
Who now by faith approach to thee,
Shall all with open face behold
In Christ the glorious Deity;
Shall see and put the Godhead on,
The nature of thy sinless Son!

4 This, this is our high calling's prize!
Thine image in thy Son I claim;
And still to higher glories rise,
Till, all transformed, I know thy name,
And glide to all my heaven above,
My highest heaven in Jesus' love.

—*Charles Wesley.*

DALEHURST. C. M. A. COTTMAN.

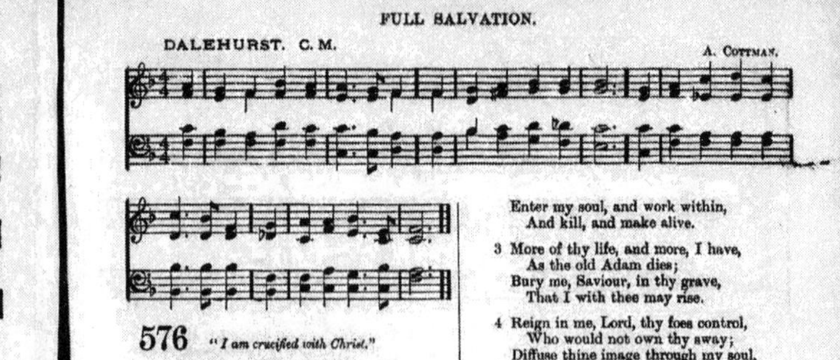

576 *"I am crucified with Christ."*

1 JESUS, my life! thyself apply,
Thy holy Spirit breathe;
My vile affections crucify,
Conform me to thy death.

2 Conqueror of hell, and earth, and sin,
Still with thy rebel strive;
Enter my soul, and work within,
And kill, and make alive.

3 More of thy life, and more, I have,
As the old Adam dies;
Bury me, Saviour, in thy grave,
That I with thee may rise.

4 Reign in me, Lord, thy foes control,
Who would not own thy sway;
Diffuse thine image through my soul,
Shine to the perfect day.

5 Scatter the last remains of sin,
And seal me thine abode;
O make me glorious all within,
A temple built by God!

—*Charles Wesley.*

HALLON. C. M. S. WEBBE.

577 *Faith for full salvation.*

1 LORD, I believe thy every word,
Thy every promise, true;
And, lo! I wait on thee, my Lord,
Till I my strength renew.

2 If in this feeble flesh I may
Awhile show forth thy praise,
Jesus, support the tottering clay,
And lengthen out my days.

3 Still let me live thy blood to show,
Which purges every stain;
And gladly linger out below
A few more years in pain.

4 Faith to be healed thou know'st I have,
From sin to be made clean;
Able thou art from sin to save,
From all indwelling sin.

5 I shall, a weak and helpless worm,
Through Jesus strengthening me,
Impossibilities perform,
And live from sinning free.

6 For this in steadfast hope I wait;
Now, Lord, my soul restore;
Now the new heavens and earth create,
And I shall sin no more.

—*Charles Wesley.*

PETERBOROUGH. C. M. REV. RALPH HARRISON.

578 Matt. vi. 10.

1 JESUS, the Life, the Truth, the Way,
In whom I now believe,
As taught by thee, in faith I pray,
Expecting to receive.

2 Thy will by me on earth be done,
As by the choirs above,
Who always see thee on thy throne,
And glory in thy love.

3 I ask in confidence the grace,
That I may do thy will,
As angels, who behold thy face,
And all thy words fulfil.

4 When thou the work of faith hast wrought,
I shall be pure within;
Nor sin in deed, or word, or thought,
For angels never sin.

5 From thee no more shall I depart,
No more unfaithful prove;
But love thee with a constant heart,
For angels always love.

6 The graces of my second birth
To me shall all be given;
And I shall do thy will on earth,
As angels do in heaven.

—*Charles Wesley.*

NASHVILLE. 6-8s. (2ND METRE.) ADAPTED BY LOWELL MASON.

579 *The sanctifying Spirit.*

1 COME, Holy Ghost, all-quickening fire!
Come, and my hallowed heart inspire,
Sprinkled with the atoning blood;
Now to my soul thyself reveal,
Thy mighty working let me feel,
And know that I am born of God.

2 Thy witness with my spirit bear,
That God, my God, inhabits there;
Thou, with the Father, and the Son,
Eternal light's co-eval beam,
Be Christ in me, and I in him,
Till perfect we are made in one.

3 When wilt thou my whole heart subdue?
Come, Lord, and form my soul anew,
Emptied of pride, and wrath, and hell;
Less than the least of all thy store
Of mercies, I myself abhor;
All, all my vileness may I feel.

4 Humble, and teachable, and mild,
O may I as a little child,
My lowly Master's steps pursue!
Be anger to my soul unknown;
Hate, envy, jealousy, be gone;
In love create thou all things new.

—*Charles Wesley.*

LUCERNE. 6-8s. (2nd Metre.) GERMAN.

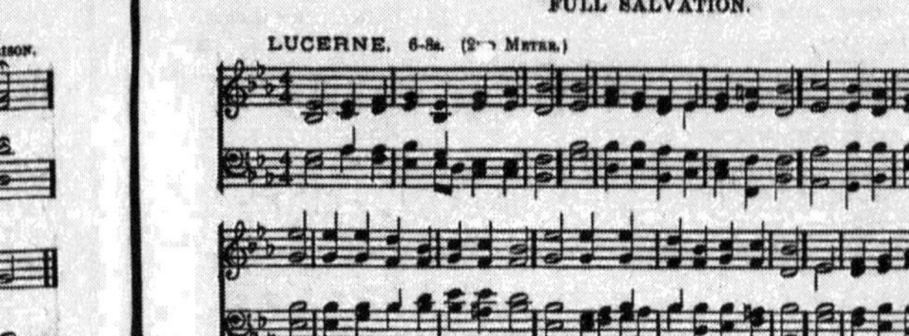

580

SECOND PART.

1 Let earth no more my heart divide,
With Christ may I be crucified,
To thee with my whole soul aspire;
Dead to the world and all its toys,
Its idle pomp, and fading joys,
Be thou alone my one desire:

2 Be thou my joy, be thou my dread;
In battle cover thou my head,
Nor earth, nor hell, I then shall fear;
I then shall turn my steady face;
Want, pain defy, enjoy disgrace,
Glory in dissolution near.

3 My will be swallowed up in thee;
Light in thy light still may I see,
Beholding thee with open face;
Called the full power of faith to prove,
Let all my hallowed heart be love,
And all my spotless life be praise.

4 Come, Holy Ghost, all-quickening fire!
My consecrated heart inspire,
Sprinkled with the atoning blood;
Still to my soul thyself reveal,
Thy mighty working may I feel,
And know that I am one with God.

—*Charles Wesley.*

NASHVILLE. 6-8s. (2nd Metre.) ADAPTED BY LOWELL MASON.

581

The mind of Christ.

1 O Jesus, source of calm repose,
Thy like nor man nor angel knows;
Fairest among ten thousand fair!
Even those whom death's sad fetters bound,
Whom thickest darkness compassed round,
Find light and life, if thou appear.

2 Lord over all, sent to fulfil
Thy gracious Father's sovereign will,
To thy dread sceptre will I bow;
With duteous reverence at thy feet,
Like humble Mary, lo! I sit;
Speak, Lord, thy servant heareth now.

3 Renew thine image, Lord, in me,
Lowly and gentle may I be;
No charms but these to thee are dear;
No anger mayest thou ever find,
No pride, in my unruffled mind,
But faith, and heaven-born peace, be there!

4 A patient, a victorious mind,
That life and all things casts behind,
Springs forth obedient to thy call;
A heart that no desire can move,
But still to adore, believe, and love,
Give me, my Lord, my Life, my All!

—*Charles Wesley.*

MIDDLESEX. 6-8s.

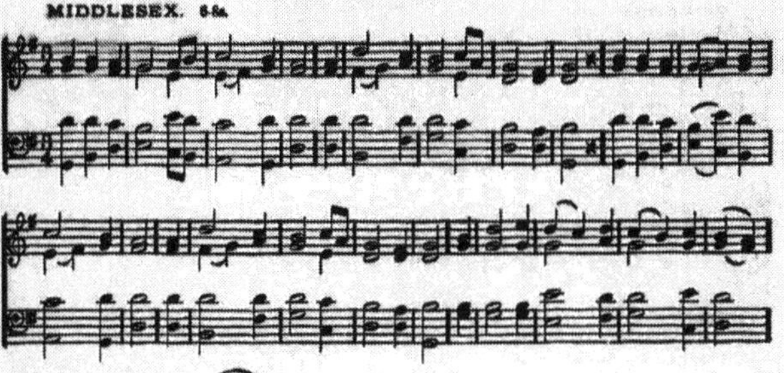

582 *Renouncing the world for Christ.*

1 Master, I own thy lawful claim,
Thine, wholly thine, I long to be!
Thou seest, at last, I willing am,
Where'er thou goest, to follow thee;
Myself in all things to deny,
Thine, wholly thine, to live and die.

2 Whate'er my sinful flesh requires,
For thee I cheerfully forego;
My covetous and vain desires,
My hopes of happiness below;
My senses' and my passions' food,
And all my thirst for creature good.

3 Pleasure, and wealth, and praise no more
Shall lead my captive soul astray;
My fond pursuits I all give o'er,
Thee, only thee, resolved to obey;
My own in all things to resign,
And know no other will but thine.

4 Wherefore to thee I all resign;
Being thou art, and Love, and Power;
Thy only will be done, not mine;
Thee, Lord, let heaven and earth adore!
Flow back the rivers to the sea,
And let my all be lost in thee!

—*Charles Wesley.*

583 *The living Sacrifice.*

1 O God, what offering shall I give
To thee, the Lord of earth and skies?
My spirit, soul, and flesh receive,
A holy, living sacrifice;
Small as it is, 'tis all my store;
More should'st thou have, if I had more.

2 Now, then, my God, thou hast my soul;
No longer mine, but thine I am;
Guard thou thine own, possess it whole;
Cheer it with hope, with love inflame;
Thou hast my spirit; there display
Thy glory to the perfect day.

3 Thou hast my flesh, thy hallowed shrine,
Devoted solely to thy will;
Here let thy light for ever shine,
This house still let thy presence fill;
O Source of life, live, dwell, and move
In me, till all my life be love!

4 Send down thy likeness from above,
And let this my adorning be;
Clothe me with wisdom, patience, love,
With lowliness and purity,
Than gold and pearls more precious far,
And brighter than the morning star.

5 Lord, arm me with thy Spirit's might,
Since I am called by thy great name;
In thee let all my thoughts unite,
Of all my works be thou the aim;
Thy love attend me all my days,
And my sole business be thy praise!

—*Charles Wesley.*

PURLEIGH. 8.8.6, 8.8.6. A. H. Brown.

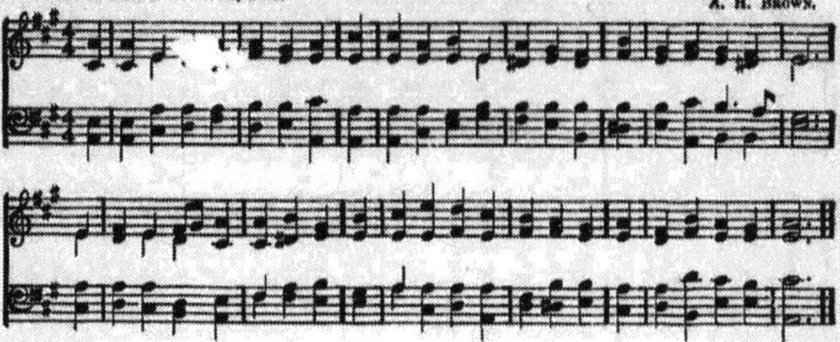

584 *"To know the love of Christ, which passeth knowledge."*

1 O Love Divine, how sweet thou art!
When shall I find my willing heart
All taken up by thee?
I thirst, I faint, I die to prove
The greatness of redeeming Love,
The love of Christ to me!

2 Stronger his love than death or hell;
Its riches are unsearchable:
The first-born sons of light
Desire in vain its depths to see;
They cannot reach the mystery,
The length, and breadth, and height.

3 God only knows the love of God;
O that it now were shed abroad
In this poor stony heart!
For love I sigh, for love I pine;
This only portion, Lord, be mine,
Be mine this better part!

4 O that I could for ever sit
With Mary at the Master's feet!
Be this my happy choice;
My only care, delight, and bliss,
My joy, my heaven on earth, be this,
To hear the Bridegroom's voice!

—Charles Wesley.

585 *The promised land.*

1 O glorious hope of perfect love!
It lifts me up to things above,
It bears on eagles' wings;
It gives my ravished soul a taste,
And makes me for some moments feast
With Jesus' priests and kings.

2 Rejoicing now in earnest hope,
I stand, and from the mountain-top
See all the land below:
Rivers of milk and honey rise,
And all the fruits of Paradise
In endless plenty grow.

3 A land of corn, and wine, and oil,
Favoured with God's peculiar smile,
With every blessing blest;
There dwells the Lord our Righteousness,
And keeps his own in perfect peace,
And everlasting rest.

4 O that I might at once go up!
No more on this side Jordan stop,
But now the land possess:
This moment end my legal years,
Sorrows, and sins, and doubts, and fears,
A howling wilderness.

5 Now, O my Joshua, bring me in!
Cast out thy foes; the inbred sin,
The carnal mind, remove;
The purchase of thy death divide!
And oh! with all the sanctified
Give me a lot of love!

—Charles Wesley.

PEMBROKE. 8.8.6, 8.8.6. J. Foster.

586

The Beatitudes.

1 Saviour, on me the want bestow,
Which all that feel shall surely know
Their sins on earth forgiven;
Give me to prove the kingdom mine,
And taste, in holiness divine,
The happiness of heaven.

2 Meeken my soul, thou heavenly Lamb,
That I in the new earth may claim
My hundred-fold reward;
My rich inheritance possess,
Co-heir with the great Prince of Peace,
Co-partner with my Lord.

3 Me with that restless thirst inspire,
That sacred, infinite desire,
And feast my hungry heart;
Less than thyself cannot suffice;
My soul for all thy fulness cries,
For all thou hast, and art.

4 Mercy who show shall mercy find;
Thy pitiful and tender mind
Be, Lord, on me bestowed;
So shall I still the blessing gain,
And to eternal life retain
The mercy of my God.

5 Jesus, the crowning grace impart;
Bless me with purity of heart,
That, now beholding thee,
I soon may view thy open face,
On all thy glorious beauties gaze,
And God for ever see!

—*Charles Wesley.*

ADMAH. 6-8s. Lowell Mason.

TUNE: ADMAH. 6-8s.

587 *"None of us liveth to himself."*

1 Saviour from sin, I wait to prove
That Jesus is thy healing name;
To lose, when perfected in love,
Whate'er I have, or can, or am:
I stay me on thy faithful word,
"The servant shall be as his Lord."

2 Answer that gracious end in me,
For which thy precious life was given;
Redeem from all iniquity,
Restore, and make me meet for heaven;
Unless thou purge my every stain,
Thy suffering and my faith are vain.

3 Didst thou not in the flesh appear,
Sin to condemn, and man to save?
That perfect love might cast out fear?
That I thy mind in me might have?
In holiness show forth thy praise,
And serve thee all my spotless days?

4 Didst thou not die that I might live
No longer to myself, but thee?
Might body, soul, and spirit give
To him who gave himself for me?
Come, then, my Master, and my God,
Take the dear purchase of thy blood.

5 Thy own peculiar servant claim,
For thy own truth and mercy's sake;
Hallow in me thy glorious name;
Me for thine own this moment take,
And change, and throughly purify;
Thine only may I live and die.
—Charles Wesley.

MURRAY. 6.6.6.6.8.8. GERMAN.

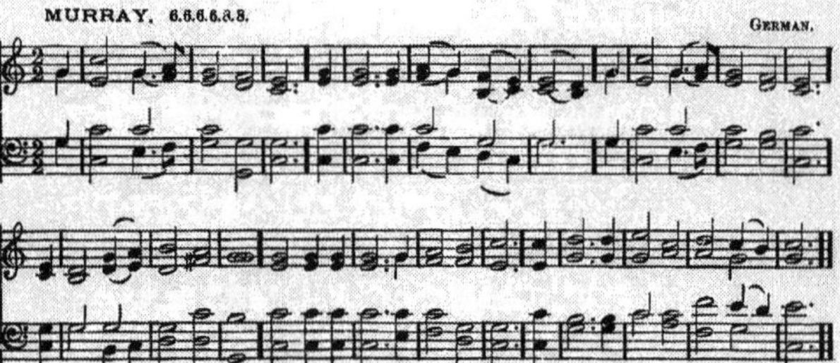

588 *Hope of full redemption.*

1 Ye ransomed sinners, hear,
The prisoners of the Lord,
And wait till Christ appear,
According to his word:
Rejoice in hope, rejoice with me,
We shall from all our sins be free.

2 Let others hug their chains,
For sin and Satan plead,
And say, from sin's remains
They never can be freed:
Rejoice in hope, rejoice with me,
We shall from all our sins be free.

3 In God we put our trust;
If we our sins confess,
Faithful he is, and just,
From all unrighteousness
To cleanse us all, both you and me;
We shall from all our sins be free.

4 The word of God is sure,
And never can remove,
We shall in heart be pure,
And perfected in love:
Rejoice in hope, rejoice with me,
We shall from all our sins be free.

5 Then let us gladly bring
Our sacrifice of praise,
Let us give thanks, and sing,
And glory in his grace:
Rejoice in hope, rejoice with me,
We shall from all our sins be free.
—Charles Wesley.

TIMNA. 8-8s.

D.C.

589 *The fountain of life.*

1 A FOUNTAIN of life and of grace
 In Christ, our Redeemer, we see;
For us, who his offers embrace,
 For all, it is open and free.
Jehovah himself doth invite
 To drink of his pleasures unknown;
The streams of immortal delight,
 That flow from his heavenly throne.

2 As soon as in him we believe,
 By faith of his Spirit we take;
And, freely forgiven, receive
 The mercy for Jesus's sake:
We gain a pure drop of his love,
 The life of eternity know,
Angelical happiness prove,
 And witness a heaven below.
—*Charles Wesley.*

ST. GEORGE. 8-7s. SIR G. ELVEY.

590 *"Be not afraid, only believe."*

1 DROOPING soul, shake off thy fears;
 Fearful soul, be strong, be bold;
Tarry till the Lord appears,
 Never, never quit thy hold!
Murmur not at his delay,
 Dare not set thy God a time;
Calmly for his coming stay,
 Leave it, leave it all to him.

2 Every one that seeks shall find,—
 Every one that asks shall have,
Christ, the Saviour of mankind,
 Willing, able, all to save;
I shall his salvation see,
 I in faith on Jesus call;
I from sin shall be set free,
 Perfectly set free from all.

3 Lord, my times are in thy hand;
 Weak and helpless as I am,
Surely thou canst make me stand;
 I believe in Jesus' name.
Saviour, in temptation thou,
 Thou hast saved me heretofore;
Thou from sin dost save me now,
 Thou shalt save me evermore.
—*Charles Wesley.*

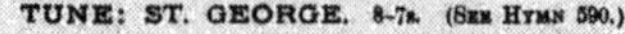

TUNE: ST. GEORGE. 8-7s. (SEE HYMN 590.)

591 *"Christ shall give thee light."*

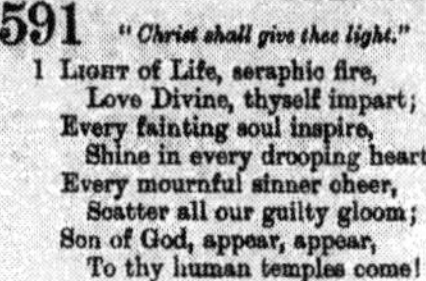

1 LIGHT of Life, seraphic fire,
Love Divine, thyself impart;
Every fainting soul inspire,
Shine in every drooping heart.
Every mournful sinner cheer,
Scatter all our guilty gloom;
Son of God, appear, appear,
To thy human temples come!

2 Come, in this accepted hour,
Bring thy heavenly kingdom in;
Fill us with the glorious power,
Rooting out the seeds of sin.
Nothing more can we require,
We will covet nothing less;
Be thou all our heart's desire,
All our joy, and all our peace.
—*Charles Wesley.*

REQUIES. 8-7s. BLUMENTHAL.

592 *Consecration.*

1 GOD of all-redeeming grace,
By thy pardoning love compelled,
Up to thee our souls we raise,
Up to thee our bodies yield;
Now our sacrifice receive;
Now accept us through thy Son,
While to thee alone we live,
While we die to thee alone.

2 Meet it is, and just, and right,
That we should be wholly thine,
In thine only will delight,
In thy blessèd service join;
O that every work and word
Might proclaim how good thou art!
"Holiness unto the Lord"
Still be written on our heart.
—*Charles Wesley.*

593 *"Ye are not your own."*

1 NOT your own, but his ye are,
Who hath paid a price untold
For your life, exceeding far
All earth's stores of gems and gold.
With the precious blood of Christ,
Ransom treasure all unpriced,
Full redemption is procured
Full salvation is assured.

2 Not your own—to him ye owe
All your life and all your love;
Live, that ye his praise may show,
Who is yet all praise above.
Every day and every hour,
Every gift and every power
Consecrate to him alone,
Who hath claimed you for his own.

3 Teach us, Master, how to give
All we have and are to thee;
Grant us, Saviour, while we live,
Wholly, only thine to be.
Henceforth be our calling high
Thee to serve and glorify;
Ours no longer, but thine own,
Thine forever, thine alone!
—*Miss Havergal.*

CHOPE. 4-7s. DR. CHOPE.

594

The new and living way.

1 HOLY Lamb, who thee receive,
Who in thee begin to live,
Day and night they cry to thee,
As thou art, so let us be!

2 Fix, O fix each wavering mind!
To thy cross our spirits bind;
Earthly passions far remove;
Swallow up our souls in love.

3 Dust and ashes though we be,
Full of sin and misery,
Thine we are, thou Son of God;
Take the purchase of thy blood!

4 Who in heart on thee believes,
He the atonement now receives;
He with joy beholds thy face,
Triumphs in thy pardoning grace.

5 Jesus, when thy light we see,
All our soul's athirst for thee;
When thy quickening power we prove,
All our heart dissolves in love.

6 Boundless wisdom, power divine,
Love unspeakable, are thine:
Praise by all to thee be given,
Sons of earth, and hosts of heaven!
—*Mrs. Dober, translated by J. Wesley.*

INNOCENTS. 4-7s. ARRANGED BY W. H. MONK.

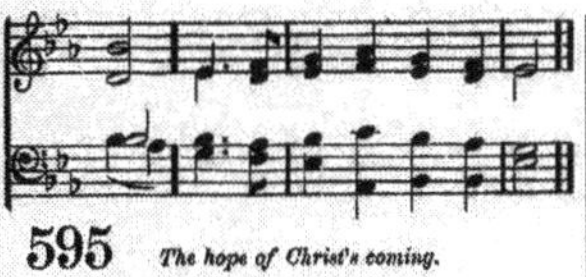

595

The hope of Christ's coming.

1 JESUS comes with all his grace,
Comes to save a fallen race;
Object of our glorious hope,
Jesus comes to lift us up.

2 He hath our salvation wrought,
He our captive souls hath bought;
He hath reconciled to God;
He hath washed us in his blood.

3 We are now his lawful right,
Walk as children of the light;
We shall soon obtain the grace,
Pure in heart to see his face.

4 We shall gain our calling's prize;
After God we all shall rise,
Filled with joy, and love, and peace,
Perfected in holiness.

5 Let us then rejoice in hope,
Steadily to Christ look up;
Trust to be redeemed from sin,
Wait, till he appear within.

6 Hasten, Lord, the perfect day!
Let thy every servant say,
I have now obtained the power,
Born of God to sin no more.
—*Charles Wesley.*

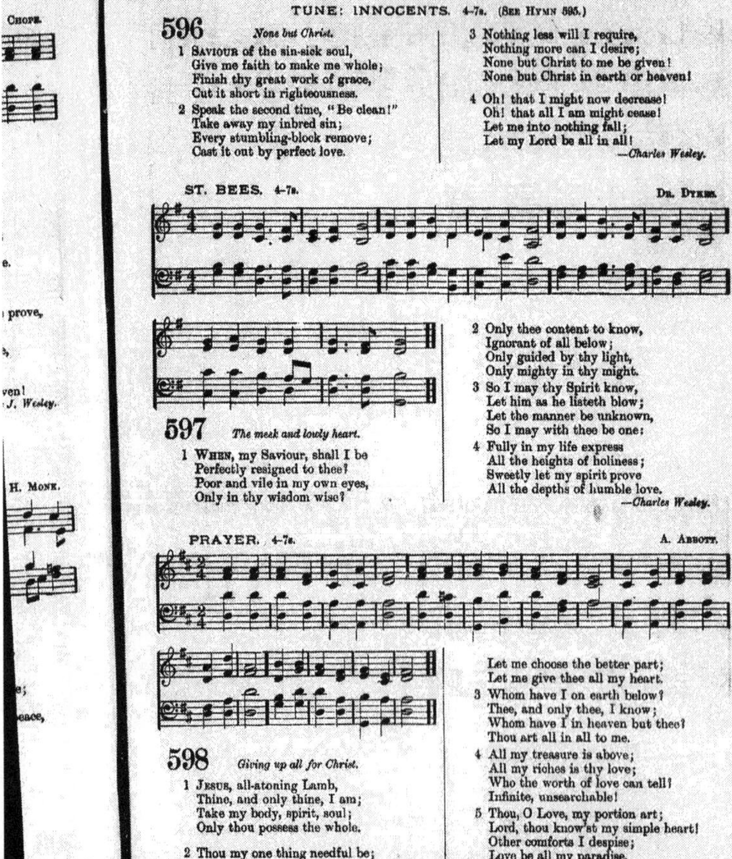

TUNE: INNOCENTS. 4-7s. (See Hymn 595.)

596 *None but Christ.*

1 Saviour of the sin-sick soul,
Give me faith to make me whole;
Finish thy great work of grace,
Cut it short in righteousness.

2 Speak the second time, "Be clean!"
Take away my inbred sin;
Every stumbling-block remove;
Cast it out by perfect love.

3 Nothing less will I require,
Nothing more can I desire;
None but Christ to me be given!
None but Christ in earth or heaven!

4 Oh! that I might now decrease!
Oh! that all I am might cease!
Let me into nothing fall;
Let my Lord be all in all!

—*Charles Wesley.*

ST. BEES. 4-7s. Dr. Dykes.

597 *The meek and lowly heart.*

1 When, my Saviour, shall I be
Perfectly resigned to thee?
Poor and vile in my own eyes,
Only in thy wisdom wise?

2 Only thee content to know,
Ignorant of all below;
Only guided by thy light,
Only mighty in thy might.

3 So I may thy Spirit know,
Let him as he listeth blow;
Let the manner be unknown,
So I may with thee be one:

4 Fully in my life express
All the heights of holiness;
Sweetly let my spirit prove
All the depths of humble love.

—*Charles Wesley.*

PRAYER. 4-7s. A. Abbott.

598 *Giving up all for Christ.*

1 Jesus, all-atoning Lamb,
Thine, and only thine, I am;
Take my body, spirit, soul;
Only thou possess the whole.

2 Thou my one thing needful be;
Let me ever cleave to thee;
Let me choose the better part;
Let me give thee all my heart.

3 Whom have I on earth below?
Thee, and only thee, I know;
Whom have I in heaven but thee?
Thou art all in all to me.

4 All my treasure is above;
All my riches is thy love;
Who the worth of love can tell?
Infinite, unsearchable!

5 Thou, O Love, my portion art;
Lord, thou know'st my simple heart!
Other comforts I despise;
Love be all my paradise.

—*Charles Wesley.*

SEYMOUR. 4-7s. C. M. Von Weber.

599 *Entire consecration to Christ's service.*

1 Take my life and let it be
Consecrated, Lord, to thee:
Take my moments and my days,
Let them flow in ceaseless praise.

2 Take my hands and let them move
At the impulse of thy love:
Take my feet and let them be
Swift and beautiful for thee.

3 Take my silver and my gold—
Not a mite would I withhold:
Take my intellect and use
Every power as thou shalt choose.

4 Take my voice and let me sing
Always, only, for my King:
Take my lips and let them be
Filled with messages from thee.

5 Take my will and make it thine,
It shall be no longer mine:
Take my heart, it is thine own;
It shall be thy royal throne.

6 Take my love, my Lord, I pour
At thy feet its treasure store:
Take myself, and I will be,
Ever, only, all for thee.

—Miss Havergal.

WARRINGTON. L. M. Rev. Ralph Harrison.

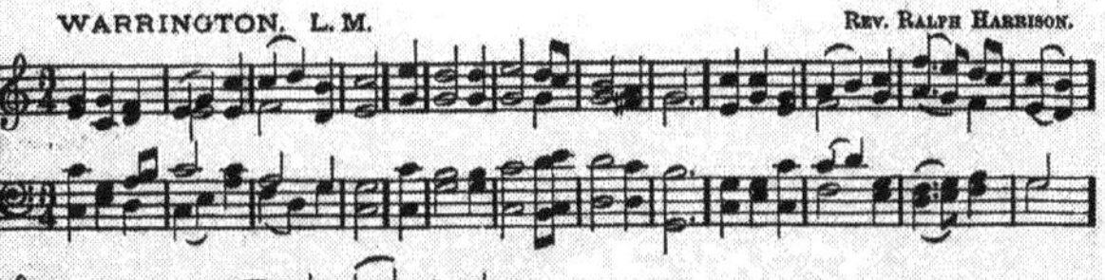

600 *Consecration sealed at the cross.*

1 Lord, I am thine, entirely thine,
Purchased and saved by blood divine;
With full consent thine would I be,
And own thy sovereign right in me.

2 Grant one poor sinner more a place
Among the children of thy grace;
A wretched sinner, lost to God,
But ransomed by Immanuel's blood.

3 Thine would I live, thine would I die,
Be thine through all eternity;
The vow is past beyond repeal,
And now I set the solemn seal.

4 Here, at the cross where flows the blood
That bought my guilty soul for God,
Thee, Lord and Master, now I call,
And consecrate to thee my all.

5 Do thou assist a feeble worm
The great engagement to perform;
Thy grace can full assistance lend,
And on that grace I dare depend.

—S. Davies.

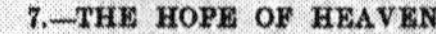
7.—THE HOPE OF HEAVEN.

ST. AGNES. C. M. — Dr. Dykes.

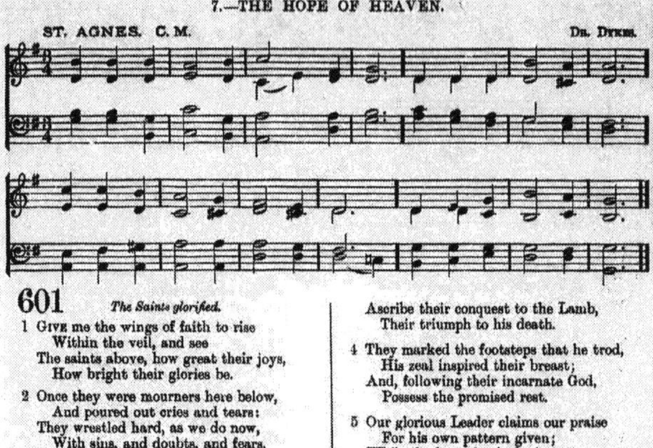

601 *The Saints glorified.*

1 Give me the wings of faith to rise
Within the veil, and see
The saints above, how great their joys,
How bright their glories be.

2 Once they were mourners here below,
And poured out cries and tears:
They wrestled hard, as we do now,
With sins, and doubts, and fears.

3 I ask them whence their victory came;
They, with united breath,
Ascribe their conquest to the Lamb,
Their triumph to his death.

4 They marked the footsteps that he trod,
His zeal inspired their breast;
And, following their incarnate God,
Possess the promised rest.

5 Our glorious Leader claims our praise
For his own pattern given;
While the long cloud of witnesses
Show the same path to heaven.

—*Isaac Watts.*

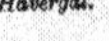

ST. PETER. C. M. — A. R. Reinagle.

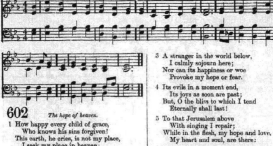

602 *The hope of heaven.*

1 How happy every child of grace,
Who knows his sins forgiven!
This earth, he cries, is not my place,
I seek my place in heaven:

2 A country far from mortal sight—
Yet, O by faith I see
The land of rest, the saints' delight,
The heaven prepared for me!

3 A stranger in the world below,
I calmly sojourn here;
Nor can its happiness or woe
Provoke my hope or fear.

4 Its evils in a moment end,
Its joys as soon are past;
But, O the bliss to which I tend
Eternally shall last!

5 To that Jerusalem above
With singing I repair;
While in the flesh, my hope and love,
My heart and soul, are there:

6 There my exalted Saviour stands,
My merciful High Priest,
And still extends his wounded hands
To take me to his breast.

—*Charles Wesley.*

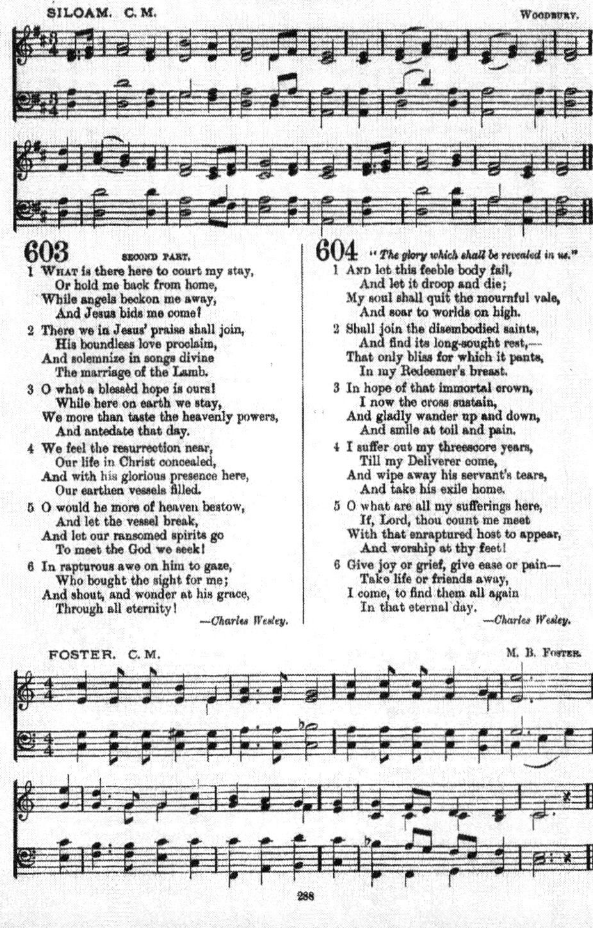

SILOAM. C. M. WOODBURY.

603

SECOND PART.

1 WHAT is there here to court my stay,
Or hold me back from home,
While angels beckon me away,
And Jesus bids me come!

2 There we in Jesus' praise shall join,
His boundless love proclaim,
And solemnize in songs divine
The marriage of the Lamb.

3 O what a blessèd hope is ours!
While here on earth we stay,
We more than taste the heavenly powers,
And antedate that day.

4 We feel the resurrection near,
Our life in Christ concealed,
And with his glorious presence here,
Our earthen vessels filled.

5 O would he more of heaven bestow,
And let the vessel break,
And let our ransomed spirits go
To meet the God we seek!

6 In rapturous awe on him to gaze,
Who bought the sight for me;
And shout, and wonder at his grace,
Through all eternity!

—*Charles Wesley.*

604

"The glory which shall be revealed in us."

1 AND let this feeble body fail,
And let it droop and die;
My soul shall quit the mournful vale,
And soar to worlds on high.

2 Shall join the disembodied saints,
And find its long-sought rest,—
That only bliss for which it pants,
In my Redeemer's breast.

3 In hope of that immortal crown,
I now the cross sustain,
And gladly wander up and down,
And smile at toil and pain.

4 I suffer out my threescore years,
Till my Deliverer come,
And wipe away his servant's tears,
And take his exile home.

5 O what are all my sufferings here,
If, Lord, thou count me meet
With that enraptured host to appear,
And worship at thy feet!

6 Give joy or grief, give ease or pain—
Take life or friends away,
I come, to find them all again
In that eternal day.

—*Charles Wesley.*

FOSTER. C. M. M. B. FOSTER.

TUNE: FOSTER. C. M.

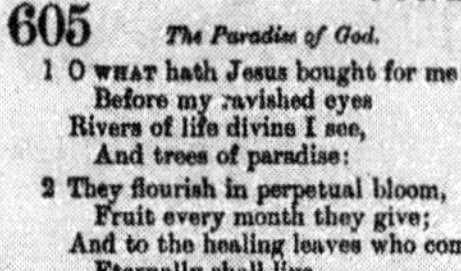

605

The Paradise of God.

1 O WHAT hath Jesus bought for me!
Before my ravished eyes
Rivers of life divine I see,
And trees of paradise:

2 They flourish in perpetual bloom,
Fruit every month they give;
And to the healing leaves who come
Eternally shall live.

3 I see a world of spirits bright,
Who reap the pleasures there;
They all are robed in purest white,
And conquering palms they bear.

4 Adorned by their Redeemer's grace,
They close pursue the Lamb;
And every shining front displays
The unutterable name.

5 They drink the vivifying stream,
They pluck the ambrosial fruit,
And each records the praise of him
Who tuned his golden lute.

6 At once they strike the harmonious lyre,
And hymn the great Three-One;
He hears, he smiles, and all the choir
Fall down before his throne.

—*Charles Wesley.*

ELLACOMBE. C. M. D. GERMAN.

606

"Of whom the whole family in heaven and earth is named."

1 COME, let us join our friends above
That have obtained the prize,
And on the eagle wings of love
To joys celestial rise.
Let all the saints terrestrial sing,
With those to glory gone;
For all the servants of our King,
In earth and heaven, are one.

2 One family we dwell in him,
One church above, beneath,
Though now divided by the stream,
The narrow stream of death:
One army of the living God,
To his command we bow;
Part of his host have crossed the flood,
And part are crossing now.

3 Ten thousand to their endless home
This solemn moment fly;
And we are to the margin come,
And we expect to die:
His militant embodied host,
With wishful looks we stand,
And long to see that happy coast,
And reach the heavenly land.

4 Our old companions in distress
We haste again to see,
And eager long for our release,
And full felicity:
Even now by faith we join our hands
With those that went before;
And greet the blood-besprinkled bands
On the eternal shore.

5 Our spirits too shall quickly join,
Like theirs with glory crowned,
And shout to see our Captain's sign,
To hear his trumpet sound.
O that we now might grasp our Guide!
O that the word were given!
Come, Lord of hosts, the waves divide,
And land us all in heaven!

—*Charles Wesley.*

JERUSALEM. C. M. S. GROSVENOR.

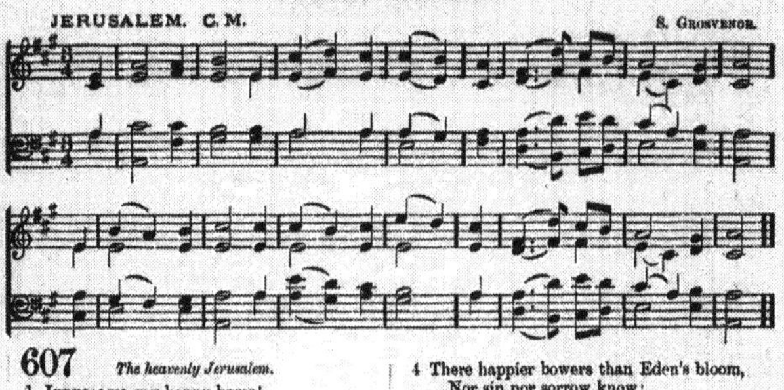

607 *The heavenly Jerusalem.*

1 JERUSALEM, my happy home!
Name ever dear to me;
When shall my labours have an end,
In joy, and peace, and thee?

2 When shall these eyes thy heaven-built walls
And pearly gates behold?
Thy bulwarks, with salvation strong,
And streets of shining gold?

3 O when, thou city of my God,
Shall I thy courts ascend,
Where congregations ne'er break up,
And Sabbaths have no end?

4 There happier bowers than Eden's bloom,
Nor sin nor sorrow know;
Blest seats, through rude and stormy scenes,
I onward press to you.

5 Apostles, prophets, martyrs, there
Around my Saviour stand;
And soon my friends in Christ below
Will join the glorious band.

6 Jerusalem, my happy home!
My soul still pants for thee;
When shall my labours have an end,
In joy, and peace, and thee?

—*Dickson.*

EVAN. C. M. REV. W. H. HAVERGAL.

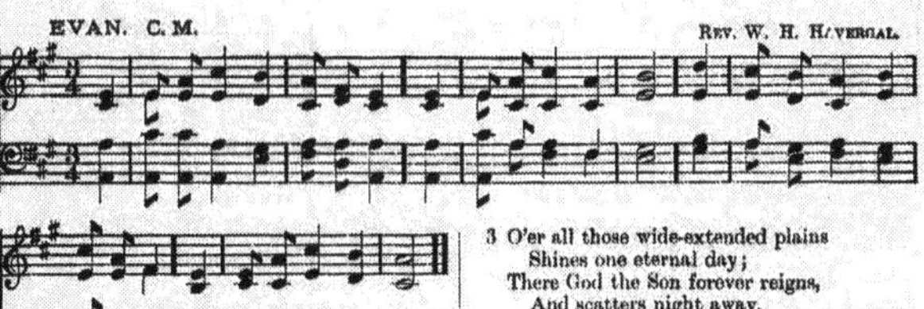

608 *The prospect of the heavenly Canaan.*

1 ON Jordan's stormy banks I stand,
And cast a wishful eye
To Canaan's fair and happy land,
Where my possessions lie.

2 Oh! the transporting, rapturous scene,
That rises to my sight;
Sweet fields arrayed in living green,
And rivers of delight.

3 O'er all those wide-extended plains
Shines one eternal day;
There God the Son forever reigns,
And scatters night away.

4 No chilling winds, or poisonous breath,
Can reach that healthful shore;
Sickness and sorrow, pain and death,
Are felt and feared no more.

5 When shall I reach that happy place,
And be forever blest?
When shall I see my Father's face,
And in his bosom rest?

6 Filled with delight, my raptured soul
Would here no longer stay;
Though Jordan's waves around me roll,
Fearless I'd launch away.

—*S. Stennett.*

BELMONT. C. M. — WEBBE.

609 *The heavenly Canaan.*

1 There is a land of pure delight,
Where saints immortal reign;
Infinite day excludes the night,
And pleasures banish pain.

2 There everlasting spring abides,
And never-withering flowers;
Death, like a narrow sea, divides
This heavenly land from ours.

3 Sweet fields beyond the swelling flood
Stand dressed in living green;
So to the Jews old Canaan stood,
While Jordan rolled between.

4 But timorous mortals start and shrink
To cross this narrow sea;
And linger, shivering on the brink,
And fear to launch away.

5 O could we make our doubts remove,
Those gloomy thoughts that rise,
And see the Canaan that we love
With unbeclouded eyes!

6 Could we but climb where Moses stood,
And view the landscape o'er,
Not Jordan's stream, nor death's cold flood,
Should fright us from the shore.

—*Isaac Watts.*

LYDIA. C. M.

610 *The joy of meeting in heaven.*

1 Our souls are in his mighty hand,
And he shall keep them still;
And you and I shall surely stand
‖:With him on Zion's hill.:‖

2 Him eye to eye we there shall see;
Our face like his shall shine:
Oh! what a glorious company,
‖:When saints and angels join!:‖

3 Oh! what a joyful meeting there!
In robes of white arrayed,
Palms in our hands we all shall bear,
‖:And crowns upon our head.:‖

4 Then let us lawfully contend,
And fight our passage through;
Bear in our faithful minds the end,
‖:And keep the prize in view.:‖

5 Then let us hasten to the day
When all shall be brought home;
Come, O Redeemer, come way!
‖:O Jesus, quickly come!:‖

—*Charles Wesley.*

MERIBAH. 8.8.6, 8.8.6. DR. MASON.

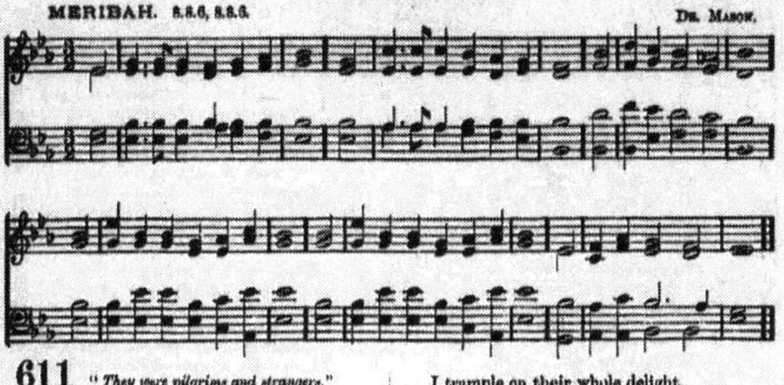

611

"They were pilgrims and strangers."

1 How happy is the pilgrim's lot!
How free from every anxious thought,
From worldly hope and fear!
Confined to neither court nor cell,
His soul disdains on earth to dwell,
He only sojourns here.

2 This happiness in part is mine,
Already saved from low design,
From every creature-love;
Blest with the scorn of finite good,
My soul is lightened of its load,
And seeks the things above.

3 Nothing on earth I call my own;
A stranger, to the world unknown,
I all their goods despise;
I trample on their whole delight,
And seek a country out of sight,
A country in the skies.

4 There is my house and portion fair,
My treasure and my heart are there,
And my abiding home;
For me my elder brethren stay,
And angels beckon me away,
And Jesus bids me come.

5 I come,—thy servant, Lord, replies—
I come to meet thee in the skies,
And claim my heavenly rest!
When life's brief pilgrimage shall end,
Then, O my Saviour, Brother, Friend,
Receive me to thy breast!

—*John Wesley.*

DARWELL. 6.6, 6.6, 8.8. REV. J. DARWELL.

TUNE: DARWELL. 6.6, 6.6, 8.8.

612 *The heavenly country.*

1 Come, all who e'er have set
Your faces Zion-ward,
In Jesus let us meet,
And praise our common Lord;
In Jesus let us still go on,
Till all appear before his throne.

2 Nearer and nearer still,
We to our country come;
To that celestial hill,
The weary pilgrim's home,
The new Jerusalem above,
The seat of everlasting love.

3 The ransomed sons of God,
All earthly things we scorn;
And to our high abode
With songs of praise return;
From strength to strength we still proceed,
With crowns of joy upon our head.

4 The peace and joy of faith
Each moment may we feel;
Redeemed from sin and wrath,
From earth, and death, and hell,
We to our Father's house repair,
To meet our elder Brother there.

5 Our Brother, Saviour, Head,
Our all in all, is he;
And in his steps who tread,
We soon his face shall see;
Shall see him with our glorious friends,
And then in heaven our journey ends.

—*Charles Wesley.*

ADMAH. 6-8s. LOWELL MASON.

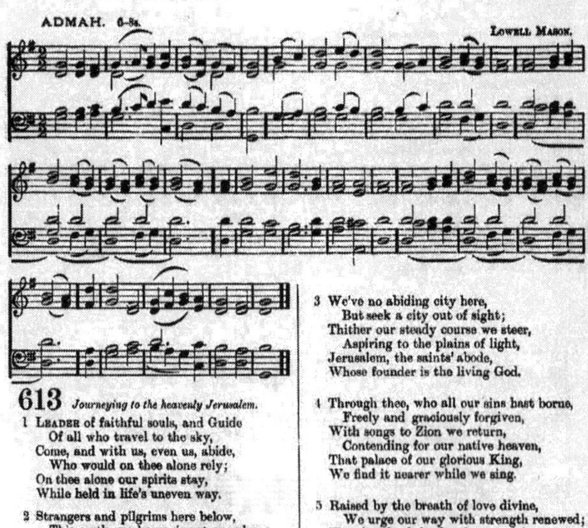

613 *Journeying to the heavenly Jerusalem.*

1 Leader of faithful souls, and Guide
Of all who travel to the sky,
Come, and with us, even us, abide,
Who would on thee alone rely;
On thee alone our spirits stay,
While held in life's uneven way.

2 Strangers and pilgrims here below,
This earth, we know, is not our place;
But hasten through the vale of woe,
And, restless to behold thy face,
Swift to our heavenly country move,
Our everlasting home above.

3 We've no abiding city here,
But seek a city out of sight;
Thither our steady course we steer,
Aspiring to the plains of light,
Jerusalem, the saints' abode,
Whose founder is the living God.

4 Through thee, who all our sins hast borne,
Freely and graciously forgiven,
With songs to Zion we return,
Contending for our native heaven,
That palace of our glorious King,
We find it nearer while we sing.

5 Raised by the breath of love divine,
We urge our way with strength renewed;
The church of the first-born to join,
We travel to the mount of God;
With joy upon our heads arise,
And meet our Captain in the skies.

—*Charles Wesley.*

STELLA. 6-8s. FROM "CROWN OF JESUS."

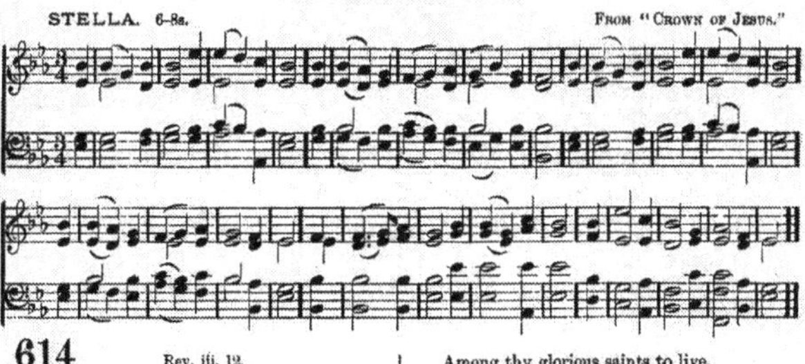

614

Rev. iii. 12.

1 SAVIOUR, on me the grace bestow,
To trample on my mortal foe;
Conqueror of death with thee to rise,
And claim my station in the skies,
Fixed as the throne which ne'er can move,
A pillar in thy church above.

2 Inscribing with the city's name,
The heavenly New Jerusalem,
To me the victor's title give,
Among thy glorious saints to live,
And all their happiness to know,
A citizen of heaven below.

3 When thou hadst all thy foes o'ercome,
Returning to thy glorious home,
Thou didst receive the full reward,
That I might share it with my Lord,
And thus thy own new name obtain,
And one with thee forever reign.

—*Charles Wesley.*

NEARER HOME. S. M. D. ISAAC WOODBURY.

615

"So shall we ever be with the Lord."

1 "FOREVER with the Lord!"
Amen! so let it be!
Life from the dead is in that word,
'Tis immortality!
Here in the body pent,
Absent from him I roam,
Yet nightly pitch my moving tent
A day's march nearer home.

2 My Father's house on high,
Home of my soul, how near!
At times, to faith's unclouded eye,
Thy golden gates appear.
Ah! then my spirit faints
To reach the land I love,—
The bright inheritance of saints,
Jerusalem above!

3 "Forever with the Lord!"
Father, if 'tis thy will,
The promise of that faithful word,
Even here to me fulfil.
Be thou at my right hand,
Then can I never fail;
Uphold thou me, and I shall stand,
Fight, and I must prevail.

4 So when my latest breath
Shall rend the veil in twain,
By death I shall escape from death,
And life eternal gain.
Knowing as I am known,
How shall I love that word,
And oft repeat before the throne,
"Forever with the Lord!"

—*Montgomery.*

LEOMINSTER. S. M. D. — G. W. Martin.

REFRAIN.
Then, O my Lord, pre-pare, My soul for that great day!
O wash me in thy precious blood, And take my sins a-way!

616

"The time is short."

1 A few more years shall roll,
A few more seasons come;
And we shall be with those that rest,
Asleep within the tomb.

2 A few more suns shall set
O'er these dark hills of time;
And we shall be where suns are not,
A far serener clime.

3 A few more storms shall beat
On this wild rocky shore;
And we shall be where tempests cease,
And surges swell no more.

4 A few more struggles here,
A few more partings o'er,
A few more toils, a few more tears,
And we shall weep no more.

5 A few more Sabbaths here
Shall cheer us on our way;
And we shall reach the endless rest,
The eternal Sabbath-day.

6 Then, O my Lord, prepare
My soul for that great day!
O wash me in thy precious blood,
And take my sins away! —*H. Bonar.*

(Use last verse as a refrain.)

TUNE: NEARER HOME. S. M. D. (See Hymn 615.)

617

"A house not made with hands, eternal in the heavens."

1 We know, by faith, we know,
If this frail house of clay,
This tabernacle, sink below
In ruinous decay,
We have a house above,
Not made with mortal hands;
And firm, as our Redeemer's love,
That heavenly fabric stands.

2 It stands securely high,
Indissolubly sure;
Our glorious mansion in the sky
Shall evermore endure.
Full of immortal hope,
We urge the restless strife,
And hasten to be swallowed up
Of everlasting life.

3 O let us put on thee
In perfect holiness,
And rise prepared thy face to see,
Thy bright, unclouded face.
Thy grace with glory crown,
Who hast the earnest given;
And then triumphantly come down,
And take our souls to heaven!
—*Charles Wesley.*

LANGTON. S. M. ADAPTED BY STREATFIELD.

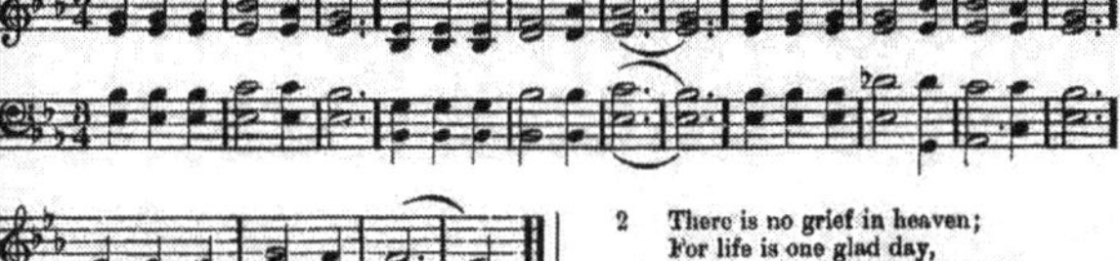

618

No night in heaven.

1 THERE is no night in heaven:
In that blest world above
Work never can bring weariness,
For work itself is love.

2 There is no grief in heaven;
For life is one glad day,
And tears are of those former things
Which all have passed away.

3 There is no sin in heaven;
Behold that blessèd throng,
All holy in their spotless robes,
All holy in their song.

4 There is no death in heaven;
For they who gain that shore
Have won their immortality,
And they can die no more.

—*Huntingdon.*

RUTHERFORD. 7.6, 7.6, 7.6, 7.6. D'URHAN.

619

"Here we have no continuing city, but we seek one to come."

1 BRIEF life is here our portion;
Brief sorrow, short-lived care;
The life that knows no ending,
The tearless life, is there.
O happy retribution!
Short toil, eternal rest;
For mortals and for sinners
A mansion with the blest!

2 And now we fight the battle,
But then shall wear the crown
Of full and everlasting
And passionless renown;
But he whom now we trust in
Shall then be seen and known;
And they that know and see him
Shall have him for their own.

3 The morning shall awaken,
The shadows shall decay,
And each true-hearted servant
Shall shine as doth the day.
There God, our King and Portion,
In fulness of his grace,
Shall we behold forever,
And worship face to face.

4 O sweet and blessèd country,
The home of God's elect!
O sweet and blessèd country
That eager hearts expect!
Jesus, in mercy bring us
To that dear land of rest;
Who art, with God the Father,
And Spirit, ever blest.

—*Bernard of Cluny.*

TUNE: RUTHERFORD. 7.6, 7.6, 7.6, 7.6. (See Hymn 619.)

620

SECOND PART.

1 For thee, O dear, dear country,
Mine eyes their vigils keep;
For very love, beholding
Thy happy name, they weep.
The mention of thy glory
Is unction to the breast,
And medicine in sickness,
And love, and life, and rest.

2 O one, O only mansion!
O paradise of joy!
Where tears are ever banished,
And smiles have no alloy;
The Lamb is all thy splendour,
The Crucified thy praise;
His laud and benediction
Thy ransomed people raise.

3 Jerusalem the glorious!
Glory of the elect!
O dear and future vision
That eager hearts expect!
Even now by faith I see thee,
Even here thy walls discern;
To thee my thoughts are kindled,
And strive, and pant, and yearn.

—Neale, from Bernard of Clugny.

EWING. 7.6, 7.6, 7.6, 7.6. ALEXANDER EWING.

621

THIRD PART.

1 Jerusalem the golden,
With milk and honey blest,
Beneath thy contemplation
Sink heart and voice oppressed;
I know not, O I know not
What social joys are there!
What radiancy of glory,
What light beyond compare.

2 They stand, those halls of Zion,
All jubilant with song,
And bright with many an angel,
And all the martyr throng;
The Prince is ever in them,
The daylight is serene;
The pastures of the blessèd
Are decked in glorious sheen.

3 There is the throne of David;
And there, from care released,
The song of them that triumph,
The shout of them that feast;
And they who, with their Leader,
Have conquered in the fight,
Forever and forever
Are clad in robes of white.

—Neale, from Bernard of Clugny.

RAPTURE. 8.6, 8.6, 6.6, 6.6. J. BARNBY.

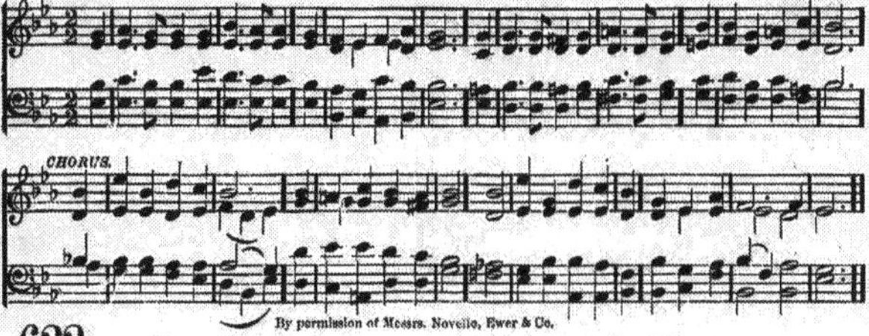
CHORUS.

By permission of Messrs. Novello, Ewer & Co.

622

The paradise above.

1 O PARADISE! O paradise!
Who doth not crave for rest?
Who would not seek the happy land
Where they that loved are blest.

CHORUS.—Where loyal hearts and true
Stand ever in the light,
All rapture through and through,
In God's most holy sight?

2 O paradise! O paradise!
The world is growing old;
Who would not be at rest and free
Where love is never cold?—CHO.

3 O paradise! O paradise!
'Tis weary waiting here;
I long to be where Jesus is,
To feel, to see him here.—CHO.

4 O paradise! O paradise!
I want to sin no more,
I want to be as pure on earth
As on thy spotless shore.—CHO.

5 O paradise! O paradise!
I greatly long to see
The special place my dearest Lord
In love prepares for me.—CHO.

—*F. W. Faber.*

ELIM. C.M. H. W. GREATOREX.

623

Rev. vii. 13-17.

1 How bright these glorious spirits shine!
Whence all their white array?
How came they to the blissful seats
Of everlasting day?

2 Lo! these are they from sufferings great,
Who came to realms of light,
And in the blood of Christ have washed
Those robes which shine so bright.

3 Now, with triumphal palms, they stand
Before the throne on high,
And serve the God they love, amidst
The glories of the sky.

4 The Lamb which dwells amidst the throne
Shall o'er them still preside;
Feed them with nourishment divine,
And all their footsteps guide.

5 In pastures green he'll lead his flock,
Where living streams appear;
And God the Lord from every eye
Shall wipe off every tear.

—*Watts and Cameron.*

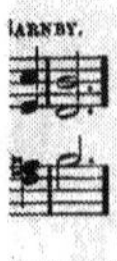

ST. GEORGE. 8-7s. SIR G. ELVEY.

624 *The glorified in heaven.*

1 Lift your eyes of faith, and see
Saints and angels joined in one;
What a countless company
Stand before yon dazzling throne!
Each before his Saviour stands;
All in spotless robes arrayed,
Palms they carry in their hands,
Crowns of glory on their head.

2 Saints begin the endless song,
Cry aloud in heavenly lays,
Glory doth to God belong;
God, the glorious Saviour, praise:
All salvation from him came;
Him who reigns enthroned on high;
Glory to the dying Lamb,
Let the morning stars reply.

3 Angel-powers the throne surround,
Next the saints in glory they;
Lulled with the transporting sound,
They their silent homage pay;
Prostrate on their face before
God and his Messiah fall;
Then in hymns of praise adore,
Shout the Lamb that died for all!

4 Be it so, they all reply,
Him let all our orders praise;
Him that did for sinners die,
Saviour of the favoured race!
Render we our God his right,
Glory, wisdom, thanks, and power,
Honour, majesty, and might;
Praise him, praise him evermore!

—*Charles Wesley.*

625 *"These are they that came out of great tribulation."*

1 Who are these arrayed in white,
Brighter than the noon-day sun?
Foremost of the sons of light,
Nearest the eternal throne?
These are they that bore the cross,
Nobly for their Master stood;
Sufferers in his righteous cause,
Followers of the Lamb of God.

2 Out of great distress they came,
Washed their robes by faith below
In the blood of yonder Lamb,
Blood that washes white as snow;
Therefore are they next the throne,
Serve their Maker day and night;
God resides among his own,
God doth in his saints delight.

3 More than conquerors at last,
Here they find their trials o'er;
They have all their sufferings past,
Hunger now and thirst no more;
God shall all their sorrows chase,
All their wants at once remove,
Wipe the tears from every face,
Fill up every soul with love.

—*Charles Wesley.*

IRENE. 6.6, 7.7, 7.7. FROM FREYLINGHAUSEN.

626

The abiding home.

1 How happy, Lord, are we,
Who build alone on thee!
What can our foundation shock?
Though the shattered earth remove,
Stands our city on a rock,
On the rock of heavenly Love.

2 A house we call our own,
Which cannot be o'erthrown;
In the general ruin sure,
Storms and earthquakes it defies;
Built immovably secure,
Built eternal in the skies.

3 High on Immanuel's land
We see the fabric stand;
From a tottering world remove
To a steadfast mansion there;
Our inheritance above
Cannot pass from heir to heir.

—*Charles Wesley.*

JUSTIFICATION. L. M. EAGLETON.

627

The redeemed in heaven.

1 Lo! round the throne a glorious band,
The saints in countless myriads stand;
Of every tongue redeemed to God,
‖: Arrayed in garments washed in blood. :‖

2 Through tribulation great they came;
They bore the cross, despised the shame;
But now from all their labours rest,
‖: In God's eternal glory blest. :‖

3 They see the Saviour face to face;
They sing the triumphs of his grace;
And day and night with ceaseless praise,
‖: To him their loud hosannas raise. :‖

4 O may we tread the sacred road
That holy saints and martyrs trod;
Wage to the end the glorious strife,
‖: And win, like them, a crown of life! :‖

—*Mary L. Duncan.*

ST. DAVID'S. 8-8s. HANDEL.

D.C.

628 Rev. xxi. 1-4.

1 AWAY with our sorrow and fear!
We soon shall recover our home;
The city of saints shall appear,
The day of eternity come:
From earth we shall quickly remove,
And mount to our native abode,
The house of our Father above,
The palace of angels and God.

2 Our mourning is all at an end,
When, raised by the life-giving word,
We see the new city descend,
Adorned as a bride for her Lord;
The city so holy and clean,
No sorrow can breathe in the air;
No gloom of affliction or sin,
No shadow of evil, is there.

3 By faith we already behold
That lovely Jerusalem here;
Her walls are of jasper and gold,
As crystal her buildings are clear;
Immovably founded in grace,
She stands, as she ever hath stood,
And brightly her Builder displays,
And flames with the glory of God.

4 No need of the sun in that day,
Which never is followed by night,
Where Jesus's beauties display
A pure and a permanent light:
The Lamb is their Light and their Sun;
And, lo! by reflection they shine,
With Jesus ineffably one,
And bright in effulgence divine!

—*Charles Wesley.*

629 *Longing for heaven.*

1 I LONG to behold him arrayed
With glory and light from above,
The King in his beauty displayed,
His beauty of holiest love:
I languish and sigh to be there,
Where Jesus hath fixed his abode;
O when shall we meet in the air,
And fly to the mountain of God!

2 With him I on Zion shall stand,
For Jesus hath spoken the word,
The breadth of Immanuel's land
Survey by the light of my Lord;
But when, on thy bosom reclined,
Thy face I am strengthened to see,
My fulness of rapture I find,
My heaven of heavens, in thee.

3 How happy the people that dwell
Secure in the city above!
No pain the inhabitants feel,
No sickness or sorrow shall prove.
Physician of souls, unto me
Forgiveness and holiness give;
And then from the body set free,
And then to the city receive!

—*Charles Wesley.*

EXCELSIOR. 5.5.5.11. D. SAMUEL WEBBE.

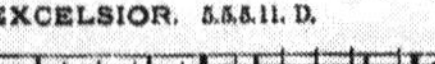

630

"Strangers and pilgrims."

1 COME, let us anew
Our journey pursue,
With vigour arise,
And press to our permanent place in the skies.
Of heavenly birth,
Though wandering on earth,
This is not our place;
But strangers and pilgrims ourselves we confess.

2 At Jesus's call,
We gave up our all;
And still we forego,
For Jesus's sake, our enjoyments below.
No longing we find
For the country behind;
But onward we move,
And still we are seeking a country above:

3 A country of joy,
Without any alloy,
We thither repair;
Our hearts and our treasure already are there.
We march hand in hand
To Immanuel's land;
No matter what cheer
We meet with on earth; for eternity's near.

4 The rougher our way,
The shorter our stay;
The tempests that rise
Shall gloriously hurry our souls to the skies.
The fiercer the blast,
The sooner 'tis past;
The troubles that come
Shall shorten our journey, and hasten us home.

—*Charles Wesley.*

COMPANION. P. M.

631

The songs of heaven.

1 COME, let us ascend, my companion and friend,
To a taste of the banquet above;
If thy heart be as mine, if for Jesus it pine,
Come up into the chariot of love.

2 By faith we are come to our permanent home;
By hope we the rapture improve;
By love we still rise, and look down on the skies,
For the heaven of heavens is love.

3 Who on earth can conceive how happy we live,
In the palace of God, the great King!
What a concert of praise, when our Jesus's grace
The whole heavenly company sing!

4 What a rapturous song, when the glorified throng
In the spirit of harmony join;
Join all the glad choirs, hearts, voices, and lyres,
And the burden is, "Mercy divine!"

5 Hallelujah, they cry, to the King of the sky,
To the great everlasting I AM;
To the Lamb that was slain, and liveth again,
Hallelujah to God and the Lamb!

6 Our foreheads proclaim his ineffable name;
Our bodies his glory display;
A day without night we feast in his sight,
And eternity seems as a day!

—*C. Wesley.*

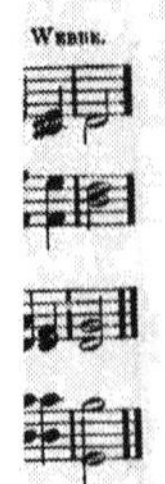

are there.

's near.

ne skies.

n us home.
Wesley.

py we live,
king?
Jesus's grace
g!
lorified

s, and lyres,
ne!"
f the sky,

veth again,
s!
e name;

s sight,
—C. Wesley.

SOLEMN THOUGHT. P.M. (First Tune.) Philip Phillips.

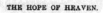

632

"Now is our salvation nearer than when we believed."

1 One sweetly solemn thought
Comes to me o'er and o'er,—
I am nearer home to-day
Than I ever have been before.

2 Nearer my Father's house,
Where the many mansions be;
Nearer the great white throne;
Nearer the crystal sea;

3 Nearer the bound of life,
Where we lay our burdens down;
Nearer leaving the cross;
Nearer gaining the crown.

4 But lying darkly between,
Winding down through the night,
Is the deep and unknown stream,
That leads at last to the light.

5 Father, perfect my trust!
Strengthen the might of my faith;
Let me feel as I would when I stand
On the rock of the shore of death.

—Phœbe Carey.

DOUBLE CHANT. P.M. (Second Tune.) W. Jacobs.

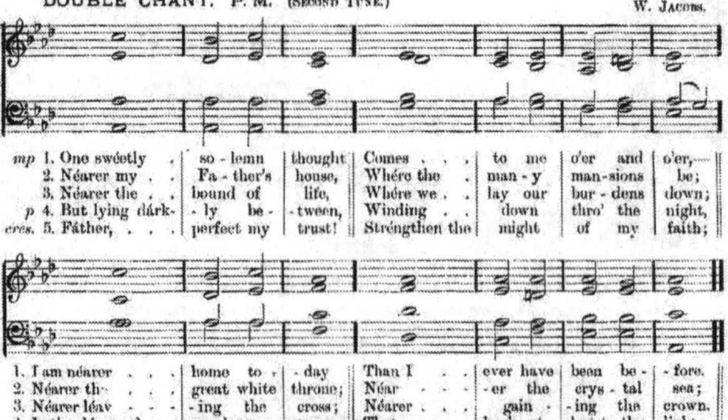
mp 1. One swéetly . . so - lemn thought Comes . . . to me o'er and o'er,—
2. Néarer my . . Fa - ther's house, Whére the . man - y man - sions be;
3. Néarer the . . bound of life, Whére we . . lay our bur - dens down;
p 4. But lying dárk- - ly be - - tween, Winding . . down thro' the night,
cres. 5. Fáther, . . . perfect my trust! Stréngthen the might of my faith;
1. I am néarer . . . home to - - day Than I . . ever have been be - - fore.
2. Néarer th- . . . great white throne; Néar . . . - er the crys - tal sea;
3. Néarer léav - - - ing the cross; Néarer . . . gain - - ing the crown.
4. Is the déep and . . un - known stream, That . . . leads at last to the light.
5. Let me feel as I would when I stand On the róck . of the shore of death.

Section VII.

CHRISTIAN ORDINANCES AND INSTITUTIONS.

1.—THE HOLY SCRIPTURES.

ERNAN. L. M. Dr. L. Mason.

633 *The excellency of Christ's religion.*

1 Let everlasting glories crown
Thy head, my Saviour and my Lord;
Thy hands have brought salvation down,
And writ the blessing in thy word.

2 In vain our trembling conscience seeks
Some solid ground to rest upon;
With long despair our spirit breaks,
Till we apply to thee alone.

3 How well thy blessèd truths agree!
How wise and holy thy commands!
Thy promises, how firm they be!
How firm our hope and comfort stands!

4 Should all the forms that men devise
Assault my faith with treacherous art,
I'd call them vanity and lies,
And bind thy Gospel to my heart.
—*Isaac Watts.*

ARNOLD. C. M. Dr. S. Arnold.

634 *The riches of God's Word.*

1 Father of mercies, in thy word
What endless glory shines!
Forever be thy name adored
For these celestial lines.

2 Here may the wretched sons of want
Exhaustless riches find;
Riches, above what earth can grant,
And lasting as the mind.

3 Here the fair Tree of Knowledge grows,
And yields a free repast;
Sublimer sweets than nature knows
Invite the longing taste.

4 Here the Redeemer's welcome voice
Spreads heavenly peace around;
And life and everlasting joys
Attend the blissful sound.

5 Divine Instructor, gracious Lord,
Be thou forever near;
Teach me to love thy sacred word,
And view my Saviour there.
—*Miss Steele.*

TUNE: ARNOLD. C. M. (See Hymn 634.)

635 *"Thy word is a lamp unto my feet."*

1 How precious is the book divine,
By inspiration given;
Bright as a lamp its doctrines shine
To guide our souls to heaven.

2 It sweetly cheers our drooping hearts,
In this dark vale of tears;
Life, light, and joy it still imparts,
And quells our rising fears.

3 This lamp, through all the tedious night
Of life, shall guide our way,
Till we behold the clearer light
Of an eternal day.

—*J. Fawcett.*

ST. MARTIN'S. C. M. TANSUR.

636 *"He shall teach you all things."*

1 Come, Holy Ghost, our hearts inspire,
Let us thine influence prove;
Source of the old prophetic fire,
Fountain of Light and Love.

2 Come, Holy Ghost, for moved by thee
The prophets wrote and spoke,
Unlock the Truth, thyself the Key,
Unseal the sacred Book.

3 Expand thy wings, celestial Dove,
Brood o'er our nature's night;
On our disordered spirits move,
And let there now be light.

4 God, through himself, we then shall know,
If thou within us shine;
And sound, with all thy saints below,
The depths of love divine.

—*Charles Wesley.*

637 *"Open thou mine eyes that I may behold wondrous things out of thy law."*

1 Father of all, in whom alone
We live, and move, and breathe,
One bright, celestial ray dart down,
And cheer thy sons beneath.

2 While in thy word we search for thee,
We search with trembling awe!
Open our eyes, and let us see
The wonders of thy law.

3 Now let our darkness comprehend
The light that shines so clear;
Now the revealing Spirit send,
And give us ears to hear.

4 Before us make thy goodness pass,
Which here by faith we know;
Let us in Jesus see thy face,
And die to all below.

—*Charles Wesley.*

EUPHONY. 6-8s. T. SINGLETON.

638 "*No prophecy of the Scripture is of any private interpretation.*"

1 COME, O thou Prophet of the Lord,
Thou great Interpreter Divine!
Explain thine own transmitted word;
To teach and to inspire is thine;
Thou only canst thyself reveal,
‖:Open the book, and loose the seal.:‖

2 Now, Jesus, now the veil remove,
The folly of our darkened heart;
Unfold the wonders of thy love,
The knowledge of thyself impart;
Our ear, our inmost soul, we bow:
‖:Speak, Lord, thy servants hearken now.:‖

3 Come, then, Divine Interpreter,
The Scriptures to our hearts apply;
And, taught by thee, we God revere,
Him in Three Persons magnify;
In each the Triune God adore,
‖:Who was, and is for evermore.:‖

—*J. Wesley, from the French of Madame Bourignon.*

639 "*Ye shall know the truth.*"

1 INSPIRER of the ancient seers,
Who wrote from thee the sacred page,
The same through all succeeding years,
To us, in our degenerate age,
The Spirit of thy word impart,
‖:And breathe thy life into our heart.:‖

2 While now thine oracles we read,
With earnest prayer and strong desire,
O let thy Spirit fr m thee proceed,
Our souls to awaken and inspire!
Our weakness help, our darkness chase,
‖:And guide us by the light of grace.:‖

3 Whene'er in error's paths we rove,
The living God through sin forsake,
Our conscience by thy word reprove,
Convince and bring the wanderers back,
Deep wounded by thy Spirit's sword,
‖:And then by Gilead's balm restored.:‖

4 The sacred lessons of thy grace,
Transmitted through thy word, repeat;
And train us up in all thy ways,
To make us in thy will complete;
Fulfil thy love's redeeming plan,
‖:And bring us to a perfect man.:‖

—*Isaac Watts.*

CAREY'S. 6-8s. HENRY CAREY.

640 *The Spirit of Truth.*

1 SPIRIT of Truth, essential God,
Who didst thy ancient saints inspire,
Shed in their hearts thy love abroad,
And touch their hallowed lips with fire;
Our God from all eternity,
World without end, we worship thee!

2 Still we believe, Almighty Lord,
Whose presence fills both earth and heaven,
The meaning of the written word
Is by thy inspiration given;
Thou only dost thyself explain
The secret mind of God to man.

—*Charles Wesley.*

MOZART. 6-8s. FROM MOZART.

641 *The study of God's Word.*

1 WHEN quiet in my house I sit,
Thy book be my companion still;
My joy thy sayings to repeat,
Talk o'er the records of thy will,
And search the oracles divine,
Till every heart-felt word be mine.

2 O may the gracious words divine
Subject of all my converse be!
So will the Lord his follower join,
And walk and talk himself with me;
So shall my heart his presence prove,
And burn with everlasting love.

3 Oft as I lay me down to rest,
O may the reconciling word
Sweetly compose my weary breast!
While, on the bosom of my Lord,
I sink in blissful dreams away,
And visions of eternal day.

4 Rising to sing my Saviour's praise,
Thee may I publish all day long;
And let thy precious word of grace
Flow from my heart, and fill my tongue,
Fill all my life with purest love,
And join me to the Church above.

—*Charles Wesley.*

2.—THE LORD'S DAY.

ST. ALBAN. L. M. St. Alban's Tune Book.

642 *The earthly and the heavenly Sabbath.*

1 Lord of the Sabbath, hear our vows,
On this thy day, in this thy house;
And own, as grateful sacrifice,
The songs which from thy servants rise.

2 Thine earthly Sabbaths, Lord, we love,
But there's a nobler rest above;
To that our labouring souls aspire,
With ardent hope, and strong desire.

3 No more fatigue, no more distress,
Nor sin nor hell shall reach the place;
No sighs shall mingle with the songs
Which warble from immortal tongues.

4 No rude alarms of raging foes;
No cares to break the long repose;
No midnight shade, no clouded sun,
But sacred, high, eternal noon.

5 O long-expected day, begin!
Dawn on these realms of woe and sin;
Fain would we leave this weary road,
And sleep in death, to rest with God.

—*Doddridge.*

LASSUS. L. M. A. H. Mann, Mus. Bac.

643 *The Sabbath a delight.*

1 Sweet is the work, my God, my King,
To praise thy name, give thanks and sing,
To show thy love by morning light,
And talk of all thy truth at night.

2 Sweet is the day of sacred rest,
No mortal cares disturb my breast;
O may my heart in tune be found,
Like David's harp of solemn sound!

3 My heart shall triumph in the Lord,
And bless his works, and bless his word;
Thy works of grace, how bright they shine!
How deep thy counsels, how divine!

4 Fools never raise their thoughts so high;
Like brutes they live, like brutes they die;
Like grass they flourish, till thy breath
Dooms them to everlasting death.

5 But I shall share a glorious part
When grace has well refined my heart;
And fresh supplies of joy are shed,
Like holy oil to cheer my head.

6 Then shall I see, and hear, and know
All I desired and wished below;
And every power find sweet employ
In that eternal world of joy.

—*Isaac Watts.*

HURSLEY. L. M. HUGUENOT MELODY.

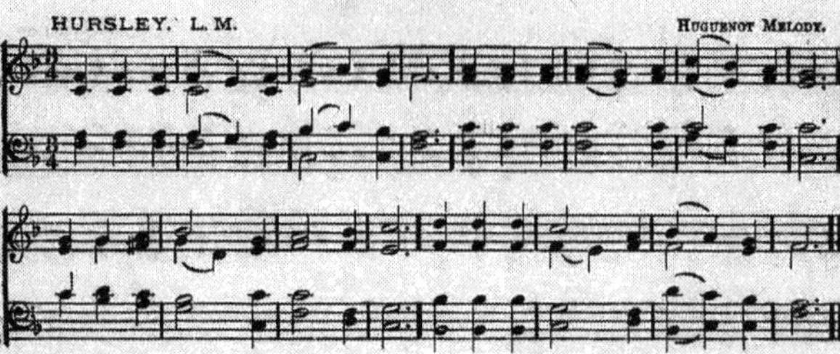

644 *Sabbath worship a foretaste of heaven.*

1 AGAIN our weekly labours end,
And we the Sabbath's call attend;
Improve, our souls, the sacred rest,
And seek to be forever blest.

2 This day let our devotions rise
To heaven, a grateful sacrifice;
And God that peace divine bestow,
Which none but they who feel it know.

3 This holy calm within the breast
Prepares for that eternal rest,
Which for the sons of God remains;
The end of cares, the end of pains.

4 In holy duties let the day,
In holy pleasures, pass away;
How sweet the Sabbath thus to spend,
In hope of that which ne'er shall end!

—*J. Stennett.*

HESPERUS. L. M. H. BAKER, Mus. Bac.

645 *The Sabbath rest.*

1 SWEET is the sunlight after rain,
And sweet the sleep which follows pain;
And sweetly steals the Sabbath rest
Upon the world's work-wearied breast.

2 Of heaven the sign, of earth the calm;
The poor man's birthright, and his balm;
God's witness of celestial things;
A sun with healing in its wings.

3 New rising in this gospel time,
And in its sevenfold light sublime,
Blest day of God! we hail its dawn,
To gratitude and worship drawn.

4 O nought of gloom and nought of pride
Should with the sacred hours abide;
At work for God, in loved employ,
We lose the duty in the joy.

5 Breathe on us, Lord! our sins forgive,
And make us strong in faith to live;
Our utmost, sorest need supply,
And make us strong in faith to die.

—*Punshon.*

SABBATH. 6-7s. DR. L. MASON.

646 *The Sabbath in the sanctuary.*

1 SAFELY through another week,
God has brought us on our way;
Let us now a blessing seek,
Waiting in his courts to-day;
‖: Day of all the week the best,
Emblem of eternal rest. :‖

2 While we pray for pardoning grace,
Through our great Redeemer's name,
Show thy reconcilèd face,
Take away our sin and shame;
‖: From our worldly cares set free,
May we rest this day in thee. :‖

3 Here we come thy name to praise;
May we feel thy presence near;
May thy glory meet our eyes,
While we in thy house appear;
‖: Here afford us, Lord, a taste
Of our everlasting feast. :‖

4 May thy gospel's joyful sound
Conquer sinners, comfort saints;
Make the fruits of grace abound,
Bring relief for all complaints:
‖: Thus may all our Sabbaths prove,
Till we join the Church above. :‖

—*J. Newton.*

STEGGALL. 6.6, 6.6, 8.8. DR. STEGGALL.

TUNE: STEGGALL. 6.6, 6.6, 8.8.

647 *Sabbath worship and praise.*

1 Awake, ye saints, awake!
And hail this sacred day;
In loftiest songs of praise
Your joyful homage pay;
Come, bless the day that God hath blest,
The type of heaven's eternal rest.

2 On this auspicious morn
The Lord of life arose;
He burst the bars of death,
And vanquished all our foes;
And now he pleads our cause above,
And reaps the fruit of all his love.

3 All hail, triumphant Lord!
Heaven with hosannas rings,
And earth, in humbler strains,
Thy praise responsive sings;
Worthy the Lamb, that once was slain,
Through endless years to live and reign.

—*Elizabeth Scott.*

WARWICK. C.M. Samuel Stanley.

648 *"This is the day the Lord hath made."*

1 Come, let us join with one accord
In hymns around the throne;
This is the day our rising Lord
Hath made and called his own.

2 This is the day which God hath blessed,
The brightest of the seven;
Type of that everlasting rest
The saints enjoy in heaven.

3 Then let us in his name sing on,
And hasten to that day
When our Redeemer shall come down,
And shadows pass away.

4 Not one, but all our days below,
Let us in hymns employ;
And in our Lord rejoicing go
To his eternal joy.

—*Charles Wesley.*

649 *Joyful Sabbath worship.*

1 With joy we hail the sacred day
Which God has called his own;
With joy the summons we obey
To worship at his throne.

2 Thy chosen temples, Lord, how fair!
As here thy servants throng
To breathe the humble, fervent prayer,
And pour the grateful song.

3 Spirit of grace, O deign to dwell
Within thy Church below!
Make her in holiness excel,
With pure devotion glow.

4 Let peace within her walls be found;
Let all her sons unite
To spread with holy zeal around
Thy gospel's glorious light.

5 Great God, we hail the sacred day
Which thou hast called thine own!
With joy the summons we obey
To worship at thy throne.

—*Harriet Auber.*

FOSTER. C. M. M. B. FOSTER.

650 *Praise to the Lord of Sabbath.*

1 THE Lord of Sabbath let us praise,
In concert with the blest,
Who, joyful, in harmonious lays
Employ an endless rest.

2 Thus, Lord, while we remember thee,
In faith and love we grow;
By hymns of praise we learn to be
Triumphant here below.

3 On this glad day a brighter scene
Of glory was displayed,
By God, the eternal Word, than when
This universe was made.

4 He rises, who mankind has bought,
With grief and pain extreme:
'Twas great to speak a world from nought;
'Twas greater to redeem!

—*S. Wesley, jr.*

CAMBRIDGE. S. M. REV. R. HARRISON.

651 *Feasting with Christ on the Lord's Day.*

1 WELCOME, sweet day of rest,
That saw the Lord arise;
Welcome to this reviving breast,
And these rejoicing eyes.

2 The King himself comes near,
And feasts his saints to-day;
Here we may sit, and see him here,
And love, and praise, and pray.

3 One day amidst the place
Where thou, my Lord, hast been
Is sweeter than ten thousand days
Of pleasurable sin.

4 My willing soul would stay
In such a frame as this,
And sit and sing herself away
To everlasting bliss.

—*Isaac Watts.*

TUNE: CAMBRIDGE. S. M. (SEE HYMN 651.)

652 *Grateful praise on the Sabbath.*

1 HAIL to the Sabbath day,
The day divinely given,
When men to God their homage pay,
And earth draws near to heaven.

2 Lord, in this sacred hour,
Within thy courts we bend,
And bless thy love, and own thy power,
Our Father and our Friend.

3 But thou art not alone
In courts by mortals trod;
Nor only is the day thine own
When man draws near to God:

4 Thy temple is the arch
Of yon unmeasured sky;
Thy Sabbath, the stupendous march
Of vast eternity.

5 Lord, may that holier day
Dawn on thy servants' sight;
And purer worship may we pay
In heaven's unclouded light.

—*S. G. Bulfinch.*

AURELIA. 7.6, 7.6, 7.6, 7.6. DR. S. S. WESLEY.

653 *"And call the Sabbath a delight, the holy of the Lord."*

1 O DAY of rest and gladness,
O day of joy and light,
O balm of care and sadness,
Most beautiful, most bright;
On thee the high and lowly,
Before the eternal throne,
Sing Holy, Holy, Holy,
To the great Three in One.

2 On thee, at the creation,
The light first had its birth;
On thee for our salvation,
Christ rose from depths of earth;
On thee our Lord victorious,
The Spirit sent from heaven;
And thus on thee most glorious
A triple light was given.

3 To-day on weary nations
The heavenly manna falls;
To holy convocations
The silver trumpet calls,
Where gospel-light is glowing
With pure and radiant beams,
And living water flowing
With soul-refreshing streams.

4 New graces ever gaining
From this our day of rest,
We reach the rest remaining
To spirits of the blest;
To Holy Ghost be praises,
To Father, and to Son;
The Church her voice upraises
To thee, blest Three in One.

—*Bishop Wordsworth.*

PATER OMNIUM. 6-8s. H. J. E. Holmes.

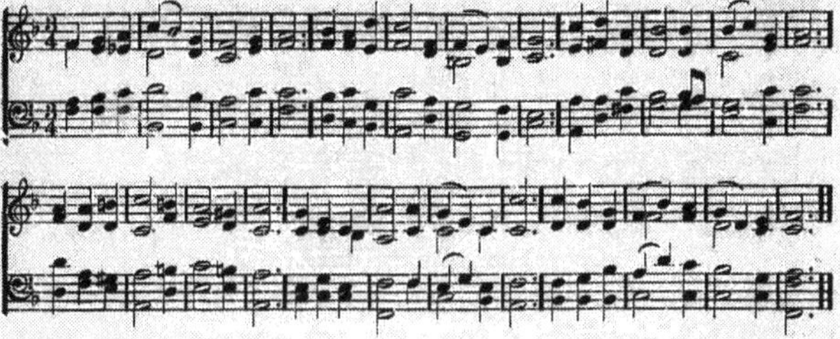

654 *Sabbath Morning worship.*

1 Great God, this hallowed day of thine
 Demands our souls' collected powers;
May we employ in works divine
 These solemn and devoted hours;
O may our souls adoring own
The grace which calls us to thy throne!

2 We bid life's cares and trifles fly,
 And where thou art appear no more;
Omniscient Lord, thy piercing eye
 Doth every secret thought explore:
O may thy grace our hearts refine,
And fix our thoughts on things divine!

3 Thy Spirit's gracious aid impart,
 And let thy word, with power divine,
Engage the ear, and warm the heart,
 And make the day entirely thine!
Thus may our souls adoring own
The grace which calls us to thy throne!

—*Miss Steele.*

GERMAN HYMN. 4-7s. Pleyel.

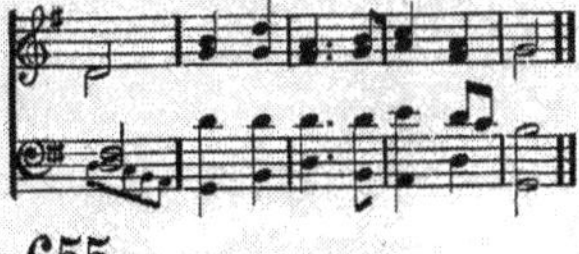

655 *Sabbath Evening worship.*

1 Softly fades the twilight ray
Of the holy Sabbath day;
Gently as life's setting sun,
When the Christian's course is run.

2 Night her solemn mantle spreads
O'er the earth as daylight fades;
All things tell of calm repose,
At the holy Sabbath's close.

3 Peace is on the world abroad;
'Tis the holy peace of God,
Symbol of the peace within,
When the spirit rests from sin.

4 Still the Spirit lingers near,
Where the evening worshipper
Seeks communion with the skies,
Pressing onward to the prize.

5 Saviour, may our Sabbaths be
Days of joy and peace in thee,
Till in heaven our souls repose,
Where the Sabbath ne'er shall close.

—*S. F. Smith.*

ELLERS. 10.10.10.10. E. J. HOPKINS.

dim.
pp

656 *Closing hymn for Sabbath Evening.*

1 SAVIOUR, again to thy dear name we raise
With one accord our parting hymn of praise;
We stand to bless thee ere our worship cease,
Then, lowly kneeling, wait thy word of peace.

2 Grant us thy peace upon our homeward way;
With thee began, with thee shall end the day;
Guard thou the lips from sin, the hearts from
shame,
That in this house have called upon thy name.

3 Grant us thy peace, Lord, through the coming
night,
Turn thou for us its darkness into light;
From harm and danger keep thy children free;
For dark and light are both alike to thee.

4 Grant us thy peace throughout our earthly life,
Our balm in sorrow, and our stay in strife;
Then, when thy voice shall bid our conflict
cease,
Call us, O Lord, to thine eternal peace.

—*J. Ellerton.*

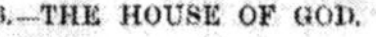

3.—THE HOUSE OF GOD.

STEGGALL. 6.6, 6.6, 8.8. DR. STEGGALL.

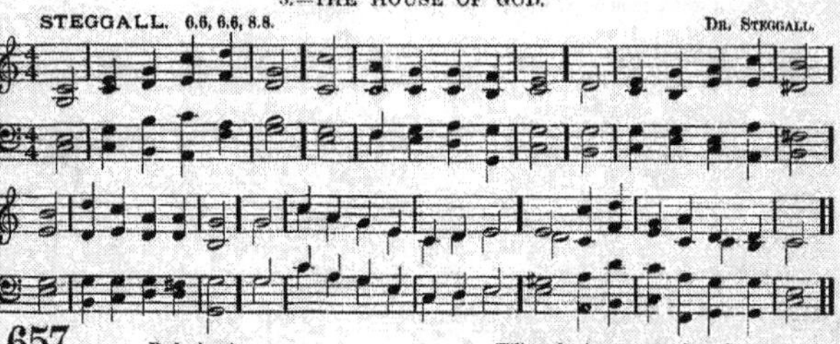

657 Psalm lxxxiv.

1 LORD of the worlds above,
How pleasant and how fair
The dwellings of thy love,
Thy earthly temples, are!
To thine abode my heart aspires,
With warm desires to see my God.

2 O happy souls that pray
Where God delights to hear!
O happy men that pay
Their constant service there!
They praise thee still, and happy they
Who love the way to Zion's hill!

3 They go from strength to strength,
Through this dark vale of tears,
Till each o'ercomes at length,
Till each in heaven appears;
O glorious seat! thou God, our King,
Shalt thither bring our willing feet.

4 God is our sun and shield,
Our light and our defence;
With gifts his hands are filled,
We draw our blessings thence:
He shall bestow upon our race
His saving grace, and glory too.

5 The Lord his people loves;
His hand no good withholds
From those his heart approves,
From holy, humble souls:
Thrice happy he, O Lord of hosts,
Whose spirit trusts alone in thee!

—*Isaac Watts.*

MILLENNIUM. 6.6, 6.6, 8.8.

658 *"One Lord, one faith, one baptism."*

1 One sole baptismal sign,
One Lord below, above,
One faith, one hope divine,
One only watchword, love;
From different temples though it rise,
One song ascendeth to the skies.

2 Our Sacrifice is one;
One Priest before the throne,
The slain, the risen Son,
Redeemer, Lord alone;
Thou who didst raise him from the dead,
Unite thy people in their Head.

3 O may that holy prayer,
His tenderest and his last,
His constant, latest care
Ere to his throne he passed,
No longer unfulfilled remain,
The world's offence, his people's stain!

4 Head of thy Church beneath,
The catholic, the true,
On all her members breathe,
Her broken frame renew:
Then shall thy perfect will be done,
When Christians love and live as one.

—*G. Robinson.*

NASHVILLE. 6-8s. (2nd Metre.) ADAPTED BY LOWELL MASON.

TUNE: NASHVILLE. 6-8s. (2nd Metre.)

659 Psalm lxxxiv.—*Another version.*

1 How lovely are thy tents, O Lord!
Where'er thou choosest to record
Thy name, or place thy house of prayer;
My soul outflies the angel-choir,
And faints, o'erpowered with strong desire,
To meet thy special presence there.

2 Happy the men to whom 'tis given,
To dwell within that gate of heaven,
And in thy house record thy praise;
Whose strength and confidence thou art,
Who feel thee, Saviour, in their heart,
The Way, the Truth, the Life of grace:

3 Who, passing through the mournful vale,
Drink comfort from the living well
That flows replenished from above;
From strength to strength advancing here,
Till all before their God appear,
And each receives the crown of love.

4 Better a day thy courts within
Than thousands in the tents of sin;
How base the noblest pleasures there!
How great the weakest child of thine!
His meanest task is all divine,
And kings and priests thy servants are.

5 The Lord protects and cheers his own,
Their light and strength, their shield and sun;
He shall both grace and glory give;
Unlimited his bounteous grant;
No real good they e'er shall want;
All, all is theirs, who righteous live.

6 O Lord of hosts, how blest is he
Who steadfastly believes in thee!
He all thy promises shall gain;
The soul that on thy love is cast
Thy perfect love on earth shall taste,
And soon with thee in glory reign.

—*Charles Wesley.*

FAITH. 7.6.7.6, 7.7.7.6. Dr. S. S. Wesley.

660 Psalm xlviii.

1 Great is our redeeming Lord,
In power, and truth, and grace;
Him, by highest heaven adored,
His Church on earth doth praise:
In the city of our God,
In his holy mount below,
Publish, spread his name abroad,
And all his greatness show.

2 For thy loving-kindness, Lord,
We in thy temple stay;
Here thy faithful love record,
Thy saving power display:
With thy name thy praise is known,
Glorious thy perfections shine;
Earth's remotest bounds shall own
Thy works are all divine.

3 See the gospel Church secure,
And founded on a rock;
All her promises are sure;
Her bulwarks who can shock?
Count her every precious shrine;
Tell, to after-ages, tell,
Fortified by power divine,
The Church can never fail.

4 Zion's God is all our own,
Who on his love rely;
We his pardoning love have known,
And live to Christ, and die.
To the new Jerusalem
He our faithful guide shall be;
Him we claim, and rest in him,
Through all eternity.

—*Charles Wesley.*

SHIRLAND. S. M. STANLEY.

661 "*The Church of the living God.*"

1 I LOVE thy kingdom, Lord,
The house of thine abode,
The Church our blest Redeemer saves
With his own precious blood.

2 I love thy Church, O God!
Her walls before thee stand,
Dear as the apple of thine eye,
And graven on thine hand.

3 For her my tears shall fall,
For her my prayers ascend;
To her my cares and toils be given,
Till toils and cares shall end.

4 Beyond my highest joy
I prize her heavenly ways,
Her sweet communion, solemn vows,
Her hymns of love and praise.

5 Sure as thy truth shall last,
To Zion shall be given
The brightest glories earth can yield,
And brighter bliss of heaven.

—*Timothy Dwight.*

ST. MARK. S. M. GEO. KINGSLEY.

662 "*God is known in her palaces for a refuge.*"

1 GREAT is the Lord our God,
And let his praise be great;
He makes his churches his abode,
His most delightful seat.

2 These temples of his grace,
How beautiful they stand!
The honours of our native place,
And bulwarks of our land.

3 In Zion God is known
A refuge in distress;
How bright has his salvation shone
Through all her palaces!

4 In every new distress
We'll to his house repair;
We'll think upon his wondrous grace,
And seek deliverance there.

—*Isaac Watts.*

TUNE: ST. MARK. S. M. (See Hymn 662.)

663

Psalm cxxii.

1 Glad was my heart to hear
My old companions say,
Come, in the house of God appear,
For 'tis an holy day.

2 Thither the tribes repair,
Where all are wont to meet,
And joyful in the house of prayer
Bend at the mercy-seat.

3 Pray for Jerusalem,
The city of our God;
The Lord from heaven be kind to them
That love the dear abode.

4 Within these walls may peace
And harmony be found;
Zion, in all thy palaces,
Prosperity abound!

5 For friends and brethren dear,
Our prayer shall never cease;
Oft as they meet for worship here,
God send his people peace!

—*Montgomery.*

AUSTRIA. 8.7, 8.7, 8.7, 8.7. F. J. Haydn.

664

Zion, the city of God.

1 Glorious things of thee are spoken,
Zion, city of our God;
He, whose word cannot be broken,
Formed thee for his own abode;
On the Rock of ages founded,
What can shake thy sure repose?
With salvation's walls surrounded,
Thou may'st smile at all thy foes.

2 See the streams of living waters,
Springing from eternal love,
Still supply thy sons and daughters,
And all fear of want remove;
Who can faint while such a river
Ever flows our thirst to assuage?
Grace, which, like the Lord, the giver,
Never fails from age to age.

3 Round each habitation hovering,
See the cloud and fire appear,
For a glory and a covering,
Showing that the Lord is near:
He who gives us daily manna,
He who listens when we cry,
Let him hear the loud hosanna
Rising to his throne on high.

—*J. Newton.*

SALVATOR. 8.7, 8.7, 8.7, 8.7. J. P. JUDSON.

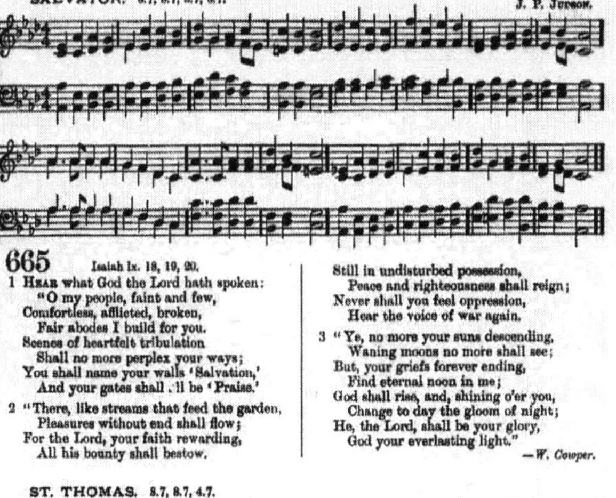

665 Isaiah lx. 18, 19, 20.

1 HEAR what God the Lord hath spoken:
"O my people, faint and few,
Comfortless, afflicted, broken,
Fair abodes I build for you.
Scenes of heartfelt tribulation
Shall no more perplex your ways;
You shall name your walls 'Salvation,'
And your gates shall all be 'Praise.'

2 "There, like streams that feed the garden,
Pleasures without end shall flow;
For the Lord, your faith rewarding,
All his bounty shall bestow.
Still in undisturbed possession,
Peace and righteousness shall reign;
Never shall you feel oppression,
Hear the voice of war again.

3 "Ye, no more your suns descending,
Waning moons no more shall see;
But, your griefs forever ending,
Find eternal noon in me;
God shall rise, and, shining o'er you,
Change to day the gloom of night;
He, the Lord, shall be your glory,
God your everlasting light."

—*W. Cowper.*

ST. THOMAS. 8.7, 8.7, 4.7.

666 *Jehovah, the defence of Zion.*

1 ZION stands with hills surrounded,
Zion, kept by power divine;
All her foes shall be confounded,
Though the world in arms combine;
||: Happy Zion, :||
What a favoured lot is thine!

2 Every human tie may perish;
Friend to friend unfaithful prove;
Mothers cease their own to cherish;
Heaven and earth at last remove;
||: But no changes :||
Can attend Jehovah's love.

3 In the furnace God may prove thee,
Thence to bring thee forth more bright,
But can never cease to love thee;
Thou art precious in his sight;
||: God is with thee, :||
God, thine everlasting light.

—*T. Kelly.*

AMSTERDAM. 7.6, 7.6, 7.8, 7.6. DR. NARES.

667 *"Then had the churches rest, and were edified."*

1 O THAT now the Church were blest
With faith and faith's increase!
Grant us, Lord, the outward rest
And true internal peace;
Build us up in holy love,
And let us walk with God below,
Serve thee as thy hosts above,
And all thy comfort know.

2 With the humble filial fear
Be mixed the joy of grace,
While we gladly persevere
In all thy righteous ways;
Thus let each in thee abide,
Let each improve the blessing given,
Till thy Church is multiplied
Beyond the stars of heaven.

—*Charles Wesley.*

WAREHAM. L. M. W. KNAPP.

668 *True worship not confined to any place.*

1 O THOU, to whom, in ancient time,
The lyre of Hebrew bards was strung,
Whom kings adored in songs sublime,
And prophets praised with glowing tongue;

2 Not now on Zion's height alone
The favoured worshipper may dwell,
Nor where, at sultry noon, thy Son
Sat weary by the patriarch's well.

3 From every place below the skies,
The grateful song, the fervent prayer,
The incense of the heart, may rise
To heaven, and find acceptance there.

4 O thou, to whom, in ancient time,
The holy prophet's harp was strung,
To thee at last in every clime,
Shall temples rise and praise be sung.

—*J. Pierpont.*

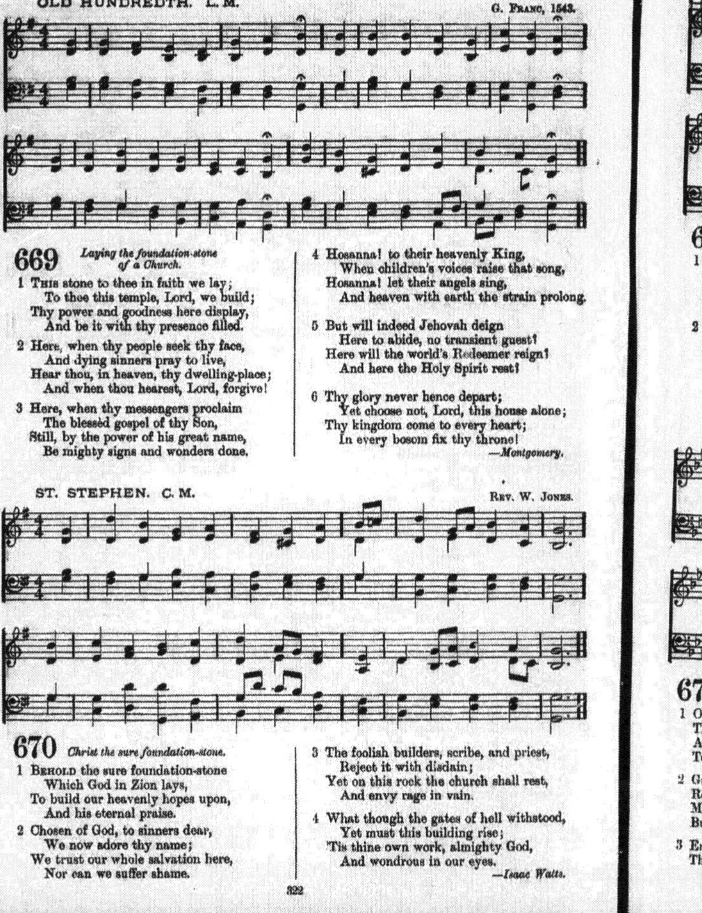

OLD HUNDREDTH. L. M. G. Franc, 1543.

669 *Laying the foundation-stone of a Church.*

1 This stone to thee in faith we lay;
To thee this temple, Lord, we build;
Thy power and goodness here display,
And be it with thy presence filled.

2 Here, when thy people seek thy face,
And dying sinners pray to live,
Hear thou, in heaven, thy dwelling-place;
And when thou hearest, Lord, forgive!

3 Here, when thy messengers proclaim
The blessed gospel of thy Son,
Still, by the power of his great name,
Be mighty signs and wonders done.

4 Hosanna! to their heavenly King,
When children's voices raise that song,
Hosanna! let their angels sing,
And heaven with earth the strain prolong.

5 But will indeed Jehovah deign
Here to abide, no transient guest?
Here will the world's Redeemer reign?
And here the Holy Spirit rest?

6 Thy glory never hence depart;
Yet choose not, Lord, this house alone;
Thy kingdom come to every heart;
In every bosom fix thy throne!

—*Montgomery.*

ST. STEPHEN. C. M. Rev. W. Jones.

670 *Christ the sure foundation-stone.*

1 Behold the sure foundation-stone
Which God in Zion lays,
To build our heavenly hopes upon,
And his eternal praise.

2 Chosen of God, to sinners dear,
We now adore thy name;
We trust our whole salvation here,
Nor can we suffer shame.

3 The foolish builders, scribe, and priest,
Reject it with disdain;
Yet on this rock the church shall rest,
And envy rage in vain.

4 What though the gates of hell withstood,
Yet must this building rise;
'Tis thine own work, almighty God,
And wondrous in our eyes.

—*Isaac Watts.*

WILTSHIRE. C. M. SIR GEORGE SMART.

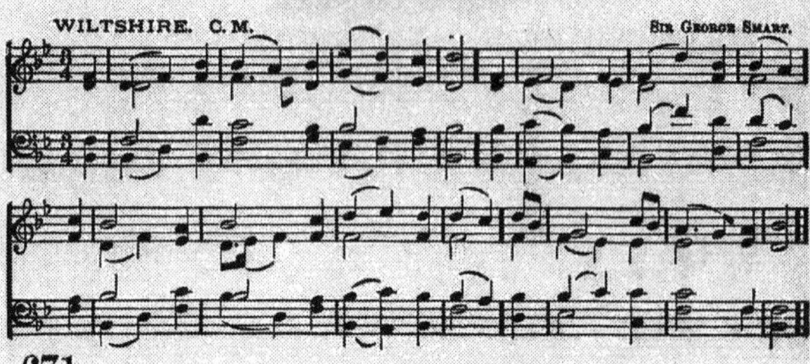

671 *Dedication of a Church.*

1 O THOU, whose own vast temple stands
Built over earth and sea,
Accept the walls that human hands
Have raised to worship thee!

2 Lord, from thine inmost glory send,
Within these courts to bide,
The peace that dwelleth without end,
Serenely by thy side!

3 May erring minds that worship here
Be taught the better way;
And they who mourn, and they who fear,
Be strengthened as they pray.

4 May faith grow firm, and love grow warm,
And pure devotion rise,
While round these hallowed walls the storm
Of earthborn passion dies.

—*W. C. Bryant.*

ABENDS. L. M. SIR H. S. OAKLEY.

672 *Laying the foundation of a Church.*

1 O LORD of hosts, whose glory fills
The bounds of the eternal hills,
And yet vouchsafes, in Christian lands,
To dwell in temples made with hands;

2 Grant that all we who here to-day
Rejoicing this foundation lay,
May be in very deed thine own,
Built on the precious Corner-stone.

3 Endue the creatures with the grace
That shall adorn thy dwelling-place;
The beauty of the oak and pine,
The gold and silver, make them thine.

4 To thee they all pertain; to thee
The treasures of the earth and sea;
And when we bring them to thy throne
We but present thee with thine own.

5 The heads that guide endue with skill;
The hands that work preserve from ill;
That we, who these foundations lay,
May raise the topstone in its day.

—*J. Neale.*

AMSTERDAM. 7.6, 7.6, 7.8, 7.6. DR. NARES.

673 *Laying a foundation-stone.*

1 Thou, who hast in Zion laid
The true foundation-stone,
And with those a covenant made,
Who build on that alone;
Hear us, architect divine,
Great builder of thy church below!
Now upon thy servants shine,
Who seek thy praise to show.

2 Earth is thine; her thousand hills
Thy mighty hand sustains;
Heaven thy awful presence fills;
O'er all thy glory reigns;
Yet the place of old prepared
By royal David's favoured son
Thy peculiar blessing shared,
And stood thy chosen throne.

3 We, like Jesse's son, would raise
A temple to the Lord;
Sound throughout its courts his praise,
His saving name record;
Dedicate a house to him,
Who, once in mortal weakness shrined,
Sorrowed, suffered, to redeem,
To rescue all mankind.

4 Father, Son, and Spirit, send
The consecrating flame;
Now in majesty descend,
Inscribe the living name;
That great name by which we live
Now write on this accepted stone;
Us into thy hands receive,
Our temple make thy throne.

—*Mrs. Bulmer.*

DUKE STREET. L. M. JOHN HATTON.

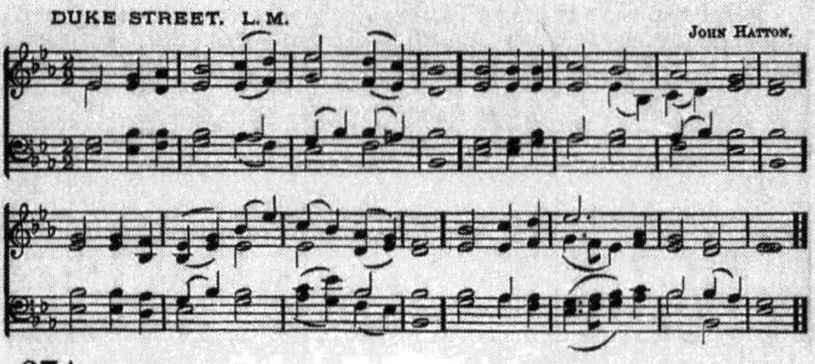

674 *The dedication of a Church.*

1 GREAT God, thy watchful care we bless,
Which guards these sacred courts in peace;
Nor dare tumultuous foes invade,
To fill thy worshippers with dread.

2 These walls we to thy honour raise,
Long may they echo to thy praise!
And thou, descending, fill the place
With choicest tokens of thy grace.

3 And in the great decisive day,
When God the nations shall survey,
May it before the world appear,
That crowds were born to glory here.

—Doddridge.

MARINERS. 4-7s.

675 *Dedication of a Church.*

1 LORD of hosts! to thee we raise
Here a house of prayer and praise;
Thou thy people's hearts prepare,
Here to meet for praise and prayer.

2 Let the living here be fed
With thy word, the heavenly bread;
Here in hope of glory blest,
May the dead be laid to rest.

3 Here to thee a temple stand,
While the sea shall gird the land;
Here reveal thy mercy sure,
While the sun and moon endure.

4 Hallelujah! earth and sky
To the joyful sound reply;
Hallelujah! hence ascend
Prayer and praise till time shall end.

—Montgomery.

MURRAY. 6.6, 6.6, 8.8. GERMAN.

676 *Dedication of a Church.*

1 Great King of glory, come,
  And with thy favour crown
This temple as thy home,
  This people as thine own;
Beneath this roof, O deign to show
How God can dwell with men below!

2 Here may thine ears attend
  Our interceding cries,
And grateful praise ascend,
  Like incense, to the skies;
Here may thy word melodious sound,
And spread celestial joys around.

3 Here may our unborn sons
  And daughters sound thy praise,
And shine, like polished stones,
  Through long-succeeding days;
Here, Lord, display thy saving power,
While temples stand and men adore.

4 Here may the listening throng
  Receive thy truth in love;
Here Christians join the song
  Of seraphim above;
Till all, who humbly seek thy face,
Rejoice in thy abounding grace.

—*B. Francis.*

DRESDEN. L. M. FROM MOZART.

677 *Dedication of a Hall of Science.*

1 The Lord our God alone is strong;
  His hands build not for one brief day;
His wondrous works, through ages long,
  His wisdom and his power display.

2 His mountains lift their solemn forms,
  To watch in silence o'er the land;
The rolling ocean, rocked with storms,
  Sleeps in the hollow of his hand.

3 Beyond the heavens he sits alone,
  The universe obeys his nod;
The lightning-rifts disclose his throne,
  And thunders voice the name of God.

4 Thou sovereign God, receive this gift
  Thy willing servants offer thee;
Accept the prayers that thousands lift,
  And let these halls thy temple be.

5 And let those learn, who here shall meet,
  True wisdom is with reverence crowned,
And Science walks with humble feet
  To seek the God that Faith hath found.

—*C. T. Winchester.*

EDEN. L. M. Dr. L. Mason.

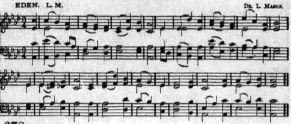

678 *The institution of the Christian ministry.*

1 The Saviour, when to heaven he rose,
In splendid triumph o'er his foes,
Scattered his gifts on men below,
And wide his royal bounties flow.

2 Hence sprung the Apostles' honoured name;
Sacred beyond heroic fame;
In lowlier forms before our eyes,
Pastors from hence, and teachers rise.

3 From Christ their varied gifts derive,
And fed by Christ their graces live;
While guarded by his mighty hand,
Midst all the rage of hell they stand.

4 So shall the bright succession run,
Through the last courses of the sun;
While unborn churches by their care
Shall rise and flourish large and fair.

5 Jesus, now teach our hearts to know
The spring whence all these blessings flow;
Pastors and people shout thy praise
Through the long round of endless days.

—Doddridge.

LASSUS. L. M. A. H. Mann, Mus. Bac.

679 *"I have not shunned to declare unto you all the counsel of God."*

1 Shall I, for fear of feeble man,
The Spirit's course in me restrain?
Or, undismayed, in deed and word
Be a true witness for my Lord?

2 Awed by a mortal's frown, shall I
Conceal the word of God most high?
How then before thee shall I dare
To stand, or how thine anger bear?

3 Shall I, to soothe the unholy throng,
Soften thy truths, and smooth my tongue,
To gain earth's gilded toys, or flee
The cross, endured, my God, by thee?

4 What then is he whose scorn I dread,
Whose wrath or hate makes me afraid?
A man! an heir of death! a slave
To sin! a bubble on the wave!

5 Yea, let men rage, since thou wilt spread
Thy shadowing wings around my head;
Since in all pain thy tender love
Will still my sure refreshment prove.

—J. Wesley, translated from Winkler.

ROCKINGHAM. L. M. — Dr. Miller.

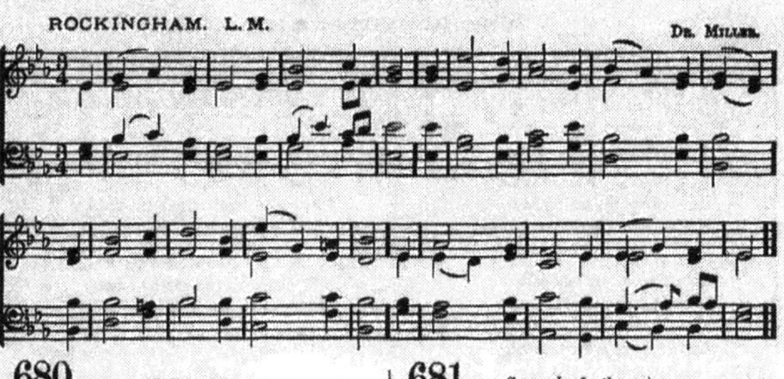

680

SECOND PART.

1 Saviour of men, thy searching eye
Doth all my inmost thoughts descry;
Doth aught on earth my wishes raise,
Or the world's pleasures, or its praise?

2 The love of Christ doth me constrain
To seek the wandering souls of men;
With cries, entreaties, tears to save,
To snatch them from the gaping grave.

3 For this let men revile my name,
No cross I shun, I fear no shame;
All hail, reproach, and welcome, pain!
Only thy terrors, Lord, restrain.

4 My life, my blood, I here present,
If for thy truth they may be spent;
Fulfil thy sovereign counsel, Lord!
Thy will be done, thy name adored!

5 Give me thy strength, O God of power;
Then let winds blow, or thunders roar,
Thy faithful witness will I be;
'Tis fixed,—I can do all through thee!

—*J. J. Winkler.*

681

Sympathy for the erring.

1 Jesus, thy wandering sheep behold!
See, Lord, with yearning pity see
The sheep that cannot find the fold,
Till sought and gathered in by thee.

2 Lost are they now, and scattered wide,
In pain, and weariness, and want;
With no kind shepherd near to guide
The sick, and spiritless, and faint.

3 Thou, only thou, the kind and good
And sheep-redeeming Shepherd art;
Collect thy flock, and give them food,
And pastors after thine own heart.

4 Open their mouth, and utterance give;
Give them a trumpet-voice, to call
On all mankind to turn and live,
Through faith in him who died for all.

5 Thy only glory let them seek;
O let their hearts with love o'erflow
Let them believe and therefore speak,
And spread thy mercy's praise below.

—*Charles Wesley.*

BOYLSTON. S. M. — Dr. Mason.

TUNE: BOYLSTON. S. M.

682

Isaiah lii. 7-10.

1 How beauteous are their feet
Who stand on Zion's hill;
Who bring salvation in their tongues,
And words of peace reveal!

2 How cheering is their voice,
How sweet the tidings are!
"Zion, behold thy Saviour King;
He reigns and triumphs here."

3 How blessèd are our ears
That hear this joyful sound,
Which kings and prophets waited for,
And sought, but never found!

4 How blessèd are our eyes
That see this heavenly light!
Prophets and kings desirèd long,
But died without the sight.

5 The watchmen join their voice,
And tuneful notes employ;
Jerusalem breaks forth in songs,
And deserts learn the joy.

6 The Lord makes bare his arm
Through all the earth abroad;
Let all the nations now behold
Their Saviour and their God.

—*Isaac Watts.*

LEEDS. S. M. SACRED HARMONY.

683

Prayer for Ministers of the Gospel.

1 JESUS, thy servants bless,
Who, sent by thee, proclaim
The peace, and joy, and righteousness
Experienced in thy name;
The kingdom of our God,
Which thy great Spirit imparts,
The power of thy victorious blood,
Which reigns in faithful hearts.

2 Their souls with faith supply,
With life and liberty;
And then they preach and testify
The things concerning thee;
And live for this alone,
Thy grace to minister,
And all thou hast for sinners done
In life and death declare.

—*Charles Wesley.*

684

Matt. ix. 38.

1 LORD of the harvest, hear
Thy needy servants' cry;
Answer our faith's effectual prayer,
And all our wants supply.

2 On thee we humbly wait,
Our wants are in thy view;
The harvest truly, Lord, is great;
The labourers are few.

3 Convert, and send forth more
Into thy church abroad;
And let them speak thy word of power,
As workers with their God.

4 Give the pure gospel word,
The word of general grace;
Thee let them preach, the common Lord,
The Saviour of our race.

5 O let them spread thy name,
Their mission fully prove,
Thy universal grace proclaim,
Thy all-redeeming love!

6 On all mankind, forgiven,
Empower them still to call;
And tell each creature under heaven,
That thou hast died for all.

—*Charles Wesley.*

BELMONT. C.M. — WEBBE.

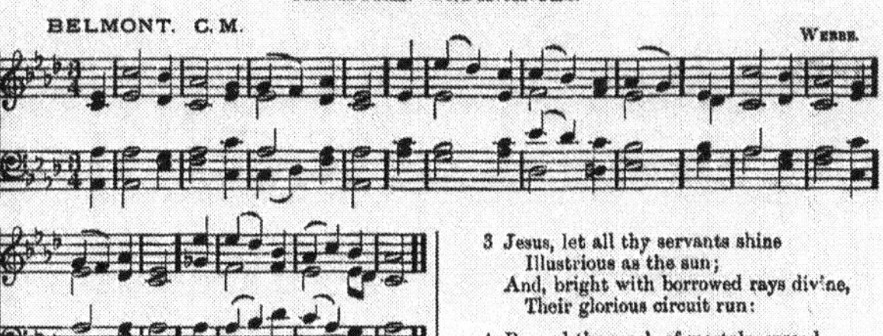

685

"Pray for us, that the word of the Lord may have free course and be glorified."

1 JESUS, the word of mercy give,
And let it swiftly run;
And let the priests themselves believe,
And put salvation on.

2 Clothed with the Spirit of holiness,
May all thy people prove
The plenitude of gospel grace,
The joy of perfect love.

3 Jesus, let all thy servants shine
Illustrious as the sun;
And, bright with borrowed rays divine,
Their glorious circuit run:

4 Beyond the reach of mortals, spread
Their light where'er they go;
And heavenly influences shed
On all the world below.

5 As giants may they run their race,
Exulting in their might;
As burning luminaries, chase
The gloom of hellish night:

6 As the bright Sun of Righteousness,
Their healing wings display;
And let their lustre still increase
Unto the perfect day.

—*Charles Wesley.*

LANCASHIRE. 7.6, 7.6, 7.6, 7.6. — HENRY SMART.

686

"I will clothe her priests with salvation."

1 LORD of the living harvest
That whitens o'er the plain,
Where angels soon shall gather
Their sheaves of golden grain;
Accept these hands to labour,
These hearts to trust and love,
And deign with them to hasten
Thy kingdom from above.

2 As labourers in thy vineyard,
Send us, O Christ, to be
Content to bear the burden
Of weary days for thee:
We ask no other wages,
When thou shalt call us home,
But to have shared the travail
Which makes thy kingdom come.

3 Come down, thou Holy Spirit!
And fill our souls with light,
Clothe us in spotless raiment,
In linen clean and white;
Beside thy sacred altar
Be with us, where we stand,
To sanctify thy people
Through all this happy land.

—*J. S. B. Monsell.*

SELENA. 6-8s. — Isaac Baker Woodbury.

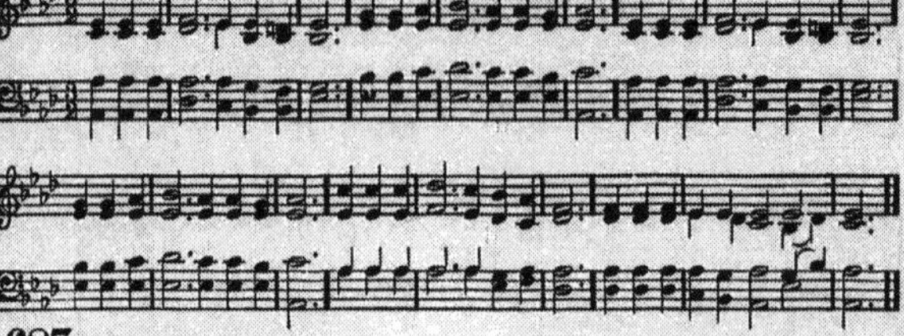

687 *"He that winneth souls is wise."*

1 Give me the faith which can remove
  And sink the mountain to a plain;
Give me the child-like praying love,
  Which longs to build thy house again;
Thy love let it my heart o'erpower,
And all my simple soul devour.

2 I want an even strong desire,
  I want a calmly-fervent zeal,
To save poor souls out of the fire,
  To snatch them from the verge of hell,
And turn them to a pardoning God,
And quench the brands in Jesus' blood.

3 I would the precious time redeem,
  And longer live for this alone,
To spend, and to be spent, for them
  Who have not yet my Saviour known;
Fully on these my mission prove,
And only breathe, to breathe thy love.

4 My talents, gifts, and graces, Lord,
  Into thy blessèd hands receive;
And let me live to preach thy word,
  And let me to thy glory live;
My every sacred moment spend
In publishing the sinner's Friend.

5 Enlarge, inflame, and fill my heart
  With boundless charity divine;
So shall I all my strength exert,
  And love them with a zeal like thine;
And lead them to thy open side,
The sheep for whom their Shepherd died.

—*Charles Wesley.*

5.—BAPTISM.

SERENITY. C. M. — W. V. Wallace.

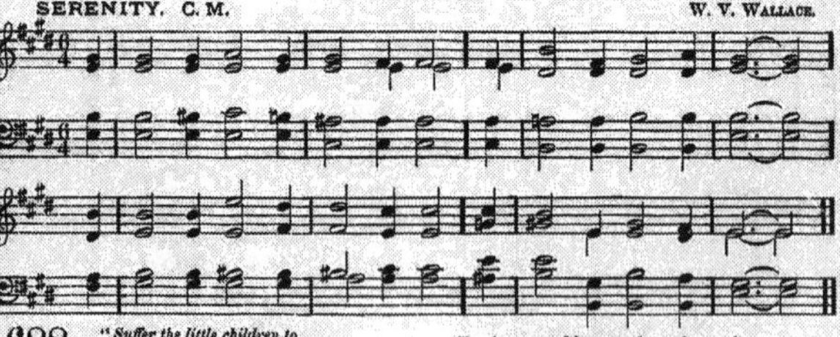

688 *"Suffer the little children to come unto me."*

1 See Israel's gentle Shepherd stand
  With all-engaging charms;
Hark how he calls the tender lambs,
  And folds them in his arms!

2 "Permit them to approach," he cries,
  "Nor scorn their humble name;
For 'twas to bless such souls as these,
  The Lord of angels came."

3 We bring them, Lord, in thankful hands,
  And yield them up to thee;
Joyful that we ourselves are thine,
  Thine let our offspring be.

—*Doddridge.*

ST. MARTIN'S. C. M. TANSUR.

689

"A God unto thee, and thy seed after thee."

1 How large the promise, how divine,
To Abr'am and his seed!
"I am a God to thee and thine,
Supplying all their need."

2 The words of his unchanging love
From age to age endure;
The Angel of the Covenant proves
And seals the blessing sure.

3 Jesus the ancient faith confirms,
To our great father given;
He takes our children to his arms,
And calls them heirs of heaven.

4 O God, how faithful are thy ways!
Thy love endures the same;
Nor from the promise of thy grace
Blots out our children's name.

—*Isaac Watts.*

ST. ANN'S. C. M. DR. CROFTS.

690

"Baptizing them in the name of the Father, and of the Son, and of the Holy Ghost."

1 O LORD, while we confess the worth
Of this the outward seal,
Do thou the truths herein set forth
To every heart reveal.

2 Death to the world we here avow,
Death to each fleshly lust;
Newness of life our calling now,
A risen Lord our trust.

3 And we, O Lord, who now partake
Of resurrection life,
With every sin, for thy dear sake,
Would be at constant strife.

4 Baptized into the Father's name,
We'd walk as sons of God;
Baptized in thine, we own thy claim
As ransomed by thy blood.

5 Baptized into the Holy Ghost,
We'd keep his temple pure,
And make thy grace our only boast,
And by thy strength endure.

—*Mary Bowly.*

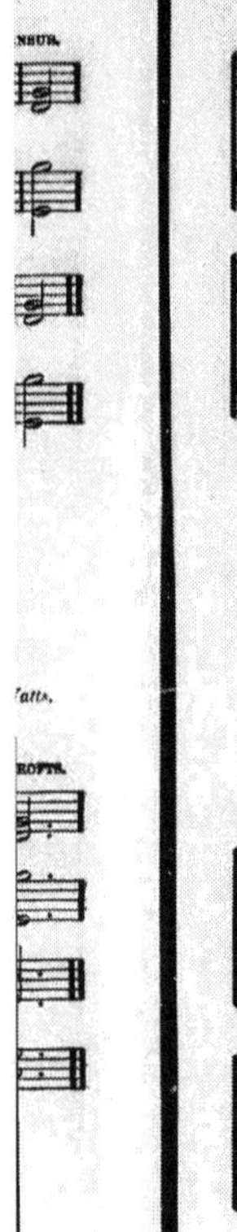

DENNIS. S. M. — H. G. NAEGELI.

691 *Prayer for spiritual baptism.*

1 FATHER, our child we place
Where we thy children kneel;
For thou hast made the sign of grace
To *him*, to us, the seal.

2 Rites cannot change the heart,
Undo the evil done,
Or with the uttered name impart
The nature of thy Son.

3 Be grace from Christ our Lord,
And love from God supreme,
By the communing Spirit poured
In a perpetual stream.

4 So cleanse our offering;
Then will we, at thy call,
This pledge accepted, daily bring
Ourselves, our house, our all.

—*W. M. Bunting.*

AJALON. 6-7s. — R. REDHEAD.

692 *Dedication of infants in baptism.*

1 LORD of all, with pure intent,
From their tenderest infancy
In thy temple we present
Whom we first received from thee;
Through thy well-belovèd Son,
Ours acknowledge for thine own.

2 Sealed with the baptismal seal,
Purchased by the atoning blood,
Jesus, in our children dwell,
Make their heart the house of God;
Fill thy consecrated shrine,
Father, Son, and Spirit divine.

—*Charles Wesley.*

HAMBURG. L. M. Dr. L. Mason.

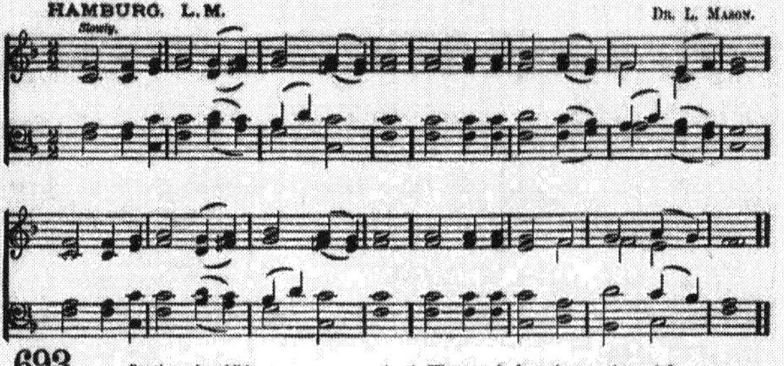
Slowly.

693

Baptism of a child.

1 This child we dedicate to thee,
O God of grace and purity!
Shield it from sin and threatening wrong,
And let thy love its life prolong.

2 O may thy Spirit gently draw
Its willing soul to keep thy law!
May virtue, piety, and truth,
Dawn even with its dawning youth.

3 We, too, before thy gracious sight,
Once shared the blest baptismal rite,
And would renew its solemn vow
With love, and thanks, and praises, now.

4 Grant that, with true and faithful heart,
We still may act the Christian's part,
Cheered by each promise thou hast given,
And labouring for the prize in heaven.

—*S. Gilman.*

WAREHAM. L. M. W. Knapp.

694

The baptism of adults.

1 Come, Father, Son, and Holy Ghost,
Honour the means ordained by thee!
Make good our apostolic boast,
And own thy glorious ministry.

2 We now thy promised presence claim,
Sent to disciple all mankind,
Sent to baptize into thy name;
We now thy promised presence find.

3 Father! in these reveal thy Son;
In these for whom we seek thy face,
The hidden mystery make known,
The inward, pure, baptizing grace.

4 Jesus! with us thou always art;
Effectuate now the sacred sign,
The gift unspeakable impart,
And bless the ordinance divine.

5 Eternal Spirit! descend from high,
Baptizer of our spirits thou!
The sacramental seal apply,
And witness with the water now!

6 O that the souls baptized therein
May now thy truth and mercy feel!
May rise and wash away their sin;
Come, Holy Ghost, their pardon seal!

—*Charles Wesley.*

6.—THE LORD'S SUPPER.

ST. MICHAEL. S. M. — DAY'S PSALTER.

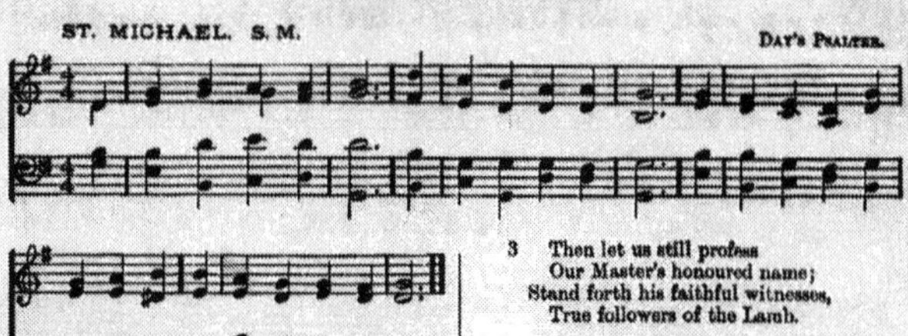

695 *"This do in remembrance of Me."*

1 Come, all who truly bear
The name of Christ your Lord,
His last mysterious supper share,
And keep his kindest word.

2 Hereby your faith approve
In Jesus crucified;
"In memory of my dying love,
Do this," he said,—and died.

3 Then let us still profess
Our Master's honoured name;
Stand forth his faithful witnesses,
True followers of the Lamb.

4 In proof that such we are,
His saying we receive,
And thus to all mankind declare
We do in Christ believe.

5 Who thus our faith employ,
His sufferings to record,
Even now we mournfully enjoy
Communion with our Lord.

6 We too with him are dead,
And shall with him arise;
The cross on which he bows his head
Shall lift us to the skies.

—*Charles Wesley.*

CASSEL. 6-7s. — FROM THE GERMAN.

696 *"One Body in Christ."*

1 All who bear the Saviour's name,
Here their common faith proclaim;
Though diverse in tongue or rite,
Here, one body, we unite;
Breaking thus one mystic bread,
Members of one common Head.

2 Come, the blessèd emblems share,
Which the Saviour's death declare;
Come, on truth immortal feed;
For his flesh is meat indeed;
Saviour, witness with the sign,
That our ransomed souls are thine.

—*Josiah Conder.*

BARNBY. 6-8s. J. BARNBY.

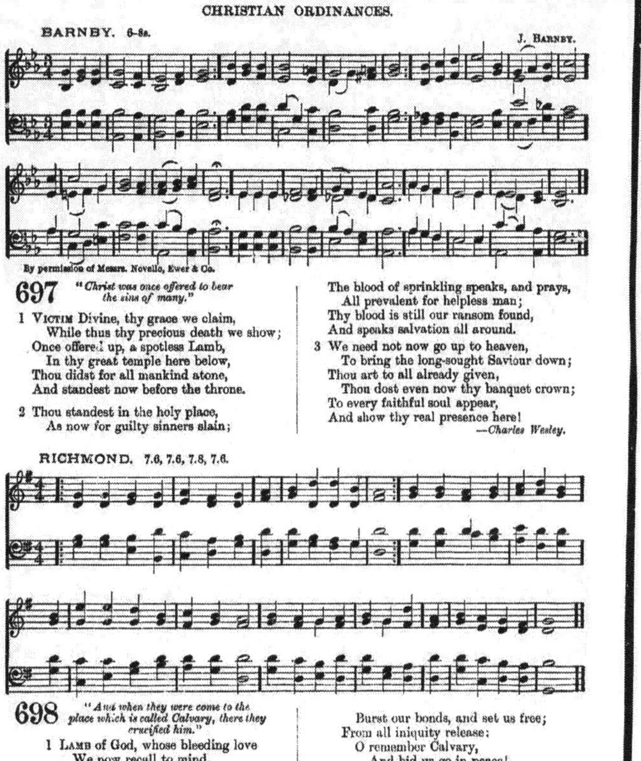

By permission of Messrs. Novello, Ewer & Co.

697

"Christ was once offered to bear the sins of many."

1 Victim Divine, thy grace we claim,
While thus thy precious death we show;
Once offered up, a spotless Lamb,
In thy great temple here below,
Thou didst for all mankind atone,
And standest now before the throne.

2 Thou standest in the holy place,
As now for guilty sinners slain;
The blood of sprinkling speaks, and prays,
All prevalent for helpless man;
Thy blood is still our ransom found,
And speaks salvation all around.

3 We need not now go up to heaven,
To bring the long-sought Saviour down;
Thou art to all already given,
Thou dost even now thy banquet crown;
To every faithful soul appear,
And show thy real presence here!

—*Charles Wesley.*

RICHMOND. 7.6, 7.6, 7.8, 7.6.

698

"And when they were come to the place which is called Calvary, there they crucified him."

1 Lamb of God, whose bleeding love
We now recall to mind,
Send the answer from above,
And let us mercy find;
Think on us, who think on thee,
And every struggling soul release:
O remember Calvary,
And bid us go in peace!

2 By thine agonizing pain
And bloody sweat, we pray,
By thy dying love to man,
Take all our sins away;
Burst our bonds, and set us free;
From all iniquity release:
O remember Calvary,
And bid us go in peace!

3 Let thy blood, by faith applied,
The sinner's pardon seal;
Speak us freely justified,
And all our sickness heal;
By thy passion on the tree,
Let all our griefs and troubles cease:
O remember Calvary,
And bid us go in peace!

—*Charles Wesley.*

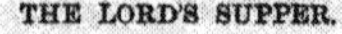

ST. MARTIN'S. C. M. TANSUR.

699 *"I am that Bread of Life."*

1 JESUS, at whose supreme command
We now approach to God,
Before us in thy vesture stand,
Thy vesture dipped in blood!

2 Obedient to thy gracious word,
We break the hallowed bread,
Commemorate thee, our dying Lord,
And trust on thee to feed.

3 Now, Saviour, now thyself reveal,
And make thy nature known;
Affix thy blessèd Spirit's seal,
And stamp us for thine own.

4 The tokens of thy dying love
O let us all receive!
And feel the quickening Spirit move,
And joyfully believe!

5 The living bread, sent down from heaven,
In us vouchsafe to be;
Thy flesh for all the world is given,
And all may live by thee.

—Charles Wesley.

BELMONT. C. M. WEBBE.

700 *The covenant sealed with blood.*

1 "THE promise of my Father's love
Shall stand forever good,"
He said; and gave his soul to death,
And sealed the grace with blood.

2 To this sure covenant of thy word
I set my worthless name;
I seal the engagement to my Lord,
And make my humble claim.

3 Thy light, and strength, and pardoning grace,
And glory shall be mine;
My life and soul, my heart and flesh,
And all my powers are thine.

4 I call that legacy my own
Which Jesus did bequeath;
'Twas purchased with a dying groan,
And ratified in death.

5 Sweet is the memory of his name,
Who blest us in his will,
And to his testament of love
Made his own life the seal.

—Isaac Watts.

DUNDEE. C. M. SCOTCH PSALTER.

701 *Grateful remembrance of Christ's death.*

1 According to thy gracious word,
In meek humility,
This will I do, my dying Lord,
I will remember thee!

2 Thy body, broken for my sake,
My bread from heaven shall be;
Thy testamental cup I take,
And thus remember thee!

3 Gethsemane can I forget?
Or there thy conflict see,
Thine agony and bloody sweat,
And not remember thee?

4 When to the cross I turn mine eyes,
And rest on Calvary,
O Lamb of God, my Sacrifice,
I must remember thee!

5 Remember thee, and all thy pains,
And all thy love to me;
Yea, while a breath, a pulse remains,
Will I remember thee!

6 And when these failing lips grow dumb,
And mind and memory flee,
When thou shalt in thy kingdom come,
Jesus, remember me!

—*Montgomery.*

ST. AGNES. C. M. DR. DYKES.

702 *"Christ our Passover is sacrificed for us; therefore let us keep the feast."*

1 In memory of the Saviour's love,
We keep the sacred feast,
Where every humble, contrite heart
Is made a welcome guest.

2 By faith we take the bread of life
With which our souls are fed,
The cup in token of his blood
That was for sinners shed.

3 Under his banner thus we sing,
The wonders of his love,
And thus anticipate by faith
The heavenly feast above.

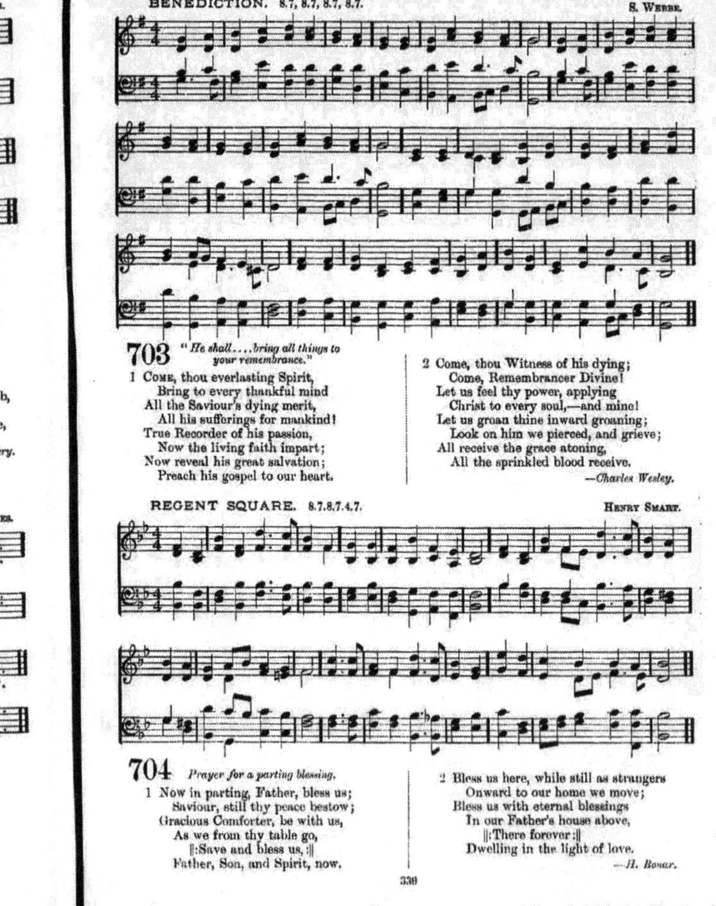

BENEDICTION. 8.7, 8.7, 8.7, 8.7. S. WEBBE.

703 *"He shall....bring all things to your remembrance."*

1 COME, thou everlasting Spirit,
Bring to every thankful mind
All the Saviour's dying merit,
All his sufferings for mankind!
True Recorder of his passion,
Now the living faith impart;
Now reveal his great salvation;
Preach his gospel to our heart.

2 Come, thou Witness of his dying;
Come, Remembrancer Divine!
Let us feel thy power, applying
Christ to every soul,—and mine!
Let us groan thine inward groaning;
Look on him we pierced, and grieve;
All receive the grace atoning,
All the sprinkled blood receive.

—Charles Wesley.

REGENT SQUARE. 8.7.8.7.4.7. HENRY SMART.

704 *Prayer for a parting blessing.*

1 Now in parting, Father, bless us;
Saviour, still thy peace bestow;
Gracious Comforter, be with us,
As we from thy table go,
‖:Save and bless us,:‖
Father, Son, and Spirit, now.

2 Bless us here, while still as strangers
Onward to our home we move;
Bless us with eternal blessings
In our Father's house above,
‖:There forever:‖
Dwelling in the light of love.

—H. Bonar.

SACRAMENT. 9.8, 9.8. EDWARD JOHN HOPKINS.

705 *Bread and wine emblems of Christ.*

1 BREAD of the world, in mercy broken!
Wine of the soul, in mercy shed!
By whom the words of life were spoken,
And in whose death our sins are dead;

2 Look on the heart by sorrow broken,
Look on the tears by sinners shed,
And be thy feast to us the token
That by thy grace our souls are fed.

—*Bishop Heber.*

SECTION VIII.

THE KINGDOM OF CHRIST.

OLD HUNDREDTH. L. M. G. FRANC.

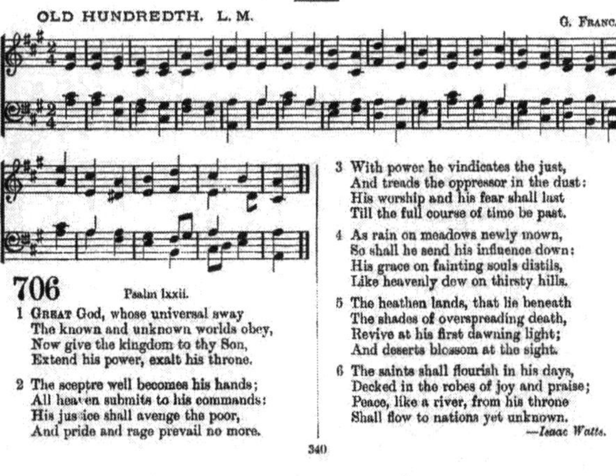

706 Psalm lxxii.

1 GREAT God, whose universal sway
The known and unknown worlds obey,
Now give the kingdom to thy Son,
Extend his power, exalt his throne.

2 The sceptre well becomes his hands;
All heaven submits to his commands:
His justice shall avenge the poor,
And pride and rage prevail no more.

3 With power he vindicates the just,
And treads the oppressor in the dust:
His worship and his fear shall last
Till the full course of time be past.

4 As rain on meadows newly mown,
So shall he send his influence down:
His grace on fainting souls distils,
Like heavenly dew on thirsty hills.

5 The heathen lands, that lie beneath
The shades of overspreading death,
Revive at his first dawning light;
And deserts blossom at the sight.

6 The saints shall flourish in his days,
Decked in the robes of joy and praise;
Peace, like a river, from his throne
Shall flow to nations yet unknown.

—*Isaac Watts.*

DUKE STREET. L. M. — John Hatton.

707

SECOND PART.

1 Jesus shall reign where'er the sun
Doth his successive journeys run;
His kingdom stretch from shore to shore,
Till suns shall rise and set no more.

2 For him shall endless prayer be made,
And praises throng to crown his head;
His name like sweet perfume shall rise
With every morning sacrifice.

3 Peoples and realms of every tongue
Dwell on his love with sweetest song;
And infant voices shall proclaim
Their young hosannas to his name.

4 Blessings abound where'er he reigns;
The prisoner leaps to lose his chains;
The weary find eternal rest,
And all the sons of want are blest.

5 Where he displays his healing power,
Death and the curse are known no more;
In him the tribes of Adam boast
More blessings than their father lost.

6 Let every creature rise, and bring
Its grateful honours to our King;
Angels descend with songs again,
And earth prolong the joyful strain.

—*Isaac Watts.*

HOME. L. M. — From Mozart.

708

Christ our conquering King.

1 The Lord is King, and earth submits,
Howe'er impatient, to his sway;
Between the cherubim he sits,
And makes his restless foes obey.

2 All power is to our Jesus given,
O'er earth's rebellious sons he reigns;
He mildly rules the hosts of heaven,
And holds the powers of hell in chains.

3 In vain doth Satan rage his hour,
Beyond his chain he cannot go;
Our Jesus shall stir up his power,
And soon avenge us of our foe.

4 Come, glorious Lord, the rebels spurn,
Scatter thy foes, victorious King!
And Gath and Askelon shall mourn,
And all the sons of God shall sing;

5 Shall magnify the sovereign grace
Of him that sits upon the throne;
And earth and heaven conspire to praise
Jehovah, and his conquering Son.

—*Charles Wesley.*

LASSUS. L. M. A. H. MANN, Mus. Bac.

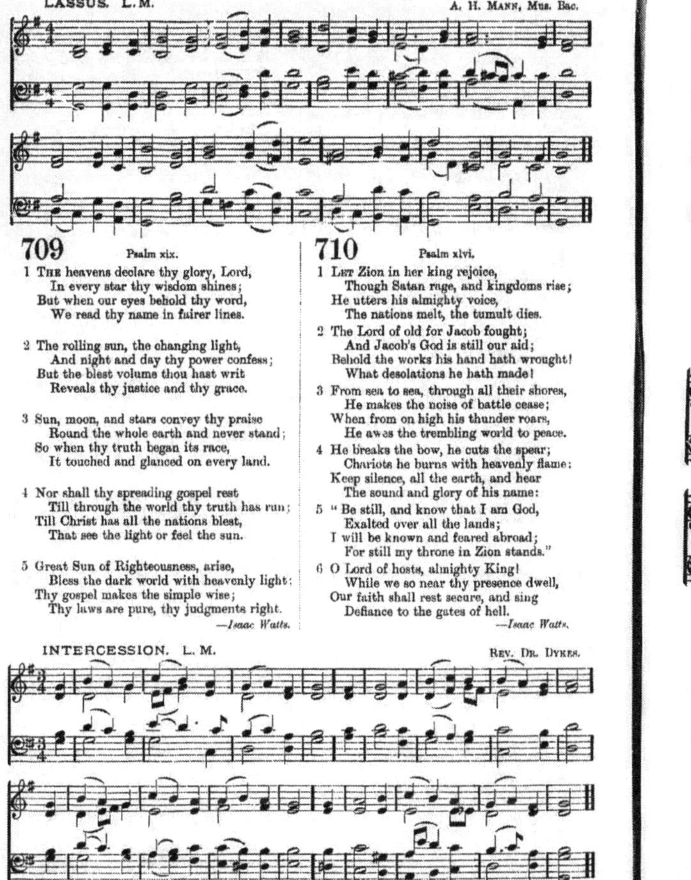

709

Psalm xix.

1 THE heavens declare thy glory, Lord,
In every star thy wisdom shines;
But when our eyes behold thy word,
We read thy name in fairer lines.

2 The rolling sun, the changing light,
And night and day thy power confess;
But the blest volume thou hast writ
Reveals thy justice and thy grace.

3 Sun, moon, and stars convey thy praise
Round the whole earth and never stand;
So when thy truth began its race,
It touched and glanced on every land.

4 Nor shall thy spreading gospel rest
Till through the world thy truth has run;
Till Christ has all the nations blest,
That see the light or feel the sun.

5 Great Sun of Righteousness, arise,
Bless the dark world with heavenly light:
Thy gospel makes the simple wise;
Thy laws are pure, thy judgments right.

—*Isaac Watts.*

710

Psalm xlvi.

1 LET Zion in her king rejoice,
Though Satan rage, and kingdoms rise;
He utters his almighty voice,
The nations melt, the tumult dies.

2 The Lord of old for Jacob fought;
And Jacob's God is still our aid;
Behold the works his hand hath wrought!
What desolations he hath made!

3 From sea to sea, through all their shores,
He makes the noise of battle cease;
When from on high his thunder roars,
He awes the trembling world to peace.

4 He breaks the bow, he cuts the spear;
Chariots he burns with heavenly flame:
Keep silence, all the earth, and hear
The sound and glory of his name:

5 "Be still, and know that I am God,
Exalted over all the lands;
I will be known and feared abroad;
For still my throne in Zion stands."

6 O Lord of hosts, almighty King!
While we so near thy presence dwell,
Our faith shall rest secure, and sing
Defiance to the gates of hell.

—*Isaac Watts.*

INTERCESSION. L. M. REV. DR. DYKES.

TUNE: INTERCESSION. L. M.

711 *Sympathy for the perishing.*

1 Shepherd of souls, with pitying eye
The thousands of our Israel see;
To thee in their behalf we cry,
Ourselves but newly found in thee.

2 See where o'er desert wastes they err,
And neither food nor feeder have,
Nor fold, nor place of refuge near,
For no man cares their souls to save.

3 Thy people, Lord, are sold for nought,
Nor know they their Redeemer nigh;
They perish, whom thyself hast bought,
Their souls for lack of knowledge die.

4 The pit its mouth hath opened wide,
To swallow up its careless prey;
Why should *they* die, when *thou* hast died,
Hast died to bear their sins away?

5 Extend to these thy pardoning grace;
To these be thy salvation showed;
O add them to thy chosen race!
O sprinkle all their hearts with blood!

6 Still let the publicans draw near;
Open the door of faith and heaven,
And grant their hearts thy word to hear,
And witness all their sins forgiven.

—Charles Wesley.

ANGELUS. L. M. J. Scheffler.

712 *"He must reign till he hath put all enemies under his feet."*

1 Eternal Father, thou hast said,
That Christ all glory shall obtain;
That he who once a sufferer bled
Shall o'er the world a conqueror reign.

2 We wait thy triumph, Saviour King;
Long ages have prepared thy way;
Now all abroad thy banner fling,
Set time's great battle in array.

3 Thy hosts are mustered to the field;
"The Cross! the Cross!" the battle-call;
The old grim towers of darkness yield,
And soon shall totter to their fall.

4 On mountain tops the watch-fires glow,
Where scattered wide the watchmen stand;
Voice echoes voice, and onward flow
The joyous shouts from land to land.

5 O fill thy Church with faith and power!
Bid her long night of weeping cease;
To groaning nations haste the hour
Of life and freedom, light and peace.

6 Come, Spirit, make thy wonders known,
Fulfil the Father's high decree;
Then earth, the might of hell o'erthrown,
Shall keep her last great jubilee.

—Ray Palmer.

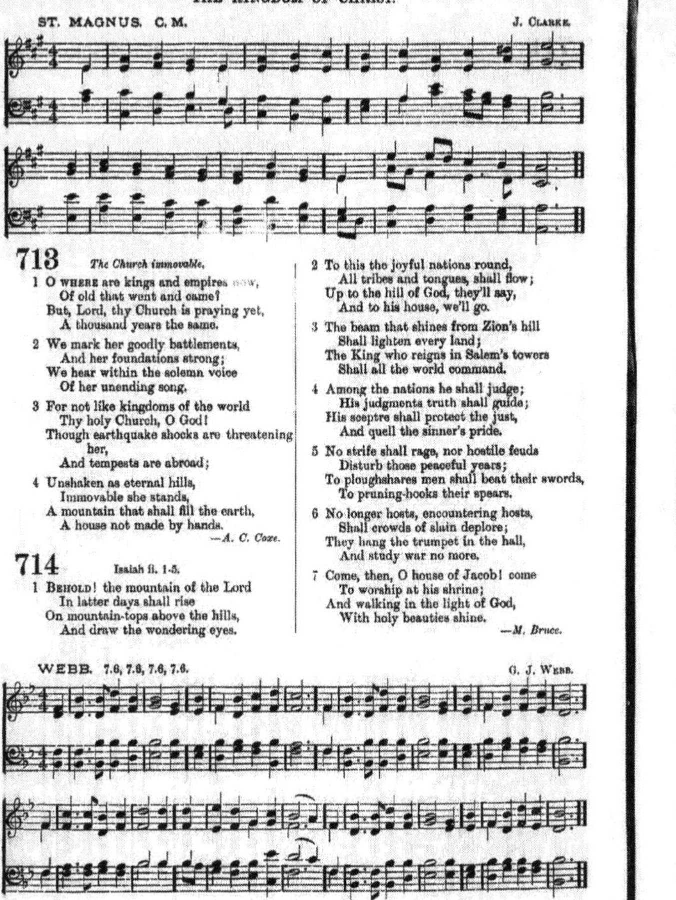
ST. MAGNUS. C.M.
J. CLARKE.
WEBB. 7.6, 7.6, 7.6, 7.6.
G. J. WEBB.

713 *The Church immovable.*

1 O WHERE are kings and empires now,
Of old that went and came?
But, Lord, thy Church is praying yet,
A thousand years the same.

2 We mark her goodly battlements,
And her foundations strong;
We hear within the solemn voice
Of her unending song.

3 For not like kingdoms of the world
Thy holy Church, O God!
Though earthquake shocks are threatening her,
And tempests are abroad;

4 Unshaken as eternal hills,
Immovable she stands,
A mountain that shall fill the earth,
A house not made by hands.

—A. C. Coxe.

714 Isaiah ii. 1-5.

1 BEHOLD! the mountain of the Lord
In latter days shall rise
On mountain-tops above the hills,
And draw the wondering eyes.

2 To this the joyful nations round,
All tribes and tongues, shall flow;
Up to the hill of God, they'll say,
And to his house, we'll go.

3 The beam that shines from Zion's hill
Shall lighten every land;
The King who reigns in Salem's towers
Shall all the world command.

4 Among the nations he shall judge;
His judgments truth shall guide;
His sceptre shall protect the just,
And quell the sinner's pride.

5 No strife shall rage, nor hostile feuds
Disturb those peaceful years;
To ploughshares men shall beat their swords,
To pruning-hooks their spears.

6 No longer hosts, encountering hosts,
Shall crowds of slain deplore;
They hang the trumpet in the hall,
And study war no more.

7 Come, then, O house of Jacob! come
To worship at his shrine;
And walking in the light of God,
With holy beauties shine.

—M. Bruce.

TUNE: WEBB. 7.6, 7.6, 7.6, 7.6.

715

"Let us go up at once and possess it, for we are well able."

1 Our country's voice is pleading,
Ye men of God, arise!
His providence is leading,
The land before you lies;
Day-gleams are o'er it brightening,
And promise clothes the soil;
Wide fields, for harvest whitening,
Invite the reaper's toil.

2 Go where the waves are breaking
Along the ocean shore,
Christ's precious gospel taking,
More rich than golden ore;
Go to the woodman's dwelling,
Go to the prairie broad,
The wondrous story telling,
The mercy of our God.

3 The love of Christ unfolding,
Speed on from east to west,
Till all, his cross beholding,
In him are fully blest.
Great Author of salvation,
Haste, haste the glorious day,
When we, a ransomed nation,
Thy sceptre shall obey!

—*Mrs. Anderson.*

ST. CRISPIN. L. M. Sir G. J. Elvey.

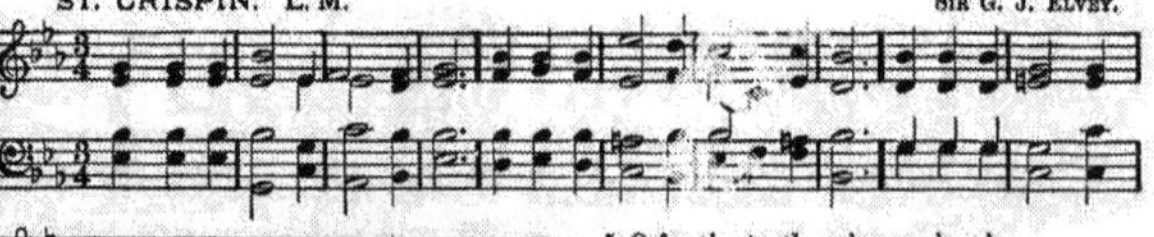

716

"The Spirit and the bride say, Come."

1 Head of thy Church, whose Spirit fills
And flows through every faithful soul,
Unites in mystic love, and seals
Them one, and sanctifies the whole;

2 "Come, Lord," thy glorious Spirit cries,
And souls beneath the altar groan;
"Come, Lord," the bride on earth replies,
"And perfect all our souls in one."

3 Pour out the promised gift on all;
Answer the universal "Come!"
The fulness of the Gentiles call,
And take thine ancient people home.

4 To thee let all the nations flow,
Let all obey the gospel word;
Let all their loving Saviour know,
Filled with the glory of the Lord.

5 O for thy truth and mercy's sake
The purchase of thy passion claim!
Thine heritage the Gentiles take,
And cause the world to know thy name.

—*Charles Wesley.*

717

"I will pour out my Spirit upon all flesh."

1 On all the earth thy Spirit shower;
The earth in righteousness renew;
Thy kingdom come, and hell's o'erpower,
And to thy sceptre all subdue.

2 Like mighty winds, or torrents fierce,
Let it opposers all o'errun;
And every law of sin reverse,
That faith and love may make all one.

3 Yea, let thy Spirit in every place
Its richer energy declare;
While lovely tempers, fruits of grace,
The kingdom of thy Christ prepare.

4 Grant this, O holy God and true!
The ancient seers thou didst inspire;
To us perform the promise due;
Descend, and crown us now with fire!

—*Charles Wesley.*

HOME. L. M. FROM MOZART.

718 *Christ, King of saints and angels.*

1 O CHRIST, the Lord of heaven, to thee,
Clothed with all Majesty divine,
Eternal power and glory be,
Eternal praise of right is thine!

2 Reign, Prince of Life! that once thy brow
Didst yield to wear the wounding thorn;
Reign throned beside the Father now,
Adored the Son of God first-born!

3 From angel hosts that round thee stand,
With forms more pure than spotless snow,
From the bright burning seraph band,
Let praise in loftiest numbers flow.

4 To thee, the Lamb, our mortal songs,
Born of deep, fervent love, shall rise;
All honour to thy name belongs,
Our lips would sound it to the skies.

5 Jesus! all earth shall speak the word;
Jesus! all heaven resound it still;
Immanuel, Saviour, Conqueror, Lord,
Thy praise the universe shall fill.

—*Ray Palmer.*

719 *Looking for Christ's coming.*

1 JESUS, thy Church, with longing eyes,
For thy expected coming waits;
When will the promised light arise,
And glory beam from Zion's gates?

2 Even now, when tempests round us fall,
And wintry clouds o'ercast the sky,
Thy words we joyfully recall,
And know that our redemption's nigh.

3 Come, gracious Lord, our hearts renew,
Our foes repel, our wrongs redress;
Man's rooted enmity subdue,
And crown thy gospel with success.

4 O come and reign o'er every land!
Let Satan from his throne be hurled,
All nations bow to thy command,
And grace revive a dying world.

5 Teach us, in watchfulness and prayer,
To wait for thine appointed hour;
And fit us by thy grace to share
The triumphs of thy conquering power.

—*W. H. Bathurst.*

DE FLEURY. 8-8s.

Fine.

D.C.

TUNE: DE FLEURY. 8-8s.

720 *"The kingdom of God is within you."*

1 All glory to God in the sky,
  And peace upon earth be restored!
O Jesus, exalted on high,
  Appear our omnipotent Lord!
Who, meanly in Bethlehem born,
  Didst stoop to redeem a lost race,
Once more to thy creatures return,
  And reign in thy kingdom of grace.

2 O wouldst thou again be made known,
  Again in thy Spirit descend,
And set up in each of thine own
  A kingdom that never shall end!
Thou only art able to bless,
  And make the glad nations obey,
And bid the dire enmity cease,
  And bow the whole world to thy sway.

3 Come then to thy servants again,
  Who long thy appearing to know;
Thy quiet and peaceable reign
  In mercy establish below;
All sorrow before thee shall fly,
  And anger and hatred be o'er,
And envy and malice shall die,
  And discord afflict us no more.

—*Charles Wesley.*

RUTHERFORD. 7.6, 7.6, 7.6, 7.6. D'Urhan.

721 Psalm lxxii.

1 Hail to the Lord's Anointed;
  Great David's greater Son!
Hail, in the time appointed,
  His reign on earth begun!
He comes to break oppression,
  To set the captive free,
To take away transgression,
  And rule in equity.

2 He comes, with succour speedy,
  To those who suffer wrong;
To help the poor and needy,
  And bid the weak be strong;
To give them songs for sighing,
  Their darkness turn to light,
Whose souls, condemned and dying,
  Were precious in his sight.

3 He shall come down like showers
  Upon the fruitful earth;
Love, joy, and hope, like flowers,
  Spring in his path to birth.
Before him, on the mountains,
  Shall peace the herald go;
And righteousness in fountains,
  From hill to valley flow.

4 Arabia's desert ranger
  To him shall bow the knee;
The Ethiopian stranger
  His glory come to see:
With offerings of devotion
  Ships from the isles shall meet,
To pour the wealth of ocean
  In tribute at his feet.

5 Kings shall fall down before him,
  And gold and incense bring;
All nations shall adore him,
  His praise all people sing:
For him shall prayer unceasing
  And daily vows ascend;
His kingdom still increasing,
  A kingdom without end.

6 O'er every foe victorious,
  He on his throne shall rest;
From age to age more glorious,
  All-blessing and all-blest.
The tide of time shall never
  His covenant remove;
His name shall stand forever,
  His changeless name of Love.

—*Montgomery.*

WELD. 7.6, 7.6, 7.7, 7.6.

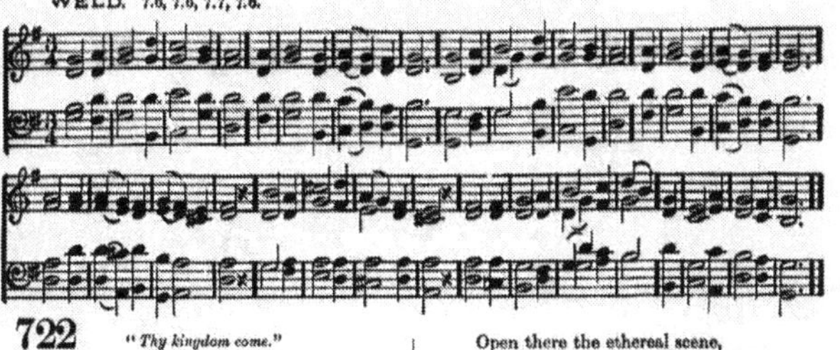

722

"Thy kingdom come."

1 Saviour, whom our hearts adore,
To bless our earth again,
Now assume thy royal power,
And o'er the nations reign;
Christ, the world's desire and hope,
Power complete to thee is given;
Set the last great empire up,
Eternal Lord of heaven.

2 Where they all thy laws have spurned,
Where they thy name profane,
Where the ruined world hath mourned
With blood of millions slain,
Open there the ethereal scene,
Claim the heathen tribes for thine;
There the endless reign begin
With majesty divine.

3 Universal Saviour, thou
Wilt all thy creatures bless;
Every knee to thee shall bow,
And every tongue confess;
None shall in thy mount destroy;
War shall then be learnt no more;
Saints shall their great King enjoy,
And all mankind adore.

—*Charles Wesley.*

NUREMBERG. 4-7s. JOHANN RUDOLF AHLE.

723

Christ's universal reign.

1 Hasten, Lord, the glorious time,
When, beneath Messiah's sway,
Every nation, every clime,
Shall the gospel call obey.

2 Mightiest kings his power shall own;
Heathen tribes his name adore;
Satan and his host, o'erthrown,
Bound in chains, shall hurt no more.

3 Then shall wars and tumults cease;
Then be banished grief and pain;
Righteousness, and joy, and peace,
Undisturbed, shall ever reign.

4 Bless we, then, our gracious Lord;
Ever praise his glorious name;
All his mighty acts record,
All his wondrous love proclaim.

—*Harriet Auber.*

VESPER HYMN. 8.7, 8.7, 8.7, 8.7. BORTNIANSKI.

724 *Christ the Light of the Gentiles.*

1 LIGHT of those whose dreary dwelling
Borders on the shades of death,
Come, and by thy love's revealing
Dissipate the clouds beneath:
The new heaven and earth's Creator,
In our deepest darkness rise,
Scattering all the night of nature,
Pouring eyesight on our eyes.

2 Still we wait for thine appearing;
Life and joy thy beams impart,
Chasing all our fears, and cheering
Every poor benighted heart:
Come, and manifest the favour
God hath for our ransomed race;
Come, thou universal Saviour,
Come, and bring the gospel grace.

3 Save us in thy great compassion,
O thou mild, pacific Prince!
Give the knowledge of salvation,
Give the pardon of our sins:
By thy all-restoring merit
Every burdened soul release;
Every weary, wandering spirit
Guide into thy perfect peace.

—*Charles Wesley.*

725 *"So shall he sprinkle many nations."*

1 SAVIOUR, sprinkle many nations,
Fruitful let thy sorrows be;
By thy pains and consolations
Draw the Gentiles unto thee;
Of thy cross the wondrous story
Be to all the nations told;
Let them see thee in thy glory,
And thy mercy manifold.

2 Far and wide, though all unknowing,
Pants for thee each mortal breast;
Human tears for thee are flowing,
Human hearts in thee would rest;
Thirsting, as for dews of even,
As the new-mown grass for rain,
Thee they seek, as God of heaven,
Thee, as man for sinners slain.

3 Saviour, lo! the isles are waiting,
Stretched the hand, and strained the sight,
For thy Spirit, new creating,
Love's pure flame, and wisdom's light;
Give the word, and of the preacher
Speed the foot, and touch the tongue,
Till on earth, by every creature,
Glory to the Lamb be sung.

—*A. C. Coxe.*

ADVENT HYMN. 8.7, 8.7, 4.7. J. TILLEARD.

cres.
f
dim.

726

The victories of the gospel.

1 O'ER the gloomy hills of darkness,
Cheered by no celestial ray,
Sun of Righteousness, arising,
Bring the bright, the glorious day!
‖:Send the gospel:‖
To the earth's remotest bound.

2 Kingdoms wide that sit in darkness,
Grant them, Lord, the glorious light;
And, from eastern coast to western,
May the morning chase the night;
‖:And redemption,:‖
Freely purchased, win the day.

3 Fly abroad, thou mighty gospel!
Win and conquer, never cease;
May thy lasting, wide dominion
Multiply and still increase:
‖:Sway thy sceptre,:‖
Saviour, all the world around!

—*W. Williams.*

727

Rev. xix. 11.

1 COME, thou Conqueror of the nations,
Now on thy white horse appear;
Earthquakes, dearths, and desolations
Signify thy coming near;
‖:True and faithful!:‖
Stablish thy dominion here.

2 Thine the kingdom, power, and glory;
Thine the ransomed nations are;
Let the heathen fall before thee,
Let the isles thy power declare;
‖:Judge and conquer:‖
All mankind in righteous war.

3 Thee let all mankind admire,
Object of our joy and dread!
Flame thine eyes with heavenly fire,
Many crowns upon thy head;
‖:But thine essence:‖
None, except thyself, can read.

4 On thy thigh and vesture written,
Show the world thy heavenly name,
That, with loving wonder smitten,
All may glorify the Lamb;
‖:All adore thee,:‖
All the Lord of hosts proclaim.

5 Honour, glory, and salvation
To the Lord our God we give;
Power, and endless adoration,
Thou art worthy to receive;
‖:Reign triumphant,:‖
King of kings, forever live!

—*Charles Wesley.*

WINCHESTER. C. M. — Este's Psalter.

728

"All nations shall call him blessed."

1 Jesus, immortal King, arise;
  Assert thy rightful sway,
Till earth, subdued, its tribute brings,
  And distant lands obey.

2 Ride forth, victorious Conqueror, ride,
  Till all thy foes submit,
And all the powers of hell resign
  Their trophies at thy feet.

3 Send forth thy word, and let it fly
  The spacious earth around,
Till every soul beneath the sky
  Shall hear the joyful sound.

4 O may the great Redeemer's name
  Through every clime be known!
And heathen gods, forsaken, fall,
  And Jesus reign alone.

5 From sea to sea, from shore to shore,
  Be thou, O Christ, adored!
And earth, with all her millions, shout
  Hosannas to the Lord.

—*A. C. H. Seymour.*

HALLON. C. M. — S. Webbe.

729

"He shall have dominion from sea to sea."

1 Light of the lonely pilgrim's heart,
  Star of the coming day,
Arise, and with thy morning beams
  Chase all our griefs away!

2 Come, blessèd Lord, let every shore
  And answering island sing
The praises of thy royal name,
  And own thee as their King.

3 Bid the whole earth, responsive now
  To the bright world above,
Break forth in sweetest strains of joy,
  In memory of thy love.

4 Jesus, thy fair creation groans,
  The air, the earth, the sea,
In unison with all our hearts,
  And cries aloud for thee.

5 Thine was the cross, with all its fruits
  Of grace and peace divine;
Be thine the crown of glory now,
  The palm of victory thine!

—*Sir E. Denny.*

RAKEM. 6-8s.

ISAAC BAKER WOODBURY.

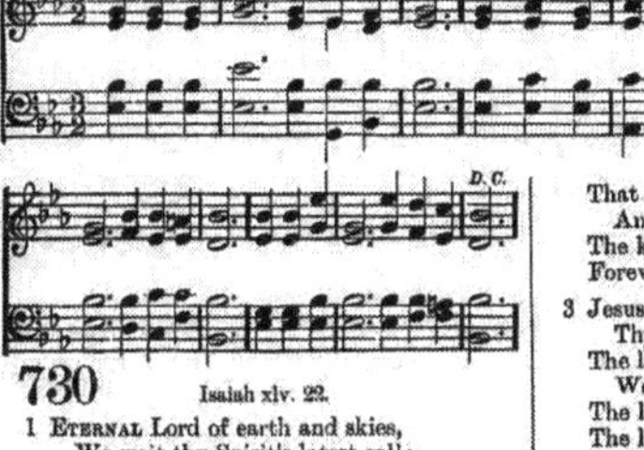
Fine.
D.C.

730

Isaiah xlv. 22.

1 ETERNAL Lord of earth and skies,
We wait thy Spirit's latest call;
Bid all our fallen race arise,
Thou who hast purchased life for all;
Whose only name, to sinners given,
Snatches from hell, and lifts to heaven.

2 The word thy sacred lips has past,
The sure, irrevocable word,
That every soul shall bow at last,
And yield allegiance to its Lord;
The kingdoms of the earth shall be
Forever subjected to thee.

3 Jesus, for this we still attend,
Thy kingdom in the isles to prove;
The law of sin and death to end,
We wait for all the power of love,
The law of perfect liberty,
The law of life which is in thee.

4 O might it now from thee proceed,
With thee, into the souls of men!
Throughout the world thy gospel spread;
And let thy glorious Spirit reign,
On all the ransomed race bestowed;
And let the world be filled with God!

—*Charles Wesley.*

LUTHER'S HYMN. 6-8s.

MARTIN LUTHER.

731

"All nations shall serve him."

1 LORD over all, if thou hast made,
Hast ransomed every soul of man,
Why is the grace so long delayed?
Why unfulfilled the saving plan?
The bliss for Adam's race designed,
‖: When will it reach to all mankind? :‖

2 Art thou the God of Jews alone?
And not the God of Gentiles too?
To Gentiles make thy goodness known;
Thy judgments to the nations show;
Awake them by the gospel call;
‖: Light of the world, illumine all! :‖

3 As lightning launched from east to west,
The coming of thy kingdom be;
To thee, by angel-hosts confest,
Bow every soul and every knee;
Thy glory let all flesh behold,
‖: And then fill up thy heavenly fold. :‖

—*Charles Wesley.*

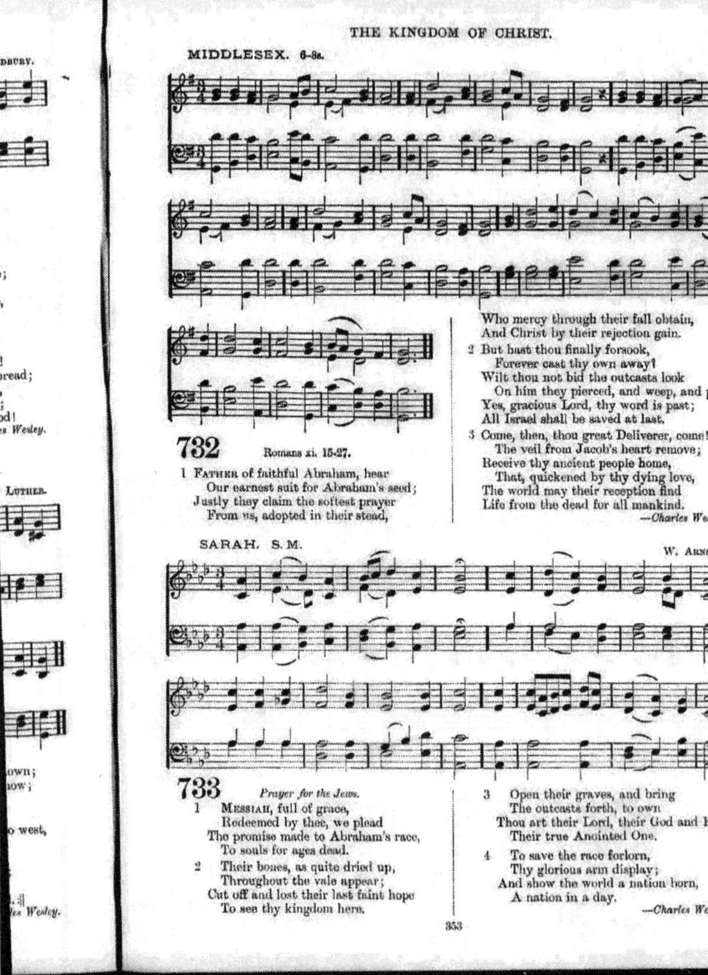

MIDDLESEX. 6-8s.

732

Romans xi. 15-27.

1 Father of faithful Abraham, hear
Our earnest suit for Abraham's seed;
Justly they claim the softest prayer
From us, adopted in their stead,
Who mercy through their fall obtain,
And Christ by their rejection gain.

2 But hast thou finally forsook,
Forever cast thy own away?
Wilt thou not bid the outcasts look
On him they pierced, and weep, and pray?
Yes, gracious Lord, thy word is past;
All Israel shall be saved at last.

3 Come, then, thou great Deliverer, come!
The veil from Jacob's heart remove;
Receive thy ancient people home,
That, quickened by thy dying love,
The world may their reception find
Life from the dead for all mankind.

—*Charles Wesley.*

SARAH. S. M. W. Arnold.

733

Prayer for the Jews.

1 Messiah, full of grace,
Redeemed by thee, we plead
The promise made to Abraham's race,
To souls for ages dead.

2 Their bones, as quite dried up,
Throughout the vale appear;
Cut off and lost their last faint hope
To see thy kingdom here.

3 Open their graves, and bring
The outcasts forth, to own
Thou art their Lord, their God and King,
Their true Anointed One.

4 To save the race forlorn,
Thy glorious arm display;
And show the world a nation born,
A nation in a day.

—*Charles Wesley.*

AURELIA. S. M. D. — Dr. S. S. Wesley.

734

"So mightily grew the Word of God and prevailed."

1 Jesus, the word bestow,
The true immortal seed;
Thy gospel then shall greatly grow,
And all our land o'erspread;
Through earth extended wide
Shall mightily prevail,
Destroy the works of self and pride,
And shake the gates of hell.

2 Its energy exert
In the believing soul;
Diffuse thy grace through every part,
And sanctify the whole:
Its utmost virtue show
In pure consummate love,
And fill with all thy life below,
And give us thrones above.

—*Charles Wesley.*

735

"There shall be one flock and one Shepherd."

1 Father of boundless grace,
Thou hast in part fulfilled
Thy promise made to Adam's race,
In God incarnate sealed.
A few from every land
At first to Salem came,
And saw the wonders of thy hand,
And saw the tongues of flame.

2 Yet still we wait the end,
The coming of our Lord;
The full accomplishment attend
Of thy prophetic word.
Thy promise deeper lies
In unexhausted grace;
And new discovered worlds arise
To sing their Saviour's praise.

3 Beloved for Jesus' sake,
By him redeemed of old,
All nations must come in, and make
One undivided fold:
While gathered in by thee,
And perfected in one,
They all at once thy glory see
In thine eternal Son.

—*Charles Wesley.*

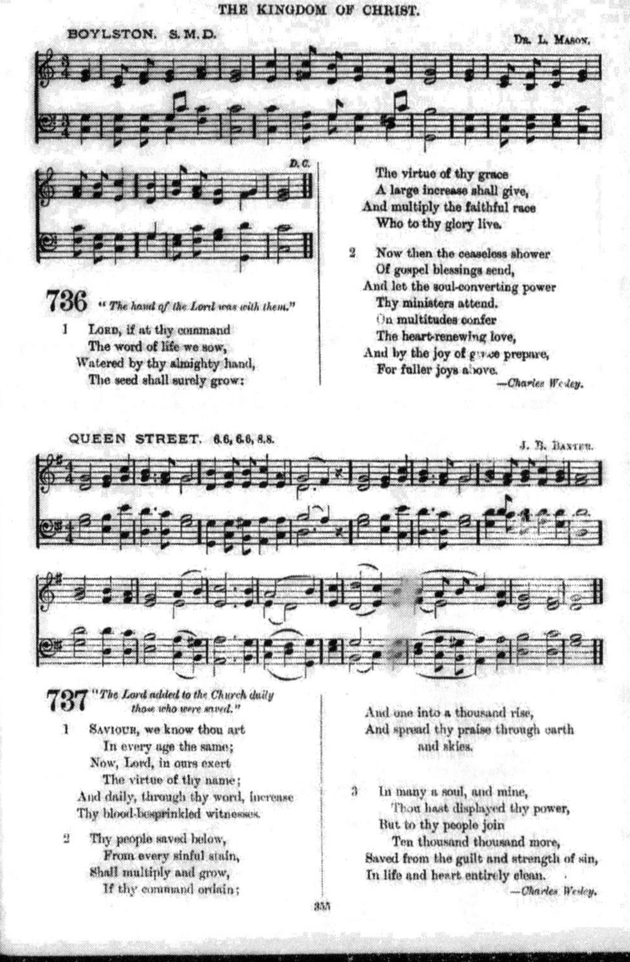

BOYLSTON. S.M.D. — DR. L. MASON.

D.C.

736 "The hand of the Lord was with them."

1 LORD, if at thy command
The word of life we sow,
Watered by thy almighty hand,
The seed shall surely grow:
The virtue of thy grace
A large increase shall give,
And multiply the faithful race
Who to thy glory live.

2 Now then the ceaseless shower
Of gospel blessings send,
And let the soul-converting power
Thy ministers attend.
On multitudes confer
The heart-renewing love,
And by the joy of grace prepare,
For fuller joys above.

—*Charles Wesley.*

QUEEN STREET. 6.6, 6.6, 8.8. — J. B. BAXTER.

737 "The Lord added to the Church daily those who were saved."

1 SAVIOUR, we know thou art
In every age the same;
Now, Lord, in ours exert
The virtue of thy name;
And daily, through thy word, increase
Thy blood-besprinkled witnesses.

2 Thy people saved below,
From every sinful stain,
Shall multiply and grow,
If thy command ordain;
And one into a thousand rise,
And spread thy praise through earth and skies.

3 In many a soul, and mine,
Thou hast displayed thy power,
But to thy people join
Ten thousand thousand more,
Saved from the guilt and strength of sin,
In life and heart entirely clean.

—*Charles Wesley.*

WATCHMAN. 8-7s. DR. MASON.

738 *"Watchman, what of the night?"*

1 WATCHMAN, tell us of the night,
What its signs of promise are.
Traveller, o'er yon mountain's height
See that glory-beaming star!
Watchman, does its beauteous ray
Aught of hope or joy foretell?
Traveller, yes; it brings the day,
Promised day of Israel.

2 Watchman, tell us of the night;
Higher yet that star ascends.
Traveller, blessedness and light,
Peace and truth, its course portends!
Watchman, will its beams alone
Gild the spot that gave them birth?
Traveller, ages are its own,
See, it bursts o'er all the earth!

3 Watchman, tell us of the night
For the morning seems to dawn.
Traveller, darkness takes its flight;
Doubt and terror are withdrawn.
Watchman, let thy wandering cease;
Hie thee to thy quiet home!
Traveller, lo! the Prince of Peace,
Lo! the Son of God is come!

—*Sir J. Bowring.*

BENEVENTO. 8-7's. S. WEBBE.

TUNE: BENEVENTO. 8-7s.

739 *The spread of Christ's kingdom.*

1 See how great a flame aspires,
Kindled by a spark of grace!
Jesus' love the nations fires,
Sets the kingdoms on a blaze;
To bring fire on earth he came,
Kindled in some hearts it is;
O that all might catch the flame,
All partake the glorious bliss!

2 When he first the work begun,
Small and feeble was his day;
Now the word doth swiftly run,
Now it wins its widening way:
More and more it spreads and grows,
Ever mighty to prevail,
Sin's strongholds it now o'erthrows,
Shakes the trembling gates of hell.

3 Sons of God, your Saviour praise!
He the door hath opened wide;
He hath given the word of grace,
Jesus' word is glorified:
Jesus, mighty to redeem,
He alone the work hath wrought;
Worthy is the work of him,
Him who spake a world from nought.

4 Saw ye not the cloud arise,
Little as a human hand?
Now its spreads along the skies,
Hangs o'er all the thirsty land:
Lo! the promise of a shower
Drops already from above;
But the Lord will shortly pour
All the Spirit of his love!

—*Charles Wesley.*

PILTON. 4-7s.

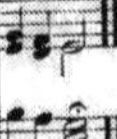

740 *"For he hath put all things under his feet."*

1 Earth, rejoice, our Lord is King!
Sons of men, his praises sing!
Sing ye in triumphant strains,
Jesus the Messiah reigns!

2 Power is all to Jesus given,
Lord of hell, and earth, and heaven,
Every knee to him shall bow;
Satan, hear, and tremble now!

3 Angels and archangels join,
All triumphantly combine,
All in Jesus' praise agree,
Carrying on his victory.

4 Though the sons of night blaspheme,
More there are with us than them;
God with us, we cannot fear;
Fear, ye fiends, for Christ is here!

5 Lo! to faith's enlightened sight,
All the mountain flames with light,
Hell is nigh, but God is nigher,
Circling us with hosts of fire.

6 Christ the Saviour is come down,
Points us to the victor's crown,
Bids us take our seats above,
More than conquerors in his love.

—*Charles Wesley.*

ST. GEORGE. 8-7s. SIR G. ELVEY.

741

"Hallelujah! for the Lord God omnipotent reigneth."

1 HARK! the song of jubilee;
  Loud as mighty thunders roar,
Or the fulness of the sea,
  When it breaks upon the shore:
Hallelujah! for the Lord
  God omnipotent shall reign;
Hallelujah! let the word
  Echo round the earth and main.

2 Hallelujah!—hark! the sound,
  From the centre to the skies,
Wakes above, beneath, around,
  All creation's harmonies:
See Jehovah's banner furled,
  Sheathed his sword: he speaks—'tis done,
And the kingdoms of this world
  Are the kingdoms of his Son.

3 He shall reign from pole to pole
  With illimitable sway;
He shall reign when, like a scroll,
  Yonder heavens have passed away:
Then the end;—beneath his rod,
  Man's last enemy shall fall;
Hallelujah! Christ in God,
  God in Christ, is all in all.

—*Montgomery.*

EXCELSIOR. 5.5.5.11. D. SAMUEL WEBBE.

ELVEY.

—'tis

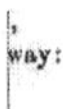

way:

omery.

WEBB.

TUNE: EXCELSIOR. 5.5.5.11. D.

742 *The triumphs of the gospel.*

1 All thanks be to God,
Who scatters abroad,
Throughout every place,
By the least of his servants, his savour of grace!
Who the victory gave,
The praise let him have,
For the work he hath done;
All honour and glory to Jesus alone!

2 Our conquering Lord
Hath prospered his word,
Hath made it prevail,
And mightily shaken the kingdom of hell.
His arm he hath bared,
And a people prepared,
His glory to show,
And witness the power of his passion below.

3 And shall we not sing
Our Saviour and King?
Thy witnesses, we
With rapture ascribe our salvation to thee.
Thou, Jesus, hast blessed,
And believers increased,
Who thankfully own,
We are freely forgiven through mercy alone.

4 O that all men might know
His tokens below,
Our Saviour confess,
And embrace the glad tidings of pardon and peace!
Then, then let it spread,
Thy knowledge and dread,
Till the earth is o'erflowed,
And the universe filled with the glory of God.

—*Charles Wesley.*

WEBB. 7.6, 7.6, 7.6, 7.6. G. J. WEBB.

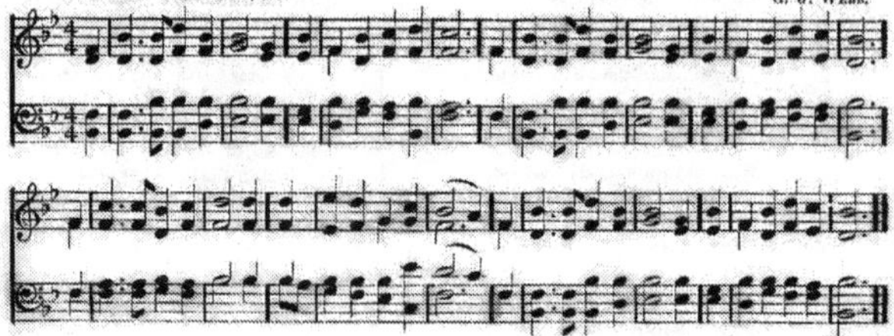

743 *The coming of Christ's kingdom.*

1 The morning light is breaking;
The darkness disappears;
The sons of earth are waking
To penitential tears;
Each breeze that sweeps the ocean
Brings tidings from afar,
Of nations in commotion,
Prepared for Zion's war.

2 See heathen nations bending
Before the God we love,
And thousand hearts ascending
In gratitude above;
While sinners, now confessing,
The gospel call obey,
And seek the Saviour's blessing,
A nation in a day.

3 Blest river of salvation,
Pursue thine onward way;
Flow thou to every nation,
Nor in thy richness stay;
Stay not till all the lowly
Triumphant reach their home;
Stay not till all the holy
Proclaim, "The Lord is come!"

—*S. F. Smith.*

MISSIONARY. 7.6, 7.6, 7.6, 7.6. DR. L. MASON.

744 *Missionary Hymn.*

1 FROM Greenland's icy mountains,
From India's coral strand,
Where Afric's sunny fountains
Roll down their golden sand,
From many an ancient river,
From many a palmy plain,
They call us to deliver
Their land from error's chain.

2 What though the spicy breezes
Blow soft o'er Ceylon's Isle,
Though every prospect pleases,
And only man is vile!
In vain with lavish kindness
The gifts of God are strewn;
The heathen in his blindness
Bows down to wood and stone.

3 Shall we, whose souls are lighted
With wisdom from on high,
Shall we to men benighted
The lamp of life deny?
Salvation! O salvation!
The joyful sound proclaim,
Till earth's remotest nation
Has learnt Messiah's name.

4 Waft, waft, ye winds, his story,
And you, ye waters, roll,
Till, like a sea of glory,
It spreads from pole to pole;
Till, o'er our ransomed nature,
The Lamb for sinners slain,
Redeemer, King, Creator,
In bliss returns to reign.

—*Bishop Heber.*

ZION. 8.7, 8.7, 4.7. DR. THOS. HASTINGS.

TUNE: ZION. 8.7, 8.7, 4.7.

745 *"The Lord shall comfort Zion."*

1 On the mountain-top appearing,
Lo! the sacred herald stands,
Welcome news to Zion bearing,
Zion, long in hostile lands:
‖: Mourning captive!
God himself shall loose thy bands. :‖

2 Has thy night been long and mournful?
Have thy friends unfaithful proved?
Have thy foes been proud and scornful,
By thy sighs and tears unmoved?
‖: Cease thy mourning;
Zion still is well beloved. :‖

3 God, thy God, will now restore thee;
He himself appears thy Friend;
All thy foes shall flee before thee;
Here their boasts and triumphs end:
‖: Great deliverance
Zion's King will surely send. :‖

4 Peace and joy shall now attend thee;
All thy warfare now is past;
God thy Saviour will defend thee;
Victory is thine at last:
‖: All thy conflicts
End in everlasting rest. :‖

—*T. Kelly.*

ST. GERTRUDE. 4-11s.
Sir Arthur Sullivan.
CHORUS.
Onward, Christian soldiers, marching as to war,
Looking unto Jesus, who is gone before!
By permission of Messrs. Novello, Ewer & Co.

746 *The Christian soldier's battle-hymn.*

1 Onward, Christian soldiers, marching as to war,
Looking unto Jesus, who is gone before!
Christ, the Royal Master, leads against the foe;
Forward into battle see his banners go.—Cho.

2 Like a mighty army, moves the Church of God;
Brothers, we are treading where the saints have trod;
We are not divided, all one body we,
One in hope and doctrine, one in charity.—Cho.

3 Crowns and thrones may perish, kingdoms rise and wane,
But the Church of Jesus constant will remain;
Gates of hell can never 'gainst that Church prevail;
We have Christ's own promise, which can never fail.—Cho.

4 Onward, then, ye people, join our happy throng;
Blend with ours your voices in the triumph song.
Glory, praise, and honour, men and angels sing,
Through the countless ages, unto Christ the King.—Cho.

—*S. Baring Gould.*

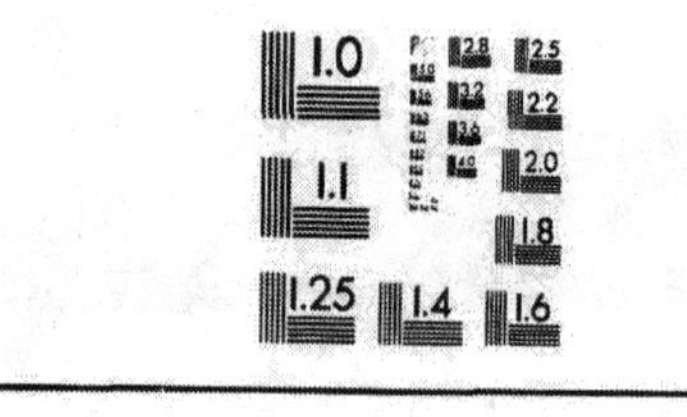
1.0
2.8
2.5
3.2
2.2
3.6
4.0
2.0
1.1
1.8
1.25
1.4
1.6
6″

SECTION IX.

SOCIAL AND FAMILY WORSHIP.

1.—CHRISTIAN FELLOWSHIP AND PRAYER.

BELMONT. C. M. WEBBE.

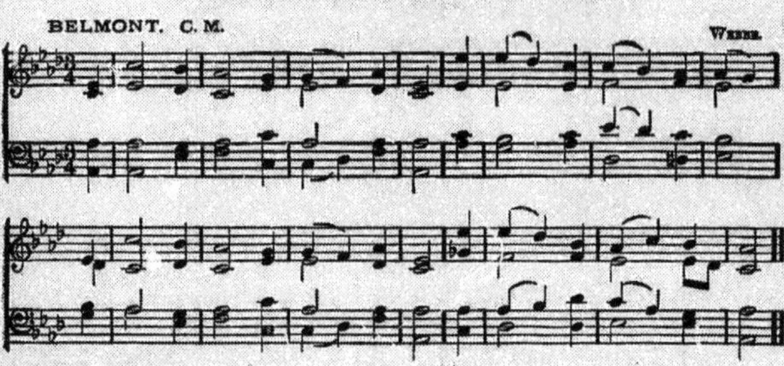

747 *The communion of saints.*

1 ALL praise to our redeeming Lord
  Who joins us by his grace,
And bids us, each to each restored,
  Together seek his face.

2 He bids us build each other up;
  And, gathered into one,
To our high calling's glorious hope,
  We hand in hand go on.

3 The gift which he on one bestows,
  We all delight to prove;
The grace through every vessel flows,
  In purest streams of love.

4 Even now we think and speak the same,
  And cordially agree;
United all, through Jesus' name,
  In perfect harmony.

5 We all partake the joy of one,
  The common peace we feel;
A peace to sensual minds unknown,
  A joy unspeakable.

6 And if our fellowship below
  In Jesus be so sweet,
What heights of rapture shall we know,
  When round his throne we meet!

—*Charles Wesley.*

748 *"There am I in the midst."*

1 SEE, Jesus, thy disciples see,
  The promised blessing give!
Met in thy name, we look to thee,
  Expecting to receive.

2 Thee we expect, our faithful Lord,
  Who in thy name are joined;
We wait, according to thy word,
  Thee in the midst to find.

3 With us thou art assembled here;
  But, O thyself reveal!
Son of the living God, appear!
  Let us thy presence feel.

4 Breathe on us, Lord, in this our day,
  And these dry bones shall live;
Speak peace into our hearts, and say,
  The Holy Ghost receive!

5 Whom now we seek, O may we meet!
  Jesus, the Crucified,
Show us thy bleeding hands and feet,
  Thou who for us hast died.

6 Cause us the record to receive;
  Speak, and the tokens show;
"O be not faithless, but believe
  In me, who died for you!"

—*Charles Wesley.*

WILTSHIRE. C.M. — SIR GEORGE SMART.

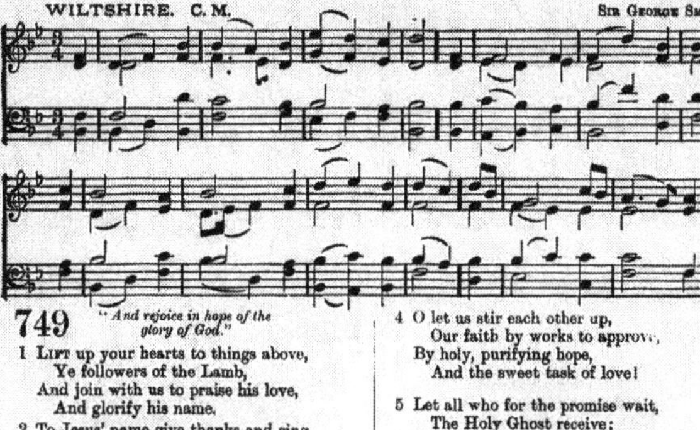

749

"And rejoice in hope of the glory of God."

1 LIFT up your hearts to things above,
Ye followers of the Lamb,
And join with us to praise his love,
And glorify his name.

2 To Jesus' name give thanks and sing,
Whose mercies never end;
Rejoice! rejoice! the Lord is King;
The King is now our Friend.

3 We, for his sake, count all things loss;
On earthly good look down;
And joyfully sustain the cross,
Till we receive the crown.

4 O let us stir each other up,
Our faith by works to approve,
By holy, purifying hope,
And the sweet task of love!

5 Let all who for the promise wait,
The Holy Ghost receive;
And, raised to our unsinning state,
With God in Eden live!

6 Live till the Lord in glory come,
And wait his heaven to share;
He now is fitting up your home;
Go on;—we'll meet you there.

—*Charles Wesley.*

PETERBOROUGH. C.M. — REV. RALPH HARRISON.

750

For a week-day service.

1 BEHOLD us, Lord, a little space
From daily tasks set free,
And met within thy holy place,
To rest awhile with thee.

2 Around us rolls the ceaseless tide
Of business, toil, and care,
And scarcely can we turn aside
For one brief hour of prayer.

3 Yet these are not the only walls
Wherein thou may'st be sought;
On homeliest work thy blessing falls
In truth and patience wrought.

4 Thine is the loom, the forge, the mart,
The wealth of land and sea;
The worlds of science and of art,
Revealed and ruled by thee.

5 Then let us prove our heavenly birth
In all we do and know;
And claim the kingdom of the earth
For thee, and not thy foe.

6 Work shall be prayer, if all be wrought
As thou wouldst have it done;
And prayer, by thee inspired and taught,
Itself with work be one.

—*J. Ellerton.*

FOSTER. C. M. M. B. Foster.

751 *Unity in separation.*

1 Blest be the dear uniting love,
That will not let us part!
Our bodies may far off remove,
We still are one in heart.

2 Joined in one spirit to our Head,
Where he appoints we go;
And still in Jesus' footsteps tread,
And show his praise below.

3 O may we ever walk in him,
And nothing know beside!
Nothing desire, nothing esteem
But Jesus crucified.

4 Closer and closer let us cleave
To his beloved embrace;
Expect his fulness to receive,
And grace to answer grace.

5 Partakers of the Saviour's grace,
The same in mind and heart,
Nor joy, nor grief, nor time, nor place,
Nor life, nor death can part.

6 But let us hasten to the day
Which shall our flesh restore,
When death shall all be done away,
And bodies part no more.
—*Charles Wesley.*

752 *The close of service.*

1 God of all consolation, take
The glory of thy grace;
Thy gifts to thee we render back
In ceaseless songs of praise.

2 Through thee we now together came,
In singleness of heart;
We met, O Jesus, in thy name,
And in thy name we part.

3 We part in body, not in mind;
Our minds continue one;
And, each to each in Jesus joined,
We hand in hand go on.

4 Subsists as in us all one soul,
No power can make us twain;
And mountains rise, and oceans roll,
To sever us, in vain.

5 Our life is hid with Christ in God;
Our Life shall soon appear,
And shed his glory all abroad
In all his members here.

6 The heavenly treasure now we have
In a frail house of clay;
But he shall to the utmost save,
And keep it to that day.
—*Charles Wesley.*

BOYLSTON. S. M. D. Dr. L. Mason.

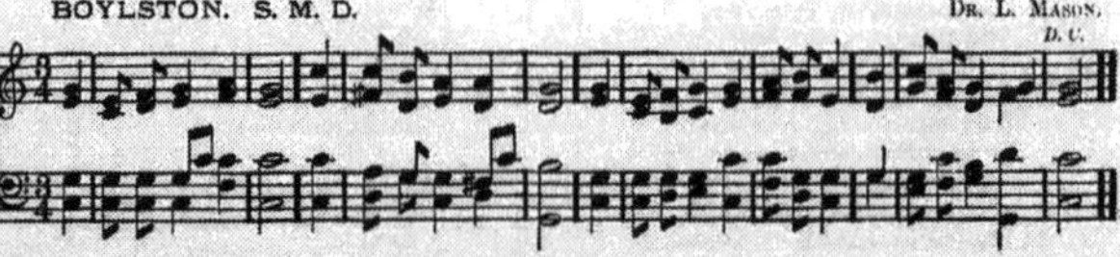
D. C.

TUNE: BOYLSTON. S. M. D.

753 *Christians meeting after separation.*

1 And are we yet alive,
And see each other's face?
Glory and praise to Jesus give
For his redeeming grace!
Preserved by power divine
To full salvation here,
Again in Jesus' praise we join,
And in his sight appear.

2 What troubles have we seen,
What conflicts have we past,
Fightings without, and fears within,
Since we assembled last!
But out of all the Lord
Hath brought us by his love;
And still he doth his help afford,
And hides our life above.

3 Then let us make our boast
Of his redeeming power,
Which saves us to the uttermost,
Till we can sin no more:
Let us take up the cross,
Till we the crown obtain;
And gladly reckon all things loss,
So we may Jesus gain.

—*Charles Wesley.*

LEEDS. S. M. Sacred Harmony.

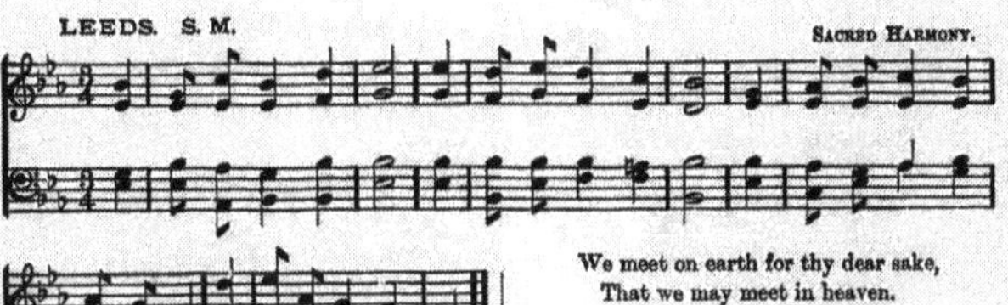

754 *United prayer for Christ's presence.*

1 Jesus, we look to thee,
Thy promised presence claim!
Thou in the midst of us shalt be,
Assembled in thy name:
Thy name salvation is,
Which here we come to prove;
Thy name is life, and health, and peace,
And everlasting love.

2 Not in the name of pride
Or selfishness we meet;
From nature's paths we turn aside,
And worldly thoughts forget.
We meet, the grace to take
Which thou hast freely given;
We meet on earth for thy dear sake,
That we may meet in heaven.

3 Present we know thou art,
But O thyself reveal!
Now, Lord, let every bounding heart
The mighty comfort feel.
O may thy quickening voice
The death of sin remove;
And bid our inmost souls rejoice
In hope of perfect love!

—*Charles Wesley.*

755 *Zeal for God.*

1 Jesus, I fain would find
Thy zeal for God in me,
Thy yearning pity for mankind,
Thy burning charity.

2 In me thy Spirit dwell,
And thy compassions move;
So shall the fervour of my zeal
Be the pure flame of love.

—*Charles Wesley.*

RHODES. S. M. H. G. Trambeth.

756 *Past mercies and future prospects.*

1 Saviour of sinful men,
Thy goodness we proclaim,
Which brings us here to meet again,
And triumph in thy name:

2 Thy mighty name hath been
Our safeguard and our tower;
Hath saved us from the world and sin,
And all the Accuser's power.

3 Awhile in flesh disjoined,
Our friends that went before
We soon in paradise shall find,
And meet to part no more.

4 O what a mighty change
Shall Jesus' sufferers know,
While o'er the happy plains they range,
Incapable of woe!

5 No slightest touch of pain,
Nor sorrow's least alloy,
Can violate our rest, or stain
Our purity of joy.

6 In that eternal day
No clouds nor tempests rise;
There gushing tears are wiped away
Forever from our eyes.

—*Charles Wesley.*

757 *Consecration.*

1 Lord, in the strength of grace,
With a glad heart and free,
Myself, my residue of days,
I consecrate to thee.

2 Thy ransomed servant, I
Restore to thee thy own;
And, from this moment, live or die
To serve my God alone.

—*Charles Wesley.*

DENNIS. S. M. H. G. Naegeli.

TUNE: DENNIS. S. M.

758 *Sympathy and mutual love.*

1 Blest be the tie that binds
Our hearts in Christian love;
The fellowship of kindred minds
Is like to that above.

2 Before our Father's throne,
We pour our ardent prayers;
Our fears, our hopes, our aims are one,
Our comforts and our cares.

3 We share our mutual woes,
Our mutual burdens bear;
And often for each other flows
The sympathizing tear.

4 When we asunder part,
It gives us inward pain;
But we shall still be joined in heart,
And hope to meet again.

5 This glorious hope revives,
Our courage by the way;
While each in expectation lives,
And longs to see the day.

6 From sorrow, toil, and pain,
And sin we shall be free;
And perfect love and friendship reign
Through all eternity.

—*J. Fawcett.*

LEOMINSTER. S. M. D. G. W. Martin.

759 *The inseparable union of saints.*

1 And let our bodies part,
To different climes repair,
Inseparably joined in heart
The friends of Jesus are.
Jesus, the Corner-stone,
Did first our hearts unite,
And still he keeps our spirits one,
Who walk with him in white.

2 O let us still proceed
In Jesus' work below;
And, following our triumphant Head,
To further conquests go!
The vineyard of their Lord
Before his labourers lies;
And, lo! we see the vast reward
Which waits us in the skies.

3 O let our heart and mind
Continually ascend,
That haven of repose to find,
Where all our labours end;
Where all our toils are o'er,
Our suffering and our pain;
Who meet on that eternal shore,
Shall never part again.

4 O happy, happy place,
Where saints and angels meet!
There we shall see each other's face,
And all our brethren greet.
The Church of the first-born,
We shall with them be blest,
And, crowned with endless joy, return
To our eternal rest.

—*Charles Wesley.*

UNITY. 6.5, 6.5, 6.6, 6.5. LOWELL MASON.

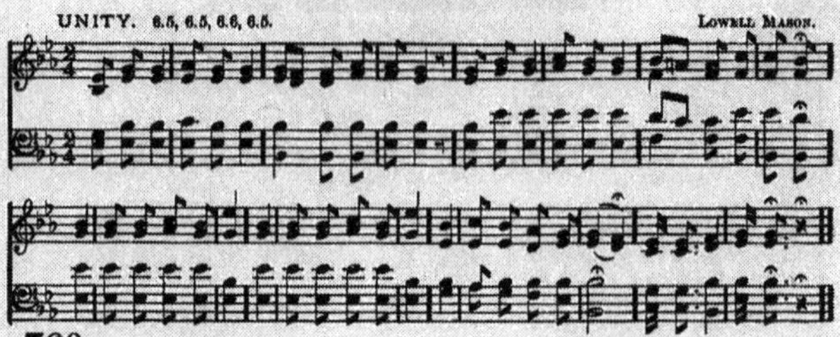

760 *Parting on earth—meeting in heaven.*

1 WHEN shall we meet again,
  Meet ne'er to sever?
When shall peace wreathe her chain
  Round us forever?
Our hearts will ne'er repose,
Safe from each blast that blows,
In this dark vale of woes,
  Never—no, never!

2 When shall love freely flow
  Pure as life's river?
When shall sweet friendship glow
  Changeless forever?
Where joys celestial thrill,
Where bliss each heart shall fill,
And fears of parting chill,
  Never—no, never!

3 Up to that world of light
  Take us, dear Saviour;
May we all there unite,
  Happy forever;
Where kindred spirits dwell,
There may our music swell,
And time our joys dispel,
  Never—no, never!

4 Soon shall we meet again,
  Meet ne'er to sever;
Soon shall peace wreathe her chain
  Round us forever;
Our hearts will then repose
Secure from worldly woes;
Our songs of praise shall close
  Never—no, never!

—*A. A. Watts.*

ERNAN. L. M. DR. L. MASON.

761 *The highway of holiness.*

1 JESUS, my all, to heaven is gone,
He whom I fix my hopes upon;
His track I see, and I'll pursue
The narrow way, till him I view.

2 The way the holy prophets went,
The road that leads from banishment,
The King's highway of holiness,
I'll go, for all his paths are peace.

3 This is the way I long have sought,
And mourned because I found it not;
My grief a burden long has been,
Because I was not saved from sin.

4 The more I strove against its power,
I felt its weight and guilt the more;
Till late I heard my Saviour say,
"Come hither, soul, I am the way."

5 Lo! glad I come; and thou, blest Lamb,
Shalt take me to thee, as I am;
Nothing but sin have I to give;
Nothing but love shall I receive.

6 Then will I tell to sinners round,
What a dear Saviour I have found;
I'll point to thy redeeming blood,
And say, "Behold the way to God."

—*J. Cennick.*

FEDERAL STREET. L. M. H. K. OLIVER.

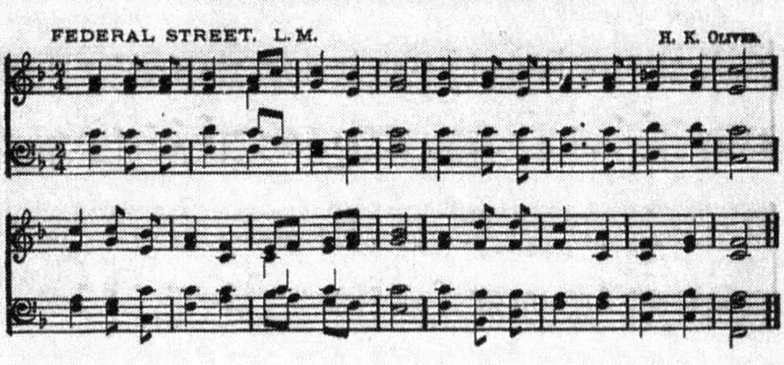

762 Psalm lvi. 13.

1 My soul, through my Redeemer's care,
Saved from the second death I feel,
My eyes from tears of dark despair,
My feet from falling into hell.

2 Wherefore to him my feet shall run;
My eyes on his perfections gaze;
My soul shall live for God alone;
And all within me shout his praise.
—*Charles Wesley.*

"GOING HOME." L. M. ARRANGED BY REV. W. McDONALD.

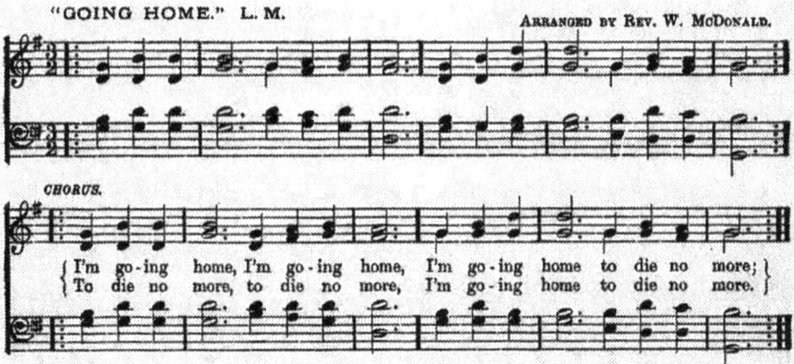

CHORUS.

{ I'm go-ing home, I'm go-ing home, I'm go-ing home to die no more; }
{ To die no more, to die no more, I'm go-ing home to die no more. }

763 *The heavenly home.*

1 My heavenly home is bright and fair;
Nor pain nor death can enter there;
Its glittering towers the sun outshine;
That heavenly mansion shall be mine.

2 My Father's house is built on high,
Far, far above the starry sky;
When from this earthly prison free,
That heavenly mansion mine shall be.

3 Let others seek a home below,
Which flames devour, or waves o'erflow;
Be mine the happier lot to own
A heavenly mansion near the throne.

4 Then fail the earth, let stars decline,
And sun and moon refuse to shine,
All nature sink and cease to be,
That heavenly mansion stands for me.
—*Wm. Hunter.*

EDEN. L. M. DR. L. MASON.

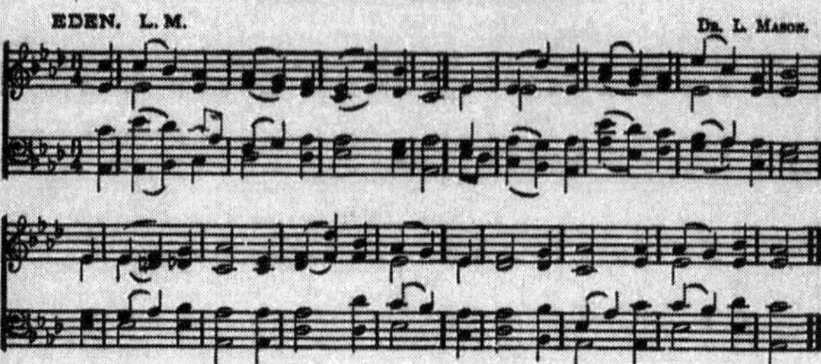

764 *Healing and comfort in Christ.*

1 At even, ere the sun was set,
The sick, O Lord, around thee lay;
O in what divers pains they met!
O with what joy they went away!

2 Once more 'tis eventide, and we
Oppressed with various ills draw near;
What if thy form we cannot see?
We know and feel that thou art here.

3 O Saviour Christ, our woes dispel!
For some are sick, and some are sad,
And some have never loved thee well,
And some have lost the love they had;

4 And some have found the world is vain,
Yet from the world they break not free;
And some have friends who give them pain,
Yet have not sought a friend in thee;

5 And all, O Lord, crave perfect rest,
And to be wholly free from sin;
And they who fain would serve thee best
Are conscious most of wrong within.

6 O Saviour Christ, thou too art man;
Thou hast been troubled, tempted, tried;
Thy kind but searching glance can scan
The very wounds that shame would hide;

7 Thy touch has still its ancient power;
No word from thee can fruitless fall;
Hear in this solemn evening hour,
And in thy mercy heal us all.

—*H. Twells.*

OLIVES' BROW. L. M. (SECOND TUNE.) W. B. BRADBURY.

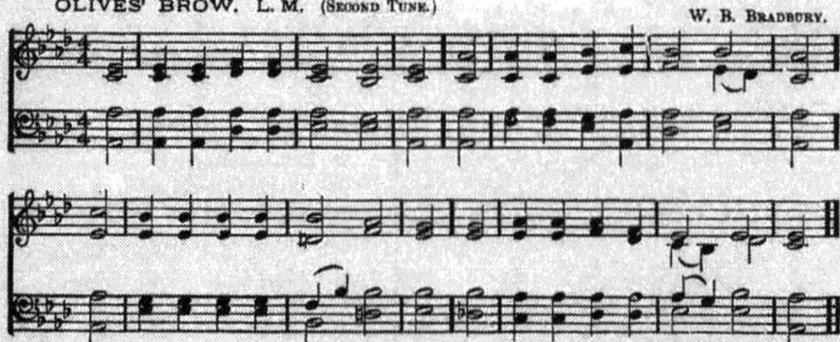

BENEVENTO. 8-7s. S. WEBBE.

765

The Love-Feast.

1 COME, and let us sweetly join,
Christ to praise in hymns divine!
Give we all, with one accord,
Glory to our common Lord;
Hands, and hearts, and voices raise;
Sing as in the ancient days;
Antedate the joys above;
Celebrate the feast of love.

2 Strive we, in affection strive;
Let the purer flame revive,
Such as in the martyrs glowed,
Dying champions for their God:
We, like them, may live and love;
Called we are their joys to prove,
Saved with them from future wrath,
Partners of like precious faith.

3 Sing we then in Jesus' name,
Now as yesterday the same;
One in every time and place,
Full for all of truth and grace;
We for Christ, our Master, stand,
Lights in a benighted land;
We our dying Lord confess;
We are Jesus' witnesses.

4 Witnesses that Christ hath died,
We with him are crucified;
Christ hath burst the bands of death;
We his quickening Spirit breathe:
Christ is now gone up on high;
Thither all our wishes fly;
Sits at God's right hand above;
There with him we reign in love.

—*Charles Wesley.*

766

SECOND PART.

1 COME, thou high and lofty Lord!
Lowly, meek, incarnate Word!
Humbly stoop to earth again,
Come and visit abject men!
Jesus, dear expected Guest,
Thou art bidden to the feast;
For thyself our hearts prepare,
Come, and sit, and banquet there.

2 Jesus, we thy promise claim,
We are met in thy great name;
In the midst do thou appear,
Manifest thy presence here!
Sanctify us, Lord, and bless,
Breathe thy Spirit, give thy peace,
Thou thyself within us move,
Make our feast a feast of love.

3 Make us all in thee complete,
Make us all for glory meet,
Meet to appear before thy sight,
Partners with the saints in light
Call, O call us each by name,
To the marriage of the Lamb;
Let us lean upon thy breast,
Love be there our endless feast!

—*Charles Wesley.*

MAIDSTONE. 8-7s. W. B. GILBERT.

767

THIRD PART.

1 LET us join, 'tis God commands,
Let us join our hearts and hands;
Help to gain our calling's hope;
Build we each the other up:
God his blessings shall dispense;
God shall crown his ordinance;
Meet in his appointed ways;
Nourish us with social grace.

2 Let us then as brethren love,
Faithfully his gifts improve,
Carry on the earnest strife,
Walk in holiness of life;
Still forget the things behind,
Follow Christ in heart and mind,
Toward the mark unwearied press,
Seize the crown of righteousness.

3 Plead we thus for faith alone,
Faith which by our works is shown;
God it is who justifies;
Only faith the grace applies;
Active faith that lives within,
Conquers earth, and hell, and sin,
Sanctifies and makes us whole,
Forms the Saviour in the soul.

4 Let us for this faith contend;
Sure salvation is its end;
Heaven already is begun,
Everlasting life is won.
Only let us persevere,
Till we see our Lord appear;
Never from the Rock remove,
Saved by faith, which works by love.

—*Charles Wesley.*

MARTYN. 8-7s. S. B. MARSH.

Fine.
D.C.

TUNE: MARTYN. 8-7s.

768 FOURTH PART.

1 Partners of a glorious hope,
Lift your hearts and voices up,
Jointly let us rise, and sing
Christ our Prophet, Priest, and King:
Monuments of Jesus' grace,
Speak we by our lives his praise;
Walk in him we have received,
Show we not in vain believed.

2 While we walk with God in light,
God our hearts doth still unite;
Dearest fellowship we prove,
Fellowship in Jesus' love:
Sweetly each, with each combined,
In the bonds of duty joined,
Feels the cleansing blood applied,
Daily feels that Christ hath died.

3 Still, O Lord, our faith increase,
Cleanse from all unrighteousness;
Thee the unholy cannot see;
Make, O make us meet for thee!
Every vile affection kill,
Root out every seed of ill,
Utterly abolish sin,
Write thy law of love within.

4 Hence may all our actions flow,
Love the proof that Christ we know;
Mutual love the token be,
Lord, that we belong to thee:
Love, thine image, love impart,
Stamp it on our face and heart;
Only love to us be given,
Lord, we ask no other heaven.
—*Charles Wesley.*

769 *Meeting in Christ's name.*

1 Glory be to God above,
God from whom all blessings flow;
Make we mention of his love,
Publish we his praise below;
Called together by his grace,
We are met in Jesus' name;
See with joy each other's face,
Followers of the dying Lamb.

2 Let us then sweet counsel take,
How to make our calling sure,
Our election how to make
Past the reach of hell secure;
Build we each the other up;
Pray we for our faith's increase,
Solid comfort, settled hope,
Constant joy, and lasting peace.

3 More and more let love abound;
Let us never, never rest,
Till we are in Jesus found,
Of our paradise possest;
He removes the flaming sword,
Calls us back, from Eden driven;
To his image here restored,
Soon he takes us up to heaven.
—*Charles Wesley.*

MERCY. 4-7s. L. M. Gottschalk.

Slowly.

770 *The sense of God's presence.*

1 When this song of praise shall cease,
Let thy children, Lord, depart
With the blessing of thy peace,
And thy love in every heart.

2 Oh! where'er our path may lie,
Father, let us not forget
That we walk beneath thine eye,
That thy care upholds us yet.

3 Blind are we, and weak, and frail,
Be thine aid forever near;
May the fear to sin prevail
Over every other fear.
—*W. C. Bryant.*

DIX. 6-7s.

C. KOCHER.

771

United in love.

1 CENTRE of our hopes thou art,
End of our enlarged desires;
Stamp thine image on our heart;
Fill us now with heavenly fires;
Joined in one by love divine,
Seal our souls forever thine.

2 Let us all together rise,
To thy glorious life restored;
Here regain our paradise,
Here prepare to meet our Lord;
Here enjoy the earnest given,
Travel hand in hand to heaven.

—*Charles Wesley.*

NETTLETON. 8.7, 8.7, 8.7, 8.7.

TUNE: NETTLETON. 8.7, 8.7, 8.7, 8.7.

772 *"Hitherto hath the Lord helped us."*

1 Come, thou Fount of every blessing,
Tune my heart to sing thy grace,
Streams of mercy, never ceasing,
Call for songs of loudest praise.
Teach me some celestial measure,
Sung by ransomed hosts above;
O the vast, the boundless treasure
Of my Lord's unchanging love.

2 Here I raise my Ebenezer;
Hither by thy help I've come;
And I hope by thy good pleasure,
Safely to arrive at home.
Jesus sought me when a stranger,
Wandering from the fold of God;
He, to rescue me from danger,
Interposed his precious blood.

3 O to grace how great a debtor
Daily I'm constrained to be!
Let thy goodness, like a fetter,
Bind my wandering heart to thee.
Prone to wander, Lord, I feel it,
Prone to leave the God I love;
Here's my heart, O take and seal it,
Seal it for thy courts above!

—R. Robinson.

FRIENDSHIP. 8.7, 8.7, 8.7, 8.7. C. C. Converse.

773 *"Casting all your care upon him."*

1 What a Friend we have in Jesus,
All our sins and griefs to bear!
What a privilege to carry
Everything to God in prayer!
O what peace we often forfeit,
O what needless pain we bear,
All because we do not carry
Everything to God in prayer!

2 Have we trials and temptations?
Is there trouble anywhere?
We should never be discouraged,
Take it to the Lord in prayer.
Can we find a friend so faithful
Who will all our sorrows share?
Jesus knows our every weakness,
Take it to the Lord in prayer.

3 Are we weak and heavy-laden,
Cumbered with a load of care?
Precious Saviour, still our refuge,
Take it to the Lord in prayer.
Do thy friends despise, forsake thee?
Take it to the Lord in prayer;
In his arms he'll take and shield thee,
Thou wilt find a solace there.

—Joseph Scriven.

PRECIOUS NAME. 8.7, 8.7 — W. H. Doane.

CHORUS.
Precious name, O how sweet! Hope of
Precious name, O how sweet!
earth and joy of heav'n. Precious name, O how sweet! Hope of earth and joy of heav'n.
Precious name, O how sweet, how sweet.

774 *The precious name of Jesus.*

1 Take the name of Jesus with you,
Child of sorrow and of woe;
It will joy and comfort give you;
Take it, then, where'er you go.—Cho.

2 Take the name of Jesus ever,
As a shield from every snare;
If temptations round you gather,
Breathe that holy name in prayer.—Cho.

3 O the precious name of Jesus,
How it thrills our souls with joy,
When his loving arms receive us,
And his songs our tongues employ!—Cho.

4 At the name of Jesus bowing,
Falling prostrate at his feet,
King of kings in heaven we'll crown him,
When our journey is complete.—Cho.

—*Mrs. L. Baxter.*

"ART THOU WEARY?" 8.5, 8.3. — E. W. Bullinger.

Slowly.

TUNE: "ART THOU WEARY?" 8.5, 8.3.

775 *Trusting Jesus fully.*

1 I AM trusting thee, Lord Jesus,
Trusting only thee;
Trusting thee for full salvation,
Great and free.

2 I am trusting thee for pardon;
At thy feet I bow;
For thy grace and tender mercy
Trusting now.

3 I am trusting thee for cleansing
In the crimson flood;
Trusting thee to make me holy
By thy blood.

4 I am trusting thee to guide me;
Thou alone canst lead;
Every day and hour supplying
All my need.

5 I am trusting thee for power;
Thine can never fail;
Strength which thou thyself dost give me,
Must prevail.

6 I am trusting thee, Lord Jesus;
Never let me fall!
I am trusting thee forever,
And for all.

—Miss Havergal.

RUTHERFORD. 7.6, 7.6, 7.6, 7.6. D'URHAN.

776 *"Without me ye can do nothing."*

1 I NEED thee, precious Jesus!
For I am full of sin;
My soul is dark and guilty,
My heart is dead within:
I need the cleansing fountain,
Where I can always flee—
The blood of Christ most precious,
The sinner's perfect plea.

2 I need thee, blessèd Jesus!
For I am very poor;
A stranger and a pilgrim,
I have no earthly store:
I need the love of Jesus
To cheer me on my way,
To guide my doubting footsteps,
To be my strength and stay.

3 I need thee, blessèd Jesus!
I need a friend like thee;
A friend to soothe and sympathize,
A friend to care for me:
I need the heart of Jesus
To feel each anxious care,
To tell my every trouble,
And all my sorrows share.

4 I need thee, blessèd Jesus!
And hope to see thee soon,
Encircled with the rainbow,
And seated on thy throne;
There, with the blood-bought children,
My joy shall ever be,
To sing thy praises, Jesus,
To gaze, my Lord, on thee.

—H. Bonar.

WEBB. 7.6, 7.6, 7.6, 7.6. G. J. WEBB.

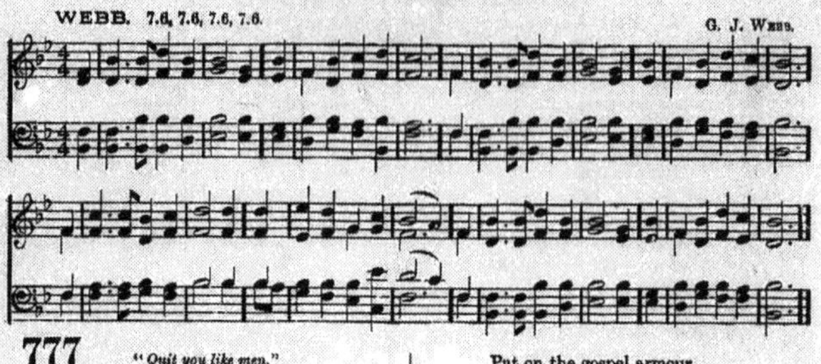

777

"Quit you like men."

1 STAND up! stand up for Jesus!
Ye soldiers of the cross!
Lift high his royal banner;
It must not suffer loss:
From victory unto victory
His army will he lead,
Till every foe is vanquished,
And Christ is Lord indeed.

2 Stand up! stand up for Jesus!
Stand in his strength alone;
The arm of flesh will fail you;
Ye dare not trust your own:
Put on the gospel armour,
And, watching unto prayer,
Where duty calls, or danger,
Be never wanting there.

3 Stand up! stand up for Jesus!
The strife will not be long;
This day the noise of battle,
The next the victor's song.
To him that overcometh
A crown of life shall be;
He with the King of glory
Shall reign eternally.

—*G. Duffield, jun.*

RUTHERFORD. 7.6, 7.6, 7.6, 7.6. D'URHAN.

778

Praise to the Saviour.

1 O SAVIOUR, precious Saviour,
Whom, yet unseen, we love!
O Name of might and favour,
All other names above:
We worship thee, we bless thee,
To thee alone we sing;
We praise thee, and confess thee
Our holy Lord and King!

2 O Bringer of salvation,
Who wondrously hast wrought,
Thyself the revelation
Of love beyond our thought:
In thee all fulness dwelleth,
All grace and power divine;
The glory that excelleth,
O Son of God, is thine.

3 O grant the consummation
Of this our song above,
In endless adoration,
And everlasting love:
Then shall we praise and bless thee,
Where perfect praises ring,
And evermore confess thee,
Our Saviour and our King!

—*Miss Havergal.*

LIFE. 6-6s. (First Tune.) P. P. Bliss.

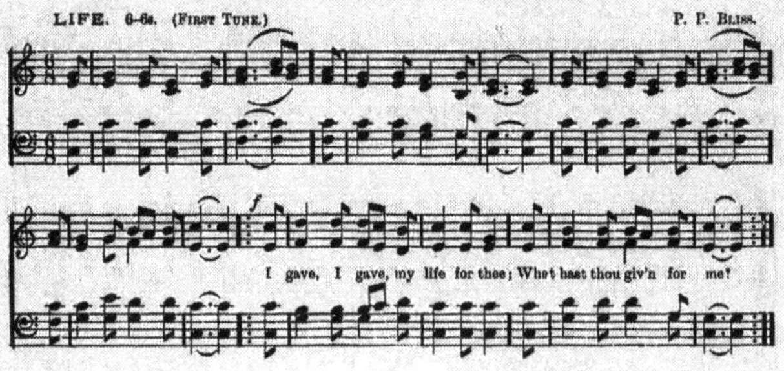
I gave, I gave, my life for thee; What hast thou giv'n for me?

779 "How much owest thou unto my Lord?"

1 I gave my life for thee,
My precious blood I shed,
That thou might'st ransomed be,
And quickened from the dead.
||:I gave my life for thee;
What hast thou given for me?:||

2 I spent long years for thee
In weariness and woe,
That an eternity
Of joy thou mightest know.
||:I spent long years for thee;
Hast thou spent *one* for me?:||

3 And I have brought to thee,
Down from my home above,
Salvation full and free,
My pardon and my love.
||:Great gifts I brought to thee;
What hast thou brought to me?:||

4 Oh, let thy life be given,
Thy years for me be spent,
World-fetters all be riven,
And joy with suffering blent.
||:I gave myself for thee;
Give thou thyself to me!:||

—*Miss Havergal.*

LIFE. 6-6s. New Arrangement. (Second Tune.)

I gave, I gave, my life for thee; What hast thou giv'n for me?

EDINBURGH. 7.6.5.5.6.4.6. REV. ROBERT LOWRY.

CHORUS.
One more day's work for Je-sus,
One more day's work for Je - sus, One more day's work for Je - sus, One less of life for me!

780 *A day's work for Jesus.*

1 ONE more day's work for Jesus,
One less of life for me!
But heaven is nearer,
And Christ is dearer
Than yesterday, to me;
His love and light
Fill all my soul to-night.—CHO.

2 One more day's work for Jesus!
How sweet the work has been,
To tell the story,
To show the glory,
Where Christ's flock enter in!
How it did shine
In this poor heart of mine!—CHO.

3 One more day's work for Jesus!
O yes, a weary day;
But heaven shines clearer,
And rest comes nearer,
At each step of the way;
And Christ in all,
Before his face I fall.—CHO.

4 O blessèd work for Jesus!
O rest at Jesus' feet!
There toil seems pleasure,
My wants are treasure,
And pain for him is sweet.
Lord, if I may,
I'll serve another day!—CHO.

—*Anna Warner.*

DEPENDENCE. 6.4, 6.4. REV. R. LOWRY.

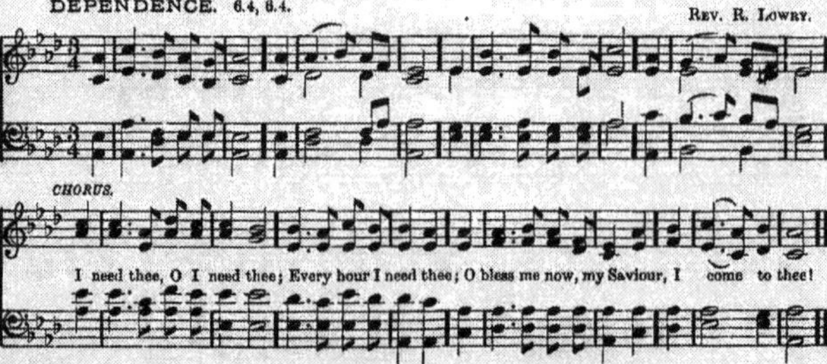
CHORUS.
I need thee, O I need thee; Every hour I need thee; O bless me now, my Saviour, I come to thee!

TUNE: DEPENDENCE. 6.4, 6.4.

781

I need thee every hour.

1 I NEED thee every hour,
Most gracious Lord;
No tender voice like thine
Can peace afford.—CHO.

2 I need thee every hour,
Stay thou near by;
Temptations lose their power
When thou art nigh.—CHO.

3 I need thee every hour,
In joy or pain;
Come quickly and abide,
Or life is vain.—CHO.

4 I need thee every hour;
Teach me thy will;
And thy rich promises
In me fulfil.—CHO.

5 I need thee every hour,
Most Holy One;
O make me thine indeed,
Thou blessèd Son!—CHO.

—*Mrs. Hawks.*

WORK. 7.6, 7.5, 7.6, 7.5. DR. MASON.

782

"The night cometh when no man can work."

mf 1 WORK, for the night is coming,
Work through the morning hours;
Work, while the dew is sparkling,
Work 'mid springing flowers;
cres. Work, when the day grows brighter,
Work in the glowing sun;
dim. Work, for the night is coming,
p When man's work is done.

mf 2 Work, for the night is coming,
Work through the sunny noon;
Fill brightest hours with labour,
Rest comes sure and soon.
cres. Give every flying minute
Something to keep in store;
dim. Work, for the night is coming,
p When man works no more.

mf 3 Work, for the night is coming,
Under the sunset skies;
cres. While their bright tints are glowing,
Work, for daylight flies.
dim. Work till the last beam fadeth,
Fadeth to shine no more;
p Work while the night is darkening,
pp When man's work is o'er.

—*Annie L. Walker.*

CECILIA. 4-10s. ADAPTED FROM FILBY.

783 "*With my song will I praise him.*"

1 SINGING for Jesus, our Saviour and King,
Singing for Jesus, the Lord whom we love;
All adoration we joyously bring,
Longing to praise as we'll praise him above.

2 Singing for Jesus, our Master and Friend,
Telling his love and his marvellous grace;
Love from eternity, love without end,
Love for the loveless, the sinful, and base.

3 Singing for Jesus, and striving to win
Many to love him, and join in the song;
Calling the weary and wandering in,
Rolling the chorus of gladness along.

4 Singing for Jesus, our Shepherd and Guide,
Singing for gladness of heart that he gives;
Singing for wonder and praise that he died,
Singing for blessing and joy that he lives.

5 Singing for Jesus, still singing with joy!
Thus will we praise him, and tell of his love,
Till he shall call us to brighter employ,
Singing for Jesus forever above.

—*Miss Havergal.*

ELLERS. 10.10.10.10. E. J. HOPKINS.

784 "*Abide with us; for it is toward evening.*"

mf 1 ABIDE wit . me, fast falls the eventide;
The darkness deepens; Lord, with me abide!
When other helpers fail, and comforts flee,
dim. Help of the helpless, O abide with me!

mp 2 Swift to its close ebbs out life's little day;
cres. Earth's joys grow dim, its glories pass away;
Change and decay in all around I see;
dim. O thou who changest not, abide with me!

mf 3 I need thy presence every passing hour;
cres. What but thy grace can foil the tempter's power?
Who like thyself my guide and stay can be?
f Through cloud and sunshine, O abide with me!

f 4 I fear no foe, with thee at hand to bless,
Ills have no weight, and tears no bitterness;
cres. Where is death's sting? where, grave, thy victory?
ff I triumph still, if thou abide with me!

pp 5 Reveal thyself before my closing eyes;
cres. Shine through the gloom, and point me to the skies,
f Heaven's morning breaks, and earth's vain shadows flee;
dim. In life and death, O Lord, abide with me!

—*H. F. Lyte.*

LYONS. 10.10, 11.11. HAYDN.

785 *Thanksgiving for infinite love.*

1 YE servants of God, your Master proclaim,
And publish abroad his wonderful name;
The name all-victorious of Jesus extol;
His kingdom is glorious, and rules over all.

2 God ruleth on high, almighty to save;
And still he is nigh; his presence we have;
The great congregation his praises shall sing,
Ascribing salvation to Jesus, our King.

3 "Salvation to God, who sits on the throne,"
Let all cry aloud, and honour the Son;
The praises of Jesus the angels proclaim,
Fall down on their faces, and worship the
Lamb.

4 Then let us adore, and give him his right,
All glory and power, all wisdom and might,
All honour and blessing, with angels above,
And thanks never ceasing for infinite love.
—*Charles Wesley.*

786 *"These are they which follow the Lamb."*

1 APPOINTED by thee, we meet in thy name,
And meekly agree to follow the Lamb,
To trace thy example, the world to disdain,
And constantly trample on pleasure and pain.

2 Rejoicing in hope, we humbly go on,
And daily take up the pledge of our crown;
In doing and bearing the will of our Lord,
We still are preparing to meet our reward.

3 O Jesus, appear! no longer delay
To sanctify here, and bear us away;
The end of our meeting on earth let us see,
Triumphantly sitting in glory with thee!
—*Charles Wesley.*

HANOVER. 10.10.11.11. DR. CROFT.

787 *United prayer and praise.*

1 ALL thanks to the Lamb, who gives us to meet!
His love we proclaim, his praises repeat;
We own him our Jesus, continually near
To pardon and bless us, and perfect us here.

2 In him we have peace, in him we have power,
Preserved by his grace throughout the dark
hour;
In all our temptations he keeps us to prove
His utmost salvation, his fulness of love.

3 O what shall we do our Saviour to love?
To make us anew, come, Lord, from above!
The fruit of thy passion, thy holiness give,
Give us the salvation of all that believe.

4 Come, Jesus, and loose the stammerer's tongue,
And teach even us the spiritual song;
Let us without ceasing give thanks for thy
grace,
And glory, and blessing, and honour, and
praise. —*Charles Wesley.*

HOUGHTON. 10.11, 10.11. (IRREGULAR). DR. GAUNTLETT.

788

Accepted in the Beloved.

1 ALL praise to the Lamb! accepted I am,
Through faith in the Saviour's adorable name;
In him I confide, his blood is applied;
For me he hath suffered, for me he hath died.

2 Not a cloud doth arise, to darken my skies,
Or hide for a moment my Lord from my eyes;
In him I am blest, I lean on his breast,
And lo! in his love I continue to rest.

—*Charles Wesley.*

DARWELL. 6.6, 6.6, 8.8. REV. J. DARWELL.

789

The blessings of unity.

1 BEHOLD, how good a thing,
It is to dwell in peace;
How pleasing to our King
This fruit of righteousness;
When brethren all in one agree,
Who knows the joys of unity!

2 Where unity takes place,
The joys of heaven we prove;
This is the gospel grace,
The unction from above,
The Spirit on all believers shed,
Descending swift from Christ our Head.

3 Grace every morning new,
And every night, we feel
The soft, refreshing dew
That falls on Hermon's hill!
On Zion it doth sweetly fall;
The grace of one descends on all.

4 Even now our Lord doth pour
The blessing from above,
A kindly gracious shower
Of heart-reviving love;
The former and the latter rain,
The love of God and love of man.

5 In him, when brethren join,
And follow after peace,
The fellowship divine
He promises to bless,
His choicest graces to bestow,
Where two or three are met below.

6 The riches of his grace
In fellowship are given
To Zion's chosen race,
The citizens of heaven;
He fills them with the choicest store,
He gives them life for evermore.

—*Charles Wesley.*

TUNE: DARWELL. 6.6, 6.6, 8.8. (See Hymn 789.)

790 *Christian unity and fellowship.*

1 Jesus, accept the praise
  That to thy name belongs;
Matter of all our lays,
  Subject of all our songs;
Through thee we now together came,
And part exulting in thy Name.

2 In flesh we part awhile,
  But still in spirit joined,
To embrace the happy toil
  Thou hast to each assigned;
And while we do thy blessèd will,
We bear our heaven about us still.

3 O let us thus go on
  In all thy pleasant ways,
And, armed with patience, run
  With joy the appointed race!
Keep us, and every seeking soul,
Till all attain the heavenly goal.

4 There we shall meet again,
  When all our toils are o'er,
And death, and grief, and pain,
  And parting are no more;
We shall with all our brethren rise,
And grasp thee in the flaming skies.

5 Then let us wait the sound
  That shall our souls release;
And labour to be found
  Of him in spotless peace,
In perfect holiness renewed,
Adorned with Christ, and meet for God.

—*Charles Wesley.*

WARSAW. 6.6, 6.6, 8.8. THOMAS CLARK.

791 *Mutual sympathy and aid.*

1 Thou God of truth and love,
  We seek thy perfect way,
Ready thy choice to approve,
  Thy providence to obey;
Enter into thy wise design,
And sweetly lose our will in thine.

2 Why hast thou cast our lot
  In the same age and place?
And why together brought
  To see each other's face?
To join with softest sympathy,
And mix our friendly souls in thee?

3 Didst thou not make us one,
  That we might one remain,
Together travel on,
  And bear each other's pain;
Till all thy utmost goodness prove,
And rise renewed in perfect love?

4 Surely thou didst unite
  Our kindred spirits here,
That we hereafter might
  Before thy throne appear;
Meet at the marriage of the Lamb,
And all thy glorious love proclaim.

5 Then let us ever bear
  The blessèd end in view,
And join, with mutual care,
  To fight our passage through;
And kindly help each other on,
Till all receive the starry crown.

—*Charles Wesley.*

MAGDALEN COLLEGE. 8.8.6, 8.8.6. WM. HAYES, Mus. Doc.

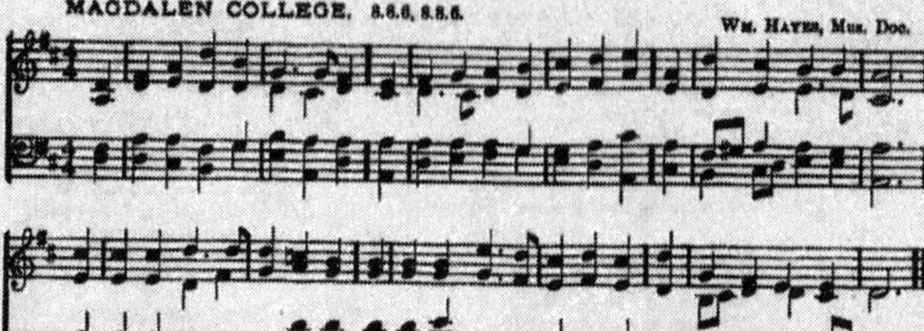

792 *The Spirit of unity and love.*

1 Come, Wisdom, Power, and Grace Divine,
Come, Jesus, in thy name to join
A happy, chosen band;
Who fain would prove thine utmost will,
And all thy righteous laws fulfil,
In love's benign command.

2 If pure essential Love thou art,
Thy nature into every heart,
Thy loving self, inspire;
Bid all our simple souls be one,
United in a bond unknown,
Baptized with heavenly fire.

3 Supply what every member wants;
To found the fellowship of saints,
Thy Spirit, Lord, supply;
So shall we all thy love receive,
Together to thy glory live,
And to thy glory die.

—*Charles Wesley.*

PATER OMNIUM. 6-8s. H. J. E. HOLMES.

793 *"Peter and John went up into the temple at the hour of prayer."*

1 Who Jesus our example know,
And his Apostles' footsteps trace,
We gladly to the temple go,
Frequent the consecrated place
At every solemn hour of prayer,
And meet the God of mercy there.

2 His offering pure we call to mind,
There on the golden altar laid,
Whose Godhead with the manhood joined
For every soul atonement made;
And have whate'er we ask of God,
Through faith in that all-saving blood.

—*Charles Wesley.*

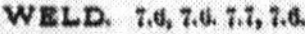
WELD. 7.6, 7.6. 7.7, 7.6.

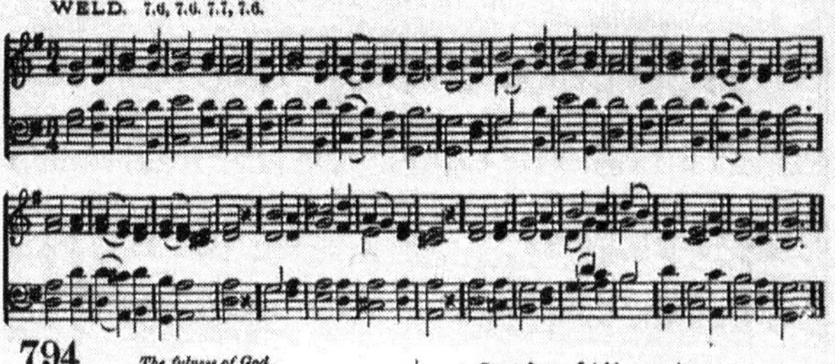

794

The fulness of God.

1 GIVE me the enlarged desire,
  And open, Lord, my soul,
Thy own fulness to require,
  And comprehend the whole;

Stretch my faith's capacity
  Wider, and yet wider still;
Then with all that is in thee
  My soul forever fill!

—Charles Wesley.

2.—THE FAMILY CIRCLE.

ARIEL. 8.8.6, 8.8.6. DR. L. MASON.

795

Family Religion.

1 I AND my house will serve the Lord;
But first obedient to his word
  I must myself appear;
By actions, words, and tempers show,
That I my heavenly Master know,
  ‖:And serve with heart sincere.:‖

2 I must the fair example set;
From those that on my pleasure wait
  The stumbling-block remove;
Their duty by my life explain;
And still in all my works maintain
  ‖:The dignity of love.:‖

3 Easy to be entreated, mild,
Quickly appeased and reconciled,
  A follower of my God,
A saint indeed, I long to be,
And lead my faithful family
  ‖:In the celestial road.:‖

4 A sinner, saved myself from sin,
I come my family to win,
  To preach their sins forgiven;
Children, and wife, and servants seize,
And through the paths of pleasantness
  ‖:Conduct them all to heaven.:‖

—Charles Wesley.

PATER OMNIUM. 6-8s. H. J. E. HOLMES.

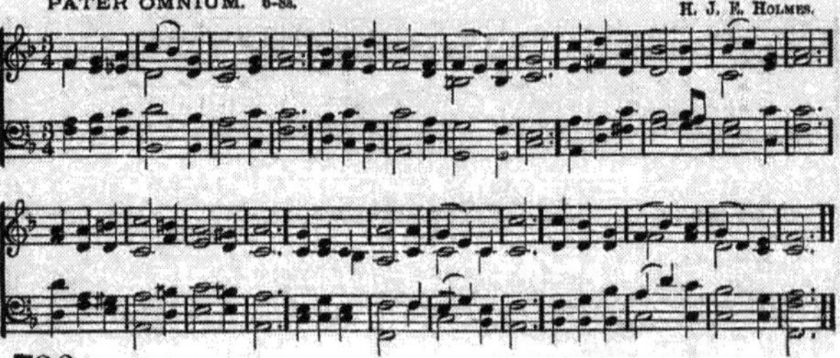

796 *Thanksgiving for life.*

1 FOUNTAIN of life and all my joy,
Jesus, thy mercies I embrace;
The breath thou giv'st, for thee employ,
And wait to taste thy perfect grace;
No more forsaken and forlorn,
I bless the day that I was born.

2 Preserved, through faith, by power divine,
A miracle of grace I stand!
I prove the strength of Jesus mine!
Jesus, upheld by thy right hand,
Though in the flesh I feel the thorn,
I bless the day that I was born.

3 Weary of life through inbred sin,
I was, but now defy its power;
When as a flood the foe comes in,
My soul is more than conqueror;
I tread him down with holy scorn,
And bless the day that I was born.

4 Come, Lord, and make me pure within,
And let me now be filled with God!
Live to declare I'm saved from sin;
And if I seal the truth with blood,
My soul, from out the body torn,
Shall bless the day that I was born!

—*Charles Wesley.*

STELLA. 6-8s. FROM "CROWN OF JESUS."

TUNE: STELLA. 6-8s.

797

Prayer for children.

1 Come, Father, Son, and Holy Ghost,
To whom we for our children cry;
The good desired and wanted most,
Out of thy richest grace supply;
The sacred discipline be given,
To train and bring them up for heaven.

2 Unite the pair so long disjoined,
Knowledge and vital Piety;
Learning and Holiness combined,
And Truth and Love, let all men see
In those whom up to thee we give,
Thine, wholly thine, to die and live.

3 Father, accept them through thy Son,
And ever by thy Spirit guide!
Thy wisdom in their lives be shown,
Thy name confessed and glorified;
Thy power and love diffused abroad,
Till all the earth is filled with God.

—*Charles Wesley.*

798

Dedication of children to Christ.

1 Captain of our salvation, take
The souls we here present to thee,
And fit for thy great service make
These heirs of immortality;
And let them in thy image rise,
And then transplant to Paradise.

2 Unspotted from the world and pure,
Preserve them for thy glorious cause,
Accustomed daily to endure
The welcome burden of thy cross;
Inured to toil and patient pain,
Till all thy perfect mind they gain.

3 Our sons henceforth be wholly thine,
And serve and love thee all their days;
Infuse the principle divine
In all who here expect thy grace;
Let each improve the grace bestowed;
Rise every child a man of God!

4 Train up thy hardy soldiers, Lord,
In all their Captain's steps to tread;
Or send them to proclaim the word,
Thy gospel through the world to spread,
Freely as they receive to give,
And preach the death by which we live.

—*Charles Wesley.*

ST. PETER. C. M. A. R. Reinagle.

799

Prayer for parents.

1 God only wise, almighty, good,
Send forth thy truth and light,
To point us out the narrow road,
And guide our steps aright:

2 To steer our dangerous course between
The rocks on either hand;
And fix us in the golden mean,
And bring our charge to land.

3 Made apt, by thy sufficient grace,
To teach as taught by thee,
We come to train in all thy ways
Our rising progeny.

4 We would persuade their hearts to obey,
With mildest zeal proceed;
And never take the harsher way,
When love will do the deed.

5 For this we ask, in faith sincere,
The wisdom from above,
To touch their hearts with filial fear
And pure, ingenuous love:

6 To watch their will, to sense inclined;
Withhold the hurtful food;
And gently bend their tender mind,
And draw their souls to God.

—*Charles Wesley.*

ST. STEPHEN. C. M. REV. W. JONES.

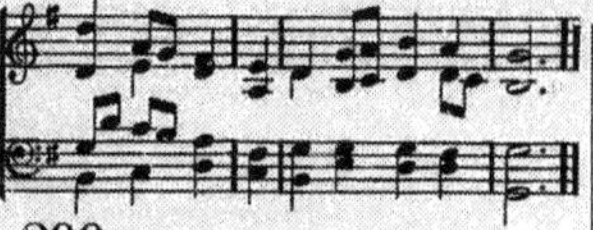

800 *Parental responsibility.*

1 FATHER of Lights! thy needful aid
To us that ask impart;
Mis rustful of ourselves, afraid
Of our own treacherous heart.

2 O'erwhelmed with justest fear, again
To thee for help we call;
Where many mightier have been slain,
By thee unsaved, we fall.

3 Our only help in danger's hour,
Our only strength, thou art;
Above the world, and Satan's power,
And greater than our heart.

4 Us from ourselves thou canst secure,
In nature's slippery ways;
And make our feeble footsteps sure
By thy sufficient grace.

5 If on thy promised grace alone
We faithfully depend,
Thou surely wilt preserve thy own,
And keep them to the end:

6 Wilt keep us tenderly discreet
To guard what thou hast given;
And bring our child with us to meet
At thy right hand in heaven.

—*Charles Wesley.*

COMPANION. P. M. 6.6.9, 6.6.9.

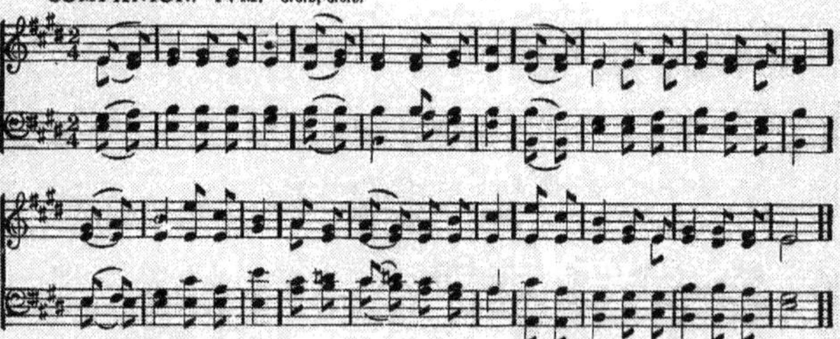

801 *Gratitude for life's mercies.*

1 AWAY with our fears!
The glad morning appears,
When an heir of salvation was born!
From Jehovah I came,
For his glory I am,
And to him I with singing return.

2 Thee, Jesus, alone,
The fountain I own,
Of my life and felicity here;
And cheerfully sing,
My Redeemer and King,
Till his sign in the heavens appear.

3 With thanks I rejoice
In thy fatherly choice
Of my state and condition below;
If of parents I came
Who honoured thy name,
'Twas thy wisdom appointed it so.

4 I sing of thy grace,
From my earliest days
Ever near to allure and defend;
Hitherto thou hast been
My preserver from sin,
And I trust thou wilt save to the end.

—*Charles Wesley.*

TUNE: COMPANION. P. M. 6.6.9, 6.6.9. (See Hymn 801.)

802

SECOND PART.

1 O the infinite cares,
And temptations, and snares,
Thy hand hath conducted me through!
O the blessings bestowed
By a bountiful God,
And the mercies eternally new.

2 What a mercy is this,
What a heaven of bliss,
How unspeakably happy am I!
Gathered into the fold,
With thy people enrolled,
With thy people to live and to die!

3 O the goodness of God
In employing a clod
His tribute of glory to raise!
His standard to bear,
And with triumph declare
His unspeakable riches of grace.

4 O the fathomless love,
That has deigned to approve
And prosper the work of my hands!
With my pastoral crook
I went over the brook,
And, behold, I am spread into bands!

5 Who, I ask in amaze,
Hath begotten me these?
And inquire, from what quarter they came?
My full heart it replies,
They are born from the skies,
And gives glory to God and the Lamb.

—Charles Wesley.

DUNDAS. 6.6.9, 6.6.9.

803

THIRD PART.

1 All honour and praise
To the Father of grace,
To the Spirit, and Son, I return!
The business pursue
He hath made me to do,
‖: And rejoice that I ever was born. :‖

2 In a rapture of joy
My life I employ,
The God of my life to proclaim;
'Tis worth living for this,
To administer bliss
‖: And salvation in Jesus's name. :‖

3 My remnant of days
I spend in his praise,
Who died the whole world to redeem;
Be they many or few,
My days are his due,
‖: And they all are devoted to him. :‖

—Charles Wesley.

HURSLEY. L. M. (First Tune). HUGUENOT MELODY.

804 *The Saviour's abiding presence.*

mf 1 Sun of my soul, thou Saviour dear,
It is not night if thou be near;
cres. O may no earth-born cloud arise,
To hide thee from thy servant's eyes!

p 2 When the soft dews of kindly sleep
My wearied eyelids gently steep,
Be my last thought, how sweet to rest
Forever on my Saviour's breast!

mf 3 Abide with me from morn till eve,
For without thee I cannot live;
cres. Abide with me when night is nigh,
dim. For without thee I dare not die.

mp 4 If some poor wandering child of thine
Have spurned to-day the voice divine,
cres. Now, Lord, the gracious work begin;
Let him no more lie down in sin.

mf 5 Watch by the sick; enrich the poor
With blessings from thy boundless store;
dim. Be every mourner's sleep to-night,
pp Like infants' slumbers, pure and light.

mf 6 Come near and bless us when we wake,
Ere through the world our way we take;
cres. Till, in the ocean of thy love,
f We lose ourselves in heaven above.

—*J. Keble.*

ABENDS. L. M. (Second Tune.) SIR H. S. OAKLEY.

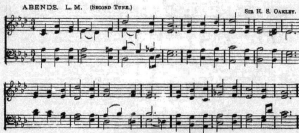

EDEN. L. M. — DR. L. MASON.

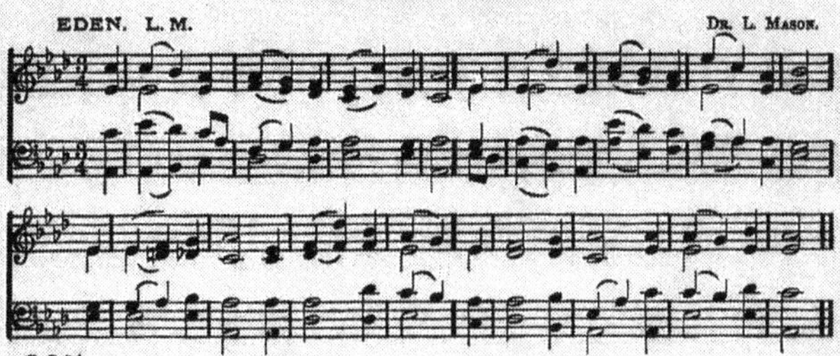

805 *Divine care and protection acknowledged.*

1 How do thy mercies close me round!
Forever be thy name adored;
I blush in all things to abound;
The servant is above his Lord.

2 Inured to poverty and pain,
A suffering life my Master led;
The Son of God, the Son of Man,
He had not where to lay his head.

3 But lo! a place he hath prepared
For me, whom watchful angels keep;
Yea, he himself becomes my guard;
He smooths my bed, and gives me sleep.

4 Jesus protects; my fears, be gone;
What can the Rock of ages move?
Safe in thy arms I lay me down,
Thine everlasting arms of love.

5 While thou art intimately nigh,
Who, who shall violate my rest?
Sin, earth, and hell I now defy;
I lean upon my Saviour's breast.

6 I rest beneath the Almighty's shade;
My griefs expire, my troubles cease;
Thou, Lord, on whom my soul is stayed,
Wilt keep me still in perfect peace.
—*Charles Wesley.*

ERNAN. L. M. — DR. L. MASON.

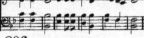

806 *Gratitude for daily mercies.*

1 New every morning is the love
Our wakening and uprising prove;
Through sleep and darkness safely brought,
Restored to life, and power, and thought.

2 New mercies each returning day
Hover around us while we pray;
New perils past, new sins forgiven,
New thoughts of God, new hopes of heaven.

3 If on our daily course our mind
Be set to hallow all we find,
New treasures still of countless price
God will provide for sacrifice.

4 Old friends, old scenes, will lovelier be,
As more of heaven in each we see;
Some softening gleam of love and prayer
Shall dawn on every cross and care.

5 The trivial round, the common task,
Will furnish all we ought to ask;
Room to deny ourselves; a road
To bring us, daily, nearer God.

6 Only, O Lord, in thy great love
Fit us for perfect rest above;
And help us, this and every day,
To live more nearly as we pray.
—*John Keble.*

MORNING HYMN. L. M. — F. H. BARTHELEMON.

807

A morning hymn.

1 AWAKE, my soul, and with the sun
Thy daily stage of duty run;
Shake off dull sloth, and early rise,
To pay thy morning sacrifice.

2 Redeem thy mis-spent moments past,
And live this day as if thy last;
Thy talents to improve take care;
For the great day thyself prepare.

3 Let all thy converse be sincere,
Thy conscience as the noon-day clear;
For God's all-seeing eye surveys
Thy secret thoughts, thy words, and ways.

4 Wake, and lift up thyself, my heart,
And with the angels take thy part;
Who all night long unwearied sing
High glory to the eternal King.

5 Praise God, from whom all blessings flow;
Praise him, all creatures here below;
Praise him above, ye heavenly host;
Praise Father, Son, and Holy Ghost.

—*Bishop Ken.*

EVENING HYMN. L. M. — THOMAS TALLIS.

808

An evening hymn.

mf 1 GLORY to thee, my God, this night,
For all the blessings of the light;
dim. Keep me, O keep me, King of kings,
p Beneath thine own almighty wings!

mf 2 Forgive me, Lord, for thy dear Son,
The ills that I this day have done;
dim. That, with the world, myself, and thee,
p I, ere I sleep, at peace may be.

mf 3 Teach me to live, that I may dread
The grave as little as my bed;
cres. Teach me to die, that so I may
f Rise glorious at the awful day.

pp 4 O let my soul on thee repose!
And may sweet sleep mine eyelids close;
cres. Sleep that shall me more vigorous make,
f To serve my God when I awake.

p 5 If in the night I sleepless lie,
cres. My soul with heavenly thoughts supply;
f Let no ill dreams disturb my rest,
No powers of darkness me molest.

mf 6 Lord, let my soul forever share
The bliss of thy paternal care;
cres. 'Tis heaven on earth, 'tis heaven above,
f To see thy face, and sing thy love.

—*Bishop Ken.*

BLOOR. L. M.
T. C. Jeffers.
RETREAT. L. M.
Thomas Hastings.

809 *Morning and evening mercies.*

mf 1 My God, how endless is thy love!
Thy gifts are every evening new;
And morning mercies from above,
dim. Gently distil like early dew.

mp 2 Thou spread'st the curtains of the night,
Great Guardian of my sleeping hours;
cres. Thy sovereign word restores the light,
And quickens all my drowsy powers.

f 3 I yield my powers to thy command;
To thee I consecrate my days;
Perpetual blessings from thy hand
dim. Demand perpetual songs of praise.

—*Isaac Watts.*

810 *Prayer for parental wisdom and grace.*

1 Father of all, by whom we are,
For whom was made whatever is;
Who hast entrusted to our care
A candidate for glorious bliss:

2 Poor worms of earth, for help we cry,
For grace to guide what grace has given;
We ask for wisdom from on high,
To train our infant up for heaven.

3 Him let us tend, severely kind,
As guardians of his giddy youth;
As set to form his tender mind,
By principles of heavenly truth:

4 To fit his soul for heavenly grace,
Discharge the Christian parents' part,
And keep him, till thy love takes place,
And Jesus rises in his heart.

—*Charles Wesley.*

811 *Family worship.*

1 Father of all, thy care we bless,
Which crowns our families with peace;
From thee they spring, and by thy hand
They are, and shall be still, sustained.

2 To God, most worthy to be praised,
Be our domestic altars raised;
Who, Lord of heaven, yet deigns to come,
And sanctify our humblest home.

3 To thee may each united house,
Morning and night present its vows;
Our servants there, and rising race,
Be taught thy precepts and thy grace.

4 So may each future age proclaim
The honours of thy glorious name;
And each succeeding race remove
To join the family above.

—*Doddridge.*

ST. ANATOLIUS. 7.6, 7.6, 8.8. A. H. Brown.

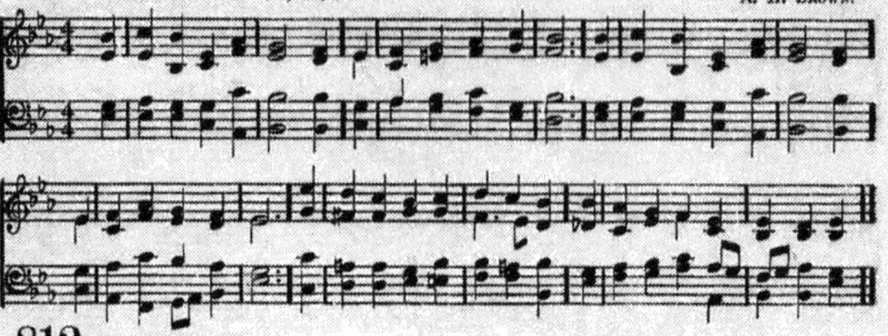

812

Protection in the darkness.

1 The day is past and over;
All thanks, O Lord, to thee!
We pray thee now that sinless
The hours of dark may be;
O Jesus, keep us in thy sight,
And save us through the coming night!

2 The joys of day are over;
We lift our hearts to thee,
And ask thee that offenceless
The hours of dark may be;
O Jesus, make their darkness light,
And save us through the coming night!

3 The toils of day are over;
We raise our hymn to thee,
And ask that free from peril
The hours of dark may be;
O Jesus, keep us in thy sight,
And guard us through the coming night!

4 Be thou our soul's preserver,
For thou, O God, dost know,
How many are the perils
Awaiting us below;
O loving Jesus, hear our call,
And guard and save us from them all!

—Dr. Neale, from Anatolius.

STEGGALL. 6.6, 6.6, 8.8. Dr. Steggall.

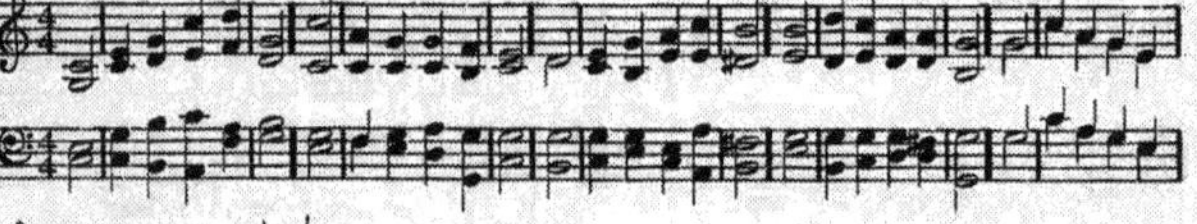

813

A birthday hymn.

1 God of my life, to thee
My cheerful soul I raise!
Thy goodness bade me be,
And still prolongs my days;
I see my natal hour return,
And bless the day that I was born.

2 A clod of living earth,
I glorify thy name,
From whom alone my birth,
And all my blessings came;
Creating and preserving grace,
Let all that is within me praise.

3 Long as I live beneath,
To thee O let me live!
To thee my every breath
In thanks and praises give!
Whate'er I have, whate'er I am,
Shall magnify my Maker's name.

4 My soul and all its powers,
Thine, wholly thine, shall be;
All, all my happy hours
I consecrate to thee;
Me to thine image now restore,
And I shall praise thee evermore.

5 Then, when the work is done,
The work of faith with power,
Receive thy favoured son,
In death's triumphant hour;
Like Moses to thyself convey,
And kiss my raptured soul away.

—Charles Wesley.

Brown.

g night!

n all!
Anatolius.

TEGGALI.

Wesley.

LANCASHIRE. 7.6, 7.6, 7.6, 7.6. HENRY SMART.

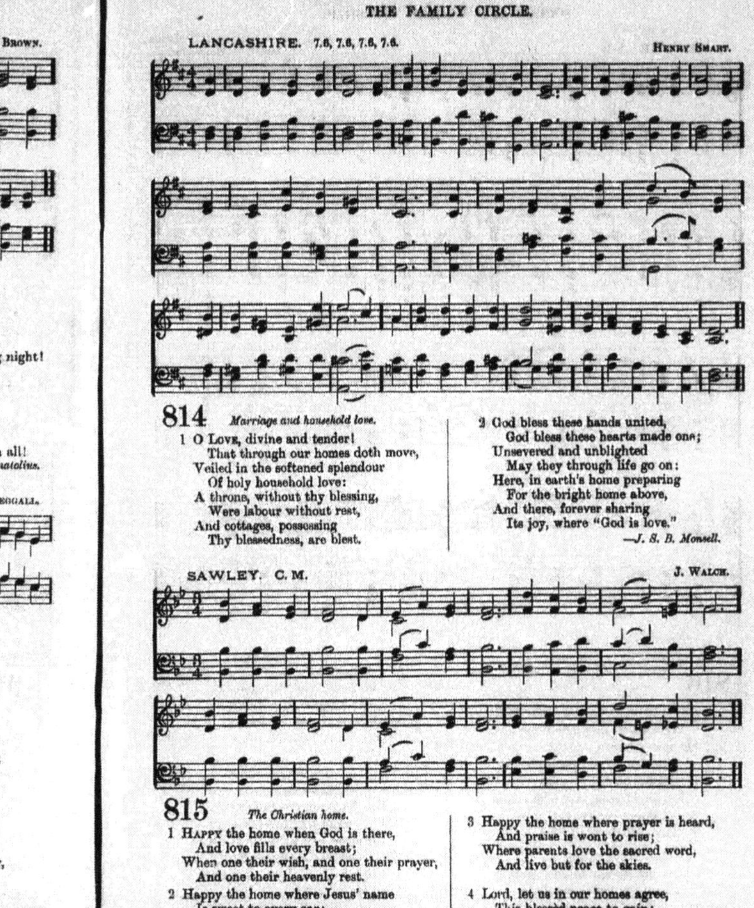

814 *Marriage and household love.*

1 O Love, divine and tender!
That through our homes doth move,
Veiled in the softened splendour
Of holy household love:
A throne, without thy blessing,
Were labour without rest,
And cottages, possessing
Thy blessedness, are blest.

2 God bless these hands united,
God bless these hearts made one;
Unsevered and unblighted
May they through life go on:
Here, in earth's home preparing
For the bright home above,
And there, forever sharing
Its joy, where "God is love."

—*J. S. B. Monsell.*

SAWLEY. C. M. J. WALCH.

815 *The Christian home.*

1 Happy the home when God is there,
And love fills every breast;
When one their wish, and one their prayer,
And one their heavenly rest.

2 Happy the home where Jesus' name
Is sweet to every ear;
Where children early lisp his fame,
And parents hold him dear.

3 Happy the home where prayer is heard,
And praise is wont to rise;
Where parents love the sacred word,
And live but for the skies.

4 Lord, let us in our homes agree,
This blessed peace to gain;
Unite our hearts in love to thee,
And love to all will reign.

REFUGE. 8-7s. JOSEPH P. HOLBROOK.

816

"Peace be to this house."

1 PEACE be on this house bestowed,
Peace on all that here reside!
Let the unknown peace of God
With the man of peace abide.
Let the Spirit now come down;
Let the blessing now take place!
Son of Peace, receive thy crown,
Fulness of the gospel grace.

2 Christ, my Master and my Lord,
Let me thy forerunner be;
O be mindful of thy word;
Visit them, and visit me!
To this house, and all herein,
Now let thy salvation come!
Save our souls from every sin,
Make us thy eternal home.

3 Let us never, never rest,
Till the promise is fulfilled;
Till we are of thee possessed,
Pardoned, sanctified, and sealed;
Till we all, in love renewed,
Find the pearl that Adam lost,
Temples of the living God,
Father, Son, and Holy Ghost!

—*Charles Wesley.*

EVENING PRAYER. 8.7, 8.7. Geo. C. Stebbins.

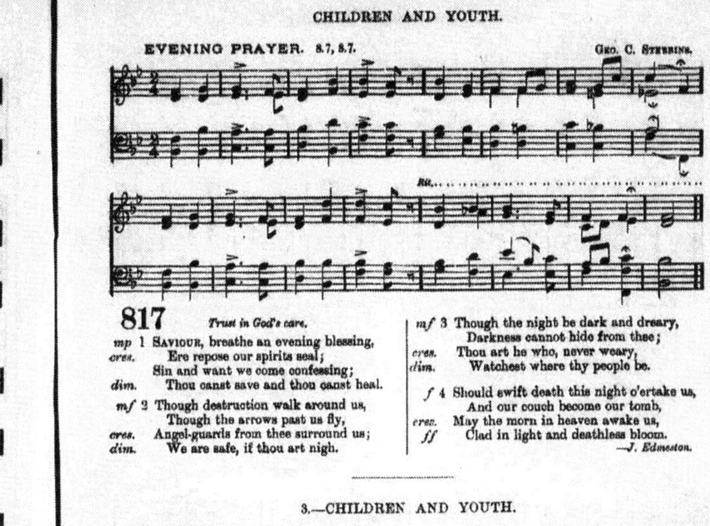
Rit.

817 *Trust in God's care.*

mp 1 Saviour, breathe an evening blessing,
cres. Ere repose our spirits seal;
Sin and want we come confessing;
dim. Thou canst save and thou canst heal.

mf 2 Though destruction walk around us,
Though the arrows past us fly,
cres. Angel-guards from thee surround us;
dim. We are safe, if thou art nigh.

mf 3 Though the night be dark and dreary,
Darkness cannot hide from thee;
cres. Thou art he who, never weary,
dim. Watchest where thy people be.

f 4 Should swift death this night o'ertake us,
And our couch become our tomb,
cres. May the morn in heaven awake us,
ff Clad in light and deathless bloom.

—*J. Edmeston.*

3.—CHILDREN AND YOUTH.

ORTONVILLE. C. M. Dr. Hastings.

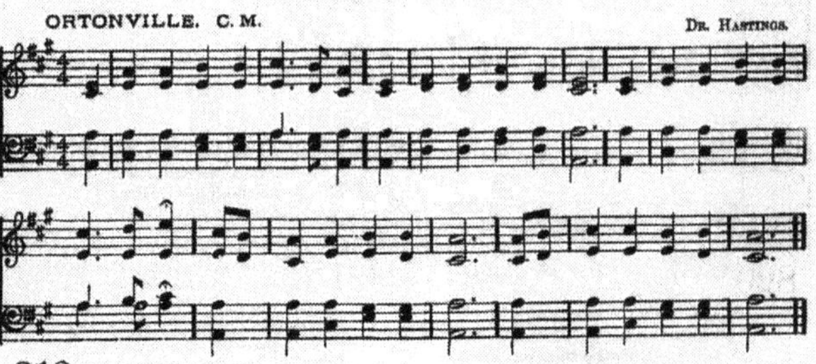

818 *Children praising Christ.*

1 Come, Christian children, come, and raise
Your voice with one accord;
Come, sing in joyful songs of praise
||:The glories of your Lord.:||

2 Sing of the wonders of his love,
And loudest praises give
To him who left his throne above,
||:And died that you might live.:||

3 Sing of the wonders of his truth,
And read in every page
The promise made to earliest youth
||:Fulfilled to latest age.:||

4 Sing of the wonders of his power,
Who with his own right arm
Upholds and keeps you hour by hour,
||:And shields from every harm.:||

SILOAM. C. M. WOODBURY.

819

The Christian child.

1 By cool Siloam's shady rill
How sweet the lily grows!
How sweet the breath, beneath the hill,
Of Sharon's dewy rose!

2 Lo! such the child whose early feet
The paths of peace have trod;
Whose secret heart, with influence sweet,
Is upward drawn to God.

3 O thou, whose infant feet were found
Within thy Father's shrine,
Whose years, with changeless virtue crowned,
Were all alike divine;

4 Dependent on thy bounteous breath,
We seek thy grace alone,
In childhood, manhood, age, and death,
To keep us still thine own.

—Bishop Heber.

MARLOW. C. M. TUCKER.

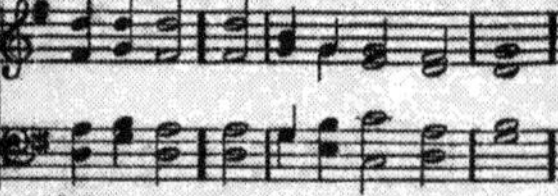

820

The children's jubilee.

1 Hosanna! be the children's song,
To Christ, the children's King;
His praise, to whom our souls belong,
Let all the children sing.

2 Hosanna! sound from hill to hill,
And spread from plain to plain,
While louder, sweeter, clearer still,
Woods echo to the strain.

3 Hosanna! on the wings of light,
O'er earth and ocean fly,
Till morn to eve, and noon to night,
And heaven to earth, reply.

4 Hosanna! then, our song shall be;
Hosanna to our King!
This is the children's jubilee;
Let all the children sing.

—Montgomery.

821

"He shall cover thee with his feathers, and under his wings shalt thou trust."

1 The morning bright with rosy light
Has waked me from my sleep;
Father, I own thy love alone
Thy little one doth keep.

2 All through the day, I humbly pray,
Be thou my guard and guide;
My sins forgive and let me live,
Lord Jesus, near thy side.

3 O make thy rest within my breast,
Great Spirit of all grace!
Make me like thee, then shall I be
Prepared to see thy face.

INNOCENTS. 4-7s. ARRANGED BY W. H. MONK.

822 *"From a child thou hast known the Holy Scriptures, which are able to make thee wise unto salvation."*

1 HOLY Bible, book divine,
Precious treasure, thou art mine;
Mine, to tell me whence I came,
Mine, to teach me what I am;

2 Mine, to chide me when I rove,
Mine, to show a Saviour's love;
Mine art thou, to guide my feet,
Mine, to judge, condemn, acquit;

3 Mine, to comfort in distress,
If the Holy Spirit bless;
Mine, to show by living faith
Man can triumph over death;

4 Mine, to tell of joys to come,
And the rebel sinner's doom;
Holy Bible, book divine,
Precious treasure, thou art mine!

—*J. Burton, sen.*

LYRA INNOCENTIS. 4-7s. KILLICK.

823 *"They brought young children to him."*

1 GENTLE Jesus, meek and mild,
Look upon a little child;
Pity my simplicity;
Suffer me to come to thee.

2 Fain I would to thee be brought;
Gracious Lord, forbid it not;
Give a little child a place
In the kingdom of thy grace.

3 Lamb of God, I look to thee,
Thou shalt my example be;
Thou art gentle, meek, and mild,
Thou wast once a little child.

4 Fain I would be as thou art,
Give me thy obedient heart;
Thou art pitiful and kind,
Let me have thy loving mind.

5 Let me, above all, fulfil
God my heavenly Father's will;
Never his good Spirit grieve,
Only to his glory live.

6 Loving Jesus, gentle Lamb,
In thy gracious hands I am;
Make me, Saviour, what thou art,
Like thyself within my heart.

—*Charles Wesley.*

PRAYER. 4-7s. A. ABBOTT.

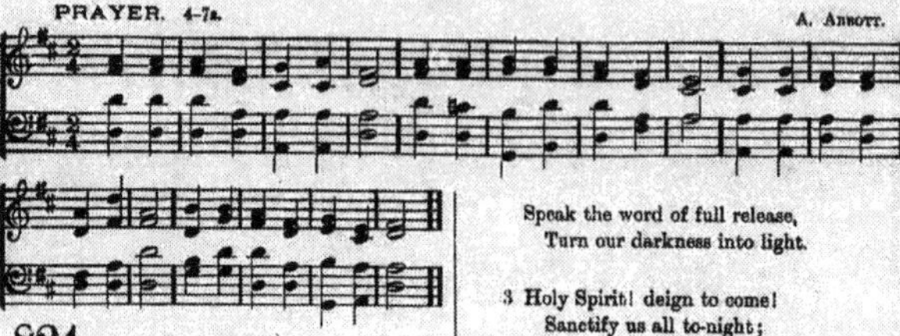

824 *Divine guardianship implored.*

1 GOD the Father! be thou near,
Save from every harm to-night,
Make us all thy children dear,
In the darkness be our light.

2 God the Saviour! be our peace,
Put away your sins to-night;
Speak the word of full release,
Turn our darkness into light.

3 Holy Spirit! deign to come!
Sanctify us all to-night;
In our hearts prepare thy home,
Turn our darkness into light.

4 Holy Trinity! be nigh!
Mystery of love adored,
Help to live, and help to die,
Lighten all our darkness, Lord.

—*G. Rawson.*

GOUNOD. 8.7, 8.7, 7.7. C. GOUNOD.

825 *Evening family worship.*

1 THROUGH the day thy love hath spared us;
Wearied we lie down to rest;
Through the silent watches guard us,
Let no foe our peace molest;
Jesus, thou our guardian be,
Sweet it is to trust in thee.

2 Pilgrims here on earth and strangers,
Dwelling in the midst of foes,
Us and ours preserve from dangers,
In thine arms may we repose;
And when life's short day is past,
Rest with thee in heaven at last.

—*T. Kelly.*

PILOT. 6-7s. J. E. Gould.

826

The guiding Star.

1 As with gladness men of old
Did the guiding star behold;
As with joy they hailed its light,
Leading onward, beaming bright;
So, most gracious Lord, may we
Ever more be led to thee.

2 As with joyful steps they sped
To that lowly manger-bed;
There to bend the knee before
Him whom heaven and earth adore;
So may we, with willing feet,
Ever seek thy mercy-seat.

3 As they offered gifts most rare,
At that manger rude and bare;
So may we with holy joy,
Pure and free from sin's alloy,
All our costliest treasures bring,
Christ, to thee our heavenly King!

4 Holy Jesus! every day
Keep us in the narrow way;
And, when earthly things are past,
Bring our ransomed souls at last
Where they need no star to guide,
Where no clouds thy glory hide.

—*W. C. Dix.*

ROCKINGHAM. L. M. Dr. Miller.

827

God our Father and Friend.

1 Great God, and wilt thou condescend
To be my Father and my Friend?
I a poor child, and thou so high,
The Lord of earth, and air, and sky?

2 Art thou my Father? canst thou bear
To hear my poor, imperfect prayer?
Or wilt thou listen to the praise
That such a little one can raise?

3 Art thou my Father? let me be
A meek, obedient child to thee;
And try in word, and deed, and thought,
To serve and praise thee as I ought.

4 Art thou my Father? then at last,
When all my days on earth are past,
Send down and take me in thy love
To be thy better child above.

—*Jane Taylor.*

AURELIA. 7.6, 7.6, 7.6, 7.6.
DR. S. S. WESLEY.
SAFETY. 7.6, 7.6, 7.6, 7.6.
W. H. DOANE.
CHORUS. Safe in the arms of Je - sus, Safe on his gentle breast, There by his love o'er-
shad - ed, Sweet - ly my soul shall rest.
Fine.

828 *The Lord's love to children.*

1 WHEN, his salvation bringing,
To Zion Jesus came,
The children all stood singing
Hosanna to his name;
Nor did their zeal offend him,
But as he rode along,
He let them still attend him,
And smiled to hear their song.

2 And since the Lord retaineth
His love to children still,
Though now as King he reigneth
On Zion's heavenly hill,
We'll flock around his standard,
We'll bow before his throne,
And cry aloud, "Hosanna
To David's royal Son."

3 For should we fail proclaiming
Our great Redeemer's praise,
The stones, our silence shaming,
Would their hosannas raise.
But shall we only render
The tribute of our words?
No; while our hearts are tender,
They too shall be the Lord's.

—*J. King.*

WESLEY.
King.
DOANE.
ove o'er-

SAFETY. *(Continued.)*

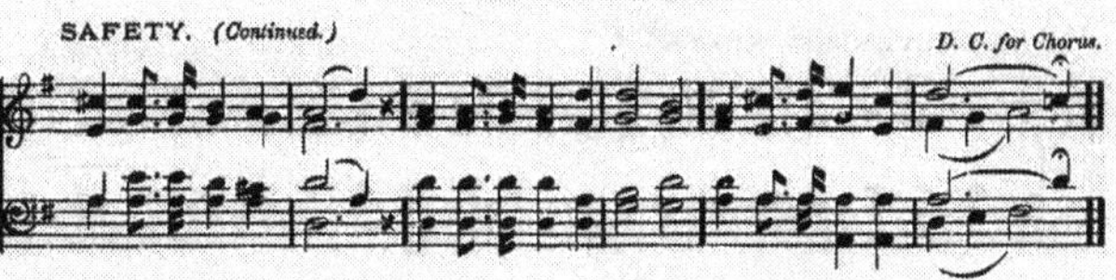

D. C. for Chorus.

829 *"He shall gather the lambs with his arm, and carry them in his bosom."*

1 SAFE in the arms of Jesus,
Safe on his gentle breast,
There by his love o'ershaded,
Sweetly my soul shall rest.
Hark! 'tis the voice of angels,
Borne in a song to me,
Over the fields of glory,
Over the jasper sea.—CHO.

2 Safe in the arms of Jesus,
Safe from corroding care,
Safe from the world's temptations,
Sin cannot harm me there.
Free from the blight of sorrow,
Free from my doubts and fears;
Only a few more trials,
Only a few more tears!—CHO.

3 Jesus, my heart's dear refuge,
Jesus has died for me;
Firm on the Rock of ages,
Ever my trust shall be.
Here let me wait with patience,
Wait till the night is o'er;
Wait till I see the morning
Break on the golden shore.—CHO.

—*Mrs. Van Alstyne.*

ST. ALPHEGE. 7.6, 7.6, 7.6, 7.6. DR. GAUNTLETT.

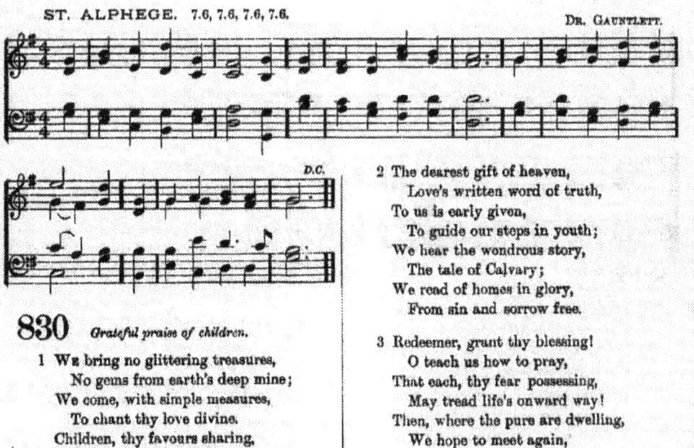

D.C.

830 *Grateful praise of children.*

1 WE bring no glittering treasures,
No gems from earth's deep mine;
We come, with simple measures,
To chant thy love divine.
Children, thy favours sharing,
Their voice of thanks would raise;
Father, accept our offering,
Our song of grateful praise.

2 The dearest gift of heaven,
Love's written word of truth,
To us is early given,
To guide our steps in youth;
We hear the wondrous story,
The tale of Calvary;
We read of homes in glory,
From sin and sorrow free.

3 Redeemer, grant thy blessing!
O teach us how to pray,
That each, thy fear possessing,
May tread life's onward way!
Then, where the pure are dwelling,
We hope to meet again,
And, sweeter numbers swelling,
Forever praise thy name.

—*Harriet Phillips.*

ST. SYLVESTER. 8.7, 8.7. REV. J. B. DYKES.

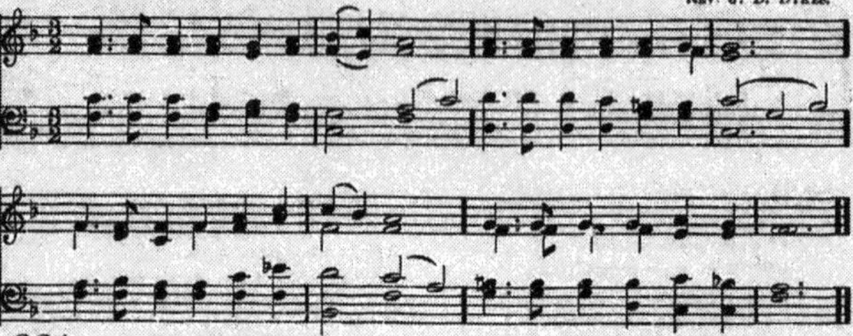

831

Child's evening prayer.

1 JESUS, tender Shepherd, hear me,
Bless thy little lamb to-night;
Through the darkness be thou near me,
Keep me safe till morning light.

2 Through this day thy hand has led me,
And I thank thee for thy care;
Thou hast warmed me, clothed, and fed me,
Listen to my evening prayer.

3 Let my sins be all forgiven,
Bless the friends I love so well;
Take me, when I die, to heaven,
Happy there with thee to dwell.

—*M. L. Duncan.*

ST. OSWALD. 8.7, 8.7. DR. DYKES.

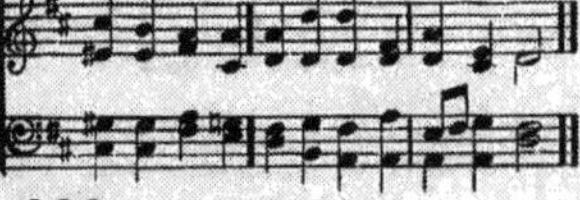

832

Youthful consecration.

1 SAVIOUR, while my heart is tender,
I would yield that heart to thee;
All my powers to thee surrender,
Thine, and only thine, to be.

2 Take me now, Lord Jesus, take me,
Let my youthful heart be thine;
Thy devoted servant make me,
Fill my soul with love divine.

3 Send me, Lord, where thou wilt send me,
Only do thou guide my way;
May thy grace through life attend me,
Gladly then shall I obey.

4 Let me do thy will or bear it,
I will know no will but thine;
Should'st thou take my life, or spare it,
I that life to thee resign.

5 May this solemn dedication
Never once forgotten lie;
Let it know no revocation,
Published and confirmed on high.

6 Thine I am, O Lord, forever,
To thy service set apart;
Suffer me to leave thee never;
Seal thine image on my heart.

—*J. Burton.*

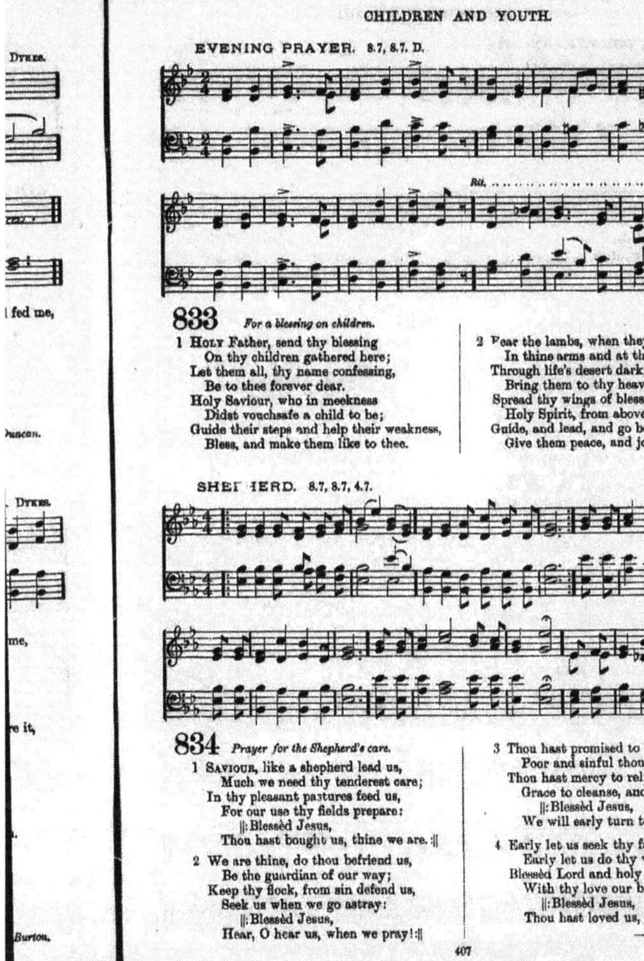

EVENING PRAYER. 8.7, 8.7. D. Geo. C. Stebbins.

Rit. D.C.

833 *For a blessing on children.*

1 Holy Father, send thy blessing
  On thy children gathered here;
Let them all, thy name confessing,
  Be to thee forever dear.
Holy Saviour, who in meekness
  Didst vouchsafe a child to be;
Guide their steps and help their weakness,
  Bless, and make them like to thee.

2 Bear the lambs, when they are weary,
  In thine arms and at thy breast;
Through life's desert dark and dreary
  Bring them to thy heavenly rest.
Spread thy wings of blessing o'er them,
  Holy Spirit, from above;
Guide, and lead, and go before them,
  Give them peace, and joy, and love.

SHEPHERD. 8.7, 8.7, 4.7. W. B. Bradbury.

834 *Prayer for the Shepherd's care.*

1 Saviour, like a shepherd lead us,
  Much we need thy tenderest care;
In thy pleasant pastures feed us,
  For our use thy fields prepare:
    ||: Blessèd Jesus,
  Thou hast bought us, thine we are. :||

2 We are thine, do thou befriend us,
  Be the guardian of our way;
Keep thy flock, from sin defend us,
  Seek us when we go astray:
    ||: Blessèd Jesus,
  Hear, O hear us, when we pray! :||

3 Thou hast promised to receive us,
  Poor and sinful though we be;
Thou hast mercy to relieve us,
  Grace to cleanse, and power to free:
    ||: Blessèd Jesus,
  We will early turn to thee. :||

4 Early let us seek thy favour,
  Early let us do thy will;
Blessèd Lord and holy Saviour,
  With thy love our bosoms fill:
    ||: Blessèd Jesus,
  Thou hast loved us, love us still. :||

—*Dorothy A. Thrupp.*

REGENT SQUARE. 8.7.8.7.4.7. HENRY SMART.

835
Early piety.

1 God has said, "Forever blessèd
Those who seek me in their youth;
They shall find the path of wisdom,
And the narrow way of truth;"
‖:Guide us, Saviour,:‖
In the narrow way of truth.

2 Be our strength, for we are weakness;
Be our wisdom and our guide;
May we walk in love and meekness,
Nearer to our Saviour's side;
‖:Naught can harm us,:‖
While we thus in thee abide.

3 Thus, when evening shades shall gather,
We may turn our tearless eye
To the dwelling of our Father,
To our home beyond the sky;
‖:Gently passing:‖
To the happy land on high.

836
Children's hymn.

1 Children, loud hosannas singing,
Hymned thy praise in olden time,
Judah's ancient temple filling
With the melody sublime;
‖:Infant voices:‖
Joined to swell the holy chime.

2 Though no more the incarnate Saviour
We behold in latter days;
Though a temple far less glorious
Echoes now the songs we raise;
‖:Still in glory:‖
Thou wilt hear our notes of praise.

3 Loud we'll swell the pealing anthem,
All thy wondrous acts proclaim,
Till all heaven and earth resounding,
Echo with thy glorious name;
‖:Hallelujah,:‖
Hallelujah to the Lamb!

—*Mrs. Steele.*

VOICE OF PRAISE. 7.7.7.5, 7.7.7.5. REV. J. BLACK.

TUNE: VOICE OF PRAISE. 7.7.7.5, 7.7.7.5.

837 *Sunday-school anniversary.*

1 Wilt thou hear the voice of praise
Which the little children raise,
Thou who art, from endless days,
Glorious God of all!
While the circling year has sped,
Thou hast heavenly blessings shed,
Like the dew, upon each head;
Still on thee we call.

2 Still thy constant care bestow;
Let us each in wisdom grow,
And in favour while below,
With the God above.
In our hearts the Spirit mild,
Which adorned the Saviour-child,
Gently soothe each impulse wild
To the sway of love.

3 Thine example, kept in view,
Jesus, help us to pursue;
Lead us all our journey through
By thy guiding hand;
And when life on earth is o'er,
Where the blest dwell evermore,
May we praise thee and adore,
An unbroken band.

—*Mrs. C. L. Rice.*

THE CHILD'S DESIRE. 11.8, 12.9.

838 *Christ blessing little children.*

1 I think, when I read that sweet story of old,
When Jesus was here among men,
How he called little children as lambs to his fold,
I should like to have been with him then.

2 I wish that his hands had been placed on my head,
That his arms had been thrown around me,
That I might have seen his kind look when he said,
"Let the little ones come unto me."

3 Yet still to his footstool in prayer I may go,
And ask for a share in his love;
And if I thus earnestly seek him below,
I shall see him and hear him above:

4 In that beautiful place he has gone to prepare
For all who are washed and forgiven;
And many dear children are gathering there,
"For of such is the kingdom of heaven."

—*Mrs. J. Luke.*

CANADA. 6.6.4, 6.6.6.4. DR. L. MASON.

839

Shepherd of tender youth.

1 SHEPHERD of tender youth,
Guiding in love and truth
Through devious ways;
Christ, our triumphant King,
We come thy name to sing;
Hither our children bring
To shout thy praise.

2 Thou art our holy Lord,
The all-subduing Word,
Healer of strife;
Thou didst thyself abase,
That from sin's deep disgrace
Thou mightest save our race,
And give us life.

3 Thou art the great High Priest;
Thou hast prepared the feast
Of heavenly love;
While in our mortal pain
None calls on thee in vain;
Help thou dost not disdain,
Help from above.

4 Ever be thou our Guide,
Our Shepherd and our pride,
Our staff and song;
Jesus, thou Christ of God,
By thy perennial word
Lead us where thou hast trod,
Make our faith strong.

5 So now, and till we die,
Sound we thy praises high,
And joyful sing;
Infants, and the glad throng
Who to thy Church belong,
Unite to swell the song
To Christ our King.

—*Clement of Alexandria.*

SECTION X.

DEATH, JUDGMENT, AND THE FUTURE STATE.

DUNDEE. C. M. SCOTCH PSALTER.

TUNE: DUNDEE. C. M.

840

Psalm xc. 1-5.

1 O God! our help in ages past,
Our hope for years to come,
Our shelter from the stormy blast,
And our eternal home:

2 Under the shadow of thy throne,
Still may we dwell secure;
Sufficient is thine arm alone,
And our defence is sure.

3 Before the hills in order stood,
Or earth received her frame,
From everlasting thou art God,
To endless years the same.

4 A thousand ages in thy sight
Are like an evening gone,
Short as the watch that ends the night,
Before the rising sun.

5 The busy tribes of flesh and blood,
With all their cares and fears,
Are carried downward by the flood,
And lost in following years.

6 Time, like an ever-rolling stream,
Bears all its sons away;
They fly forgotten, as a dream
Dies at the opening day.

7 O God! our help in ages past,
Our hope for years to come,
Be thou our guard while life shall last,
And our perpetual home.

—*Isaac Watts.*

MARTYRDOM. C. M. Hugh Wilson.

841

Shortness and uncertainty of life.

1 Thee we adore, eternal Name!
And humbly own to thee,
How feeble is our mortal frame,
What dying worms we be!

2 Our wasting lives grow shorter still,
As days and months increase;
And every beating pulse we tell
Leaves but the number less.

3 The year rolls round, and steals away
The breath that first it gave;
Whate'er we do, where'er we be,
We're travelling to the grave.

4 Dangers stand thick through all the ground,
To push us to the tomb;
And fierce diseases wait around,
To hurry mortals home.

5 Infinite joy, or endless woe,
Attends on every breath;
And yet how unconcerned we go
Upon the brink of death!

6 Waken, O Lord, our drowsy sense,
To walk this dangerous road!
And if our souls be hurried hence,
May they be found with God.

—*Isaac Watts.*

IRISH. C. M. ARRANGED FROM ISAAC SMITH.

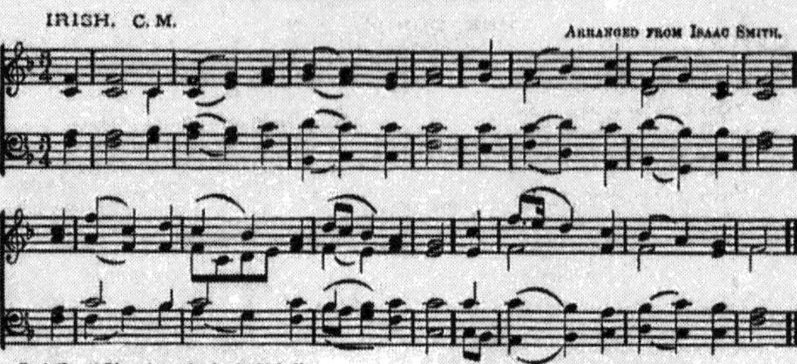

842

"Blessed are the dead which die in the Lord."

1 HEAR what the voice from heaven proclaims
For all the pious dead!
Sweet is the savour of their names,
And soft their dying bed.

2 They die in Jesus, and are blest;
How calm their slumbers are!
From sufferings and from woes released,
And freed from every snare:

3 Till that illustrious morning come,
When all thy saints shall rise,
And, decked in full immortal bloom,
Attend thee to the skies.

4 Their tongues, great Prince of Life, shall join
With their recovered breath,
And all the immortal host ascribe
Their victory to thy death.

—*Isaac Watts.*

BELMONT. C. M. WEBBE.

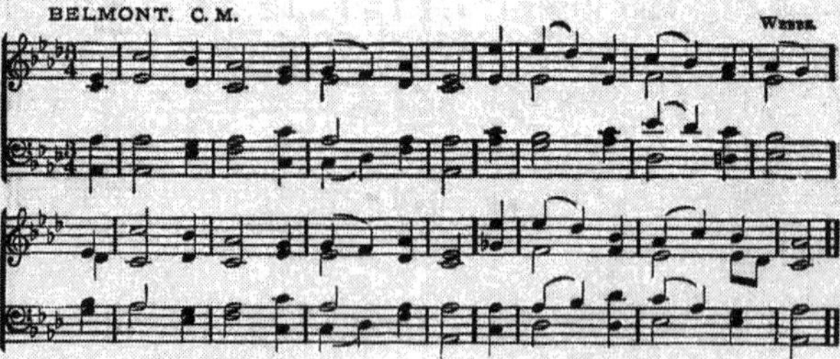

843

"That ye sorrow not, even as others that have no hope."

1 WHY do we mourn departing friends,
Or shake at death's alarms?
'Tis but the voice that Jesus sends,
To call them to his arms.

2 The graves of all his saints he blessed,
And softened every bed;
Where should the dying members rest
But with their dying Head?

3 Thence he arose, ascending high,
And showed our feet the way;
Up to the Lord our flesh shall fly,
At the great rising-day.

4 Then let the last loud trumpet sound,
And bid our kindred rise;
Awake, ye nations under ground;
Ye saints, ascend the skies.

—*Isaac Watts.*

SAWLEY. C. M. J. Walch.

844 *"The valley of the shadow of death."*

1 Earth, with its dark and dreadful ills,
Recedes and fades away;
Lift up your heads, ye heavenly hills,
Ye gates of death, give way!

2 My soul is full of whispered song;
My blindness is my sight;
The shadows that I feared so long
Are all alive with light.

3 The while my pulses faintly beat,
My faith doth so abound;
I feel grow firm beneath my feet
The green immortal ground.

4 That faith to me a courage gives,
Low as the grave to go;
I know that my Redeemer lives—
That I shall live, I know.

5 The palace walls I almost see
Where dwells my Lord and King;
O Grave! where is thy victory!
O Death! where is thy sting!

—*Alice Carey.*

HAMBURG. L. M. Dr. L. Mason.

Slowly.

845 *"We all do fade as a leaf."*

1 The morning flowers display their sweets,
And gay their silken leaves unfold,
As careless of the noontide heats,
As fearless of the evening cold.

2 Nipt by the wind's unkindly blast,
Parched by the sun's directer ray,
The momentary glories waste,
The short-lived beauties die away.

3 So blooms the human face divine,
When youth its pride of beauty shows;
Fairer than spring the colours shine,
And sweeter than the virgin rose.

4 Or worn by slowly rolling years,
Or broke by sickness in a day,
The fading glory disappears,
The short-lived beauties die away.

5 Yet these, new rising from the tomb,
With lustre brighter far shall shine;
Revive with ever-during bloom,
Safe from diseases and decline.

6 Let sickness blast, and death devour,
If heaven must recompense our pains;
Perish the grass, and fade the flower,
If firm the word of God remains.

—*S. Wesley, jun.*

GERMANY. L. M.

BEETHOVEN.

846 *"Mine age is as nothing before thee."*

1 Almighty Maker of my frame,
Teach me the measure of my days,
Teach me to know how frail I am,
And spend the remnant to thy praise.

2 My days are shorter than a span;
A little point my life appears;
How frail, at best, is dying man!
How vain are all his hopes and fears!

3 Vain his ambition, noise, and show;
Vain are the cares which rack his mind;
He heaps up treasures mixed with woe,
And dies, and leaves them all behind.

4 O be a nobler portion mine!
My God, I bow before thy throne;
Earth's fleeting treasures I resign,
And fix my hope on thee alone.

—Isaac Watts.

MONTGOMERY. L. M.

STANLEY.

847 *"Whom I shall see for myself, and mine eyes shall behold, and not another."*

1 I know that my Redeemer lives,
He lives, and on the earth shall stand;
And though to worms my flesh he gives,
My dust lies numbered in his hands.

2 In this re-animated clay
I surely shall behold him near;
Shall see him in the latter day
In all his majesty appear.

3 I feel what then shall raise me up,
The eternal Spirit lives in me;
This is my confidence of hope,
That God I face to face shall see.

4 Mine own and not another's eyes
The King shall in his beauty view;
I shall from him receive the prize,
The starry crown to victors due.

—Charles Wesley.

EUCHARIST. L. M. J. B. WOODBURY.

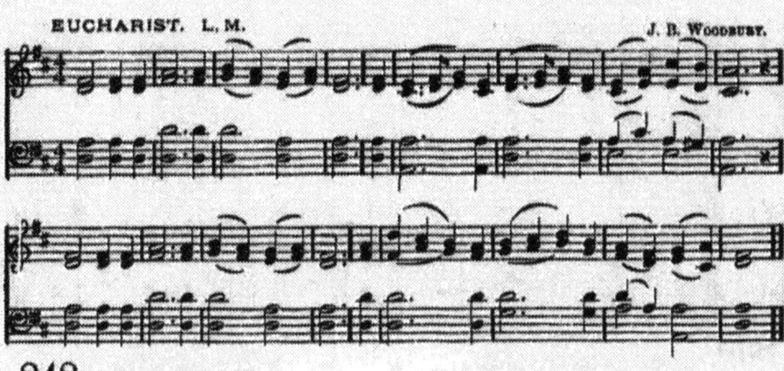

848 *Christ's presence in death.*

1 WHY should we start, and fear to die?
What timorous worms we mortals are!
Death is the gate to endless joy,
And yet we dread to enter there.

2 The pains, the groans, the dying strife,
Fright our approaching souls away;
And we shrink back again to life,
Fond of our prison and our clay.

3 O would my Lord his servant meet,
My soul would stretch her wings in haste,
Fly fearless through death's iron gate,
Nor feel the terrors as she passed.

4 Jesus can make a dying bed
Feel soft as downy pillows are,
While on his breast I lean my head,
And breathe my life out sweetly there.

—*Isaac Watts.*

HURSLEY. L. M. HUGUENOT MELODY.

849 *"Now lettest thou thy servant depart in peace."*

1 THE hour of my departure's come,
I hear the voice that calls me home;
At last, O Lord, let trouble cease,
Now let thy servant die in peace!

2 Not in mine innocence I trust;
I bow before thee in the dust,
And through my Saviour's blood alone
I look for mercy at thy throne.

3 I leave the world without a tear,
Save for the friends I held so dear;
To heal their sorrows, Lord, descend,
And to the friendless prove a friend.

4 I come, I come at thy command,
I yield my spirit to thy hand!
Stretch forth thy everlasting arms,
And shield me in the last alarms.

5 The hour of my departure's come,
I hear the voice that calls me home;
Now, O my God, let trouble cease;
Now let thy servant die in peace!

—*M. Bruce.*

FEDERAL STREET. L. M. H. K. Oliver.

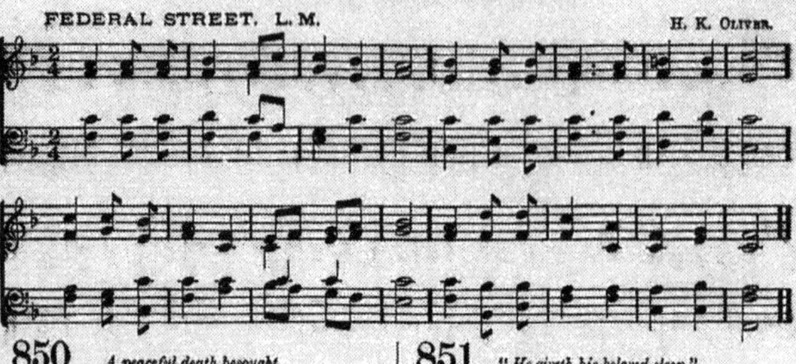

850 *A peaceful death besought.*

1 Shrinking from the cold hand of death,
I soon shall gather up my feet;
Shall soon resign this fleeting breath,
And die, my fathers' God to meet.

2 Numbered among thy people, I
Expect with joy thy face to see;
Because thou didst for sinners die,
Jesus, in death remember me!

3 O that without a lingering groan
I may the welcome word receive;
My body with my charge lay down,
And cease at once to work and live!

4 Walk with me through the dreadful shade,
And, certified that thou art mine,
My spirit, calm and undismayed,
I shall into thy hands resign.

5 No anxious doubt, no guilty gloom,
Shall damp whom Jesus' presence cheers;
My Light, my Life, my God is come,
And glory in his face appears.
—*Charles Wesley.*

851 *"He giveth his beloved sleep."*

1 Unveil thy bosom, faithful tomb;
Take this new treasure to thy trust,
And give these sacred relics room
To slumber in the silent dust.

2 Nor pain, nor grief, nor anxious fear
Invade thy bounds; no mortal woes
Can reach the peaceful sleeper here,
While angels watch the soft repose.

3 So Jesus slept; God's dying Son
Passed through the grave, and blest the bed;
Rest here, blest saint, till from his throne
The morning break, and pierce the shade.

4 Break from his throne, illustrious morn!
Attend, O earth, his sovereign word!
Restore thy trust; a glorious form
Shall then ascend to meet the Lord.
—*Isaac Watts.*

OLIVES' BROW. L. M. W. B. Bradbury.

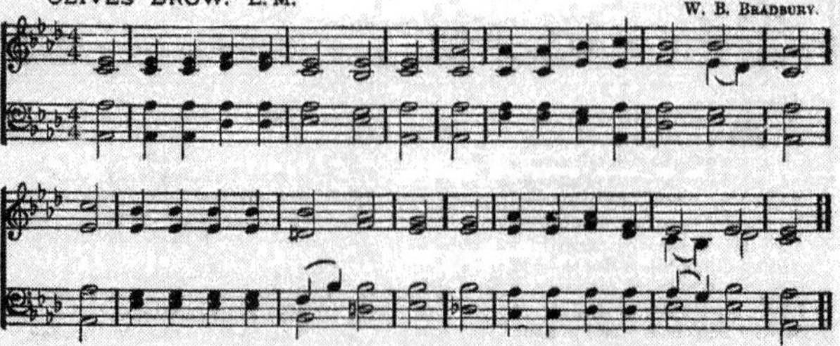

TUNE: OLIVES' BROW. L. M.

852

Asleep in Jesus.

1 Asleep in Jesus! blessèd sleep,
From which none ever wakes to weep!
A calm and undisturbed repose,
Unbroken by the last of foes.

2 Asleep in Jesus! O how sweet
To be for such a slumber meet!
With holy confidence to sing
That Death hath lost his venomed sting.

3 Asleep in Jesus! peaceful rest,
Whose waking is supremely blest!
No fear, no woe, shall dim that hour
That manifests the Saviour's power.

4 Asleep in Jesus! O for me
May such a blissful refuge be!
Securely shall my ashes lie,
Waiting the summons from on high.

5 Asleep in Jesus! far from thee
Thy kindred and their graves may be;
But thine is still a blessèd sleep,
From which none ever wakes to weep.

—*Mrs. Mackay.*

LEOMINSTER. S. M. D. G. W. MARTIN.

853

"It is appointed unto men once to die, but after this the judgment."

1 And am I born to die?
To lay this body down?
And must my trembling spirit fly
Into a world unknown—
A land of deepest shade,
Unpierced by human thought,
The dreary regions of the dead,
Where all things are forgot?

2 Soon as from earth I go,
What will become of me?
Eternal happiness or woe
Must then my portion be;
Waked by the trumpet's sound,
I from my grave shall rise,
And see the Judge with glory crowned,
And see the flaming skies.

3 How shall I leave my tomb?
With triumph or regret?
A fearful or a joyful doom,
A curse or blessing, meet?
I must from God be driven,
Or with my Saviour dwell;
Must come at his command to heaven,
Or else—depart to hell.

4 O thou that wouldst not have
One wretched sinner die;
Who diedst thyself, my soul to save
From endless misery!
Show me the way to shun
Thy dreadful wrath severe;
That when thou comest on thy throne
I may with joy appear!

5 Thou art thyself the Way;
Thyself in me reveal;
So shall I spend my life's short day
Obedient to thy will;
So shall I love my God,
Because he first loved me,
And praise thee in thy bright abode,
To all eternity.

—*Charles Wesley.*

BOYLSTON. S. M. DR. L. MASON.

854

Triumph over death.

1 AND must this body die!
This well-wrought frame decay!
And must these active limbs of mine
Lie mouldering in the clay!

2 God, my Redeemer, lives,
And ever from the skies
Looks down, and watches all my dust,
Till he shall bid it rise.

3 Arrayed in glorious grace
Shall these vile bodies shine;
And every shape and every face
Be heavenly and divine.

4 These lively hopes we owe,
Lord, to thy dying love;
O may we bless thy grace below,
And sing thy power above!

5 Saviour, accept the praise
Of these our humble songs,
Till tunes of nobler songs we raise
With our immortal tongues.

—*Charles Wesley.*

855

The conqueror crowned.

1 SERVANT of God, well done!
Thy glorious warfare's past;
The battle's fought, the race is won,
And thou art crowned at last;

2 Of all thy heart's desire
Triumphantly possessed;
Lodged by the ministerial choir
In thy Redeemer's breast.

3 In condescending love,
Thy ceaseless prayer he heard;
And bade thee suddenly remove
To thy complete reward.

4 With saints enthroned on high,
Thou dost thy Lord proclaim,
And still to God salvation cry,
Salvation to the Lamb!

5 O happy, happy soul!
In ecstasies of praise,
Long as eternal ages roll,
Thou seest thy Saviour's face.

6 Redeemed from earth and pain,
Ah! when shall we ascend,
And all in Jesus' presence reign
With our translated friend!

—*Charles Wesley.*

LEOMINSTER. S. M. D. G. W. MARTIN.

TUNE: LEOMINSTER. S. M. D.

856 *"We must all appear before the judgment seat of Christ."*

1 Thou Judge of quick and dead,
Before whose bar severe,
With holy joy, or guilty dread,
We all shall soon appear;
Our cautioned souls prepare
For that tremendous day,
And fill us now with watchful care,
And stir us up to pray:

2 To pray, and wait the hour,
That awful hour unknown,
When, robed in majesty and power,
Thou shalt from heaven come down,
The immortal Son of man,
To judge the human race,
With all thy Father's dazzling train,
With all thy glorious grace.

3 To damp our earthly joys,
To increase our gracious fears,
Forever let the Archangel's voice
Be sounding in our ears;
The solemn midnight cry,
"Ye dead, the Judge is come;
Arise, and meet him in the sky,
And meet your instant doom!"

4 O may we thus be found
Obedient to his word;
Attentive to the trumpet's sound,
And looking for our Lord!
O may we thus ensure
A lot among the blest;
And watch a moment to secure
An everlasting rest!

—Charles Wesley.

PILOT. 7.7, 8.8, 7.7. (Irregular.) J. E. Gould.

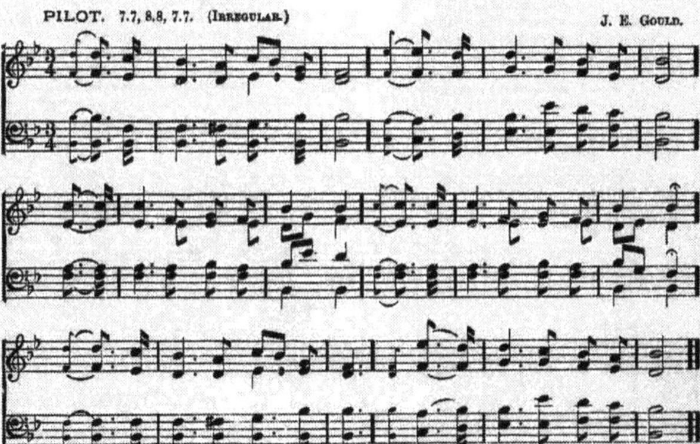

857 *The dying Christian to his soul.*

1 Vital spark of heavenly flame,
Quit, O quit this mortal frame!
Trembling, hoping, lingering, flying,
O the pain, the bliss of dying!
Cease, fond nature, cease thy strife,
And let me languish into life.

2 Hark! they whisper; angels say,
"Sister spirit, come away!"
What is this absorbs me quite—
Steals my senses, shuts my sight,
Drowns my spirit, draws my breath?
Tell me, my soul, can this be death?

3 The world recedes—it disappears;
Heaven opens on my eyes; my ears
With sounds seraphic ring!
Lend, lend your wings! I mount! I fly!
"O Grave! where is thy victory?
O Death! where is thy sting?"

—A. Pope.

MEINHOLD. 7.8, 7.8, 7.7. GERMAN.

858

On the death of a little child.

1 TENDER Shepherd, thou hast stilled
Now thy little lamb's brief weeping;
Ah, how peaceful, pale, and mild
In its narrow bed 'tis sleeping!
And no sigh of anguish sore
Heaves that little bosom more.

2 In this world of care and pain,
Lord, thou wouldst no longer leave it;
To the sunny heavenly plain
Thou dost now with joy receive it;
Clothed in robes of spotless white,
Now it dwells with thee in light.

3 Ah! Lord Jesus, grant that we
Where it lives may soon be living,
And the lovely pastures see
That its heavenly food are giving;
Then the gain of death we prove,
Though thou take what most we love.

—*From the German.*

AJALON. 6-7s. R. REDHEAD.

859

Death of a child.

1 WHEREFORE should I make my moan,
Now the darling child is dead?
He to early rest is gone,
He to paradise is fled;
I shall go to him, but he
Never shall return to me.

2 God forbids his longer stay;
God recalls the precious loan;
God hath taken him away,
From my bosom to his own;
Surely what he wills is best;
Happy in his will I rest.

3 Faith cries out, "It is the Lord,
Let him do as seems him good!"
Be thy holy name adored;
Take the gift awhile bestowed;
Take the child no longer mine;
Thine he is, forever thine.

—*Charles Wesley.*

DIX. 6-7s. (IRREGULAR.)

860

The debt unknown.

1 When this passing world is done,
When has sunk yon glowing sun,
When we stand with Christ in glory,
Looking o'er life's finished story;
Then, Lord, shall I fully know,
Not till then, how much I owe.

2 When I stand before the throne,
Dressed in beauty not my own;
When I see thee as thou art,
Love thee with unsinning heart;
Then, Lord, shall I fully know,
Not till then, how much I owe.

3 When the praise of heaven I hear,
Loud as thunders to the ear,
Loud as many waters' noise,
Sweet as harp's melodious voice;
Then, Lord, shall I fully know,
Not till then, how much I owe.

—*McCheyne.*

LUCCA. 6.6, 8.6, 8.8. J. H. SCHEIN.

861

Friends separated by death.

1 Friend after friend departs;
Who hath not lost a friend?
There is no union here of hearts
That finds not here an end;
Were this frail world our only rest,
Living or dying, none were blest.

2 Beyond the flight of time,
Beyond this vale of death,
There surely is some blessèd clime
Where life is not a breath,
Nor life's affection transient fire,
Whose sparks fly upward to expire.

3 There is a world above,
Where parting is unknown;
A whole eternity of love,
Formed for the good alone;
And faith beholds the dying here
Translated to that happier sphere.

4 Thus star by star declines,
Till all are passed away,
As morning high and higher shines,
To pure and perfect day;
Nor sink those stars in empty night;
They hide themselves in heaven's own light.

—*Montgomery.*

SOLEMNITY. 6.6.4, 6.6.4. E. L. WHITE.

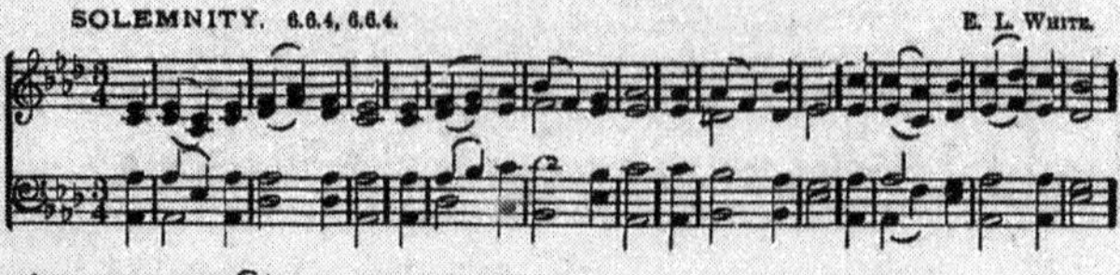

862

God our stay in death.

1 LOWLY and solemn be
Thy children's cry to thee,
Father divine!
A hymn of suppliant breath,
Owning that life and death
Alike are thine.

2 O Father, in that hour,
When earth all helping power
Shall disavow;
When spear, and shield, and crown,
In faintness are cast down;
Sustain us, thou!

3 By him who bowed to take
The death-cup for our sake,
The thorn, the rod;
From whom the last dismay
Was not to pass away;
Aid us, O God!

4 Tremblers beside the grave,
We call on thee to save,
Father divine!
Hear, hear our suppliant breath,
Keep us in life and death,
Thine, only thine.

—*Mrs. Hemans.*

VERNON. 8-8s. GERMAN.

Fine. *D.C.*

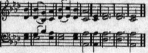

863

The death of a brother.

1 WEEP not for a brother deceased,
Our loss is his infinite gain;
A soul out of prison released,
And free from its bodily chain;
With songs let us follow his flight,
And mount with his spirit above,
Escaped to the mansions of light,
And lodged in the Eden of love.

2 Our brother the haven hath gained,
Out-flying the tempest and wind;
His rest he hath sooner obtained,
And left his companions behind,
Still tossed on a sea of distress,
Hard toiling to make the blest shore,
Where all is assurance and peace,
And sorrow and sin are no more.

3 There all the ship's company meet,
Who sailed with the Saviour beneath;
With shouting each other they greet,
And triumph o'er trouble and death;
The voyage of life's at an end,
The mortal affliction is past;
The age that in heaven they spend,
Forever and ever shall last.

—*Charles Wesley.*

TUNE: VERNON. 8-8s. (See Hymn 863.)

864 *"Having a desire to depart and to be with Christ."*

1 O when shall we sweetly remove,
O when shall we enter our rest,
Return to the Zion above,
The mother of spirits distrest!
That city of God the great King,
Where sorrow and death are no more;
But saints our Immanuel sing,
And cherub and seraph adore!

2 Not all the archangels can tell
The joys of that holiest place,
Where Jesus is pleased to reveal
The light of his heavenly face;
When caught in the rapturous flame,
The sight beatific they prove,
And walk in the light of the Lamb,
Enjoying the beams of his love.

3 Thou know'st, in the spirit of prayer,
We long thy appearing to see,
Resigned to the burden we bear,
But longing to triumph with thee;
'Tis good at thy word to be here,
'Tis better in thee to be gone,
And see thee in glory appear,
And rise to a share in thy throne.

—*Charles Wesley.*

EMS. 13.11.13.12. GERMAN CHORALE.

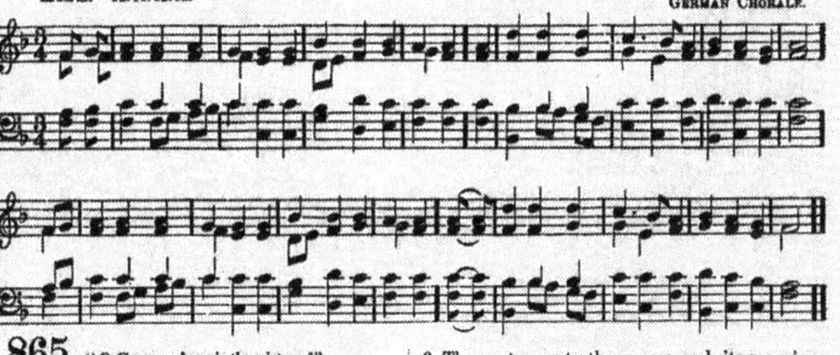

865 *"O Grave, where is thy victory?"*

1 Thou art gone to the grave; but we will not deplore thee,
Though sorrows and darkness encompass the tomb;
Thy Saviour has passed through its portal before thee,
And the lamp of his love is thy guide through the gloom.

2 Thou art gone to the grave; we no longer behold thee,
Nor tread the rough path of the world by thy side;
But the wide arms of mercy are spread to enfold thee,
And sinners may die, for the Sinless hath died.

3 Thou art gone to the grave; and, its mansion forsaking,
Perchance thy weak spirit in fear lingered long;
But the mild rays of Paradise beamed on thy waking,
And the sound which thou heardst was the seraphim's song.

4 Thou art gone to the grave; but we will not deplore thee;
Whose God was thy ransom, thy guardian, and guide;
He gave thee, he took thee, and he will restore thee;
And death has no sting, for the Saviour has died

—*Bishop Heber.*

GIESSEN. 8-8s.

866 *"Into thy hands I commend my spirit."*

1 Jesus, was ever love like thine?
Thy life a scene of wonders is;
Thy death itself is all divine,
While, pleased thy spirit to dismiss,
Thou dost out of the flesh retire,
And like the Prince of Life expire.

2 Thy death supports the dying saint;
Thy death my sovereign comfort be;
While feeble flesh and nature faint,
Arm with thy mortal agony;
And fill, while soul and body part,
With life, immortal life, my heart.

3 O let thy death's mysterious power,
With all its sacred weight, descend,
To consecrate my final hour,
To bless me with thy peaceful end;
And, breathed into the hands divine,
My spirit be received with thine!

867 *A last wish.*

1 In age and feebleness extreme
Who shall a sinful worm redeem?
Jesus! my only hope thou art,
Strength of my failing flesh and heart,
O could I catch one smile from thee,
And drop into eternity!

—Charles Wesley.

MARTYN. 8-7s. S. B. Marsh.

Fine.
D.C.

TUNE: MARTYN. 8-7s.

868 Revelation xiv. 13.

1 Hark! a voice divides the sky,
Happy are the faithful dead!
In the Lord who sweetly die,
They from all their toils are freed.
Them the Spirit hath declared
Blest, unutterably blest;
Jesus is their great Reward,
Jesus is their endless Rest.

2 Followed by their works, they go
Where their Head hath gone before;
Reconciled by grace below,
Grace hath opened Mercy's door;
Justified through faith alone,
Here they knew their sins forgiven;
Here they laid their burden down,
Hallowed, and made meet for heaven.

3 Who can now lament the lot
Of a saint in Christ deceased?
Let the world, who know us not,
Call us hopeless and unblessed;
When from flesh the spirit freed,
Hastens homeward to return,
Mortals cry, "A man is dead!"
Angels sing, "A child is born!"

4 Born into the world above,
They our happy brother greet;
Bear him to the throne of Love,
Place him at the Saviour's feet;
Jesus smiles, and says, "Well done,
Good and faithful servant thou;
Enter, and receive thy crown,
Reign with me triumphant now."

—*Charles Wesley.*

TICHFIELD. 8-7s. R. W. Beaty.

869 *"Death is swallowed up in victory."*

1 Blessing, honour, thanks, and praise,
Pay we, gracious God, to thee;
Thou, in thine abundant grace,
Givest us the victory;
True and faithful to thy word,
Thou hast glorified thy Son,
Jesus Christ, our dying Lord,
He for us the fight hath won.

2 Lo! the prisoner is released,
Lightened of his fleshly load;
Where the weary are at rest,
He is gathered into God:
Lo! the pain of life is past,
All his warfare now is o'er,
Death and hell behind are cast,
Grief and suffering are no more.

3 Yes, the Christian's course is run,
Ended is the glorious strife;
Fought the fight, the work is done,
Death is swallowed up of life!
Borne by angels on their wings,
Far from earth the spirit flies,
Finds his God, and sits and sings,
Triumphing in Paradise.

4 Join we then, with one accord,
In the new, the joyful song;
Absent from our loving Lord
We shall not continue long;
We shall quit the house of clay,
We a better lot shall share,
We shall see the realms of day,
Meet our happy brother there.

—*Charles Wesley.*

ST. SYLVESTER. 8.7, 8.7. REV. J. B. DYKES.

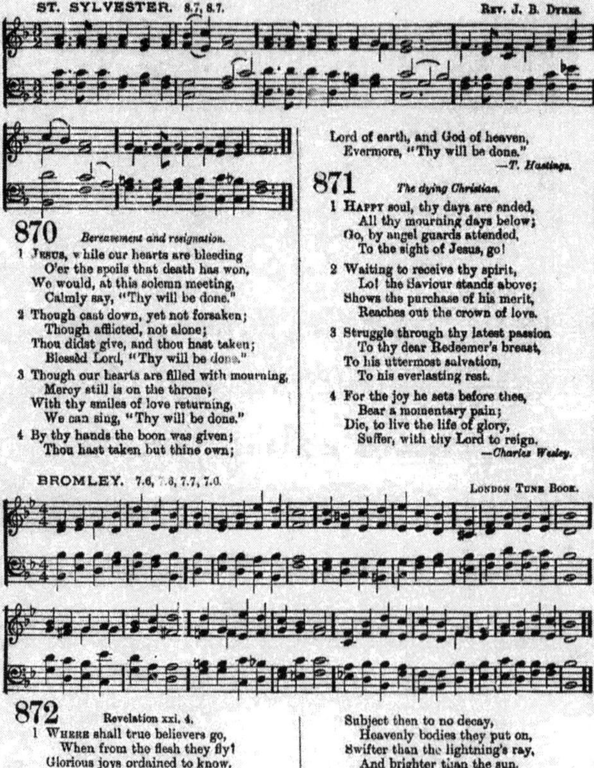

870 *Bereavement and resignation.*

1 JESUS, while our hearts are bleeding
O'er the spoils that death has won,
We would, at this solemn meeting,
Calmly say, "Thy will be done."

2 Though cast down, yet not forsaken;
Though afflicted, not alone;
Thou didst give, and thou hast taken;
Blessèd Lord, "Thy will be done."

3 Though our hearts are filled with mourning,
Mercy still is on the throne;
With thy smiles of love returning,
We can sing, "Thy will be done."

4 By thy hands the boon was given;
Thou hast taken but thine own;
Lord of earth, and God of heaven,
Evermore, "Thy will be done."
—*T. Hastings.*

871 *The dying Christian.*

1 HAPPY soul, thy days are ended,
All thy mourning days below;
Go, by angel guards attended,
To the sight of Jesus, go!

2 Waiting to receive thy spirit,
Lo! the Saviour stands above;
Shows the purchase of his merit,
Reaches out the crown of love.

3 Struggle through thy latest passion
To thy dear Redeemer's breast,
To his uttermost salvation,
To his everlasting rest.

4 For the joy he sets before thee,
Bear a momentary pain;
Die, to live the life of glory,
Suffer, with thy Lord to reign.
—*Charles Wesley.*

BROMLEY. 7.6, 7.6, 7.7, 7.6. LONDON TUNE BOOK.

872 Revelation xxi. 4.

1 WHERE shall true believers go,
When from the flesh they fly?
Glorious joys ordained to know,
They mount above the sky,
To that bright celestial place;
There they shall in raptures live,
More than tongue can e'er express,
Or heart can e'er conceive.

2 When they once are entered there,
Their mourning days are o'er;
Pain, and sin, and want, and care,
And sighing are no more;
Subject then to no decay,
Heavenly bodies they put on,
Swifter than the lightning's ray,
And brighter than the sun.

3 But their greatest happiness,
Their highest joy, shall be,
God their Saviour to possess,
To know, and love, and see;
With that beatific sight
Glorious ecstasy is given;
This is their supreme delight,
And makes a heaven of heaven.
—*Charles Wesley.*

873

TUNE: BROMLEY. 7.6, 7.6, 7.7, 7.6. (SEE HYMN 872.)

"Behold the Bridegroom cometh."

1 Hearken to the solemn voice,
The awful midnight cry!
Waiting souls, rejoice, rejoice,
And see the Bridegroom nigh;
Lo! he comes to keep his word,
Light and joy his looks impart;
Go ye forth to meet your Lord,
And meet him in your heart.

2 Ye whose loins are girt, stand forth!
Whose lamps are burning bright,
Worthy, in your Saviour's worth,
To walk with him in white;
Jesus bids your hearts be clean,
Bids you all his promise prove;
Jesus comes to cast out sin,
And perfect you in love.

3 Wait we all in patient hope,
Till Christ, the Judge, shall come;
We shall soon be all caught up
To meet the general doom;
In an hour to us unknown,
As a thief in deepest night,
Christ shall suddenly come down,
With all his saints in light.

4 Happy he whom Christ shall find
Watching to see him come;
Him the Judge of all mankind
Shall bear triumphant home;
Who can answer to his word?
Which of you dares meet his day?
"Rise, and come to judgment!" Lord,
We rise, and come away.

—*Charles Wesley.*

LEAMINGTON. 7.6, 7.6, 7.8, 7.6. J. B. Sale.

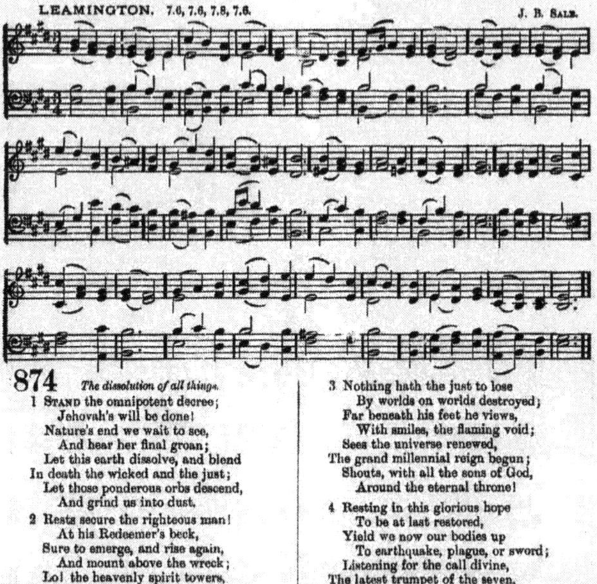

874

The dissolution of all things.

1 Stand the omnipotent decree;
Jehovah's will be done!
Nature's end we wait to see,
And hear her final groan;
Let this earth dissolve, and blend
In death the wicked and the just;
Let those ponderous orbs descend,
And grind us into dust.

2 Rests secure the righteous man!
At his Redeemer's beck,
Sure to emerge, and rise again,
And mount above the wreck;
Lo! the heavenly spirit towers,
Like flame, o'er nature's funeral pyre,
Triumphs in immortal powers,
And claps his wings of fire!

3 Nothing hath the just to lose
By worlds on worlds destroyed;
Far beneath his feet he views,
With smiles, the flaming void;
Sees the universe renewed,
The grand millennial reign begun;
Shouts, with all the sons of God,
Around the eternal throne!

4 Resting in this glorious hope
To be at last restored,
Yield we now our bodies up
To earthquake, plague, or sword;
Listening for the call divine,
The latest trumpet of the seven,
Soon our soul and dust shall join,
And both fly up to heaven.

—*Charles Wesley.*

BRIDEHEAD. 8.8.6, 8.8.6. A. H. D. TROYTE.

875 *Death and Judgment.*

1 AND am I only born to die?
And must I suddenly comply
With nature's stern decree?
What after death for me remains?
Celestial joys, or hellish pains,
To all eternity!

2 How then ought I on earth to live,
While God prolongs the kind reprieve,
And props the house of clay!
My sole concern, my single care,
To watch, and tremble, and prepare
Against the fatal day!

3 No room for mirth or trifling here,
For worldly hope, or worldly fear,
If life so soon is gone;
If now the Judge is at the door,
And all mankind must stand before
The inexorable throne!

4 No matter which my thoughts employ,
A moment's misery, or joy;
But O! when both shall end,
Where shall I find my destined place?
Shall I my everlasting days
With fiends or angels spend?

5 Nothing is worth a thought beneath
But how I may escape the death
That never, never dies;
How make mine own election sure,
And, when I fail on earth, secure
A mansion in the skies.

6 Jesus, vouchsafe a pitying ray,
Be thou my Guide, be thou my Way
To glorious happiness;
Ah! write the pardon on my heart,
And whensoe'er I hence depart,
Let me depart in peace.

—*Charles Wesley.*

MERIBAH. 8.8.6, 8.8.6. DR. MASON.

TUNE: MERIBAH. 8.8.6, 8.8.6.

876

Time and Eternity.

1 Thou God of glorious majesty,
To thee, against myself, to thee,
A worm of earth, I cry;
A half-awakened child of man;
An heir of endless bliss or pain;
A sinner born to die!

2 Lo! on a narrow neck of land,
'Twixt two unbounded seas I stand,
Secure, insensible;
A point of time, a moment's space,
Removes me to that heavenly place,
Or shuts me up in hell.

3 O God, mine inmost soul convert!
And deeply on my thoughtful heart
Eternal things impress;
Give me to feel their solemn weight,
And tremble on the brink of fate,
And wake to righteousness.

4 Before me place, in dread array,
The pomp of that tremendous day,
When thou with clouds shalt come
To judge the nations at thy bar;
And tell me, Lord, shall I be there
To meet a joyful doom?

5 Be this my one great business here,
With serious industry and fear
Eternal bliss to ensure;
Thine utmost counsel to fulfil,
And suffer all thy righteous will,
And to the end endure.

6 Then, Saviour, then my soul receive,
Transported from this vale to live
And reign with thee above;
Where faith is sweetly lost in sight,
And hope in full supreme delight,
And everlasting love.

—Charles Wesley.

ST. THOMAS. 8.7, 8.7, 4.7.

877

The last Judgment.

1 Lift your heads, ye friends of Jesus,
Partners in his sufferings here;
Christ, to all believers precious,
Lord of lords, shall soon appear;
‖: Mark the tokens :‖
Of his heavenly kingdom near!

2 Close behind the tribulation
Of the last tremendous days,
See the flaming revelation,
See the universal blaze!
‖: Earth and heaven :‖
Melt before the Judge's face!

3 Sun and moon are both confounded,
Darkened into endless night,
When, with angel-hosts surrounded,
In his Father's glory bright,
‖: Beams the Saviour, :‖
Shines the everlasting Light.

4 See the stars from heaven falling,
Hark, on earth the doleful cry,
Men on rocks and mountains calling,
While the frowning Judge draws nigh,
‖: "Hide us, hide us, :‖
Rocks and mountains, from his eye!"

5 With what different exclamation
Shall the saints his banner see!
By the tokens of his passion,
By the marks received for me,
‖: All discern him, :‖
All with shouts cry out, "'Tis he!"

—Charles Wesley.

REGENT SQUARE. 8.7.8.7.4.7. HENRY SMART.

878 Titus ii. 13.

1 CHRIST is coming! let creation
Bid her groans and travail cease;
Let the glorious proclamation
Hope restore and faith increase;
‖:Christ is coming!:‖
Come, thou blessèd Prince of peace!

2 Earth can now but tell the story
Of thy bitter cross and pain;
She shall yet behold thy glory
When thou comest back to reign;
‖:Christ is coming!:‖
Let each heart repeat the strain.

3 Long thy exiles have been pining,
Far from rest, and home, and thee;
But, in heavenly vesture shining,
Soon they shall thy glory see;
‖:Christ is coming!:‖
Haste the joyous jubilee.

4 With that "blessèd hope" before us,
Let no harp remain unstrung;
Let the mighty advent chorus
Onward roll from tongue to tongue;
‖:Christ is coming!:‖
Come, Lord Jesus, quickly come!

—*J. R. Macduff.*

ADVENT HYMN. 8.7, 8.7, 4.7. (FIRST TUNE.) J. TILLEARD.

cres.
dim.

879 *"Then shall they see the Son of man coming in a cloud, with power and great glory."*

1 Lo! he comes with clouds descending,
Once for favoured sinners slain;
Thousand thousand saints attending,
Swell the triumph of his train;
‖:Hallelujah!:‖
God appears on earth to reign.

2 Every eye shall now behold him
Robed in dreadful majesty;
Those who set at naught and sold him,
Pierced and nailed him to the tree,
‖:Deeply wailing,:‖
Shall the true Messiah see.

3 The dear tokens of his passion
Still his dazzling body bears;
Cause of endless exultation
To his ransomed worshippers;
‖:With what rapture:‖
Gaze we on those glorious scars!

4 Yea, Amen! let all adore thee,
High on thy eternal throne;
Saviour, take the power and glory,
Claim the kingdom for thine own;
‖:Jah, Jehovah,:‖
Everlasting God, come down!

—*Charles Wesley.*

HELMSLEY. 8.7, 8.7, 4.7. (SECOND TUNE.) REV. THOMAS OLIVER.

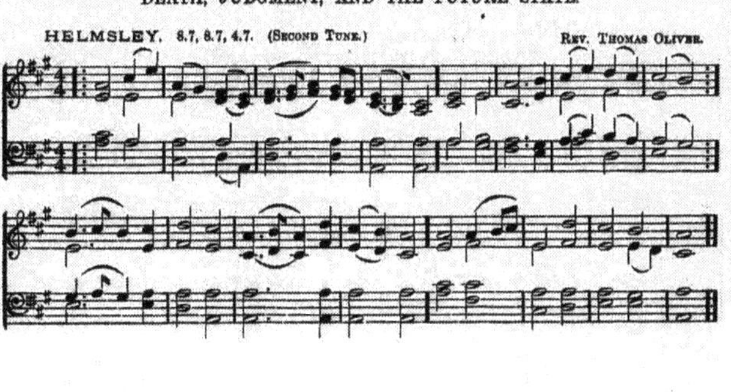

CALEDON. 6.6, 6.6, 8.8.

880 *Watching for the Bridegroom's coming.*

1 YE virgin souls, arise,
With all the dead awake!
Unto salvation wise,
Oil in your vessels take;
Upstarting at the midnight cry,
"Behold the heavenly Bridegroom nigh!"

2 He comes, he comes, to call
The nations to his bar,
And raise to glory all
Who fit for glory are;
Made ready for your full reward,
Go forth with joy to meet your Lord.

3 Go, meet him in the sky,
Your everlasting Friend;
Your Head to glorify,
With all his saints ascend;
Ye pure in heart, obtain the grace
To see, without a veil, his face!

4 Ye that have here received
The unction from above,
And in his Spirit lived,
Obedient to his love,
Jesus shall claim you for his bride;
Rejoice with all the sanctified.

5 The everlasting doors
Shall soon the saints receive,
Above yon angel powers
In glorious joy to live;
Far from a world of grief and sin,
With God eternally shut in.

6 Then let us wait to hear
The trumpet's welcome sound;
To see our Lord appear,
Watching let us be found;
When Jesus doth the heavens bow,
Be found—as, Lord, thou find'st us now!

—*Charles Wesley.*

LUTHER'S HYMN. 8.7, 8.7, 8.8.7. MARTIN LUTHER.

881

The end of all created things.

1 GREAT God! what do I see and hear!
The end of things created!
The Judge of man I see appear,
On clouds of glory seated;
The trumpet sounds; the graves restore
The dead which they contained before;
Prepare, my soul, to meet him!

2 The dead in Christ shall first arise,
At the last trumpet's sounding,
Caught up to meet him in the skies,
With joy their Lord surrounding;
No gloomy fears their souls dismay,
His presence sheds eternal day
On those prepared to meet him.

3 But sinners, filled with guilty fears,
Behold his wrath prevailing;
For they shall rise and find their tears
And sighs are unavailing;
The day of grace is past and gone,
Trembling they stand before the throne,
All unprepared to meet him.

4 Great God! what do I see and hear!
The end of things created!
The Judge of man I see appear,
On clouds of glory seated;
Low at his cross I view the day
When heaven and earth shall pass away,
And thus prepare to meet him.

—*B. Ringwaldt.*

CELANO. 8-7s.

TUNE: CELANO. 6-7s.

882

The Day of wrath.

1 Day of wrath, O dreadful day!
When this world shall pass away,
And the heavens together roll,
Shrivelling like a parchèd scroll,
Long foretold by saint and sage,
Psalmist's harp, and prophet's page.

2 Day of terror, day of doom,
When the Judge at last shall come!
Through the deep and silent gloom,
Shrouding every human tomb,
Shall the archangel's trumpet tone
Summon all before the throne.

3 Then the writing shall be read,
Which shall judge the quick and dead;
Then the Lord of all our race
Shall appoint to each his place;
Every wrong shall be set right,
Every secret brought to light.

4 O just Judge, to whom belongs
Vengeance for all earthly wrongs,
Grant forgiveness, Lord, at last,
Ere the dread account be past!
Lo, my sighs, my guilt, my shame!
Spare me for thine own great name.

5 Thou, who bad'st the sinner cease
From her tears and go in peace;
Thou, who to the dying thief
Spakest pardon and relief;
Thou, O Lord, to me hast given,
E'en to me, the hope of heaven.

—Dean Stanley, from Thomas of Celano.

ANGELUS. L. M. J. Scheffler.

883

"For the trumpet shall sound, and the dead shall be raised incorruptible."

1 The great archangel's trump shall sound,
While twice ten thousand thunders roar,
Tear up the graves, and cleave the ground,
And make the greedy sea restore.

2 The greedy sea shall yield her dead,
The earth no more her slain conceal;
Sinners shall lift their guilty head,
And shrink to see a yawning hell.

3 But we, who now our Lord confess,
And faithful to the end endure,
Shall stand in Jesus' righteousness,
Stand, as the Rock of ages sure.

4 We, while the stars from heaven shall fall,
And mountains are on mountains hurled,
Shall stand unmoved amidst them all,
And smile to see a burning world.

5 The earth, and all the works therein,
Dissolve, by raging flames destroyed,
While we survey the awful scene,
And mount above the fiery void.

6 By faith we now transcend the skies,
And on that ruined world look down;
By love above all height we rise,
And share the everlasting throne.

—Charles Wesley.

STIRLING. L. M. R. HARRISON.

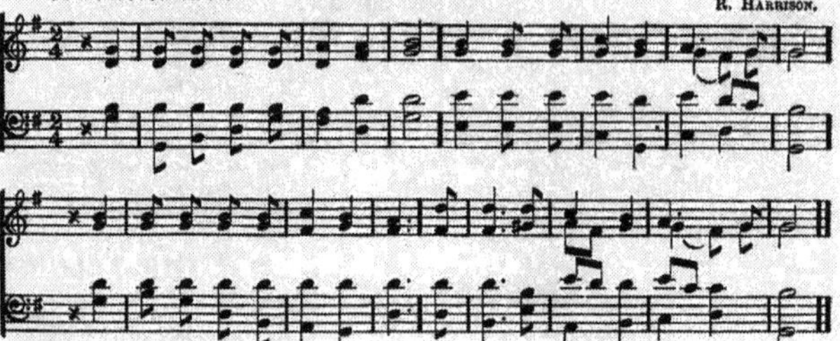

884 *"Dust thou art, and unto dust shalt thou return."*

1 TREMENDOUS God, with humble fear,
Prostrate before thy awful throne,
The irrevocable word we hear,
The sovereign righteousness we own.

2 'Tis fit we should to dust return,
Since such the will of the Most High;
In sin conceived, to trouble born,
Born only to lament and die.

3 Submissive to thy just decree,
We all shall soon from earth remove;
But when thou sendest, Lord, for me,
O let the messenger be love!

4 Whisper thy love into my heart,
Warn me of my approaching end;
And then I joyfully depart,
And then I to thy arms ascend.

—*Charles Wesley.*

WARD. L. M. DR. L. MASON.

Slowly.

885 *The Day of Judgment.*

1 THE day of wrath, that dreadful day,
When heaven and earth shall pass away!
What power shall be the sinner's stay?
How shall he meet that dreadful day?

2 When, shrivelling like a parchèd scroll,
The flaming heavens together roll;
And louder yet, and yet more dread,
Swells the high trump that wakes the dead!

3 O on that day, that wrathful day,
When man to judgment wakes from clay,
Be thou, O Christ, the sinner's stay,
Though heaven and earth shall pass away!

—*Sir W. Scott.*

LASSUS. L.M. — A. H. MANN, MUS. BAC.

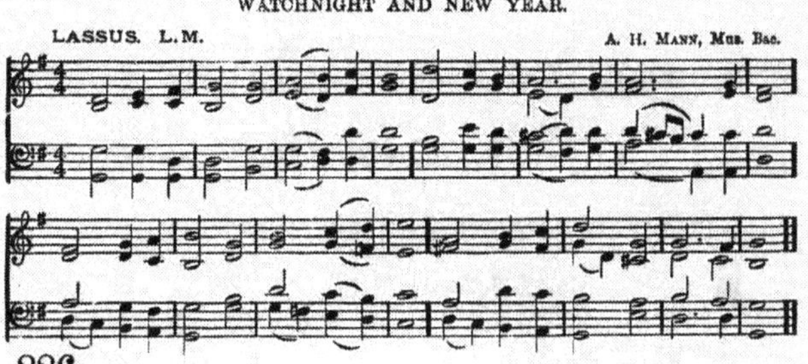

886 *Christ the Judge of all.*

1 He comes! he comes! the Judge severe!
The seventh trumpet speaks him near;
His lightnings flash; his thunders roll;
How welcome to the faithful soul!

2 From heaven angelic voices sound;
See the Almighty Jesus crowned!
Girt with omnipotence and grace,
And glory decks the Saviour's face.

3 Descending on his azure throne,
He claims the kingdoms for his own;
The kingdoms all obey his word,
And hail him their triumphant Lord.

4 Shout, all the people of the sky!
And all the saints of the Most High;
Our Lord, who now his right obtains,
Forever and forever reigns.

—*Charles Wesley.*

SECTION XI.

SPECIAL OCCASIONS.

1.—WATCHNIGHT AND NEW YEAR.

SELENA. 6-8s. — ISAAC BAKER WOODBURY.

887 *Opening of Watchnight service.*

1 How many pass the guilty night
In revellings and frantic mirth!
The creature is their sole delight,
Their happiness the things of earth;
For us suffice the season past;
We choose the better part at last.

2 We will not close our wakeful eyes,
We will not let our eyelids sleep,
But humbly lift them to the skies,
And all a solemn vigil keep;
So many years on sin bestowed,
Can we not watch one night for God!

3 We can, O Jesus, for thy sake,
Devote our every hour to thee;
Speak but the word, our souls shall wake,
And sing with cheerful melody;
Thy praise shall our glad tongues employ,
And every heart shall dance for joy.

4 O may we all triumphant rise,
With joy upon our heads return,
And far above those nether skies,
By thee on eagles' wings upborne,
Through all yon radiant circles move,
And gain the highest heaven of love!

—*Charles Wesley.*

EVAN. C. M. REV. W. H. HAVERGAL.

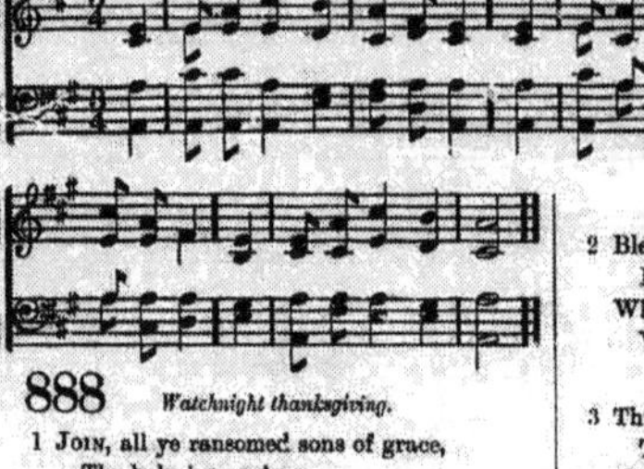

888 *Watchnight thanksgiving.*

1 JOIN, all ye ransomed sons of grace,
The holy joy prolong,
And shout to the Redeemer's praise
A solemn midnight song.

2 Blessing, and thanks, and love, and might,
Be to our Jesus given,
Who turns our darkness into light,
Who turns our hell to heaven.

3 Thither our faithful souls he leads,
Thither he bids us rise,
With crowns of joy upon our head,
To meet him in the skies.

—Charles Wesley.

DUKE STREET. L. M. JOHN HATTON.

889 *New year adoration.*

1 ETERNAL Source of every joy,
Well may thy praise our lips employ,
While in thy temple we appear,
Whose goodness crowns the circling year.

2 The flowery spring, at thy command,
Embalms the air, and paints the land;
The summer rays with vigour shine,
To raise the corn, and cheer the vine.

3 Thy hand in autumn richly pours
Through all our coasts redundant stores;
And winters, softened by thy care,
No more a face of horror wear.

4 Seasons, and months, and weeks, and days,
Demand successive songs of praise;
Still be the cheerful homage paid
With opening light, and evening shade.

5 Here in thy house shall incense rise,
As circling Sabbaths bless our eyes;
Still will we make thy mercies known
Around thy board, and round our own.

6 O may our more harmonious tongue
In worlds unknown pursue the song;
And in those brighter courts adore,
Where days and years revolve no more.

—Doddridge.

EVANGELIST. C. M. From Mendelssohn.

890

New year thanksgiving.

1 Sing to the great Jehovah's praise!
All praise to him belongs;
Who kindly lengthens out our days,
Demands our choicest songs.

2 His providence hath brought us through
Another various year;
We all with vows and anthems new
Before our God appear.

3 Father, thy mercies past we own,
Thy still continued care;
To thee presenting, through thy Son,
Whate'er we have or are.

4 Our lips and lives shall gladly show
The wonders of thy love,
While on in Jesus' steps we go
To see thy face above.

5 Our residue of days or hours
Thine, wholly thine, shall be,
And all our consecrated powers
A sacrifice to thee:

6 Till Jesus in the clouds appear
To saints on earth forgiven,
And bring the grand sabbatic year,
The Jubilee of heaven.

—*Charles Wesley.*

MILLENNIUM. 6.6, 6.6, 8.8.

891

New year confession.

1 The Lord of earth and sky,
The God of ages, praise:
Who reigns enthroned on high,
Ancient of endless days:
Who lengthens out our trial here,
And spares us yet another year.

2 Barren and withered trees,
We cumbered long the ground;
No fruits of holiness
On our dead souls were found:
Yet doth he us in mercy spare
Another and another year.

3 When justice bared the sword,
To cut the fig-tree down,
The pity of our Lord
Cried, "Let it still alone:"
The Father mild inclines his ear,
And spares us yet another year.

4 Jesus, thy speaking blood
From God obtained the grace,
Who therefore hath bestowed
On us a longer space:
Thou didst on our behalf appear,
And, lo, we see another year!

5 Then dig about our root,
Break up the fallow ground,
And let our gracious fruit
To thy great praise abound:
O let us all thy praise declare,
And fruit unto perfection bear!—*C. Wesley.*

DERBE. 10.5.11. (First Tune.) Sacred Harmony.

892 *New year consecration.*

1 Come, let us anew our journey pursue,
‖:Roll round with the year,:‖
‖:And never stand still:‖ till the Master appear.

2 His adorable will let us gladly fulfil,
‖:And our talents improve,:‖
‖:By the patience of hope,:‖ and the labour of love.

3 Our life is a dream; our time, as a stream,
‖:Glides swiftly away;:‖
‖:And the fugitive moment:‖ refuses to stay.

4 The arrow is flown; the moment is gone;
‖:The millennial year:‖
‖:Rushes on to our view,:‖ and eternity's here.

5 O that each in the day of his coming may say,
‖:"I have fought my way through;:‖
‖:I have finished the work:‖ thou didst give me to do."

6 O that each from his Lord may receive the glad word,
‖:"Well and faithfully done!:‖
‖:Enter into my joy,:‖ and sit down on my throne."

—*Charles Wesley.*

EXCELSIOR. 10.5.11. D. (Second Tune. Without Repeats.) Samuel Webbe.

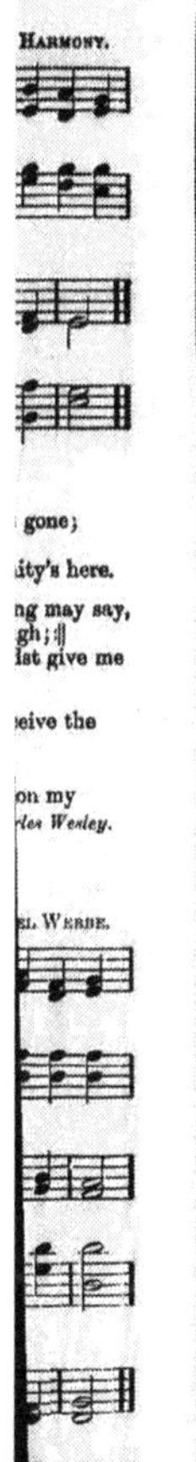

LEAVITT. 8-7s. JOSEPH P. HOLBROOK.

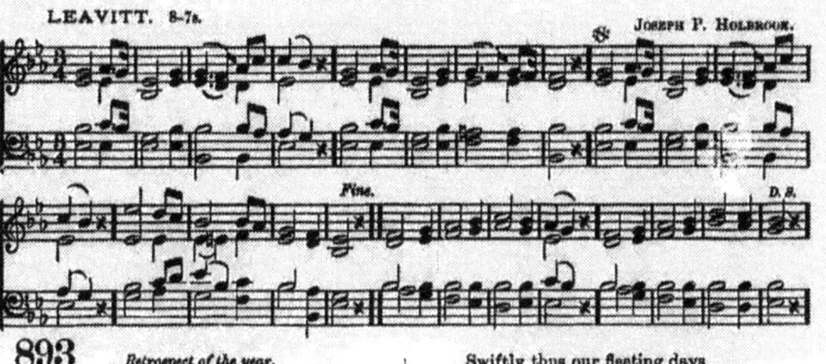

Fine.
D.S.

893 *Retrospect of the year.*

1 WHILE, with ceaseless course, the sun
Hasted through the circling year,
Many souls their race have run,
Never more to meet us here;
Fixed in an eternal state,
They have done with all below;
We a little longer wait,
But how little—none can know.

2 As the wingèd arrow flies
Speedily the mark to find;
As the lightning from the skies
Darts, and leaves no trace behind;
Swiftly thus our fleeting days
Bear us down life's rapid stream;
Upward, Lord, our spirits raise;
All below is but a dream.

3 Thanks for mercies past receive;
Pardon of our sins renew;
Teach us henceforth how to live
With eternity in view;
Bless thy word to young and old;
Fill us with a Saviour's love;
And when life's short tale is told,
May we dwell with him above.

—*J. Newton.*

2.—COVENANT SERVICE.

BRIGHTON. 6-8s.

894 *Renewing the covenant.*

1 O GOD! how often hath thine ear
To me in willing mercy bowed!
While worshipping thine altar near,
Lowly I wept, and strongly vowed;
But, ah! the feebleness of man!
Have I not vowed and wept in vain?

2 Return, O Lord of hosts, return!
Behold thy servant in distress;
My faithlessness again I mourn,
Again forgive my faithlessness;
And to thine arms my spirit take
And bless me for the Saviour's sake.

3 This day the covenant I sign,
The bond of sure and promised peace;
Nor can I doubt its power divine,
Since sealed with Jesus' blood it is;
That blood I take, that blood alone,
And make the covenant peace mine own.

4 But, that my faith no more may know
Or change, or interval, or end,
Help me in all thy paths to go,
And now, as e'er, my voice attend,
And gladden me with answers mild,
And dwell, O Father, with thy child!

—*W. M. Bunting.*

EVAN. C.M. — Rev. W. H. Havergal.

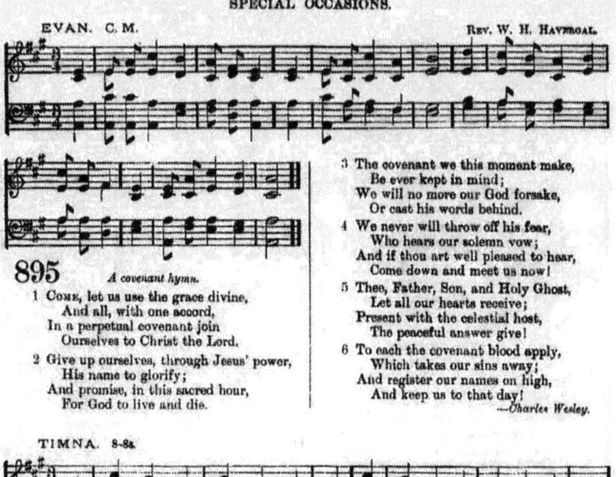

895

A covenant hymn.

1 Come, let us use the grace divine,
And all, with one accord,
In a perpetual covenant join
Ourselves to Christ the Lord.

2 Give up ourselves, through Jesus' power,
His name to glorify;
And promise, in this sacred hour,
For God to live and die.

3 The covenant we this moment make,
Be ever kept in mind;
We will no more our God forsake,
Or cast his words behind.

4 We never will throw off his fear,
Who hears our solemn vow;
And if thou art well pleased to hear,
Come down and meet us now!

5 Thee, Father, Son, and Holy Ghost,
Let all our hearts receive;
Present with the celestial host,
The peaceful answer give!

6 To each the covenant blood apply,
Which takes our sins away;
And register our names on high,
And keep us to that day!

—*Charles Wesley.*

TIMNA. 8-8s.

D.C.

896

After the renewal of the covenant.

1 O how shall a sinner perform
The vows he hath vowed to the Lord?
A sinful and impotent worm,
How can I be true to my word?
I tremble at what I have done;
O send me thy help from above!
The power of thy Spirit make known,
The virtue of Jesus's love!

2 My solemn engagements are vain,
My promises empty as air;
My vows, I shall break them again,
And plunge in eternal despair;
Unless my omnipotent God
The sense of his goodness impart,
And shed by his Spirit abroad
The love of himself in my heart.

3 O Lover of sinners, extend
To me thy compassionate grace;
Appear, my affliction to end,
Afford me a glimpse of thy face!
That light shall enkindle in me
A flame of reciprocal love;
And then I shall cleave unto thee,
And then I shall never remove.

4 O come to a mourner in pain,
Thy peace in my conscience reveal!
And then I shall love thee again,
And sing of the goodness I feel;
Constrained by the grace of my Lord,
My soul shall in all things obey,
And wait to be fully restored,
And long to be summoned away.

—*Charles Wesley.*

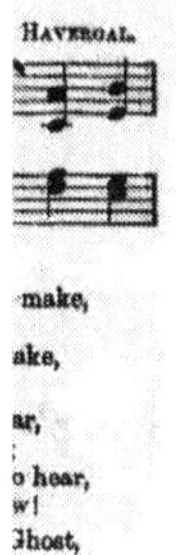

HEBRON. L. M. (First Tune.) Dr. L. Mason.

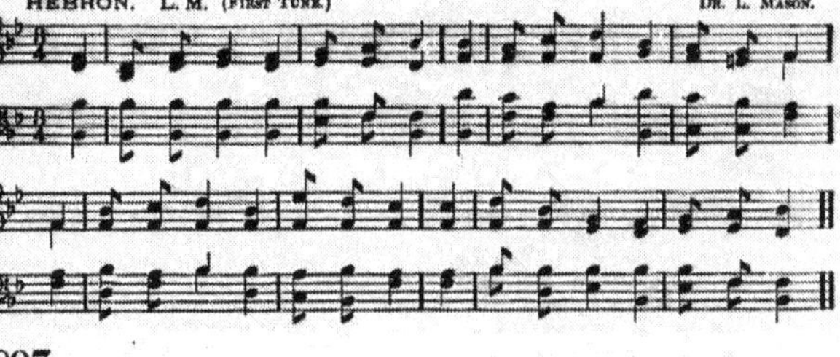

897

Renewal of self-dedication.

1 O HAPPY day that fixed my choice
On thee, my Saviour and my God!
Well may this glowing heart rejoice,
And tell its raptures all abroad.

2 O happy bond, that seals my vows
To him who merits all my love!
Let cheerful anthems fill his house,
While to that sacred shrine I move.

3 'Tis done, the great transaction's done,
I am my Lord's, and he is mine;
He drew me, and I followed on,
Charmed to confess the voice divine.

4 Now rest my long-divided heart;
Fixed on this blissful centre, rest;
Nor ever from thy Lord depart,
With him of every good possest.

5 High Heaven, that heard the solemn vow,
That vow renewed shall daily hear,
Till in life's latest hour I bow,
And bless in death a bond so dear.

—*Doddridge.*

HAPPY DAY. L. M. (Second Tune.)

CHORUS.
Hap-py day, Hap-py day, When Je-sus washed my sins a-way,
Fine.
D. S.
He taught me how to watch and pray, And live re-joic-ing ev-'ry day.

REDHEAD. 4-7s. R. REDHEAD.

898

Abjuration of sin.

1 God of truth, and power, and grace,
Drawn by thee to seek thy face,
Lo! I in thy courts appear,
Humbly come to meet thee here;

2 Trembling at thine altar stand,
Lift to heaven my heart and hand,
Of thy promised strength secure,
All my sins I now abjure.

3 All my promises renew,
All my wickedness eschew,
Chiefly that I called my own,
Now I hate, renounce, disown.

4 Never more will I commit,
Follow, or be led by it;
Only grant the grace I claim,
Arm my soul with Jesus' name.

5 Sure I am it is thy will,
I should never yield to ill,
Never lose thy gracious power,
Never sin or grieve thee more.

6 What doth then my hopes prevent?
Lord, thou stay'st for my consent;
My consent through grace I give,
Promise in thy fear to live.

7 Father, Son, and Holy Ghost,
Present with thy angel host,
While I at thy altar bow,
Witness to the solemn vow.

8 Now admit my bold appeal,
Now affix thy Spirit's seal,
Now the power from high be given,
Register the oath in heaven.

—*Charles Wesley.*

3.—RECEPTION OF NEW MEMBERS.

MELCOMBE. L. M. S. WEBBE.

899

A fraternal welcome.

1 Brethren in Christ, and well-beloved,
To Jesus and his servants dear,
Enter, and show yourselves approved;
Enter, and find that God is here.

2 Welcome from earth; lo, the right hand
Of fellowship to you we give!
With open hearts and hands we stand,
And you in Jesus' name receive.

3 Jesus, attend, thyself reveal!
Are we not met in thy great name?
Thee in the midst we wait to feel,
We wait to catch the spreading flame.

4 Thou God that answerest by fire,
The Spirit of burning now impart;
And let the flames of pure desire
Rise from the altar of our heart.

5 Truly our fellowship below
With thee and with the Father is;
In thee eternal life we know,
And heaven's unutterable bliss.

—*Charles Wesley.*

EAGLEY. C.M. J. WALCH.

900 "Come thou with us, and we will do thee good."

1 COME in, thou blessed of the Lord,
Stranger nor foe art thou;
We welcome thee with warm accord,
Our friend, our brother, now.

2 The hand of fellowship, the heart
Of love, we offer thee;
Leaving the world, thou dost but part
From lies and vanity.

3 Come with us; we will do thee good
As God to us hath done;
Stand but in him, as those have stood
Whose faith the victory won.

4 And when, by turns, we pass away,
As star by star grows dim,
May each, translated into day,
Be lost and found in him.

—*Montgomery.*

4.—PATRIOTIC HYMNS.

HULL. 8.8.6, 8.8.6. OLD MELODY.

901 *Prayer for the Sovereign.*

1 LORD, thou hast bid thy people pray
For all that bear the sovereign sway,
And thy vicegerents reign,
Rulers, and governors, and powers;
And, lo! in faith we pray for ours,
Nor can we pray in vain.

2 Cover *her* enemies with shame,
Defeat their every hostile aim,
Their baffled hopes destroy;
But shower on *her* thy blessings down,
Crown *her* with grace, with glory crown,
And everlasting joy.

3 To hoary hairs be thou *her* God;
Late may *she* reach that high abode,
Late to *her* heaven remove;
Of virtues full, and happy days,
Accounted worthy by thy grace
To fill a throne above.

4 Secure us, of *her* royal race,
A man to stand before thy face,
And exercise thy power;
With wealth, prosperity, and peace,
Our nation and our churches bless,
Till time shall be no more.

—*Charles Wesley.*

MELCOMBE. L. M. S. WEBBE.

902

A prayer for the Queen.

1 O KING of kings, thy blessing shed
On our anointed Sovereign's head!
And, looking from thy holy heaven,
Protect the crown thyself hast given.

2 Her may we honour and obey,
Uphold her right and lawful sway;
Remembering that the powers that be
Are ministers ordained of thee.

3 Her with thy choicest mercies bless,
To all her counsels give success;
In war, in peace, thine aid be seen,
Thy strength command—God save the
Queen!

4 And oh! when earthly thrones decay,
And earthly kingdoms fade away,
Grant her a throne in worlds on high,
A crown of immortality.

CANADA. 6.6.4, 6.6.6.4. DR. L. MASON.

903

Our native land.

1 GOD bless our native land!
Firm may she ever stand,
Through storm and night;
When the wild tempests rave,
Ruler of wind and wave,
Do thou our country save
By thy great might!

2 For her our prayer shall rise
To God, above the skies;
On thee we wait;
Thou who art ever nigh,
Guarding with watchful eye,
To thee aloud we cry,
God save the State!

3 And not this land alone,
But be thy mercies known
From shore to shore;
Let all the nations see
That men should brothers be,
And form one family
The wide earth o'er.

—*J. S. Dwight.*

"GOD SAVE THE QUEEN." 6.6.4, 6.6.6.4. HENRY CAREY.

904 *"And all the people shouted, and said, God save the king."*

1 God save our gracious Queen,
Long live our noble Queen,
God save the Queen;
Send her victorious,
Happy and glorious,
Long to reign over us;
God save the Queen.

2 Thy choicest gifts in store
On her be pleased to pour,
Long may she reign;
May she defend our laws,
And ever give us cause
To sing with heart and voice
God save the Queen.

905 *"The king trusteth in the Lord."*

1 Lord, thy best blessings shed
On our loved monarch's head;
Round her abide.
Teach her thy holy will,
Shield her from every ill,
Guard, guide, and speed her still,
Safe to thy side.

2 Through every changing scene,
O Lord, preserve our Queen,
Long may she reign!
Her heart inspire and move
With wisdom from above,
And in the nation's love
Her throne maintain!

3 Under thy mighty wings,
Keep her, O King of kings;
Answer her prayer;
Till she shall hence remove
Up to thy courts above,
To dwell in light and love,
Evermore there.

—*Charles Wesley.*

ABRIDGE. C. M. ISAAC SMITH.

906 *Prayer for our native land.*

1 Lord, while for all mankind we pray
Of every clime and coast,
O hear us for our native land,—
The land we love the most!

2 O guard our shores from every foe!
With peace our borders bless,
Our cities with prosperity,
Our fields with plenteousness.

3 Unite us in the sacred love
Of knowledge, truth, and thee;
And let our hills and valleys shout
The songs of liberty.

4 Lord of the nations, thus to thee
Our country we commend;
Be thou her refuge and her trust,
Her everlasting friend.

—*Wreford.*

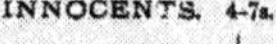

INNOCENTS. 4-7s. ARRANGED BY W. H. MONK.

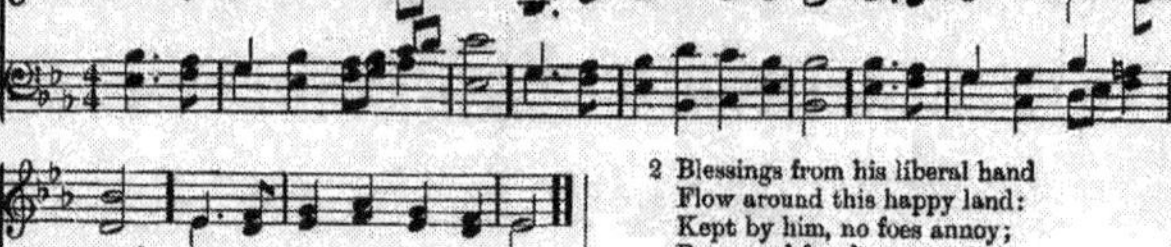

907

National thanksgiving.

1 SWELL the anthem, raise the song;
Praises to our God belong;
Saints and angels join to sing
Praises to the heavenly King.

2 Blessings from his liberal hand
Flow around this happy land:
Kept by him, no foes annoy;
Peace and freedom we enjoy.

3 Here, beneath a virtuous sway,
May we cheerfully obey;
Never feel oppression's rod,
Ever own and worship God.

4 Hark! the voice of nature sings
Praises to the King of kings;
Let us join the choral song,
And the grateful notes prolong.

—*N. Strong.*

5.—THANKSGIVING SERVICES.

LANCASHIRE. 7.6, 7.6, 7.6, 7.6. HENRY SMART.

908

Praise to the Lord of harvest.

1 SING to the Lord of harvest!
Sing songs of love and praise!
With joyful hearts and voices
Your hallelujahs raise;
By him the rolling seasons
In fruitful order move;
Sing to the Lord of harvest
A song of happy love.

2 By him the clouds drop fatness,
The deserts bloom and spring,
The hills leap up in gladness,
The valleys laugh and sing;
He filleth with his fulness
All things with large increase,
He crowns the year with goodness,
With plenty, and with peace.

3 Heap on his sacred altar
The gifts his goodness gave,
The golden sheaves of harvest,
The souls he died to save;
Your hearts lay down before him
When at his feet ye fall,
And with your lives adore him
Who gave his life for all.

4 To God, the gracious Father,
Who made us "very good,"
To Christ, who, when we wandered,
Restored us with his blood,
And to the Holy Spirit,
Who doth upon us pour
His blessed dews and sunshine,
Be praise for evermore!

—*J. S. B. Monsell.*

SERENITY. C. M. W. V. WALLACE.

909

"He crowneth the year with his goodness."

1 FOUNTAIN of mercy, God of love,
How rich thy bounties are!
The rolling seasons, as they move,
Proclaim thy constant care.

2 When in the bosom of the earth
The sower hid the grain,
Thy goodness marked its secret birth,
And sent the early rain.

3 The spring's sweet influence, Lord, was thine;
The plants in beauty grew;
Thou gav'st refulgent suns to shine,
And the refreshing dew.

4 These various mercies from above
Matured the swelling grain;
A kindly harvest crowns thy love,
And plenty fills the plain.

5 We own and bless thy gracious sway;
Thy hand all nature hails;
Seed-time nor harvest, night nor day,
Summer nor winter, fails.

—*Mrs. Flowerdew.*

ST. GEORGE. 8-7s. SIR G. ELVEY.

910

Harvest-home festival.

1 COME, ye thankful people, come,
Raise the song of harvest-home;
All is safely gathered in,
Ere the winter storms begin;
God our Maker doth provide
For our wants to be supplied;
Come to God's own temple, come,
Raise the song of harvest-home!

2 We ourselves are God's own field,
Fruit unto his praise to yield;
Wheat and tares together sown,
Unto joy or sorrow grown;
First the blade, and then the ear,
Then the full corn shall appear;
Grant, O harvest Lord, that we
Wholesome grain and pure may be.

3 For the Lord our God shall come,
And shall take his harvest home;
From his field shall in that day
All offences purge away;
Give his angels charge at last
In the fire the tares to cast;
But the fruitful ears to store
In his garner evermore.

4 Then, thou Church triumphant, come,
Raise the song of harvest-home!
All are safely gathered in,
Free from sorrow, free from sin;
There forever purified,
In God's garner to abide;
Come, ten thousand angels, come,
Raise the glorious harvest-home!

—*Dean Alford.*

6.—DAYS OF NATIONAL HUMILIATION.

BEDFORD. C. M. *Slowly.* W. WHEALL.

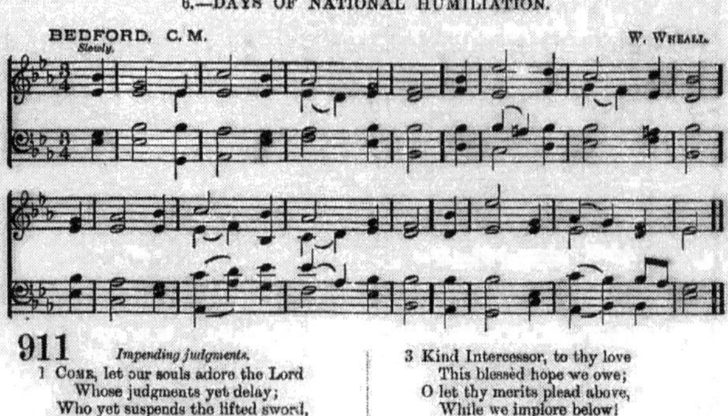

911 *Impending judgments.*

1 COME, let our souls adore the Lord
Whose judgments yet delay;
Who yet suspends the lifted sword,
And gives us time to pray.

2 Great is our guilt, our fears are great,
But let us not despair;
Still open is the mercy-seat
To penitence and prayer.

3 Kind Intercessor, to thy love
This blessed hope we owe;
O let thy merits plead above,
While we implore below!

4 Though justice near thy awful throne
Attends thy dread command,
Lord, hear thy servants, hear thy Son,
And save a guilty land.

—*Anne Steele.*

BYZANTIUM. C. M. W. JACKSON.

912 *National confession.*

1 GREAT King of nations, hear our prayer,
While at thy feet we fall,
And humbly, with united cry,
To thee for mercy call.

2 The guilt is ours, but grace is thine,
O turn us not away!
But hear us from thy lofty throne,
And help us when we pray.

3 Our fathers' sins were manifold,
And ours no less we own,
Yet wondrously from age to age
Thy goodness hath been shown.

4 When dangers, like a stormy sea,
Beset our country round,
To thee we looked, to thee we cried,
And help in thee was found.

5 With one consent we meekly bow
Beneath thy chastening hand,
And, pouring forth confession meet,
Mourn with our mourning land.

6 With pitying eye behold our need,
As thus we lift our prayer;
Correct us with thy judgments, Lord,
Then let thy mercy spare.

—*J. H. Gurney.*

WHEALL.

throne
hy Son,
ane Steele.

. JACKSON.

ea,
rried,
ow
d,
neet,
nd.
ed,
Lord,
Gurney.

MARTYRDOM. C. M. HUGH WILSON.

913

Prayer in time of pestilence.

1 In grief and fear, to thee, O Lord,
We now for succour fly,
Thine awful judgments are abroad,
O shield us, lest we die!

2 The fell disease on every side
Walks forth with tainted breath;
And pestilence, with rapid stride,
Bestrews the land with death.

3 O look with pity on the scene
Of sadness and of dread,
And let thine angel stand between
The living and the dead!

4 With contrite hearts to thee, our King,
We turn, who oft have strayed;
Accept the sacrifice we bring,
And let the plague be stayed.

—*Bullock.*

NEWTON FERNS. 8.7, 8.7. SAMUEL SMITH.

914

Pardon for national sins.

1 Dread Jehovah! God of nations!
From thy temple in the skies,
Hear thy people's supplications,
Now for their deliverance rise.

2 Lo! with deep contrition turning,
In thy holy place we bend;
Hear us, fasting, praying, mourning;
Hear us, spare us, and defend.

3 Though our sins, our hearts confounding,
Long and loud for vengeance call,
Thou hast mercy more abounding;
Jesus' blood can cleanse them all.

4 Let that mercy veil transgression;
Let that blood our guilt efface;
Save thy people from oppression;
Save from spoil thy holy place.

BRIGHTON. 6-8s.

915

National humiliation.

1 O God, thy righteousness we own;
Judgment is at thy house begun!
With humble awe thy rod we hear,
And guilty in thy sight appear;
We cannot in thy judgment stand,
But sink beneath thy mighty hand.

2 Our mouth as in the dust we lay,
And still for mercy, mercy pray;
Unworthy to behold thy face,
Unfaithful stewards of thy grace,
Our sin and wickedness we own,
And deeply for acceptance groan.

3 We have not, Lord, thy gifts improved,
But basely from thy statutes roved,
And done thy loving Spirit despite,
And sinned against the clearest light,
Brought back thy agonizing pain,
And nailed thee to thy cross again.

4 Yet do not drive us from thy face,
A stiff-necked and hard-hearted race;
But, oh! in tender mercy break
The iron sinew in our neck;
The softening power of love impart,
And melt the marble of our heart.

—*Charles Wesley.*

HEBRON. L. M. Dr. L. Mason.

916

National repentance.

1 O let us our own works forsake,
Ourselves and all we have deny;
Thy condescending counsel take,
And come to thee, pure gold to buy.

2 O might we, through thy grace, attain
The faith thou never wilt reprove;
The faith that purges every stain,
The faith that always works by love!

3 O might we see, in this our day,
The things belonging to our peace,
And timely meet thee in thy way
Of judgments, and our sins confess!

4 Thy fatherly corrections own:
With filial awe revere thy rod;
And turn, with zealous haste, and run
Into the outstretched arms of God.

—*Charles Wesley.*

SHAWMUT. S. M. — Arranged by Lowell Mason.

917 *The evils of intemperance.*

1 Mourn for the thousands slain,
  The youthful and the strong;
Mourn for the wine-cup's fearful reign,
  And the deluded throng.

2 Mourn for the tarnished gem—
  For reason's light divine,
Quenched from the soul's bright diadem,
  Where God had bid it shine.

3 Mourn for the ruined soul—
  Eternal life and light
Lost by the fiery, maddening bowl,
  And turned to hopeless night.

4 Mourn for the lost,—but call,
  Call to the strong, the free;
Rouse them to shun that dreadful fall
  And to the refuge flee.

5 Mourn for the lost,—but pray,
  Pray to our God above,
To break the fell destroyer's sway,
  And show his saving love.

INVITATION. C. M. — Thomas Hastings.

918 *"Dead in trespasses and sins."*

1 Life from the dead, Almighty God,
  'Tis thine alone to give;
To lift the poor inebriate up,
  And bid the helpless live.

2 Life from the dead! For those we plead
  Fast bound in passion's chain,
That, from their iron fetters freed,
  They wake to life again.

3 Life from the dead! Quickened by thee,
  Be all their powers inclined
To temperance, truth, and piety,
  And pleasures pure, refined.

4 And may they by thy help abide,
  The tempter's power withstand;
By grace restored and purified,
  In Christ accepted stand.

919 *Prayer for the intemperate.*

1 'Tis thine alone, almighty Name,
  To raise the dead to life,
The lost inebriate to reclaim
  From passion's fearful strife.

2 What ruin hath intemperance wrought!
  How widely roll its waves!
How many myriads hath it brought
  To fill dishonoured graves!

3 And see, O Lord, what numbers still
  Are maddened by the bowl,
Led captive at the tyrant's will,
  In bondage, heart and soul.

4 Stretch forth thy hand, O God, our King,
  And break the galling chain;
Deliverance to the captive bring,
  And end the usurper's reign.
—*E. F. Hatfield.*

8.—WORKS OF CHARITY.

ST. MICHAEL. S. M.

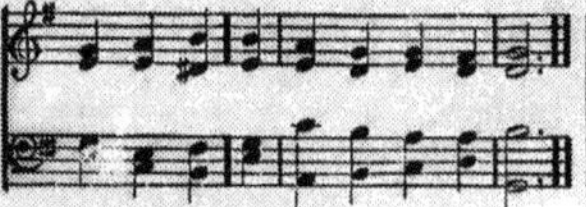

920 *Christian sympathy.*

1 O PRAISE our God to-day,
His constant mercy bless,
Whose love hath helped us on our way,
And granted us success.

2 His arm the strength imparts
Our daily toil to bear;
His grace alone inspires our hearts,
Each other's load to share.

3 O happiest work below,
Earnest of joy above,
To sweeten many a cup of woe,
By deeds of holy love!

4 Lord, may it be our choice
This blessed rule to keep,
"Rejoice with them that do rejoice,
And weep with them that weep."

5 God of the widow, hear,
Our work of mercy bless;
God of the fatherless, be near,
And grant us good success.

—Sir H. W. Baker.

ST. GEORGE. S. M. H. J. GAUNTLETT, Mus. Doc.

921 *"Ye have done it unto Me."*

1 WE give thee but thine own,
Whate'er the gift may be;
All that we have is thine alone,
A trust, O Lord, from thee.

2 May we thy bounties thus
As stewards true receive,
And gladly as thou blessest us,
To thee our first-fruits give.

3 O, hearts are bruised and dead,
And homes are bare and cold,
And lambs for whom the Shepherd bled
Are straying from the fold

4 To comfort and to bless,
To find a balm for woe,
To tend the lone and fatherless
Is angels' work below.

5 And we believe thy word,
Though dim our faith may be;
Whate'er we do for thine, O Lord,
We do it unto thee.

—W. W. How.

ST. THOMAS. 8.7, 8.7, 4.7.

922

Home missionary hymn.

1 Now, O Lord, fulfil thy pleasure;
Breathe upon thy chosen band;
And with pentecostal measure,
Send forth reapers o'er our land—
‖:Faithful reapers,:‖
Gathering sheaves for thy right hand.

2 Feebly now they toil in sadness,
Weeping o'er the waste around,
Slowly gathering grains of gladness,
While their echoing cries resound,
‖:"Pray that reapers:‖
In God's harvest may abound."

3 Broad the shadow of our nation;
Eager thousands hither roam;
Lo! they wait for thy salvation;
Come, Lord Jesus! quickly come;
‖:By thy Spirit:‖
Bring thy ransomed people home.

4 Soon shall end the time of weeping,
Soon the reaping time will come,
Heaven and earth together keeping
God's eternal Harvest Home;
‖:Saints and angels!:‖
Shout the world's great Harvest Home.

PRESCOTT. C. M.

923

The Box of Spikenard.

1 She loved her Saviour, and to him
Her costliest present brought;
To crown his head, or grace his name,
No gift too rare she thought.

2 So let the Saviour be adored,
And not the poor despised;
Give to the hungry from your hoard,
But all, give all to Christ.

3 Go, clothe the naked, lead the blind,
Give to the weary rest;
For sorrow's children comfort find,
And help for all distressed;

4 But give to Christ alone thy heart,
Thy faith, thy love supreme;
Then for his sake thine alms impart,
And so give all to him.

—*W. Cutter.*

9.—EDUCATIONAL MEETINGS.

NURENBERG. 4-7s. JOHANN RUDOLF AHLE.

924 *Asking a blessing for teachers.*

1 MIGHTY One, before whose face
Wisdom had her glorious seat,
When the orbs that people space
Sprang to earth beneath thy feet.

2 Source of truth, whose beams alone
Light the mighty world with mind;
God of love, who from thy throne
Kindly watchest all mankind;

3 Shed on those who in thy name
Teach the way of truth and right,
Shed that love's undying flame,
Shed that wisdom's guiding light.

—*W. C. Bryant.*

INVITATION. C. M. THOMAS HASTINGS.

925 *Christian education.*

1 FATHER supreme, by whom we live,
Thou who art God alone,
Our songs of grateful praise receive,
And make our hearts thy throne.

2 Creation vast reveals thy name;
The earth, the heavens above,
With one unceasing voice proclaim
Thy wisdom, power, and love.

3 We bless thee for thy works, all bright
With tokens of thy skill;
But more for reason's sacred light,
By which we read thy will:

4 For not on brightest orbs, which roll
Through space at thy decree,
Hast thou bestowed the thinking soul,
To know and worship thee.

5 May every science, every truth,
Our eager minds explore,
Lead us, alike in age and youth,
Thy wisdom to adore.

6 May those who teach, and those who learn,
Walk in the narrow road;
In every sphere of thought discern
An ever-present God.

—*E. H. Dewart.*

ST. PETER. C.M. — A. R. Reinagle.

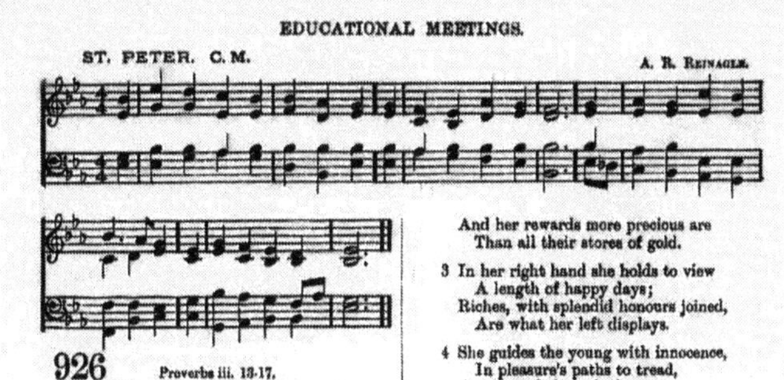

926

Proverbs iii. 13-17.

1 O happy is the man who hears
Instruction's warning voice;
And who celestial Wisdom makes
His early, only choice.

2 For she has treasures greater far
Than east or west unfold;
And her rewards more precious are
Than all their stores of gold.

3 In her right hand she holds to view
A length of happy days;
Riches, with splendid honours joined,
Are what her left displays.

4 She guides the young with innocence,
In pleasure's paths to tread,
A crown of glory she bestows
Upon the hoary head.

5 According as her labours rise,
So her rewards increase;
Her ways are ways of pleasantness,
And all her paths are peace.

—*Isaac Watts.*

HURSLEY. L.M. — Huguenot Melody.

927

Prayer for teachers and students.

1 O Thou who hast, in every age,
Thy trusting people safely led,
On us, who in thy work engage,
Thy Spirit's guiding influence shed.

2 As moon and stars their beams unite,
To gild and gladden every zone,
So blend thy word and works their light,
To make thy grace and glory known.

3 Though thou art holy, wise, and great,
And we are sinful worms of clay,
Thou dost regard our low estate,
And bend to listen while we pray.

4 On those who sow in youthful minds
The seeds of harvests yet to be,
Bestow the living faith, which binds
The heart in loyal love to thee.

5 Protect our youth from every foe,
And lead in paths of truth and peace;
As they in age and knowledge grow,
May faith and holiness increase.

6 So to thy Church, in wisdom taught,
May men of nobler life be given;
Until, by holy deed and thought,
This world is lifted nearer heaven.

—*E. H. Dewart.*

IMAGE EVALUATION
TEST TARGET (MT-3)

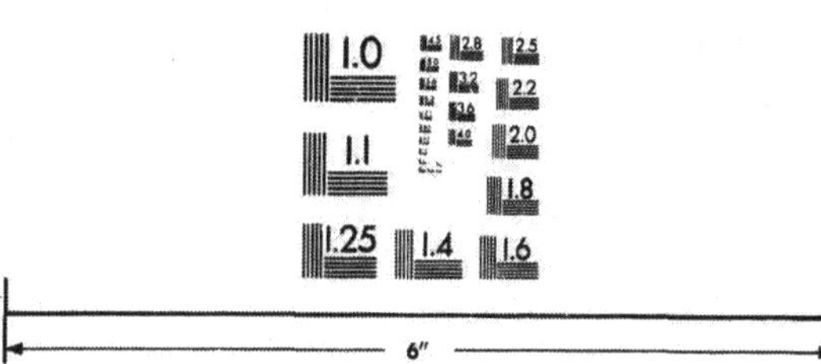

WARRINGTON. L. M. REV. RALPH HARRISON.

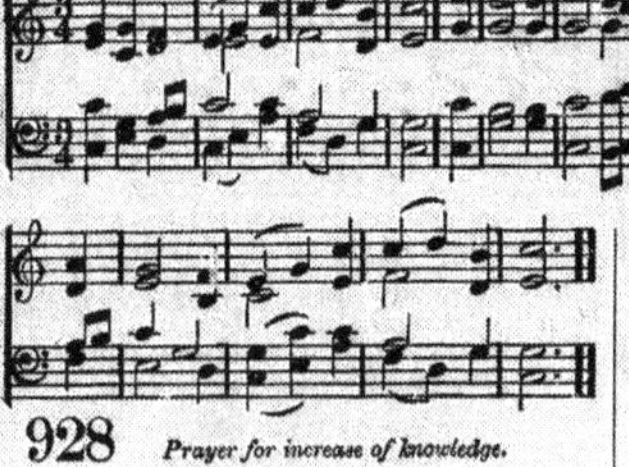

928 *Prayer for increase of knowledge.*

1 STRONG Son of God, immortal Love,
Whom we, that have not seen thy face,
By faith, and faith alone embrace,
Believing where we cannot prove;

2 Our little systems have their day;
They have their day and cease to be;
They are but broken lights of thee,
And thou, O Lord, art more than they.

3 We have but faith: we cannot know;
For knowledge is of things we see;
And yet we trust it comes from thee,
A beam in darkness: let it grow.

4 Let knowledge grow from more to more,
But more of reverence in us dwell;
That mind and soul, according well,
May make one music as before.

—*Tennyson.*

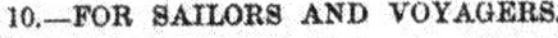

10.—FOR SAILORS AND VOYAGERS.

MARINERS. 4-7s.

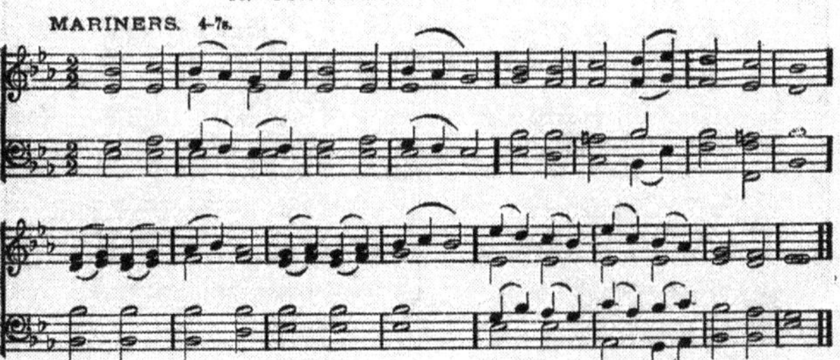

929 *On going on shipboard.*

1 LORD, whom winds and seas obey,
Guide us through the watery way;
In the hollow of thy hand
Hide, and bring us safe to land.

2 Jesus, let our faithful mind
Rest, on thee alone reclined;
Every anxious thought repress,
Keep our souls in perfect peace.

3 Keep the souls whom now we leave;
Bid them to each other cleave;
Bid them walk on life's rough sea;
Bid them come by faith to thee.

4 Save, till all these tempests end,
All who on thy love depend;
Waft our happy spirits o'er;
Land us on the heavenly shore.

—*Charles Wesley.*

BROMLEY. 7.6, 7.6, 7.6, 7.6. LONDON TUNE BOOK.

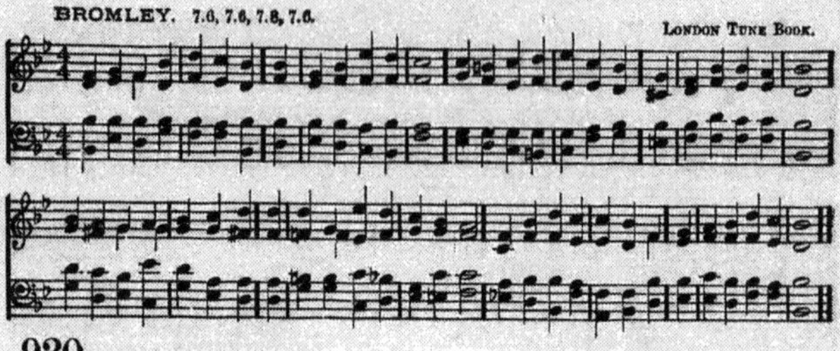

930

Divine protection on the sea.

1 Lord of earth, and air, and sea,
Supreme in power and grace,
Under thy protection, we
Our souls and bodies place.
Bold an unknown land to try,
We launch into the foaming deep;
Rocks, and storms, and deaths defy,
With Jesus in the ship.

2 Who the calm can understand,
In a believer's breast?
In the hollow of his hand
Our souls securely rest;
Winds may rise, and seas may roar,
We on his love our spirits stay;
Him with quiet joy adore,
Whom winds and seas obey.

—*Charles Wesley.*

BLOOR. L. M. T. C. JEFFERS.

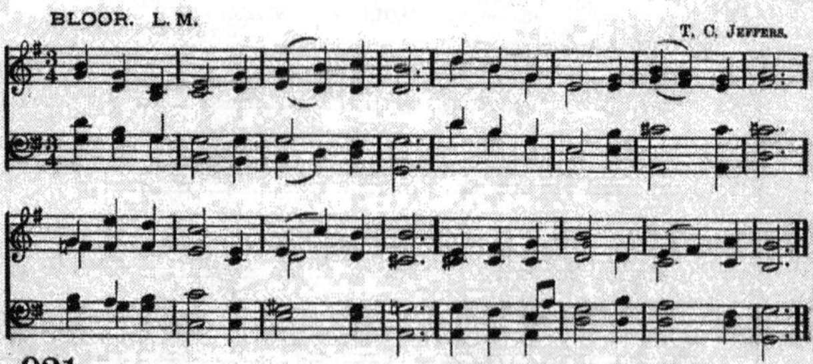

931

"Thy way is in the deep."

1 Lord of the wide, extensive main,
Whose power the wind, the sea controls,
Whose hand doth earth and heaven sustain,
Whose Spirit leads believing souls:

2 For thee we leave our native shore,
We whom thy love delights to keep,
In other climes thy works explore,
And see thy wonders in the deep.

3 'Tis here thine unknown paths we trace,
Which dark to human eyes appear;
While through the mighty waves we pass,
Faith only sees that God is here.

4 Throughout the deep thy footsteps shine,
We own thy way is in the sea,
O'erawed by majesty divine,
And lost in thy immensity.

5 Thy wisdom here we learn to adore,
Thine everlasting truth we prove;
Amazing heights of boundless power,
Unfathomable depths of love.

—*Charles Wesley.*

ABENDS. L. M. Sir H. S. Oakeley.

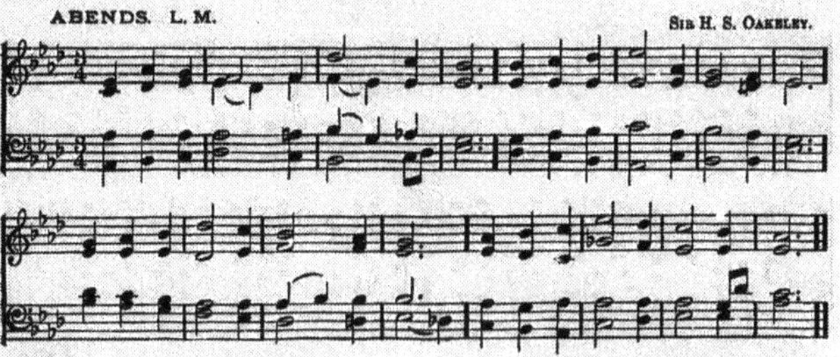

932

Prayer for those at sea.

1 While o'er the deep thy servants sail,
Send thou, O Lord, the prosperous gale;
And on their hearts, where'er they go,
O let thy heavenly breezes blow!

2 If on the morning's wings they fly,
They will not pass beyond thine eye;
The wanderer's prayer thou bend'st to hear,
And faith exults to see thee near.

3 When tempests rock the groaning bark,
O hide them safe in Jesus' ark!
When in the tempting port they ride,
O keep them safe at Jesus' side!

4 If life's wide ocean smile or roar,
Still guide them to the heavenly shore;
And grant their dust in Christ may sleep,
Abroad, at home, or in the deep.

—*Burgess.*

ST. PETERSBURG. 6-8s. Dimitri S. Bortniansky.

933

Intercession for those at sea.

1 Eternal Father! strong to save,
Whose arm doth bind the restless wave,
Who bidd'st the mighty ocean deep
Its own appointed limits keep:
O hear us when we cry to thee
For those in peril on the sea!

2 O Saviour! whose almighty word
The winds and waves submissive heard,
Who walkedst on the foaming deep,
And calm amidst its rage did sleep:
O hear us when we cry to thee
For those in peril on the sea!

3 O Sacred Spirit! who didst brood
Upon the chaos dark and rude,
Who bad'st its angry tumults cease,
And gavest light, and life, and peace:
O hear us when we cry to thee
For those in peril on the sea!

4 O Trinity of love and power!
Our brethren shield in danger's hour;
From rock and tempest, fire and foe,
Protect them wheresoe'er they go;
And ever let there rise to thee
Glad hymns of praise from land and sea.

—*W. Whiting.*

TALLIS' ORDINAL. C. M. — Thomas Tallis.

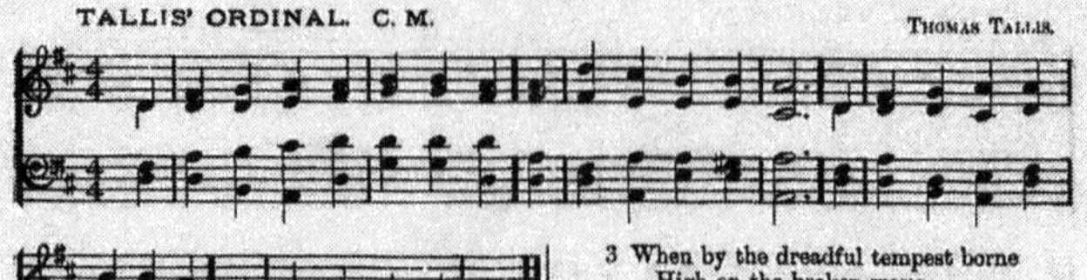

934

Travellers' hymn.

1 How are thy servants blest, O Lord!
How sure is their defence!
Eternal Wisdom is their guide,
Their help Omnipotence.

2 In foreign realms, and lands remote,
Supported by thy care,
Through burning climes they pass unhurt,
And breathe in tainted air.

3 When by the dreadful tempest borne
High on the broken wave,
They know thou art not slow to hear,
Nor impotent to save.

4 The storm is laid, the winds retire,
Obedient to thy will;
The sea, that roars at thy command,
At thy command is still.

5 In midst of dangers, fears, and deaths,
Thy goodness we'll adore;
We'll praise thee for thy mercies past,
And humbly hope for more.

6 Our life, while thou preserv'st that life,
Thy sacrifice shall be;
And death, when death shall be our lot,
Shall join our souls to thee.

—*Addison.*

SALVATOR. 8.7, 8.7, 8.7, 8.7. — J. P. Judson.

935

Mariner's evening hymn.

1 Out on life's dark heaving ocean,
Winds and waves around us rave;
In the tempest's wild commotion,
Friend of sinners, shield and save!
Vain are all our weak endeavours—
Thou our Guide and Helper be!
Star of Hope! in danger cheer us;
Help can only come from thee.

2 When the storms of fierce temptation
Wildly sweep across our way,
And the night of fear and sorrow
Quenches every starry ray,
Let thy presence, great Redeemer,
Banish all our guilty fear;
And the joy of thy salvation
Every fainting spirit cheer.

3 When the mists of doubt and passion
Hide the reefs and shoals from sight,
God of love protect and save us,
Be our Refuge and our Light;
Be our sure unerring Pilot,
Guide us safely to the shore,
Where the waves of sin and sorrow
Beat upon the soul no more.

—*E. H. Dewart.*

STELLA. 6-8s. (First Tune.) From "Crown of Jesus."

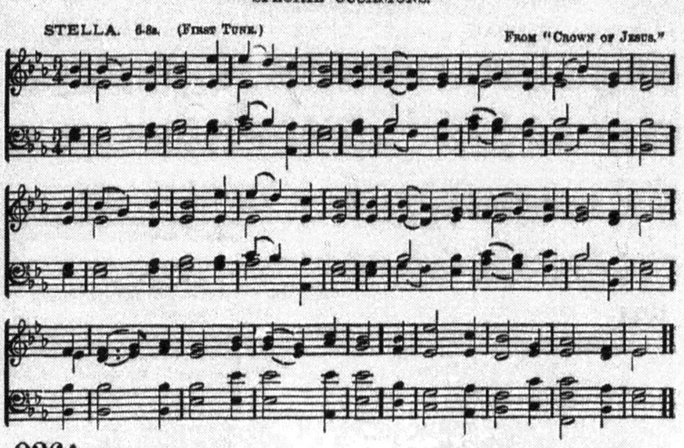

936*

1 And can it be that I should gain
An interest in the Saviour's blood?
Died he for me, who caused his pain?
For me, who him to death pursued?
Amazing love! how can it be,
That thou, my God, shouldst die for me?

2 'Tis mystery all! The immortal dies!
Who can explore his strange design?
In vain the first-born seraph tries
To sound the depths of Love Divine!
'Tis mercy all; let earth adore,
Let angel minds inquire no more.

3 He left his Father's throne above;
(So free, so infinite his grace!)
Emptied himself of all but love,
And bled for Adam's helpless race:
'Tis mercy all, immense and free,
For, O my God, it found out *me!*

4 Long my imprisoned spirit lay
Fast bound in sin and nature's night;
Thine eye diffused a quickening ray;
I woke: the dungeon flamed with light;
My chains fell off, my heart was free,
I rose, went forth, and followed thee.

5 No condemnation now I dread;
Jesus, and all in him, is mine!
Alive in him, my living Head,
And clothed in righteousness divine,
Bold I approach the eternal throne,
And claim the crown through Christ my own.

—*Charles Wesley.*

* *This hymn was accidentally omitted in the earlier editions.*

BRIGHTON. 6-8s. (Second Tune.)

SECTION XII.

DOXOLOGIES, BENEDICTIONS, AND CHANTS.

1 TUNE: ST. ANN'S. C.M.
(SEE HYMN 90.)

1 To Father, Son and Holy Ghost,
The God whom we adore,
Be glory, as it was, is now,
And shall be evermore!

2 TUNE: ST. ANN'S. C.M.
(SEE HYMN 90.)

1 To Father, Son, and Holy Ghost,
Who sweetly all agree,
To save the world of sinners lost,
Eternal glory be!

3 TUNE: OLD HUNDREDTH.
L. M. (SEE HYMN 7.)

1 PRAISE God, from whom all blessings flow;
Praise him, all creatures here below;
Praise him above, ye heavenly host;
Praise Father, Son, and Holy Ghost

4 TUNE: BELMONT. C.M.
(SEE HYMN 109.)

1 BE known to us in breaking bread,
But do not then depart;
Saviour abide with us, and spread
Thy table in our heart.

5 TUNE: HURSLEY. L. M.
(SEE HYMN 804.)

1 BE present at our table, Lord,
Be here and everywhere adored,
These creatures bless, and grant that we
May feast in Paradise with thee.

6 TUNE: HURSLEY. L. M.
(SEE HYMN 804.)

1 WE thank thee, Lord, for this our food,
But more because of Jesus' blood;
Let manna to our souls be given,
The Bread of life sent down from heaven.

7 TUNE: AUTUMN. 8.7, 8.7, 8.7, 8.7.
(SEE HYMN 95.)

1 MAY the grace of Christ our Saviour,
And the Father's boundless love,
With the holy Spirit's favour
Rest upon us from above!
Thus may we abide in union
With each other in the Lord;
And possess, in sweet communion,
Joys which earth cannot afford.

8 TUNE: MAIDSTONE. 8-7s.
(SEE HYMN 767.)

1 HOLY Father, fount of light,
God of wisdom, goodness, might;
Holy Son, who cam'st to dwell
God with us Emmanuel;
Holy Spirit, heavenly Dove,
God of comfort, peace, and love;
Evermore be thou adored,
Holy, Holy, Holy Lord. Amen.

9 TUNE: AUSTRIA. 8.7, 8.7, 8.7, 8.7.
(SEE HYMN 664.)

1 LET the voice of all creation,
Earth and heaven's triumphant host,
Praise the God of our salvation,
Father, Son, and Holy Ghost.
See the heavenly elders casting
Golden crowns before his throne;
Hallelujahs everlasting
Be to him, and him alone. Amen.

10 TUNE: REGENT SQUARE.
8.7, 8.7, 4.7. (SEE HYMN 835.)

1 PRAISE the Father, throned in heaven;
Praise the everlasting Son;
Praise the Spirit freely given;
Praise the blessed Three in One.
‖:Hallelujah!:‖
Long as ceaseless ages run. Amen.

11 TUNE: PRAYER. 4-7s.
(SEE HYMN 598.)

1 FATHER, live, by all things feared;
Live the Son, alike revered;
Equally be thou adored,
Holy Ghost, eternal Lord.

2 Three in person, one in power,
Thee we worship evermore;
Praise by all to thee be given,
Endless theme of earth and heaven.

12 TUNE: BENEDICTION. 7.8, 7.8, 7.8, 7.8. (See Hymn 703.)

1 Lord, dismiss us with thy blessing,
Bid us now depart in peace;
Still on heavenly manna feeding,
Let our faith and love increase;
Fill each breast with consolation;
Up to thee our hearts we raise;
When we reach yon blissful station,
Then we'll give thee nobler praise!
Hallelujah!

ST. THOMAS. 8.7, 8.7, 4.7.

13

1 Lord, dismiss us with thy blessing,
Fill our hearts with joy and peace;
Let us each, thy love possessing,
Triumph in redeeming grace;
‖: O refresh us, :‖
Travelling through this wilderness!

2 Thanks we give, and adoration,
For thy gospel's joyful sound;
May the fruits of thy salvation
In our hearts and lives abound;
‖: May thy presence :‖
With us evermore be found.

3 So, whene'er the signal's given
Us from earth to call away,
Borne on angels' wings to heaven,
Glad the summons to obey,
‖: May we ever :‖
Reign with Christ in endless day.

14 TUNE: EPIPHANY. 11.10, 11.10. (See Hymn 146.)

The infinity of God.

1 Holy and Infinite! Viewless, Eternal!
Veiled in the glory that none can sustain,
None comprehendeth thy being supernal,
Nor can the heaven of heavens contain.

2 Holy and Infinite! limitless, boundless,
All thy perfections, and power, and praise!
Ocean of mystery! awful and soundless
All thine unsearchable judgments and
ways!

3 King of Eternity! what revelation
Could the created and finite sustain,
But for thy marvellous manifestation,
Godhead incarnate in weakness and pain!

4 Therefore archangels and angels adore thee,
Cherubim wonder, and seraphs admire;
Therefore we praise thee, rejoicing before
thee,
Joining in rapture the heavenly choir.

5 Glorious in holiness, fearful in praises,
Who shall not fear thee and who shall not
laud?
Anthems of glory thy universe raises,
Holy and Infinite, Father and God!

15 TE DEUM LAUDAMUS. Sir F. A. G. Ouseley.

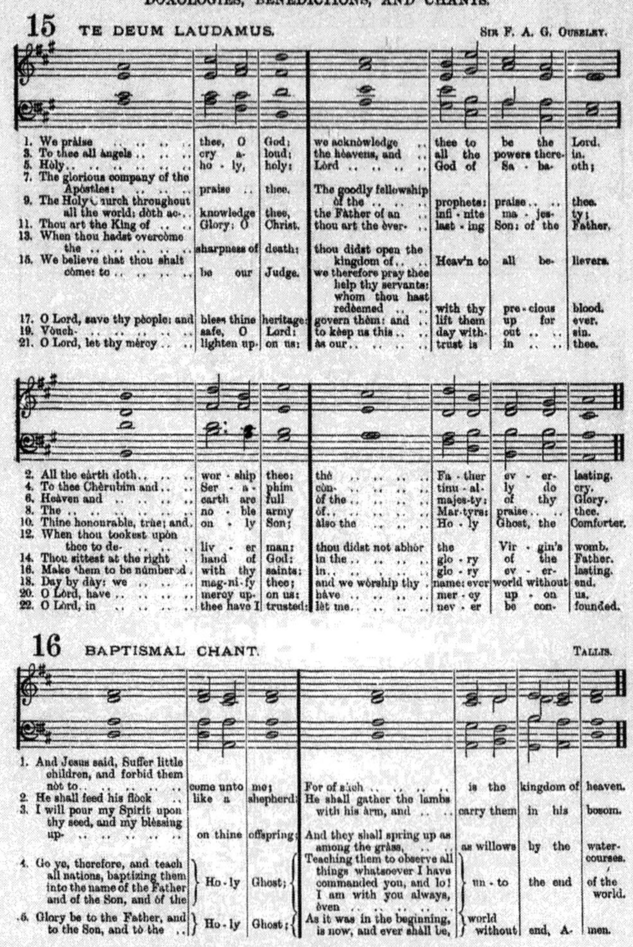

1. We pràise	thee, O	God;	we acknòwledge ..	thee to	be the	Lord.
3. To thee all àngels	cry a-	loud;	the hèavens, and ..	all the	powers there-	in.
5. Hòly..	ho - ly,	holy;	Lòrd	God of	Sa - ba-	oth;
7. The glorious company of the Apòstles:	praise ..	thee.	The goodly fellowship òf the	prophets:	praise	thee.
9. The Holy Church throughout all the world: dòth ac- ..	knowledge	thee,	the Fàther of an ..	infi - nite	ma - jes-	ty;
11. Thou art the King of	Glory: O	Christ.	thou art the èver- ..	last - ing	Son: of the	Father.
13. When thou hadst overcòme the	sharpness of	death:	thou didst open the kingdom of	Heav'n to	all be-	lievers.
15. We believe that thou shalt còme: to	be our	Judge.	we therefore pray thee help thy servants: whom thou hast redèemed	with thy	pre - cious	blood.
17. O Lord, save thy pèople: and	bless thine	heritage:	govern thèm: and ..	lift them	up for	ever.
19. Vòuch-	safe, O	Lord:	to kèep us this	day with-	out	sin.
21. O Lord, let thy mèrcy	lighten up-	on us:	às our	trust is	in	thee.

2. All the eàrth doth	wor - ship	thee:	thè	Fa - ther	ev - er-	lasting.
4. To thee Chèrubim and	Ser - a -	phim	còn-	tinu - al-	ly do	cry.
6. Heàven and	earth are	full	òf the	majes-ty:	of thy	Glory.
8. The	no - ble	army	òf..	Mar-tyrs:	praise	thee.
10. Thine honourable, trùe; and.	on - ly	Son;	àlso the	Ho - ly	Ghost, the	Comforter.
12. When thou tookest upòn thee to de-	liv - er	man:	thou didst not abhòr	the	Vir - gin's	womb.
14. Thou sittest at the right .	hand of	God:	in the	glo - ry	of the	Father.
16. Make them to be nùmbered .	with thy	saints:	in	glo - ry	ev - er-	lasting.
18. Day by dày: we	mag-ni-fy	thee;	and we wòrship thy .	name: ever	world without	end.
20. O Lòrd, have	mercy up-	on us:	hàve	mer - cy	up - on	us.
22. O Lòrd, in	thee have I	trusted:	lèt me	nev - er	be con-	founded.

16 BAPTISMAL CHANT. Tallis.

1. And Jesus said, Suffer little children, and forbid them nòt to	come unto	me;	For of sùch	is the	kingdom of	heaven.
2. He shall feed his flòck ..	like a	shepherd:	He shall gather the lambs with his àrm, and	carry them	in his	bosom.
3. I will pour my Spirit upon thy seed, and my blèssing up-	on thine	offspring:	And they shall spring up as among the gràss, ...	as willows	by the	water-courses.
4. Go ye, therefore, and teach all nations, baptizing them into the name of the Father and of the Son, and òf the	Ho - ly	Ghost;	Teaching them to observe all things whatsoever I have commanded you, and lo! I am with you always, èven	un - to	the end	of the world.
5. Glory be to the Father, and to the Son, and tò the ..	Ho - ly	Ghost;	As it was in the beginning, is now, and ever shàll be,	world without	end, A-	men.

(Read across the

17 *"All thy works praise thee, O Lord."*

1. THE strain upraise .. .. of | joy and praise, | Al - le - lu - | ia.

2. And the chòirs that .. .. .. | dwell on high, | Al - le - lu - | ia,
3. They in the Rest of Pàra- .. .. | dise who dwell, | Al - le - lu - | ia,
4. The planets beaming òn their .. | heaven - ly way, | Al - le - lu - | ia,
5. Ye clòuds .. .. that | on - ward sweep, | Ye winds on pin - ions | light,
6. In swèet .. .. con- | sent u - nite | Your Al - le - lu - | ia.

7. Ye flòods .. .. and | o - cean billows, | Ye storms and win - ter | snow,

8. Ye gròves .. .. that | wave in spring, | Al - le - lu - | ia,
9. First let the birds, with pàinted | plum - age gay, | Al - le - lu - | ia,
10. Then let the beasts of èarth, with | vary - ing strain, | Al - le - lu - | ia,
11. Here let the mountains thunder fòrth so- | nor - - ous | Al - le - lu - | ia.
12. Thou jubilant abỳss of .. .. | o - cean, cry | Al - le - lu - | ia.

13. To God, who àll cre- .. .. .. | - a - tion made, | Al - le - lu - | ia,

14. This is the stràin, the e- .. .. | ter - nal strain, | The Lord Al - might - y | loves:
15. Àl- .. .. le- | lu - - ia, | Al - le - lu - | ia,
16. Wherefore we sing, both heart and vòice a- | wak - - ing, | Al - le - lu - | ia.
17. Now from àll men .. .. .. | be out - poured | Al - le - lu - | ia,
18. With Allelùia .. .. | e - ver - more, | Al - le - lu - | ia,
19. Praise be dòne .. .. to the | Three in One. | Al - le - lu - | ia,

two pages.)

REV. J. B. DYKES.

To the glory of their King shall the ransomed | peo - ple sing | Al - le - lu - | ia.
Shall re-ècho .. .. | through the sky | Al - le - lu - | ia.
The blessed ones, with jòy the .. | cho - rus swell. | Al - le - lu - | ia.
The shining constellàtions .. .. | join, and say | Al - le - lu - | ia.
Ye thunders, èchoing .. .. .. | loud and deep, | Ye lightnings wild - ly | bright,
Àl - - - - - - - le - | lu - - ia; | Al - le - lu - | ia.
Ye dàys .. .. of | cloud - less beauty, | Hoar frost and sum - mer | glow,
And glòrious .. .. | for - ests, sing | Al - le - lu - | ia.
Exalt their great Creàtor's .. .. | praise, and say | Al - le - lu - | ia.
Join in creation's hýmn, and .. .. | cry a - gain | Al - le - lu - | ia.
There let the valleys sing in gèntler | cho - - - rus | Al - le - lu - | ia.
Ye tracts of earth and cònti - | nents, re - ply | Al - le - lu - | ia.
The frequent hýmn be .. .. .. | du - ly paid: | Al - le - lu - | ia.
This is the sòng, the | heaven-ly song, | That Christ the King ap - | proves:
Àl - - - - - - - le - | lu - - ia, | Al - le - lu - | ia.
And children's voices echo, ànswer | mak - - ing, | Al - le - lu - | ia.
Allelùia .. .. | to the Lord; | Al - le - lu - | ia.
The Son and Spirit | we a - dore. | Al - le - lu - | ia.
Àl - - - - - - - le - | lu - - ia, | Al - le - lu - | ia.

18 Psalm lxvii.

FROM SPOHR.

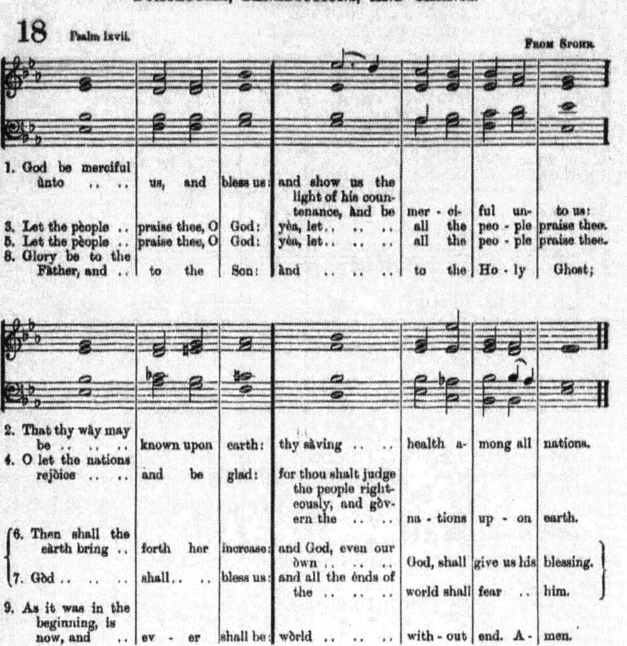
1. God be merciful unto .. .. | us, and | bless us: | and show us the light of his countenance, and be | mer - ci- | ful un- | to us:
3. Let the pèople .. | praise thee, O | God: | yèa, let.. .. .. | all the | peo - ple | praise thee.
5. Let the pèople .. | praise thee, O | God: | yèa, let.. .. .. | all the | peo - ple | praise thee.
8. Glory be to the Fàther, and .. | to the | Son: | ànd .. .. .. | to the | Ho - ly | Ghost;
2. That thy wày may be .. .. .. | known upon | earth: | thy sàving .. .. | health a- | mong all | nations.
4. O let the nations rejòice .. .. | and be | glad: | for thou shalt judge the people righteously, and gòvern the .. .. | na - tions | up - on | earth.
6. Then shall the eàrth bring .. | forth her | increase: | and God, even our òwn .. .. .. | God, shall | give us his | blessing.
7. Gòd .. .. .. | shall.. .. | bless us: | and all the ènds of the .. .. .. | world shall | fear .. | him.
9. As it was in the beginning, is now, and .. | ev - er | shall be | wòrld .. .. .. | with - out | end. A- | men.

19 "GLORIA IN EXCELSIS."

ARRANGED BY W. H. W. DARLEY.

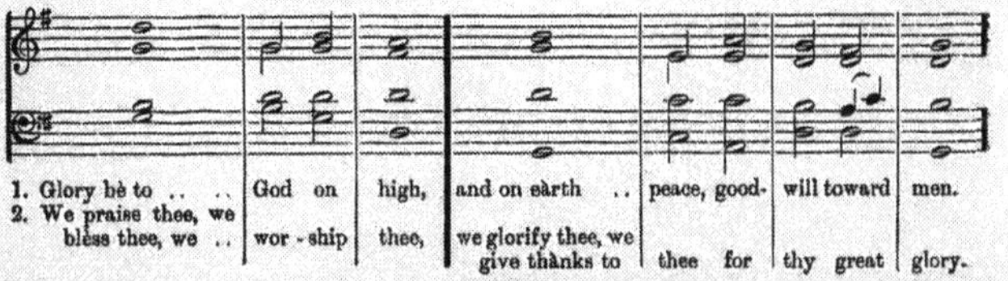

1. Glory bè to .. .. | God on | high, | and on eàrth .. | peace, good- | will toward | men.
2. We praise thee, we blèss thee, we .. | wor - ship | thee, | we glorify thee, we give thànks to | thee for | thy great | glory.

"GLORIA IN EXCELSIS"—*Continued.*

3. O Lord Gȯd, ... | heaven-ly | King, | Gȯd the .. .. | Fa - ther | Al- .. | mighty.
4. O Lord, the only begotten Sȯn, .. | Je - sus | Christ: | O Lord God, Lamb of Gȯd, ... | Son .. | of the | Father,

5. That takest away the | sins of the | world, | hȧve .. .. .. | mercy up- | on .. .. | us.
6. Thou that takest awȧy the .. .. | sins of the | world, | rė - .. .. .. | ceive .. | our .. .. | prayer.
7. Thou that sittest at the right hȧnd of | God the | Father, | hȧve .. .. .. | mercy up- | on .. . | us.

8. For thou ȯnly | art .. | holy; | thou .. .. | on - ly | art the | Lord;
9. Thou only, O Christ, with the .. .. | Ho - ly | Ghost, | art most high in the .. | glory of | God the | Father. | A - men. | A - men.

INDEX TO THE HYMNS.

INDEX TO THE HYMNS.

INDEX TO THE HYMNS.

DOXOLOGIES, BENEDICTIONS AND CHANTS.

INDEX TO EACH VERSE,

EXCEPTING THE FIRST ONE OF EVERY HYMN.

The Figures denote the Number of the Hymn.

INDEX OF SUBJECTS.

INDEX OF SUBJECTS.

INDEX OF SCRIPTURE TEXTS.

INDEX OF SCRIPTURE TEXTS.

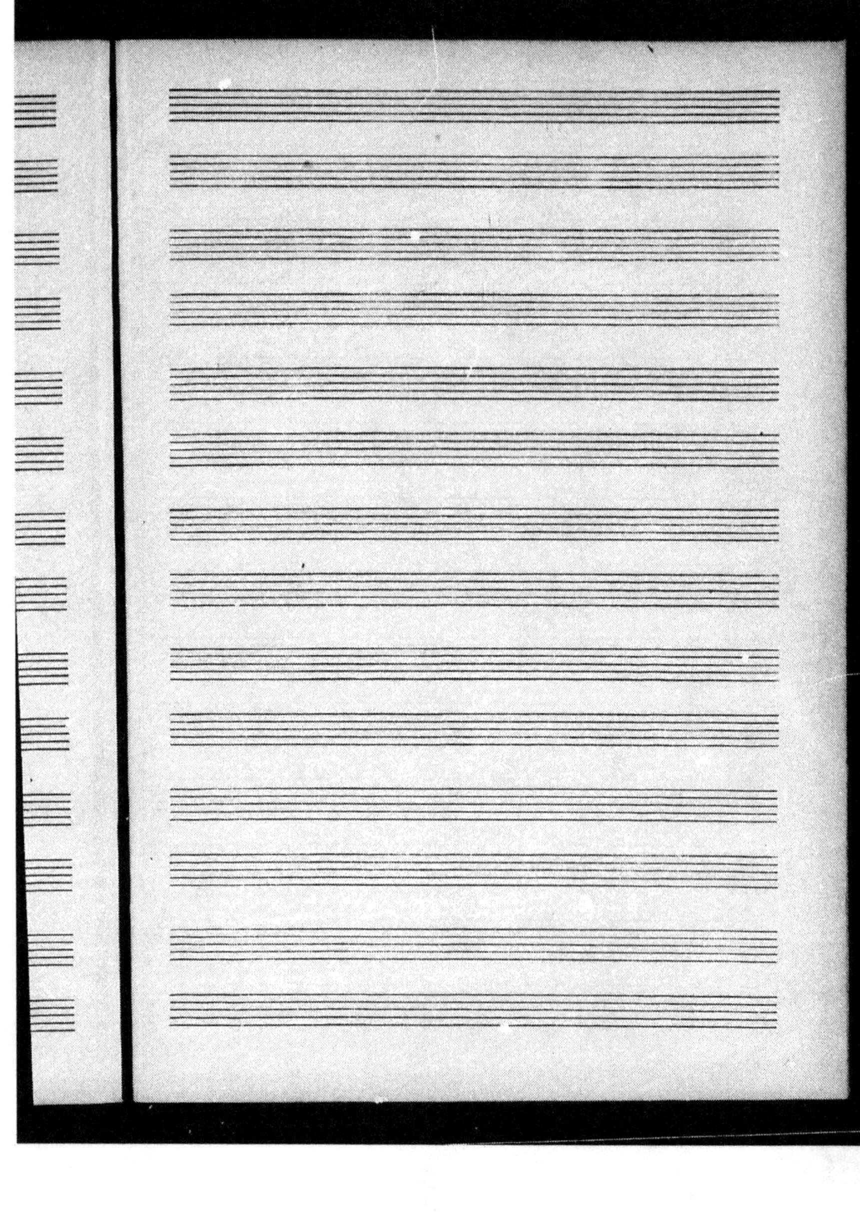

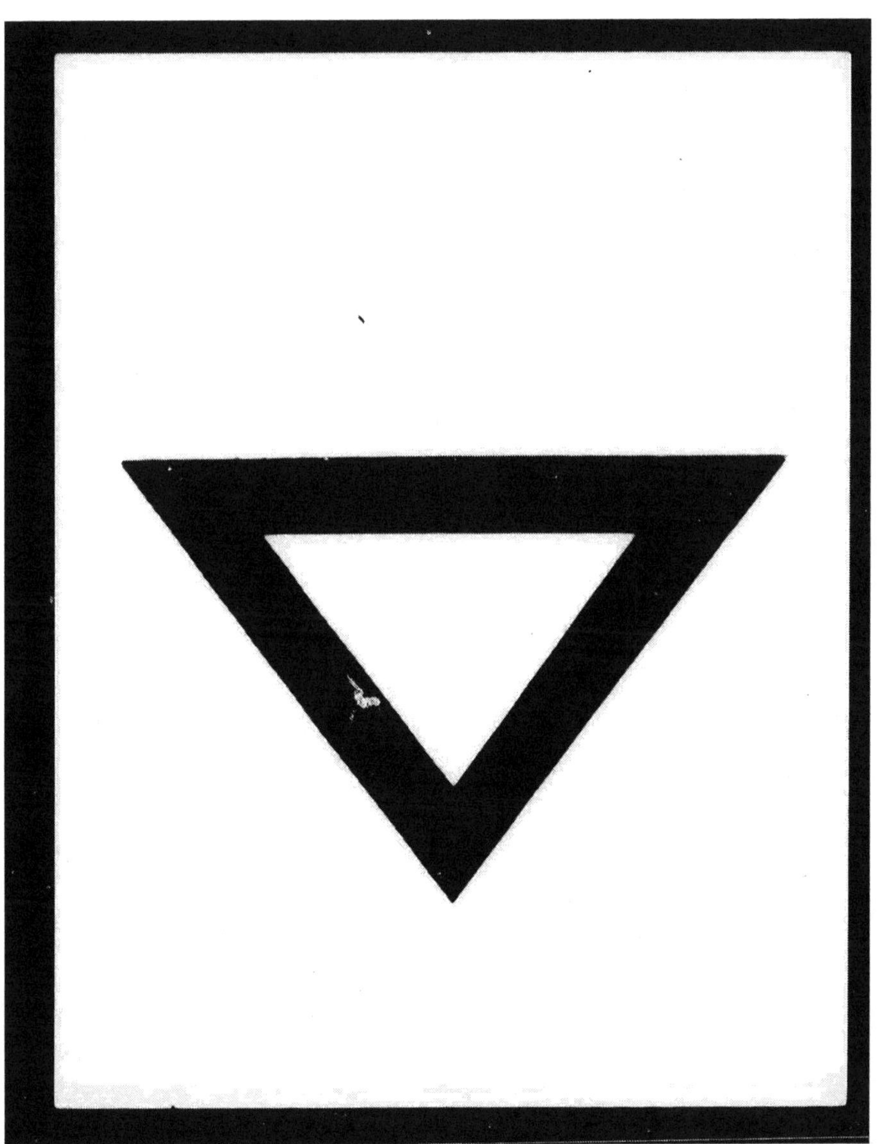

CPSIA information can be obtained
at www.ICGtesting.com
Printed in the USA
LVHW081342160122
708708LV00002B/20

9 781013 324154